ALSO BY JACQUELINE JONES

Creek Walking:
Growing Up in Delaware in the 1950s

A Social History of the Laboring Classes
from Colonial Times to the Present

American Work:
Four Centuries of Black and White Labor

The Dispossessed:
America's Underclasses from the Civil War to the Present

Labor of Love, Labor of Sorrow:
Black Women, Work, and the Family from Slavery to the Present

Soldiers of Light and Love:
Northern Teachers and Georgia Blacks, 1865–1873

Saving Savannah

Saving Savannah

THE CITY AND THE CIVIL WAR

Jacqueline Jones

ALFRED A. KNOPF · NEW YORK

2008

THIS IS A BORZOI BOOK
PUBLISHED BY ALFRED A. KNOPF

Library of Congress Cataloging-in-Publication Data

Jones, Jacqueline, [date]
Saving Savannah : the city and the Civil War / by Jacqueline Jones.
p.   cm.
Includes bibliographical references and index.
ISBN 978-1-4000-4293-7 (alk. paper)
1. Savannah (Ga.)—History—19th century.
2.   Georgia—History—Civil War, 1861–1865.
3.   Savannah (Ga.)—Race relations—History—19th century.
4.   African Americans—Georgia—Savannah—History—19th century.
5.   Freedmen—Georgia—Savannah—History—19th century.
6.   Slavery—Georgia—Savannah—History—19th century.
7.   Savannah (Ga.)—Social conditions—19th century.
8.   Elite (Social sciences)—Georgia—Savannah—History—19th century.
9.   Social classes—Georgia—Savannah—History—19th century.   I.   Title.
F294.S2J65 2008
975.8'03—dc22   2008011508

Manufactured in the United States of America
First Edition

For my students

CONTENTS

MAPS

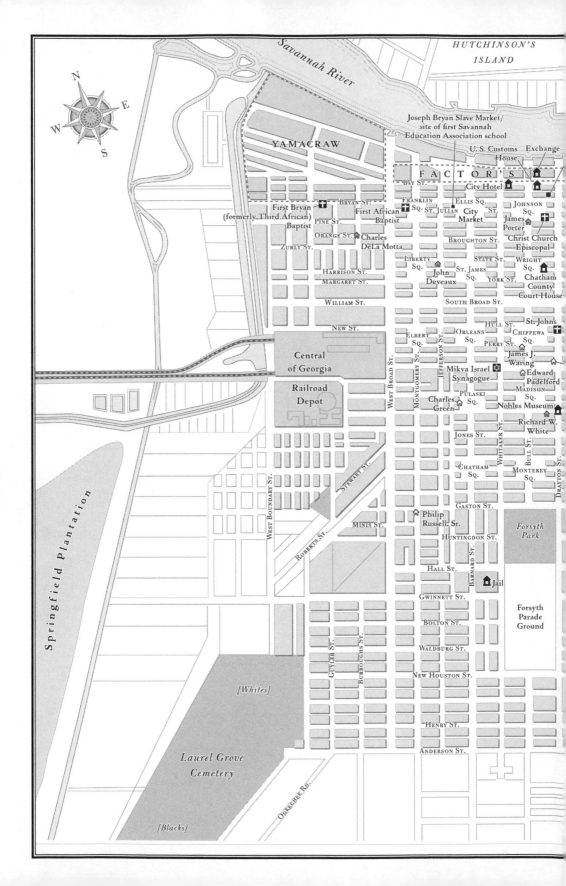

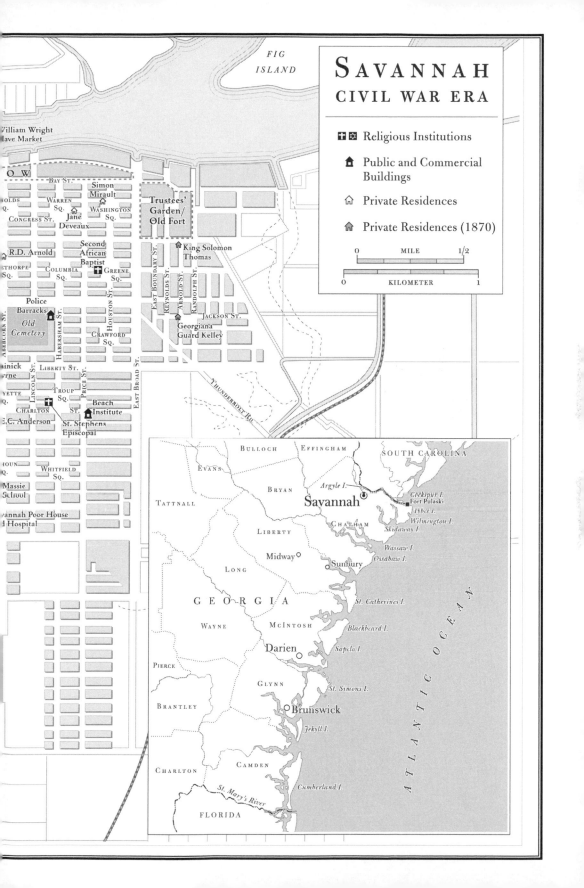

FIG
ISLAND

SAVANNAH
CIVIL WAR ERA

✝✡ Religious Institutions

🏠 Public and Commercial
Buildings

🏠 Private Residences

🏠 Private Residences (1870)

```
0          MILE          1/2

0          KILOMETER          1
```

William Wright
Slave Market

OW

BAY ST.

Simon
Mirault

OLDS
Q.

WARREN
Q.

Washington
Sq.

CONGRESS ST.

Jane
Deveaux

Trustees'
Garden/
Old Fort

R.D. Arnold

Second
African
Baptist

King Solomon
Thomas

THORPE
Q.

COLUMBIA
SQ.

GREENE
Sq.

EAST BOUNDARY ST.

REYNOLDS ST.

ARNOLD ST.

RANDOLPH ST.

Police
Barracks

Old
Cemetery

HABERSHAM ST.

HOUSTON ST.

CRAWFORD
SQ.

JACKSON ST.

Georgiana
Guard Kelley

ABERCORN ST.

EAST BROAD ST.

THUNDERBOLT RD.

ainick
yrne

LIBERTY ST.

LINCOLN ST.

PRICE ST.

FAYETTE
Q.

TROUP
SQ.

Beach
Institute

E.C. Anderson

CHARLTON
ST.

St. Stephens
Episcopal

HOUN
Q.

WHITFIELD
SQ.

Massie
School

annah Poor House
d Hospital

BULLOCH

EFFINGHAM

SOUTH CAROLINA

EVANS

BRYAN

Argyle I.

Cockspur I.
Fort Pulaski

Savannah

Tybee I.

TATTNALL

Wilmington I.

CHATHAM

Skidaway I.

LIBERTY

Wassaw I.

LONG

Midway

Sunbury

Ossabaw I.

GEORGIA

St. Catherines I.

WAYNE

McINTOSH

Blackbeard I.

Darien

Sapelo I.

PIERCE

GLYNN

St. Simons I.

BRANTLEY

Brunswick

Jekyll I.

ATLANTIC OCEAN

CHARLTON

CAMDEN

Cumberland I.

St. Mary's River

FLORIDA

✥ ANTEBELLUM ✥

-◦❦| PROLOGUE |❦◦-

I Am in the Hands of Kidnappers

ON FEBRUARY 21, 1851, a young enslaved bricklayer named Thomas Simms stowed away on a ship scheduled to set sail from Savannah, Georgia, the following morning. In planning the time and place of his liberation, Simms had calculated well. That Friday the docks were humming with the sights and sounds of the river port's high season. Weary seafaring passengers disembarked, gingerly stepping onto dry land and marveling at the commotion around them. Tied up at the wharves were fourteen steamers and more than three times that many tall ships—barques, brigs, and schooners, their masts rising far above the muddy waters of the Savannah River. Clutching bills of lading, young clerks shouted out to ship captains, and invoked the names of the city's prominent cotton factors and merchants. Along the docks, draymen positioned their heavy wooden two-wheeled carts laden with staples transported from the railroad depot on the west side of town. Enslaved laborers lifted their voices in the backbreaking rhythms of call-and-response work songs, punctuated with cries and groans—"Hooray, 'o-ray!" Together with white longshoremen, they strained to stow piles of wooden planks, bushels of rice, and bales of cotton into the holds of ships bound for ports as far away as England and France. Private conveyances, from simple hacks to resplendent carriages, awaited those new arrivals who could afford a ride up the steep cobblestone drayways to the city perched atop the bluff above. The weather was mild, delightful, and the docks were bustling—a perfect day for a fugitive bent on freedom.[1]

In the midst of this busy Friday, a docked steamship was the site of a brief but novel ceremony. That afternoon, a preacher from the Mariner's Church descended the bluff to the docks and boarded the *Florida*. There on deck the clergyman administered baptism to an infant who had been

3

born on the ship en route from New York three days before. Using a miniature lifeboat as a baptismal basin, he christened the baby Florida, the name her parents had chosen for her. Of the child, one of the ship's officers observed, "she first opened her eyes to the light of heaven on the water, an emblem of purity," a sign that her "voyage through life would be as successful as those of the noble steamship after which she was called, had thus far been."[2]

It was around this time that Thomas Simms furtively boarded the brig *M. & J. C. Gilmore*. The ship had been in port for eighteen days, and now it was fully loaded and ready to sail. The following day, Saturday, the vessel left for Boston; Thomas Simms had freed himself. The *Gilmore* would take him eighteen miles down the Savannah River, conduit of spirits and source of life for the Georgia lowcountry, and then bear him up the coast to Boston and free soil. Tucked away for two weeks, Simms had no chance to see the "light of heaven on the water" that had greeted the little white girl named Florida; but he had managed to embark on a new life, however short-lived his triumph.

Simms's escape that day in February bore all the marks of shrewd planning, a long-standing plot to be executed at the precise time when conditions were right. Just a few days earlier had come initial, sketchy reports about the rescue of a fugitive slave in Boston by a group of daring abolitionists. In the columns of Savannah newspapers and on the city's street corners, "the late disgraceful proceedings in Boston" vied for people's attention with reports that a touring circus celebrity had been arrested recently by the local police. Tom Thumb, a fifteen-pound, twenty-eight-inch-high eighteen-year-old, had been drumming up business for his show by driving his miniature carriage around town. When he veered onto a city sidewalk, the police arrested him for violating local ordinances, much to the amusement of nearly everyone but the mayor and chief of police. For his part, Tom Thumb could not have hoped for better publicity.[3]

Of the seven ships that left Savannah and went to sea on Saturday the 22nd, others were bound for New York, Providence, and Baltimore. But clearly, Simms had chosen Boston as his destination for a reason. By this time all of Savannah was talking about the rescue of the black man Shadrach Minkins, as the local papers gave over increasing numbers of column inches to detailed reports of the incident and its political fallout. On Saturday, February 15, Boston authorities had arrested the runaway slave, now in violation of the 1850 Fugitive Slave Act, passed by Congress and designed to turn all Northerners into slave catchers. Later that day a group of black Bostonians had assumed the role of unruly liberators when they stormed the federal courthouse and, in the middle of a judicial hearing, seized Minkins and swiftly rushed him to safety. When Thomas Simms left Savannah one week later, Minkins was already in Canada. Savannah authorities condemned the "Boston riot," with a "negro mob" flouting federal law and depriving law-abiding Southerners of their slave property. The editor of the Savannah *Republican* could hardly find the words, or the typeface, to express his outrage: "*The City of Boston is a black speck on the map—disgraced! By the lowest—the meanest,* THE BLACKEST *kind of* NULLIFICATION!!!" Boston stood condemned for "nullifying" a law of Congress.[4]

The Minkins rescue no doubt inspired Thomas Simms with hope for a future in Boston as a free man. Too, it was likely that even before this he had heard of another slave fugitive—Henry, who escaped in December 1849 by securing the job of a "French cook" on board a brig that sailed between Savannah and Boston. In March of the following year, when the ship returned to the Georgia port, Henry was still on board; his subsequent capture represented a modest triumph for Savannah authorities and one that garnered headlines in the local papers. One published account of Henry's recklessness suggested a larger conspiracy that made the water route between Savannah and Boston a surreptitious pathway to freedom. Noted a reporter: "[Henry's] return to Savannah can only be accounted for in his desire to carry off some of his comrades or relations." In a foreshadowing of the Simms incident, "when arrested [Henry] affected to have no knowledge whatever of his master—We are informed that the Captain of the vessel was entirely unacquainted with the fact of the man being a slave."[5]

On the morning of Saturday, February 22, 1851, a local street celebration provided the diversion Thomas Simms needed to make good his waterborne escape from Savannah. The day after he had secreted himself aboard the *Gilmore*, virtually the whole city was basking in sunshine and watching the annual Washington's Birthday parade. Simms could hear the sounds of gun salutes and the roar of the crowd not far away—up on the Bay (as the street was called), where throngs were lining the parade route in front of the three-story brick warehouses and offices called Factors' Row. On display were the disciplined, smartly outfitted militias, including the Savannah Volunteer Guards, Chatham Artillery, Irish Jasper Greens, and German Volunteers, all paying tribute to Savannah's martial tradition. A reporter later remarked upon the sweet sounds of "national airs performed by the effective military bands" composed of enslaved musicians who may or may not have been aware of the patriotic send-off they were at that moment giving one of their own. No one could deny that all of Savannah loved a parade, and that for now at least no one would be searching for a bricklayer gone missing.[6]

Still, Simms had put into motion a series of events he could not control. A little more than five weeks later, around 9 p.m. on the night of April 3, the flickering street lamps of Boston offered him no cover. Suddenly a group of white men emerged out of the shadows of Endicott Street and seized him, but not before he put up a fierce fight, stabbing one of them and calling out, "I am in the hands of kidnappers!" Yet his captors, a deputy United States marshal and several Boston police officers, had nabbed a rich prize—the twenty-seven-year-old slave owned by James Potter, one of the wealthiest rice planters in the Georgia lowcountry. Despite Simms's effort to defend himself, the men pushed him into a carriage waiting nearby and drove him from the city's North End to the federal courthouse, the site of Shadrach Minkins's rescue two months before. Fearing more in the way of criminal theatrics from the Boston black community, local officials turned the courthouse into a jail; they incarcerated Simms on the third floor, and then encircled the whole building with a massive chain. Outside, abolitionists watched in horror as, one by one, eminent judges and lawyers "bowed and stooped and bent and cringed and curled and crouched down, and crawled under the chain," in effect prostrating themselves before the slave South: a court of justice had become a cage for slaves.[7]

In the course of his life, Simms would prove himself a resilient man, an escape artist of uncommon courage and ingenuity. But on Friday, April 4, Thomas Simms, the runaway slave of slender build and delicate features, was in the process of becoming Thomas Sims, 7 Cushing 285 (Mass. 1851), a legal test case challenging the Fugitive Slave Act. (In Savannah, the Simms family spelled their name with two *m*s; authorities in Boston, and historians since, dropped one of them.) Charged with being "a fugitive from service in the state of Georgia," Simms had no legal rights. And the Commonwealth of Massachusetts had no jurisdiction in the case, except to the extent that state and local officials were obliged to defer to a federal commissioner, bound to take the word of any white person who could present evidence, credible or not, that Simms was indeed his slave. Southern politicians demanded that the North recognize their unfettered right to hold human beings as property anywhere in the country—in other words, to eliminate the northern states as a haven for fugitive slaves, once and for all.[8]

In April 1851, Boston was gaining notoriety for just that reason. Six months earlier, soon after the passage of the Fugitive Slave Act, a warrant had been issued for an enslaved couple, William and Ellen Craft, who had escaped from Macon, Georgia, and found their way to Boston. The daughter of her owner, the light-skinned Ellen had disguised herself as a young white man—skin color was no sure sign of legal status—while her husband, William, posed as the personal servant of this "gentleman." A newly formed anti-slavery group, the Boston Committee of Vigilance and Safety, launched a successful campaign of public harassment and legal intimidation aimed at the slave catchers sent to fetch the Crafts. By the time Thomas Simms arrived in Boston, the couple had fled to England; there, taunting slaveowners from afar, they spoke before mass audiences and condemned the United States for treating human beings "like the beasts of the field, subject to be bought and sold, and separated from each other at any time, and at the mere will of their master." Even more humiliating to U.S. authorities was the startling rescue of Shadrach Minkins, a Virginia runaway who also sought refuge in Boston's black community.[9]

Coming just a few weeks after the Minkins debacle—or triumph, depending on one's point of view—the capture of Simms galvanized the full spectrum of Boston's abolitionists, a small but committed group of black and white men and women. Together, they moved quickly, huddling behind closed doors and clustering on street corners to denounce the villains in the drama: the Boston police, U.S. Marshal Charles Devens and his deputies, U.S. Circuit Court commissioner George Ticknor Curtis, and justices of the Massachusetts Supreme Judicial Court. Trembling with indignation, opponents of slavery congregated in Tremont Temple and on Boston Common to rail against the southern "slavocracy," with its insatiable thirst for money and power, abetted by its craven minions on the Supreme Court and in Congress and the White House.[10]

Commissioner Curtis intended to dispatch Simms south to his owner as soon as possible—in the parlance of the day, to effect a slave rendition. On April 4, Curtis initiated hearings into the circumstances of Simms's escape aboard the *M. & J. C. Gilmore* and, more generally, into this crime against the property of James Potter. In an effort to prove that Simms was indeed his slave, Potter had sent north from Savannah a delegation of white men, including his personal agents and a white bricklayer named Edward Barnett, age twenty-four. Barnett testified that he knew Simms well; recently the two men had worked together, sharing the same bricklayer's scaffold. Barnett said he had first laid eyes on the black man ten months earlier, at a "fancy ball" where Simms appeared (according to one transcription, "in the character of a sailor," but according to another, "he was there as a waiter"). The fancy ball, or "blow-out," was a popular form of entertainment in Savannah, a masquerade with guests costumed as exotic peoples: "The dark Peruvian, and the Naples Maid / Fly through the waltz or down the gallopade / Spain's haughty Grandee seeks the Gipsey Girl / and Greek and Moslem join the airy whirl." Regardless of whether Thomas Simms was there in disguise or serving food and wine, Barnett could credibly claim to have encountered the slave in the normal course of both his workdays and his evenings.[11]

Although Barnett did not know all the details, Thomas Simms was in fact the son of James Simms and Minda Campbell. Minda was born in 1793 and owned by James Potter, a planter who presided over vast holdings in slaves and land north of Savannah. She had once belonged to the grandmother of Potter's wife, Sarah Grimes Potter. At some point, after the enslaved woman became the property of the Potter family, she managed to negotiate relatively favorable treatment for her sons. Accordingly, James Potter arranged for Thomas Simms (born in 1824) and his older brother James Meriles Simms (born in 1823) to be trained as skilled artisans, Thomas as a bricklayer and James as a carpenter. The two young men were allowed to live with or near their mother in Savannah, but they were required to turn over their wages to her so that she could give the money to Potter. Yet Thomas apparently defied this arrangement and kept his earnings for himself. Apprenticed to a master builder in Savannah, he was making a decent wage, an estimated $1.50 to $2.50 a week, before he fled north.[12]

During the hearings in Boston, the captain of the *Gilmore* and two of the ship's seamen offered their version of the events leading to the capture of the fugitive. According to their testimony, sometime after the ship docked in Savannah on February 3, the young black man had approached John Ball, a sailor on board, and asked him if the cook needed an assistant. When Ball replied in the negative, Simms disappeared, but returned to stow away on February 21, the day before the ship set sail. Another seaman, Cephas J. Ames, testified that it was he who discovered Simms two weeks later, near the end of the trip, just as the ship was about to enter Boston harbor. Ames claimed that on March 6 he found Simms in the ship's forecastle, hiding under a bed in the wedge-shaped compartment that served as the crew's quarters. Ames alerted Captain Kimball Eldridge, who ordered that Simms be held overnight in a locked stateroom, with two men posted outside the door. But the guards either fell asleep or "were out of the way," because apparently Simms made off with the ship's rowboat that night or early the next morning.[13]

This story was no doubt a fiction concocted by white men bent on avoiding criminal prosecution for any part they might have played in Simms's successful getaway. In all likelihood, Simms had bribed one or more of the *Gilmore*'s crew members to help him escape. Certainly he had enough money to ensure the full cooperation of his coconspirators. It was his wages then that financed the clandestine sea voyage, covering bribes for men who fed him, watched out for him—in their own quarters, no less—and ultimately unlocked the stateroom door and helped lower the rowboat into the water. The "deeply mortified" Captain Eldridge failed to state the obvious: that, in the words of a Savannah reporter, Simms had required the "connivance of someone on board."[14]

For elites both northern and southern, the image of white laborers sheltering runaway slaves was a frightening one. Yet Savannah, city of enterprise, had a hard time keeping track of the whereabouts of its workers regardless of their color or legal status. Situated forty feet above the Savannah River, the city was small by today's standards, with a population of 15,312 in 1850. That number included 7,000 slaves and 686 free people of color. Yet these relatively modest numbers belied the river port's vibrant commercial economy. To reach the docks, Thomas Simms would have left his home on the fringe of the city, one of the congested neighborhoods of low-lying wooden tenements, and set out through streets arranged in a tight grid pattern. Founded in 1733, Savannah was meant to serve as a buffer between the English colony of Carolina to the north and its Spanish enemy, the colony of Florida, to the south; the city's defensive role gave shape to the grid plan, which resembled nothing so much as a military encampment. The outpost, planted in the Georgia woods, was soon dubbed "Forest City," notable for its uniform house lots and its twenty-four parklike public squares. Inscribed in this plan were the ideals of the colony's founder, James Oglethorpe—to ensure equality among its homesteaders of modest means, and thereby carve social order out of a forested wilderness. To that end, the founders were determined to ban liquor, slaves, and lawyers from the young colony.[15]

Nevertheless, the Savannah of 1851 was no all-white utopia of sober family farmers. When Simms descended the bluff to the river that day in February, he saw men and women of all colors and statuses mingling in profusion. Nearly 80 percent of the city's export economy relied on cotton, some of it grown as far away as Tennessee and Alabama, and much of it transported by the Central of Georgia Railroad, and then compressed into bales for shipment to the North and Europe. On River Street he brushed past black women balancing immense burdens of firewood and laundry on their heads, and dodged black teamsters urging on mules winded from pulling a ton of wagon and rice through the city's sandy streets. On the docks, the ranks of black longshoremen included slaves owned or hired by white contractors, and a small number of free men who worked for wages. The whites were mostly Irish (and some French Canadian) immigrants who came to Savannah for the busy season, from November through May, and then returned home to New York City (and Quebec). Waterfront warehouses, cotton presses, and rice mills brought together bookkeepers, sailors, teamsters, and loaders, all doing their work, or rather the work of their masters and employers. Coming and going were rough crews of black and white men who had guided rafts made of lumber down the river from the interior, and enslaved pilots who had brought in flatboats laden with rice from the surrounding creeks and canals. Schooners that plied coastal waters disgorged loads of raw, long-staple cotton from the Georgia Sea Islands. Steamships from the North deposited hats, shoes, and calico fabric, along with invalids seeking to luxuriate in Savannah's mild winter climate.[16]

Simms could assume that no white person would take notice of a black man casually—nervously?—sauntering up to a sailing ship, especially a black man so familiar with city ways. He counted on finding at least a couple of seamen whose scruples could easily be compromised by the flash of bills or the jingle of coins. When he arrived in Boston in March, he paid for lodgings in a seamen's boardinghouse, on Ann Street in the southern part of the city. When he was caught on the night of April 3, he was walking the streets of the city's North End, where workers made their living on or near the docks. Many other fugitive slaves also took their leave from the slave South by water, out of Baltimore or Charleston or Savannah. The most famous runaway of all, Frederick Douglass, eluded officials by disguising himself as a seaman; a Baltimore ship caulker, he adopted the lingo and dress of a sailor.[17]

Still, neither Commissioner Curtis nor any of the other officials at the Boston hearings chose to pursue the obvious fabrications of the *Gilmore* captain and crew members. At some point in March an unknown informant had tipped off Potter about Simms's whereabouts. The planter in turn alerted Boston authorities. Now the compelling issue was not how Thomas Simms got to Boston, but rather how quickly he could be sent back.

Over the nine days that Simms was held in Boston's federal court-house, the efforts to free him emerged as overlapping strategies pursued by the runaway himself, his attorneys, and members of the Vigilance Committee. Simms attempted to devise an alternative identity, first by claiming that he was a free man named Joseph Santina; that he was born in St. Augustine, Florida, the son of a Spaniard and an enslaved woman; and that his father had purchased his freedom when he was a child. He said he had never heard of James Potter: He had traveled to Savannah and remained there for a year, in order to see a certain young woman; but as a free person of color, he was liable for a fine of $100 for entering the state (and indeed, this would have been the case had this story been true). Simms further maintained that, when the woman's jealous lover threatened to report him, he fled north.[18]

This tale and variations on it reappeared in a "Petition of Thomas Sims" submitted to the Massachusetts legislature, and in an affidavit submitted to Commissioner Curtis, both documents prepared by Simms's attorneys on his behalf. Indeed, the young man had the benefit of Boston lawyers outspoken in their abolitionist sympathies and resourceful in manipulating local, state, and federal law. Besides promoting the Santina story, they argued that the black man could not be sent south because Boston police needed him to appear in criminal court to answer assault charges for stabbing the Boston police officer the night of his capture. The attorneys also managed to have two of Potter's emissaries—his lawyer, John E. Bacon, and a Savannah police officer, M. S. DeLyon— arrested on kidnapping charges.[19]

Using a scattershot approach, the lawyers argued that Simms was entitled to a trial by jury, presided over by a judge; and they petitioned the Massachusetts Supreme Court to issue a writ of habeas corpus in order to safeguard what they claimed were Simms's basic rights as a resident of the commonwealth. The Fugitive Slave Act was unconstitutional, they held, because it gave judicial power to a federal commissioner who was not a judge. Further, the law abrogated the rights of all citizens of the northern states, any of whom could be torn from their families and dragged south into slavery on the word of men or women who need undergo no cross-examination in a court of law. With grudging admiration, one New York journalist noted, "The abolitionists certainly leave no stone unturned to achieve [their] object, and the same energy in a better cause would be highly commendable."[20]

Outside the Boston federal courthouse, other schemes surfaced, and then went awry. A dozen members of the Boston Vigilance Committee plotted to free Simms by violent means if necessary. Leading the way was the clothier Lewis Hayden, himself a fugitive slave (from Kentucky) and one of the militant masterminds who had protected the Crafts and rescued Minkins. (For the latter effort Hayden was arrested, tried, and acquitted.) Convinced that direct action was the only meaningful anti-slavery strategy, Hayden and others arranged to have the Reverend William Grimes, also a runaway, visit Simms in his third-story cell on the evening of Friday, April 11. At the appointed time, Grimes was to encourage Simms to take a literal leap of faith—to cross the room and jump out of a window onto mattresses that committee members had placed on the sidewalk below. But at dusk, a few hours before the plan was to be set in motion, a group of workmen began to fit Simms's window with iron bars. Wrote a bitterly disappointed conspirator, the young Unitarian minister Thomas Wentworth Higginson, "Whether we had been betrayed, or whether it was simply a bit of extraordinary precaution, we never knew."[21]

By this time, the Massachusetts Supreme Judicial Court had rendered its decision that the Fugitive Slave Act was legal and that all officers of the commonwealth were compelled to obey it. The court held that the law was a legitimate effort on the part of Congress to contain the slave question within legislative and judicial bounds. For the most part, both of the national political parties, the Democrats and the Whigs, preferred to ignore the issue in an effort to retain constituencies in the North as well as the South. Chief Justice Lemuel Shaw wrote, "In this spirit [of compromise], and with these views steadily in prospect, it seems to be the duty of all judges and magistrates to expound and apply these provisions in the Constitution and laws of the United States." Most whites in Boston, and throughout the United States, agreed with this view; and in fact, in 1851, the majority of free white citizens either acquiesced in or actively supported the oppression of slaves.[22]

Although Simms's supporters were relatively small in number, his case highlighted the ability of Boston-area abolitionists to force a national debate over slavery; it was these Northerners who documented, in the words of Henry David Thoreau, "this moral earthquake." From outdoor platforms, church pulpits, and editorial offices came a rhetorical cascade of outrage on the part of anti-slavery activists. The enemy of justice was silence, according to the lawyer Richard Henry Dana: "Our officers are slave-hunters, and the voice of the old law of the state is hushed into silence before this fearful slave-power which has got such entire control of the Union." In the space of one week, preachers, lawyers, writers, and ordinary citizens offered up speeches and resolutions, prayers, hymns, sermons, newspaper articles and editorials, legal briefs, petitions to the state legislature, and street-corner harangues. The court hearing itself covered four days and consisted of more than forty thousand words spoken by Commissioner Curtis and the lawyers for Simms and Potter.[23]

But in truth, many abolitionists felt constrained by vocabularies they considered unequal to the task of condemning slavery, a practice that seemed to originate in some fiendish netherworld, a practice nourished by mysterious and unspeakable evil. Upon hearing of the Simms rendition, Frederick Douglass cried, "Let the Heavens weep and let Hell be merry!" The captured slave was but a human sacrifice to "the most infernal propensities of man's malicious heart." The Reverend Theodore Parker exclaimed that in order to understand slaveowners, this "brood of monsters," he must "open the graves, and bring up the most hideous tyrants from the dead!" According to the common-school reformer Horace Mann, "The southern planter seems to possess some wizard art, unknown to the demonology of former times." In response, supporters of slavery tried without much success to block out a cacophony of insults, catcalls, songs, and ringing church bells. Thoreau condemned the speech of slavery's supporters; he said such speech percolated through the mainstream Boston press with "the gurgling of the sewer through every column."[24]

These anti-Simms newspapers were giving voice to Boston elites who did business with southern planters and merchants, and to the white laboring classes eager to keep slaves in the South and northern blacks out of paid jobs. John H. Pearson, the owner of the *Gilmore* and a fleet of packet ships that made regular runs between Savannah and Boston, put up $8,000 in bail money for the Savannahians DeLyon and Bacon when they were arraigned on kidnapping charges. Contemplating the commercial links between port cities, North and South, William Lloyd Garrison, a founder of the American Anti-Slavery Society, and the editor of the *Liberator*, claimed that "the Boston of 1851 is not the Boston of 1775. Boston has now become a mere shop—a place for buying and selling goods; and I suppose, also, of *buying and selling men*."[25]

Not all who wanted to speak about the Simms case had their say. The young black man himself lacked a public voice of his own. Indeed, the Fugitive Slave Act expressly prohibited the alleged runaway from testifying in his or her own behalf, on the assumption that no black person should be allowed to directly contradict the word of a white person: "In no trial or hearing under this Act shall the testimony of such alleged Fugitive be admitted as evidence." In newspaper accounts of the controversy, Simms spoke only through other people. The seaman Cephas Ames of the *Gilmore* testified that the fugitive had cried, "Have we got up? [Have we arrived?]" when Ames pulled him out of the forecastle. The *Liberator* reported that, on the night of his arrest, Simms's "transfer was performed too speedily to afford him an opportunity to make much of a speech."[26]

Before dawn on the morning of Saturday, April 12, a force estimated at 150 men marched into Boston's Court Square and assembled in the shape of a hollow square. Among them were U.S. Marshal Charles Devens and his deputies; members of the city watch, armed with clubs and hooks; and police shouldering swords. Simms was roused from his cell, brought outside, and placed in the middle of the square, which then proceeded to move forward, toward Long Wharf and a waiting ship, the brig *Acorn*. Gathering at the site of the Boston Tea Party seventy-eight years before, the early morning crowd became increasingly angry. Someone called out to the departing fugitive, "Sims, preach Liberty to the slaves!" In honor of the occasion, the *Acorn* had been outfitted with two cannon—a necessary precaution considering the Vigilance Committee had debated sending one of its own members, a Cape Cod sea captain, to capture the ship on the high seas. Eager to protect his own good name, John Pearson, the owner of the *Gilmore*, had agreed to pay all expenses incurred in returning Thomas Simms to his owner.[27]

Back in Savannah, members of the city council pointedly refrained from making a public statement about the case; they busied themselves with long-winded debates over building a new waterworks, draining the swamplands surrounding the city, attaching a workhouse to the jail, and cracking down on thefts of loose cotton by establishing a wharf police. Still, no one could deny that the escapes of Simms and the Crafts had proved embarrassing for the state of Georgia. In referring to Simms, the city newspapers only belatedly used his last name, breaking with a custom that decreed slaves should be identified by their first name exclusively. Yet politicians and newspaper editors could look forward to the day when the young bricklayer would once more stand on the docks of Savannah, this time in shackles.[28]

By mid-April, the *Daily Morning News* could smugly report, "The fiery denunciations, the fanatical appeals, and the insane ravings of the orators, have fallen coldly upon the ears of the people at large, and resistance to the law is evidently an unpopular doctrine." The editors expressed disgust with the stench of abolitionists' words, "gas let off by these tongue-valiant agitators." Meanwhile, the city's whites were mightily impressed by the fact that James Potter expressed no interest in Simms the slave, but keen interest in Simms the legal test case: indeed, Potter told an editor, he had "not been influenced by pecuniary considerations in his pursuit of the slave, but [had] been actuated by principle alone," determined to test the constitutionality of the Fugitive Slave Law. The planter even had to fend off rumors that he had staged Simms's escape himself in order to set the legal process in motion and reaffirm Southerners' rights.[29]

Potter could well afford to profess no interest in Thomas Simms the slave. As one of the lords of the lowcountry Georgia Rice Kingdom, he owned hundreds of human beings and thousands of acres of land. Rice lands were among the most valuable kinds of real estate in the antebellum South, for they were the result of the arduous labors and considerable engineering skills of enslaved workers. And by 1850, planters on the lower Savannah River had developed a form of rice cultivation that proved extraordinarily profitable.[30]

The founders of the new colony of Georgia had banned slavery on the theory that reliance on the labor of people of African descent would discourage English settlers from working hard themselves. In 1736, William Byrd II, a wealthy Virginia tobacco planter, went further and warned leaders of the colony that slaves posed an inherent threat to any community that aspired to harmony and industry: "They blow up the pride, & ruin the industry of our white people, who seeing a rank of poor creatures below them, detest work for fear it should make them look like slaves." The neighboring colony of South Carolina, which early on relied heavily on slave labor, presumably placed itself in mortal danger, for a black man "of desperate courage" could easily "kindle a servile war . . . before any opposition could be formed against him, and tinge our rivers as wide as they are with blood."[31]

Despite these warnings, most Georgia colonists wholeheartedly embraced slavery, convinced that the swamps were impossible for any white householder and his family to clear and cultivate, especially in the heat and humidity of a lowcountry summer. The colony legalized bondage in 1750, seventeen years after its founding. About this time, rice growers along the Georgia coastal riverways, in the Ogeechee region west of Savannah and the Altamaha Delta near the border with Florida, began to rely on enslaved workers to perfect a hydraulic system of irrigation. This system used river and marshland tidal flows to flood rice fields with fresh water, flows regulated by intricate systems of dikes, trunks, and canals. Lowcountry planters favored slaves imported from Sierra Leone, men

and women familiar with rice cultivation in a way that Europeans were
not. By 1849, the 550 great rice planters of the Georgia lowcountry were
profiting from 25 million pounds of clean rice each year; that figure would
double over the next ten years.

Among these men were the brothers James and Thomas Potter and
their neighbors, father and son Charles and Louis Manigault. Both
extended families owned rice plantations a few miles upriver from Savannah. It was the intense, hardheaded ambition of these men that helped
fuel the boom in rice culture during the 1850s. Both families sought to
enlarge and consolidate their holdings, buying up the lands of smaller
neighboring planters through outright sales as well as through foreclo-
sure proceedings. The slave-labor equation seemed straightforward
enough: each able-bodied man or woman could produce 240 bushels of
rice a year, and so each slave could earn the master $324 a year. The most
successful planters were constantly buying more slaves, both to expand
crop production and to replace the large number of laborers who died
from disease and overwork each year. Within six years of the Thomas
Simms affair, James Potter would own between 400 and 500 slaves and
5,257 acres, 1,253 in rice, and would build one of the Rice Kingdom's
most magnificent mansions on his Colerain plantation. At the same time,
Savannah was exporting nearly 400,000 bales of cotton (worth $8 mil-
lion) a year, and serving as the center of Georgia's domestic slave trade.[32]

In siding with principle, Potter eventually relinquished a bricklayer
who was bound to become even more valuable in the coming years.
When Thomas Simms ran away, Savannah was entering a period of
explosive growth that was highly unusual compared to other southern
cities at the time. Between 1850 and 1860, the city's population grew by
50 percent, to 22,292 residents, driven by the completion of three railroad
lines that linked the port to the state's interior and diverted trainloads of
upcountry cotton away from its archrival, Charleston. And in fact, the
economic prosperity of the Georgia Rice Kingdom found expression in
the region's newly built landscape during the 1850s. Lowcountry planters
needed engineers and artisans to construct steam threshing mills, slave
quarters, stables, storage barns, smokehouses, and grand residences, as
well as complex irrigation systems. Savannah's own building spree
included an extensive railroad depot complex (rendered in a combination of Gothic Revival, Classical Revival, and Italianate styles), new
waterworks, schools, churches, firemen's halls, army and police barracks,
boardinghouses for workers, and stately mansions of brick and stucco.
Among the grandest of these residences was the one built by British-born

merchant Charles Green, beginning in 1851. (An admiring reporter described the imposing structure, with its Gothic and Italianate elements, as "very rich in details, but simple and chaste, yet imposing.") The high demand for skilled construction workers indicated that the lower Savannah River, together with the six coastal counties—which included the Georgia Sea Islands—made up a unified regional economy fueled by the production and distribution of cotton, rice, and lumber.[33]

On Saturday, April 19, the *Acorn* entered the mouth of the Savannah River at Tybee Lighthouse, and then proceeded northwestward, past the formidable brick octagon Fort Pulaski, and on toward Savannah. Aboard the boat were four deputy U.S. marshals and four other "special officers and assistants," an official entourage designed, in the words of one Savannah paper, "to satisfy the southern mind, that this particular [Fugitive Slave] law shall be maintained and carried out with all the power and dignity of the Government." As the *Acorn* navigated the shallow river and avoided perilous mudflats and sandbars, the several native New Englanders on board were no doubt struck by the beauty of the flat, expansive green marshlands that stretched to the horizon.[34]

Anticipating an audience with James Potter himself, the officials could expect to find much to admire, and much that was familiar, in the planter. Not only did he possess the kind of acquisitive spirit that also animated the lords of industry in the New England and Mid-Atlantic states, he was part of a lowcountry elite that maintained close ties with many concentric groups of Northerners—college classmates and former professors, steamship company owners, merchants and creditors, fellow politicians, friends and extended kin. For the Massachusetts visitors then, the trip to Georgia was not so much a voyage into a foreign place as a trip to an exotic climate that showcased the achievements of a distinctive group of prosperous and thoroughly American men.

In contrast, for lowcountry blacks, the lower Savannah River was a sacred landscape that formed the heart of Africa-America, the Gullah-Geechee culture of the South Carolina and Georgia coastal and Sea Island region. (Gullah usually refers to West African traditions in South Carolina, Geechee to those traditions in Georgia; however, regardless of these artificial state boundaries, Africans and their descendants throughout the region shared many cultural beliefs and practices.) Linking the profane and spiritual worlds of the slaves were the waterways that laced the lowcountry. The river of life-giving properties had carried Simms away, but the river of death and disease had returned him to Savannah; for the rice swamps spawned gastrointestinal and respiratory diseases that regularly killed horrific numbers of black men, women, and children. Toiling in standing water during the spring planting season and drinking water polluted by ocean tides and nearby privies, rice slaves paid for the fabulous wealth of their masters and mistresses with their lives.

Gullah-Geechee people shared an intimate relation with land and water. The natural surroundings evoked their ancestral homelands in West Africa and in the process helped to create and reinforce an emerging African-American culture that shaped patterns of work, family feeling, and religious faith. Together black men and women slogged around in the muck-filled rice fields; tended the cattle that ranged freely through isolated hammocks of dark cedars, live oaks, and myrtle trees; contended daily with the insect pests and snakes that lived in the marshes; fished and gathered crabs, shrimp, and oysters; and used plants and wood to make all manner of useful things, from medicines to furniture and canoes. Runaways who had managed to survive for weeks at a time in the marshlands, and pilots who had guided canoes, flatboats, and skiffs through the maze of creeks, canals, and "cuts," could map wide swaths of the lowcountry. And waterways not only nourished the crops, offered up food, and provided escape routes for fugitives and haunts for nighttime revelers; according to West African tradition, rivers and streams hosted spirits, and enabled the dead to circulate among the living. The Christian rite of baptism reinforced African beliefs that water was all-powerful, nourishing the soul as well as the body.[35]

Enslaved men and women thus folded their spirituality into the natural contours of the landscape, where the cosmic and material worlds were fused, the line between them blurred. African rituals marked the change of seasons and stages of rice and cotton crops; the annual harvest was celebrated with "ring shouts" of dance and prayer. African folktales about crocodiles took root and became African-American "trickster" tales pitting crafty rabbits against gullible alligators, tales limned with violence, cruelty, and deceit. Traditional African stories—about people who could fly away from suffering and pain, and about the magic hoe that "goes ahead and cultivates the gahden [sic] without anyone touching it"—took on a new life in the lowcountry slave quarters. Enslaved men and women, then, found the coastal soil to be fertile ground for transplanting not only specific crops, herbs, and medicinal plants native to West Africa, but also distinctive ways of looking at the world. In the process they challenged whites' contention that the land was primarily a commodity to be bought and sold, a place of profit making only.[36]

Potter's economic interests and the burdens shouldered by his slaves intersected in the rice fields, where the task system of labor prevailed. This system mandated that each person complete a daily task: one quarter acre per day per man, slightly less per woman (although age and strength could trump male-female distinctions). The system also provided that workers could labor on behalf of themselves and their families after their task was completed. At the same time, task completion often required heroic exertions on the part of individual slaves, many of them ill or incapacitated from overwork; after ten hours of field labor, only the strongest had energy to work for themselves and their families. On Potter's Colerain and Tweedside plantations, the slaves were allowed to trade among themselves and market their wares in Savannah; and also, as one former slave recalled later, "by industry and economy" they could accumulate cows, chickens, mules, turkey, hogs, horses, and even racehorses. Thomas Butler, a cooper and miller in charge of the Colerain water-powered rice mill, stockpiled rice and honey; he and his wife kept their own flatboat and tended 300 fowl, which they fed waste from the mill. They also planted corn and potatoes. By giving a slave the "liberty of trading and trafficking for himself," planters such as Potter lessened their own obligation to provide their workers with food and other necessities, thus forcing black men and women to rely more on themselves, and on each other. Though he lived and worked in the city, Thomas Simms revealed the contradictions embedded in this system. James Potter's task system and hiring-out policies did not soften Thomas Simms's determination to be free.[37]

Wealthy slaveowners and overworked, malnourished slaves represent seemingly polar opposites not only in political power and economic and physical well-being, but also in cultural sensibilities. In this view, James Potter saw the lowcountry mainly as a vast water-driven machine to make rice, and he trafficked in the currency of money, slaves, and land. His language was English, literal and direct, his worldview scientific, rational. In contrast, the field hands spoke Geechee, a pidgin of English and West African languages, and they communicated through metaphors and indirection. Their currency came in the form of mediation between the spiritual and material worlds. Where the planters were individualistic and ambitious, the slaves valued collective effort and the preservation of African traditions.

Yet cultures rarely exist in relation to each other as polarities. Consider, for example, the wide spectrum of beliefs and practices among slaves and free people, black people and white, poor people and rich. In the city, many slaves and free people of color labored, ate, fought, and slept with white workingmen and -women. A few free blacks owned slaves, in some cases at least suggesting that people of enterprise regardless of skin color could see human bondage as a means of running a profitable business. Throughout the lowcountry, enslaved men and women struggled to grow and accumulate small surpluses that could then be marketed in the city; they valued the money they could earn through hard work. Although some black preachers eschewed the African beliefs and practices that informed the religious faith of many slaves, in fact their Christianity represented a blend of West African and European elements. Many blacks in Savannah as well as in the countryside lived in a world populated by spirits and ghosts, a world interpreted by conjurers and root doctors; but then, so too did some poor whites. And finally, many blacks and whites were related by blood, though these most fundamental of human ties were rarely acknowledged in public, and never acknowledged in law. Thus lowcountry cultures defied urban-rural, black-white, enslaved-free distinctions.

There exists no record of the means by which Simms was conveyed from the Savannah docks to the Chatham County jail. Savannahians delighted in processions of all kinds, but apparently city officials were reluctant to turn the young man's enforced homecoming into a provocation. He spent the next few weeks lodged in the Chatham County jail, a forbidding two-story structure; built five years before, it resembled a medieval fortress, with its crenellated parapets and thick brick walls. Here languished Savannah's most vulnerable people, men and women destined to serve out sentences in fetid, cramped quarters—black seamen required by law to remain imprisoned while their ships were docked at the city's wharves; recalcitrant slaves sent in from plantations to be whipped; and fugitives awaiting punishment, and, in all likelihood, sale. Here too were large numbers of white laborers, mostly Irish immigrants arrested for public drunkenness and fighting, for stealing and for cavorting with slaves. For his treachery, Simms received thirty-nine stripes of the lash, the maximum allowed by the law at any one time. He later told a reporter that "he would have been more severely punished but for the sympathy manifested for him at the North."[38]

IT WAS AROUND this time that Simms's older brother, twenty-eight-year-old James, was in the process of earning for himself a mixed reputation as a skilled carpenter and a headstrong young man. Small and slender, James apparently resembled his brother in physical appearance. He was known as quick-witted and verbally dexterous; an admirer would call him a son of Boanerges, the god of thunder—"quick, brainy, shrewd, brilliant at repartee." Soon after he was baptized as a member of Savannah's independent First African Baptist Church, the leaders of the church excommunicated the seventeen-year-old for (in the words of one preacher) "continued neglect of Christian duties" and his "very presumptuous and defiant" demeanor. Embracing a life of music and conviviality, James had refused to give up playing the fiddle at exuberant city blow-outs, where he and the members of his band were fixtures for many years. In the process James ran up against church elders, stern enforcers of morality among the members of their congregation. By 1851 James was still outside the church, but he was now the husband of Margaret, age twenty-seven, and the father of Susan, age two. Whether he admired, resented, or pitied his younger brother that spring remains a mystery.[39]

Before they left for home, the Boston marshals enjoyed a lavish dinner hosted by James Potter. Together they all hoisted their glasses in a toast: "*The North and the South*—May the links of the chain that binds their union be stronger than ever—the abolitionists pitched into h——l, and Bunker Hill monument rolled against the gate." The Bostonians left Savannah in late April and thus avoided the giant biting insects called gallinippers, and the deadly lowcountry summer vapors so feared by the white population. With the departure of its honored guests, Savannah directed its attention to other amusements that week, including a mesmerist who could convince a subject that he was "tormented by fleas and mosquitoes."[40]

The Simms case reverberated throughout the North and South. In Boston, the Vigilance Committee tightened its organization, enlisting dozens of black men and women to assist sixty-nine runaways in the year 1851 alone. Within the next few weeks, in Pennsylvania and upstate New York, bold rescues of fugitive slaves confirmed that the fight against slavery was entering a new and violent phase. Runaway slaves and free blacks alike felt vulnerable. In New York City, a young woman named Harriet Jacobs feared showing her face outside; springtime might bring mild weather, but that was also "when snakes and slaveholders make their appearance," she noted. Jacobs's own daring escape from bondage would become legendary; beginning in 1835, for seven long years she had hidden in an Edenton, North Carolina, attic, a tiny space seven feet wide, nine feet long, and three feet high, before making her way north on a Philadelphia-bound schooner. In 1851 the thirty-eight-year-old was living in New York City and working as a governess for a white family. Since the burden of proof fell on black people to document their freedom, Jacobs noted, "many a poor washerwoman, who, by hard labor, had made herself a comfortable home, was obliged to sacrifice her furniture, bid a hurried farewell to friends, and seek her fortune among strangers in Canada." And so the northern free family shared with the southern enslaved family a terrible uncertainty—that at any moment parents might be separated from children, husbands from wives.[41]

The Simms controversy prompted Georgia politicians of all stripes to ponder the viability of the Union itself: what future for the land-hungry system of slavery? In Savannah, Union supporters sparred with extremists who favored "non-intercourse" with the North. Irish immigrants tended to side with the Unionists, and so did those elites who profited from the economic ties between Savannah and Philadelphia, New York, and Boston. Among Savannah's most vocal "Union Democrats" was the ambitious northern-educated physician Richard D. Arnold, who believed the Compromise of 1850 would hold: "My ardent desire was to see the nationality of the Democratic Party preserved." The Simms rendition seemed to prove the strength of that "nationality," and, at least for now, to vindicate Arnold and other Union Democrats. At the same time, Arnold believed, correctly, that "the old party lines" between Whigs and Democrats were insufficient to contain the explosive issue of slavery.[42]

Within a matter of weeks of his return to Savannah, Thomas Simms was sold away to Vicksburg, Mississippi. At the time he could not have known that his own desperate bid for freedom had deeply touched many black and white men and women, some of whom would reappear in his life, and in the life of his brother James, over the next quarter century. A dozen years after his first attempt, Thomas would manage another remarkable escape from slavery. In the meantime, James remained in Savannah, biding his time until he too seized the chance to flee the South. But unlike his brother, James would soon return to Savannah and cast his lot permanently with the black people living and working there. And in time James would break his own silence, claiming that "the white race had never understood or known us perfectly; because we have always dissimulated. This was a natural result of tyranny—of the tyranny of slavery." Over the course of his lifetime (he died in 1912) James would work as a preacher, missionary, labor agent, attorney, judge, leader of Freemasons, publisher, and politician. Though a product of the city, he became a forceful advocate for the lowcountry rice hands freed from slavery; these were men and women "Loath to Leave their old Homes and [who] often Speak of their Relations for the Lands . . . their Fathers and Mothers cleared these Swamps and Marshes, and made them the Fruitful Rice Fields they are." When he finally had an opportunity to declaim in public, Simms took nearly everyone by surprise. Remarked one awestruck listener, "His clear, musical voice, distinct enunciation, and elegant and beautiful style of delivery impressed every one, and greatly astonished those who had never heard him speak before."[43]

THIS BOOK is about the conflict over slavery that claimed almost 700,000 lives, and in the process transformed forever the world inhabited by Sarah and James Potter, Richard Arnold, Edward Barnett, and Minda Campbell and her sons Thomas and James. Above all, it is a story about the larger African-American freedom struggle, and about the way that struggle shaped the streets and households of Savannah and the rice and cotton fields of lowcountry Georgia. I first encountered some of the people in this book more than thirty years ago, when I began researching the history of the northern teachers of the Georgia freedpeople in the eight years after the Civil War.[44] At the time I was struck by the speed with which Savannah's black leaders organized a system of schools right after Union general William Tecumseh Sherman captured the city in December 1864; the success of their efforts was no doubt due to the fact that the antebellum community possessed independent black institutions such as mutual aid societies and self-governing Baptist churches. The Savannah case seemed emblematic of a larger story about the former slaves' fight to integrate themselves fully into the nation's body politic, and also to win for themselves some measure of self-determination in their homes, workplaces, churches, and schools. Throughout the South, blacks' religious faith offered a compelling narrative of liberation and redemption, a narrative promoted by strong-willed preachers and teachers in both public and surreptitious settings. The Reverend Andrew Bryan, founder of First African Baptist Church (in 1788), assured his congregants, "God is no respecter of persons, but in every nation he that feareth him and worketh righteousness, is accepted with him."[45]

In the months and years immediately following emancipation, the former slaves and free people of color in Savannah and the Georgia lowcountry aggressively pressed for full citizenship rights; they educated themselves, petitioned the federal government for protection, and eagerly entered the fray of partisan politics. Yet seven years after the end of the Civil War, they lacked political power in any meaningful sense of the word. As a group, they remained impoverished, disenfranchised, and

excluded from jury service, the judiciary, the police force, and local elective offices of all kinds. This book seeks to tell the story of why that
was so.

In the two decades after the capture of Thomas Simms, wealthy white
men of Savannah sought to save the city from economic depression,
pestilence, war, occupation by a hated enemy army, and the destruction of
slavery. But the most compelling challenge faced by these men was to
stave off the forces of equality and democracy sweeping through their
region. To maintain a brutal form of white supremacy, planters, bankers,
cotton factors, merchants, and clergymen were forced to act creatively
and violently, in the process enlisting the support of whites of modest
means. This project was complicated by the fact that Savannah lacked a
white middle class, men and women who might lend respectability to
institutionalized discrimination and outright terror. Yet during the postwar period elites received surprisingly strong validation from an unexpected quarter: the northern missionaries and U.S. government agents
and military officials who for their own reasons sought to stall if not obliterate the drive for black self-determination. Why such divergent groups
of white people found so threatening the quest of blacks for basic forms of
equality and cultural integrity constitutes the heart of this story.

As well as any two individuals perhaps, Thomas and James Simms
demonstrated that, for all their wealth, Savannah's white leaders lacked
absolute power. Together with other African Americans, the brothers
helped to lead a series of civil wars that spilled out of the confines of a single plantation, city, or section of the country. These wars were presaged,
and then ignited, when Thomas Simms found his way onto the *Gilmore,*
and when James Simms found his voice.

-❦| CHAPTER ONE |❦-

Sell and Buy and Sell and Buy

IN EARLY SEPTEMBER 1854, Savannah was diseased, dying. At dusk, tar fires kindled in the public squares threw a plume of acrid smoke into the air, an immense black shroud that settled over the desolate, oppressively hot and humid city. The lush, tree-lined thoroughfares were nearly deserted, the hush broken only by the muffled sounds of a horse-drawn hearse plodding through the sandy streets. The usually raucous marketplace was empty, stately homes were abandoned, schools and hotels shuttered. Many people had fled, most to the interior of Georgia or to the North. Behind closed doors, the ill, unattended, lay side by side with the dead, and in poorer areas of the city, human corpses mingled with refuse piled in back alleyways. Deprived of supplies from either the surrounding countryside or from arriving ships, the river port risked slow starvation. "How changed is our beautiful, growing, healthy city, lately full of enterprise, noise, and business," despaired one of the city's clergymen, exhausted from ministering to the ill. Racked with fever, chills, and convulsions, hundreds of all ages were succumbing to the "black vomit," more commonly known as yellow fever.[1]

Savannah was dying, and Richard Arnold, M.D., could do nothing to stem the plague. The stricken city was in fact playing unwilling and unwitting host to *Aedes aegypti*, the carrier mosquito for yellow fever. Breeding most freely in manmade receptacles such as barrels and culverts, the insect proved the bane of commercial ports from the West African coast to New Orleans. The illness spread rapidly, not because it was contagious but because infected mosquitoes carried it from victim to victim. When the epidemic hit, Arnold was still mourning the death of his thirty-five-year-old wife, Margaret, from tuberculosis four years earlier. Nevertheless, beginning in August 1854, the doctor spent his every wak-

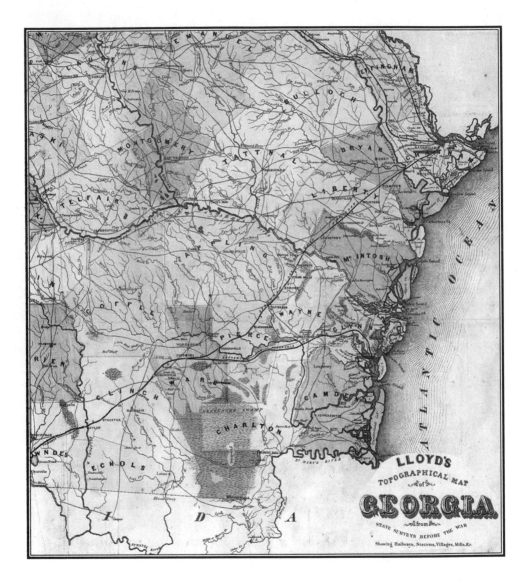

LLOYD'S
TOPOGRAPHICAL MAP
of
GEORGIA
from
STATE SURVEYS BEFORE THE WAR

Showing Railways, Stations, Villages, Mills, &c.

ing hour with patients, crisscrossing the city in his carriage and losing all sense of time. Trying not to panic in the midst of so much misery, he wrote on September 2, "my mind is calm, for I have a duty to perform in staying here." Under these conditions, he believed, the physician was akin to a soldier, albeit one denied the requisite glory: the doctor "goes into the very dens of infection, he inhales the reeking effluvia of filth & disease, *he is most exposed to catch disease himself in those very cases which will bring him neither money nor credit.*"[2]

For forty-six-year-old Richard Arnold, the yellow-fever epidemic of 1854 represented a crisis of multiple dimensions—a crisis destructive not only of the physical and fiscal health of the city he loved, but also of his own good name as a man of science and as an exemplar of civic virtue. Born in Savannah, the son of a Rhode Island merchant, Arnold had graduated from the College of New Jersey (later renamed Princeton University) and received his medical degree from the University of Pennsylvania. Settling in the place of his birth, he served in a variety of elected and appointed posts related to municipal governance and education. Like other elite Savannahians, Arnold well understood that the river port thrived to the extent it could attract not only investors and merchants, but also hundreds of seasonal, unskilled northern workers annually. Yet the city suffered from a stubborn reputation as an unhealthy place plagued by fevers bred in rotting vegetation and polluted water, and by a vaguely defined but lethal form of "miasma," or poisonous air. Savannah's boosters were always on the defensive; some blamed the high mortality rate on large numbers of northern invalids dying an untimely death in the city en route to their final destination in Florida. Now the "yellow jack" epidemic of 1854 threatened not only Savannah's good name, but also its very survival.[3]

Arnold and Savannah's other physicians did well financially in their everyday business. As a group they helped ensure the "soundness" of the enslaved rural coastal population in Chatham, Bryan, Liberty, McIntosh, Glynn, and Camden counties—thirty-five thousand blacks who planted, harvested, and processed vast quantities of cotton and rice each year. Arnold also served as the physician for the region's largest industrial slaveowner, the Central of Georgia Railroad. At the same time, his doctor's salary seemed chronically insufficient to afford him the gracious life of a wealthy merchant, banker, or lawyer, a constant irritant given his appreciation for fine wines, champagne, sherry, sauterne, and Madeira. And now in this disease-ridden city Arnold could not help but wonder why he was putting himself in mortal danger day in and day out, coming face-to-face with failure as he left the home of each dying patient—for *"neither money nor credit."*[4]

In early August, the sickly cast of yellow fever had made its first appearance in Yamacraw, the northeastern neighborhood that was home to many Irish immigrants (70 percent of all foreigners living in Savannah). At the first sign of the outbreak, Arnold and other physicians had joined with politicians, businessmen, and newspaper editors in a public relations campaign that was part wishful thinking and part cynical manipulation. As in past epidemics, they feared that rumors would give way to hysteria, which in turn would lead to a quarantine of all vessels leaving Savannah. The city's trade would be crippled, its archrival Charleston enriched. A correspondent for the *Savannah Morning News* tried to reassure readers with the claim that northeast winds had carried the disease exclusively to newcomers living on the edges of the city in wretched wooden tenements. These were presumably men, women, and children "who do not enjoy the comforts of life, and have no regard for cleanliness." On August 10, Mayor John E. Ward, a former U.S. attorney and prominent Democrat, ordered the board of health to cease listing yellow fever as the cause of death on its mortality reports; the mayor's aim was to protect "the reputation and interest of the city." Richard R. Cuyler, president of the Central of Georgia Railroad and Banking Company, published a letter in the *New York Times* maintaining that of the 392 whites employed by the railroad, almost all continued to "go out and come in, in the night, and many are exposed to the burning sun" without contracting the illness. Like others, Cuyler assumed that both night air and direct sunlight were causes of yellow fever.[5]

Yet the mounting death toll spoke louder than the bland pronouncements uttered by businessmen and parroted in the city's newspapers. By the last week in August a full-blown exodus from the city was under way. The sight of dozens of Savannah families crowded in mail packets going south and in steamer ships headed north laid bare the deep fear that had overtaken the city. Prodded by the outrage spread in whispered street conversations and in newspapers of nearby towns, authorities began to react. Dominick O'Byrne, an alderman and lawyer of Irish descent, offered a resolution authorizing the committee on health and cemeteries to spend a largely symbolic $1,000 for the alleviation of suffering among the city's poor. Meanwhile, the mayor and other leaders found themselves gratefully accepting cash donations from cities as far away as Boston. Contingents of physicians and nurses arrived from Mobile and New Orleans.[6]

Above all else, Savannah's leaders prized prosperity and public order, and on both counts the epidemic was devastating. Not until the late nineteenth century would the medical-scientific establishment link mosquitoes to yellow fever. Still, physicians did know enough to associate deadly illnesses with weed-choked rice-field ditches and with undrained city streets. Indeed, as early as 1817 the city council had established a dry culture committee; its purpose was to pay the owners of private lands adjacent to the city to drain their fields of scum-covered stagnant water. The city also funded a board of health charged with monitoring conditions in each of the city's thirty wards, a health officer to inspect incoming ships for signs of infectious disease among crew members, a scavenger department of black men who cleared the streets of refuse and animal carcasses, a pest house to segregate impoverished ill people from the general population, and a dispensary to distribute medicines to the ailing. Nevertheless, the 1854 epidemic eventually claimed the lives of more than 6 percent of the city's total population—a loss comparable to that of 400,000 lives in New York City today.[7]

Savannah was dying, and whites were its chief victims. To a large degree, lowcountry blacks did not contract mosquito-borne illnesses; the paired genetic trait that made West African groups vulnerable to sickle-cell anemia also provided them with relative immunity to yellow fever and malaria. In caring for the ill, Arnold probably relied on the assistance of black nurses such as forty-three-year-old Georgiana Guard, a free woman of color. Over the previous few years Guard had helped the widower Arnold care for his daughter, Ellen, and he had served as the black woman's guardian. (All free blacks in the city were required to have a white male "guardian" to represent them in legal matters.) During the epidemic, black men and women left food at the doorstep of infected households, and otherwise attended to those bereft of other caretakers. Throughout the ordeal, few Savannahians, enslaved or free, could escape the conclusion that this scourge afflicted primarily white folk.[8]

To add to the city's distress, on September 8 a ferocious hurricane slammed into coastal Georgia. With its fierce winds and torrential rains, the gale was the region's most destructive storm in three decades, ripping off roofs, smashing windows, and leveling the city's exotic mix of jasmines, Spanish daggers, magnolias, palmettos, and Pride of India trees. The streets of the elegant Forest City were now virtually impassable, littered with tree limbs, tin, shingles, and pieces of slate. Disrupted gas service snuffed out the lamps in the two dozen grassy, shaded public squares that dotted the city. On the riverfront, floodwaters carried off whole lumberyards, drove vessels into the wharves, and tore the city's dry dock from its moorings. Across from the city, in the Savannah River, Hutchinson's Island was submerged under twelve feet of water, a watery grave for an estimated one hundred enslaved men, women, and children. Along the Ogeechee River, a center of Georgia's rice industry, the force of wind and water destroyed the intricate systems of embankments, ditches, and dams that regulated irrigation of the fields. Much of the entire region's rice crop was lost, the small amount already harvested carried off by swollen rivers and creeks, the maturing plants choked by rising seawater.[9]

On the morning of Sunday, September 10, throughout the lowcountry enslaved workers slowly emerged from their quarters, small cabins made of wood or tabby (a mixture of oyster shells, lime, and sand), to survey the damage. Up and down the 118-mile coastline, men and women found that their year's worth of work had been destroyed by the storm. On the Elizafield rice plantation in Glynn County, the "Dreadful Gale" had drowned whole fields and "blown and washed away" the entire recent harvest of six thousand bushels of rice. Under dark skies still heavy with heat and moisture, the slaves there and on other plantations spent the day not in their customary way, holding worship services and tending to their own gardens, but toiling in the fields. At Elizafield, Scipio, Frederick, London, and other men labored to repair breaks in the dikes, while Nancy, Matilla, and Mary Ann and other women waded through the boggy soil to salvage what rice was left.[10]

The storm obliterated not only the cash crops of the master class, but also the slaves' vegetable gardens, livestock, and stores of staples—the product of their own strenuous labors in the quarters after they had completed their daily tasks in the fields. Pushed to the limit of human endurance, enslaved families were forced to grow their own rice and corn in order to survive. Some rendered their own lard, kept turkeys and hogs, and crafted quilts, wooden utensils, and baskets. Rainwater and floods carried away beehives, jars of honey, pots, and other goods displayed in neatly swept yards in front of the slave cabins. On many plantations, then, the storm brought a double load of grief to lowcountry slaves—longer days of toil to repair the fields and rescue the rest of the rice and cotton, but also the ruin of their own stores of food and household goods.[11]

Over the next few days with clearing skies came blistering heat. In Savannah, people continued to die. Four days after the storm, a group of prominent men formed the Young Men's Benevolent Association (YMBA). The association set up soup kitchens for the city's poor whites, dispensing bread and serving medicinal teas brewed from snakeroot and flaxseed. Like other private charity groups, the YMBA ignored the black population, on the assumption that masters would care for the city's 7,500 slaves, and that the 900 free people of color were by definition unworthy of aid of any kind. In any case, the fact that relatively few blacks contracted the disease seemed to confirm the notion that they could fend for themselves.[12]

By the end of September, only 12,000 residents remained: an estimated 4,000 whites and almost all of the blacks. Among those who fled were the city marshal, the city constable, and Mayor Ward. An alderman, Dr. James P. Screven, physician, planter, and president of the Savannah, Albany and Gulf Railroad, assumed the position of mayor pro tem. Many of the wealthiest left their slaves behind. Because enslaved men and free men of color formed the core of the city's fire department, few whites objected to the new black majority in their midst. Reeling from the combined effects of illness, floods, and high winds, this city of lumber mills, cotton warehouses, and wooden boardinghouses could ill risk fire as well.[13]

Meanwhile, Richard Arnold stayed at his post, worked twenty-hour days, treated hundreds of patients, and managed to survive. But his triumph was bittersweet at best. The unseemly manner with which some of his colleagues suffered from "*Stampede* Fever" brought disrepute on the whole profession, he thought. In mid-September, he mourned the deaths of "two noble young men," his protégés. The weekly interment reports and obituaries featured names of a cross section of the white population—Burroughs, Sheftall, Hannemeyer, Gallagher. The city's three cemeteries, for Protestants, Catholics, and Jews, were daily engorged with fresh corpses: "Death has had a full harvest," mourned the doctor.[14]

Arnold and his colleagues at Savannah Medical College considered themselves scientists; they dissected cadavers, recorded observations of their patients, and published their findings in journals such as the *Savannah Journal of Medicine* and the *Charleston Medical Journal and Review*. Yet these white men hardly dominated the medical business in Savannah. The city board of health authorized burning tar fires at night and pine fires during the day in an effort to "purify" the sickly air; beyond these measures there existed little agreement about cures for yellow fever. Some people advocated sniffing camphor, taking cold baths in the morning, and lining shoes with garlic. Arnold watched in disgust as a relative newcomer to the city, Dr. Philo H. Wildman, founder of the upstart Georgia General Hospital, prescribed twenty to sixty drops of tincture of iron administered every two hours for his yellow-fever patients. A local paper endorsed Wildman as "a great enemy to quackery in all its forms"; but after he contracted the disease, medicated himself, and then died, his "specific" fell into disfavor.[15]

Arnold also resented a well-established system of medicine dominated by Savannah's African-American women. In the middle of the epidemic, the physician had assumed responsibility for Diana, a slave owned by his friend, the merchant Solomon Cohen. The Cohen family had escaped to Philadelphia, leaving their slaves behind. Suffering from typhoid fever, Diana relied primarily on the care provided by her husband, but after a week and a half, Arnold noted, "some of her Sisters in the Church began to drop in to gossip & to have the impertinence to advise her husband not to give my medicine." Arnold was outraged: the women thought he was trying to kill the patient. (He was probably unfamiliar with a lowcountry song, "Ball the Jack," that told the story of an ill slave woman, Aunt Dinah, who was told by the attending white physician, "Get up Dinah / You ain't sick / All you need / Is a hickory stick.") In treating Diana themselves, the church sisters perhaps prescribed a traditional African-American remedy for typhoid—medicine derived from boneset, a plant that grew in the coastal swamps. These women treated illness as a sign of some specific disruption in the everyday relations among human beings, whether living or dead. Whereas Arnold worked alone to heal, the church sisters visited together; whereas he placed his faith in specific medicines, the church sisters saw health in holistic terms, encompassing the patient's spiritual as well as bodily well-being. Nevertheless, Diana died.[16]

Arnold contended with black healers under his own roof and with "wiseacres" on the street, people who loudly ridiculed his "old-fashioned & prejudiced" cures: bleeding his patients and administering a mercury-based purgative called calomel in an effort to cleanse the body of its "bad" blood and fluids. The hecklers gave voice to a more general breakdown in social order. As the city had grown and prospered over the previous two decades, Savannah's civic leaders sought to restrain their boisterous workforce—slaves, free blacks, and immigrants who hauled lumber, rice, and cotton from flatboat or railroad car to warehouse and processing mill and then loaded it onto ships at the docks. Of the city's regulatory and coercive mechanisms, a northern visitor observed in 1854, "here is strong government," noting its "tonic, bracing effect" upon all residents. In the early fall of 1854, that strong government faltered.[17]

Some people, and not only enterprising purveyors of patent medicines, either turned the disaster to their own advantage or showed callous indifference toward the sufferers. In early September, one of Arnold's own slaves, George, seized upon his master's distracted state of mind and "went off," finding temporary refuge in the labyrinth of Savannah's back alleys and lanes. Elsewhere in the city, landlords unceremoniously tossed destitute widows and children into the streets, prompting the YMBA to place ads in the local paper condemning these "unchristian, unmanly, and inhuman acts." The Right Reverend Francis Xavier Gartland, first bishop of the Catholic diocese of Savannah (and later a victim of the epidemic), warned his parishioners that a "stranger" priest was abroad, a "public scoundrel" who came to prey upon and not to pray with the faithful of Savannah. As foot patrolmen fell ill or left the city, the public police presence melted away. Arsonists and thieves grew bolder. A few intrepid passersby interrupted burglaries in progress in abandoned homes and shops, prompting the robbers to make a hasty exit out windows and back doors.[18]

In mid-October, with the fever still raging, city officials became alarmed at the sight of passenger ships en route from New York and other northern ports bearing loads of foreign immigrants. What was normally a predictable autumn phenomenon, the arrival of Irish from the North and smaller numbers of French Canadians from Quebec, now inspired fear; authorities condemned the newcomers as "adventurers," persons who "have, beyond a doubt, been attracted hither by the hope of reveling in idleness upon the funds which have been so bounteously bestowed for the succor of our own suffering and dying poor." The travelers were welcome to use the city as a way station on their trip to the Georgia interior; but for those who tarried, "*to stay is death*; let it be proclaimed to all who follow them, that *to come is death!* DEATH!! nothing but DEATH!!!" The city of boosters now publicized itself as a vast graveyard.[19]

Gradually the epidemic abated. At the end of October, authorities began to take stock: a total of 1,049 dead, 943 whites and 106 blacks. Almost two-thirds were natives of foreign countries, most of them Irish. The city's economy lay in shambles; the value of cotton shipped from the interior to Savannah via the Central Railroad had fallen by more than half in September and October 1854 compared to the same period the year before. More broadly, the epidemic sparked an intense, ongoing debate over its causes and meanings. Observers variously cited the unseasonably hot weather; mud dredged from the Savannah River and piled on the wharves; rotting vegetation and animal carcasses in and near the city; the open privies and "unaccountable amount of filth" in the poorest neighborhoods; and ill seamen aboard the Danish ship *Charlotte Hague*, moored at one of the city docks. And what lessons did white Savannahians learn from this disaster? The YMBA lauded the generosity of spirit, at home and elsewhere, that produced nearly $60,000 in contributions to its relief fund. The council authorized construction of a new drainage system to replace the open sewers that coursed through the streets. Up and down the coast white people exhorted each other, "Let us try & live more worthy of God's mercy." The Reverend Thomas Rambaut, pastor of the First Baptist Church, took to task city residents awash in arrogance, those who wished desperately for Savannah to become the "depot of a great trade," those who believed that the dry culture committee or the board of health could stem God's will as expressed through "the Saffron Monster." Rambaut asked, "Have we not in this city provoked God by pride?" Richard Arnold drew his own conclusion: "the epidemic has convinced me how utterly impossible it is for the white Race to do the outdoor work in this hot climate."[20]

Over the next two and a half years Savannah and the lowcountry would struggle with the aftershocks of widespread illness and physical devastation, a struggle that took place in the midst of a rapidly shifting political landscape. The city, already burdened by rapid population growth, found itself squeezed between declining revenues due to crippled business activity and increased costs associated with the storm and epidemic—the extraordinary expenses of digging paupers' graves, installing a new sewer system, repairing public buildings, and planting new trees in the city's now denuded public squares. Recent municipal improvements, including gas street lamps and public waterworks, were proving costly to maintain. In the early fall, the city council went ahead with plans to open Savannah's first free school, intended to get poor white children off the streets. Funded with city, county, and state money, this venture was a noble one, local leaders agreed, but also an unwelcome financial commitment considering the city's limited resources.[21]

Throughout coastal Georgia, the epidemic left in its wake a collective outpouring of grief. The afflictions visited upon the Charles Colcock Jones family of Liberty County were emblematic of the losses suffered by wealthy white households. The Joneses were part of a thick tangle of inbred planter kin networks. Together with the Dunwodys, Mallards, Quartermans, Maybanks, and Robarts, they were notable for the cousin marriages suggested by their names—Maybank Jones, Dunwody Jones, Charles Colcock Mallard. A prominent slaveowner-planter and Presbyterian minister, the Reverend Charles Colcock Jones had gained renown for his conviction that white Southerners should instruct their slaves in Christianity—or rather, in a peculiar form of Christianity that justified the raw exploitation of one group of people by another. Jones's duty, as he saw it, was to further "the peace and order of society" by preaching among the slaves a gospel of obedience to "all those whom God, in his providence, has placed in authority over them." He himself was painfully aware of all the ways his enslaved listeners rejected the message—by stomping out of his sermons, by conducting their own worship services at night, by daily rejecting his pleas for enforced servility. Nevertheless, he persisted in reaching out to his white neighbors, even "ungodly planters," assuring them that they could make more money from a slave who believed in God.[22]

In the aftermath of the September storm, Jones's own enslaved work-force, by this time well catechized, was forced to contend with the damage to the family's three Liberty County plantations—the flattened cotton house, barn, and shuck house at Monte Video (near the Newport River) and corn house and rice house at Arcadia (at the village of Midway); the downed trees and broken windows at Maybank (just inland from St. Catherines Island); the ruined rice crops at all three places. At Maybank, the Joneses set the talented seamstress Phoebe to rubbing the damp and mildew from the household's extensive library of books.[23]

For Jones and his wife, Mary (who was also his first cousin), it was the deaths of so many in their wider circle of kin and friends that made this a season of darkness. In the words of Mary Jones: "The Angel of Death has visited and swept every class." Studying law at Harvard, their dutiful son Charles Junior took to heart the sad letters from home chronicling in fulsome detail the "weeping and lamentation" that echoed through the Rice Kingdom. Surely, the younger Jones wrote, the region's tribulations could only be compared with "that dread night of sorrow when the Death Angel passed over and smote all the firstborn in the land of Egypt," a time when "*there was not one house where there was not one dead.*"[24]

Mourners' lamentations were not confined to the city of Savannah that fall and early winter. One day in December, on a plantation on Argyle Island (eight miles north in the Savannah River), a young man named Abel Hunt writhed on the ground, calling out in his grief for his recently deceased mother and father. Abel apparently could see and hear his parents, and so he sang a plaintive funeral hymn to comfort them or perhaps to placate them in their anger. Old George and his wife had shed their earthly shells, but in the eyes of their son and the other slaves on Argyle Island, the departed continued to inhabit the land of the living, keeping sorrow alive. Abel's grief was compounded by the deaths of six of his other relatives, men, women, and children. All were members of the thirteen-person extended Hunt family recently bought and brought to two Argyle Island plantations, Gowrie and East Hermitage (not far from James Potter's holdings), both owned by a wealthy Charleston planter, Charles Manigault. Charles and his son Louis, the plantation manager, seemed mystified by Abel's anguish. The young black man they considered "almost like a Crazy person," his wailing a source of anxiety for the other slaves, and a severe breach in plantation discipline.[25]

In the rice swamps, the enslaved working population was always dying. In the fall of 1854, the September hurricane led to even more deaths. White visitors to the region were constantly reassured that the slaves who labored in the rice fields enjoyed "uninterrupted health." Certainly blacks' relative immunity to mosquito-borne malaria and yellow fever bolstered white perceptions, both popular and scientific, that, in Richard Arnold's words, only blacks were able "to do the outdoor work in this hot climate." Yet rice cultivation was hazardous by any standard. Slaves were forced to maintain networks of ditches and canals, working in the wet, mucky fields to plant, weed, and harvest the crop, and in the frozen wetlands during the winter to repair dams and embankments. "It is awful work," recalled one former enslaved rice hand, John Brown. In the summer, the stench was unbearable, as "muddy soil . . . sends up the foulest smell and vapour," and the water, reflecting intense sunlight, "is intolerably painful, frequently bringing on giddiness and sunstroke. Then the feet get water-poisoned, or you take the toe or ground-itch, when the flesh cracks and cankers." Chiggers burrowed into the skin, "causing a great lump to swell up, and an unendurable irritation." Snakes and other water reptiles lurked under the marshy grasses and bit bare legs and feet.[26]

In the humid swamps, slaves fell prey to bacteria and viruses transmitted to humans from mosquitoes, flies, rats, and waterborne protozoa. Cholera, hepatitis, typhoid, dysentery, and scarlet fever afflicted slaves of all ages. The proximity of privies to sources of drinking water produced intestinal diseases that carried off large numbers of people. (Not surprisingly, many planters either lived elsewhere year-round, or deserted the lowcountry in the hottest months for higher ground and cooler climes.) Work in the damp fields in the winter as well as summer months led to high rates of tuberculosis and other respiratory diseases among enslaved workers. Pregnant women were forced to continue to stand and walk, and to hoe, carry, and thresh rice for up to ten hours a day through their second trimester. The rice fields were killing fields, producing high rates of miscarriage. Exhausted new mothers came under stern pressure from planters to wean their infants at an early age, thus depriving babies of the women's natural antibodies. And few infants could survive a steady diet of dirty drinking water.[27]

Rice planters sought to replenish their workforces periodically with slaves bought on the open market. Elsewhere in the South owners could often count on natural reproduction to add to the numbers of their bound laborers. Not so in lowcountry Georgia. During the first seven years of East Hermitage, 115 slaves died and less than a third of that number were born. Between 1833 and 1855, the infant mortality rate at Gowrie was 89 percent. These grim facts of life and death held true for the entire region; black babies born to a rice-slave mother had only a slight chance of survival. It was no wonder that many Gullah-Geechee mothers lived in perpetual fear of the malevolent spirits they believed haunted the slave quarters.[28]

Near the coast, rising floodwaters from the September hurricane introduced disease-causing bacteria into plantation drinking supplies, a problem exacerbated on the Savannah River by "freshets," or floods, that swept down from the interior of the state to the sea. That fall, rains and record high tides submerged Savannah River plantations under saltwater, the worst flood in fifty years, coating fields and living quarters with foul-smelling mud. The Manigaults' two Argyle Island plantations lost fully three-quarters of the year's rice crop, harvesting just 8,000 bushels instead of the anticipated 32,000 that fall. It was about this time that Abel and other members of the extended Hunt family had begun work at Gowrie, sold by a South Carolina Pee Dee River planter to Charles Manigault for an average of $800 each.[29]

Among the family were the nineteen-year-old twins, Cain and Abel, their sisters Nancy and Fanny, and their mother and their father, Old George, a "trunk minder" who maintained the drainage system in the fields. Charles Manigault considered the Hunts a "truly fine family & well worth" the money he paid for them, but they proved a poor investment; eight of the thirteen family members had died within the year, half of them from what the Manigaults called the "Asiatic cholera" of December 1854. Most of the slaves who perished in that Argyle Island epidemic probably succumbed to some sort of enteric disease; their symptoms included diarrhea and fever, suggesting a chronic illness exacerbated by polluted floodwater coursing through the rice-field ditches. On December 10 the Manigaults had brought in a physician, William G. Bulloch of

Savannah, and soon afterward they began to move all their slaves to an upland camp in the pine woods nine miles from Savannah. Bulloch blamed some of the deaths on the slaves themselves, for not obeying his orders to refrain from eating: "negroes! they will overeat themselves." As for the deaths of the babies more generally, the overseer thought it "more the mother fault than any thing else[,] buy night Leting them get uncovered in those coold nights of last week."[30]

Now separated by two hundred miles from his kin who remained on the Pee Dee River plantation, Abel suffered the shock of dislocation, uprooted from the place he considered home. At Gowrie, he witnessed the deaths of babies, young adults, middle-aged, and elderly alike, surely a catastrophe in any small community. Suddenly bereft of the persons closest to him, including his twin brother, he could only speculate on the causes of his own misfortune—another man or woman at this strange new place, a conjurer intent on doing him harm? He mourned the loss of a familiar community—his extended kinfolk, the established healers and preachers. The uneasy spirits of the recently deceased would continue to roam the Gowrie and East Hermitage plantations, though no white person could see or feel them. Meanwhile, the Manigaults rendered the stench of death in terms of dollars lost. Recording the loss of thirteen people (out of a total of one hundred) in December, Louis noted they were "Slaves no longer on the Plantation Books."[31]

In Savannah, the yellow-fever epidemic claimed its first political casualties during the fall municipal elections. A substantial number of mourners were also voters, resentful of city officials' initial efforts to downplay the severity of the crisis. And so in November, mayor John E. Ward lost his bid for reelection, and nine of twelve aldermen were replaced (though several of the newly elected had held the office previously). Still, the turnover revealed little about the vitality of the Democratic party per se: the Democrats were supreme, but bitterly divided.

During the early 1850s, the demise of the nationalistic Whig Party had strengthened the Democrats' hold over Georgia politics in cities like Savannah and in the state's rural hinterland. Richard D. Arnold, long drawn to those elements of Whig ideology that associated commercial trade with prosperity, abandoned that party and joined the Democrats in 1852. Arnold had rejected calls in 1850 for the South to secede from the Union; like other members of Savannah's elite, he believed the city's economy was too dependent on foreign and domestic trade to indulge the overheated rhetoric of a few South Carolina slaveholders who were alarmed by the emerging congressional power of northern states. The

Democrats stood for the white laboring classes and for slavery, for "progress," profits, and states' rights. Who among white men could object?[32]

Nevertheless, Democratic campaign slogans masked the enduring challenge of the party's elite: how to maintain the support of the poor-white laboring classes in the larger project of white supremacy within a vibrant commercial economy. No sleepy backwater, Savannah served as the financial center for the Georgia cotton boom, and eagerly invested tax-payers' money in railroads, banks, and internal improvements. The white population of the port was relatively diverse in terms of ethnic and religious identities. Interlocking networks of wealthy Protestant families dominated lowcountry politics and economics, yet those few families shared power with anyone rich enough to exploit enslaved workers and to afford the French bonnets, silk umbrellas, and leather-bound books sold at the city's exclusive shops. Among the city's Jews were the prosperous descendants of the original settlers of 1733. The Russell family—siblings Philip and Waring, and Philip's sons Isaac and Philip Junior—constituted an increasingly influential bloc in the city's politics. The siblings Octavus and Solomon Cohen and Moses and Joseph Solomons all hailed from South Carolina, but gained prominence in the rarefied circles of Savannah's elite. A few well-to-do Catholics, some native-born and some immigrants, also wielded influence in factorage houses, banks, attorneys' offices, and dry-goods stores. Many German and Irish laborers—who by 1860 made up about half of the total white population of the city—further distinguished Savannah from the more homogeneous countryside, where native-born Protestants predominated.

At the same time, to put the matter bluntly, Savannah possessed only one class, the very wealthy. (Here a class is defined as a group of people who not only recognize their own collective interests but are capable of acting upon them.) Though they represented perhaps only 1 percent or so of the city's population, Savannah's bankers, planters, railroad officials, physicians, attorneys, merchants, and cotton factors controlled the local government—but only as long as they could maintain the support of the white laborers who were their constitutents. And many of these workers—probably hundreds—were highly transient, coming south for the winter and spring months to work on the docks and raise hell in the poor neighborhoods of Old Fort and Yamacraw. The richest Savannahians were forced to acknowledge that they owed not just their livelihood but also their political power to the poorest whites in the city.[33]

Savannah had long boasted volunteer associations that promoted fellow feeling among all whites by knitting together the white stevedores and merchants, the Protestants and Jews and Catholics, and the recent immigrants and long-established families. The Union Society and the Needle Woman's Society offered venues for wealthy men and women, respectively, to ameliorate some of the social ills flowing naturally from an economy that relied on such a large proportion of seasonal, low-wage workers. Social groups such as the Hibernians and the Irish Union Society included men of Irish descent, regardless of income. The Catholic Church counted among its parishioners the native-born as well as German and Irish immigrants. Volunteer militia companies and fire companies gave expression to male bravado and a peculiarly southern martial spirit. Jury service brought together white male citizens from all walks of life—laborers, shipping masters, carpenters, dry-goods merchants' clerks, police officers, and grocers hailing from other states and from western Europe. But the Democratic Party represented the most successful cross-sectional alliance of all, a testament to the mutual if wildly unequal dependence of the planter-merchant-lawyer elite on large numbers of teamsters, dockworkers, and sawmill hands.[34]

City Democrats were virtually unbeatable. But in fact the party was deeply divided between those men who advocated turning a blind eye on grog-shop owners and profaners of the Sabbath, and those who insisted on rigorous public enforcement of personal morality. Richard Arnold, a self-interested authority on local politics if there ever was one, stated the cardinal rule of Savannah politics: "The Mayor and & [city] Marshall . . . regulate the shopkeepers politically by *not* regulating them as to the Law." In other words, the way to appeal to immigrants and laborers was to allow them considerable leeway in their off-hours behavior, as long as they remained steady and sober on the job. The fact of the matter was that economic prosperity came at the expense of public order.[35]

In the mid-1850s the moralistic reformers were joined by the Know-Nothings, a small but rising political party that resented the zeal with which Irish immigrants in particular had entered the ranks of the Democratic Party and received in return jobs as public-works laborers and police officers. Of Savannah's immigrant Democratic faithful, one observer noted sardonically, "In a twinkling, he masters the science of government and winds his way without a light through all the labyrinths of politics." Indeed, the Irish proved adept at Savannah's political game. In order to vote in municipal elections, a white man had only to be twenty years old, a resident of the state of Georgia for one year, and a resident of Savannah for four months. Overlapping Catholic and Irish constituen-

cies used their numbers to good advantage at the ballot box. The ranks of
the city aldermen included at least one Catholic every year between 1849
and 1877; wealthy men like Dominick O'Byrne served as cultural and
political mediators between the Irish working class and the Protestant
elite. Spurred by famine back home, in the late 1840s and early 1850s an
upsurge in Irish immigration translated into many new names on Savannah's list of registered voters. As a group, the Irish readily joined in
election-day clashes, their weapon of choice the shillelagh in contrast to
the bowie knife, brick, and pistol favored among raucous native-born
voters.[36]

At the same time, holding public office remained the purview of relatively few men, a tight-knit directorate of merchants, bankers, planters,
physicians, and lawyers. From 1850 to 1860, of the 143 slots for mayor and
twelve aldermen each year, only 136 different men ran for office. Drawn
mostly from the 13 percent of adult whites who owned slaves, three-
fourths of the candidates identified themselves as Democrats. An at-large
system of representation defused the power of any one of the city's neighborhoods, with the exception of the downtown brick-walled compounds
of the wealthy. Some prominent families created intergenerational dynas-
ties of great political influence. White voters from the poorer neighborhoods rarely set the agenda for any municipal election.[37]

Members of a loose coalition called the People's Party, or Reform
Party, seized upon the multiple traumas of the fall of 1854 to gain control
of the city. Ironically, John Ward, the outgoing mayor, had been something of a reformer himself; the centerpiece of his 1853–54 administration
was the swift and unforgiving enforcement of the Sunday blue laws,
which mandated that all business activity, and all drinking of spirits, cease
on the Sabbath. Ward had also helped to organize a new, mounted police
patrol force. The reformers taking office in December 1854 aimed to
extend Ward's program by cracking down on vices such as brawling in
the streets, trading with slaves, and selling liquor without a license. However, over the next few months, the new mayor, Edward C. Anderson,
provoked an outcry among voters who charged him with overreaching;
apparently even little old white ladies serving sherry in their parlors on
Sunday afternoons were not safe from the long arm of the mayor's law.
Anderson, a forty-year-old native of Savannah and recently retired navy
lieutenant, also beefed up the police force and pressed for the licensing of
all slaves who worked as porters and draymen without the supervision of
their owners.[38]

Anderson targeted the illicit businesses with which Irish and German workers, employers, and shopkeepers supplemented their legitimate livelihoods. These businesses thrived because the demand for their services was high. Forced to grow their own food, rice slaves were eager to market their small surpluses in town, and exchange those surpluses for clothing and alcohol via a lively underground economy. Some enterprising boardinghouse owners made a living by "abducting" disgruntled seamen and then helping them find employment elsewhere, a practice that gave the city a bad name among ship captains up and down the East Coast. Some shop owners facilitated the hiring or "entertaining" of runaway slaves. Savannah was a favorite destination among coastal fugitives, and labor-hungry dock masters and housewives were inclined to employ any able-bodied black person they could find, no questions asked, no identification papers or passes required. After a hard day's work on the wharves, at the railroad depot, or in a sawmill, laborers retreated to Yamacraw in Oglethorpe ward, or Currytown in the southwestern part of the city, eager to slake their thirst with a pint of ale, or to risk their hard-earned wages on a game of dice. Their compatriot shopkeepers were more than willing to provide liquor and a fiddler's tune, and perhaps a prostitute as well, for evening or Sabbath-day customers. Late-night carousing was presumably the province of white workingmen, for all blacks were supposed to abide by a curfew, 8 p.m. in the winter and an hour later in the summer. Yet the police force was neither numerous nor vigilant enough to enforce the curfew. Indeed, Savannah's commercial spirit remained stubbornly resistant to traditional southern hierarchies that were meant to enforce, and reinforce, caste lines between white and black, free and slave.[39]

For the most part, city elites tried to accommodate themselves to the disreputable, disruptive behavior of immigrants and other poor whites, and to keep those men within the white-supremacist fold. The formal site of this accommodation was the Exchange, a building on the bay built in 1799 and home to various municipal offices. Fittingly, the structure resembled a church, with a portico, steeple, and bell tower, signifying a place where city officials worshipped the spirit of enterprise.

Throughout the 1850s, the city council, composed of twelve aldermen and the mayor, routinely devoted the beginning of their biweekly meetings to a curious ritual: after the council president gaveled the meeting to order, members settled back and prepared for the evening's entertainment—lawbreakers recently convicted in mayor's court were appealing their fines. (Convening his "court" daily, the mayor had the authority to impose fines on individuals arrested for minor crimes.) Typically, the defendants had surnames such as Egan, Kelly, and Gleason. They represented a cross section not of the Savannah population, but of the city's Irish immigrants, hailing from the counties of Limerick, Cork, Donegal, Roscommon, Galway, Kerry. Some, like Patrick Gleason, a fifty-five-year-old from Limerick, were laborers, but most operated modest businesses in the city—John McAuliffe, thirty-five, from Cork, was a grocer and barroom keeper; and William Dunn, twenty-seven, from Roscommon, the keeper of a seaman's boardinghouse. The defendants were charged with "entertaining" seamen deserters and slave runaways; with serving alcohol to blacks after curfew, fencing stolen goods, keeping a brothel, making a ruckus on the Sabbath. And many of the witnesses testifying against the defendants, in mayor's court and later before the council, were policemen, Irish immigrants themselves.[40]

The evening's real drama came in the form of the "defense" offered by each man's attorney. Among the lawyers representing these men were John McPherson Berrien, former judge of the Eastern Circuit Court of Georgia, state senator, U.S. senator (1825–29, 1841–52), and attorney general under President Andrew Jackson; Alexander R. Lawton, president of the Augusta and Savannah Railroad (1849–54); Edward J. Harden, former judge of the city court; and Mordecai Sheftall, an officer in the local U.S. Custom House. These distinguished attorneys predictably defended their clients by offering a spirited if spurious defense, a variation on the theme that the apprehension itself violated local or state law. In representing John F. Tucker, convicted of disorderly conduct and resisting arrest, Berrien "stated that he considered the arrest illegal, being made in obedience to an illegal order emanating from the Mayor, and the defendant had a right to resist it." In another case, Harden argued against the $100 fine levied on a shipping master, twenty-five-year-old Christopher Hussey (for "enticing and harbouring seamen from the barque *Mary E. Dunworth*"), by claiming "that the council had no jurisdiction, inasmuch as the Constitution requires every criminal to be tried by a jury of his peers." In response to this novel view, one alderman proceeded to read aloud an 1849 statute from the Laws of Georgia authorizing city courts to handle routine petty crimes. The council then voted to confirm Hussey's fine.[41]

Hearings like these were actually highly charged political rituals. The lawyers performed a "defense" of men and women of the white laboring and petty-proprietor classes, and urged the aldermen—their own peers, not the peers of the defendants—to drop the charges or at least reduce the fines. Many of the attorneys had political ambitions. In 1855, Lawton, for example, had just completed a stint as railroad president and launched a campaign for the state legislature; he served as representative from 1855 to 1856 and as senator from 1859 to 1860. At the same time, for any aspiring politician, these performances could be problematic when the strategy relied on impeaching the testimony of an Irish police officer. Policemen received half of each fine levied on the men and women they arrested; a successful appeal deprived the arresting officer of that income. Aldermen were unpredictable in passing judgment on defendants who managed to retain savvy, well-connected counsel. Yet these rituals allowed elites to curry favor among potential constituents, immigrants accused of petty crimes.

Not everyone relished this biweekly city council charade. Joining the offices of former mayor John Ward in early 1855, the newly minted lawyer Charles Colcock Jones Jr. found himself serving as defense counsel to poor Catholic immigrants. To his sister Mary, Jones confided a recent disappointing encounter with a client and complained that "the Irish were not to be trusted." Possessed of a strong streak of self-righteousness, Charles had inherited his minister father's anti-Catholicism. "What a religion for the masses is popery!" the senior Jones had exclaimed at one point. "It is a religion that . . . rules them by superstition and brute force, sanctifies them in sin, and gives them rigorous lords, temporal and spiritual, and no redemption save by revolution." As an aspiring politician, however, Charles confined his views on Irish Catholics to his inner family circle.[42]

White laborers were not the only group to resist the elites' fervent call for public order and decorum. Slaves and free blacks consistently and openly challenged efforts to subordinate them. And the new year of 1855 brought an impending disaster: the rumored sailing of a ship sponsored by the American Colonization Society (ACS) from the port of Savannah to Liberia. Founded in 1817, the ACS sponsored the removal of American blacks to an American colony in West Africa, Monrovia (later, after freedom in 1847, the Republic of Liberia). The founders of the ACS maintained that, regardless of the value of slavery as an institution, blacks and whites simply could not live in America together. In the northern states, many abolitionists scorned the ACS, claiming that the society catered to the prejudices of whites rather than promoting the welfare of blacks. Black leaders in particular reacted defensively against the ACS. Though they often affixed the name "African" to their independent churches and schools, they did not renounce their quest for American citizenship, nor did they consider themselves a "race" yearning to settle in a putative homeland that they had never seen. As early as 1832, in New Brunswick, New Jersey, a well-educated young black man, Tunis G. Campbell, formed an anti-colonization society and spent the next two decades condemning the ACS and declaring "never to leave this country until every slave was free on American soil."[43]

From its founding, the ACS had claimed among its active Georgia supporters both blacks and whites. Yet the nature of that support was complicated. Some free people of color hoped to sponsor Christian missions to benighted Liberians, American and African-born. Among the earliest Savannah black Baptists were Loyalists who left the United States after the American Revolution and founded similar congregations in Canada, the Caribbean, and later, the first ACS colony, Sierra Leone. Subsequent generations of black Georgians also saw the ACS as a vehicle for proselytizing. In 1851, a forty-year-old slave, a Methodist named Hardy Mobley, expressed alarm that the black Baptists of Augusta, Georgia, had started a missionary society that attracted donations from members of his own denomination; he was hoping to begin a rival Methodist society that would send its own missionary "to africa to preach to the people of that Land." Within two years, Mobley had earned $5,000 through his work as a porter and through his appeals to "friends" of the ACS, implying if not promising that he himself and his family would go to Liberia as missionaries. Mobley used the money to buy himself and his enslaved wife, Susan, and their two daughters; then he immediately moved his family to Brooklyn, where they betrayed their sponsors and made a new life for themselves.[44]

Some Georgia masters and mistresses, some suffering lifelong pangs of conscience and others undergoing deathbed conversions, manumitted their slaves, who were then forcibly dispatched to Africa. By the 1850s, Georgia had passed increasingly harsh laws to discourage such manumissions as well as the in-migration of free people of color. Slaves who managed to purchase themselves and family members confronted a terrible dilemma: to make the dangerous voyage to Liberia, only to risk death by starvation or tribal warfare once they got there; or to find refuge in the North; or to face reenslavement in Georgia. Still, the successful emigration of some black Savannahians—including men who had worked their way up to prosperity and to positions of leadership in Liberia—inspired others to go. In the late 1840s, Charles DeLaMotta, an enslaved ship carpenter, had eagerly embraced the role of ACS agent in Savannah, selling subscriptions to the society's journal, *African Repository*. By that time his own wife, Martha, had moved to Liberia, where she was, in his words, "injoying hur freedom in a free land, which affords me much plesur." Of all southern states, Georgia claimed the third-highest number of emigrants to Liberia (behind Virginia and North Carolina); and between the late 1840s and the mid-1850s, Savannah served as embarkation point for nearly one thousand emigrants bound for the African country.[45]

Meanwhile, white Savannah was losing its patience with the triumphant send-offs that had become a hallmark of ACS departures. In 1849 the noisy farewell for the ACS-sponsored ship *Huma* had caused consternation among authorities, who vowed to prevent a similar occurrence in the future. On May 15 of that year, a crowd of blacks, estimated at several thousand, had assembled to see 117 emigrants off at the dock. The festivities included a round of speeches, and a steamship bearing two local black church choirs and a band accompanying the *Huma* on its way down the river to the sea. Whites were appalled by the spectacle. One self-described "citizen and a slaveholder" suggested in a letter to a local paper "that *forever hereafter in this city*, no such furor and excitement among our blacks, free or slave, should be allowed to be gotten up." The writer objected to the fact that prospective emigrants had spent several days in the city waiting for the ship to arrive; they had "been swaggering among our black population, to no benefit of the morals of the latter, you may be assured." The thousands of "negro idlers huzzahing to negro harangues, and shouting to Yankee Doodle from a band of music" did little but inspire in other black men and women "a very improper dissatisfaction" with their lot in life. In response to the *Huma* incident, a grand jury convened and recommended the city forbid free people of color from sailing from Savannah; but the council demurred, reluctant to interfere with the crews of ships coming in and out of the port.[46]

The ACS's *General Pierce* did sail from Savannah on January 5, 1855, and its departure revealed a tangle of motivations among the emigrants and their patrons. A master in Columbus, Georgia, stipulated in his will that his own children, conceived with an enslaved woman, be sent to Liberia; he did not want his offspring sold into slavery after his death. The wealthy Liberty County planter-politician Charlton Hines enlisted the help of his neighbor, the Reverend Charles Jones, in soliciting $1,500 from local citizens to free the carpenter Harry Bacon, owned by Thomas Mallard. Hines intended to send several of his own slaves, including Harry's wife and seven children, to Liberia.[47]

Over the years Harry Bacon had struggled mightily to earn enough money to free himself, but in the winter of 1854 he was still short $450 of his purchase price. His story highlights the lowcountry enslaved men and women who by hard work might eventually earn enough money to buy themselves and their families. Neither planters nor city masters could afford to waste talent with impunity, and they allowed some slaves considerable latitude in making money. Cato Keating, a slave who worked as an engineer for two Savannah rice mills, won at least grudging respect from his master and other whites; they "looked upon [him] as a very responsible man." His master granted him a weekly allowance of $4. His wife, a washerwoman, also earned modest sums. The couple managed to buy hogs, selling them for a profit: "sell and buy and sell and buy" was Keating's motto.[48]

The slaves Hardy Mobley, Harry Bacon, and Cato Keating sought to control and profit from their own labor. That spirit of enterprise extended to many free people of color as well. Born in 1823 to a woman who had been freed by her master, the Liberty County blacksmith Tony Axon plied his trade and earned $20 per month. He put away half that sum, "as living was cheap in the country." Axon opened his own shop in the town of Riceboro, and purchased land from another black man who was moving to Liberia. Known for the high quality of his work, the blacksmith gained the patronage of prominent planters; by the 1850s he had accumulated an impressive amount of livestock, tools, clothes, and household belongings. Edward J. Delegal, a planter-physician, owned Axon's wife, Nellie, and allowed her to buy and sell things as she pleased. Years later, Tony Axon would exclaim of his own holdings, "I got this property by the sweat of my brow, hard licks, Sir!"[49]

Though relatively small in number—only 900 documented in the mid-1850s (12 percent of the city's black, and 5 percent of the total population)—Savannah's free blacks demonstrated entrepreneurial impulses that whites well understood but tolerated only grudgingly. The city was Georgia's center of free black population (about 20 percent of the state's total of 2,932 in 1850), and these men and women were integrated fully into the local economy; indeed, the men were overrepresented among skilled artisans. Prominent in the building trades was Isaac Deveaux, like James M. Simms a carpenter. Simon Mirault, descended from French-speaking émigrés from St. Domingue, was a bricklayer; by 1852 he had made enough money to build his family a snug but substantial story-and-a-half frame house in Troup Ward, a rapidly expanding area in the southern part of the city. Jackson Sheftall came from an extended family of butchers. Active in the city's transportation economy were draymen such as Andrew C. Marshall, pastor of First African Baptist Church, and Jeremiah Kelly, who in the late 1850s took as his bride the nurse Georgiana

Guard. Isaac Deveaux, Simon Mirault, and Jackson Sheftall were so light-skinned that they were not readily identifiable as members of Savannah's lower caste of "black" people. Their light color revealed that they shared far more with elite whites than a spirit of enterprise. Indeed, many free blacks, in addition to the Sheftalls, carried the names of prominent slave-owners who were their own but routinely unacknowledged kin—the Middletons, DeLaMottas, Gouldings, Laws.[50]

Yet even the most financially secure free person of color was subjected to the indignities of guardianship. For example, the patriarch of a wealthy family, Anthony Odingsells, had received a bequest of land and slaves from his former owner. Now in the mid-1850s, the sixty-five-year-old Odingsells owned Little Wassaw Island, consisting of two thousand acres, as well as considerable livestock. He sold large quantities of meat, milk, hides, and wool in the Savannah market. Like all free people of color, he and his family had to register with city authorities annually and have their names, along with the names of their guardians, published in local newspapers. Odingsells managed to conduct his plantation opera-tions without oversight from a white man, though he had a formal guardian. But many would-be black entrepreneurs ran up against laws that restricted their ability to own and operate certain kinds of busi-nesses, including grogshops and groceries.[51]

Anthony Odingsells listed himself as a "planter," and by the 1850s he owned thirteen slaves, a relatively large number that suggests that, like his white counterparts, he saw human bondage primarily as a system of labor exploitation. In 1850, eighteen free people of color in Savannah owned a total of thirty-six slaves, but those numbers dwindled in the course of the decade, reflecting increasing restrictions on the kinds of property that free blacks could own. (In 1830, twenty-nine free people of color in Savannah had owned a total of eighty-two slaves.) In the lowcountry, slaves were a means to more efficient businesses of all kinds; and some people of color abided by those facts of economic life. And yet the precise meaning of black slaveholders remains elusive; some might have owned kin who, if freed, would have been forced to migrate out of state or to Liberia. For these families, bondage was a means of preserving family connections in the face of increasingly harsh state legislation that aimed to curtail the numbers of free blacks.[52]

Thus the lines between slavery and freedom blurred; regardless of their legal status, all persons identifiable by their African heritage shared a harsh reality imposed by the caste system. During her visit to the city in the mid-1850s, the Englishwoman Barbara Bodichon elicited divergent though revealing responses from the free people of color she talked to. One woman said, "I'd rather live all my days on a crust of bread as I am than be a slave. I was born free." But other blacks considered their guardian to be a "nominal owner," and so, in Bodichon's words, felt "it is hardly worth while to be free—the laws are so hard on them now." Slaves and free blacks intermarried and worshipped and worked together, their households and workplaces testaments to the proximity of bondage and freedom. Yet while blacks enslaved and free shared the liabilities of caste, many also shared with middling whites the desire to operate small businesses and to thrive accordingly.[53]

People of color born free were immune to the state laws that decreed that any slave freed by himself or herself or by a master must leave the state or face reenslavement. Anthony Sherman, a Savannah slave liberated through the efforts of the ACS, noted the "Stir about Liberia" among "a great many who is trying to purchase themselves and cannot remaine after they have finish payed." For many enslaved men and women, then, emigration was a necessary consequence of purchased freedom. And so prominent on the *General Pierce* passenger list of January 1855 were wheelwrights, blacksmiths, and carpenters, men who, like Bob Brewer, had earned a considerable amount of cash "for the purchase of his children and relations—& done it with almost a lifetime's labor and self-denial." Slaveholders were willing to put a price tag on almost anything, even the freedom of a few skilled slaves.[54]

For a tiny number of Georgia blacks, ACS sponsorship provided an escape from slavery; yet unlike Thomas Simms, Liberia-bound emigrants had no choice but to abandon the country of their birth in the hope of an uncertain future in an alien land. For whites, the sailing of the *General Pierce* signified a host of ominous developments: the continued, if limited, success of a national organization devoted to liberating enslaved men and women; the collusion in that project of slaveowners who were at least ambivalent about the institution of bondage; the strenuous efforts of some slaves to free themselves; and the out-migration of skilled and talented tradesmen valuable to a growing economy.

As the year 1854 receded into the past, many Georgians were inclined to bid it a less than fond farewell. For one cruel season, the yellow-fever epidemic of late summer and early fall had brought a degree of suffering to lowcountry whites that enslaved laborers endured year in and year out. Indeed, in the Rice Kingdom, the prosperity of a few rested on a foundation of human misery among the many. Meanwhile in Savannah, commercial activity spawned the constant threat of disorder in the grogshops and alleys of poor neighborhoods. From this regional economy then flowed a series of dilemmas confronted by elites: How best to promote a vibrant spirit of enterprise and at the same time enforce white-black and rich-poor distinctions? How best to maintain public order year-round within an economy that relied on large numbers of rowdy seasonal and unskilled workers? In other words, how to save Savannah from itself? Over the next few years these questions would yield some unsettling answers.

CHAPTER TWO

Our Common Master in Heaven

IN THE MID-1850S, the casual visitor to Savannah would have had difficulty discerning the city's legal distinctions between enslaved and free persons. Black and white workers toiled together on the docks and streets, in iron foundries, and in steam mills processing rice, cotton, and lumber. Given the wide range of skin colors on display throughout the city, even black and white social identities were sometimes invisible to the eye, shaped by custom and family heritage, rather than phenotype. But for the invalid seeking warm weather in the wintertime, or the New York merchant visiting cousins and business customers, Savannah did present itself as a divided city in at least one striking way: on the basis of wooden and nonwooden buildings.

An early painting of Georgia's first city shows a neat grid of tiny houses bordered on the north by the Savannah River and surrounded on the other three sides by a dense, dark green forest. By the middle of the nineteenth century, the settlement had grown in people and in acres; but its core still consisted of houses surrounded by wood, in the form of wooden tenements and boardinghouses in the neighborhoods of Currytown, Yamacraw, and Trustees' Garden. In the center of town, fire-resistant warehouses, banks, and mansions showcased the wealth of their owners, including commercial factors, lawyers, and planters. These buildings were made of terra cotta, brownstone, or red and white brick, as well as colorful materials unique to Savannah—a pinkish stucco, and a gray brick from the kilns of nearby Hermitage plantation. Imposing homes boasted limestone trim, copper finials and copings, marble steps, cast-iron balconies and railings, and solid stone foundations. The vast majority of Savannahians lived in wooden firetraps; the privileged showed their status with fire-resistant materials.[1]

Among the most magnificent public buildings was the gray granite United States Customs House, on the corner of Bull and Bay streets across from the Exchange. Designed by the architect John S. Norris, the massive structure took four years to complete and cost the nation's taxpayers almost $170,000. Adorned with a three-story portico of six Temple-of-the-Winds Corinthian capitals, it was made out of granite imported at great expense from Quincy, Massachusetts. Norris, a native New Yorker, designed other notable Savannah buildings—including homes for the merchants Charles Green and Andrew Low, and the military leader Hugh Mercer—in a number of styles, such as Gothic Revival, Federal, Italianate, and Second Empire. Yet the federal Customs House was rendered in a style popular among New England and southern architects alike during this period: Greek Revival, with its connotations of a proud republic impervious to all manner of threats, not the least of which was fire.[2]

Early spring of 1855 brought signs that Savannah's commercial economy was rebounding from the awful autumn before. The federal government played a key role in the city's recovery. In March, at the request of the city, the U.S. Congress appropriated $160,000 to remove obstructions in the Savannah River and to make other improvements to the shallow waterway, which was used by so many oceangoing steamships. The city council rejoiced at the news, for logs, submerged vessels, swelling deposits of mud and oyster shells, and debris from the previous September's storm were choking the river, hindering "the progress and prosperity of our commerce, foreign and domestic, to the great detriment of the City of Savannah." Indeed, in and around the city the federal government was a palpable presence. It maintained the military barracks used by the city as a police station, as well as nearby Forts Jackson and Pulaski, and the lighthouse downriver on Fig Island. A number of loyal Democrats made a comfortable living working in the Customs House, which also provided space for a post office and courtroom. In addition, the Poor House and Hospital for destitute and impoverished foreign and domestic seamen received federal support; more than five hundred men were admitted for care in 1854. Under the direction of Dr. Richard Arnold, the institution also served as a teaching hospital for medical students. The larger significance of these federal subsidies to the city's well-being, financial and otherwise, would become painfully obvious over time.[3]

Savannah authorities took money where they could get it, and they were particularly resourceful in cobbling together public and private funding for projects that facilitated trade. Between 1835 and 1860, the city itself invested $2.75 million (over half the total amount raised) in the Central of Georgia and the Savannah, Albany and Gulf railroads; these commitments paid off handsomely for storage and shipping businesses, which in turn replenished the city coffers with their taxes. In the mid-1850s, Savannah ranked third in the nation as a cotton port, behind New Orleans and Charleston; by the end of the decade it would surpass its South Carolina rival. Still, the river port remained at a disadvantage compared to saltwater competitors. En route upstream, sailing ships and steamships had to fight the strong current of the Savannah River and steer clear of mudflats and debris; when vessels ran aground, frustrated passengers and crew members could only wait for currents, tides, and winds to dislodge them. If reliable schedules were the hard currency of the shipping trade, then the Forest City seemed perpetually in debt.[4]

The northern journalist (and, later, landscape architect) Frederick Law Olmsted visited Savannah and described what he considered its liabilities as a commercial center: first, "the expense, delays, and dangers attending the shipment of cotton" from the port, due to "loss and obstructions in the river below the town"; and second, "the dead weight of a numerous unproductive class of exceedingly ignorant, unambitious indolent people." Olmsted recommended that the state of Georgia invest in mining and manufacturing, which, he believed, would offer steady wage work and "infuse new life and spirit among the poor." The city should also provide "facilities for general popular instruction . . . *in loco parentis* to the innumerable white-headed children, that themselves will soon be a part of the State." Savannah's lively daytime street scene, with its large number of mischief-making boys, gave proof of the city's failure to require a common-school education of all its "white-headed children."[5]

And so the March 1855 public examination of the pupils attending the new tuition-free Savannah Free School represented a breakthrough of sorts, the city's first experience "in the application of the Public school system—so popular in the Northern states" (according to the *Morning News*). Principal Bernard Mallon led the boys and girls, ages seven to fourteen, through their recitations, a standard nineteenth-century end-of-school-year celebration. Authorities remained sensitive to Northerners like Olmsted who chided the city for its lack of public schooling. More generally, Georgia slaveholders were becoming increasingly agitated by northern "freedom shriekers" who caricatured the South as a land of degraded slaves, shiftless and illiterate poor whites, and dissolute planters. At the same time, common-school reform Savannah-style stemmed more from a fear of streetwise white children causing mischief during daylight hours than from a desire that all white children partake of common opportunities for social advancement through literacy.[6]

In 1855, the Savannah Free School was one among several systems of education in the region. Throughout the lowcountry prosperous planters paid for tutors to teach their children at home, and some boys and girls went on to private academies, some boys to military schools. Many of the children of the elite attended college and professional school in the North. In 1850, 35 percent of white Savannah children had attended some sort of school, either paying their way at private Chatham Academy, receiving charity from the Sisters of Mercy or other parochial schools run by Catholics and Episcopalians, or attending the so-called Free School, which at that point charged a modest tuition. In the proportion of its children schooled, Savannah lagged behind its northern counterparts, but outdistanced most other cities in the South.[7]

Savannah blacks ran their own clandestine school "system," a patchwork of formal and informal instruction and stolen chances for learning. In 1817 the city had outlawed schooling for slaves as well as for free people of color. However, some blacks working for white craftsmen or merchants became literate. For any number of reasons, some mistresses taught enslaved children how to read and write. Black preachers, eager to read the Bible and write down their Sunday sermons, taught themselves. As a community, blacks sought to learn, as well as earn, on their own terms.[8]

In Savannah, religious faith was both an incentive and a cover for black schooling, which remained intertwined with the churches, the largest, most powerful institutions in the black community. By the mid-1850s the city boasted five self-governing independent black churches: First African Baptist (founded in 1788, the first black Baptist church in the country), Second African Baptist (1802), and Third African Baptist (1833), as well as the Methodists' Andrew Chapel (1835) and St. Stephen's Episcopal (1855). Biracial congregations such as the Presbyterians and Catholics enforced segregated seating arrangements and excluded black members from leadership positions. But virtually all of the city's churches sponsored some sort of religious education for black children. On Sunday morning, black girls and boys scurried through the city streets clutching hymnbooks on their way to Sunday school. There they learned catechisms, Bible stories, basic literacy skills, and classroom decorum.

A handful of black men and women had conducted clandestine black schools since the late eighteenth century. Throughout the 1850s, several such schools were in operation. One of them was taught by James Porter.

Born a free man in 1826 in Charleston, as a youth he suffered a crippling accident but went on to learn the tailor's trade. Intellectually hungry, he managed to receive a classical education, becoming proficient in several foreign languages and mastering vocal and instrumental music. Soon after the founding of St. Stephen's, the first urban free black Episcopal church in the United States, in 1855, Porter arrived in Savannah to teach the music of the Anglican Communion to its congregants. By day Porter offered private music lessons in violin, piano, and voice. In the evenings he operated a secret school, complete with trapdoor for rapid escapes. Elsewhere in the city a free woman of color named Jane Deveaux, the wife of the carpenter Isaac, taught secret classes in her home; as a child she had helped her mother, Catherine, instruct black boys and girls in the Bible.[9]

While white children were filing into the Savannah Free School each weekday morning, a little black girl named Susie Baker was also on her way to school, swinging a bucket and looking over her shoulder for eagle-eyed policemen. She knew if she got caught going to school, not only would she lose the chance to learn, but also her grandmother would suffer an offical reprimand, or worse. Born in 1848 on an Isle of Wight plantation off the Georgia coast, Susie had arrived in Savannah as a seven-year-old, along with her younger brother and sister, to live with their maternal grandmother, Dolly Reed. Soon after, the little girl began attending a school on Bay Lane run by a free woman, Mary Woodhouse, a widow, and her daughter Mary Jane, both congregants of St. Stephen's along with James Porter. Susie and twenty-five to thirty other black children entered Mrs. Woodhouse's kitchen, one at a time, "with our books wrapped in paper to prevent the police or [other] white persons from seeing them." They remained undetected because the "neighbors believed the children were learning trades." Within a few years Susie would learn from another black teacher, Mary Beasley; from a playmate named Katie O'Connor; and from her landlord's son, a high school student.[10]

Susie's grandmother, Dolly Reed, was one of many lowcountry black women possessed of market-savvy energy and industry. (It is unknown whether she was enslaved or free.) Whenever Reed made routine visits to see her daughter, Susie's mother, Hagar Ann, on the Isle of Wight, she would hire a wagon to carry bacon, tobacco, flour, molasses, and sugar to trade with the rural people, and then return to the city with eggs, chickens, or cash. Through this trade as well as laundry work and cleaning "some bachelor's rooms," Reed managed to put away several thousand dollars, some of which she used to buy schoolbooks for her granddaughter. In turn, Susie was able to forge the passes that enabled Dolly Reed to travel after the nighttime curfew.[11]

In all probability Susie would not have attracted much attention day or night; Savannah, with its semitropical climate, encouraged outdoor activity of all kinds, and its city squares and thoroughfares were endowed with a high degree of round-the-clock theatricality. The marketplace, streets, and parks were sites of commerce, social conflict, and public spectacle. Modeled on the open-air central markets of early modern England, and similar to those in West Africa, the public marketplace in Ellis Square consisted of stalls under a pillared roof. There servants and slaves shopped for their masters' fresh meat every morning at stalls presided over by white butchers. Enslaved women who had arrived early from the countryside would be chewing sugarcane and waiting for customers to buy shad, oysters, poultry, and fruit. (White visitors were confounded by the Geechee speech of these women. "Such a gibberish—enough to craze a man!" exclaimed one Northerner.) Mingling with the crowds were white farm folk who had traveled for miles in rude wooden bull carts laden with trade items such as honeycombs, melons, fresh vegetables, shellfish and finny fish, meats, and mops and other housewares.[12]

Savannah residents met in the squares to use the public water pumps and to see and be seen. Women showed off their headgear—the wives of merchants their fashionable beaver-fur hats trimmed with ostrich feathers, black wives and mothers their tightly wound white cambric turbans, each a perfectly smooth "structure a foot or more high" trimmed with dainty colored stripes. The center of the city attracted foreign and domestic tourists eager to promenade along the main streets under lush, leafy archways. But few respectable visitors would venture into the poorer wards of the city. There and along the docks and parts of the Bay, places "thronged by sailors, slaves and rowdies of all grades and color," no "ladies" could be found. With few exceptions the streets throughout the city, which was situated in a plain of sand, remained largely unpaved through the mid-nineteenth century. As a result, longtime residents developed a distinctive gait—shoulders forward, haunches back—from years of shuffling through the deep sand, "as one would walk through a bed of tough brick mortar," noted an amused visitor.[13]

Coming to the city from the countryside, enslaved workers and wealthy planters alike were struck by the general cacophony. In alleys, lanes, and avenues, chimney sweeps called out to potential customers. Strolling fiddlers and other musicians offered impromptu serenades, while hawkers rudely accosted passersby with cakes, brooms, and goods of dubious origin and ownership. Pedestrians often took to the middle of the street so they would not have to trip over open cellar doors and the barrels and carts littering the city's sidewalks. Careening around corners were frantic clerks rushing to deliver bills of lading, young men relieved to escape for a few minutes from what they considered the humdrum, mind-deadening work of the office. Tanners and butchers appropriated space in lanes and alleys outside their shops to dry hides and slaughter pigs. Housewives and hotel kitchen workers threw dirty dishwater out windows, adding to the offal, rubbish, and stinking water that befouled the streets. And accidents were part of open-air street life: Laborers suffered crushed limbs when loads of iron spilled out of wagons. Runaway horses sent loads of lumber crashing into pedestrians.[14]

In the heart of the city, young men from planter families pursued the "fast life," racing their fancy carriages in the streets and generally causing mayhem. One visitor was minding his business, standing on the sidewalk outside the Marshall House Hotel, when he was forced to duck a shower of heavy cut-glass tumblers and plates, as well as knives, small articles of furniture, and a large platter—all tossed out the hotel window by a group of young Kentucky men, well lubricated from celebrating a recent sale of horses and mules. Many other wealthy men spent much of their time at the bar of James Foley's City Hotel, "the gathering place for the convivially inclined." These were members of "the sporting crowd," sampling the brandies, whiskeys, and vintage European wines from Foley's famous cellar, and then stumbling outside to wreak havoc on innocent bystanders. Charged $500 for damages incurred during one of his rampages, a fast young man paid up, laughing, "Cheap enough! . . . I have had a good frolic!"[15]

In the spring of 1855, Savannah was embracing the sounds and signs of economic recovery, including the public processions that were such a significant part of the city's popular culture. Apparently almost any event could and should be marked with a parade: Washington's Birthday, an upcoming political campaign, a Sunday school picnic, funerals of local dignitaries, the dedication of a new monument or fountain, the Jewish Feast of Tabernacles, the arrival of Van-Amburg's menagerie, with an elephant leading the procession. Among the largest and most lively of these parades were the ones marking St. Patrick's Day on March 17 and the firemen's parade held the last Friday in May. Organized by the Hibernians, an Irish benevolent society founded in 1812, the annual St. Patrick's Day parade attracted huge numbers of spectators, not just persons claiming a heritage from the Emerald Isle. In the afternoon, an array of Irish and Catholic groups, including benevolent societies and the Jasper Greens militia, marched from Foley's City Hotel to the Cathedral of St. John for a high mass, and later ended the day with a grand banquet, where devotees of St. Patrick and others "drown[ed] the shamrock in mountain dew." The day's lively proceedings could not help but remind the city's predominantly Protestant elite of the political clout of overlapping groups of Irish immigrants, Catholics, and the laboring classes.[16]

The annual "Colored Fire Companies parade" affirmed a different sort of political reality—in this case, the role of black men, enslaved and free, in protecting the largely wooden city against fire. The Savannah Fire Department operated on the principle that black men would respond reliably and well to financial incentives. In return for exemption from the annual city head tax of $6.25, all free black men between the ages of fifteen and sixty were required to serve as firefighters. The law also stipulated that slaves who were tradesmen must serve, and they received payment; the fifty most senior members of each company each earned 12.5¢ an hour to extinguish blazes. The first black man to arrive at the fire station after the alarm was sounded was rewarded with $1, the next two with 50¢ each. The department was organized into seven black engine companies, two black hose companies, and one black hook and ladder company, most of which consisted entirely of either slaves or free men of color, and each of which was under the direct supervision of a white manager. In the mid-1850s, 487 slaves and 140 free men of color made up the Savannah Fire Department. Supplementing the black firefighters, under control of the fire department, were the white volunteer companies organized as fraternal orders.[17]

On the last Friday in May, the black fire companies assembled in front of the Exchange, where the mayor and aldermen reviewed their ranks; each company wore a uniform consisting of white pants and loose black shirts trimmed in its own distinctive color. Then they processed, dragging their engines behind them, as many as seven hundred strong, singing loudly "as the sound of many waters," in the words of one observer, wending their way up the street to the intersection of West Broad and Bay. There the various companies—Warren, Pulaski (named for the Revolutionary War hero who died defending Savannah), Neptune, Niagara, Tomochichi (named for the Indian ally of Georgia founder James Oglethorpe)—engaged in a distinctly masculine competition: to see whose engine hose could throw the longest stream of water.[18]

Relying on black men to render prompt and efficient service in the chaotic midst of burning buildings might have seemed risky. Traditionally, southern whites believed that disgruntled slaves naturally posed a severe threat—the women were thought to favor poison and the men the arson's torch. Northern visitors to the city professed amazement that blacks would be given "the largest liberty at times when general consternation and confusion would afford them the best opportunities to execute seditionary and murderous purposes." Even native white Savannahians marveled that the system "placed us entirely at their mercy. At any time they might have allowed the whole city to be burnt to the ground without taking active part themselves." Yet the policies of the fire department suggested the power of money in regulating the behavior of the black population as a whole. The city gained a stable firefighting force, and African-American men—no doubt at times reveling in the general excitement provoked by fires—affirmed their place as an integral part of the larger urban community. Denied citizenship rights, they nonetheless contributed to the common good, and many of them either earned wages or received tax abatements in return.[19]

On the night of July 4, 1855, members of the Young America engine company no. 5 engaged in "conduct unbecoming a fire company," and clashed with black firemen who were trying to quench a blaze. Tensions had erupted periodically between the blacks and several white engine companies, including two Irish groups—Washington (founded in 1847) and Young America (1848)—and a German group, Germania (1853). In 1850, all of the white companies had petitioned the city council that only they, and not the blacks, should be permitted to wear distinctive firefighters' uniforms. The council rejected the demand, noting that the uniforms enhanced morale among black as well as white men, and reminding the white companies that they remained subject to the authority of the fire department. Elites would continue to manipulate and benefit from animosities between black and white firefighters.[20]

On this Fourth of July, members of Young America, apparently consisting of the "rough element of the community," were merely continuing their Independence Day celebration by taunting the black men. Within days of the incident, the city council divested Young America of its engine and horse cart. However, over the next few months some members of the council sought to put the matter to rest, arguing that it was only natural that "the fierce and fearless spirit of the white firemen" brought them "into collision" with the black men. Thus the council found itself torn between, on the one hand, the established order, which mandated that the Savannah Fire Department maintain strict control over all firefighting efforts, and, on the other, the political muscle of Irish workers organized in the Young America company.[21]

Indeed, Irish immigrants wielded considerable power over annual municipal elections. In the fall of 1855, U.S.-born voters retained a slight numerical edge in city politics, and this edge helps to account for the reelection of Mayor Anderson, whose candidacy was sponsored by the Know-Nothing Party. The Know-Nothings consisted of a loose coalition of former Whigs, now bereft of any formal party apparatus, and those righteous Democrats who resented the growing Irish influence in virtually all aspects of public life. Though Anderson retained his seat as mayor, the city council showed a surprising turnover rate; only one incumbent was reelected. The coalition's platform, such as it was, could be summed up in its slogan: "Freedom for foreigners, but supremacy for ourselves; foreigners may ride but [Uncle] Sam must drive." By "foreigners" the party probably meant "Irish immigrants," since its 1855 slate for municipal elections included John B. Gallie, a former Whig who was born in Scotland. Over the coming years, the council would seesaw between the reformers and the anti-reformers as candidates' positions on brothels and grogshops set the standard for voters of various stripes.[22]

MEANWHILE, lowcountry planters were anticipating a banner growing season. To many of the wealthiest slaveholders, prosperity was contingent not merely on sustaining levels of crop production, but on increasing harvests year after year: buy more land, buy more slaves, grow more rice, sell more rice. Throughout the winter of 1855, Charles Manigault kept his eye out for other Argyle Island plantations that might come on the market. He was also eager to buy twelve more prime hands, men and women who could replenish his chronically ailing workforce. Manigault had spent the fall fretting about the price of rice, a figure determined by its quality and its destination. The profits he made were essential to the gracious living, in Charleston and abroad, that defined the social status of the Francophile Manigault clan.[23]

The Manigaults also depended upon free white workers. The steam-powered threshers and pounding mills used on the plantations needed constant attention, and only skilled artisans could provide it. In early 1856, Charles, exasperated, spent a great deal of time and energy trying to track down three specific white workmen, two mechanics and a brick-layer. He also pursued a mulatto man, Ellick, who knew much about the operation of steam threshers but was "a slippery dodging fellow," impossible to lure to the island. Adding to Manigault's frustration was the fact that the lowcountry produced none of its own agricultural machinery; he had to place each order with a Philadelphia manufacturer and wait for the machine's delivery.[24]

More time-consuming than finding slippery workmen was finding and hiring a responsible overseer who knew something about the intricacies of rice cultivation. Like most other planters in the region, the Manigaults put their ultimate faith in an experienced black (enslaved) driver, in this case forty-one-year-old Robert; as Charles reminded his son Louis, "You can't go wrong with Roberts experience." However, state law mandated that each plantation of any size employ a full-time white overseer. The family's former employee, Stephen F. Clark, had been on Argyle Island for only two years before he sickened and died of tuberculosis in early December 1855. In January Charles interviewed a number of prospects for the overseer's position, but none met his standards. He was looking for someone who understood rice cultivation and who would be willing to bring his family to live on Argyle Island. One promising candidate was rejected because his wife was "a Charleston woman who has never resided in the swamp." Manigault also shied away from men with long-standing ties in the region, for he had learned from hard experience that they would incline toward "visiting & going away &c" rather than attending to their duties on the plantation. One candidate planned to keep his family in Savannah: Manigault considered that a deal breaker. Finally, after several weeks of corresponding with and interviewing candidates, Charles settled upon Leonard F. Venters, a twenty-four-year-old bachelor.[25]

Venters dutifully signed the elaborate contract originally drawn up for Stephen F. Clark in January 1853. The document stipulated that the overseer must not hire out the plantation's slaves to other whites in the area, and must ensure that the carpenters and other skilled workers be kept busy year-round. The overseer must not "interfere too much" in the working of the steam thresher and rice mill, "as the Negroes in charge have experience therein." In contrast to their neighbor James Potter, the Manigaults forbade their overseers (as well as their slaves) to keep horses, hogs, or chickens, on the theory that confusion inevitably developed over whether the animals were owned by slaves or overseer. Venters, like Clark before him, was encouraged to transact business in Savannah via letter "sent by a boy in a canoe" rather than make the short trek to the city himself. Of Venters, Charles told his son, "Keep him as ignorant of Savannah as you can, &c."[26]

In January and February, Abel and the other Argyle Island slaves labored to clear and repair the fields and prepare for spring planting. Men cut wood and split rails, dug ditches and repaired trunks. Women cleared the ditches, cleaned manure out of cow pens, and pulled up cornstalks. Together men and women raked the stubble from last year's crop and burned it in large piles, a difficult job at any time, but an especially disagreeable one during the winter of 1855–56, when temperatures dropped as low as six degrees Fahrenheit. The threat of early spring freshets rushing down from the interior meant that all hands had to help repair breaks in the banks that protected the fields from the river. Abel and other prime field hands would have each been responsible for one-quarter acre of planting each day, from mid-March, when the season commenced, until all the plants were in the ground in early May. In the spring and summer, a series of "flows" irrigated the fields through the regulation of river waters lowered and raised by the effect of ocean tides on the river. Hands cleared the canals of weeds, hoed the areas around the young plants, and kept the floodgates in good repair. Regardless of the season, the tasks assigned to rice slaves were designed to maximize their output, and those tasks remained fixed regardless of mitigating factors such as the weather or the health of the worker.[27]

The division of labor at Gowrie and Argyle suggested the extent of specialized work assignments: Enslaved women worked as field hands and as cooks, nurses, laundresses, and servants for Louis Manigault and the overseer. (On large plantations with a resident mistress, enslaved women also worked as producers—of thread and cloth and clothes as well as cooked meals and preserved foods.) Enslaved men worked as field hands and as chimney sweeps, drivers, trunk minders, engineers, carpenters, and firemen (to stoke the steam engines). Abel's sister Nancy was now preparing Leonard Venters's hominy, rice, and bacon, and another sister, Fanny, had been sent to Charleston to work as a lady's maid. Men and women operated the steam-powered threshing mill, a task that was hazardous ("George's Betty got caught in the end of the convaying claught") and vulnerable to sabotage: "if they think they are not watched" Betty and Cathrina "will let the Beater wear itself out in turning uselessly," thus subjecting expensive machinery to needless damage. The Manigaults tried to abide by a strict schedule for planting, hoeing, and irrigating, but they did not know from day to day how many enslaved workers would be available for field labor. In the summer and early fall of 1855, two women and four children died. Venters was suffering from his own health problems, finding "this sun and dew" more than he could safely take.[28]

Moreover, two enslaved women—Judy, age twenty-eight, and Julia, forty—had absconded for several weeks. Louis seemed to accept these disruptions as routine: "Judy has walked off, but I hope that she will feel rested and will walk back in a few days as G. Jack did." Other planters, too, seemed to accept "runaway frolics" as a matter of course; for weeks and months at a time men and women braved marshland snakes and alligators, secreting themselves in the swamps, living by stealing cattle or "slyly abetted by those of their family at home." A rash response to a runaway could cost an owner more than a hand's lost time: when one Liberty County master shot and wounded a fugitive, he decreased the man's value by $1,500—from $2,000 to $500. Far better from an economic standpoint was a severe flogging, especially if the runaway was forced to spend some time anticipating it. In December 1855, when Judy and Julia returned, Louis sent them to jail, presumably in either Charleston or Savannah, to "bring them to holesome conclusions."[29]

Though weakened in body and spirit, Venters joined with his employers in anticipating a bumper harvest that would signal the rebounding of the region's rice economy. At the same time, most whites understood that they inhabited a rapidly shifting national political landscape. The Republican Party, founded in the spring of 1854 in Wisconsin, had brought together a potent alliance of critics of slavery. Among its supporters were radical abolitionists but also, more significantly, anxious New England farmers distressed at the prospect of competing with slaveholders for land and labor in the western territories. In Savannah, the local papers were covering the escalating civil war between pro-slavery and anti-slavery settlers in Kansas; the blood flowed on both sides as a series of raids and counterattacks claimed dozens of lives. The papers also featured stories about the brutal attack on the abolitionist Charles Sumner, the "foul mouthed Massachusetts senator," by a South Carolina congressman, Preston Brooks. (Sumner had won election to the Senate in the aftermath of the Thomas Simms affair of 1851.) A Savannah paper asked its readers to consider the "Ability of the South for Self-Defense" in case Republicans forced "that rupture [with the South] they seemed determined to bring about."[30]

According to the popular press, "nigger worship" was "rampant" in the North, a sure sign of estrangement between the two sections of the country. It is true that, all over the Northeast, black men and women were finding their political voice. By the 1850s, Tunis G. Campbell, founder of the anti-colonization society in New Jersey, had actively taken up not only the abolitionist standard, but also the cause of temperance and moral reform. In addition to his day job as a hotel waiter and steward, Campbell labored as a Methodist preacher. He harvested souls in New York City's notorious Five Points neighborhood, relying on a police escort to get him in and out of temperance meetings every Monday night. In the process he gained the attention not only of the thieves of Five Points, but of local philanthropists who believed his work to be good and useful.[31]

It was against this backdrop that, in the early summer of 1856, the American Colonization Society prepared to send another ship to Liberia, which would stop in Savannah to pick up passengers. The sailing of the *Elvira Owen* highlighted new and perilous times. Throughout the state of Georgia a dwindling cadre of white ACS supporters lamented the rising animosity toward anti-slavery activity of any kind, the fact that "the political pro-slavery party was the mouthpiece of so-called popular opinion—and all the rest deem it prudent to join in the cheer or be silent."[32]

In June, an ACS official, William McLain, arrived to arrange for the ship's sailing. He was shocked to discover seventy-six of the emigrants languishing in the city jail. Some had come so early to the city that Mayor Anderson ordered them confined until their departure. Over the next few days, McLain tried to negotiate with Anderson, but to no avail. Even local white clergy berated the ACS agent, demanding that he "stop this shipping *Negroes* from the city." McLain finally won the detainees' daytime release, but he spent the next two weeks, until the ship arrived on June 19, in a state of fear and sleeplessness: a dead wind had stalled all oceangoing sailing ships in the area. The *Elvira Owen* finally got under way, with a total of 321 passengers (including, in the end, 142 from Savannah); ahead of them lay a fifty-day journey, during which many of the passengers would contract measles and diarrhea. McLain left the city knowing that this would be the last ACS voyage to sail from Savannah for the foreseeable future. And in fact, that summer the city council slapped a prohibitive $200 tax on all future emigrants who left the river port for Liberia.[33]

Within the year the Georgia Supreme Court would halt virtually all ACS operations in Georgia, by ruling, first, that the society could not inherit slaves from remorseful owners, but rather must limit its emigrants to free people of color; and second, that slaves could no longer labor to earn money for passage to Africa. In this second decision, justices asked, "Can it be denied, that . . . these slaves are working for themselves?"

What kind of slavery had Georgia wrought, that slaves could work for themselves and not for their masters?[34]

And so in the early fall of 1856, rabble-rousers in the North, defamers of the South's good name in the U.S. Congress, abolitionist sharpshooters loose in Kansas, African colonizationists in their midst: in its struggle to regain its economic footing after 1854, white Savannah had not anticipated this alarming turn of events. Yet to most lowcountry planters, the burden of slavery was less political than personal, less national than local. Around this time, one eighteen-year-old fugitive exposed the moral contradictions of the institution of bondage for the family of the Reverend Charles C. Jones. Jane had run away from Maybank plantation in the late summer. Her brother John had died recently, a personal tragedy that probably exacerbated her stubborn defiance toward her owners. The elder Charles Jones advertised widely for Jane, and, acting on a tip, a Savannah policeman picked her up on the last day of September. During her brief sojourn she had evidently not tasted the bread of idleness, for she had changed her name to Sarah, gained some weight, acquired flashy earrings and finger rings, and found a job that paid $6.50 a month. She was working for Susan C. Dunham, a forty-four-year-old widow whose eagerness to find a domestic servant had prompted her to dispense with the required documentation in the form of written permission from Jane's owner. Dunham accepted the young woman's story that she belonged to an upcountry planter who was allowing her to keep her own wages—"a very common thing in this city," all could agree.[35]

The minister advised his son to have Jane confined in the pen of William Wright, a slave trader, while the family contemplated their next move. They decided to pay the policeman a $30 reward, $5 above the advertised amount, because he had enlisted the services of an informant for $15 and also because rewards for runaway slaves were "running quite high" at the time. They agreed that Jane should never be allowed to return to Maybank, for her "tales of Savannah and of high life in the city would probably not have the most beneficial effect upon her peers." After some soul-searching they decided not to sue Dunham for her role in the sorry affair; litigation would tend "to make the matter notorious."[36]

Jane's transgressions prompted the Joneses to solve a problem that had plagued their household for years. Not only was Jane herself impudent, but she also belonged to a family that had refused to abide by plantation conventions and show gratitude toward their master and mistress. Mary Jones had reached the limits of her patience with Jane's mother, Phoebe, who happened to be an excellent seamstress but was apparently more trouble than she was worth. Phoebe exerted a bad influence on her husband, Cassius, or Cash, who had started using "bad words" and avoiding prayer services. With all this in mind, Charles Junior began to look around for a buyer for the whole family: Cassius, age forty-five, a field hand, basket maker, and all-around handyman; his wife, Phoebe, forty-seven; and their children Jane; LaFayette, twelve; Victoria, fourteen; Cassius Junior, twenty; Prime, sixteen; and Titus, twenty-nine. The estimated price for all together: $6,700.[37]

For several weeks the younger Charles worked hard at selling the slaves. As a matter of religious principle, the Joneses would keep the family as a group, even though they could make more money by selling them separately. However, they did decide to hold on to one of the younger sons, who would serve as valet to Charles Junior's brother Joseph, a physician. Slave trader William Wright, who charged 25¢ a day to keep and feed each person, assured the Joneses that potential buyers would be favorably impressed by the slaves' "size, soundness of teeth, etc." Charles convinced himself that he need not disclose the family's troublesome qualities. He advertised Jane as "a house servant, good seamstress, and field hand." Meanwhile, his father calculated and recalculated the family's value in dollars, mulling over a number of estimates from different traders.[38]

Fearing idle gossip—the Reverend Mr. Jones's catechizing efforts gone supremely awry!—Charles Junior sought to sell the slaves "in the least public way and the most speedy." He hoped to send Cassius and Phoebe and their children far from home, both to prevent any of them from returning to the community at Maybank, and to avoid drawing attention to the sale among their neighbors. After going back and forth between buyers who would not pay in cash, and buyers who lived too close, the Joneses settled on a man from Macon who would pay $4,500 in cash for six of them (LaFayette and Titus had been removed from the group at the last minute). Father and son congratulated themselves on a sale well consummated.[39]

THAT FALL, Charles Junior noted that "politics forms the all-absorbing topic at present" in the city of Savannah. The Know-Nothing mayor, Edward C. Anderson, went down to defeat at the hands of a pro-immigrant ticket. The Democrats, together with a faction called the Anti–Know Nothing Party, elected a new mayor, Dr. James P. Screven (he had filled in for Mayor Ward during the yellow-fever epidemic), and ten new aldermen (out of twelve), including James P. Foley, proprietor of the City Hotel. Meanwhile, national political tensions were edging out local issues at the ballot box, as, Charles noted, "Disunionist sentiments are already entertained to a very general extent." Walking home from his law office one evening in October, Charles overheard two black men "in close confab beneath a lamp in the streets," expressing support for the Know-Nothings. What could the future hold, now that "negroes are talking politics in the streets"? Though the Democrat James Buchanan won the presidency that November, the Republicans found themselves two states short of carrying the electoral college and winning the White House.[40]

A few weeks later, white Savannahians proudly hosted the Southern Commercial Convention, which brought one thousand delegates from ten southern states into the city, filling the hotels to overflowing and prompting wealthy households to throw open their doors to guests. The days leading up to the convention had been marred by a couple of potentially embarrassing developments. The first week in December, the city's native-born, Irish, and French Canadian dockworkers had struck for higher wages, and employers immediately called for black replacements, enslaved and free. Over the next month it became clear that the number of available black workers was insufficient to fill the strikers' places. This temporary cessation of activity on the docks challenged Savannah's view of itself as a well-run port, where all white workers knew their place.[41]

Meanwhile, many city residents seemed to care less about the plight of the striking workers and more about the so-called "Greatest Exhibition in the World" sponsored by Colonel Wood's Museum, now on view at one of the local halls. Savannahians appreciated traveling entertainers, including clairvoyants, hot-air balloonists, strongmen, jugglers, and minstrels. Now the museum, with its exhibit of eight extraordinarily short and extraordinarily tall people, attracted curiosity-seekers young and old. Among the customers were many people of color, who were admitted at the reduced rate of 25¢ each. Yet the exhibit caused a minor scandal when blacks insisted on pushing their way to the front to get a better look at these "most wonderful living curiosities." White women especially found the jostling most unpleasant, complaining that the presence of so many blacks had become "a positive nuisance." The consensus seemed to be that 25¢ entitled any black person to indulge his or her curiosity in the exhibit, but that Colonel Wood should "appoint a separate hour for the negroes to be admitted, or else keep them from monopolizing the space around his big and little people."[42]

Meanwhile, delegates to the commercial convention debated the role of internal improvements, trade, manufacturing, and agriculture in a future bid for southern "commercial independence" from the North. They discussed whether or not southern white men should be discouraged from marrying northern white women, and whether the slave states should ban all journals and magazines published in the North. The meeting's liveliest debate came in response to a resolution offered by a native son, William B. Gaulden, a forty-year-old planter from Liberty County who had served previously as a state legislator and a local judge. Addressing the Democratic National Convention in Charleston six years earlier, Gaulden had delivered an impassioned speech in favor of reopening the foreign slave trade, and now he repeated that performance at the commercial convention. "Slavery was an institution from God," he claimed. No planter objected to buying his slaves in Georgia or Virginia, so why the opposition to purchasing more in West Africa? Some delegates agreed, arguing that the border states lacked a sufficient labor supply, now that so many slaves had been drained off by the cotton states, and white workingmen had proved such miserable employees and such active voters. Others countered that while slavery was right, the slave trade was wrong, and that the South could well rely on natural reproduction rather than the foreign slave trade. (This last argument would fail to impress planters from the deadly rice swamps.) In response to a committee formed to study and presumably promote the matter, the Reverend Charles Jones and his son both expressed disgust at the "abominable resolution," the despicable spawn of fire-eaters bent on disunion.[43]

Soon after the last delegates departed, the whole city paused to observe the funeral of the Reverend Andrew Cox Marshall, venerable pastor of the First African Baptist Church. Marshall was a nephew of Andrew Bryan, whose ordination in 1788 marked the founding of the first independent African-American Baptist church in the United States. Born a slave in South Carolina one hundred years before, Marshall had purchased his freedom in the early nineteenth century ("as the more industrious of our slaves" often do, noted the city paper). Over the years, he and his sons built a successful drayage business in Savannah, and he owned considerable property, and, for a time, as many as eight slaves. He assumed leadership of First African in 1826 at the age of seventy. Blacks and whites alike reckoned his long career in numerical terms—3,800 men, women, and children baptized in the Ogeechee Canal west of the city; 2,000 couples married. By the mid-1850s First African could claim 4,000 members, a significant proportion of whom were scattered in small rural congregations throughout the lowcountry. Marshall died in Richmond, on his way home from a trip to New York, where he had raised money for a new sanctuary for First African.[44]

Like many black preachers in the antebellum South, Marshall was skilled in the art of circumspection. Each Sunday he preached to hundreds of people, white visitors in addition to the enslaved and free congregants who paid his salary and otherwise supported the church through pew rents and subscriptions. Many whites shared Charles Jones's views that Christianity was of use to the slaves as long they imbibed its lessons of meekness and obedience. Yet by tolerating these self-governing institutions—with their Sunday schools, mutual aid and missionary associations, and vibrant forms of leadership and cultural expression—white people badly miscalculated. The Baptist faith in particular provided both a training ground and a forum for black leaders, male and female. Its lack of institutional hierarchy and its emphasis on literacy and on the equality of all souls offered both a material and an implicitly political challenge to the slaveholders' ideology of black dependence and inferiority. Encoded in the weekly sermons of Marshall and others was an emotional message of hope for the day of reckoning, the dawn of freedom. Marshall compared himself to Moses: "The Lord shall be revealed in all the grace and glory of the Redeemer, and the king," he preached one day in May 1855, to a congregation of more than eight hundred people, "but these aged eyes of mine will not continue their sight until that day." Though prideful now, Satan would soon be vanquished: "Our skins are dark but our souls are washed white in the blood of the Lamb. . . . How many of those to whom we are subject in the flesh have recognized our common Master in Heaven, and *they are our masters no longer?*" This call for deliverance, embraced so fervently by slaves and free people of color alike, was more dangerous to the tenets of white supremacy than white people understood. The Reverend Charles C. Jones might have approved of Marshall's words, but only because he failed to comprehend their meaning for the slaves.[45]

On December 14, 1856, the city of Savannah acknowledged Marshall's many years of devoted service to his church. Funerals afforded one of the few opportunities for black people to assemble on their own terms, and the commemoration of Marshall's life combined religious devotion with a political statement in the form of an impressive spectacle. In the morning, "an immense throng" of blacks and whites assembled at First African, "the floor, aisles, galleries and even steps and windows of which were densely packed." Those who could not squeeze inside waited outside on the surrounding streets, now congested with horse-drawn carriages.

After the sermon, the crowd formed in procession behind the "neat metallic coffin." The marchers offered testament to the size and vitality of Savannah's black religious establishment—deacons and other church officers in front, followed by representatives of the city's Colored Female Missionary Society, Colored Temperance Society, burial and benevolent societies, then fifty carriages filled with mourners.[46]

Missing from this procession was one of the persons most stricken by Marshall's death: thirty-three-year-old carpenter James M. Simms, still suffering from the public disgrace of excommunication from the church. At some point he abandoned his carefree ways, settled down, and taught himself how to read; indeed, in his later years he would cultivate and exude a distinctly professorial air of reasoned deliberation. But he continued to chafe at insults, real and imagined, directed at him. Recently, Simms had attempted to return to First African, one day standing humiliated outside the church in the pouring rain, waiting to be summoned inside; but the call did not come. In anger he confronted Marshall and reportedly declared, "When I ask you all to take me in again, you will do it." Simms would later cite the old preacher's death as a turning point in his own life, a time of reflection and remorse; the young man was, in the words of another preacher, "one of the bitterest weepers at Mr. Marshall's funeral." Soon after, Simms would embark on a mission of linking his renewed religious faith to active engagement with a wider, intensely political world. And few mourners appreciated more than he the larger significance of slaves coming together and speaking to one another, even in circumspect terms; the newly devout carpenter understood that funerals and worship services were the only forms of slave assemblies that white officials would tolerate, and that the church building itself offered a haven, no matter how fleeting, from an unjust world.[47]

White observers failed to gauge the depth of feeling that Marshall's passing stirred among black people. A reporter for the *Savannah Morning News* noted approvingly that the funeral procession "was a most solemn and imposing spectacle," testament to the fact that Marshall "was greatly respected by all our citizens." And many whites saw in the orderly demeanor of the mourners and onlookers confirmation of a timeless caste system, a Savannah way of life safely under control.[48]

They were wrong.

CHAPTER THREE

A Demon Ready with
Knife and Torch

DURING CHRISTMAS WEEK, it was customary for Savannah to offer up a rousing tribute to the carnivalesque. Calling themselves the Mysterious Fantasticals, mounted men in costume galloped through downtown streets, scattering pedestrians in their wake. Street musicians serenaded velvet-jacketed young men rushing from house to house for holiday parties; there in plush, darkened parlors young hostesses waited eagerly, their hair smooth and glistening with oil, their silk dresses fashioned in the new hoop-skirt style. In back alleys and in basements of fine houses, enslaved workers and free people of color danced to their own tunes. In the center of town, black and white men and boys made merry by setting off firecrackers, and by igniting wads of cotton soaked in kerosene and then throwing the blazing fireballs back and forth to one another. Smells of saltpeter and kerosene wafted through the air: it was Christmastime in Savannah.[1]

At least that was the tradition. In 1856, however, the city council made an effort to enforce a half-century-old ban on Christmas-week fireworks. Abolitionists were afoot, also in disguise, and even a temporary lapse in public decorum—especially one that brought unsupervised males together in the streets to play with explosives and make "a devil of a noise"—seemed too much to risk. Early on Christmas Day the customary crowds assembled in the streets, yelling, blowing tin horns, fraying the nerves of older people indoors. But then after dark, boys and young men defiantly let loose with firecrackers, skyrockets, and Roman candles "blazing and popping in almost every street." That night policemen rounded up a few of the lawbreakers: Thomas Murtagh, a forty-year-old native of Ireland, got hauled into court and fined for allowing his sons to set off firecrackers. But these rambunctious souls posed less of a threat than James Marshall, a native Northerner arrested downtown while he was "delivering an abolition speech . . . , giving to a few little niggers, his opinion of Southern institutions," as the *Morning News* reported the incident. The police also took into custody another man "of the same stripe" who was exhorting people near the public market; soon both he and Marshall would be sent north, "and should be thankful each at having escaped a coat of tar and feathers."[2]

Meanwhile, in the countryside outside Savannah, nameless, mysterious strangers were traveling from one plantation to the next, drawing crowds of the curious. A prominent Presbyterian minister, Robert Quarterman Mallard, expressed the anxieties of many planters: Out of their sight and earshot, might these intruders possess sinister motives and aim to "tamper with our negroes"? All white residents must remain "on their guard" as long as these men tarried in the neighborhood. Though claiming to be show masters, opera singers, or peddlers, the outsiders were in fact, according to Mallard, "having frequently clandestine intercourse with our slaves, and infusing dangerous notions, telling them, amongst other things, that they ought to be free." Presumably, then, with or without a trained monkey in tow, such persons might well be anti-slavery fanatics in disguise. It was said that lowcountry whites would welcome into their midst a thief or an arsonist before they would tolerate an abolitionist. The simple "vagrant" wending his way around the countryside appeared now as a potential insurrectionist.[3]

Between Christmas and New Year's Day, coastal rice and cotton planters allowed their workers an annual three- or four-day respite from toil. To mark the occasion, some masters plied their workforces with enormous amounts of rum or whiskey, and proceeded to "give out Christmas"—plugs of chewing tobacco, sides of pork, fruits and candies, and, to each man, woman, and child, a new blanket or pair of shoes. In the quarters, black men and women harkened back to West African celebratory traditions, strumming stringed instruments made out of horsehair and animal bladders, and beating out rhythms on drums of raccoon hide stretched over hollow logs. Revelers moved and swayed to the music, dancing the buzzard lope and the camel walk, in a rare show of release in the daylight of a weekday—in this case, Thursday, December 25, 1856.[4]

For generations, whites throughout the Georgia lowcountry had remained on high alert during the freewheeling festivities of Christmas week. Planters cast a suspicious eye on any social gathering that featured African drums or dance styles, gatherings marked by "the sports and amusements with which the benighted & uncivilized children of nature,

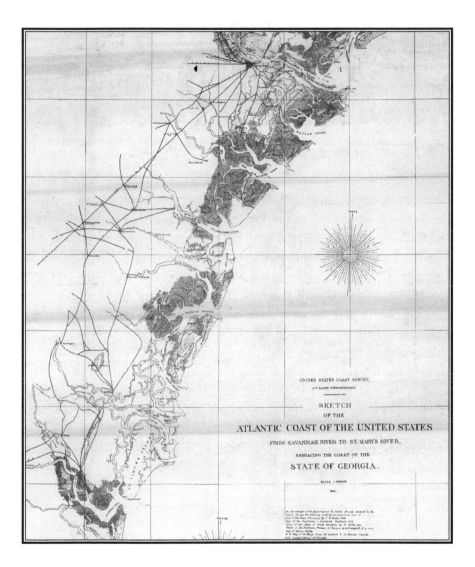

UNITED STATES COAST SURVEY,
A.D.BACHE SUPERINTENDENT.

SKETCH
OF THE
ATLANTIC COAST OF THE UNITED STATES
FROM SAVANNAH RIVER TO ST. MARY'S RIVER,
EMBRACING THE COAST OF THE
STATE OF GEORGIA.

SCALE 1:296660
1861.

divest themselves . . . distorting their frames into the most unnatural figures and emitting the most hideous noises in their dancing," in the words
of one observer. Whites associated these exotic musical and dance forms
with disaster—in too many cases, barns, machinery, sawmills, and barrels
of rice were all consumed by a fire started by "careless" revelers during
the end-of-year holidays. And then there was the inevitable "demoralizing" effect of so much drinking and carousing among workers expected
to head compliantly back to the fields on New Year's Day. Louis Manigault put the matter succinctly when he noted, "Christmas is always a
very bad time for Negroes."[5]

Christmas and New Year's celebrations only highlighted the pervasive
West African influence on black life in the quarters. Much of the work the
Gullah-Geechee did for themselves derived from African customs.
Descended from peoples of present-day Sierra Leone and Angola, slaves
along the Georgia coast tended small garden plots with vegetables native
to Africa—groundnuts, benne (sesame), and gourds. At night outside
their cabins, weary wives and mothers rhythmically pounded corn into
hominy, using a traditional mortar and pestle. They might steal some
time from sleep to weave cloth or sew clothes. By day, enslaved men made
furniture and wove baskets from sweetgrass, and they appropriated their
owners' canoes and flatboats to fish for oysters and the luscious white
mullet; by night they hunted for opossums and raccoons. Within the
quarters, then, time was a most precious commodity, allowing slaves to
provide for themselves in ways that honored the memory of their forebears. Well into the twentieth century, lowcountry blacks continued to
sing funeral songs in African languages such as Mende, and they pep-
pered their speech with the Africanisms incorporated into the pidgin language called Geechee—*seraka* for rice cake, *juba halta* for water bucket,
wah-hoo bahk for slingshot.[6]

At times planters expressed amusement and amazement at slaves' cultural and subsistence activities that evoked West African practices. The
Reverend Robert Mallard marveled at the practice of "churning," a sport
perfected by black men who trolled the creeks and canals with flour barrels stripped of their tops and bottoms. Moving in unison through the
waterway, a half-dozen boys and men would trap fish in their barrels and
then toss each one onto land, where waiting youngsters "quickly strung it
up upon stripped branches of the sea myrtle tree." Mallard observed,
"How they managed to handle the cat fish, with its sharp and poisonous
spines, I cannot imagine; perhaps their horny hands were impervious to
them." But more often white people expressed profound misgivings

about African cultural forms, especially religious and musical traditions that were foreign to them. The sound of nighttime drumbeats, which whites feared signalled an imminent slave insurrection, could send planters all over the lowcountry scrambling for their revolvers.[7]

In the late 1850s, elites worried that the seemingly resilient system of lowcountry slavery had become more vulnerable than ever to insidious "outside influences." Slavery was a profitable, generations-old political and economic system that nevertheless might be brought down by the machinations of a single perambulating organ-grinder or some other conniving "stranger": this was the contradiction that plagued white people all over the South, including Robert Mallard and his well-to-do neighbors. Some planters defended human bondage as the foundation of Christian civilization, while others dispensed with the moralizing and declared that they would take more black bodies wherever they could find them—on the block of the local slave market, surely, but even from the far reaches of West Africa if need be. Planters and their allies debated ways to expand slavery in order to silence its critics. In Savannah during the 1850s this debate focused on the buying of people at home or abroad.

For their part, the Charles C. Jones family had no desire to fuel the wretched excesses of the domestic slave trade. By selling five members of Jane's family together in the fall of 1856, the Joneses believed they had demonstrated that "conscience is better than money." On March 18, 1857, Charles Jones Sr. fulfilled his final duty to Jane's father, Cash, when he instructed his son Charles to send the family's new master a check for $84.75, the amount realized from the recent sale of a horse owned by the black man. The minister hoped "there may be certainty of Cassius' getting his money." And so just a few days later, a few months after the sale was finalized, the Joneses were shocked to learn that the new owner had turned around and sold Cash and Phoebe and the three children to a New Orleans slave trader, a man under no obligation to keep the family together. In a letter to his father, Charles Junior sputtered with indignation: "The revelation confirms me in hitherto unshaken conviction that no confidence whatever can be placed in the word of a Negro trader. It is the lowest occupation in which mortal man can engage, and the effect is a complete perversion of all that is just, honorable, and of good report among men."[8]

Writing from New Orleans, Cash offered his own view of the sale in a letter to one of Jones's neighbors, Frederick R. Lyons. Reporting that Jane had died the first of February, and that the other daughter and a son had been ill with the measles, Cash noted bitterly that his family had been "sold for spite." Moreover, despite their self-congratulatory disclaimers, the Joneses themselves had done a poor job of respecting family ties. They had retained a son, Titus, as a manservant for their own son Joseph, and they had ignored a wider circle of relatives close to Cash and Phoebe. Lyons's plantation was home to two of Cash's other daughters, Clarissa and Nancy, and another son, James, as well as sons-in-law and grandchildren, Phoebe, Mag, Chloe, John, Judy, and Sue among them. Also owned by Lyons were Cash's brother Porter, his wife, Patience, and assorted aunts, uncles, and cousins. Cash's family was not alone in their anger and grief; throughout the lowcountry, severed black families gave testimony to the planters' self-interest, variously defined.[9]

Upon hearing the news of the resale, the elder Jones could do little but condemn "how the game has been played." By this time his wife, Mary, had resigned herself to making do without the troublesome Phoebe, and began calculating the cost of buying a sewing machine, a major investment at $100. Meanwhile, her daughter Mary Sharpe Jones remained preoccupied with her upcoming marriage to Robert Mallard, pastor of the nearby Walthourville Presbyterian Church.[10]

By convincing themselves that they had followed the moral high road in selling Cash's family, the Joneses revealed a major split within the planter class—a split between frankly irreligious slaveowners on the one hand and slaveowners who professed religious conviction on the other. Most elite men and women considered themselves Christians; however, a minority attained a high level of righteousness—many friends and neighbors would have termed it self-righteousness—in their zeal to monitor the behavior not only of their slaves but also of others within their own tight-knit social circle. Resented for their religious enthusiasm and their "bigoted" ways, some of the zealous busybodies on the Savannah social scene felt free to insult prominent citizens who embraced the convivial life of high society. Even the physician Richard D. Arnold, a Unitarian, was not immune to their insults: he was told to his face that he "was sure to be damned" for his love of fine foods and wines over his devotion to God.[11]

The Charles Joneses disapproved of their "ungodly" neighbors who abused their slaves with impunity, separated black families on a whim, and favored a reopening of the African slave trade. Charles Senior well understood that his appeal to the Christian conscience of slaveholders was an enterprise "of exceeding delicacy." Certainly most planters paid no attention to religious appeals, whether those appeals emanated from abolitionists in the North or from neighbors down the road. Looking to buy a dozen or so field hands in early 1857, Charles Manigault favored "gangs" of slaves from the same plantation, at least some of whom were likely to be related to each other. But he cared little for black family life per se: When individuals were bought and thrown "all together among strangers, they don't assimilate and they ponder over former ties of family, &c and all goes wrong with them"—in other words, they acclimated to the job only slowly, or, in some cases, they took ill and died. When it came to growing rice, Manigault suggested, moral sentiment made sense only when it dovetailed with hard-nosed practicality.[12]

Planters who considered themselves godly believed that the line between right and wrong was well demarcated: On the other side were people fond of drinking and dancing, gambling and horse racing, novel reading and theatergoing, card playing and billiards. Ungodly men challenged their rivals to duels and treated enslaved women like their concubines. However, the line was by no means drawn cleanly between households. Indeed, many a privileged son from a "good" family slipped out of respectability and into the "fast life" before he reached his twenties. Mary Jones placed the blame squarely on alcohol; she was convinced that "the social glass, sipped at first in a genteel way, has brought ruin to many souls and sorrow to many hearts." Jones was especially anxious for her son Charles, an eligible bachelor still awaiting his own religious conversion; until then he was making the rounds of Savannah blow-outs, mingling with women dressed as gypsy girls, Neapolitan peasants, and Jewesses.[13]

Mary Jones endured the humiliation inflicted upon her own family by their alcoholic kinsman, the widower Joseph William Robarts, who was dismissed from his job as Savannah city treasurer in 1855. Within a few years Robarts would marry a nineteen-year-old girl. His mortified kin were sickened "that he should sink, despite powerful and opposing influences, to such a depth of degradation and foul infamy, and so openly and impudently," in the words of the Reverend Charles Jones. Charles Junior agreed that "language and thought fail to express or conceive the depth of infamy into which he voluntarily plunged himself." Mary also saw early warning signs in her nephew, James Dunwody Jones. The son of her brother, the Reverend John Jones, Dunwody (as he was called) had had a peripatetic and indifferent school career, quite unlike his ambitious, well-educated cousins Charles and Joseph. In his early teens Dunwody was showing an alarming fondness for shooting guns and tormenting his little cousins by sticking pins in them. When the boy was sixteen, his own father said, "The truth is, Dunwody is a bad boy."[14]

In their certainty about right and wrong, planters like the Charles

Joneses were confounded by the African-American culture that flour-
ished not far from the "big house," in the quarters. Much of slave community life remained hidden from whites, especially rich ones, and what they
did see they could not or would not fully comprehend. One lowcountry
white woman remarked that black people in general did not "easily reveal
themselves to the white race"; they were "an emotional people outwardly
but often with deep hidden motives," motives that were expressed in
"queer ways." Charles Jones Sr. sadly concluded that blacks of all ages
were congenital liars—"deception . . . is characteristic of them"—and
that slaves in general represented "a distinct class in community and keep
very much *to themselves*." Too often slave congregants like the willful
Cash and Phoebe proved resistant, if not downright hostile, toward white
preachers who presumed to minister to them. For planters who craved
from their slaves heartfelt gratitude, evidence of "familiar and affectionate
relations," such inscrutable behavior was disappointing at best, maddening at worst.[15]

Everyday relations between masters and slaves were complicated by
the considerable dissembling that took place on both sides. In the parlance of the day, owners did not sell, but rather "sent away" troublemakers; defiant slaves did not run away, but were "enticed" away by persons
of evil influence. For the most part white men and women spoke to the
slaves they called "our people" or "our servants" by issuing orders, prod-
ding, and threatening; such wildly unequal power relations were hardly
conducive to conversing. At the same time, blacks avoided talking to
whites when they could help it, feeding their owners a steady diet of
rhetorical treacle when they had to. Speaking among themselves, many
plantation slaves used Geechee. Born in Africa and snatched from the
Guinea coast when she was a girl, one rice hand greeted the journalist
Frederick Law Olmsted with words he could barely comprehend; but
when she wanted to be understood, she turned to her master and said, "I
lubs 'ou mas'r, oh, I lubs 'ou. I don't want to go 'way from 'ou."[16]

And it was common for slaveholders and whites in general to misread
black people's verbal expressions, especially their songs. Whites took
pleasure in hearing workers singing while hoeing in the fields, and boatmen singing while guiding a flatboat through the creeks; in these songs
white people discerned contentment, not lament. After the death of a
master, the sounds of slaves wailing were routinely interpreted as an
expression of their intense grief, when in fact many rightly feared the sales
and separation of kin that would inevitably follow. A visitor from the
North concluded that the blacks he encountered said what they thought

whites wanted to hear, forced to make "false representations . . . for their own security." In response to a white woman who asked, "Well, how do you get along," a black mother who rarely saw her five children answered, " 'Oh, splendidly—of course must get along, you see, there ain't no other way—splendidly!" The white woman interpreted these remarks this way: "I . . . cannot say that [the slaves] are unhappy even when their circumstances are unhappy."[17]

Most planters, like Charles Manigault and his son Louis, believed that black people's thoughts and desires were worth understanding only to the extent that they affected the ability of enslaved men, women, and children to live together and labor efficiently. Some strong-willed personalities, like the Gowrie plantation cook Martha—she of the "eternal & untireing tongue"—provoked, or perhaps intimidated, or perhaps frightened, their co-workers. Too, unnamed slave customs might interfere with crop and household production. In April 1857, Louis hurried to install the Gowrie driver in a house that stood empty because of the recent death of its former occupant, for he believed that if no one occupied the house right away "the Negroes will get up a story of its being haunted, & none will wish to go there." If the mourners failed to sprinkle turpentine on the floor as the corpse was carried out, for instance, that oversight was believed to make the dwelling vulnerable to the spirits of the dead. The Manigaults also noted what they considered blacks' inscrutable attitude toward certain objects, fetishes; their slaves were "too fond of casting things aside, or swapping them away." Clothing, household wares, work implements—all might possess some sort of talismanic quality unknown to whites. More generally, when rice planters replenished their workforces with experienced rice hands from other parts of the lowcountry, they unwittingly helped to solidify not only work patterns in the fields, but Gullah-Geechee beliefs and customs in the quarters as well.[18]

Also hidden from whites were powerful spheres of influence that shaped relations among slaves. Armed with laws, firearms, and bullwhips, many whites considered themselves the ultimate authority over their plantation "households." And to a large extent they were. But within the quarters a number of different personalities held sway—the root doctor, knowledgeable in the use of healing herbs; the midwife, skilled in birthing babies and interpreting signs pointing toward life or death; and the conjurer, keeper of spells that would ward off "hants" (ghosts and spirits), hags, and witches. The younger Charles Jones knew little about the web of relations among slaves, only that planters endured "difficulty and annoyance" as a result of "the interference of these old negro

women—conjurers—who, in plying their secret trade, gave rise to disturbances and promoted strife and disquietude."[19]

To some extent influences overlapped, with individual black men
and women seeking to mediate between the spiritual and material realms,
and coming into conflict with church leaders—watchmen, elders,
preachers—in the process. In some cases preachers railed against traditional African beliefs, condemning those who put their faith in amulets
and other objects with mysterious qualities. And it was not merely a matter of formal religious leaders arrayed against competing systems of
belief; on the Sea Islands, some elderly Africans, and their children, preserved Muslim religious beliefs, foods, seasonal ceremonies, and public
prayers—all in opposition to the pervasive influence of Christians. In
other areas, these two religions blended to produce syncretic folkways
that shaped rituals of prayer and worship and that preserved secret societies in the West African tradition. Some of these societies were gender-
specific, but they all adhered to customs that punished transgressors and
otherwise regulated the behavior of slaves as individuals and as a collective. Their extent, and their pervasive influence, would emerge in sharp
relief only after emancipation.[20]

In Savannah, the independent black churches played a powerful role
in disciplining wayward congregants such as James Simms. In addition,
missionary, temperance, and mutual-aid associations—all composed of
members from both the enslaved and the free black communities—
acknowledged formal patterns of leadership that for the most part
remained outside the purview of white masters and authorities. In 1851,
Charles DeLaMotta, American Colonization Society agent and enslaved
carpenter, was serving as president of the Beneficial Social Society and a
leader in the Carpenters Mechanic Society, two associations among the
apparently many in the city. But, like all systems of authority, black systems reflected local politics and bitter personality conflicts. The revered
preacher Andrew Marshall never sought membership in his own church;
he remained on the rolls of Second African so that the congregation he
preached to each Sunday could never formally discipline him for any
alleged infraction he might commit against God—or any of them.[21]

IN THE EARLY SPRING of 1857 the United States Supreme Court rendered a decision of more than passing interest to the people of the Georgia lowcountry. On March 6, the Court held that a slave named Dred
Scott could not legitimately gain his freedom by traveling to or residing in

a free state. In fact, the Court went so far as to rule that a slave was a slave no matter where he or she lived—and that black people had no rights "that white people were bound to respect." Of the nine justices on the Court, seven owed their appointment to pro-slavery presidents, and five came from slaveholding families. The Dred Scott decision confirmed the right of slaveowners to transport or claim their human property wherever they pleased.

Savannah watched anxiously as fugitive slaves and their black liberators continued to make headlines in the North. In 1854, when Boston police arrested a Virginia runaway, Anthony Burns, the northern city seemed to be setting the stage for a replay of the Thomas Simms case three years before. Among the observers at Burns's court hearing was Charles Jones Jr., taking time from his studies at Harvard Law School. Jones's sojourn in Cambridge suggested that a young man from a slaveholding family could live very well in the North without embracing its anti-slavery heresies. He welcomed his mother's homey gifts of muskcluster roses and sprigs of verbena, and impressed his new college friends by showing off Georgia alligator skins and other lowcountry artifacts. The Burns proceedings, with their aggressive defense lawyers combined with the "infernal machinations" of the black man's supporters, left Jones "tired, downhearted, and vexed." Meanwhile, members of the Vigilance Committee, including the fugitive Lewis Hayden and the minister Thomas Wentworth Higginson, were scheming to free Burns by force. Like the plot on Simms's behalf, this one failed. And yet abolitionists all over the country took heart from the outcry raised on Burns's behalf.[22]

By this time other black refugees from Georgia were blending discreetly into northern neighborhoods. The industrious slave Hardy Mobley, who purchased himself and his family with the help of American Colonization Society supporters, had fled Augusta in 1853 and was now living quietly in Brooklyn. He had opened a little store of knickknacks and was studying to become a minister while his wife worked as a seamstress and his children attended school. And at this point few if any Savannahians had heard of Aaron A. Bradley. Born in 1815 in Edgefield District, South Carolina, Bradley had been owned by Francis Pickens, a prominent planter and politician. The young black man worked as a shoemaker in Augusta before escaping to the North in the mid-1830s. In 1848, he was practicing law in Brooklyn and in the process sparking a wider debate about whether or not a former slave had the right to enter the legal profession. Within two years he had moved to Massachusetts and become a member of the Suffolk County bar, but he was disbarred

(in October 1856) for withholding money from a client. Bradley's controversial legal career in New York and Massachusetts foreshadowed his turbulent sojourn in Georgia several years later; there, with his impressive
store of legal knowledge and his defiant demeanor, he would become
lowcountry white people's worst nightmare.[23]

Meanwhile, in the 1850s, an increasing number of fugitives were
choosing to go public with their denunciations of slavery. Frederick Douglass had gained an international reputation for his eloquence on the stage,
as a speaker and fundraiser, and for his eloquence on the page—in his
autobiography, *Narrative of the Life of Frederick Douglass, An American
Slave,* and in a series of periodicals he edited. Among the emerging cadre
of prominent black abolitionists making a living by speaking and writing
was the fugitive Harriet Jacobs. By any measure, her story of hiding for
seven long years in an Edenton, North Carolina, attic was a compelling
testament to the power of the prospect of freedom. Of her determination
to elude her master, Jacobs later wrote, "I resolved to match my cunning
against his cunning." Jacobs finally managed to escape; she was later
reunited in New York with her daughter Louisa and son Joseph, both of
whom had preceded her to the city. In the mid-1850s Harriet Jacobs was
finding her distinctive public voice by writing for anti-slavery publications and by addressing audiences throughout the Northeast. In March
1857, she took time from her work to react to the *Dred Scott* decision:
"When I see the evil that is spreading throughout the land my whole soul
sickens— . . . this poor heart that has bled in slavery—is often wrung
most bitterly to behold the injustice the wrongs—the oppression—the
cruel outrages inflicted on my race."[24]

Dred Scott provided cold comfort to Savannah bankers, merchants,
and slaveholders in the summer and fall of 1857. When a national financial crisis dried up the sources of credit necessary to the cotton trade, the
city's many businesses suffered a severe blow; among the failures were
eighty-two factorage houses, thirteen insurance companies, the main
office of the Bank of Georgia, and branches that represented nine of
Georgia's twenty-five other banks. In response to the crisis, Georgia and
South Carolina bankers suspended specie payments, a violation of state
law, forcing planters to pay the price for what Charles Jones Jr. called a
"wild spirit of extravagance and reckless speculation." Among the most
notable offenders in this regard was the wealthy lowcountry heir Pierce
Butler, owner of two large plantations, one on the northern part of St.
Simons Island (Hampton Point) and the other along the Altamaha River
(Butler's Island). Butler owned nearly a thousand enslaved men, women,

and children. In several respects his financial woes were typical of those of other coastal planters. He maintained an elegant town house in Philadelphia and lived a high life of gambling, traveling, and partaking of expensive food and wines. By 1856 his plantations were hemorrhaging money, and he was forced to relinquish management of his own affairs to three trustees. Now the nationwide contraction of credit in 1857 pushed Butler over the edge into bankruptcy.[25]

Nevertheless, Butler's plight was unique in that he was also responsible for paying his former wife alimony of $1,500 a year. Married in 1834, Frances Anne Kemble and Pierce Butler made a glamorous couple; she was an accomplished British Shakespearean actress, he the scion of a wealthy plantation family. In December 1838, Butler brought his wife to live on his St. Simons cotton plantation. Kemble was appalled at the living and working conditions of the black people there—slaves of all ages routinely beaten and overworked, the women ill and sexually abused, many of the children dying at an early age, the rest growing up malnourished, ragged, despondent. The manager of Hampton, Roswell King Jr., oversaw an enslaved workforce that included several of his own children by the slave women Betty, Judy, Scylla, and Minda.[26]

Herself the mother of two daughters, Frances and Sarah, Fanny Kemble saved some of her most biting comments for her lowcountry counterparts, planters' wives and daughters: "I pity them for the stupid sameness of their most vapid existence, which would deaden any amount of intelligence, obliterate any amount of instruction, and render torpid and stagnant any amount of natural energy and vivacity." Certainly slaveholding women had their own burdens to bear, but some took out their frustrations on the most vulnerable people on the plantation. Learning of the birth of her husband's enslaved children by Judy and Scylla, Roswell King's wife had had the two women whipped and sent to the estate's "penal colony."[27]

The Butler-Kemble divorce of 1849 had been a messy one, made even more newsworthy by Fanny's increasingly outspoken abolitionist sentiments. Pierce Butler was surprised to find himself the object of some bad press, and decided that he could redeem himself in the public eye by joining an Episcopal church in Philadelphia. His aunt Eliza expressed skepticism: "I think he must be crazy," she said. "None of the Butlers ever had any religion."[28]

Influential Savannah bankers shed few tears over Pierce Butler's financial woes, justifying their decision to withhold specie payments as sound fiscal policy. However, in the fall of 1857, the newly elected governor of Georgia, Joseph E. Brown, inspired fear among financiers all over the state. Hailing from Canton, Cherokee County (just north of the frontier city of Atlanta), Brown was an attorney, a slaveholder, a speculator in mineral rights, and a circuit judge. Throughout his life he remained enamored of the state-sponsored railroad, the Western and Atlantic, which, he claimed, had transformed remote Cherokee County from "a wild, uncivilized region, into one of the most interesting and prosperous sections of our State." Though Brown was a political novice, his pro-slavery stance, combined with the chronic underrepresentation of the upcountry in state Democratic affairs, had made him an acceptable candidate for his party's nomination. He received the nod over former Savannah mayor John E. Ward.[29]

Brown had a moralistic streak that made him the butt of ridicule and suspicion among lowcountry elites. The great coastal planters had always claimed more of a cultural kinship with their urban counterparts on the eastern seaboard, North and South, than with their crude neighbors in the state's interior. Brown hated bankers and drinkers in equal measure. In the fall 1857 campaign, journalists played up the humble origins of the "*Mountain Boy* . . . the ploughboy judge." His critics, including Savannah's business leaders, called him "a third rate lawyer, an unscrupulous demagogue and little more than a conceited upstart." Yet Brown beat the established politician Benjamin H. Hill (favored by the nativist Know-Nothing Party) by a respectable margin, 57,568 to 46,826. In his belief that the railroad was a great force of economic regeneration, in his home-spun qualities, in his lawyerly skills and his consistent ability to confound the critics who underestimated him, Brown would emerge as the southern counterpoint to one of his northern contemporaries—an Illinois lawyer-politician and rising star in the Republican Party named Abraham Lincoln.[30]

The day after he took office on November 6, Brown delivered an address that blamed the state's banks and their freewheeling credit policies for the current financial crisis. He proposed legislation that would force all lawbreaking banks (those that withheld hard currency from customers who demanded it) to forfeit their state charters—in other words, to give up their business and close their doors. However, within days of the speech, the state legislature had yielded to the pleas of bankers and their lobbyists; the result was legislation that mandated fines rather than charter forfeitures for offending institutions. In turn, Brown vetoed the bill, invoking the interests of ordinary hardworking people, Georgia's debtors. But John Ward, now serving as president of the state assembly, delivered a "thrilling speech," an oratorical masterpiece comparable to "a Damascus scimitar, as keen as it was polished," in the words of one admirer. Inspired, the legislators overrode Brown's veto and approved the more lenient bank bill. Back in Savannah, Ward's supporters shifted uneasily as they realized that the state's chief executive was capable of raising mundane financial issues to the level of class warfare.[31]

That fall of 1857, Democrats held tight control over city politics. A few days before the municipal election, the executive committee of the American, or Know-Nothing, Party announced they "have determined to nominate no ticket, preferring to let our citizens learn by another year's experiences [of] the evils of Democratic rule." Nevertheless, a group of dissenters within the party, "Young American friends," considered inaction, no matter how principled, a dubious strategy at best; under the banner of the Young Men's Independent Ticket, they nominated their own slate of candidates for mayor and aldermen. All thirteen men went down to defeat. Out of the city's approximately 2,500 registered voters, 1,580 cast ballots, with each of the Democrats receiving at least 930 votes; none of the individual independent candidates could muster more than 600. Mayor Screven relinquished power to another physician, Richard Wayne, a former U.S. Army surgeon, now elected to the mayoralty for the sixth time in his career. Among the twelve aldermen taking the oath of office were eight newcomers, including the president of a bank and a railroad, assorted merchants and lawyers, and William Wright, the slave trader.[32]

Members of the city council had their work cut out for them. In the midst of Savannah's explosive growth, they now contended with an outmoded form of municipal government, one that was run by committees of aldermen. Decreased tax revenues, a consequence of the current financial panic, compounded the crisis. The most pressing single problem, though, was the disgraceful condition of the city jail, one of the chief means by which the city conducted its quest for elusive stability and order. Housed in the decrepit former U.S. Army barracks building, the city jail posed a chronic health threat to the prisoners, an amalgamation of slaves, free people of color, and white rowdies. (After 1856, the city ceased incarcerating free black seamen in port with their ships; the requirement that such men be held in the city jail for up to forty days, with a bond of $200, had proved too irksome to ship captains.)

One of the abiding complaints about the jail was the sorry performance of the man in charge of it, Edwin L. Hollis. In November 1857 the city council heard charges that Hollis was "guilty of negligent and improper conduct in the management" of the place. He lived off the premises, which made the task of guarding his charges problematic at best. He failed to keep accounts of the prisoners when they were admitted and discharged, and whether or not they had paid their fines. It was rumored that he had recently engineered the escape of three men in exchange for a bribe. He had also apparently "suffer[ed] Negroes and other Criminals to go at large, and sending such persons to work in his place"—in short, he was profiting from the labor of the inmates while Savannah taxpayers footed the bill. In May 1858, he absconded, taking $756 of the city's money with him.[33]

A report commissioned by the council in 1856 had noted that the large number of inmates held for crimes of "drunkenness, sleeping in the streets, improper conduct, contempt, vagrancy and like offenses" were proving to be a drain on the city treasury. For men who could not pay their fines, a few weeks in jail, "free from labor and expence," held "but few terrors." Now that the jail was becoming more and more a place where disorderly white men could rest and recuperate, the number of slave inmates was dropping precipitously, and so were the municipal revenues from fines and confinement fees paid by slaveowners. Private "pens" catering to slaveholders offered a more secure alternative to the dank, unventilated city jail. In an advertisement in the *Republican* in February 1858, William Wright boasted that his "jail and yard [were] the largest, safest, and most comfortable in the city, if not in the state."[34]

The many hues of skin color within the jail revealed the challenge faced by Savannah elites determined to distinguish between enslaved and free people, "blacks," and "whites." Complicating this project of "racial" and caste distinction was the fact that black and white men and women of the lower orders in many cases not only worked together; they also drank, gambled, traded, and slept with each other. Savannah authorities had always reserved whipping for black people as a way of highlighting their legal vulnerability compared to whites. But by the 1850s the city confined flogging to the jail yard. Making a spectacle of brutal forms of punishment not only served as a provocation to the black population; it also brought disrepute to a city eternally trying to burnish its public image. Most tourists were in town to enjoy the mild weather and the leafy thoroughfares, not to watch a black person beaten bloody before a crowd of gawkers. And so authorities attempted to preserve distinctions between blacks and whites in other ways, though they did not always have the muscle, the manpower, or even the willpower to enforce those distinctions in consistent or systematic ways.

Incentives such as cash rewards for firefighting offered to slaves and free people of color helped to extract a measure of compliance from them, but coercion and public humiliation formed the core of the city's caste system. Free blacks were required to register with the city each year, and the published list announced to everyone the fact that grown men and women, some with prosperous businesses, possessed white male guardians. Slaves who hired out their time were required to wear badges that showed their owners had given them the requisite permission, and paid the requisite fees, to allow them to work on their own. The scavenger department put blacks to work on the city streets, cleaning up trash, animal carcasses, and the waste left by oxen, mules, and horses. Free people of color throughout the lowcountry were subject to up to twenty days of forced labor each year, toiling on public works projects. After 1857, free black men and women who moved to Savannah had to either pay a $100 fine or work off the fine by laboring on the city streets, the men for 100 days, the women for 125 days. Whippings; badges; dirty, disagreeable work on the streets; newspaper notices of the sale of black bodies; these forms of public humiliation set all blacks apart from all whites.[35]

In Savannah, the geography of labor and housing attested to the elites' efforts to enforce a caste system, but also to their difficulties in doing so. The city market served as a work site not only for white male butchers, but also for enslaved women who came in from the countryside to tend their stalls selling seafood and vegetables. Black people were an integral part of the city's transportation, construction, and service sectors. Among the largest slaveowners were painters and other building contractors, owners of foundries and steam-powered mills, the railroads, and physicians. (Blacks were by law barred from working as printers, typesetters, and pharmacists, on the theory that literate slaves were just as dangerous as those with a knowledge of poisons.) The streets of the city were clogged with black women hawking goods and carrying bulky loads of laundry to customers and food to market. Ironically, slaves and free people of color represented a uniquely stable presence in the regional labor market. Blacks, for example, dominated the jobs of wagoner, drayman, and porter; transient Irish workers had fewer opportunities to invest in the animals and wagons necessary for this kind of business. More generally, one's legal status was not readily apparent to people at the time, or historians since. Ulysses L. Houston, who would become pastor of the Third African Baptist Church, was a butcher by trade. Hiring his own time and paying his master $50 a month, Houston regularly went out into

the countryside to buy cattle, selling the meat and hides from his residence in the city. He had a freedom of movement that belied his status as
a slave.[36]

Many of the city's foreign-born population, which accounted for more
than half the adult white males in 1860, worked with blacks on the docks,
and in the brickyards, rice mills, cotton presses, sawmills, and depot and
yards of the Central of Georgia; together, mechanics and laborers made
up more than one-quarter of the city's white workforce. Seven percent of
all white men, most of them members of the stable immigrant population,
owned small businesses and shops throughout the city. This group
included the grocer John H. Stegin, born in Hanover, with a wife from
Saxony and two young children born in Savannah; and Henry Blun, from
Hesse-Darmstadt, a merchant living in a boardinghouse with several of
his compatriots. Anthony Basler, born in France, kept a barroom. These
men were able to advertise their businesses not only through storefront
signs, but also in the local papers. Some immigrant women, too, owned
shops, taught school, and offered music lessons. For their dresses,
millinery, ribbons, and other dry goods, fashion-conscious consumers in
the city and nearby plantation districts patronized shopkeepers such as
Mrs. Winberg, Mrs. Blumensweig, and Mrs. Silberg. Widows in straitened circumstances opened their parlors to paying students for instruction in piano, guitar, and fancy sewing. Lower down on the social scale
were entrepreneurs like Mrs. McBride, who was arrested for violating the
Sabbath by entertaining customers in her Bay Street barroom, and Mary
Williams, who was forced to appear in mayor's court for drying hides in
the street outside her house.[37]

Residential patterns provided only an imperfect means of enforcing
racial and legal differences among poor people. Blacks were well integrated throughout the city's wards, though by the 1850s they were beginning to concentrate in the poorer areas on the city's fringes—Oglethorpe,
Currytown, and Yamacraw on the west, and Old Fort and Trustees' Gardens on the east. About two out of five slaves lived in the backyard of the
house of their owner, but the rest found lodging on their own in congested neighborhoods of low-lying wooden tenements with grogshops,
groceries, and brothels packed tightly together. In 1860, of 3,200 free
white households, only 21 percent were nuclear families, which made up
17 percent of the white population. Only about one-fifth of white laborers
were heads of nuclear households. The overwhelming majority of whites
lived either in a boardinghouse, a hotel, or an institution such as Abram's
Widow Home, the Sisters of Mercy Convent, Female Asylum, Poor

House and Hospital for seamen, an orphanage, a brothel, or the jail. The boardinghouses were largely segregated by color, and many brought together under one roof men and women working in a certain trade—groups of seamen, fishermen, laborers, gas-works employees, painters, tinners, carpenters, and tailors all resided together in their respective boardinghouses, for example. Some housed only Irish or only Germans, but others were remarkably multicultural. The neighboring brothels owned by Elizabeth Jaudon and Fanny Fall employed a total of eighteen women ages sixteen to thirty-two who hailed from New York, Boston, Baltimore, Philadelphia, Jersey City, Richmond, Montreal, and the Irish cities of Dublin, Waterford, and Limerick.[38]

Most black workers living apart from their masters resided in non-white households. Women headed more than seven out of ten households of free blacks. William J. Cleghorn, a mulatto and free man of color, presided over a household atypical in terms of its head (male) and composition (blacks and whites together). A master baker, he operated an establishment that included his two daughters and one son and four bakers—three German-born and one from England.[39]

Domestic service revealed another blurred division of labor. Irish-born women such as thirty-year-old Ann McCann and Julia McAuliffe, twenty-eight, had opportunities to keep boardinghouses while black women for the most part did not. Within the city, one thousand white working-class women, an equal number of enslaved women, and two hundred free women of color crowded the ranks of servants, nursemaids, cooks, seamstresses, and washerwomen. And at the lowest echelons of the female workforce, the lines among paid and enslaved black women and paid white women were by no means clearly defined. The George Kollock family expended a great deal of time and energy trying to find domestic "help" for their Savannah home. They considered hiring Englishwomen as housekeepers, cooks, and governesses for their children; one likely candidate "is also *fond of children* (She also does Starches)." A "little Protestant Irish girl," fresh off the boat, seemed promising as an all-purpose wage-earning servant because "she has the good sense to suit herself to her new sphere" of reduced circumstances.[40]

THE SAVANNAH building boom of the 1850s enabled some skilled slaves to earn enough money to free themselves, and James Simms was one of them. (According to Simms, the other chief means by which a black person became free was the decision of a master to manumit his slave "on account of blood"—that is, because he was the person's father.) Within a year of the death of the Reverend Andrew Marshall, Simms had bought his own freedom, for $740. After periodically seeking readmission to First African, he finally achieved success in October 1858, and that December, a few days before his thirty-fifth birthday, he was elected a clerk and a deacon of the church. By this time his wife, Margaret, thirty-four, a free woman of color and a native of Charleston, was working as a washer and ironer. The couple had two daughters, Susan, nine, and Isabella, five. There is some evidence that James and Margaret also had responsibility for their nephew, William Henry Sikes, the thirteen-year-old son of James's sister Cornelia and her husband, William G. Patterson.[41]

No doubt impressed by his increased family responsibilities, Simms decided that the best way for him to atone for his sins would be to seek a close connection with Marshall's successor, First African's new preacher, the Reverend William J. Campbell, forty-six. Campbell was now overseeing construction of a new sanctuary, an enduring monument to his predecessor. The seven-hundred-seat brick building cost $26,000, an impressive sum that was raised by black Savannahians and their northern supporters. Along with ACS agent Charles DeLaMotta, Simms served as a member of the building committee, and he contributed his skills as master carpenter to the project. In what was a community endeavor, enslaved congregants donated their time after they had finished working for their owner each day. Black women did their part by using their aprons to carry bricks from an on-site kiln to men working on scaffolds. The finished building was the largest brick edifice in Georgia owned by black people. And Simms was now free, and back in the fold, his life infused with a new purpose that had little to do with fiddling or merrymaking.[42]

The heroic exertions of Simms and others in earning money suggests that it was not work in general that bondmen and women shirked, but rather a particular kind of work: jobs carried out under the close supervision of whites. Like Jane, the Joneses' runaway, many fugitives who made their way to Savannah lost little time finding wage labor, the women as domestics, the men as laborers on the wharves; if they must toil for white people, they wanted to get paid for it. This impulse united free people of color and slaves who hired themselves out in Savannah with their rural counterparts.

The countryside furnished abundant evidence of the slaves' own spirit of enterprise. Chickens and eggs, vegetables gathered from large gardens, hanging moss for mattress stuffing, handicrafts made of wood and reeds, lard, fish oil, and oysters and eels pulled from marshland creeks: all found ready customers among masters and mistresses, neighbors in the quarters, and shoppers in Savannah's bustling marketplace. On some plantations, eggs were a form of currency that facilitated exchanges of all kinds. So nearly universal was the practice of petty trading among lowcountry slaves that the few planters who imposed restrictions on their own workers felt compelled to make amends in some way. In Charles Manigault's negotiations with prospective overseers, he found that a major sticking point was his demand that the successful candidate not grow any crops or keep any livestock of his own. Manigault allowed the slaves on Gowrie and East Hermitage to raise only a few chickens "to attach them to their homes." But as a result, he observed, "our negroes have a hard time of it—no perquisites whatever, or facilities to plant an inch of land for themselves." By imposing the same restriction on his employee, Manigault eliminated disputes over property ownership common on plantations where slaves and overseers all kept gardens and tended the same kinds of animals, but these prohibitions violated lowcountry norms.[43]

Manigault's policies stemmed from a chronic problem affecting plantations up and down the Savannah River: an illicit, waterborne traffic in alcohol and stolen goods. Peddlers and grogshop owners were eager to exchange alcohol, and in some cases a noxious mixture of tobacco and whiskey, for cotton, rice, produce, tools, and anything else purloined from the plantation. In 1846, to counter "the extensive and growing traffick unlawfully carried on with slaves by white persons and chiefly by Retailers of Spiritous Liquours," planters between Savannah and Augusta had formed the Savannah River Anti-Slave Traffick Association. They all feared that slaves saw every chicken and ham, every dinner plate, piece of silverware, scrap of cotton and cast-off piece of iron piping as an item to be sold for money or traded for whiskey. In these cases, according to the organizers of the association, "the negro ceases to be a moral being, holding a position in the framework of society, and becomes a serpent knawing at [society's] vitals or a demon ready with knife and torch to demolish its foundation." Throughout the lowcountry, planters claimed that whites who traded with blacks were "practical abolitionists," men and women intent on obliterating the caste system and thus just as dangerous to the legal basis of southern society as the anti-slavery fanatics of the North. At the same time, illicit trading was integral to the livelihood of the region's non-slaveholding whites in Savannah and the surrounding countryside, prompting the founders of the association to acknowledge that "it has been said that ours was a combination to oppress the poor."[44]

In fact, many poor whites made a living by trading food and liquor with slaves. A few enterprising whites even parlayed an illicit trade with slaves into profits that enabled them to buy bondmen and -women of their own. Scattered throughout the lowcountry and interspersed among the great rice estates were white men and women of modest means who partook of neither staple-crop agriculture nor the urban trades. In coastal Georgia, whites amounted to one-fourth the total population, and half of them were non-slaveholders. Living the hardscrabble life of self-sufficient farmers were backwoods folk in the "Old Canoochee" region, where the Canoochee River flowed into the Ogeechee, ten miles southwest of Savannah. Inhabiting the banks of the marshland waterways were fishermen who plied creeks and streams on flatboats, eking out a meager existence for their families.[45]

These impoverished people, variously and derogatorily termed "crackers," "clay eaters," and "sandhill tackeys" by their social betters, lacked the political clout wielded by immigrant workers in Savannah. Wealthy whites rarely encountered modest rural folk and paid them even less attention, except when they emerged from remote areas to work as ferryboat operators, to market goods in Savannah, or to appear on the doorstep of the big house, unkempt and unwelcome intruders. Journalists and other visitors to the lowcountry portrayed these whites as colorful foils to the great planters who dominated the area. Female "drudges," dressed in simple homespun, toiled as field hands alongside their children and menfolk. Frederick Law Olmsted entertained northern readers of the *New York Times* with his tales of landless whites on the Georgia rice coast, men and women of "high cheek bones and sunken eyes," people "still coarse and irrestrainable in appetite and temper."[46]

Of indeterminate status between the planter and the poor white squatter was the plantation overseer, typically regarded as a man who lacked the requisite inheritance money, talent, ambition, or sobriety to enable him to possess a plantation of his own. The Manigaults' employees learned quickly that the job was too often a thankless one, and the employer an unforgiving taskmaster. Charles Manigault considered overseers "an outcast set in general." Some planters dispensed with overseers altogether, on the theory that no matter how skilled they were in crop management, few white men had the inclination either to live or to labor on the plantation full-time. Overseers were perpetually locked in a contest of wills with the enslaved workers they managed, and in an attempt to establish their authority they used too much force, or too little. Doing the bidding of haughty men and women who measured their own worth in fine clothing and carriages, books, and pianos, their white employees lived in rude cabins that were drafty and sparsely furnished. With their own well-being tied to annual harvest levels, overseers remained forever at the mercy of the weather as well as that of a largely unpredictable, hostile workforce.

Plantations throughout the lowcountry marked the beginning of the new year with annual contract negotiations between overseers and owners; and in January 1858, young Leonard Venters lost his job managing Gowrie and East Hermitage. Charles and Louis Manigault were unequivocal in their disappointment with Venters's performance. For the past two years he had overseen only middling harvests. Yet it was not his deficiencies in the field that were his undoing. Apparently the overseer was "elated by a strong and very false religious feeling," one that "began to injure the plantation a vast deal." Venters placed "himself on a par with the Negroes, even by joining them at prayer meetings, breaking down long established discipline, which is so difficult in every Case to preserve." In disputes, he took sides "with the people, against the [black] Drivers," the strong-willed George and Ralph. Most alarming of all, according to Louis, Venters had caused "numerous grievances which I now have every reason to suppose my Neighbours know; & perhaps I was laughed at and ridiculed for keeping in my employ such a Man."[47]

Apparently, Venters was not just praying with the Manigaults' slaves; before the year was out, a twenty-year-old slave named Harriet had given birth to his child, a baby she called James. Conventional wisdom held that an overseer, like a jailer, should "always be a man of family" because his own household (wife, children, chickens, for example) would remind him what was his and what belonged to his employer (wife, children, chickens, land, slaves). When Leonard Venters entered into the Argyle Island slave community, he must have known his days as an overseer were numbered.[48]

Though powerless compared to their landed betters, poor whites remained a preoccupation of elites in their public discussions about the nature of southern society, discussions that became increasingly heated in the late 1850s. Conspicuous for their absence from these debates were middle-class voices. Indeed, Savannah possessed only the barest outlines of a middle class. And therein lay a difficulty for wealthy men determined to maintain a caste system, for they lacked allies among a solid group of middling folk who could lend respectability and moral power to the cause of white supremacy. Missing were the mediators who could help overseers and planters, longshoremen and cotton factors, find common ground.

Compared to many northern and some southern cities at the time, Savannah had few substantial groups associated with an emerging middle class. In 1860, compared to Charleston, Norfolk, and Richmond, for example, a smaller percentage of Savannah white males twenty years and older owned or hired slaves (24 percent in 1860), but those who did own slaves tended to own larger numbers—more than 25 percent owned ten or more. Banking and commercial-house clerks and bookkeepers made up fully 13 percent of the city's white male workers, but they were not a separate class of householders. Rather, most were either the sons of the elite—young men living with their parents who would eventually rise to become partners in the great factorage houses—or they were bachelors living in boardinghouses or boarding with families. In 1860, nearly two-thirds of Savannah's clerks were forty-two years old or under, and only 16 percent of the total number headed their own households.[49]

The city's white artisanal community consisted of a handful of successful master craftsmen, many of whom owned slaves and also housed their own journeymen and apprentices. In presiding over large augmented households, artisans such as butchers, carpenters, and bakers departed from two main nineteenth-century middle-class ideals: the nuclear family and the separation of residence and workplace, with fathers going outside the home to earn cash wages. The vast majority of shopkeepers sold liquor and groceries; many of these men were deeply enmeshed in the shadow economy that provided illicit services to enslaved and free people alike. In contrast to the large dry-goods stores, shops of master craftsmen, and other places that catered to the wealthy, the vast majority of businesses were tiny grogshops with a boisterous clientele, hardly the haven of middle-class respectability. The number of newspaper editors, clergy, and teachers was too small to constitute a class in and of itself: together they made up less than 2 percent of white workers in 1860. In Savannah, social reform consisted of providing charity for the poor, rather than promoting social change in the form of abolition, women's rights, labor unions, or a comprehensive system of common schools. In 1859–60, the city was exporting annually more than $18 million worth of staples from the hinterland but importing less than $800,000 worth of goods for the wealthy, indicating that this was a region with many slaves and white laborers subsisting outside a consumer economy. Elites therefore wielded power and influence through traditional, patriarchal means, by presenting governance by the well-born as the natural basis of social order.[50]

During the winter and early spring of 1858, Savannahians began to debate the potential pitfalls of a white men's democracy, both at home and in the halls of Congress. Echoing the concerns of slaveholders settling in the strife-torn territory of Kansas, elites feared democracy if it meant yielding to a popular will that was potentially anti-slavery. The firebrand editor of the *Morning News*, William T. Thompson, was uncompromising in his denunciation of Illinois senator Stephen Douglas, purveyor of the idea of "popular sovereignty" as a means of settling the slavery question in the western territories. Douglas and other "Recreant Northern Democrats and Southern Traitors," Thompson charged, were breaking with southern principles to do the bidding of Kansas abolitionists who had mere numbers on their side.[51]

The Kansas crisis represented in microcosm the South's larger dilemma. Minnesota, Kansas, and Oregon were about to enter the Union as free states. For decades the South had retained the upper hand in the federal government: because of the notorious three-fifths clause, which for purposes of representation counted every slave as three-fifths of a person, the South had sent more than its fair share of congressmen to Washington over the generations. The Supreme Court and the executive branch remained in the hands of slaveholders or their northern "doughface" (pro-slavery) allies. But now the numbers were working against slavery. Not only were new states tipping the congressional balance in favor of the North, but each year as many as half a million foreigners arrived in the North to operate its machines and harvest its crops. Demographic trends made political outcomes easy to calculate, if, for slaveholders, terrifying to contemplate: the 1860 Electoral College would consist of 306 delegates, 186 from non-slaveholding states and 120 from slaveholding states.[52]

Events in Savannah during the spring of 1858 suggested the baneful effects of an excess of "democracy" dominated by non-slaveholding white men. Many wealthy people worried that poor whites simply could not be trusted to side with their social betters on the issue of slavery. Might not the widespread, underground trade between blacks and poor whites eventually yield a political alliance among men who realized that they had certain economic interests in common?

It was within this context that *Morning News* editor Thompson offered a series of articles proposing that the African slave trade be reopened. The arguments in favor of such a move were obvious. In order to keep pace with northern growth, which was spurred by both natural increase and foreign immigration, the South must continually replenish its resources of enslaved workers; this was all the more urgent because (lowcountry) slaveowners were plagued by high slave mortality rates. The new territories of the West offered fertile soil for an expanded slave system. As the repository of Christian values and civilization, the South had an obligation to assume responsibility for ever more heathens from Africa. Class differences would recede with an infusion of more slaves: "Every white man of capacity will own his slave. Every man of enterprise will own his labor." Members of the "ruling race" would meet at the ballot box, and "cast their vote from the same position; as well at home as abroad they will have a common cause." And finally, only a misguided sense of morality prevented the reopening of the slave trade. Once the South was released from "the brand of reprobation," it would continue to thrive, free from the interference of northern fanatics. Not long after the series ran, Illinois Republicans nominated the anti-slavery lawyer Abraham Lincoln as a candidate for the U.S. Senate. In his acceptance speech, Lincoln warned, "A house divided against itself cannot stand," a prophecy lost in the moment.[53]

The "house" that Lincoln had in mind was, of course, the federal union. But in 1858 Savannah authorities might well worry more about putting in order their own house, defined variously as the city itself, or Georgia, or the South. Elite men and women had good reason to doubt the loyalty of the white longshoreman who, in the company of black co-workers, endured a tongue-lashing from a boss on the docks each day; the white husband whose wife "did starches" for a wealthy family; the German shopkeeper who made a living, and a comfortable one at that, from trafficking with slaves; the overseer who slept with enslaved women; the petty thief who cared less about the color of the skin of his partner in crime and more about the color of cash pilfered during break-ins and back-alley muggings. As a defense against the northern Republicans' siren song, unity among all whites remained in desperately short supply.

-•❊| CHAPTER FOUR |❊•-

Let's See Her Face

O N JUNE 28, 1858, Savannah paused from normal Monday business to observe what one resident called "confessedly the grandest funeral pageant ever witnessed in our city." And a grand "pageant" it was, even by Savannah standards. Mayor Richard Wayne had died in office at the age of fifty-four, his life a testament to all the values held dear by the city's commercial and professional elite. Wayne had received his undergraduate degree from Union College in New York, and he had completed his medical education at the University of Pennsylvania. The voters first elected him mayor in 1844, and then rewarded him with reelection five more times.[1]

Episcopal bishop Stephen Elliott conducted the funeral service at Christ Church, a graceful Classical Revival building on Johnson Square, the earliest of the city's five parks on Bull Street. After the service, mourners assembled on the street and formed a procession, estimated to be almost a mile long, bound for Laurel Grove Cemetery in the southwestern part of the city. Behind the horse-drawn hearse were Wayne's widow, Henrietta, and the couple's three daughters in a carriage, accompanied by the family's slaves on foot. Next marched the volunteer militia companies—the Republican Blues, Oglethorpe Light Infantry, and the Georgia Hussars, a mounted cavalry unit. Following were a truly remarkable number and variety of groups to which Wayne had belonged or claimed some affiliation—the white fire companies and fraternal orders including the United Ancient Order of Druids, Solomon's Lodge of the Masons, the Odd Fellows, and the Sons of Malta. Then came representatives of the charitable Union Society, various Irish fraternal and benevolent groups, members of the city council, contingents of physicians and judges, foreign consuls and U.S. government officials, and the "citizens generally." Bells at the Exchange and the different churches tolled in ecumenical unison. Flags atop public buildings and on ships anchored in the river flew at half-mast. As many as ten thousand onlookers lined the sidewalks, jostled each other on front stoops, and watched from windows.[2]

When the mourners arrived at the northern end of Laurel Grove Cemetery (where white people were buried), they experienced a "most interesting and affecting incident," in the words of Charles Colcock Jones Jr.—the *singing of the Negroes.* More than a hundred members of the First African Baptist Church had gathered at the grave site, lifting their voices "with their own peculiar fervor and impressiveness" as they sang, "We are passing away." A reporter for the *Republican* surveyed the scene with some satisfaction and noted that "it was a spectacle which one large section of our Union might have contemplated to their profit."[3]

In fact, some northern visitors did contemplate Savannah's processions and found in them the foundation and symbol of what on the surface at least appeared to be a remarkably stable civil order. Based on his own observations, a prominent Boston clergyman, the Reverend Nehemiah Adams, believed the city apparently lacked an "underswell . . . [,] the motley crowd of men and boys of all nations which gather in [northern cities] on public occasions"—gangs of ruffians and ne'er-do-wells determined to make their mark on the streets. Missing were the "mobs . . . that fearful element in society, an irresponsible and low class"—the ugly demonstrations of unemployed workers, the pitched battles between Catholic and Protestant and between immigrant and native-born workers. According to Adams's view (which prompted cries of outrage from New England abolitionists), in place of civil strife the Georgia river port offered parades, highly choreographed displays of overlapping systems of power and influence—the volunteer militias and fire companies, the charities, churches, fraternal orders, professional groups, and political parties.[4]

The collective discipline that marked the largest city processions was but an extension of the martial spirit that was coming to dominate Savannah's public life. Active in the elite Chatham Artillery, Charles Jones Jr. would later claim that "no American city has had a more brilliant military history than Savannah." By the 1850s, virtually all white men belonged to some sort of military organization; native-born members of the laboring classes formed ragtag bands of volunteer home guards, and the Irish sponsored the Jasper Greens and the Montgomery Guards. The wealthy joined independent companies such as the richly attired Republican Blues, Georgia Hussars, Chatham Artillery, or Oglethorpe Light Infantry, each complete with its own marching band of African-American musicians—the soldiers' "step enlivened, their spirits cheered by them," in the words of a northern observer. Together with the fire companies, the militias provided white men with the near-universal experience of parading and drilling, and provided many bankers and hotel keepers with the title of lieutenant or colonel—testament to the overwhelming physical force that undergirded the system of slavery. The more exclusive companies traveled to other cities, where they offered drill exhibitions and enjoyed the camaraderie of their fellow armed and uniformed volunteers. At the same time, the companies dominated by immigrants unabashedly put ethnic pride on display; at one point, city Democrats managed to quash an attempt by Know-Nothings to ban German and Irish flags from home guard and militia parades.[5]

It was among these militiamen that several pro-slavery adventurers found ready recruits in Savannah during the 1850s, when some of these "filibusters" led an expedition to Cuba in the summer of 1855, and others attempted to establish a new republic for slavery in Nicaragua in 1857 and 1858. The city also sent money and men to establish a slaveowners' colony in Kansas, though that venture faltered when, at the end of 1856, the settlers disbanded and dispersed, most retreating to Kansas City, Missouri.[6]

The martial spirit intensified as white Savannahians increasingly feared that enemies, both black and white, lived and labored among them. In July, the principal of Massie School came under fire for hiring one Miss Mason while "knowing her to be an abolitionist." (Only recently completed in 1857, the impressive two-story Massie School had been built with $5,000 bequeathed to the city sixteen years earlier by Peter Massie of Glynn County.) Hailing from the North, Miss Mason "began to show her fondness for the colored people of the South," and went so far as to engage in "injudicious talk at the public table," according to Richard Arnold. The school principal, Bernard Mallon, denied that he had been aware of Miss Mason's seditious tendencies when he hired her, and as soon as her indiscretions became the subject of gossip—once she became "so notorious"—he fired her. Now all teachers had to prove their "Native Americanism" if they expected to keep their jobs.[7]

The Mason incident highlighted Savannah's increasingly ambivalent stance toward all things and all people northern. By the late 1850s, about one-sixth of the city's white men had been born in the North. Of course some of the region's most prominent planters and professionals came from the North, and many, like Arnold, Charles Jones Jr. and his brother

Joseph, and Richard Wayne, had attended school there. They and their families summered in Philadelphia, Princeton, Saratoga Springs, and New York City, where they visited friends and relatives and escaped the heat, fevers, and sand flies of the lowcountry. They subscribed to northern newspapers and designed their Federalist brick homes with northern-style front stoops and dormer windows. They prized not only northern-made luxury goods, but also beef and sturdy shoes shipped down from Massachusetts. And they routinely employed Northerners as the teachers of their children.[8]

Soon after the indiscreet Miss Mason caused such a stir, another northern-born woman was adjusting to Savannah as her new home and enjoying a warm welcome from the city's wealthiest families. Twenty-three-year-old Eleanor Kinzie hailed from Chicago. Her father, fluent in the language of the Winnebago, had gained some renown as a government Indian agent in the late 1820s. He had also made a fortune working for John Jacob Astor's American Fur Company. Eleanor grew up imbibing Chicago's rough-hewn heritage, learning to make her own clothes and shoes as any self-respecting housewife was expected to do, but also, together with her five brothers and the seven cousins adopted by her parents, enjoying a life of rare privilege. The Kinzies entertained celebrities such as Fanny Kemble Butler and the Swedish writer Frederika Bremer. They visited West Point, where Eleanor's uncle David Hunter was paymaster, and made a stop at the White House, where the little girl exchanged pleasantries with President Zachary Taylor. Eleanor met her future husband, William Washington Gordon, a Savannah native, when she visited friends in New Haven, where he was a student at Yale. The two were married in Chicago in December 1857 and settled in Savannah the following spring. Like other young men of the elite class, William started out as a clerk and later became a partner in his family's cotton factorage business. Eleanor was always a high-spirited girl; family legend had her sliding down a banister (the first time her future husband laid eyes on her) and riding a wild horse owned by a well-known fixture on the Savannah social scene, Captain Charles A. L. Lamar.[9]

The story about "Nellie" Gordon taming Charley Lamar's horse might have been apocryphal; if so, it was no doubt intended to suggest how quickly and thoroughly members of Savannah's elite had embraced the newcomer, for the Lamars were a family of great wealth and distinction. As a fourteen-year-old, Charles Lamar and his father, the powerful banker and businessman Gazaway Bugg Lamar, had survived the sinking of the oceangoing steamer *Pulaski*. The disaster took Charles's mother and five of his siblings to a watery grave, but failed to dampen the young man's enthusiasm for saltwater sailing. By the time Nellie Gordon moved to Savannah, Charley Lamar had a family and an established career as a commission merchant and politician. Yet a renegade streak lay not far below the surface of his social respectability.[10]

With an increasing number of influential lowcountry politicians, journalists, and planters, Lamar aggressively promoted the idea that Georgia's prosperity depended on the reopening of the African slave trade. But unlike most ideologues, Lamar had the money to act upon his convictions, and the inclination to make even more money by doing so. Recently stymied by federal authorities in his efforts to bring African "apprentices" to Georgia, in 1858 Lamar set about secretly building a large schooner called *Wanderer* in Sekauket, New York. Supposedly built as a luxury vessel, the 243-ton *Wanderer* cost the substantial sum of $25,000. After a trial run to New Orleans that summer, Lamar had the ship outfitted with tanks large enough to hold 15,000 gallons of water—a sign that the ship was destined for more than just pleasure jaunts around Long Island Sound. Lamar spent little time fretting over the legality of what he was about to do; at one point he had boasted that he had nothing to fear from the authorities or a jury: "That is the advantage of a small place [Savannah]. A man of influence can do as he pleases."[11]

In the early fall of 1858, the *Wanderer* sailed to the western coast of Africa, where the captain purchased as many as six hundred blacks captured from settlements along the Congo River. The ensuing journey back to the United States encapsulated all the horrors of the Middle Passage, with men, women, and children packed tightly in the ship's hold. In November, the ship discharged its human cargo of 409 Africans on Jekyll Island, off the South Carolina coast. Among the terrified and exhausted group were many boys ages twelve to eighteen. (Soon all of the captives would receive new names—Zow Uncola would become Tom Johnson, Mabiala would become Uster Williams, and Manuella, Katie Noble.) Federal authorities were not far behind, seizing and impounding the ship in January, and Lamar scrambled to sell the Africans quickly. Wary of investing in this particular kind of property, most of his lowcountry neighbors passed on the chance to enhance their own workforces with people who might very well bring federal marshals to their plantation gates. Lamar was so successful in scattering individuals to Mobile, Memphis, Vicksburg, and beyond that false rumors circulated for months that a new, clandestine slave trade was bringing enormous numbers of African slaves to the South.[12]

In Savannah, people reacted to the *Wanderer* scandal with divergent and predictably strong opinions. Charles Junior condemned Lamar as a "dangerous man," notable primarily for his "recklessness and lawlessness." While William Thompson of the *Savannah Morning News* supported Lamar's venture, the more cautious editor of the *Republican*, James Roddy Sneed, suggested "the people of the South are to-day the freest, happiest and most prosperous on earth—in Heaven's name, why will not the politicians allow them to remain as they are?" Sneed was the true conservative in this debate, opposed to the radical, even revolutionary, sentiments of those in favor of the reopened trade. He warned that local politicians should avoid issues on which Southerners themselves "are known to be conscientiously and hopelessly divided." In February 1859, only the *Republican* carried the notice that Charley Lamar had been expelled from the New York Yacht Club, truly an insult to such a wealthy and well-connected man.[13]

To most men of the commercial elite, Lamar "was a man who became life, and life became him"—vigorous, resourceful, defiant of the federal laws that would stifle lowcountry economic development. In contrast, some slave traders argued that a reopening of the trade would harm their lucrative business of trafficking in U.S.-born men, women, and children. A reopened trade also amounted to an explicit threat to white workers, since one of Lamar's aims was to flood the lowcountry with fresh imports of hundreds if not thousands of Africans. Because of this new "abundance of negroes," according to a letter published in the *Republican* (probably written by Sneed), the "poor white man will stand no chance at all to make a support . . . and the poor would grow poorer while the rich grew richer." Lamar himself was unapologetic in his desire to make the South less dependent on white laborers; in Savannah, undisciplined Irish dockworkers set a perpetually bad example in the grogshops and brothels of the city. Contradicting Thompson, who believed that fresh imports of African slaves would bring more poor whites into the body politic, Lamar argued that all workers, regardless of legal status or skin color, should be disenfranchised; that way they would be "more susceptible of government than the hireling labor of the Democratic [northern] states." Lamar and others thus offered a pointed critique of the city's current labor market, which they believed consisted of too many white workers who were vulnerable to the blandishments of free-soil Republicans.[14]

Slaveholders worried specifically about the threat posed by the native-born workers who formed the backbone of the small but outspoken nativist Know-Nothing Party. By 1860, foreigners would constitute fully

50 percent of the city's total white adult males, having contributed to the 40 percent growth in the white population since 1850. Because of the increase in working-class newcomers, the number of slaves in the city, though stable, dropped as a proportion of the total population, from 45 percent in 1850 to 38 percent in 1860. A smaller percentage of white households now had a material stake in the slave system. At the same time, immigrants dominated the city's small businesses—dry-goods stores, groceries, saloons, cigar and tobacco shops, bakeries. Loyal to the Democrats, Irish and German newcomers were enjoying the fruits of political patronage, sealing their allegiance to the party and to the "southern way of life." Roman Catholic church leaders had recruited Irish laborers for the Central of Georgia Railroad in the early 1840s, and they remained eager to ingratiate themselves with the Protestant elite.[15]

Democratic politicians routinely associated the Know-Nothings with abolitionist tendencies: would native-born white artisans eventually act on their frustrations, squeezed as they were between slaves and free blacks on the one side and burgeoning numbers of Irish on the other? White casual laborers knew very well that they were in constant danger of being replaced by enslaved workers. Moreover, the 30 percent of Savannah white workers who were skilled also found themselves competing with slaves and free men of color as machinists, engineers, coopers, masons, carpenters, barbers, blacksmiths, plasterers, bricklayers, waiters, tailors, cabinetmakers, butchers, pastry cooks, and tinners. Responding to the complaints of white butchers, the council had passed regulations supposedly intended to restrict the activities of their black counterparts, but the alderman made no effort to enforce such restrictions, rendering them meaningless. Few white workers were immune to the baneful effects of the city's commercial economy, which was based on the processing of rice, lumber, and cotton and which relied on large numbers of blacks who were forced to labor for little or no pay. Even relatively privileged workers found only seasonal employment in Savannah; the welfare of their families depended on the rhythm of the cotton and rice cultivation and the vicissitudes of market prices.[16]

At the same time, lowcountry white laborers showed little evidence that they possessed either the will or the strength to act in their own economic self-interest in opposition to the town and country lords of the lash. Had they struck for higher wages, they would probably have been replaced by black workers in the trades and in the city's largest industries. Some craftsmen, including typographers, master bootmakers, and journeyman tailors, did organize in the antebellum period, but these associations more nearly resembled fraternal orders than labor unions. In the mid-1850s, groups of white workers struck for higher wages: in 1853, carpenters and mechanics working for the Central of Georgia Railroad; in 1856, laborers working for the same railroad; and, in the same year, the city's dockworkers. In each case employers moved swiftly to fire the striking workers and bring in blacks. Complicating the situation was the incremental upward mobility experienced by a few, albeit highly visible, members of the white laboring classes, most notably Irish immigrant men who won jobs as foot patrolmen in the police force, and shopkeepers who worked their way into the planter class. In 1850, more than half of all Irish immigrants were laborers; ten years later the proportion was one-third, though this suggestion of upward mobility might reflect the relatively high skill levels of newcomers as a group, and not the improving fortunes of individual immigrants who had lived in the city for the previous decade. But many whites believed that as long as the city reserved certain jobs for whites exclusively, even the poor could aspire to a better life.[17]

In early 1859 Charles Lamar was still trying to sell the last of the *Wanderer* Africans. Buyers remained wary. Some of the captured men and women bore tribal scars, or had their teeth filed to a point, distinguishing them from native-born blacks. Few slaveholders wanted to risk hard cash on a slave who might later be seized as part of a federal court case. In December 1858, the boat's crew were charged with piracy and remanded to jail to await trial during the next term of the U.S. district court, a development that Charles Jones Jr. hailed as "one which should call for rejoicing at the mouths of all humanity-loving and law-abiding citizens." Lamar expressed his displeasure with these developments by physically assaulting the jailer in charge of the *Wanderer* crew.[18]

The African slave trade issue resonated with so many lowcountry planters and merchants because the domestic slave trade remained a vital part of the urban and regional economy. Coffles of handcuffed black men, women, and children were a routine sight in Savannah streets, being transported twice a week from pens owned by traders (invariably referred to as "brokers") such as William Wright, to auction houses such as Joseph Bryan's, located near the city market, on Johnson Square. On her way to school in the morning, Susie Baker would watch these grim processions, the source of livelihood for the wealthiest men in the city.[19]

In late February 1859, a plantation carpenter named Primus and his wife, Daphne, with their baby and their three-year-old daughter, Dido, were forced into a freight car at Darien, a Georgia coastal town, and transported north to Savannah. From there they were taken to the Ten Broek racetrack, three miles outside the city. For the next week they and nearly 440 other slaves remained confined in sheds normally used for the horses and carriages of racetrack patrons: Pierce Butler was liquidating part of his estate. His inherited fortune, worth approximately $700,000, had dwindled, squandered by (in the words of one of his close friends) Butler's "sheer folly and infatuation." Nearly one-half of all the slaves on Hampton Point and Butler's Island—blacksmiths, carpenters, field hands, sawyers, and engineers among them—would be auctioned off to the highest bidder. Meanwhile, slave traders and planters' agents from Richmond to New Orleans were converging on Savannah in anticipation of the sale, one of the largest in recent memory. Between shots of whiskey at the City Hotel and the Pulaski House, the speculators argued over the worth of the Butler slaves, and debated the possible effects of the *Wanderer* on their own business. Writing under his pen name "Doesticks," a reporter for the *New York Tribune,* Mortimer Thomson, described the men as "a rough breed, slangy, profane and bearish." Joseph Bryan was set to preside over the sale. William Wright was there, and so was fellow alderman and slave trader George Wylly.[20]

The Butler slaves had to wait for several days, penned, before the auction got under way. They had brought with them bundles of household wares, tin dishes and gourds, and small stores of rice, beans, bacon, and corn bread. They had arrived dressed in their best, the women wearing earrings and yellow and blue beads, their heads covered with turbans adorned with ribbons. Later they and their descendants would refer to the big sale as the "weeping time."[21]

In the 1830s, Fanny Kemble had observed that the slaves on the two Butler plantations had deep roots there. And so the auction of March 1859 represented the violation of two long-standing communities, their members bound to one another by common traditions and by extended kinship. Though buyers were required to purchase "families," those units were often torn away from the complex social relationships that sustained the Butler slaves. Even before the sale, it was common knowledge among Butler's friends and associates that "brothers & sisters of mature age, parents & children of mature age, all other relations & ties of home & long association will be violently severed."[22]

The slaves put up for sale did not include several children who had a white father. For example, the Butler family retained Daphne, thirty-four, the daughter of the overseer Roswell King Jr. and the slave Minda, and Jim Valient, forty-four, son of King and the slave Judy. Perhaps the estate's trustees did not want to provide too much fodder for the gossips who would inevitably leer at the mulattoes from this seemingly closed community of slaves. Or perhaps the estate's trustees squirmed at the thought of a white man's children being auctioned off to the highest bidder.[23]

The two-day sale took place on March 2 and 3 in a driving rain. Individual men, women, and children stood on a platform two and a half feet high while prospective buyers examined them for their "soundness," a catchall term meant to convey a man's capacity for field work and a woman's capacity for field work and for bearing children. Posing as a trader, Thomson the reporter circulated through the crowd, taking notes. He described the scene before the sale, a peculiar southern performance reenacted countless times in the antebellum period: "The Negroes were examined with as little consideration as if they had been brutes indeed; the buyers pulling their mouths open to see their teeth, pinching their limbs to find how muscular they were, walking them up and down to detect any signs of lameness, making them stoop and bend in different ways that they might be certain there was no concealed rupture or wound; and in addition to all this treatment, asking them scores of questions relative to their qualifications and accomplishments." When Primus's wife, Daphne, stood on the block, she pulled her shawl tight around her, protecting her two-week-old baby from the downpour. The onlookers demanded, "Pull off her rags and let us see her . . . Who's going to bid on that nigger, if you keep her covered up. Let's see her face."[24]

In the end, the sale netted the Butler estate more than $300,000, an average of $716 a person. Joseph Bryan earned a 2.5 percent commission and billed the estate the money he had spent on advertising—a total of $8,000. Pierce Butler had put in an appearance, at one point extending a gloved hand to the now former members of his "plantation family," distributing to each adult four silver quarters newly minted in Philadelphia. As the buyers popped champagne corks (courtesy of Bryan), the slaves were transported to railroad depots and the Savannah wharves; many were bound to the interior of Georgia.[25]

After reading Mortimer Thomson's account in the *New York Tribune,* William Thompson, the *Savannah Morning News* editor, fumed, "While the article is well suited to impose on the willing credulity and excite the mawkish sentimentality of the abolition fanatics of the North, for whose edification it was written, it can induce in the minds of Southern readers only feelings of scorn and contempt." By this time, editor Thompson and others could take satisfaction from what they considered a successful closure of the *Wanderer* case. (Reporter Thomson had observed that within the city of Savannah generally, the reopening of the African slave trade was "devoutly to be wished.") Prosecutors of the *Wanderer* crew had had a difficult time finding witnesses; the Africans were of no use here, since they were barred by law from testifying against a white person. And so in the spring of 1859 U.S. authorities would enter a *nolle prosequi,* a formal notice that the prosecution would end its proceedings against the defendants. Lamar lost little time in buying back the impounded *Wanderer* at auction. He was proposing to sponsor another voyage, this one to China, where the ship would pick up "coolies" who could be sold in Cuba for as much as $350 each. Presumably Chinese indentured servants were just as vulnerable as African slaves, and could be exploited in the rice and cotton fields accordingly. Had Lamar followed through with this venture, he would have encountered John E. Ward, the attorney and former mayor, now serving as U.S. minister to China and charged with overseeing the international trade in Chinese indentured labor.[26]

In May 1859 Liberty County planter William B. Gaulden, a longtime proponent of a reopened African slave trade, saw an opportunity to reclaim the public's attention. He rented out Savannah's St. Andrews Hall and invited "the citizens of Chatham County" to hear him speak on this and other issues of the day. If importing Africans was a risky business venture, talking about it offered some possibility of moneymaking. Gaulden was joined in the call by Charles Lamar; Philip M. Russell, clerk of the city court and father of the new jailer, Waring Russell; Joseph Bryan, the slave trader; and Thompson of the *Morning News.* More appealing to the mass of Savannahians, though, was an encore performance of the "Great Attraction," a circus that featured the "General Wade Hampton" sideshow. Hampton was a black man, forty-seven years old and weighing thirty-eight pounds. One satisfied ticket holder described him as "an intelligent fellow, [who] converses freely, and is quite entertaining."[27]

The fuss surrounding Wade Hampton recalled the visit of Tom Thumb, the tiny circus performer who had appeared in the city eight years before. Yet white Savannahians believed themselves living daily in the midst of a public sideshow on the streets and in the squares, and they were not always amused by the spectacle. In June the grand jury of Chatham County Superior Court protested against allowing black men and women "to ride about in carriages on the public streets in the city, and on the drives in the country, and to walk and parade in the Park and on the side walks frequented by our wives and daughters to their great annoyance." Whites had always insisted that blacks take the outside of the sidewalk, where pedestrians were more likely to get dirty from the animal waste and general filth of the streets; now black people seemed to be claiming the inside space as their own. Moreover, too many black women were "richly dressed & nothing on their heads," relinquishing the traditional, modest-colored turban or kerchief in favor of hats, veils, or, most shocking, nothing. Complaints about black women centered on the gradual disappearance of a caste-based dress code; indeed, with black women wearing so much fine jewelry, and attaching false braids and curls to their hairdos, "at a little distance a [white] lady cannot be distinguished in dress from a servant!"[28]

Some visitors from the North and Europe contrasted the finery of a few Savannah blacks with the wretched appearance of the many; for every bejeweled mulatto in a horse-drawn carriage were many barefoot rice slaves, ill-clad servants and dock laborers, and hotel workers beaten and "dulled by overwork." The visiting northern clergyman Nehemiah Adams speculated about the larger social meaning of dress in a slave society. At church services on Sunday, he took careful note of "slaves with broadcloth suits, well-fitting and nicely-ironed fine shirts, polished boots, gloves, umbrellas for sunshades, the best of hats, their young men with their blue coats and bright buttons, in the latest style, white Marseilles vests, white pantaloons, brooches in their shirt bosoms, gold chains, elegant sticks, and some old men leaning on their ivory and silver-headed staves." Gazing upon this novel sight, Adams "fell into some reflections upon the philosophy of dress as a powerful means of securing respect." He wrote, "how impossible it must soon become to treat with indignity men who respected themselves, as these men evidently did." However, Adams was mistaken in his assumption that a well-dressed slave could not be "violently separated from his family, . . . or abused with impunity."[29]

The municipal elections of October 1859 brought a shake-up to city government as the Democratic Party collapsed under the weight of its own power, splitting into two factions. Charging the old guard with corruption, the dissidents nominated Richard Arnold for mayor and the younger Charles Jones for one of the alderman slots. Members of the Know-Nothing Party knew they remained outnumbered, even though "the Democracy [is] torn asunder and at war." Of Arnold they had few kind things to say: "Ever since we have been a party who has abused us more than Dr. Arnold? Who has done it oftener? Who with as much bitterness and acrimony? Yea, with more delight?" On October 10, the reformers achieved a clean sweep; at the head of the balloting were Jones and Wallace Cumming, banker and railroad president, who tied with 907 votes each. Now married (to the former Ruth Berrien Whitehead) and the father of a little girl, Jones had embarked on what he hoped would be a career in the service of social order and public morality.[30]

A week after the election, on October 16, the nation was stunned by the news that a northern abolitionist named John Brown had led a raid on the federal arsenal at Harpers Ferry, Virginia. Brown received financial backing from a group of abolitionists calling themselves the Secret Six; among them was the minister Thomas Wentworth Higginson, who had long been determined to play a direct role in the destruction of slavery. Brown and his twenty-two white and black accomplices, including his sons, had intended to seize weapons, arm slaves in the area, and incite a large-scale rebellion throughout the South. In the aborted raid, Brown and his men killed seven people before they themselves were captured. Eight of the raiders, including two of Brown's sons, lay dead, slain by federal troops under the command of Colonel Robert E. Lee from Virginia. In Savannah, editor Thompson condemned "these insane abolitionists," this "band of fanatical demons," who "attempted to force the slaves of Virginia into servile insurrection, and to deluge the Southern States in blood." Yet as southern whites rose up to excoriate Brown, they feared that the real threat lay in his ability to speak their own language—the conviction that the slavery question would be resolved by those willing to kill and be killed over it.[31]

John Brown stood trial, charged with treason, multiple counts of murder, and inciting a slave insurrection. He was convicted on all counts, and was hanged on December 2, 1859, but not before claiming martyrdom: "Now, if it is deemed necessary that I should forfeit my life for the furtherance of the end of justice, and mingle my blood further with the blood of my children and with the blood of millions in this slave country whose rights are disregarded by wicked, cruel, and unjust enactments, I say, let it be done." In response, white Southerners renewed their focus on suspected traitors in their midst: free people of color and Northerners of modest means. In December the Georgia legislature passed laws to end deathbed emancipations of slaves, to bar nonresident free blacks from the state, and to sell into slavery any free blacks found "wandering or strolling about, or leading an idle, immoral or profligate course of life." Distinctions between free and enslaved persons receded as caste lines hardened: now it was African heritage, rather than skin color or legal status, that rendered a whole group of people vulnerable to the depredations of law and extralegal violence. Planters scuttled plans to send their children north to school that coming fall. Throughout the lowcountry, new "vigilance com-mittees" and militias such as the Phoenix Riflemen in Savannah orga-nized and took up arms. On December 1, a Savannah mob subjected a Massachusetts-born shoe dealer to a painful tar-and-feathering for his anti-slavery sentiments, for his "too free expression of opinions not suited to this latitude." The following month a Savannah court ordered that John Taylor, a free black seaman, receive 128 lashes for assaulting one of his shipmates. The judge regretted that the law prevented him from meting out a harsher sentence. Gone was the custom of limiting lashings to thirty-nine at a time.[32]

Upriver from Savannah, the city of Augusta began an all-out campaign against the 386 free people of color who lived there. In January 1860, Robert Campbell, a lawyer and longtime supporter of the American Col-onization Society, wrote to the Augusta *Chronicle and Sentinel* decrying the city's attempt to tax and harass the class of free blacks out of exis-tence. Campbell considered the ACS a vehicle to promote the emigration of free people of color; the group, he believed, was the "Safety-Valve of the Slave States and as such should be cherished." James Harper, another prominent white man and a life member of the ACS, served as a local agent of the society and, in the spring, helped to coordinate preparations for a Liberia-bound voyage scheduled for late April or early May. Among the prospective emigrants was Silas Pope, forty-seven years old; Pope had paid his former owner $1,072 to free himself some time ago, and had recently purchased his wife, Louisa, and daughter, Eliza, for $667.[33]

It was the so-called "Cuthbert Conspiracy" that infused the 1860 ACS sailing with high drama. Alfred Cuthbert Jr., a large landowner in Jasper County, near Augusta, had decided to free the seventy-three slaves he had inherited from his father, a former U.S. senator, and send them to Liberia. He planned to move his own family to Paterson, New Jersey, immediately after the ship sailed. The "conspiracy," notable for its coded messages sent between Augusta and the North, had been under way since 1853. With his wife, Annie, Cuthbert had donated $4,000 to the ACS to ensure his slaves' safe passage to Liberia. Cuthbert and James Harper devised a plan to send the group down the Savannah River by steamer to Tybee Lighthouse. The party would thus avoid the port of Savannah, which had recently imposed a $200 fee on all blacks emigrating to Liberia, and the U.S. Customs agent, who was prepared to deny the group clearance. In late April, William McLain of the ACS once again found himself in Savannah, staying indoors, out of the public eye, biding his time and waiting for the arrival of the ACS ship *M. C. Stevens*. It pained McLain that, when he saw old acquaintances on the street, "they said nothing and I did the same." He added, "It grieves me to find my colored friends afraid to be seen speaking to me." The ship's arrival on April 30 brought relief all around; responding to a telegram and following the secret plan, the Cuthberts sent their group via steamer to meet the ship waiting at the mouth of the Savannah River. Wrote Cuthbert in the midst of feverish preparations to get the emigrants out of the country, "God has thus far signalled that he blesses the plan."[34]

ON THEIR WAY downriver toward freedom, and toward hardship in another form in the raw country of Liberia, the ACS emigrants, including the Cuthbert slaves, slipped past Argyle Island. There the slaves at Gowrie and East Hampton were contending with the third overseer in as many years. By January 1858, the Manigaults had finally found someone to replace the disgraced Leonard Venters. The new overseer, a married man named William H. Bryan, promptly installed his family at the "camp," a pineland settlement a dozen miles from Argyle Island. But he soon "turned out wretchedly," insisting on visiting his family nearly every day and neglecting "all things" in the process. Meanwhile, pneumonia and dysentery had swept through the plantations in the summer and fall of 1858, causing the deaths of several slaves. Bryan had decided that his best course was to take himself out of harm's way and retreat to the camp, leaving the slaves to fend for themselves. The Manigaults fired Bryan at the end of 1858, only to learn that he was contaminating the small pool of potential replacements by spreading "all sorts of nonsense" about the miserable working conditions on Argyle Island.[35]

In early 1860 they hired Louis's third cousin William Capers, "a man of high standing & experience," though unfortunately burdened by debt and a host of lawsuits against him. Before signing the elaborate contract put in front of him, Capers absorbed advice about dealing with workers "inclined to be unruly." Among the East Hermitage and Gowrie slaves, Martha, Joe, Dublin, and Stepney had all recently been sent to a jail yard to be flogged. The Manigaults wanted to keep this information quiet, knowing that it would hurt the resale value of each person; and they assigned Martha, the cook, to the new overseer without telling him about her disturbing history. Charles advised Capers to assemble all the hands, then line up potential troublemakers with their hands tied behind their backs and "preach them a short sermon on the propriety of conduct." The new overseer lost little time forcing the slaves to dig a new irrigation canal.[36]

Discipline problems continued to plague the Argyle Island plantations throughout the spring of 1860. In June, George the driver threatened to punish a young hand named London. But London managed to break free, heading for the river and vowing to drown himself before he would be whipped. Later, Capers found London's corpse floating in a canal on Gowrie plantation, and ordered the body left there: "this I have done to let the negroes see when a negro takes his own life they will be treated in this manner." By denying the rest of the Gowrie and East Hermitage community the opportunity to give London's body a proper burial, Capers sought to establish his own authority once and for all. Regarding George as a culprit in the unfortunate affair, he advised the Manigaults to sell the slave "in a quiet manner" for "he is of no use to you as a driver and is a bad negro."[37]

Meanwhile, all of white Georgia remained on edge, still reeling from the Harpers Ferry bloodbath. Meeting in Chicago in May, the Republicans had just nominated as their candidate for president the avowedly anti-slavery Abraham Lincoln. In Georgia, delegates to the Democratic state nominating convention split over possible presidential candidates. One group favored Senator Stephen Douglas of Illinois; the other group, "bolters," determined to uphold congressional protection for slavery in the territories, planned to nominate a native son, the planter Alexander Stephens. This faction would eventually support Stephens's fellow pro-slavery ideologue John C. Breckinridge.[38]

The spring and summer brought a welter of mixed signals as residents contemplated the future of the federal union. With its customary nationalistic overtones, the annual St. Patrick's Day celebration retained a certain timeless quality; at their banquet, members of the Irish Union society offered toasts to President Buchanan and the U.S. Army and Navy, in addition to honoring the martyrs of Ireland, Pope Pius IX, and woman ("To her yoke alone the true man bows his neck a submissive captive").[39]

Richard Arnold embodied the conflicting impulses of devotion to country and defiance toward northern abolitionists. In June, he delivered the keynote address at the fourth National Quarantine and Sanitary Convention in Boston, a national meeting of public health officers. Arnold praised "this Republican Union . . . the most successful instance of self government which [God] has ever to be shown on his earth." Of his hometown, Savannah, he opined, "May the health-seeking wish that associates her today with Boston, be a type of future mutual study to secure a healthful union of good-will and friendship." Arnold concluded by expressing his gratitude to his hosts, holding up a glass of champagne and noting that several years before in the same city, the founders of the American Medical Association (of which he was a charter member) had served only cold water to their disappointed guests; but then he went on to laud the distinctive nature of the southern economy and society: "We are not a manufacturing people; we don't want to be."[40]

On a muggy Fourth of July, in towns all over Georgia, volunteer militia companies paraded through the streets and fired salutes in honor of the day. The Savannah celebration took place at six in the morning, so that the men, wearing caps and heavy wool uniforms, could avoid the heat of midday. Unnoticed amid the excitement was the arrival of the enslaved George from Argyle Island. William Capers had brought him to the city and then paid $4 to the Adams Express Company to have him delivered to Charleston, where he was bound to fetch at least $1,500 from a buyer.[41]

Back on the island a few days later, Capers wrote his employer a letter that began: "A more painful task than this has not been my lot for some time." On Saturday, July 7, a mighty storm of hail and rain had flattened the ripening rice crop, producing a sight truly "melancholy to behold." In the slave quarters, "the white wash on the Houses look [sic] as if the House had been Shot at with Balls." At the time, no one could have anticipated the truly monumental whirlwind of destruction on the way, what a future president would call "a John Brown raid, on a gigantic scale."[42]

IN BELLO

-◦❧┤ CHAPTER FIVE ├❧◦-

An Abiding Hope in Every Breast

O N A STEAMY FRIDAY in July 1860, military companies representing the city of Savannah and the city of New York met in a historic encounter. That morning, the 20th, the steamship *Florida* had entered New York harbor, cut its engines, and waited. Arrayed on its decks were ninety uniformed Savannah Republican Blues standing at attention. When the tugboat *Satellite* pulled alongside the ship, an artillery salute rang out, a band struck up a march, and crew members on both sides waved their caps and cheered. With great ceremony, representatives of the New York City Guards transferred from the *Satellite* to the *Florida* and welcomed their guests from Georgia. Lieutenant Colonel Ferris of the City Guards delivered the first of many speeches the Blues would hear (and endure) during their five-day visit. According to a reporter present, Ferris told the Blues "that hospitality was not a plant of Northern or of Southern growth exclusively, but alike the product of both sections of the Union." The City Guards aimed to show their guests, in Ferris's words, "that they were true friends—in short, that they were white men."[1]

On board the *Satellite*, the Blues partook of "sundry timely glasses of claret and bushels of sandwiches" en route to the dock at North Moore Street, where they disembarked. A crush of onlookers crowding the sidewalks followed the men as they marched through the streets of Manhattan. Carrying knapsacks and outfitted in woolen uniforms and caps, weary from the long voyage and perhaps too many glasses of claret, the militia members nonetheless maintained remarkable military discipline. New Yorkers took particular note of three members of the Blues' entourage, slave musicians, who, it was rumored, "are too much attached to the company and their masters to be in any danger of yielding to the temptations to desertion which will undoubtedly be held out to them."[2]

A front-page article in the *New York Times* heralded the Blues' arrival and extolled the illustrious military company, which boasted "some of the wealthiest and most honored citizens of Savannah." The company's leader was Captain John W. Anderson, a cotton merchant and the older brother of former mayor Edward C. Anderson. Other members included the sons of prominent businessmen, as well as a number of civic leaders, men who rotated on and off the city council. Over the next few days, the Blues enjoyed a whirlwind of ceremonial dinners and private receptions. They spent one day touring the Randall's Island orphanage and the Blackwell's Island workhouse, almshouse, hospital, and penitentiary complex. Resplendent in their tall plumed bearskin caps, dark blue dress coats, and white pants, the company drilled to the delight of large crowds. With expenses shared by guests and hosts, this type of military exhibition was not unprecedented in antebellum cities—the Chicago Zouaves had visited New York earlier that summer—but never had a southern company ventured so far north.[3]

The Blues and their hosts indulged in a show of "white men's" solidarity that seemed to belie the fears of Southerners and Northerners who, like Charles Jones Jr., had been "somewhat inclined to doubt the policy of the trip just at this time." Tongue in cheek, a *Times* reporter compared the Blues' social activities to a benevolent military maneuver: "Their strategy was developed in pacification, their artillery practice, in the firing of welcome salutes." During formal dinners, the Blues and the City Guards "made 'war to the knife,'—with the butter knife and fruit knife; they charged freely—not upon each other—but upon sundry stores of provisions; their cannonade consisted mainly of the popping of corks; and the smoke of the battle arose from thousands of 'best Havanas [cigars].' " In elaborate toasts, the citizen soldiers pledged that "both were equally ready to fight for mutual rights," and that "they would know no North or South as far as these two companies were concerned." At a banquet on Monday, the Blues and their hosts lifted their glasses to George Washington, Andrew Jackson, and other generals who were also political leaders ("We claimed a part of their common glory"); to Woman ("Her virtues are the object of a soldier's idolatry"); and to the Constitution (most treasured was its "protection of personal property").[4]

The Blues' formal visit came to an end on July 25, but not before the corps had posed for a stereopticon portrait at J. Gurney & Son on Broadway. Marring their otherwise triumphal tour was the unsuccessful attempt by an unknown person to persuade one of the slaves "to elope," now that he "was on free soil." The black man resisted this appeal, according to the *Times,* claiming "that he was at liberty to leave when he chose, and was too well treated by his master to wish any further freedom." On the day of their departure, Captain Anderson thanked his hosts for their hospitality and invited them to Savannah—"a visit which he hoped would not be long delayed." Then, as cannon boomed and well-wishers waved farewell, the *Florida* departed. Only fifty-four Blues sailed for Georgia that day; the rest stayed behind for "business or for pleasure."[5]

Among those remaining was George A. Mercer, who headed to the popular vacation spot Saratoga Springs. Though a proud member of the Blues, Mercer was more inclined to opera and fine literature than military rituals. An attorney in the firm of John E. Ward and Charles Jones, the twenty-five-year-old Mercer suffered from a persistent crisis of self-confidence. His fear of public speaking was intense; his first address to the Blues, the year before, had unnerved him. Mercer was convinced that "a morbid, emasculating diffidence, which it appears impossible to overcome, presents the greatest impediment to my legal success." Nevertheless, the excursion to New York had left the young man deeply satisfied; indeed, the "very late hours, rich food and plenty of champagne, the attendant excitement and pleasant company" had done him "great good," he believed.[6]

The Blues returned home to a city in turmoil. As early as the midsummer of 1860, the outcome of the upcoming presidential election appeared a foregone conclusion. The national Democratic Party had split in two, with some Northerners fielding Stephen Douglas, proponent of the now discredited idea of sectional compromise on slavery; and radical Southerners bolting the party to endorse their own staunchly pro-slavery candidate, John C. Breckinridge. Complicating the contest for the White House was a coalition of Know-Nothings and former Whigs who had cobbled together the Constitutional Union Party; their presidential candidate, John C. Bell, favored ignoring the issue of slavery altogether and preserving the Union at all costs. With the Democrats hopelessly divided along both regional and ideological lines, the Republican Lincoln was virtually assured of victory. Throughout the South, speculation swirled around the ways an abolitionist chief executive might strangle the institution of slavery—by nominating anti-slavery fanatics to the Supreme Court, by outlawing bondage in the territories, by bolstering a southern wing of the Republican Party through political appointees. In Savannah, on street corners, in well-appointed parlors, and in the city council chambers, blustery talk of secession from the Union filled the air.[7]

The prospect of Lincoln's election united in fellow feeling the hot-headed slave smuggler Charley Lamar with the cautious physician Richard D. Arnold and the righteous young lawyer Charles Jones Jr. But not all Savannah white men came together under the banner of the southern slavocracy. The Liberty County planter William B. Gaulden, who not long ago had had a falling-out with local Democratic Party leaders, declared his intention of "stumping the State industriously" on behalf of Douglas. Mayor Arnold successfully solicited political contributions for Breckinridge from a cross section of the city's wealthiest Jews, Catholics, and Protestants; but he confided to a correspondent in August, "I am sorry to say that there are a great many adopted Irish citizens that are strongly inclined to Douglas."[8]

Adding to the unease that midsummer was the "bread excitement" sweeping the city. Journeymen bakers had struck for higher wages and then resorted to arson and riotous protests when they did not get their way. The bakers were incensed by price-fixing on the part of the city treasury, what they called an "unjust, unconstitutional law" that kept the price of a loaf of bread constant even when the price of flour rose. The bakers tried to shrink their loaves in order to maintain a steady profit margin, prompting retaliation by the city council, followed by another round of charges and countercharges. Would the wealthy now be cast as oppressors of white wage earners?[9]

Meanwhile, Savannah whites of all classes were stunned by the news of "a most diabolical plot to destroy the country," a plot centered in Texas and reportedly instigated by abolitionist preachers. Though hundreds of miles away, the so-called "Texas Troubles" served as a sinister backdrop to even routine transgressions on the part of Savannah slaves—black men and women absconding from their owners "without a pass or any cause," fugitives now "lurking about the city" and plundering storehouses and ships. On Argyle Island, the overseer William Capers reluctantly informed his employer, Louis Manigault, that the slaves Hector and Daniel had run off—one probably to Savannah, the other to "the Crackers" living nearby: "all negroes must be watched," Capers warned ominously. The ghost of John Brown seemed to settle upon the lowcountry.[10]

Responding to perceived threats both internal and external, the city fathers spent the summer and early fall of 1860 attempting to establish social order and at the same time to distance themselves from the ascendant "Black Republicans" of the North. By late September the council had approved a measure to create a homegrown insurance company and thus free the city from the $70,000 premiums paid annually to northern insurance companies, businesses "whose antagonism to the South, Southern Institutions, and Principles are well known." The council also renewed its efforts to beef up the city's small, undisciplined police force, which was no longer a match for drunken rowdies and gangs of "professional burglars." Aldermen vowed to crack down on brothels and taverns that entertained blacks and whites together, targeting foreign-born shopkeepers. By this time the city had completed construction of a broad new parade ground at the south end of Forsyth Park, landscaped and graded at a cost of $65,000, to accommodate the regimental drills that were becoming an ever more prominent feature of everyday life. In the words of Mayor Arnold, "Our citizen soldiery, our pride in peace, will be our safeguard in time of danger." Home militias, including the Republican Blues, Jasper Greens, and Chatham Artillery, were taking on new members.[11]

Yet daily displays of martial force called forth some unintended consequences. Early in the summer the council had noted the tendency of "negroes to congregate upon the side walks, in the streets, and squares . . . to attend, follow, and precede" military drills and parades. The throngs of black curiosity-seekers aggravated white passersby and disturbed the "quietude of the neighborhood." In what would amount to a fruitless gesture, the council ordered the city marshal to arrest and confine all black people who attended the parades (with the exception of the musicians who took part in them), and to outlaw the peddling of alcohol in the vicinity of such processions. Three-quarters of a century later, George Carter (in 1860 one of Arnold's slaves) vividly recalled stopping his master's carriage to watch the volunteers "march an' drill in duh square. Dey wuz a pritty sight." Carter's delight highlighted a central irony: military mobilization was beginning to spawn the sorts of disorder it was meant to eliminate.[12]

Such turbulent times demanded a leader of firm resolve, an energetic man of sound principles and unquestioned moral rectitude. And so on October 8 the voters of Savannah chose the twenty-nine-year-old attorney Charles C. Jones Jr. as their mayor. Jones lost little time fulfilling his supporters' expectations; within two weeks he had ordered the arrest of several free black sailors on the charge of "tampering with our Negroes [slaves] and attempting to induce them to leave the state." The new mayor also vowed to address the city's most pressing problem: the fact that blacks in general "have forgotten their places—are guilty of gambling, smoking in the streets, drinking, and disorderly conduct generally." Behind this breakdown of order were "those offenders of foreign birth, the rum-sellers, who at the corners of our streets in their shops are demoralizing our servants and ruining them in every point of view." The Reverend Charles Jones Sr. and his wife, Mary, took pride in the fact that their son was now in a position to put Christian principles into practice by upholding the system of slavery and eradicating the horrors of drink. The elder Jones urged the new mayor to "avoid excitement and too frequent speaking on public occasions," advice that the young man would choose to ignore.[13]

In early November, the rivals Savannah and Charleston conducted a public, if largely symbolic, reconciliation as they celebrated the recent completion of a one-hundred-mile railroad linking the two ports. Charlestonians hoped that the rail route, which had been in the works for six years, would help them capture some of the lucrative upcountry cotton trade from the Forest City. On November 2, a delegation of Charleston businessmen inaugurated the new line by taking the train to Savannah, where they were greeted by Mayor Jones. Later that evening, the festivities concluded with a banquet in the Pulaski House; there Savannahians and Charlestonians affirmed their fraternal ties as white Southerners. In a speech that night, one of the hosts, Francis S. Bartow, gave a cautious endorsement to the burgeoning South Carolina secession movement. Bartow, a lawyer, politician, and head of the Oglethorpe Light Infantry, declared that Georgians "pledge that we will defend South Carolina, rash though we think her, precipitate though we deem her, with all the energy and courage of a brother." Bartow added, "But my counsel to you is not to do it." The guests took from this less than enthusiastic endorsement of their own radical politics the conviction that, if and when South Carolina seceded from the Union, Georgia would not be far behind. Gratefully, the Charlestonians invited their hosts to visit the South Carolina city on November 9. A few days after their visitors returned home, the Savannah council resolved "to purchase a suitable quantity of fixed ammunition for each active member of the Volunteer Corps of this city."[14]

On November 8, the Republican Abraham Lincoln won a plurality of 1,865,593 of the popular vote (and a projected 180 electoral votes), defeating both Democrats—Douglas (1,382,713) and Breckinridge (848,356)—and the Constitutional Unionist, Bell (592,906). Fully two-thirds of Chatham County voters cast their ballots for Breckinridge. The Georgia state legislature immediately called for a secession convention to meet in January, and the city of Savannah proceeded to throw itself into a "perfect turmoil." On the day after the election, the Republican Blues unveiled in public what they called a secession flag, a banner similar to one adopted by the colonists during the Revolutionary War. Imprinted on the flag was a coiled snake and the words "Don't Tread on Me." (In fact, the rattlesnake as a symbol of swiftness and fierceness boasted a long lowcountry history, stretching back to prehistoric Mississippian Indian culture.)[15]

That day a delegation of Savannah bankers, businessmen, and planters traveled to Charleston for another round of speech making and fire-eating. Still apparently hedging his bets, Francis Bartow once again addressed the glittering gathering of dignitaries, declaring in one breath, "I am a Union man"; but in the next, as for the gathering storm: "Put it not off until tomorrow . . . we shall not be stronger by waiting." That night Charleston politicians telegraphed the state capital that Georgians "have pledged their state." They hoped to seal the deal a few days later by heaping praise on their former rivals, now presumed soon-to-be allies in secession. Sending a resolution to Mayor Jones and the Savannah city council, the Charlestonians highlighted the economic prosperity and progress that marked the elegant river port: "Magnificent buildings that bespeak the character of their inhabitants! Railroads that would do honor to any nation on the globe! Steamers that bring distant places almost hourly to your doors!" South Carolina, Charleston seemed to be saying, was fully prepared for independence on its own terms. But the state eagerly seized on the prospect that its neighbor would also choose to defy the perfidious northern abolitionists.[16]

Quickly the white population of Savannah apparently coalesced around the idea of southern independence. A series of grand torchlight processions and "citizens' meetings" fanned the flames of rebellion. "I trust that we may soon see a Southern confederacy," wrote Mayor Jones on November 13, and his mother responded that, if war should come, it "would be preferable to submission to Black Republicanism, involving as it would all that is horrible, degrading, and ruinous." Their support for Douglas by now a distant memory, white laborers were swept up in the frenzy of the moment, carried away by the speeches of fire-eaters and the fevered pitch of public meetings: for German and Irish Democrats especially, to be an American now was to close ranks with other southern white men in defiance of northern abolitionists. At a mass meeting on December 12, the Catholic priest Jeremiah O'Neill gave his blessing to the secessionists and exhorted his fellow Irish immigrants to join the cause; indeed, "he would be the first to *lade* them into battle, he would!" (The priest's enthusiasm prompted Mayor Jones to remark, "Popery and republicanism make a funny figure together.") One observer claimed that

Savannah was now of "one mind, and that mind is resistance to our oppressors!" Nevertheless, later developments would suggest that a wide array of groups—rich and poor, native-born and immigrant, male and female, black and white—felt compelled to mask their misgivings in the midst of so much public posturing by an influential segment of the white male population.[17]

To their consternation, Savannah merchants, lawyers, and planters soon realized that the rush to southern independence might well exact from them a high price in both money and power. As early as November they were expressing anxiety about the "Stagnant State of business," now that political uncertainty was taking a toll on the city's economy. A host of new questions about the future relations between Savannah and its northern creditors, its domestic and foreign customers, and the federal government was paralyzing activity in the mills, in the warehouses, and on the docks. Immigrant men had recently arrived from the North to process, haul, and load the region's cotton, rice, and timber; but now they found themselves without work, "many becoming the inmates of our poor houses and hospital," complained the city council. Banks began to curtail their operations and some stores closed their doors. Reports circulated that "the Irish draymen, rail road employees, and all depending on the transportation of cotton are out of employment." In December the U.S. Treasury Department pointedly refused to recognize the claims of the Savannah Poor House and Hospital for its care of ill and disabled seamen. Savannah would pay a price for its treasonous breast-beating, if federal authorities had any say in the matter. As business contracted, the fate of the hospital would be in the hands of private donors, men and women already feeling the strain of financial uncertainty.[18]

The city, which had incurred large new debts for its recent initiatives—not only the new parade ground but also an updated sewer system—now had to contend with rapidly shrinking tax revenues. Plans for a new jail and workhouse would have to wait. The economic downturn put a crimp in an emerging southern patriotism among some of the elite. Hiram Roberts, the president of the Merchants and Planters Bank, was not inclined to respond favorably to Governor Joseph Brown's appeal that banks raise a $1 million military appropriation by purchasing state bonds. However, in an effort to avoid charges of disloyalty, Roberts downplayed the substance of the governor's request and focused instead on the way it was delivered. Responding to Brown, Roberts observed that the directors of his own bank were "not disposed to obey your *threat*."[19]

Meanwhile, unruly paramilitary organizations were forming in the

city. Some of the new militias seemed less interested in military prepared-
ness and more in intimidating blacks and suspect whites. In November, a
mob attacked a light-skinned free black carpenter, Joseph Ribero, thirty-
one, charging that he had told slaves that Lincoln would free them. Calling themselves "jurors," they whipped Ribero and shaved his head before
they sent him out of the city. (The fact that he was married to a white
woman born in London probably heightened his vulnerability; the family
eventually settled in Chelsea, Massachusetts, and became "white.")
Three of the new vigilante groups—the Rattlesnake Club, Savannah
Rifles, and Blue Caps—reportedly consisted of "all the rowdies in town."
The Rattlesnakes claimed responsibility for tarring and feathering a
British sea captain in the presence of his horrified wife on board his own
ship. The captain had invited a black crew member to dine at his table. A
northern mechanic who received the unwanted attention of the Rattlesnake Club claimed that, although its members called themselves
"minutemen," the group was little more than a ring of racketeers, offering
to protect "members" from the wrath of the mob.[20]

The formal secession of South Carolina from the United States on
December 20 propelled Savannahians outdoors for an immense torchlight procession, described by the *Republican* with predictable hyperbole as "the most imposing spectacle ever witnessed in our city." (In a
moment of candor the paper noted, "There may be some who would
have preferred for the gallant Palmetto state to have acted at a later day, to
have obtained more simultaneous secession," but quickly added, "now
that that Rubicon had been crossed, there are none who will utter or
cherish a wish but for her welfare and prosperity.") Led by a contingent of
Savannah Volunteer Guards, the marchers held high their torchlights,
banners, and transparencies while onlookers "swarmed the street and
gave vent to their enthusiasm." Fireworks lit up the street to reveal an
imposing flower-bedecked carriage drawn by four magnificent grays; the
passengers were several young white women representing the "sisters of
the Southern Confederacy." Not all Savannahians thrilled to this display of
nascent nationalism, however; George Mercer noted disapprovingly that
the carriage was too much like "the custom in France and the North, and
inconsistent with that exalted sense of character which has distinguished
southern ladies," a vulgar sign of "declension in our manners." Yet Mercer's misgivings represented a contrarian view in the midst of so many
loud and colorful public performances on behalf of white solidarity.[21]

On New Year's Day Governor Brown arrived in Savannah to make a
dramatic move against the U.S. government: he ordered the seizure of

Fort Pulaski on Cockspur Island at the mouth of the Savannah River. Charley Lamar, ignoring the dictates of older and cooler heads, including those of his Unionist father, was making noises about taking over the fort with his own band of vigilantes. The governor wanted state troops to occupy the fort before Lamar or Union soldiers could get there first. And so on a stormy January 3, members of the Chatham Artillery, Savannah Home Guards, and Oglethorpe Light Infantry departed from the city docks, urged on by a crowd of drenched well-wishers. Regarding their mission as less a military maneuver than a holiday excursion, the troops traveled downriver to Cockspur Island, and, "with drums beating colors flying and hearts swelling," marched over the drawbridge and claimed the federal fort for the state of Georgia. The lone U.S. Army sergeant and his few assistants waiting inside offered no resistance. All in all, it was a very satisfactory venture; George Mercer, one of the fort's occupiers, enjoyed himself immensely: "I found the life pleasant and healthful; the discipline is not too rigid to be inconsistent with enjoyment; the fare is plain but abundant; and the spirit and excitement of military life compensate for all hardships." The men lost no time setting a contingent of slaves to work digging out the weed-choked moat that surrounded the fort. The structure was an engineering marvel consisting of bricks floating on mud bolstered by wooden pilings and oyster shells. (Begun in 1829, its construction had been overseen by a young military engineer named Robert E. Lee.) Local "patriotic planters" had proffered the services of the black men at no cost to the state. Within a few weeks, however, the governor had sent to each slaveholder a check representing a "gratuity . . . of fifty cents per day" for each laborer, which was to be distributed to the slaves as payment. Secession would afford moneymaking opportunities in some unexpected quarters.[22]

The day before Pulaski's fall to the state of Georgia, lowcountry voters had braved the bad weather to vote for delegates to the upcoming state secession convention. Most counties fielded two slates of candidates—those in favor of immediate secession, and those in favor of cooperating with other southern states in a wait-and-see position. Chatham County put forth only one set of delegates, those in the former category. In the state as a whole, the immediate secessionists won 55,000 supporters in contrast to the cooperationists' 37,000. It was no surprise, then, that on Saturday, January 19, the convention, meeting in the state capital of Milledgeville, overwhelmingly passed a secession ordinance and ordered the governor to begin raising two regiments of troops. Delegates also resolved to reconvene in Savannah in March and write a new state constitution, one befitting Georgia's new independent status. In Savannah, whites greeted the news that night with a celebration of fireworks and cannon salutes: *"We are a free and independent people!"*[23]

Over the next month, the whole city seemed to come unhinged, with "fights and weddings" the order of the day. Day and night, a nearly continuous celebration of brass bands, bonfires, and fireworks filled the city streets. New volunteer companies formed on a moment's notice and began drilling on the parade ground. Residents reported an increase in gun accidents as teenage boys hastily shouldered firearms. State troops seized Oglethorpe Barracks, the federal installation long used as a jail and police headquarters. Fearing for his safety, the United States engineer in charge of dredging the Savannah River suspended operations and discharged his employees. There was speculation that Georgia would annex Florida to create a vast empire of rice and cotton.[24]

In Savannah and its environs, black men and women were anticipating a Lincoln presidency. As early as January 1861, observers noted that Savannah's well-educated, well-dressed blacks "are as familiar with current events as the whites themselves, and really expect to be made free by the incoming administration." Whites perceived in slaves a rising militancy: "impertinent and insubordinate," black men and women were demonstrating a new level of restlessness in the city and its environs. On January 19 Charles Manigault acknowledged to his son Louis that the Savannah River region was becoming the refuge of more and more runaways, slaves who "have very generally got the idea of being emancipated when 'Lincon' comes in." The elder Manigault blamed rumors of liberation on "house Negroes" and ordered that "no overseer, or Planter should speak on such subjects even before a small house boy, or girl, as they communicate all they hear to others."[25]

Throughout the lowcountry, slaves and free people of color bore the brunt of white people's fears. In Savannah, whippings of slaves became more frequent and more extreme. Some whites called for an end to the widespread practice of slaves hiring themselves out and of slaves carrying "to market *any produce* given them for sale on commission"—both practices that enriched individual owners but, elites feared, undermined public order. In the countryside, the days of waiting patiently for runaways to return was over: now shotgun-toting white men ventured into the swamps and quickly retrieved the fugitives. Charles Manigault ordered his son to shoot in the leg "or in a vital part if necessary, any negro who attempts to resist or escape after being caught."[26]

On February 11, Georgia joined with South Carolina, Mississippi,

Florida, Alabama, Louisiana, and Texas to form the Confederate States of America (CSA). Savannah marked the momentous event with a parade of military companies and marching bands, combining the traditional Washington's Birthday observance with a celebration of southern independence. Around this time, the governor of New York decided to hold a cache of muskets that Georgia and Alabama had deposited in a New York arsenal. From Milledgeville, Governor Brown retaliated by seizing all New York–owned ships tied up in Savannah harbor. In response, New York released the guns and sent them south.[27]

Georgia's secession delegates reconvened in Savannah on March 7 and proceeded to ratify the new Confederate constitution and revise their own. A highlight of the convention was the famous "cornerstone of the Confederacy" speech delivered by Georgia native Alexander H. Stephens, the newly elected Confederate vice president. Succinctly, Stephens went to the heart of the difference between North and South: the United States, he claimed, adhered to the idea that "all men are created equal." In contrast, "Our new government is founded upon exactly the opposite idea; . . . its cornerstone rests upon the great truth, that the negro is not equal to the white man; that slavery—subordination to the superior race—is his natural and normal condition." A statement of first CSA principles, Stephens's speech would prove a problematic source of inspiration in wartime. The call—Will you not die so that slaveowners shall retain their property?—would lack staying power over the next four long, bloody years.[28]

The revised Georgia constitution, approved by the delegates 270–0, not only preserved slavery but also diminished the influence of the state's white male democratic base. The new document reduced by one-third the number of state senators, stripped the state legislature of its power to revise the constitution (in favor of a new body called for that purpose), and mandated that judges of the superior courts be appointed by the state legislature and not elected by the voters. The *Morning News* promptly labeled the proposed constitution the vehicle of a "double revolution," presumably one that would protect planters' interests from avowed abolitionists and also from the state's white majority—the non-slaveholding classes consisting of yeoman farmers and urban workingmen. Alarmed at the "anarchical spirit introduced into the community" by recent events, some prominent Savannahians regretted that the document left intact the system of electing judges of inferior (local) courts; for, in the words of George Mercer, "universal suffrage is found by sad experience to be inapplicable to the judiciary." Elites watched uneasily as a popularly elected judge, a "notorious member of the lawless rattle-snake club," presided over a city court, "dispensing his own brand of justice."[29]

In the early morning of April 12, the federal Fort Sumter in Charleston harbor fell to Confederate forces. And so the war began. It would take another month for the CSA to coalesce with its new member states—the essential Virginia on April 17, Tennessee on April 25, Arkansas on May 6, and North Carolina two weeks later. Dampening the palpable sense of relief and exhilaration among many white Savannahians were the immediate jurisdictional disputes that divided local, state, and Confederate authorities. The questions of who would accept responsibility for defending the city, mobilizing the city's volunteers, and controlling its arms would prove divisive and enduring. For their part, officials found themselves caught between, on the one hand, the Confederate capital of Richmond, with its voracious appetite for men and war matériel, and, on the other, Milledgeville, where Governor Brown was determined to uphold the principle of states' rights and resist Richmond's moves toward military and bureaucratic centralization. In the ensuing rush to safeguard the lowcountry, the official lines of authority were by no means clear, leaving plenty of room for Mayor Jones, Governor Brown, and military officers to clash with one another. Among the last group were General Alexander R. Lawton, the CSA officer in charge of Savannah fortifications; Commodore Josiah Tattnall, commander of a "mosquito fleet" off the coast; and General Henry Jackson, head of the state's land forces.

White men in Savannah rushed to volunteer, with a mixture of motives and emotions. Like other Southerners, they acted out of pro-slavery principle and anti-black prejudice; but they also embraced the exuberance and "manliness" embedded in the call to arms. Some feared charges of cowardice if they did not volunteer, but many others had been prepared for this day by the routine marching, drilling, and parading sponsored by the city's several militias, organizations that provided their members with a "white" identity and with a source of pride. Many years later, Nellie Gordon looked back on those tumultuous days and offered a reason why so many whites raised the rebels' rallying cry so quickly, and why so many seemed to accept armed conflict so enthusiastically: "Fortunately, no one realized what lay in the future, but thought two or three months soldiering would settle the matter, and that our boys would come marching home, like conquering heroes." Certainly many secessionists believed that, by fighting a purely defensive war, the South might not only dispatch northern aggressors, but secure its own way of life once and for all, with a minimum of bloodshed.[30]

Though unable to vote or serve as soldiers, the wives and daughters of Savannah's wealthy white men threw themselves into preparations for war. They proudly sported rattlesnake badges on their jackets, and they organized a ladies' soldiers' aid society on behalf of the troops in the field and the families at home. Coming together in groups to work and gossip, women of all ages filled sandbags for fortifications, sewed flannel shirts, knitted socks, and made haversacks. They made cartridges for muskets and cannon, filling paper cups with gunpowder and "tieing up the missiles of death," in the process rendering their workplaces, the city's parlors and military-company drill rooms, unsafe for smoking. Over cups of tea they planned elaborate fairs and "tableaux vivants"—staged scenes from the Bible, mythology, or history—that would bring in thousands of dollars over the course of the war. For some women, at least, devotion to the cause went well beyond badges and fundraisers, becoming an all-consuming obsession with battlefield strategy and military hardware. In recounting to her son Charles the details of Fort Sumter's fall, Mary Jones betrayed her newfound fascination with the technology of war: "The barbette gun designed to play upon the iron battery recoiled at the first fire and was rendered useless, and the outer metallic doors to the magazines became so warped that they could not be opened."[31]

The challenge of defending the city provoked conflicts among amateur and professional strategists and politicians alike. General Lawton soon came under rhetorical fire for scattering troops along the coast rather than concentrating them in Savannah and at Fort Pulaski. In an early face-off with the state's military companies, Governor Brown declared that he would keep all Georgia regiments at home, despite appeals from CSA president Jefferson Davis to send them to the battlefront in Virginia. However, in May, Savannah's Francis Bartow, now a representative to the Confederate Congress, outmaneuvered the governor on this issue. Bartow was instrumental in gaining the congress's authorization for the CSA to accept military companies that volunteered for the "period of the war" (instead of the customary six to twelve months). This new provision allowed companies to bypass the state and sign on directly with the CSA. On May 21, Bartow's Oglethorpe Light Infantry was mustered into Confederate service over the protests of Brown, and the men immediately departed for Virginia. In explaining his allegiance to the CSA, the newly commissioned colonel sent a defiant letter to the governor, dismissing his objections and declaring, "Your opinions do not in the least disturb me."[32]

Many of the established military companies of the city became part of the First Georgia Volunteers—the Savannah Volunteer Guards, Oglethorpe Light Infantry, Republican Blues, Jasper Greens, Irish Volunteers, and German Volunteers, to name a few. Early recruitment patterns suggest that the sons of Savannah's elite quickly shouldered arms, apparently tapped for their positions as officers by other militia leaders, rather than by the vote of the men they would command. William S. Basinger, thirty-three, an attorney; Thomas P. Scriven, twenty-five, a physician; George W. Stiles, thirty, a planter; and Edward Padelford Jr., twenty-seven, a cotton merchant, all served as officers in the Savannah Volunteers. Basinger and Stiles were both living with their widowed mothers when they joined the army. Philip M. Russell Jr., eighteen, an attorney and the son of the longtime clerk of the city court, was an officer in the Republican Blues. Some groups were a part of the city's history, and others were new, such as the Savannah Blues, founded in May 1861; yet together they represented a cross section of the city's stable population, both native-born and immigrant, as well as rural men drawn from the vicinity of the railroad lines leading to the coast. Joining the German Volunteers was John H. Stegin, twenty-one, a police officer and son of a German-born grocer; and Jacob Fleck, twenty-nine, a grocer and an immigrant from Germany. Other volunteers included George Giebelhouse, twenty-six, a baker; and Henry Blun, twenty-seven, a commission merchant living in a boardinghouse with other Germans. The Germans also welcomed into their ranks Anthony Basler, forty-five, a French-born barroom keeper, and Michael Grace, twenty-nine, a native of Ireland.[33]

The Second Republican Blues drew native-born men from the upper echelons of Savannah society, as well as tradesmen and skilled workers. Included among its officers were William H. Davis, fifty-five, a butcher; George W. Anderson, sixty-two, president of Planters' Bank; and Daniel Olcott, thirty, a book dealer. This company also had within its ranks two cabinetmakers, a plasterer, five grocery-store clerks, a police officer, a tinsmith, two custom-house clerks, a machinist, two pilots, a mariner, two engineers, a student, two painters, a tobacco dealer, a printer, a cooper, a carpenter, an attorney, a boardinghouse keeper, and a bookbinder. Of a sample of thirty-six volunteers, twenty-five were born in either Georgia or South Carolina, nine in the North or in a border state, and two abroad. Typical was Henry Snyder, twenty-four, a native of Savannah and a grocery-store clerk, who was living with his mother and siblings when the war broke out; Aldolphus Marmelstein, twenty-two, a boat pilot born in Baltimore, boarding with a married couple; and Augustus LaRoche, eighteen, a student living with his parents. It was not unusual for kin to volunteer together: among the Second Republican Blues were Benjamin Purse, eighteen, and his brother William C., both sons of Thomas Purse, a railroad official and merchant; and Edward J. Purse, forty-three, probably the uncle of the two youths.[34]

In the late spring of 1861 military mobilization was transforming the cityscape. New structures sprouted almost overnight—gun sheds in various neighborhoods, tents on the new parade ground. Most dramatic was the great churning of population that gave the city an appearance of liveliness, if not sheer panic. Of the northern job-seekers who had migrated south that spring, Mayor Jones later claimed, disingenuously, that the beginning of the war brought "a strong and growing influx into our City of paupers from the Northern States, who, escaping from the destitution and lack of employment encountered at home, sought here better fortunes and brighter skies." In a move that echoed the city's reaction to the appearance of Irish migrants during the yellow-fever epidemic in 1854, council members prohibited vessels from unloading any steerage passengers at the Savannah docks. For good measure, they also paid for the return passage of the more than "three hundred paupers"—disappointed longshoremen—back to New York.[35]

While northern workers were barred from entering the city, thousands of other people were arriving—as many as five thousand soldiers, among others, by midsummer. In May two hapless U.S. Army officers, tuberculosis patients staying at the Pulaski House, came under suspicion as Yankee spies. Barely managing to disperse a menacing crowd that had gathered outside the hotel, Mayor Jones promised "the poor fellows" safe passage out of the city as they endeavored "to recruit their enfeebled constitutions" to their ultimate destination, Florida. Remarked the exasperated mayor, "If there is one thing which I detest more than another, it is the exhibition of mob law."[36]

Meanwhile, in customary fashion, wealthy men raised their own companies by appealing to young men throughout the interior of Georgia, offering to arm, feed, and clothe individual recruits (usually forty-five men at a time). Because companies were similar to fraternal orders, the recruitment process reflected the status—or the notoriety—of the recruiter. The slave smuggler Charley Lamar had little difficulty raising a company for combat. In contrast, the former Douglas supporter William B. Gaulden advertised in vain in the local paper for men to report to his

Liberty County "camp of instruction." Promising to outfit each man, Gaulden urged potential recruits not to arrive in their own homemade uniforms, which created confusion on the battlefield and led to men "firing on each other." Some wealthy young men, like the mayor's obstreperous nineteen-year-old cousin Dunwody Jones, found that they lacked the influence and stature to form their own company; Dunwody swallowed his pride and enlisted as a private. Others pranced and preened about town; writing from the Oglethorpe Barracks to his mother in April, Edward R. Harden noted, "I shall go to the Presbyterian Church today in my splendid uniform," adding, "I was the only officer in the Baptist Church last Sabbath."[37]

That spring, troops from all over the state trudged into the city—weary, grime-covered young men eager to volunteer for service and to see the river port and sample its pleasures. At any point in the war, between 1,800 and 14,000 soldiers were stationed in or around Savannah, most of them men in their teens and early twenties, fresh from the countryside. Among these was William H. Andrews of Fort Gaines, in the southwestern corner of Georgia. Andrews began his enlisted life in Savannah in March 1861 as a member of the Georgia Regulars. There he got his hair "shingled" and for the first time tasted the fare of a foot soldier—Yankee bean soup and "pickled pork, so fat you could hold it up and see through it." For Andrews, the initial excitement of camp life soon wore off. He contracted pneumonia, and within a few weeks was sent to Fort Pulaski, where he and a hundred other soldiers came down with the measles. Illness soon became a fact of wartime life for civilians and military personnel alike. Swelling concentrations of slaves working on fortifications and soldiers awaiting orders taxed the city's freshwater supply and primitive sewer system. The scavenger department could hardly keep up with the mounting animal carcasses and garbage rotting in the streets. Under these conditions, diseases of all kinds spread quickly.[38]

As long as he was up and about, Andrews was mightily impressed with what he heard and saw in Savannah. Other newly arrived soldiers and first-time visitors commented on the majestic live oaks laden with hanging moss, the parade ground carpeted with Bermuda grass, the jumble of low-lying residences in the poorer sections of town. Not all newcomers were charmed with the place or its people: a seventeen-year-old from Athens, Georgia, informed his kinfolk at home that the city was "an old-looking place with ill-shapen houses and narrow streets on which the sand was about a foot deep . . . [The residents are] a set of stuck up know nothing fools." Arriving in late April, William Howard Russell, correspondent for *The Times* of London, also marveled at "the deepest sand in the streets I have ever seen," as well as "a busy, well-clad gaily attired race of negroes." Russell gushed over merchant Charles Green's recently completed Gothic Revival mansion: "Italian statuary graced the hall; finely carved tables and furniture, stained glass, and pictures from Europe set forth the sitting rooms, and the luxury of bathrooms and a supply of cold fresh water, rendered it an exception to the general run of Southern edifices."[39]

During his brief stay, Russell attended services at Christ Church and heard a sermon delivered by its famous pastor, the Reverend Stephen Elliott, Episcopal bishop of Georgia. Shocked by Elliott's aggressive defense of human bondage, Russell told his readers, "I rather revolted at hearing a Christian prelate advocating the institution on scriptural grounds." Yet many Savannahians embraced the war in religious terms, though those terms carried radically divergent meanings for different groups. Meeting in the city in May, the Southern Baptist Convention gave its blessing to the Confederacy and condemned the United States for "letting loose hordes of armed soldiers to pillage and desolate the entire South." Not surprisingly, Mayor Jones could sound like his preacher father at times, praising the Almighty's "marked interposition in our behalf; infusing into the breasts of our people a generous, high-toned patriotism; touching the lips of our clergy with a live coal from off the altar . . . inspiring our soldiers with valor, and granting us victory upon the field of battle."[40]

In Savannah and throughout the lowcountry, blacks also saw the hand of God in the war, but they were forced to encode in hymns and prayers their fervent hopes for freedom. For them, the destruction of slavery would mark the culmination of a generations-long spiritual journey. Wartime religious services in the black community—conducted in modest "praise houses" on rice plantations no less than in the substantial independent churches of the city—afforded a safe place for black men and women to link the progress of Union armies to their own eventual liberation from bondage. Still, circumspection prevailed. Later James M. Simms would recall that the outbreak of war prompted "great caution in our churches." Slaves and free blacks alike abided by the watchword: "Be ye wise as serpents and harmless as doves." Some prominent black preachers kept their own counsel. In the spring of 1861, the white Southern Baptist convention appointed Ulysses L. Houston church leader of the First Bryan Baptist Church (formerly Third African); accordingly, Houston made a conscious decision to refrain from mentioning the war directly in his sermons. Simms noted, "But the secret thoughts belong to God, and from the beginning of the war to its close there was an abiding hope in every breast that God would in the end grant us freedom." In sermons and songs, then, "de Lord" could mean "de Yankees," the day of judgment, the day of liberation.[41]

One evening early in the war Susie Baker's grandmother Dolly Reed attended a worship service in a small church in an outlying area of the city. There she lifted her voice with other church congregants and sang:

> *Yes we shall all be free*
> *Yes we shall all be free*
> *Yes we shall all be free*
> *When the Lord shall appear.*

Alarmed that old hymns were taking on new meanings, city police raided the church and arrested everyone for "planning freedom." Independent black churches, once considered handmaidens of the slave system, now served as outposts of disloyalty within the Confederacy.[42]

Nevertheless, city and military officials tended to take at face value black people's highly public display of initial, apparent support for the war. In April sixty free men of color offered their services to Governor Brown, but he demurred. In contrast, the labor-hungry General Lawton accepted the men's offer and set them to work on defenses below the city along the Savannah River. The city council gave its blessing to the arrangement, but placed a cap on the number who could go: because black men in general formed the backbone of the fire company, "it was thought best not to spare them [additional volunteers] from the city." Among the group was the bricklayer Simon Mirault; George Jones, a tailor; and carpenters' and engineers' apprentices. At the same time, free women of color began a sewing project with the aim of outfitting one hundred soldiers. Among the thirty-five seamstresses were Jane Deveaux, longtime teacher of a clandestine school; Georgiana Guard Kelley, the nurse; Elizabeth Mirault, wife of Simon; and Susan Densler (Denslow). Several of the women were neighbors, kin, or members of the same households. Both the *Republican* and the *Morning News* lauded blacks' "public spirit," seemingly oblivious to the possibility that these calculated gestures might be suspect just because they were so public. As life became more precarious for all blacks, enslaved and free, open displays of support for the Confederacy would buy them precious time to watch and wait.[43]

Building on its prewar corporate ethos, the city rapidly systematized efforts to distribute charity efficiently and to regulate an increasingly chaotic marketplace. In the late spring of 1861, the council passed an ordinance aimed at speculators who went to the market early in the morning and then resold articles for a tidy profit later in the day. The Union Society and the Savannah Benevolent Society (the latter formed during the yellow-fever epidemic of 1854) continued to meet, but their rolls were diminished because several active members had enlisted in the army. Consequently older men in the community formed a new association, the Committee of Thirteen, to coordinate contributions for the relief of families of impoverished soldiers. This new group was headed by Richard D. Arnold and supported by a familiar roster of wealthy men, including Gazaway Bugg Lamar, Hiram Roberts, Richard R. Cuyler, and Solomon Cohen.[44]

Mayor Jones enjoyed the ceremonial aspects of his job—he was an inveterate speech maker—but he endured several personal and professional blows in the summer and early fall of 1861. In July his eighteen-month-old daughter Julia succumbed to scarlet fever, and his wife, Ruth, who had given birth to another baby in late June, died of childbirth complications. Jones was still in mourning when he had to contend with a home-brewed scandal affecting his own father. Nine months earlier, while a guest in the senior Jones's home, a respected schoolteacher from Columbus, Georgia, William States Lee, had apparently impregnated one of the family's slaves, Peggy, age eighteen. In an angry letter to the teacher's home congregation, Charles Senior cited evidence of the crime: the young woman's confession, the timing of the white man's visit and that of the birth, and the child—*"a mulatto, now sometime born; and there is a resemblance to you beyond mistake."* Through officers of his church, Lee disputed the charges and ridiculed the idea that a slave woman, and an unchaste one at that, could impugn the character of any white man. The matter ended there, officially at least; but the presence of the mulatto child would continue to mock the Joneses' high-minded ideals linking slavery to religious piety.[45]

Around this time the young mayor faced another embarrassing affront to his moral principles. The year before, the city jailer, Waring Russell, had issued a dueling challenge to another man, and then-mayor Arnold had fired him; dueling was against the law. Now on Charles Jones's watch, Russell sued to get his job back; he was eventually vindicated by Judge W. B. Fleming of the Eastern District Court of Georgia. (It certainly did not hurt Russell's case that he was the brother of Philip M. Russell, powerful clerk of the city court.) Fleming noted that Waring Russell's violation of the dueling law did not in and of itself make him an unfit jailer: would the mayor fire a man from his job if that man was "a bad citizen or a bad husband, a bad father, a bad Master?" Whatever his shortcomings outside the jail, Russell had met his public service obligations within it. As part of the legal settlement, the city had to pay Russell $3,415, the salary accrued since his dismissal. The young mayor was outraged at one more case of vice rewarded, or at least tolerated.[46]

On July 27, Charles wrote to his parents: "It seems to me that I am living in a graveyard." Labor was so scarce he could not even find a worker to make a headstone for his departed wife and daughter. With the rest of white Savannah, he rejoiced that the South had just won a great victory at Manassas, in Virginia, not far from Washington, D.C. Still, that victory came at the price of the deaths of a number of Savannahians, including the defiant Colonel Bartow. The body of the fallen officer was brought home, where it lay in state and attracted hushed crowds of mourners. At Christ Episcopal Church on Sunday, July 28, Bishop Elliott preached a sermon on the war, taking Exodus 15:1–19 (the story of Pharaoh's chariots drowned in the Red Sea) as his text. Elliott divined God's will in forging disparate elements of the southern army into an effective fighting force. Coming together were "young men, trained up in the lap of luxury and known at home, many of them, only as idlers of fashion" along with "backwoodsmen . . . with no preparation save the few weeks drilling of a disorderly camp." Somehow these unlikely warriors had together been able to vanquish a formidable foe, Northerners who have "labored all their days with the hammer and the axe and every tool of iron, amid furnaces and forges [with] their muscles like brass and their sinews as cords of steel." After services, a funeral cortege brought the city to a standstill; sixteen different military companies, all based in Savannah, marched in the procession.[47]

In August a group of well-to-do white men formed a new group called the Savannah Vigilance Committee. Their avowed purpose was to aid city, state, and Confederate authorities in rooting out the "spies against and traitors to the South [who] are residing among us, fattening upon southern patronage." Aiming to monitor people, letters, and parcels leaving Savannah, members of the committee nevertheless apprehended few disloyalists: "We have tried in every possible honorable way to catch them in their traitorous acts, but (Yankee-like) so cunningly and cautiously devised have they carried out their plans, that detection has been impossible." A British national who fled the city around this time testified to the fear that had gripped the white community, where, he reported, a "reign of terror worse than that of the French Revolution, hangs over the people, like a sable pall." Posted on street lamps and tacked on the sides of buildings were the numerous warnings of vigilantes, including, "I am a rattlesnake, if you touch me I will strike," and "I am a wildcat! Beware, etc."[48]

Keeping track of friend and foe in Savannah was no easy matter, for the city was a major staging area for Confederate troops, a lively hub of military and economic activity, and a pass system did little to stem traffic in and out of it. The state maintained a munitions arsenal and relied upon an active gunboat-building business located in the river port. A dry-goods merchant, Henry Lathrop, a native of Massachusetts and now a resident of the Pulaski House Hotel, received a contract from the CSA and hired women to make Confederate uniforms. In place of the traditional rice-cotton-lumber trade emerged a speculators' economy based on smuggling and blockade running. Off the South Carolina coast, the U.S. Navy was engaged in a less than successful effort to close the port of Savannah. In mid-September the steamer *Bermuda* from Liverpool managed to elude federal forces and deposit its cargo on the city's docks: rifled cannon, Enfield rifles, ammunition, shoes, blankets, morphine, dried shrimp, and red potatoes. Later in the fall the ship would return to England loaded with one thousand bales of cotton. Among the wartime profiteers was Gazaway Bugg Lamar.[49]

In October, state and municipal elections indicated that Savannah voters lacked unity of conviction when it came to selecting men to lead them in wartime. Jones did not run again that August; he had enlisted as senior first lieutenant in the Chatham Artillery, First Volunteer Regiment, Georgia Artillery. Running for mayor, Thomas Purse, a fifty-nine-year-old railroad official and merchant, bested his opponent, Richard D. Arnold—but only after neither man won a majority of votes and the choice fell to the city council. In state elections, Chatham County voted narrowly (811–772) to reject Joseph Brown in favor of his challenger, Judge Eugenius A. Nisbet, leader of the state's secession convention earlier that year. White Savannahians were becoming increasingly nervous about their own defense, convinced that Brown was wasting precious time bickering with the CSA; but the rest of Georgia elected the governor to his third term by a substantial vote of 46,593 to 32,802.[50]

It had been less than a year since the Republican Blues marched down the streets of lower Manhattan, hailed by their compatriots, the New York City Guards. And indeed, for the Blues, for Georgia, and for Confederates generally, secession from the Union was fraught with irony. Before the war, elites of the North and South acknowledged they were conjoined by educational and kinship ties, by business interests and by their common identity as "white men"; now they were combatants. To defend states' rights, white Southerners mobilized for war by centralizing military and political operations, a move that prompted outspoken dissent among those more principled than practical. In the process, class fissures emerged within the white population, calling into question the united front that was the presumed hallmark of the Confederate cause. In addition, the institution of slavery was now coming under daily attack from the very people who, according to antebellum southern ideology, benefited from it: supposedly contented, childlike black men and women. That development was as threatening to the Confederate cause as were the Yankee gunboats positioned at the mouth of the Savannah River. Now blacks enslaved and free prepared to fight the notion that this was a war between white men only.

-⊷| CHAPTER SIX |⊶-

As Traitors, They Go
Over to the Enemy

GOVERNOR JOSEPH BROWN had little use for CSA president Jefferson Davis or the unceasing demands of the would-be new country he led. Early in the war Brown showed that he would resist in equal measure the incursion of Yankees into Georgia and the demands of Richmond, the CSA capital, for men and arms. Defiantly consistent in his states' rights principles, the Georgia governor assumed responsibility for guarding the state's 118-mile coastline, as well as its hundreds more miles of inland waterways and swamplands. He was eager to advance and entertain any number of suggestions for defense measures, believing that Georgia's fate rested on the military prowess of Georgia's soldiers. In an address to the "Mechanics of Georgia," he roused the troops by declaring, "We are left to choose between freedom at the end of a desperate and heroic struggle and submission to tyranny, followed by the most abject and degraded slavery to which a patriotic and generous people were ever exposed." In answer to the question, "What shall be done in this emergency?" he urged all soldiers to shoulder the "Georgia pike," a three-pound, six-foot staff, with an eighteen-inch blade as a side knife, since many of the enlistees who flooded the coast lacked arms. Brown assured his men that "hand to hand, the pike has vastly the advantage of the bayonet," and yet it was unclear how the pike could be used against federal gunboats menacing the state from offshore. (By this time, among the boats patrolling the Atlantic coast was the former civilian steamship *Florida*, as well as the former slave ship *Wanderer*, which had been seized from its new owner, who had bought it from Charley Lamar.) A plan more in keeping with the actual military threat posed by the federal navy was offered to the governor by a Georgia woman: she proposed that state forces dump a thousand barrels of turpentine into the lower Savannah

River at night, ignite the watery mix, and then watch flames engulf the federal fleet and immolate sleeping crewmen.[1]

Although Brown held to a romantic view of warding off Yankee invaders with hand-to-hand combat, the fact was that the coastline remained Georgia's major vulnerability, not only to Union forces but also to homegrown sources of subversion. In their determination to liberate themselves, slaves and free people of color opened up a second front in the war, and neither pikes nor rifles could stem their advance. Soon enough Georgia whites discovered that they had to contend with their own rebels, enemies within, and that they must wage this war on black people's own territory and even, to a certain extent, on black people's own terms.

IN LATE OCTOBER Charles Colcock Jones Jr. assumed his official duties with an engineering corps nine miles below the city on the Isle of Hope. There he joined thousands of other men, many of them Savannah residents, in the service of defending Georgia. Virtually no volunteers sought a coastal assignment; rumors of a yellow-fever outbreak in the area prompted fears that marshland diseases were more deadly than offshore Yankees. Still, initially, some found the semitropical environment pleasing, the rigors of camp life entertaining. Stationed on Sapelo Island in October, John W. Hagan of Berrien County enjoyed the camaraderie for at least a few days: "some of the Boyes are writing Some Singing Some fiddleing Some dancing Some cooking Some play cardes & Some are at work cleaning off our perade ground & places to pitch our tents." Yet he and others soon became disillusioned by the combination of heat, biting insects, and miserable food. A few men fashioned havelock helmets with linen flaps to protect heads and necks from sunburn, and rigged gauze netting on a wire frame in an effort to keep sand flies away from their faces. But these defensive measures could not change the fact that the well water tasted "brackish and almost unpalatable" and the daily ration of greasy bacon and a pound of crackers amounted to "a very poor diet." The Savannah Volunteers, assigned to the coast, for the most part did battle exclusively with various fevers and agues; at one point 140 of their 250 men were ill and largely incapacitated.[2]

Camped out on Tybee Island and recovering from his various illnesses, William H. Andrews endured "hard drilling" every afternoon, with no whiskey to ease the mind-numbing boredom. Night guard duty, with nothing but the sound of lapping waves for company, proved the

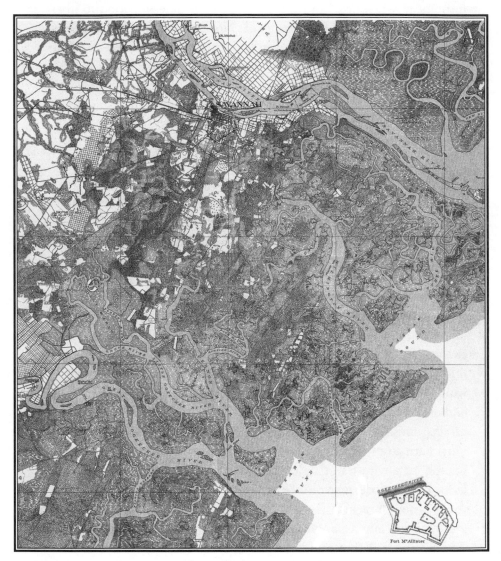

*Map illustrating the defense of Savannah, Ga. and the operations resulting
in its capture by the army commanded by Maj. Genl. W. T. Sherman*

worst assignment of all. Consequently, according to Andrews, "We are all more than anxious to be sent to the front, preferring an active campaign to remaining here doing coast duty and being ate up by the mosquitoes and sand flies. Besides, the heat of the noonday sun upon the sand is terribly distressing." Enforced inaction took its toll among foot soldiers and specialized troops alike. Stationed in batteries along the coast, men assigned to the Signal Corps under the command of Joseph Manigault (son of Charles and brother of Louis) demonstrated little aptitude for signaling with flags; and they had no patience for guard duty, which required them to look through spyglasses at least once every two minutes, day and night.[3]

Together with impoverished men from the city and the interior, sons of the wealthy suffered from the sand flies and mosquitoes, but they shouldered an extra burden: the conviction, rooted in slaveholders' ideology, that white men could not survive on the coast, at least not in hot weather. At the same time, a considerable number of officers believed that "no Yankee dare put his foot" in this section of the country because of its unhealthfulness; indeed, the South's greatest weapons against the invaders were "Providence, sand flies, musquitoes, & sickness." Nevertheless, a contingent of elite Southerners found themselves assigned to batteries located, according to George Mercer, in "low swampy fields, where the insects are terrible[,] the air close and fetid and full of miasma and death."[4]

Cohabiting with their social inferiors in less than desirable circumstances—"in the rain & dew, [with] bad water to drink, amidst poisonous airs & rank weeds"—men such as Jones and Mercer enjoyed privileges that eased the pain of isolation and physical discomfort. Many went back and forth between camp and Savannah, going to town to "take a scrub," enjoy a hearty breakfast, and attend to business. In camp, they entertained visitors with meals of roasted oysters prepared by the slaves or Irish cooks they had brought from home. Most officers had slaves to wash their clothes, though Jones counted on his mother to send him clean laundry. She also sent him a cornucopia of fresh food: peppers, groundnuts, corned beef, sausages, melons, boiled ham, biscuits, and oranges, as well as blackberry cordial "prepared for medicinal use (excellent for all *bowel affections*—prepared with *brandy,* consequently a *strong article*)." Spending most of his time writing long letters to his parents and enjoying tasty meals, Charles had little to complain about. He turned down an offer to head the Oglethorpe Light Infantry, which was bound for the battlefront, preferring (as of October 1862) his position as chief of artillery for the military district of Georgia, under General Henry Jackson in Savannah. His parents agreed that he should remain near home, where he could assume their protection as his personal responsibility.[5]

Upcountry soldiers stationed in the lowcountry were intrigued by the sight of so many black men laboring on defensive fortifications along the coast. Here slaves from all over the state mingled in a common workplace for the first time, exchanging information and news with one another. By September 1861, owners in Chatham, Bryan, and Liberty counties had volunteered as many as three hundred bondsmen to Confederate military authorities in the vicinity of Savannah. A few worked at Fort Pulaski, but the majority labored on the earthworks (fortified with sandbags, sod, and fascines, bundles of branches and straw used to fill ditches) built in a southeastern arc encircling the city, and on sand batteries on the banks of the Savannah River and along the coast and on the Sea Islands.[6]

Meanwhile, few soldiers and seamen grasped the full import of the fact that they had set up camp in the heart of Africa-America. Before the war, the region had been home to a decisive black majority; by the winter of 1861–62, many of the whites had fled inland, some taking their slaves with them. The black men and women who remained possessed a familiarity with and a mastery of the land in ways that would assume heightened political and military significance as the war dragged on. White men on both sides remained interlopers in alien territory.

Early in the conflict, the coast became bitterly contested military terrain. On November 7, 1861, the Federals captured Hilton Head Island, an island off South Carolina only a few miles northeast of Savannah. Many whites in Chatham County took the fall of the island as their cue to flee, with seemingly all of Savannah "mounting in hot haste, and running away from town." Wealthy men scrambled to send their wives, children, slaves, bales of cotton, silver, banknotes, and kegs of silver into the interior. Displaced by the Yankee invaders on the South Carolina coast, thousands of retreating troops flooded into the city. At that point Governor Brown reluctantly agreed to cede defense of the city and its environs to Confederate authorities, but not before warning the CSA that Georgia troops "are not cattle, to be bought and sold in the market."[7]

The fear of invasion, combined with high prices and shortages of necessities, prompted angry finger-pointing. After the Yankees captured Hilton Head, one CSA officer, a Savannahian, condemned the South Carolina fire-eaters as long on bluster and short on military competence: "Something more than mere words and deep hatred will be wanting now—firm determination and prompt action are now wanting," he concluded glumly. In the city, slaves were becoming burdensome to owners poised to flee at any moment: "It is a dreadful time to be having young negroes," lamented Henrietta Wayne, widow of the late mayor Richard, referring to a pregnant slave. Indeed, a number of prewar values were being called into question. George Mercer took to denouncing Jewish immigrants: they were, he believed, "the worst people we have among us; their exemption from military duty, their natural avarice, and their want of principle in this contest, render them particularly obnoxious; they are all growing rich, while the brave soldier gets poorer and his family starve." Mercer conveniently ignored the Jewish men who had volunteered for service, and the Christians (like Gazaway Lamar) who were bent on making money off the war. But the young lawyer's words suggest that any antebellum ecumenical consensus was now unraveling in the face of wartime pressures.[8]

On November 11 whites in Savannah hailed the arrival of General Robert E. Lee, who was charged with protecting a large swath of low-country stretching from South Carolina to Florida. Lee visited Savannah periodically but remained based in Coosawhatchie, South Carolina. He immediately became embroiled in jurisdictional disputes with General Lawton. And he won few friends among Savannahians when he warned that their city might fall now that its military defenders were being sent to the Virginia battlefront. On November 13, the *Fingal* arrived at Savannah bearing Enfield rifles, rifled cannon, revolvers, sailors' uniforms, and sabers; it was piloted by a native son, Edward C. Anderson, former mayor and U.S. naval officer. But by this time, not even this spectacular feat of blockade running could stem the round of recriminations among Brown, Lee, and Lawton over whether or not Savannah was worth saving.[9]

Up and down the coast, planters hastened to "refugee" their slaves— to send their able-bodied male slaves, and in some cases their entire workforce, inland and upcountry, out of the reach of Yankee soldiers and Confederate impressment agents alike. Passing through Savannah en route to Argyle Island, Charles Manigault found the city in "quite a Panic." Meanwhile, on the Savannah River, his slave Ishmael had stolen powder and shot, "confessing it was his intention to go with the Yankees." Manigault arranged to "refugee" ten slaves from the island to South Carolina; among them were Abel and a prized boatman, Hector; the latter had repaid Manigault's trust by showing signs that he "would have hastened to the embrace of his Northern Brethren, could he have foreseen the least prospect of a successful escape." Three of the refugeed slaves had to be handcuffed, so fierce was their refusal to leave Argyle

Island. Elsewhere, other owners too decried slaves who were perfecting "the art of the villain" to keep from being refugeed, impressed, sold, or otherwise separated from their families.[10]

Many black men and women resisted this forced migration for any number of obvious reasons, among them reluctance to leave their kin and homes, and resentment over losing their stores of pigs and chickens. Because planters were most likely to refugee healthy men, slave families were separated and whole communities disrupted in the process. In Savannah, according to James Simms, the several Baptist Church congregations registered the effects of these migrations: "many of her members were run up the country by their owners . . . causing sad separations and the breaking up of family ties . . . some of the male members absconded rather than be carried away," seeking refuge behind Union lines. And men and women alike feared, rightly, that removal to the interior would result in the loss of their stores of food, livestock, and household items accumulated through hard work over the years. Some owners bent on refugeeing won grudging compliance from their slaves not by using force, but by purchasing the slaves' property at market value. When it came time for Charles Jones the younger to refugee his family's slaves, he found the move complicated by their attachment to their own belongings: "If they have hogs we will purchase them; and we will have to make the best arrangements we can in reference to their little matters of property." Yet some slaves absconded at the first rumor of refugeeing. Faced with the problems of chronic runaways and intransigence from those who remained behind, Louis Manigault believed the larger lesson was clear: "This war has taught us the perfect impossibility of placing the least confidence in any Negro. In too numerous instances those we esteemed the most have been the first to desert us."[11]

In November, federal troops overran Tybee Island, a scant one mile from Fort Pulaski. Both northern and southern military officials quickened their efforts to reconfigure the landscape to their advantage. Southern troops worked feverishly to fell trees along the roads running from the coast to Savannah, so that invaders could not launch an ambush from the brush. Both sides rushed to obstruct the Savannah River and thus block access—for blockade runners as well as federal gunboats—to Savannah. Confederates ripped up city paving stones along the bay, towed them downriver, and dumped them in the water. In December the Union sent south a "stone fleet" consisting of twenty old ships, including decrepit whalers, loaded with six thousand tons of stone; by December 20, northern naval forces had sunk the entire fleet off Cockspur Island, sealing the river from blockade runners once and for all.[12]

Commodore Samuel F. DuPont, commander in charge of U.S. naval operations along the South Carolina and Georgia coast, appreciated the lush beauty of the lowcountry, the sight and smell of roses and geraniums in winter. And indeed, many northern soldiers and seamen waxed eloquent in their diaries and letters home about the unfamiliar birds and plants that thrived in the coastal area. However, for the most part Union gunboat officers considered the physical environment a major hindrance to military operations. In December, the rebels began abandoning their batteries along the coast—impressive structures constructed not long before at great effort by ragged soldiers who did more digging with shovels than drilling with arms. Meanwhile, Union soldiers expressed frustration with the "soft, unctuous mud, free of grit and sand," soil incapable of supporting cannon and other heavy munitions. Engineering officers groped for words and metaphors to describe the reed-covered marshes that presented such a challenge to work crews: "the substratum being a semi-fluid mud, which is agitated like jelly by the falling of even small bodies upon it, like the jumping of men or the ramming of earth."[13]

Forced to maneuver within an alien land- and waterscape, federal military officials welcomed the assistance they received from fugitive slaves (who were called "contraband" early in the war). At the same time that Savannah blacks were petitioning the city council for permission to hold a fundraiser for Confederate soldiers' families, black boatmen were showing federal navy captains how to use sidewheel steamers to open a low-country channel aptly named Mud River. A group of enslaved men forced to labor on saltworks near the Savannah River made their way to Union lines and then described to navy officers the size and location of bridges in the area. Even more useful were the black pilots who "knew every foot of the river," including Isaac Tatnall, a slave from Brunswick whose "forte," according to DuPont, "is the Georgia waters." Formerly a pilot for the CSA's *St. Marys,* Tatnall was, according to Union officials, "thoroughly acquainted" with local batteries and waterways, a pilot who could be "perfectly relied upon" to guide gunboats through the obstructions and narrow channels that made the Savannah River so difficult to navigate.[14]

More generally, the whole lowcountry region was like a giant sieve, with whites as well as blacks streaming out of Confederate territory and into Union lines. In December, William Barr, twenty-two, who identified himself as "a native of Ireland and a citizen of Philadelphia," deserted his post at Fort Pulaski by stealing a raft. Federal authorities found him to be "particularly intelligent and anxious to be useful"; he provided estimates of CSA troop strength at the fort and in and around Savannah. Increasingly, men like Barr, disillusioned with the southern cause for whatever reason, were hijacking flatboats, canoes, and rafts to make their escape from southern batteries and encampments. It was these men, and slaves like Isaac Tatnall, who helped the Federals in planning their upcoming assault on Fort Pulaski, the brick pentagon guarding the Savannah River.[15]

Early spring brought fresh woes to Savannah. Jefferson Davis had recalled Lee to Richmond, where the general would serve as the president's assistant. State and local officials began to fret over the upcoming first anniversary of the war's beginning in mid-April, when many volunteers would finish their one year of service and no doubt head back home. From his perch on the coast, Charles Jones Jr. could see disaster looming on the horizon: when the conflict started, he noted, men flocked to the cause because "the earliest and strongest tide of patriotism throb[bed] in their veins." Now, fearing a long war, these same men were eager to escape a wretched existence—the "Wet tents, thin blankets, scanty rations, heavy marches, sleepless nights beneath the canopy of a dripping sky, and long hours of sickness and pain." Not to mention the specter of death and destruction at the hands of a well-armed and surprisingly disciplined enemy. In March, General Joseph Johnston withdrew his troops from Manassas to Richmond and prepared for an attack by the Federals, who began moving north toward the CSA capital in early April.[16]

Taking these factors into account, Confederate lawmakers set April 16 as the date for the first military draft in the history of North America; under its provisions all white men age eighteen to thirty-five became liable for a three-year term of service. For $300 a drafted man could buy a substitute from a pool of men exempt from duty. However, the Confederate Congress was anxious to avoid forcible conscription wherever possible, and so it offered incentives—a $50 bounty and a sixty-day furlough—to anyone who volunteered before the law went into effect. Under this plan, new enlistees (or reenlistees) were also promised the privilege of electing their own company officers. But in Savannah, ordinary folks as well as members of the elite joined in a chorus of protests; noted Edward R. Harden, "I find everybody opposed to this tyrannical conscription law."[17]

In early March, Savannahians witnessed yet another public spectacle, one that left few whites rejoicing. Chatham County had sent thirty-one companies into service by that time, but a CSA quota system required that they send more. Military officials called for able-bodied men to report to the parade ground on March 4. A reporter for the Charleston *Courier* recorded the scene, as an estimated 1,500 people gathered in "a high state of excitement." The recruiting officer, a Georgia colonel, stepped before the crowd, declaring the very idea of conscription a disgrace to his home state. He stressed the cash bonus that awaited men of conviction and courage, "and on the strength of these considerations, invited everybody to walk three paces in front. Nobody did it. An ugly pause ensued, worse than a dead silence between the ticking of a conversation." At some point, to the cheers of the assembled throng, forty Irish immigrants came forward to form a new company, the Mitchell Guards. Gradually, fifty-six more men volunteered, and then the volunteering ended. When the exasperated officer called out for those who possessed legitimate exemptions from service, he was mobbed: "Did you ever see a crowd run away from a falling building at a fire, or toward a dog fight or a side-show? . . . Hats were crushed, ribs punched, corns smashed, and clothes torn." Stable hands and dry-goods clerks pressed forward, clutching certificates that attested either to their infirmity or their indispensability on the job. Some men claimed physical disabilities—"as variously and heterogeneously as by any procession of pilgrims that ever visited the Holy Land." Others were German and Irish immigrants who within the previous few months had taken an oath of nonintention to become citizens. Ten hours later, the colonel had met his quota—but only because those men threatened with the draft "volunteered" so they could qualify for the cash bounty.[18]

On March 25, Governor Brown sought to impress upon CSA secretary of war Judah P. Benjamin the fact of Savannah's vulnerability, now that more and more coastal territory was coming under control of the enemy. Brown had initially resisted sending Georgia forces to the Virginia front, claiming they must defend their own soil first; but he was beginning to realize that the state's soldiers were insufficient to the task, and begged the CSA for at least another eight thousand troops, in addition to the six thousand already stationed in and around the city.

Nevertheless, many feared that the future of Savannah depended less upon the number of soldiers defending it and more upon their morale and discipline. Critics argued that, for all their expert marksmanship, backwoods recruits by nature despised authority and resisted orders. In this view, the recent recruitment plan that allowed men to elect new company officers only exacerbated the problem. Jones worried that would-be leaders would be forced to engage in "low, petty electioneering," and he claimed that new officers—"in very many instances mere noses of wax, to be molded and controlled at will by the men whom they should govern—have been entrusted with the command." George Mercer charged that soldiers naturally chose the "most notoriously incompetent men," proving that democracy in the ranks amounted to a kind of "savage freedom," a "thorough curse" incompatible with civilized society. These recent recruits were always complaining about something—the bad food, the leaky tents; clearly they lacked the "passive qualities which are expected of a soldier in camp." The soldier should obey his officer the same way a slave obeys his master. In Charley Lamar's company, discipline was so lax that the officers actually took to scrubbing clothes and cooking meals for the troops, so cravenly did they seek the approval of their own men. Meanwhile, rumors circulated of "mutinies" among restless troops languishing on the coast.[19]

With all of white Savannah on edge, even some wealthy residents came under suspicion of disloyalty. One native Savannahian in particular faced pointed accusations, though he came from a distinguished family. Dr. James Johnstone Waring was the son of Dr. William Richard Waring, longtime colleague and friend of Richard Arnold. Like both of these older men, James had graduated from the Medical College of the University of Pennsylvania. Yet he showed little enthusiasm either for his studies or for his subsequent career as a physician. As a young student he wrote, "Medicine is certainly not an easy study. It requires an immense outlay of time & toil without any definite prospect of a return. We get along . . . as Virgil says, 'like wounded snakes dragging our slow lengths along.' " Eventually, Waring would find the contentious world of partisan politics more appealing than the practice of medicine.[20]

At the outbreak of war the thirty-one-year-old Waring was living in Washington, D.C. That summer he returned briefly to Savannah to retrieve his wife and small children and hasten back to the U.S. capital. Passing through Nashville, he was arrested after charges circulated that he had provided military secrets to the Yankees. Though subsequently released, Waring knew full well that many in Savannah considered him disloyal. (The Reverend Charles Jones said simply, "He is a spy.") With a public flourish, the physician-landlord announced that he would donate the considerable profits from his store rentals to a soldiers' fund, a gesture that the city council accepted in December 1861. By this time Waring was serving as a CSA surgeon in a hospital in Goldsboro, North Carolina. In March 1862 one of his co-workers filed a complaint charging him with dereliction of duty; apparently, when the hospital came under fire from Union troops, Waring lost his composure and fled, leaving behind a patient on the operating table. Narrowly avoiding a court-martial on a technicality, he returned to Savannah and launched an aggressive campaign to restore his good name. Within a few months the city council had declined to receive any more rent money from its suspect donor.[21]

Most of the Savannah elites who claimed both commercial and family ties with Northerners prudently chose to downplay those connections during the war. Certainly the Chicago-born Nellie Kinzie Gordon did not endear herself to her neighbors when, on the frenzied night of Georgia's secession from the Union, she made a symbolic gesture of disapproval by extinguishing all the lights in the family residence—only to have her mortified husband, William, order them turned back on. Within a few months, he was serving with General J. E. B. Stuart's cavalry in Virginia, while her uncle General David Hunter, with her brother Lieutenant Arthur M. Kinzie on his staff, were stationed with U.S. forces off the South Carolina coast. Nellie spent most of the war in Savannah, dutifully sewing and knitting for rebel soldiers, and enduring the resentment of her irritable mother-in-law and sister-in-law. To a comment from a Savannah neighbor, who said that she hoped Arthur Kinzie would soon be shot dead, the cowed Nellie had responded, "Thank you." But a few weeks later, after hearing that this woman's own brother had been wounded in battle, Nellie famously "remarked loudly and pleasantly, 'By the way, Mrs.——; I hear your brother has been shot in the back; mine is very well, thank you!' "[22]

Over the next few months, Uncle David did little to make his niece's life any easier. In early April Hunter took the dramatic step of seeking approval from the War Department "to arm such loyal men as I can find in the country." He intended to launch an immediate conscription of men ages eighteen to forty-five (presumably all blacks) residing in Union-occupied territory in South Carolina, Georgia, and Florida, a region now called the Department of the South. Hunter got no further than ordering uniforms, including "50,000 pairs of scarlet pantaloons," before coordinating an assault on Fort Pulaski with (now) Admiral DuPont.[23]

At 8 a.m. on April 10, Union forces under Hunter's command on Tybee Island commenced firing on Fort Pulaski, bringing to an end the tranquil if dull and flea-bitten existence of Confederate troops who had served there for the last fifteen months. Though long anticipated, the actual assault took the fort's defenders by surprise, since the aggressors chose not to storm the structure but rather to launch an attack from batteries across the water on Tybee Island. The days preceding the attack were ones of feverish preparation. Wrote Theodorick Monfort, a lieutenant in the Twenty-fifth Georgia Volunteer Regiment, on March 31, "the floor is covered around each gun with sand not for health or cleanliness but to drink up human blood as it flows from the veins & hearts of noble men, from the hearts of those that love & are beloved." And then on the morning of the 10th, shelling proceeded at five-minute intervals, rattling windows and nerves as far away as Savannah. After thirty hours, the high-powered, long-range rifled cannon mortars began gnawing away at the fort's southeast corner. Fearing that the magazine would explode and take with it the fort's 383 men, Colonel Charles Olmstead, age twenty-five, surrendered on the afternoon of April 11. With so many native sons defending Pulaski, in the next few weeks white Savannahians would take personally outsiders' intense criticism of Olmstead's decision; the fall of the fort had piled "disgrace upon disgrace," in the words of the Augusta *Chronicle and Sentinel.*[24]

Union forces quickly took possession of the fort and its forty-five cannon, and shipped off nearly four hundred prisoners of war (accompanied by their Irish-born Catholic chaplain) to Governor's Island in New York City. But not all CSA soldiers accepted prisoner of war status; the German-born George Giebelhouse, twenty-six, a baker from Savannah, was one who seized the opportunity to desert, an option that all U.S. forces offered to prisoners of war.

The loss of Fort Pulaski dramatically transformed the war along the Georgia coast. Within the next few weeks Confederates would shift their focus from defending Savannah to defending Augusta, the site of an essential gunpowder works and textile factories as well as a communications link to the interior of the Confederacy. Savannahians reacted indignantly to this change in strategy, for few could abide the newfound glory of a city that Nellie Gordon and others called that "horrid hole." By this time, the thrill and romance of blockade running had come to an abrupt halt, and although Confederate officials continued to maintain a navy yard in Savannah, they moved the arsenal to the safer location of Macon. Confederate engineers began to obstruct the river north of Savannah, apparently all but inviting a Yankee invasion of the city, assuming the Union navy could sail past its own "stone fleet" obstructing the river. With yet another wave of civilians retreating inland, the city's appearance evoked the mournful days of the yellow-fever epidemic in 1854: according to the *Morning News*, "A strange, mysterious weird quietude reigns perpetually. Stagnation and paralysis obstruct the channels where business briskly flowed." In May, with Savannah more vulnerable than ever, General Lawton took five thousand of his troops and headed north toward Virginia; replacing him was Hugh Mercer, George's father, a banker and graduate of the U.S. Military Academy.[25]

In a provocative move, General Hunter proceeded to "confiscate" blacks along the coast, intending not only to arm the men but to liberate the entire slave population. On May 9 he announced that slaves in the Department of the South "heretofore held as slaves, are therefore declared forever free." Hunter also ordered that black men "capable of bearing arms" be brought forward "under guard" so that they could be forcibly inducted in the Union army. This measure prompted an outcry from Hilton Head blacks; some feared they were to be shipped off to Cuba, and all resented Hunter's strong-arm tactics. A few days later, Lincoln rescinded Hunter's order. The president was still bent on reassuring southern planters that his army was not intent on destroying slavery.[26]

The fall of Fort Pulaski inspired black people hungry for freedom throughout the lowcountry. On April 1 Dolly Reed had sent her granddaughter Susie out of Savannah and back to her extended family on Great Farm plantation, on the Isle of Wight in Liberty County. Twelve days later, Susie's uncle assembled his family of seven, including his niece, and escaped to St. Catherines Island, where the family found refuge behind Union lines. By the end of the month, the federal gunboat *Potomska* had deposited the party on St. Simons, a ten-mile-long island that guarded access to Brunswick harbor. They and other refugees took up residence on the now-abandoned Retreat plantation, formerly owned by Massachusetts-born Thomas Butler King. By May, with the encouragement of Union officers, the fourteen-year-old Susie had established a school on the island for both children and adults; her supplies included schoolbooks and Bibles sent from the North.[27]

Over the next few months the African-American settlement established at St. Simons became a sanctuary for scores of black refugees. Unlike Port Royal, South Carolina, its permanent, larger, and more famous counterpart to the north, St. Simons failed to attract the zealous white missionaries and cotton agents who aimed to showcase free black labor in the cotton fields; instead, the Georgia island served primarily as a recruiting ground and provisioning base for U.S. military forces and as an exercise in self-sufficiency for the black people who settled there.[28]

As early as March 1862, the U.S. Navy had enlisted a number of men from the lowcountry, including Alexander Parland, a twenty-five-year-old from Brunswick, and Jacob Smith, a twenty-two-year-old from St. Mary's. The ranks of black seamen would swell over the course of the war. In all, 417 African-American men from Georgia served in the U.S. Navy between 1862 and 1865. Many of the recruits were young men hailing from Savannah and the lowcountry. Their surnames, in many cases identical to those of their owners, reveal the extent and nature of Union raids along the coast—Ellis, Madison, Richard, and Jacob Scarlet from Darien; Abram, Bob, John, March, and Samuel Spaulding from St. Simons. Some, like Charles Tatnell from Brunswick, listed their occupation as "pilot," but the group as a whole reflected the range of tasks assigned to male slaves: blacksmiths, dockworkers, waiters, coal heavers, hostlers, cooks, carpenters, and shoemakers, as well as field hands. They served on gunships and steamships; among the latter was the *Alabama*, recently captured and now flying the U.S. flag.[29]

Admiral DuPont believed that General Hunter had unnecessarily aroused passions on both sides with the declaration that each slave who came to Union lines was a "practically free man." However, DuPont was inclined to agree with Hunter that blacks served as highly effective guerrillas in the fight against the Confederacy: these men, he noted, were "our friends [and] . . . they had the knowledge of locality, of the forests, or the waters; for no white man in the South can handle a *skiff*, are stupid and awkward on the water, while the Negroes are skillful and daring." With St. Simons as their base, black men led Union officials to small boats, laden with blankets and shoes, lurking in creeks and trading with local people. Blacks also formed raiding parties to capture wild cattle and strip their masters' plantations of foodstuffs. One such raid, to Scarlet's plantation on Colonel's Island, netted the colony and Union seamen 150 bushels of corn as well as peas and sweet potatoes. In June, thirty black men helped to seize the rebel schooner *Southern Belle* and used it to transport 3,000 bushels of rice back to St. Simons.[30]

The colony was unique, a place largely controlled by black people themselves. Covering land owned by Thomas Butler King, Pierce Butler, and James E. Couper, it eventually consisted of a network of small villages with a total of six hundred people, mostly women and children; many had escaped from nearby coastal plantations, but at least some had journeyed far distances from the Georgia interior. Flight from slavery was increasingly a family affair; more than eight out of ten of the hundreds who made their way to the Georgia Sea Islands in 1862 traveled in groups of three or more. On St. Simons, they immediately set about planting crops and soon had eighty acres of corn, plus potatoes and beans, under cultivation.[31]

All parties involved hoped to see the settlement become "self-supporting," but in a foreshadowing of postwar developments, when whites insisted that blacks grow cotton exclusively, refugees and U.S. military officials differed on the meaning of the term. DuPont acknowledged the blacks' "great dislike to do the work they have been accustomed to—that seems to make their condition the same as before. They will sit up all night and fish and catch crabs and go and catch horses and wild cattle and cross to the mainland in sculls and get corn and so on," but they resisted the enforced pace of fieldwork. Still, officers exhorted blacks "to plant cotton and thus become of use to themselves," going so far as to place in irons the carpenters who refused to labor in the fields. Referring to the people's resistance to slavery-like work discipline, one official deplored the "idleness, improvidence, theft and a disposition to vagrancy [that] are the besetting sins of the contraband race on the island." But then in the next breath this same official detailed the efforts of St. Simons blacks to cut wood for use by the steamer *Darlington*, noting that those efforts were "to be paid for at a certain rate."[32]

Soon after arriving on the island, black men and women initiated a lively trade with U.S. seamen and officers, taking advantage of the Northerners' inability to exploit the region's natural abundance: "We tried to catch some fish for dinner, but failed," wrote DuPont at one point. A "tariff of prices to be charged to officers' messes and sailors for articles purchased of negroes on the island of St. Simon's, Georgia" was published on July 1, 1862. The list reflected the variety of foodstuffs and services that blacks were supplying to Union troops—milk (4¢ a quart), chickens (12¢ each), eggs (12¢ a dozen), corn (5¢ a dozen), watermelons (5 to 15¢ each), okra (20¢ a peck), beans (10¢ a peck), squash (two for 3¢), cantaloupes (1–3¢ each). Men cut wood and sold it to steamship captains; they caught terrapins, rabbits, shrimp, and fish "in bunches." Women gathered whortleberries and worked as laundresses, charging 50¢ per dozen of "large pieces when soap and starch furnished." Seamstresses abided by the following tariff: "The prices of making pantaloons or shirts shall not be over 50 cents each; coats, 75 cents each, where the materials are furnished." Thus did black workers begin to attach a monetary value to tasks they had been compelled to perform under slavery. The trade operated in the other direction as well; one U.S. officer came under fire from his superiors for racking up profits of 200 percent by selling "hoops, calicoes, trinkets etc. for women" in the area.[33]

Gradually, the crops grew "finely" and a new way of life took shape on the island. A Union chaplain, the Reverend Mansfield French, appeared periodically before Susie Baker's classes and lectured on such topics as "Boston and the North." French also officiated at marriages of longtime couples, and baptized children in ceremonies that reflected both enduring family ties and the necessity of reshaping those ties to accommodate a refugee population. One day in July the white minister presided over a baptism that included not only nuclear families—fathers and mothers with their children—but also "children presented by [distant] relatives or strangers, the parents being sold" or still enslaved. Life was not necessarily easy on St. Simons; the historical record is silent on possible conflicts among the refugees over food and other scarce resources, and between longtime residents of the island and newcomers from the interior, men, women, and children who arrived with little more than the clothes on their backs.[34]

The St. Simons colony chose its own leader, Charles O'Neal, who organized a defensive unit of men armed with old-fashioned flintlock muskets (provided by Union officers) to guard against night attacks from the Confederates. Among the defenders were nearly forty men who had responded to Hunter's call for volunteers in the spring. In June, these men and others from the island, led by O'Neal and two fugitives (John Brown and Edward Gould), joined with a group from the mainland and skirmished with Confederates in the swamps near Brunswick. Brown and O'Neal were killed and several others were wounded, possibly the first African-American military casualties of the war.[35]

This force of fighting men served as the foundation of Companies A and E of the First South Carolina Volunteers. Formed in November at Hilton Head by New Jersey–born Captain Charles T. Trowbridge, it was the first official all-black unit of the Union army. (Eventually, a total of 3,500 black Georgians, most from coastal regions, served as U.S. soldiers.) Susie Baker recalled the men's dismay at donning their first uniforms, the scarlet tops and pants chosen by Hunter: "The rebels see us, miles away," they noted. By this time the St. Simons settlement had been dismantled; together with other Georgia Sea Islands, it had become increasingly vulnerable to the rebels. Most of the women and children, including Susie Baker, were transported by Union gunboat to Hilton Head.[36]

The most explicit acknowledgment of blacks' service on behalf of the Union cause came not from northern military men but from southern planters. In July, the Reverend Charles Jones wrote to his son Charles and detailed the sad state of affairs in Liberty County, where more than fifty slaves had recently absconded ("Your Uncle John has lost five. *Three* are said to have left from your Aunt Susan's and Cousin Laura's.") He concluded that no slave "may be absolutely depended on," for "the temptation of *cheap goods, freedom, and paid labor* cannot be withstood." Implicit in this and other descriptions of mass runaways was the rapid disintegration of plantation discipline, and the collapse of production in the fields and the master's house, a collapse effected by black men and women alike. Around this time a Liberty County delegation of planters traveled with military escort to St. Simons and demanded the forced return of the black people there, claiming they were "noncombatants." In this case, the white men left empty-handed. In other cases, Union officers were all too eager to comply with planters' demands. However, lowcountry whites in general were coming to recognize that blacks were acting very much like combatants indeed. Increasingly, planters condemned runaway slaves as cunning spies and traitors, as "inteligent beings" intent on passing along "information well calculated to aid the enemy." Gradually disappearing was the antebellum image of blacks as passive, childlike, obedient; in its place was emerging the idea of blacks as freedom fighters aiming to undermine the Confederacy—and yearning for *"cheap goods, freedom, and paid labor."*[37]

On August 1, a group of Liberty County planters headed by the Reverend Robert Q. Mallard, Charles Jones Sr.'s son-in-law, composed a lengthy letter to General Hugh W. Mercer, now serving as Savannah's defender. The writers complained of the "constant drain" of blacks escaping from the coastal areas to Union forces—since the start of the war, perhaps as many as twenty thousand people valued at a total of $12 to $15 million. "The absconding Negroes hold the position of Traitors," wrote the petitioners, "since they go over to the enemy & afford him aid & comfort, by revealing the condition of the districts and cities from which they come, & aiding him in erecting fortifications & raising provisions for his support." Blacks were engaged in spying activities, "since they are employed in secret expeditions for obtaining information, by transmission of newspapers & by other modes; and act as guides to expeditions on the land & as pilots to their vessels on the waters of our inlets and rivers." Indeed, "they have proved of great value, thus far, to the Coast operations of the enemy."[38]

Contending with "a lawless set of runaways"—men who left the plantation for the coast, only to return later, intent on retrieving their families and "corrupting the Negroes that remain faithful"—the planters urged stern measures. They recommended that military officials make an example of those blacks apprehended and charged with "furnishing the enemy with aid & comfort, & for acting as Spies and Traitors." Swift retribution in the form of public executions would deter miscreants in the future and at the same time bypass the slow workings of the civil judicial system, not to mention the misguided objections of individual slaveowners. In essence, argued Mallard and his neighbors, slaves "constitute a part of the Body politic, *in fact*; and should be made to know their duty." The only alternative was vigilante justice, which the planters also feared. In response, General Mercer agreed that "the evil alluded to may grow into frightful proportions." At the same time he resisted the idea that army officers should assume the duty of executing slaves and thus destroying slaveholders' property. Preoccupied with moving troops out of Savannah and north into Charleston that summer, he passed the letter on to the Confederate secretary of war. And so it had come to this: White men in defense of a slaveholders' republic advocating the summary execution of slaves—blacks who were now deemed members of the "body politic."[39]

Around this time, more and more whites refused to yield up their own slave property to preserve the institution of slavery. Later, reflecting on the war, Mallard would write that "planters, who cheerfully surrendered their sons to the army, protested against the use of their slaves in the trenches!" And indeed, in the summer and fall of 1862, planters throughout the state were in an uproar over Confederate efforts to appropriate both slaves and free men of color for fatigue work routinely performed by white soldiers. In August of that year, approximately 1,500 blacks were at work on fortifications in and near Savannah, constructing a semicircular line of defense around the city. In the absence of a legislative or executive mandate to impress slaves, the governor authorized General Mercer to find the necessary number of bodies by whatever means—cajoling, threatening, forcing their owners. Black men and women did their best to thwart this process; they feigned illness, hid, ran away. Nevertheless, Mercer insisted that each county yield up 20 percent of its able-bodied slaves (he was willing to accept women to make up that number); the CSA would pay transportation and supply rations, but owners must furnish each person with a shovel. Throughout the interior, slaveowners at first tried to ignore the order, and then, forced to comply, objected to the pretense that their compliance was voluntary. Writing directly to the secretary of war in September, a Laurens County planter charged that wealthier counties were avoiding the call-up; he concluded, "We must have equality in this confederacy or it will blow up—If this is to be a free-will offering upon the altar of our country, I wish to be placed on an equal footing with the people of other counties."[40]

The planters' deep resistance was understandable. In and near Savannah, some slaves were forced to toil throughout the day, sweltering in the noon sun, while others waited listlessly, lacking shovels and wheelbarrows to keep busy. Of the seven Jones slaves sent to work on the city's fortifications, three died that summer and early fall, as many of the 1,200 slaves held in the city and throughout the countryside succumbed to measles, typhoid, dysentery ("river cholera"), and unnamed maladies. Mary Jones noted that Joe, "one of our most young and active and athletic men," and others seemed "to have taken some poison from water, food, or atmosphere into their systems which defies the ordinary remedies." Rumor had it that army agents hired slaves at low prices and then turned around and rented them to private contractors at inflated prices. Some owners objected less to their slaves going than to their returning. A planter in Dougherty County resisted the impressment order, fearing that if his slaves spent any time in Savannah, "an opportunity will thus be afforded to them of talking with one another of their wants & wishes & their situations—their minds will be inflamed by the vicious ['negroes & traitorous white men'] with false & mischevous notions."[41]

In October Thomas Purse prefaced his 1862 mayor's report with the observation, "as a city we have been comparatively more exempt from the desolating effects of the war than many of our Southern seaport cities." It was true that, unlike Hampton, Virginia, or New Orleans, Savannah remained free of Union occupiers. Yet Purse's claim blithely ignored the emotional and physical toll the war was taking not only on blacks separated from kin and pressed into fatigue labor, but also on white Savannahians killed, wounded, or maimed for life, and their families. Some of the wounded were sent home, where they drew their last breath at the CSA hospital. Very few fallen soldiers received a lengthy, emotion-laden obituary in the local paper; that kind of public recognition was reserved for officers like Bartow and for soldiers like Charles A. Goulding, son of a prominent Liberty County Presbyterian minister who was also a Confederate chaplain. Published in the *Morning News* after his death in December 1862, at the battle of Second Manassas, the obituary chronicled young Goulding's decision to enlist in the war; he had dashed home from a trip abroad in England and fought his way through enemy lines to find

Colonel Bartow in the summer of 1861. Yet for the kin of fallen soldiers, grief could not be measured in column inches of the *Morning News*.[42]

More generally, although Savannah had thus far escaped from playing host to Union soldiers, the war effort itself had disrupted the city mightily. In the fall of 1862, when forty-seven-year-old mayor-elect Thomas Holcombe (owner of a successful wholesale grocery business) assumed office, he confronted a city in chaos. The mayor's court could not keep up with, and the jail could hardly accommodate, the escalating number of black lawbreakers. September saw the return of southern troops captured during the assault on Fort Pulaski, and recently exchanged for their northern counterparts; until they could find their way home or into another regiment, they remained at loose ends, needy and restless. Drunken army recruits brawled with civilians, cavorted in the Forsyth Park fountain, trampled flower beds, and pilfered from private gardens. A March 1862 military order officially closing Savannah's grogshops had done little to alleviate the widespread problem of public intoxication. Rising to the increased demand, enterprising distillers produced alcohol made out of dried peaches and even potatoes and peas. The army hospital in Savannah did not help matters: it prescribed whiskey to all of its inmates during the unhealthy season, a practice that no doubt contributed to the alcohol dependence that fueled so much destructive behavior. On the streets Savannahians could catch glimpses of court-martialed men hobbled by balls and chains and seven-pound leg bars; these were men who had been caught rebelling against the hardships of camp life, or trying to return to their families on the home front, or resenting the fact that they had tasted (in the words of George Mercer) "little of the poetry and romance of war." More and more, regular troops provoked the contempt of elites, who feared that these young men were incapable of "energetic heroic action," that they were useful mainly because they "understand how to use the spade" (in the words of Charles Jones Jr.).[43]

During Mayor Purse's term the CSA ran up an unpaid debt of $2,610 to the Savannah jail for detaining "prisoners of war" (i.e., deserters) until they could be reclaimed by their commanding officers. Meanwhile, the city was reeling from a whole host of new and ballooning expenses: the police, grave diggers, "Irish day laborers," and health officers were all clamoring for pay increases. The city also found itself responsible for providing "refreshments" for soldiers passing through, for sinking obstructions in the Savannah River, and for arming the elderly and infirm Home Guards called up for duty.[44]

The Savannah Poor House and Hospital, the temporary home of

impoverished and ill seamen and city residents, had lost its federal government subsidy, but the Confederate government refused to provide it with any support. In response to a plea for aid, in 1862 the CSA's treasury secretary counseled local officials to pare the hospital's expenses and fire most of its staff. He also lectured the city to look to its own residents, rather than to Richmond, in matters of social welfare: charity, he wrote, should be "administered by the people, from the impulses of their own feeling, and to place the sick and infirm of all classes and occupations on the same footing, private charity everywhere makes ample provision for the sick and disabled." Yet the crushing financial burdens imposed by the war, burdens felt by individuals no less than the municipal government, rendered quaint the notion that private citizens must accept the alleviation of widespread poverty and distress as their own civic responsibility.[45]

The shortage of goods and food combined with the cheapness of Confederate currency and the "spirit of speculation" produced an inflationary spiral that threatened to reduce all but the wealthiest to beggary. Eyeing twenty-dollar bushels of potatoes at the city market, the widow Henrietta Wayne decided to hire out her slaves to a factory owner in Macon and thereby improve her cash flow. George Mercer, now serving as an aide to his father, believed that the "nefarious practices" of speculators were "inflicting more injury upon us than the Yankees themselves." Even the well-to-do felt exploited by different groups determined to use the crisis to their advantage. Landowners in the interior of the state were charging outrageous rates to planters seeking a place for their refugeed slaves. In November, Charles Junior bought such a plantation one hundred miles northwest of the city, in Burke County. In addition to paying for the start-up costs of corn, mules, and meat, he found himself forced to negotiate with his own slaves for the purchase of their hogs.[46]

Where lowcountry whites saw disorder, blacks saw opportunity. On September 22 President Lincoln declared his intention to make an emancipation proclamation on January 1, 1863. Reacting to the Union victory at Antietam Creek in Maryland, the bloodiest single day in history on U.S. soil, Lincoln maintained that the proclamation was "a fit and necessary war measure." Though the proclamation would free no slaves—it "liberated" only those slaves still within Confederate territory—Lincoln's announcement prompted an anxious vigil among Savannah blacks over the next thirteen weeks. Wrote James Simms, "Who, then, could estimate or describe with tongue or pen the struggle in their hearts between *hope and fear*? Who can measure the prayer offered in secret at this period and know its effects?" For their part, whites condemned, in the words of Charles Junior, Lincoln's calculated, "fiendish purpose," his "direct bid for insurrection, . . . to incite flight, murder, and rapine on the part of our slave population."[47]

On Thursday, November 27, General Rufus Saxton proclaimed a day of Thanksgiving throughout the Department of the South. At Fort Pulaski, the occupying federal troops welcomed military and civilian guests from Hilton Head to a grand celebration on a day that was "propitious and cool." Morning religious services included an oration by General Saxton, who told his black listeners, "The Lord has come to you, and has answered your prayers." The afternoon was devoted to a variety of amusements and competitions, including target practice, a rowing match, a foot race, a hurdle sack race, greased-pole climbing, and a wheelbarrow race (with blindfolded contestants). A highlight of the day's festivities was the "meal feat," a competition "exclusively for the contrabands." Hands tied behind their backs, each of the six contestants rooted for a $5 gold piece dropped in a tub of corn meal. Crowded on the fort's ramparts, spectators roared with pleasure "when one of the wooly-headed contraband boys raised the $5 from the flour," according to one observer. The day's events concluded with a "burlesque dress parade," entertainment by a minstrel band, and a feast of oysters, pies, and lemonade.[48]

The "meal feat" and minstrel show notwithstanding, lowcountry blacks sought to claim control over their own fighting energies no less than over their own labor. In the fall of 1862, uniformed black soldiers, members of the newly organized, 550-strong First South Carolina Volunteers, began a series of forays up the rivers and creeks of coastal Georgia and Florida. In organizing the raids, General Saxton aimed to seize lumber, destroy rebel saltworks and picket stations along the coast, and "prove the fighting qualities of the negroes (which some have doubted)." Not only did the men successfully skirmish with the enemy, they also devised military strategy "on account of the greater facility with which they can effect landings through the marshes and thick woods which line the banks of the streams."[49]

In some instances black men chose targets on their own, in defiance of Union military officials. In the fall, several of Robert Stafford's slaves returned to his Cumberland Island plantation to exact their due from him. One of the largest slaveowners in the state, Stafford had held more than one hundred people in bondage, including several children he had had with a slave named Elizabeth. When the war broke out, the planter made money by leasing enslaved workers to businesses on the mainland in nearby Fernandina, Florida. In September 1862, nine of them returned, armed with guns and clubs and accompanied by "a number of strange negroes." Unlike many of his white neighbors along the coast, Stafford had refused to leave the island, probably because he intended to safeguard from arsonists and plunderers the forty thousand pounds of ginned cotton stored on his plantation. As early as spring 1862, some planters in occupied Union areas had begun trading with northern cotton agents, a sign that profit-making trumped Confederate patriotism.[50]

A Navy officer on the USS *Alabama* reported that black men were terrorizing Stafford, "their conduct being of riotous and threatening character, refusing to submit to any control, killing the cattle and overrunning the private dwelling." Fearful for his life and the safety of his valuable property, Stafford convinced Union officers to round up the blacks and place them in irons. In a report to his superiors, one officer made note of the stockpile of arms on the place—"several guns and pistols and a quantity of ammunition." When Stafford declared that he had relinquished his claim to them as slaves, the prisoners requested that they be accepted as crew members on the *Alabama*. They thus joined a number of other former Stafford slaves—Dennis, Hayes, Jack, Prince, Roger, and Stephen, all born on Cumberland Island and mustered into Union naval service two months before.[51]

In coastal swamplands and on the streets of Savannah, in African-American churches and workplaces of all kinds, black people emerged as traitors to the Confederate cause. Still, they were not necessarily and always aligned with the Union, the enemy of their enemy.

-❧| CHAPTER SEVEN |❧-

Are We Free?

O N NEW YEAR'S EVE 1862, the Savannah city council held its regular biweekly session and debated routine proposals—a pay hike for the grave diggers at Laurel Grove Cemetery, and a standing reward of $1,000 for the apprehension of arsonists, past, present, and future. Meanwhile, not far away, at their sanctuary on Franklin Square, members of the First African Baptist Church were holding their traditional December 31 "watch-meeting." Outwardly, the service seemed unremarkable, the prayers and songs customary for this end-of-year service. Soon after midnight, when Wednesday gave way to Thursday, the congregants exchanged greetings with one another, and then parted. The meeting had proceeded peacefully, undisturbed by city authorities. And yet secretly the members of First African had just celebrated a promise of freedom: the Emancipation Proclamation of January 1, 1863.[1]

James Simms considered the church service a miracle of sorts, a quiet affair honed by long years of verbal restraint and by one hundred days of painful anticipation. Looking back, Simms recalled of slavery times: "The tongue must be dumb upon that theme; it was the soul that sung [sic]." That night the choir offered up familiar hymns; only in their hearts did these "gospel trumpeters" herald "the year of Jubilee," for the music of the soul "was not for earth's ears, but it was heard in heaven." On New Year's Day black clergy from all over the city held a celebratory but equally subdued dinner. The Reverend John Cox of Second African and the Reverend Ulysses L. Houston of First Bryan led prayers on the theme "that God would permit nothing to hinder Mr. Lincoln from issuing his proclamation." (Cox himself had been free since 1849, when he paid his master $1,100.) Of the dinner itself, we know little more, except that James Porter, choirmaster and warden of St. Stephen's Episcopal, "delivered an excellent address on the proclamation"—an address recounted by the anonymous author of Porter's obituary, published in a black newspaper, the *Savannah Tribune,* thirty-two years later.[2]

Off the coast of South Carolina, the New Year's celebration at the U.S. military camp near Beaufort was a livelier affair, filled with pageantry and surprises. The night before, while First African congregants were holding their watch-meeting, troops at Camp Saxton (named for Rufus Saxton, commander of the Department of the South) were roasting ten oxen in an open pit, the flames casting "a thousand fantastic shadows among the great gnarled oaks," in the words of one army officer. The next morning an estimated three thousand black people arrived, many dressed in their Sunday best. By 11:30 the festivities were under way. White and black troops (the latter in their red uniforms) had gathered expectantly under a grove of trees, some sitting, some standing, near the podium filled with white women teachers, federal military officials, and other dignitaries. The Reverend Mansfield French was in the process of presenting a stand of flags, a gift from a New York City church, to an officer newly arrived from Massachusetts, Colonel Thomas Wentworth Higginson. And then suddenly an elderly black man and two black women began to sing: "My country 'tis of thee, Sweet land of Liberty, of thee I sing!"[3]

Momentarily taken aback, the white onlookers were uncertain how to react to this spontaneous departure from the scripted program. However, upon reflection, most seemed to agree with the camp surgeon that "nothing could have been more unexpected or more inspiring." Sergeant Prince Rivers and Corporal Robert Sutton—who just a few months ago had been slaves, and were now Union officers—delivered brief remarks to the crowd. The formal ceremony closed with a feast of the roasted oxen, washed down with a mixture of molasses, water, vinegar, and ginger. Like other former St. Simons colonists, Susie Baker savored the day's events. She believed the meat was "not served as tastily or correctly as it would have been at home," but she appreciated the spirit of the occasion, and noted that the meal "was enjoyed with keen appetites and relish."[4]

In the absence of the traditional New Year's ruckus in the city streets, and despite the brilliant sunshine, Savannah whites sensed foreboding. The day was "filled with disquietudes," in the words of Lieutenant Charles C. Jones. On January 1, the *Republican* carried news about the tremendous bloodletting at Fredericksburg (on December 13). And now a huge battle was raging at Stones River, near Murfreesboro, Tennessee, while Confederates continued to fend off Union forces at Vicksburg, Mississippi. In the end, these winter battles took an enormous toll in lives: at

Fredericksburg the North suffered 13,000 casualties, compared to 5,000 for the Confederates. At Stones River nearly one-third of all the U.S. soldiers engaged were either killed or wounded, and the South lost 1,500 troops in a single hour as the two massive armies fought to a standstill. Cast in a defensive role at both these places, the Confederates lost fewer men but gained little for their victories. Even the most defiant Confederates—and there were many in Savannah—could see no end to the carnage.[5]

City authorities remained preoccupied with renegades of various stripes. On January 1, President Lincoln had appended a paragraph to his proclamation, authorizing emancipated slaves to "be received into the armed service of the United States to garrison forts, positions, stations, and other places, and to man vessels of all sorts in said service." This statement represented a dramatic shift from the Union's initial policy against the use of black military personnel. In the Georgia lowcountry, however, the proclamation merely hastened and formalized a recruitment effort that had been well under way since General David Hunter's initiatives in the spring of 1862. Enslaved men continued to offer their services to U.S. forces. Born in Savannah, the Parlin brothers, Isaac, a twenty-five-year-old laborer, and Robert, twenty-nine, a carpenter, celebrated that New Year's Day on board the U.S. store ship *Brandywine*, where they had been serving since October. George Robbenberry, a Savannah-born nineteen-year-old, had enlisted in the navy the day after Christmas 1862, and received an assignment as a "third class boy" on the *Colorado*. A stream of black fugitives—including, at some point in the war, Susie Baker's father—replenished the ranks of the U.S. Navy.[6]

During the first week of January 1863, the advertising pages of the local newspapers were filled with descriptions of many men with a price on their heads. The twenty-six-year-old "quick-spoken" Frank had absconded from work on Savannah's fortifications, and was probably hiding out somewhere near his former owner in the city, where the rest of his family was still living. Other ads described Manly, five feet, six inches tall, thirty-two years old, missing one eye; James, five-foot-nine, about twenty-two years old; and Louis, also five-foot-nine, fifty-one years old, with "a prominent nose" and a stout build (he "speaks very broken English"). Twenty-eight-year-old John, five feet, nine inches, had a slight stoop and looked and acted older than his age. It was suspected that he had sought refuge with his wife in Savannah.[7]

However, except for Frank, all these runaways were white men, deserters from the Confederate army. The usual reward of $30 awaited the captor of Manly Hart, a carpenter, and John Makin, an Irish-born baker, both of whom had fled from the Savannah Volunteer Guards, and of James Caulfield, a member of Phoenix Rifles Company B. In contrast, for some unknown reason, the "apprehension and delivery" of Louis Longe would earn the successful bounty hunter a munificent $200. By this time, ads for runaway soldiers were far outpacing ads for runaway slaves. The spring of 1863 would bring a rash of desertions, some among immigrant compatriots who had enlisted together and then fled together, including a group of German-born bakers, butchers, and gardeners who had signed up with the First Battalion Georgia Sharpshooters on June 5, 1861, and deserted en masse one year and eleven months later. Some soldiers sent out to retrieve their fugitive comrades failed to return as well. The war's grim statistics told a larger story of widespread fear in the ranks: a sampling of regiments raised in Savannah suggests that, out of every hundred men, forty-three would return home as honored veterans, while twenty-five would desert and thirty-three would die of disease or battle wounds.[8]

Quartered in the Forest City, some white soldiers who neither marched off to battle nor avoided service took a middle way: they bided their time but then pillaged livestock and stole vegetables from the gardens of city residents; or they went off on benders for days at a time, returning hungry and dirty to their barracks to face confinement or hard labor. In addition to the advertising sections of the newspapers, the jail register signaled a dramatic breakdown in military discipline, even among men whose lives were not in immediate danger. The jail was now packed tight with deserters held for "safe keeping" until their commanding officers could retrieve them.[9]

For most working-class whites, wartime Savannah afforded little in the way of new and expanded economic opportunities since the able-bodied at least were supposed to be in military service. In contrast, some black men and women were making a bold bid for independence in the form of wage work and other moneymaking enterprises. Behind southern lines or in the Union's Department of the South, they provided for their own families by trafficking in scarce goods and services, literally taking advantage of absent masters and distracted mistresses. Union troops rewarded the daring men and women who sold animal pelts, cotton, and corn, or performed a variety of services such as cooking and laundering, paying them from $10 to $50 a month and rations. Enslaved men found their way through picket lines to deliver precious letters and packages from Savannah to soldiers stationed on batteries south of the city. Referring to blacks up and down the Georgia coast, James Henry Gooding, an African-

American soldier from the North, observed admiringly, "The slaves, hereabouts, are working for the government mostly, although they can make a pretty snug little sum, peddling among the soldiers, selling fruit, &c."[10]

Free persons of color responded to cash incentives when they worked in any number of Confederate war-related industries—sawmills, brick-making establishments, railroads, the hospital, and saltworks outside the city. Even slaves hired out by their owners took advantage of a daily task system that included overtime pay. In 1863 Engineer Bureau slaves impressed to work on railway roadbeds dug out twelve to fifteen cubic yards by noon or so; after that, they earned a "premium" of 15¢ per additional cubic yard excavated. Enslaved railroad hands, boatmen, and teamsters also worked on a modified task system that offered cash wages.[11]

Many slaves and free people of color found new and potentially profitable sources of income in and around the city. In Liberty County, Tony Axon, the free blacksmith, continued to work at his trade during the war. Axon decided to accept provisions in return for his services, so that when the war was over, "I would have something which would do me more good than Confederate money." By the end of 1864 he reckoned he had accumulated horses, wagons, and buggies, as well as eight cows, eight hogs, 20 bushels of salt, 150 bushels of corn, and 1,000 pounds of fodder. The well-to-do Anthony Odingsells went into business selling fish, oysters, and meat and other provisions to Confederate soldiers stationed in and around Wassaw Island.[12]

In the city, stable keepers, skilled construction workers, and draymen were especially in demand. Georgiana Guard had recently married a teamster, Jeremiah Kelley, who was working hard and investing his earnings in a fine horse, "a pretty 'critter'—large, strong." The slave Rachel Bromfield hired her own time and that of her two daughters; together they kept a boardinghouse in Savannah and rented out rooms. Other black men and women responded to the heightened demand for food by raising chickens and hogs and tending vegetable gardens. The slaves Moses Stikes and Binah Butler formed a partnership to cultivate a seven-acre garden in the city; Moses paid his master $21 and Dinah hers $10 a month for the privilege. Together they "worked there two years raising all kinds of Garden *truck* for the market" and selling chickens. The two also managed to stockpile 50 bushels of potatoes and 2,500 pounds of fodder and hay.[13]

Jackson B. Sheftall, the butcher, was among the most enterprising of Savannah blacks during the war. Born free, Sheftall looked white; his mother was a slave, his father a white man. Asked later to account for the favoritism he received from Confederate authorities, he replied, "I had been doing business here [in Savannah] a long time and was generally thought a great deal [of] among the whites here." Reviewing Sheftall's record of wartime profit making (if not profiteering), one Union official later noted disapprovingly that the butcher had realized that "there was a large profit in it, and . . . went in zealously." Sheftall claimed that the Confederate government had forced him to do the work: "Well, if you was a butcher you had to butcher for the Government, and if you were a cook you had to cook for them." Still, the specific arrangement he negotiated with the authorities proved to be a highly lucrative one. Each day, the twenty-nine-year-old drove cattle from the railroad to a pen; but after he finished that work he was "allowed all the balance of the time to do my own." He received permission from CSA officials to keep as many of his own cows and pigs as he wished. He also retained the offal, as well as the hides, livers, and tongues of cattle, which he sold at a profit to other businesses. In early 1862 Sheftall managed to buy his wife, Elizabeth, from her owner, paying $2,600 in cash for her freedom. Based on his impressive stores of poultry, corn, beef tallow, rice, flour, fodder, and hay—not to mention a full array of butchering utensils and scales—Sheftall was among Savannah's best-provisioned persons, black or white.[14]

Free black men were embedded in the city's wartime economy; they were working as (in order of numerical significance) carpenters, wagoners, bricklayers, laborers, coopers, butchers, and masons. Smaller numbers found jobs as machinists, barbers, blacksmiths, plasterers, engineers, and cabinetmakers. The women labored mainly as domestic servants, laundresses, nurses, and seamstresses. Forced to register annually with the city, some reported jobs other than the work they routinely performed; the choirmaster and teacher James Porter listed himself as a tailor, and the teacher Jane Deveaux gave pastry cook as her occupation. Confederate war imperatives did not lessen the burdens among black workers, but those burdens were shifting away from slavery and toward self-determination.[15]

IN THE LATE WINTER and early spring of 1863, privileged white people continued to enjoy a busy social life, one evocative of the antebellum years but to a degree tempered by the rising death toll that affected a cross section of the city. On February 12 the Georgia Historical Society marked its twenty-fifth anniversary with speeches followed by "a sumptuous repast, prepared by that excellent caterer, Sam Whaley of the Beauregard Restaurant." Wartime weddings, even lavish ones, had become a fixture on the city's social scene. The wealthy enjoyed excursions to the out-skirts of the city, picnicking on the batteries lining the river, and touring CSA gunboats. In the courtyards of imposing mansions and townhouses, parents indulged their children with tea parties of custard and cake.[16]

In fact, Savannah high society adjusted quickly to wartime. Before 1861, the theater scene had been shaped by an eclectic mix of touring lec-turers, actors, singers, instrumentalists, and novelty performers. Now, with a population swollen by military personnel, theatricals of all kinds offered patrons an added touch of glamour and rewarded managers and performers handsomely. And so a large number of intrepid singers, pianists, magicians, and acting troupes made their way through the South and onto the stage at the Savannah Theatre, St. Andrew's Hall, and Masonic Hall. Politicians came to town, lecturing on "What Made Seces-sion the Necessary Policy of the Civil War" and "Fatal Defects in the Civ-ilization of the U.S.A." Also attracting audiences in the spring of 1863 were Blind Tom, "Negro Boy Pianist"; Mago del Mage, the wizard; and the comic singer Mr. Sloman with his daughters Anna and Elizabeth, vir-tuosos of the harp, piano, and organ. Ticket-price increases failed to dampen that year's March–April high season, when the Queen Sister troupe played 79 nights, giving 146 performances of 52 different plays. These productions had broad appeal, prompting complaints from well-heeled patrons about other members of the audience—the "crowd of rude and ill-bred boys turned loose to do as they pleased," and the blacks who, shouting, whistling, and spitting tobacco juice, "must be taught that they are in the presence of white superiors."[17]

By attending benefit productions, theatergoers could contribute to the Confederate cause while enjoying a night out. Lectures and plays raised funds for the "Fredericksburg sufferers" and for the impoverished families of slain and wounded soldiers. Wealthy lowcountry folk discov-ered that they could still partake of rich foods and merrymaking, as long as they did so to honor their men in uniform. On a Liberty County plan-tation, the visit of an army captain and his men called forth "a bountiful repast consisting of turkey, ham, ducks, and chickens, breads, cakes, boiled custard, syllabub, etc." And much of the Savannah social scene revolved around military officers. On February 21, the city witnessed a "grand military display" as long lines of troops, brandishing their bayonets and sabers, moved to the center of the city from their various encampments. That evening at the Pulaski House Hotel, Savannah women sponsored a "spirited and *recherché* entertainment" in honor of General P. G. T. Beauregard and his staff. To the strains of a "fine band," the general "moved among the 'pretty faces and costly laces' with as much coolness and ease as if he were among the sterner duties of the battlefield, and seemed to partake fully of the occasion." After the initial reception, the guests feasted on food both rich and plentiful. The party broke up at a late hour. Apparently flirting, dancing, and overeating had their place in wartime, as long as there was a Confederate officer nearby. It was no wonder that some wealthy women resisted the entreaties of their husbands to move upcountry for the duration of the conflict: the glamour and the gossip were just too delicious to relinquish.[18]

These same women turned fundraisers into opportunities for socializing. They came together in the Soldiers' Relief Committee, Ladies' Association in Aid of the Military, Ladies' Knitting Society, Georgia Relief and Hospital Society, Widows' Society, Ladies' Military Association for the Relief of Sick and Wounded Soldiers, German Ladies' Association, and St. John's Episcopal Church Aid Society. These groups and others sponsored *tableaux vivants*, fairs, concerts, and balls. The women worked at not just knitting socks and sewing shirts, but also outfitting the blockade-running steamer *Fingal* (renamed *Atlanta*) as an ironclad. In February, rumor had it that the vessel had ventured perilously and irresponsibly close to enemy gunships just "to satisfy the Savannah ladies, who insisted something must be done." Volunteers also donated funds to the Wayside Home for Wounded Soldiers, where each beneficiary needed to show "that he was absent from his command by proper authority." Savannah women helped to support a Confederate hospital in their own city, and another hospital in Richmond, the Chimborazo. There a native of the Forest City and volunteer nurse, Phoebe Yates Pember, combated disease, infection, and the prejudices of surgeons who disapproved of women's presence in the wards. Pember's labors seemed far removed from the conviviality enjoyed by many wealthy women in Savannah.[19]

Some residents expressed if not disapproval, at least misgivings about the seeming frivolity of the city's social scene. Henrietta Wayne kept track of invitations to extravagant receptions, weddings, and parties. In early 1863 she was moved by the sight of one of her relatives, Sandy Wayne, home on furlough from his post in Virginia. The young man had survived thirteen battles, and, noted Henrietta, though "acting most nobly, he looks very thin and all the gay spirits he used to have seems gone but he is very grave[;] I never saw anyone so changed." Throughout that spring, waves of smallpox, diphtheria, and scarlet fever swept through the city, afflicting many of the thousands of soldiers awaiting deployment to Charleston. In April the widow Wayne was taken with news of an upcoming wedding, a "grand affair" with four hundred invited guests. But she also remarked, "I think it seems so heartless having such large entertainments in these dreadful war times." By now she was convinced that "we shall be ruined if this dreadful war lasts."[20]

Faced with widespread distress among the white laboring classes, the city council stepped up its charitable efforts during the first half of 1863. Aldermen ordered one hundred cords of wood cut and distributed to the poor at city expense, and they appropriated emergency funds for the Board of Health, Episcopal Orphan Home, Savannah Female Orphan Asylum, and Widow's Society. The council also secured an interest-free loan of $10,000 from the Marine Bank to open up a city store that would buy and sell basic provisions at cost. City leaders were reacting to spiraling inflation provoked by chronic petty offenders like the German-born George Ehrlich, a self-described "speculator and peddler," who showed up at the city market at dawn and bought potatoes, then sold them later in the day for a profit. Rapidly escalating fines leveled at Ehrlich had failed to curtail his early-morning ventures, which were no doubt an effort to support his wife and seven children. That spring, aldermen watched nervously as bread riots swept the South, in Richmond and in major Georgia cities, including Columbus, Macon, and Augusta. Arming themselves with pistols, hatchets, and sticks, impoverished women looted stores and rioted to protest inflated food prices. Municipal authorities justified the city store as an effort to tamp down the "spirit of speculation," which hurt the poor most, though they admitted it had "become a competitor and dealer in articles of prime necessity." Before long the store had received a total of $75,000 in bank loans and had begun distributing large quantities of bacon, rice, flour, molasses, meal, sugar, and peas.[21]

THE LATE WINTER and early spring brought sporadic land and water skirmishes alarmingly close to Savannah. In February General Hugh Mercer had warned, "All indications point to an early attack on this city." But Mercer remained stymied in his efforts to secure and retain the requi-

site number of impressed slaves to labor on fortifications; he wanted
1,500, but they were hard to come by. The CSA's chief engineer in Savannah complained repeatedly about the stubborn refusal on the part of both
the governor and the state legislature to authorize compulsory impress-
ments. Throughout the lowcountry, slaveholders registered official complaints and concerns about the well-being of their slave property. In
South Carolina, General Beauregard was forced to respond to angry
queries from planters and politicians: impressed slaves, he wrote to one
state legislator, "you may rest assured, as a rule, are as well fed and sheltered as our brave soldiers, and moreover, have good medical attention."
The general also had to beat back a suggestion that "troops recruited
from the upper districts" (that is, poor whites) "would cheerfully volunteer to do the work now conducted almost entirely by slave labor"—as
long as they could earn a dollar to a dollar and a half per day over their
base pay. Both Beauregard and Mercer believed that southern soldiers
already performed too much fatigue work, and that such suggestions
were ploys by planters to safeguard their own slaves.[22]

In March the Union's ironclad *Montauk* sank the CSA's *Nashville* in
the Great Ogeechee River. Charles Junior dismissed the debacle: the
Nashville was better off destroyed, he claimed, its "drinking captain
and . . . rough crew" a disgrace to the South and a nuisance to the neighborhood. Within the week, Confederate troops had repulsed a federal
assault on Fort McAllister, an earthworks only a few miles south of the
city on the Ogeechee. Jones hailed "the good and great God of Battles"
that had kept Fort McAllister safe for the South. But during this period
the young officer remained largely distracted with family matters. He was
refugeeing his father's slaves to Burke County, and irritated that his aunt
Susan refused to sell the slave Kate and her children so that they could be
reunited with Kate's husband, William, on the upcountry plantation.
Wrote Charles to his father, "William begged me very earnestly to try and
purchase his wife and children, for whom he appears to cherish a strong
attachment"; but Aunt Susan remained unmoved. And then in mid-
March, just a few days after Charles's sister Mary gave birth to her first
child, a daughter, Charles Senior died in his sleep. The death of the fifty-
nine-year-old minister prompted an outpouring of grief among an extensive lowcountry network of kin, friends, congregants, and neighbors, and
among planters throughout the South drawn to his notions of a religious
education designed specifically for the slaves. His widow, Mary, took
comfort from letters such as the one written to her by her younger

brother, the Reverend John Jones, remembering her husband's "hopeful, cheerful words always encouraging to duty and pointing to God as our father, Saviour, and Almighty Helper."[23]

Now in her mid-fifties and feeling old, Mary had to fend largely for herself, managing the plantation and caring for her daughter Mary, the baby, and Charles's young daughter, Mary Ruth, in the absence of her two sons (Joseph was serving as a physician in the Confederate army). Trying to maintain a brave face for her children, she nonetheless could not help lament the "loneliness and isolation of my situation." Through family tragedy and happenstance, the war had left her bereft and vulnerable. So she was particularly pleased when visitors came to call. In April she welcomed her twenty-year-old nephew Dunwody, John's son, who wanted to pay his last respects to his "sainted" uncle, "the best man he ever knew." By this time the erstwhile ne'er-do-well had redeemed himself through military service. When he presented himself to his aunt Mary, he was limping, battle-hardened after several major engagements, including First Manassas and the protracted Virginia Peninsula campaign of 1862. Subsequently reassigned to Georgia, he had returned home with a promotion and accolades for his bravery. The impetuous Dunwody found army life appealing: in a letter home from the front he wrote, "I like this kind of life first-rate; it suits me, for you know, I always wanted to wander about." He would soon take up the task of hunting down Confederate deserters in Decatur County, an untamed region in the southwestern corner of the state, and guarding starving Union prisoners at Andersonville prison.[24]

With the two local papers publishing, the city council meeting regularly, the Bryan Slave Mart conducting business, and the private and public schools in session, Savannah struggled to maintain a normal institutional life. At the same time, the city had become a more raw, unpredictable place. Fights broke out on the street in front of the Marshall House, with young men—soldiers and civilians, officers and enlisted men—drawing knives and pistols against each other. The *Republican* advised that they "keep their blades and bullets for real and not imaginary enemies." More dramatically, slaves and free people of color pursued all sorts of illicit activities, and at the same time pushed the boundaries of public decorum and the law. Jane Deveaux and James Simms taught classes in secret, although apparently at some point in 1863 Simms's Berrien Street school was discovered by the authorities and closed down. Under conditions that remain mysterious, he managed to flee north to Boston, apparently by water, more than two decades after his younger brother's escape by the same route. James Simms later said he sought to evade a new CSA policy that would impress into service all free men of color without offering them any compensation.[25]

On April 24, 1863, the Boston papers made a startling announcement. A former celebrity had arrived unexpectedly in the city the night before: Thomas Simms had once more escaped from slavery. Simms arrived with his wife and eight-year-old daughter; in the last three weeks they had traveled all the way from Vicksburg, Mississippi. Soon after his forced return to Savannah in April 1851, he had been sold to a master in Vicksburg, and for many years he had worked as a bricklayer there. With his family and three other men (whether they were enslaved or free, black or white, is unknown) Simms had slipped away in a dugout canoe that they had stolen and then hidden from authorities. Thomas Simms told a reporter that "he was allowed to go in and out of the city without restraint, and having hired a horse he went out at night and got his wife and child," who were living on a nearby plantation. Because he had spent the previous two years "peddling among the soldiers, having bought his time of his master," he was familiar with troop movements in the area. Simms's appearance in Boston no doubt caused a sensation among abolitionists, some of whom had tried without success to purchase him from his original owner, James Potter, before Potter sold him to Mississippi. The details of a presumed Simms brothers reunion in Boston are not known. Toward the end of the war came reports that Thomas was in Nashville, working as a recruiter for the Union army. He had applied for and received an exemption from Union military service during the summer of 1863.[26]

In Savannah, a great roiling of the black population—with runaways coming and going, and with an influx of laborers impressed to work on nearby fortifications—thwarted the efforts of whites to keep close track of slaves as well as free people of color. Between 1862 and 1864, the number of black offenders appearing in the mayor's court increased fourfold; most were charged with resisting arrest, larceny, assault, and "improper conduct." In public, black men and women alike were reportedly going out of their way to jostle white passersby on the sidewalks and to show off their fancy clothes. White outrage had its limits, however, so integral was the labor of blacks to the welfare of the city; in early summer the clerk of the Savannah Fire Company requested that the council increase the per fire pay of black firemen to 20¢ from 12½¢. Aldermen approved the request, acknowledging that black men, regardless of legal status, would respond to incentives, even inflated currency, in sorting out their options for wage earning.[27]

Yet it was the coastal area that represented the epicenter of Gullah-Geechee self-liberation, the site of dramatic individual and collective escapes. In the interior, a seventy-year-old grandmother, "erect as a pine tree," gathered together twenty-two members of her extended family. Balancing precariously on a castoff flatboat, the group floated down the Savannah River to freedom; when seamen pulled her to safety aboard a Union gunboat, the woman marveled, "My God! Are we free?" The elderly Uncle Peter took the same watery route, clinging to a huge log and watching for alligators; he found refuge at Fort Pulaski. His son, also a fugitive, made his way to the Union army; he enlisted and died later that summer. One black man, known as "Uncle York" to the federal surgeon who recorded his story, guided several other Darien slaves to the Union lines, using sheepskin to muffle his oars so he could navigate the coastal creeks at night, "when de moon was berry shine." When they reached a Union vessel, "I *whoop*," he recalled, and "den I make de rowers raise a sing."[28]

In June 1863, the Department of the South included three African-American regiments: the First South Carolina Volunteers (with remnants of General Hunter's force organized the year before), under Colonel Thomas Wentworth Higginson; the Second South Carolina Volunteers (also composed of lowcountry fugitives), under Colonel James Montgomery; and the 54th Massachusetts Volunteer Infantry (with free men of color from the northern states), commanded by Robert Gould Shaw. By this time a newly formed central Bureau of Colored Troops was coordinating the mandatory conscription of black men in coastal South Carolina and Georgia.[29]

Throughout the North, the mobilization of troops galvanized black men and women, some of whom before long would take their place in the city of Savannah. Among the volunteer recruits of the 55th Massachusetts Regiment were 222 men from Ohio, including a twenty-two-year-old, Richard W. White. Light-skinned enough to pass for white, the South Carolina native had attended Oberlin College before taking up teaching school in Salem, a small town in Ohio. He enlisted as a private on May 23, 1863, in Company D of the regiment. The 55th embarked for the South from Boston in June. The month before, the city had provided a rousing send-off for the 54th, retracing the steps of the fugitive slave Simms, who had been marched through the city to the wharf. Among the recruiters for the 54th was Lewis Hayden, the Boston abolitionist, who had been able to turn his energies from rescuing fugitive slaves to raising a black regiment for the Union. Attending the farewell festivities was Harriet Jacobs, who exclaimed, "How proud and happy I was that day, when I saw the 54th reviewed on Boston Common! How my heart swelled with the thought that my poor oppressed race were to strike a blow for freedom! Were at last allowed to help in breaking the chains, which their kindred had so hopelessly worn!"[30]

Commanding a regiment of black recruits proved controversial for white Unionists; like their southern counterparts, many northern officers believed blacks unworthy of the honor that soldiering conferred on men. Still, Higginson, Montgomery, Shaw, and other anti-slavery men agreed with the recruiter who declared that "it can be no 'sacrifice' to any man to command in a service which gives Liberty to Slaves, and Manhood to Chattels, as well as Soldiers to the Union." Higginson's passion to fight was born of abolitionist fervor and not just Unionist sentiment. In contrast, Robert Gould Shaw, from a wealthy Boston family, accepted the invitation to command the 54th Massachusetts more out of duty than conviction; yet he believed that black men's essentially pliable nature meant they had at least the potential to become good soldiers. James Montgomery had served with John Brown himself on the bloody fields of Kansas. Like Brown, Montgomery was skilled in the scorched-earth tactics of the bushwhacker, impatient with notions of "civilized" combat, and committed to the use of violence as a form of moral regeneration. Higginson and Shaw were alternately appalled and fascinated by their fierce colleague, who was "Indian in his mode of warfare." Noted Shaw of Montgomery, "He never drinks, smokes or swears, & considers that praying, shooting, burning & hanging are the true means to put down the Rebellion." Though devoted to the destruction of slavery, in June 1863 Montgomery had executed an alleged black deserter without bothering with the formality of a court-martial.[31]

Higginson had a keen eye for the dramatic moment, recording the reaction of white men and women who encountered black men in uniform for the first time. In his raids up Georgia coastal rivers, he drew freely on the expertise of the pilot Robert Sutton, formerly a slave and now a corporal in the United States army. Though illiterate, Sutton possessed a "meditative and systematic intellect" and physique—a "tall straight and brawnly muscled body"—that made him a natural leader of men, in Higginson's estimation. In January 1863, Sutton guided the First South Carolina in an expedition to his home territory, up the St. Mary's River at the southernmost part of the Georgia coast. By night he led troops over paths he had blazed as a slave, and by day he piloted the steamer *John Adams*, carrying several hundred men, through waterways entangled with driftwood and low-lying trees.[32]

Passing by the plantation where Sutton had been enslaved, Higginson decided to stop and present his credentials to the mistress of the house. With the black man by his side, he introduced himself to the white woman and casually said "that I believed she had been previously acquainted with Corporal Robert Sutton?" And then: "I never saw a finer bit of unutterable indignation than came over the face of my hostess, as she slowly recognized him." With some effort, her words like "so many drops of nitric acid," she managed to exclaim, "Ah, *we* called him Bob!" In response, the corporal "simply turned from the lady," touched his hat to Higginson, and asked if he "would wish to see the slave-jail, as he had the keys in his possession." Sutton thereby defused the situation, which, Higginson believed, encapsulated the "whole drama of the war." Taking leave of the woman, the two men proceeded to view a tiny outbuilding, a cramped "villainous edifice" outfitted with rusty chains and stocks. Nearby was another building where "a person once imprisoned in it could neither stand, nor lie, but must support the body half raised, in a position scarcely endurable." Corporal Sutton said little.[33]

After this episode, one in April seemed almost anticlimactic. Stationed aboard the CSA ship *Pocotaligo*, General W. S. Walker sought to retrieve from federal forces the southern soldiers who had been wounded, as well as the remains of the fallen. Walker sent out a flag of truce and a message to that effect, expecting a Union officer to come and negotiate with him about the matter. The Union emissary happened to be Higginson, piloted in a rowboat by "a negro in the full uniform of a sergeant of infantry" (probably Color Sergeant Prince Rivers, described by Higginson as "a natural king among my dusky soldiers"). Walker was taken aback at this "offensive and insulting" sight, incensed that Union authorities had chosen for the mission someone "obnoxious to the well-known sentiments" of Confederate officers. He sent Higginson back without talking to him. The CSA had a policy against recognizing any officers of a "negro regiment," white men whom they considered criminals. Wrote one wealthy Savannahian of the federal recruitment effort among blacks in early 1863, "I thought it was bad enough to enlist the scum of Europe to fight their battles, but this last act exceeds everything else & is worthy only of savages." In May the CSA Congress announced that if captured on the battlefield white officers of black regiments, together with their men, would be summarily executed.[34]

For black soldiers, Camp Saxton represented a middle place between slavery and freedom. Despite the insistent entreaties of military recruiters, many men first needed time to recuperate from their ordeal under bondage. Physicians noted pervasive and chronic health problems among the refugees, some of whom had still-painful scars from whippings, some with shriveled limbs and other effects of long-term confinement in chains. Compared to their white counterparts, black recruits suffered disproportionately from lung diseases, including pneumonia, pleurisy, and tuberculosis. Of a comrade who seemed mentally slow, one soldier told the attending surgeon of the First South Carolina Volunteers that "he had been overworked in the Georgia rice swamps and that 'he be chilly minded, not brave and expeditious like me.' "[35]

On the South Carolina Sea Islands, a new cadre of black preacher-politicians emerged, including James Lynch, an African Methodist Episcopal missionary from Baltimore; and Tunis G. Campbell of New York City. By this time Campbell had gained a considerable reputation for himself in the New York City area as both a preacher to prostitutes and thieves and as a staunch foe of colonization. During the 1850s he had appeared several times on the speakers' platform with Frederick Douglass and other luminaries in the anti-slavery community, and he had served as a delegate to periodic "colored national conventions." For many years Campbell had supported his family by working as a principal waiter, first in New York's Howard Hotel and then at Adams House in Boston. When the war began, he was a partner and general agent in a New York City bread-manufacturing company. For a time he was employed by the chief quartermaster of the Union army on Staten Island.[36]

Rebuffed in his attempt to join the army in 1861, Campbell wrote to President Lincoln two years later, offering to move south and "to organize civil government, to improve the colored people in the South wherever I could do it." Though Lincoln did not reply directly to the petition, in late summer 1863 Campbell received a commission from the War Department to report to General Saxton at Port Royal. Accompanying Campbell were his wife, Harriet, his daughter, Harriet, his son, Tunis Jr., and an adopted son, Edward E. Howard. The family brought with them several thousand dollars in savings. On the island, Campbell took note of the work of northern white cotton agents, men who seemed less interested in facilitating black self-sufficiency than in harnessing black labor to a revived cotton staple-crop economy.[37]

Black recruits were eager to cast off their ragged slave clothing and don the uniforms of U.S. servicemen—blue uniforms rather than the target-red attire that Hunter had chosen for them. Many former slaves became "abecedarians" for the first time. One of them was a Georgia carpenter, Sergeant Edward King, who was drawn to the precocious young teacher, Susie Baker. The two had been acquainted before the war, and in late 1862 or early 1863, they married; she was only fourteen. Of the troops of the First South Carolina Volunteers, she noted, "nearly all were anxious to learn." The men debated the meaning of the war and sought to provide for themselves and their families. Military drills represented a new kind of discipline—not the degraded rhythm of fieldwork but an exercise in dignity and self-respect. At the same time, white soldiers and federal policy makers alike seemed bent on reminding black recruits that their citizenship status would remain decidedly second-class. Black soldiers received monthly wages of $7, in contrast to the whites' $13; by late spring of 1863 Hunter's men had not received any pay at all. Black men could not aspire to a command of white men, regardless of their talents or ambition, and they were more often relegated to digging trenches and latrines and building fortifications than assigned to combat positions. For their part, white troops chafed at enforced association with their black counterparts. In camp they ridiculed black soldiers, jeered their drilling, picked fights with them. In their resentments, these whites no doubt took their cue from the Union general who declared that "he would rather the Union cause should be lost than be saved by black soldiers."[38]

Throughout the spring of 1863, Union raiding parties sought to recruit black men for military service, handing out copies of the Emancipation Proclamation to any slaves they encountered. These parties also foraged for food, and seized stores of lumber, resin, and iron. Federal vessels ventured up coastal rivers in South Carolina and Georgia, and returned laden with chickens, alive and dead, hanging from the mainmasts, and geese and pigs scrambling around the decks. On June 17, the recently arrived Fifty-fourth Massachusetts entered the largely deserted coastal town of Darien, twenty miles north of St. Simons, in what appeared to be, in Colonel Shaw's words, just one more of "these little miserable expeditions" designed to "keep up the spirits of our men." On Colonel Montgomery's orders, the troops "pretty thoroughly disembowelled" the place of furniture, carting off a spinet piano, mirrors, and bedspreads together with grain, salt pork, livestock, and resin.[39]

Montgomery then ordered the town torched; his intent, he said, was to make the South feel the fact that "this was a real war." Flames consumed houses, a sawmill, the courthouse, and white churches; but the men spared a black Methodist church. The soldiers could hardly hold their own guns, the barrels were so hot from the nearby conflagration. Shaw recoiled with horror at the sight of the billowing black smoke rising from the town. He had hoped that this modest foray would prove the fighting abilities of his black soldiers, and now he feared that whites would perceive his men as barbarians, and himself a looter and a vandal— and all because Montgomery aimed to humiliate and eviscerate a small town with no military significance.[40]

Black soldiers saw the burning of Darien differently. Corporal James Henry Gooding of the Fifty-fourth filed regular reports for a newspaper, the New Bedford, Massachusetts, *Mercury*, detailing the daily life of soldiers forced to pick their way through "stink weed, sand, rattlesnakes, and alligators" during expeditions along the coast. Gooding expressed personal satisfaction when dwellings belonging to "notorious rebels were burned to the ground." He noted that Confederate forces routinely sank U.S. boats, civilian or military, proving that private property was fair game for either side. He ridiculed press releases that claimed that the tiny, deserted town of Darien was equivalent to Rome or Athens as a center of regional culture or politics. Even the *New York Times* ran a story provided by a Georgian, a rant against the supposed injury inflicted "upon unarmed and defenceless private citizens," the fruits of "Yankee negro valor." But another Fifty-fourth soldier who sent home an account of the raid described it primarily in terms of the sheep, cattle, and hogs seized for the camp larder.[41]

In accounting for the actions of black soldiers and runaways, southern whites were forced to reckon with antebellum ideologies that held that enslaved workers were grateful and contented. Now new, emerging ideas reflected the hopes and anxieties of specific groups of white people. One notion held that childish, duped black fugitives were suffering abuse at the hands of the Yankees. In February, the Savannah merchant Solomon Cohen had called in his neighbors, including the Mercers, father Hugh and son George, "to hear the narrative" of his slave David, recently returned from a "spy" mission to Beaufort. To the listeners' delight, David reported that the "Yankee troops are in bad spirits and expect to be defeated; the negroes are badly treated and many very discontented; the Yankee soldiers indulge in the most shameful license with the negro women; and such a picture of Yankee morals as David drew can hardly be conceived." With "intense interest," George Mercer listened to David's "simple tale," convinced that "few have experienced such a chapter in this war as that related by this honest, faithful negro slave." Little did these whites know that, in African-American culture, storytelling was a fine art; in this case David's audience was reacting to his convincing performance as much as to his reassuring words. Savannah newspapers picked up this theme; the *Republican* publicized the plight of what it considered misguided black fugitives who were now pining for their former life on the plantation. According to the paper, blacks who initially sought refuge behind Union lines were now awakening "from their fatal dream, only to sigh for the happy and contented homes they have left behind them." Planters should now welcome with open arms the dark-skinned prodigals finding their way back to slavery.[42]

Juxtaposed with the image of the loyal slave was that of the armed, bloodthirsty black man breaking loose from his bonds to take his revenge on whites—and especially white women. Certainly the generic rebel "Nat" had figured prominently in antebellum slaveholder ideology: Nat, like Nat Turner, was the exception that proved the rule, the conniving slave who sought to twist the contented black masses into a murderous horde. Now Nat had reappeared (most recently at Darien) in the form of "fiendish and devilish" musket-toting black fugitives manipulated by northern military officers. Governor Brown and other officials expressed fear for white wives and mothers at "the mercy of negro invaders, who may insult and plunder them at pleasure." Gradually over the course of the conflict, the southern "cause" was metamorphosing from the preservation of slavery to the protection of home, hearth, and southern white womanhood, all supposedly vulnerable to the depredations of black men in Union uniforms. This newfound "cause" diverged dramatically from the original one, which had emphasized the harmony of the southern household, with its black and white dependents loyal to a white father-master.[43]

At the same time, northern military officers were revising—or, in some cases, reaffirming—their own racial ideologies as they encountered southern black people for the first time. Shaw pronounced southern black people "perfectly childlike . . . no more responsible for their actions than so many puppies." At Beaufort, one surgeon saw the First South Carolina Volunteers drill in formation daily, when they were not raiding coastal settlements; yet he persisted in calling black people in general "children of the tropics": "A more childlike, devotional, musical, shrewd, amusing set of beings never lived." Higginson appreciated the bravery of the black soldiers under his command, men who boldly carried "the proclamation of freedom to the enslaved," and he considered Robert Sutton and Prince Rivers to be models of leadership and personal integrity. Yet he still described blacks in general as "the world's perpetual children, docile, gay, and lovable, in the midst of this war for freedom on which they have intelligently entered." Simple as children but brave in battle, eager for freedom but pliant and "amusing" in their odd ways: these were the contradictory notions of black people's temperament and character—their "race"—developed by Department of the South officials during the war.[44]

With the summer of 1863 came severe and ultimately fatal setbacks to the Confederacy's military and diplomatic fortunes. Savannah suffered another blow to its pride on June 17, when the refurbished *Atlanta* grounded itself in Wassaw Sound and waited helplessly while the Union monitor *Weehawken* approached and then destroyed it; the debacle sent two steamboats full of disappointed Savannah women scurrying back home. Their much-touted "gunboat fund" had come to an ignominious end.[45]

The following month brought little in the way of good news for even the most die-hard supporters of the Confederate nation. In early July, 51,000 men (28,000 of them Southerners) suffered wounds, went missing, or lost their lives at the monumental three-day battle of Gettysburg. General Robert E. Lee's bold thrust into Union territory had failed, forcing his previously invincible army to retreat into Virginia. And then, just a few days later, the Federals finally pierced the defenses of Vicksburg on the Mississippi River. As a result of these hard-won Union victories, England decided once and for all not to extend diplomatic recognition to the Confederacy. The bloodred tide of war had finally turned in favor of the United States.[46]

In Savannah and along the coast, whites tried to cheer themselves with the news that on July 10 Confederate forces had successfully repulsed an assault on Battery Wagner, an earthworks guarding Charleston harbor. Pivotal to the attack, the Fifty-fourth Massachusetts lost half its men, with nearly all its officers wounded or killed, including Robert Gould Shaw, who was shot dead soon after he ascended the parapet of the fort. A few northern papers lauded the bravery of black soldiers on display at Fort Wagner, and Lincoln taunted his Democratic rivals, "You say you will not fight to free negroes. Some of them seem willing to fight for you, but no matter." In the absence of more substantial military victories, southern whites derived a measure of satisfaction from news that Shaw's lifeless body had been dumped into an open grave with that of his men: "We have buried him with his niggers."[47]

That summer an acquaintance of Shaw's family published a provocative book that gained wide attention in England and the United States. Frances Kemble, former wife of Pierce Butler, released her *Journal of a Residence on a Georgian Plantation*, a heart-wrenching account of her stay on St. Simons during the winter of 1838–39. Kemble had delayed the journal's publication while her former husband retained legal control over the couple's younger daughter, Frances, who had turned twenty-one in 1859. (Kemble feared that if the book was published prematurely, Butler would not allow her to see Frances at all.) Now living in England, Kemble was determined to answer the "sentimental apologists" for slavery in her own country, as well as "the ignorant and mischievous nonsense I was continually compelled to hear upon the subject of slavery in the seceding states." The book became a sensation in northern abolitionist circles. With its stress on the abuse of enslaved women as wives and mothers, and on the routine separation of families, Kemble's factual account echoed Harriet Beecher Stowe's fictional rendering published eleven years earlier, *Uncle Tom's Cabin*. Of Kemble's book, *Harper's Weekly* opined, "There is nothing strained or extravagant in it. It is the plain story of the most hideous state of society that has existed anywhere in a normal Christian land."[48]

Publication of the *Journal* also highlighted a painful split within the Kemble-Butler family; the couple's older daughter, Sarah, now twenty-eight and married to a Pennsylvania physician, had remained loyal to her divorced mother and to her mother's abolitionist principles throughout the war. The younger, Frances, now twenty-five, shared her father's strong pro-slavery sentiments. In an effort to redeem herself from her mother's public humiliation of the Butler family, Frances herself would before long inject herself into the drama unfolding along the Georgia coastline.[49]

The war provoked equally bitter rifts within other families, North and South; and as the conflict entered its third year, the South was forced to reckon with dissent within its own ranks, dissent so pervasive and violent that it rivaled the threat posed by the Union army. In Savannah, Confederate deserters joined fugitive slaves to challenge Savannah's sense of itself as a well-ordered city united against northern aggressors. At the same time, enterprising black men and women, enslaved and free, sought to profit from the strains of war, while the white laborers became ever more resentful of the ostentatious displays of well-being among their social betters. But the Union army, too, registered the contradictions inherent in its own fight, now that emancipation was a stated goal of its war against the South. The army's discriminatory treatment of black troops foreshadowed future political developments that would shape the United States for generations to come: Many white Northerners hated slavery, but like their Confederate adversaries, they also felt contempt for the slave.

-◄❙ CHAPTER EIGHT ❙►-

We Have Dyed the Ground with Blood

I N THE SUMMER and fall of 1863, the Confederacy's stalled drive for independence was mirrored in Savannah's wretched condition, which evoked the disastrous yellow-fever epidemic of 1854. In July, growing piles of corpses rotting in the railroad yard—remains of victims of scarlet fever, typhoid, and smallpox—prompted aldermen to order immediate mass burials. With no gas, the city was using a pinewood distillate as an illuminant for its street lamps; the sticky stuff emitted a smoky, eerie light from cracked and dusty panes. The council noted that the pitch-black nighttime darkness meant residents must endure "grasping along the streets not knowing at what time an enemy be encountered," further unnerving an exhausted citizenry. Aldermen debated the propriety of publishing the names of landlords who evicted soldiers' wives and war widows for nonpayment of rent. In the absence of aggressive action by the dry culture committee, the canals surrounding the city were now choked with foul-smelling weeds and filled with standing water. Most painful of all, Confederate officials had ordered cannon and munitions removed from Savannah to Charleston, leaving residents to bemoan their "defenseless condition."[1]

The city's threadbare appearance bespoke widespread shortages of labor and resources throughout the region, leading to a home-industry revival of sorts among mistresses on even the largest plantations. When enslaved women ran away or otherwise deserted plantations, they took with them the major source of household labor—in the kitchen, the laundry, the parlor, the garden; there they had performed such tasks as weaving cloth and sewing clothes, cooking food, preserving meats and produce, and cleaning and scrubbing the surfaces of things and people. Now in wartime slaveholding households, white wives and daughters learned to produce dyes from trees—the color gray from the sweet gum, black from gall berry, and brown from walnut—and to plait palmetto leaves into hats. With so many slaves refugeed upcountry, impressed into Confederate service, or fleeing to Union lines, white women and girls found themselves weaving their own homespun, knitting their own socks, and sewing their own underwear. With the shelves of Savannah's fancy-goods stores bare, white housewives made candles from beeswax and boiled myrtle berries, castor oil from beans, soap from lard, and boot-black from soot and boiled chinaberries with the oil skimmed off. Women throughout the region responded to a call from the Savannah CSA sur-geon urging them to cultivate garden poppies; the "unadulterated opium" would not only relieve the suffering of ill soldiers but also reward the gardener with "a remunerative income."[2]

Not all shortages could be alleviated with a burst of household enthu-siasm. In Savannah, the Catholic bishop Augustin Verot worried about the church's lack of olive oil, which was necessary for holiday rituals. Verot had concocted his own test for genuine olive oil—it congealed in "moderately cold weather"—and he finally received a small supply of the precious liquid from the bishop of Charleston. By this time the Savannah cleric was making do with shabby church vestments and altar furniture, though he felt self-conscious ministering to his parish attired in ragged clothing and standing before tables covered with dirty linens. Mean-while, his own support for the war was waning. Within a few weeks of the olive-oil crisis, he confided to his Charleston counterpart, "It is my per-sonal impression that things have come to such a pass, & the sufferings of the people have reached such a height, that there is no impropriety, nay good & urgent cause for the clergy to do what they can to stop the awful bloodshed that has now stained the land for three long years." Verot was convinced that the South's fortunes depended on France's intervening in the war, "in the name of humanity, civilization, & liberty." The Confeder-acy, "once so prosperous & now plunged in unspeakable sufferings," was now worthy only of Europe's pity.[3]

In the countryside, a lack of basic necessities forced some slavehold-ers to modify their long-standing convictions about the need for black subordination. During the fall of 1863, Mary Jones was contending with an enslaved workforce in disarray. Yet another laborer, Adam, had recently died as epidemics swept through the barracks that housed black men impressed to build fortifications along the Savannah River. Colds and the measles were afflicting the women, children, and elderly still residing on Arcadia plantation. Other Jones slaves were joining periodic

GENL. SHERMAN'S CAMPAIGN WAR MAP.

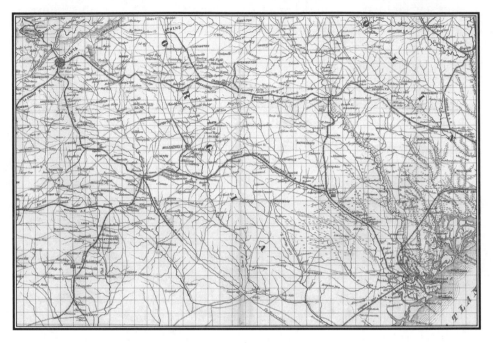

"stampedes" away from the plantations and toward the coast. It was against this background that in mid-September Mary Jones noted the return home of Tom, a young slave whom she had sent away to work for a family friend, Elijah McRae, in Montgomery County. Tom had spent four months on the McRae place learning how to make shoes. When he returned home, Jones noted that "he has quite the air of a *graduated tradesman*, and is tanning and making lasts preparatory to making shoes." She was eager to get him to make shoes for her extended family.[4]

Before long Mary Jones learned that Tom had proved less than satisfactory as an apprentice; though he "learned his trade so fast they were greatly pleased with him," he had a habit of stealing leather and sneaking out of the slave quarters at night. McRae admitted that he had sent Tom back to Jones because he "was known to have made shoes at night and sold them." The widow believed that Tom had always been "an unfaithful boy," giving the Joneses "much trouble" even before the war, when he worked as a messenger for the family; and now she was reluctant to keep such a person on the plantation, "*situated as I am*"—that is, alone. But she did keep him, since he proved so useful and apparently accommodating; in October she dispatched him and another slave, Gilbert, to Savannah, entrusting them with trunks and boxes of books and other articles bound for the new living quarters fitted out for her son Charles, who had recently married again, to Eva Berrien Eve of Augusta. Mary Jones was even willing to put up with Tom's disgusting new habit of chewing tobacco, although she believed it made him "sick and stupid." Eventually she hired the young man out to make shoes for her neighbor Edward Delegal at the rate of two dollars a day, a not insignificant sum. With his wanton ways, Tom would have proved a liability to a widowed woman before the war; now he could redeem himself by providing a steady income and making new shoes.[5]

Living in Augusta, Louis Manigault too made concessions to newly assertive slaves. Louis's cook and washerwoman Dolly ran away in the spring of 1863, fearing that she would be sent back to Gowrie. She had told another slave, " 'There is Mr. Lewis—he is Courting me.' " Mr. Lewis, the black driver of a hotel omnibus in Augusta, apparently hid her well, for the Manigaults never retrieved Dolly, though they went to considerable trouble advertising for her, even affixing a studio-portrait daguerreotype of her to a handwritten notice. (The picture shows a young woman in a prim white cap sitting in a richly carved wooden chair.) In the fall of 1863 Louis tried to bring the slave Jenny, along with her infant, to Augusta from Gowrie to make up for the loss of Dolly. When

Jenny learned that she would have to leave at home her four-year-old daughter, she informed the overseer, William Capers, that she planned to bolt before anyone could pack her off to Augusta. Capers advised his employer to exercise some flexibility in the matter: "In these times [we mus]t be carefull with Negroes. There is so many chan[ces for] them to make their way to the Yankees." Manigault allowed Jenny to bring both children to the city. For a good house servant one might moderate one's principles on slave discipline.[6]

In October 1863, Richard Arnold was elected mayor of Savannah, besting his two rivals, incumbent Thomas Holcombe and merchant-politician Solomon Cohen. The city, together with Chatham County, sent back to Congress Julian Hartridge, an outspoken critic of Jefferson Davis. Born in Savannah and educated at Brown and Harvard, Hartridge had served as junior first lieutenant in the Chatham Artillery. In a further rebuke to the administration in Richmond, a majority of Savannah voters cast their ballots for Governor Brown (1,630–1,216) in the fall elections. (Brown swept the state, winning 36,700 votes to his two opponents' combined total of 28,000; soldiers voted for him two to one.) This outpouring of states' rights fervor did not prevent the city from putting on a patriotic show when Davis came to town on October 31. The newly elected mayor, perhaps fearing an outburst of localist sentiment, reminded Savannahians that the president should be accorded a warm welcome "as the guest of the city." A soldier stationed in the city thrilled to the band music and the torchlight parade that welcomed the CSA president, but refused to try to shake hands with him, "for I detest running after the big folks of the land."[7]

THAT FALL, Union troops stationed at Fort Pulaski waited impatiently for orders to advance up the Savannah River. Preoccupied with massive campaigns elsewhere, federal officials were reluctant to attack a city that at this point in the war lacked much in the way of strategic value. And so the men at Fort Pulaski settled into a routine. They took considerable pleasure welcoming deserters from nearby Confederate batteries, dirty, hungry men with baggy homespun clothes hanging limply from their thin frames. Many had run away from the Georgia First Regulars, escaping in crude dugout canoes and using their shirts to muffle the sound of their oars, slipping past the river batteries manned by, among others, the increasingly exasperated naval hero Edward C. Anderson. The deserters claimed they were "happy in again coming under the national flag," joining with black men and women who were also "feeling their way across the vast marshes to our outposts," subsisting on oysters along the way.[8]

In December, two divergent celebrations within and outside the walls of the fort gave voice to the two separate Unionist societies encamped there. A group of white soldiers had formed themselves into the Eagle Opera Troupe, and on December 10 they offered a day of free entertainment—a concert, a minstrel show, and a masquerade ball. The production included songs, dances, and violin solos, as well as skits with white men dressed as women and as black people with such names as "Angelina Baker" and "Pompey Snow." One interlude featured an act called "Nigger in the Bag." Such shows had gained wide popularity in the antebellum North; now, with their broad caricatures of buffoonish black women and men, they were painfully at odds with the ongoing freedom struggle in the lowcountry.[9]

Two weeks later black men and women gathered outside the fort to celebrate Christmas Eve, praying and offering songs of rejoicing. Some of the songs struck the white listeners as incomprehensible, while other "hymns of a higher order" echoed traditional Protestant church music. One white observer could make little sense of this curious gathering, a "religious carnival" that he thought blended the serious with the "well-nigh ludicrous." The blacks seemed to believe that on Christmas Eve all animals on earth "as by an inspiration kneel down and bellow or bleat, or moan in a sort of adoration, thanksgiving and praise, in recognition of the world's Deliverer, the Savior of the lost." The white man concluded, "Of the history of this superstition we were never informed." Many northern whites would remain deeply ambivalent about African-American religious traditions that contained familiar elements—appeals to Moses, Abraham, and Jesus—but found expression in strange stories ("superstitions") and in strange music, West African songs with their unfamiliar melodies and insistent rhythms.[10]

That winter the federal soldiers on Cockspur Island luxuriated in the sight and smell of thick grasses, prickly pears, and fragrant flowers, and expressed wonder at the sound of songs sung by the former slaves: "He will have freedom, on Souf Carolina shore." Yet not far away a drama of great political import was rocking the Department of the South. Whether they hailed from the North or South, many black soldiers were growing increasingly resentful over their meager wages, knowing that their families back home were struggling to survive in their absence. For the men of the Fifty-fourth Massachusetts, who had fought bravely and saw their comrades die in great numbers at Battery Wagner in July, unequal compensation mocked their sacrifices. Generals Hunter and Saxton had recruited slaves with the promise of equal pay as soldiers, and the South Carolina regiments had earned the regular rate until the War Department announced its discriminatory policy in the summer of 1863; after that, the men in those regiments faced reductions of $6 per month. Black non-commissioned officers could not hope to earn more than that rate, which was less than the amount accorded white privates.[11]

The pay issue was only one part of a larger set of betrayals that angered black soldiers. They found themselves pitching camp for white soldiers, who in other places, absent black labor, performed the work themselves. In September, the white commander of the "African Brigade" on Folly Island, off the coast of South Carolina, reported that "the fatigue duty of my regiment has been incessant and trying" to the point that many black men had fallen ill; he protested "against the imposition [by his superiors] of labors which by principle of custom or right devolve upon my command." Despite their exertions in the service of the Union army, his men were derided as "d——d Niggers . . . by so-called 'gentle-men' in uniform of U.S. Officers." In the course of the war, one out of five black soldiers died from disease or from overwork at the battlefront; the rate for white soldiers was one out of ten.[12]

Corporal James Henry Gooding, who had served under Colonel Robert Gould Shaw at Darien and at Battery Wagner, linked the griev-ances of discriminatory pay and work assignments in a letter to President Lincoln in September 1863. "Now the main question is," he wrote, "Are we *Soldiers*, or are we LABOURERS." While their wives faced depriva-tion at home, "the patient Trusting Decendants of Afics Clime, have dyed the ground with blood, in defense of the Union, and Democracy." After fighting their way into the Union army, black men faced a galling prejudice from their superiors, while "all we lack, is a paler hue, and a better acquaintance with the Alphabet." Gooding asserted that the free black men who joined the army should "be assured that their service will be fairly appreciated, by paying them as american SOLDIERS, not as menial hirelings." Though spurned by their country, they were honor-bound and "sworn to serve her."[13]

That fall, men of the Fifty-fourth Massachusetts decided that as a mat-ter of principle they would refuse the lower pay, an action that bordered on mutiny. But it was former slaves who pressed the issue. On November 19, Sergeant William Walker of the Third South Carolina Volunteers led his fellow black soldiers in a protest against the pay policy: they stacked their arms before the tent of their commander, and refused further duty.

Later, during his court-martial, Walker defended his actions, informing the court that he had served as a pilot under DuPont on the federal gunboat *Wissahican*, and joined the army only later, "on the promise solemnly made by some who are now officers in my regiment, that I should receive the same pay and allowances as were given to all soldiers in the U.S. Army." Walker minced no words: "Nine-tenths of those now in service there [in the Third South Carolina Volunteers] will be my witness that it has been tyrannical in the extreme, and totally beneath the standard of gentlemanly conduct which we were taught to believe as pertaining to officers wearing the uniform of a government that had declared 'freedom to all' as one of the cardinal points of its policy." Walker told the court that his men had no "wilful desire to violate the law."[14]

Higginson and other sympathetic officers tried to frame the issue in legal terms: "It is not a matter of dollars and cents only; it is a question of common honesty,—whether the United States Government has sufficient integrity for the fulfillment of an explicit business contract." However, the military judges who heard the case decided otherwise, and in February 1864 Walker was executed by firing squad as the members of his brigade were forced to watch. In June of that year Congress reversed the policy of the War Department and authorized equal pay, retroactive to January 1, 1864, for all black soldiers who had been free at the start of the war, but the South Carolina regiments composed of former slaves gained nothing for their service before that date.[15]

Savannah remained oblivious to this dispute within the Department of the South, but the city was feeling the effects of its own mutiny of sorts: the shocking actions of poor women made desperate by a seemingly endless war. During the previous spring, the river port had escaped the women's bread riots that swept through many southern cities. However, by mid-April 1864, conditions in Savannah had deteriorated to the point that a group of armed women conducted a "daring robbery" in the downtown area, raiding at least four different stores and seizing bacon and other items. Some shopkeepers sought to preempt the looting by handing out free supplies of rice and sugar. The Chatham County sheriff arrested three women: Mary Welsh, for robbery, and Anne McGlin and Julia McLane (all probably Irish-born) for disorderly conduct. City authorities decided not to prosecute them, prompting the aggrieved store owners to petition the council (unsuccessfully) for reimbursement for stolen goods.[16]

The women were soldiers' wives, and their plight reflected the heavy burdens borne by impoverished families. Food, jobs, and cash: those things, in combination or singly, were increasingly hard to come by. Throughout Georgia, farmers found that they could make more money distilling their corn into liquor rather than selling it for food. Some planters persisted in growing cotton exclusively, hoping to reap a windfall with a harvest of the increasingly precious commodity. In Savannah, distress among poor white women was acute. When the city lost Confederate defense industries to the interior of the state, jobs for seamstresses sewing tents and uniforms went with them. The military monopolized transportation along the river, disrupting trade networks and stemming the flow of food into the marketplace. And in any case the needs of the army diverted staples and other supplies away from the civilian population. Governor Brown saw this as a propitious moment to lambaste wealthy planters who, he believed, were spurning self-sacrifice; in a letter to Major General Howell Cobb he praised "the hardy wayworn veterans of Georgia," hungry, ragged men "who left their wives and little ones to defend your large inheritance."[17]

By this time it was apparent that the absence of a wage-earning husband spelled disaster for many ordinary families. And therein lay a central irony of the southern cause, which had metamorphosed into a defense of white households from Yankee invaders: in some cases, when a soldier's wife wrote to her husband at the front, describing the emaciated condition of their children and begging him to help them, he abandoned his post and returned home, only to be seized by the authorities and jailed, or in some cases shot, for desertion. The result was widespread suffering among women and children. Stung by the actions of the "mob" of wives and mothers during the bread riot, the Savannah city council proposed a few days later to establish a "free market" that would distribute supplies to the poor free of charge. The earlier city market project, which had resold food at a price, had failed the women who had no cash at all.[18]

During the summer and into the early fall of 1864, Savannah registered a series of internal shocks to its increasingly fragile system. Beginning in late July, the port served as an entrepôt for Union prisoners of war on their way to be exchanged or incarcerated elsewhere. The move came too late for many prisoners of war, including James Henry Gooding; wounded in battle in March, he died in July 1864 at Andersonville, the infamous prison camp near Americus in Sumter County. Some of Gooding's compatriots were transferred out when the Andersonville authorities realized they could not stem the spread of diseases—scurvy, diarrhea, intestinal disorders, and typhoid—in the crowded, rain-soaked, mosquito-plagued holding pen.[19]

Among the attending physicians at Andersonville that early fall was Dr. Joseph Jones, the brother of Charles Jones Jr., and a graduate of the University of Pennsylvania Medical School. Like his new assistant, Louis Manigault, Joe Jones recoiled when he saw the conditions under which Union soldiers were dying or just barely living: nearly a quarter of them were seriously ill. The sight would forever haunt Jones, as would "the ghastly corpses with their glazed eyeballs, staring up into vacant space, with the flies swarming down their open and grinning mouths." In the midst of the suffering he was perhaps surprised to see his cousin Dunwody standing guard over so many emaciated men. (For his part, Dunwody no doubt chafed at guard duty, a secure enough position, but one that could hardly compare to fighting Yankees or capturing deserters.) Dunwody later brushed off denunciations of Andersonville, claiming that it was no worse than other prisons, North or South. And certainly the guards themselves to some degree aggravated the appalling conditions; among them were members of the Fifty-fourth Georgia Regiment, men who had staged a mutiny on the coast earlier in the year, and now resentfully accepted an assignment at Andersonville as penance for their collective disgrace. Between August and September, the number of men held at Andersonville fell from 31,693 to 8,218; some prisoners died, but most were shipped to Charleston and Savannah in an effort to ease congested conditions.[20]

In early September, CSA officials stationed in Savannah panicked at reports that up to ten thousand prisoners were on their way from Andersonville. Wrote one officer to his superiors on September 8, "There must be some strange misconception as to the force in this district and the location" of the holding pen. The large number failed to materialize, but before long as many as 4,500 men were being held in a new five-acre stockade at the corner of Hall and Whitaker streets. "Level as a pancake" and "as hot as an oven," the site lacked running water and shade from the sun. The prisoners, most of whom were still ailing from maladies contracted at Andersonville, remained exposed to the elements—heat that periodically gave way to a driving rain, followed by swarms of green flies. When the weather turned cold in October, dozens died of exposure. Among the officers in charge was Colonel Edward C. Anderson, the blockade runner and former mayor. Anderson was stunned to see Union soldiers in such "a pitiable condition"—"dirty & half clad & . . . filled with vermin." Here in Savannah of all places was "the most squalid gathering of humanity." The South, where white soldiers from both sides were to meet on a field of honor, had degenerated into a collection of death camps.[21]

Efforts on the part of the city's civilian population to relieve the prisoners' suffering became legendary. Arriving in Savannah at the end of July, one prisoner, Lieutenant Allen O. Abbott of the First New York Dragoons, observed that blacks predominated in the crowd that gathered to see the men, and he commented on their ability to communicate so much while using so few words: "They seemed to understand our feelings, and had respect for them, saying very little to us, while many of them manifested an interest in us such as we had not seen in any city of the South." Georgiana Guard Kelley collected loaves of bread from friends and from young boys who solicited donations throughout the black community. In turn she dispatched the youngsters to "ride past the stockade and throw them [the prisoners] a bag of bread." Though they risked being jailed for their efforts, "the colored people made it their business to help the prisoners."[22]

Daniel G. Kelley, captured at the battle of Cold Harbor in June 1864, was among the hundreds of prisoners transferred from Andersonville at the end of September. He later recalled that the "citizens of Savannah" brought clothing and bread to distribute to the men, but that guards turned them away. On October 12, when Kelley was herded into a railroad car bound for another camp, in Millen, a white boy appeared with a loaf of bread and attempted to hand it over to one of the prisoners. When a guard intervened, a black man stepped up, seized the loaf, and threw it into the railroad car full of prisoners. He was promptly arrested. Within a few weeks Confederate officials had brought Kelley and others back to Savannah, and this time white and black women gave them water and wheat bread while they were incarcerated. A guard, William Andrews, reported an incident in which "between 500 and 1000 women and children visited the stockade carrying baskets of provisions." So intense was their rush forward the guards could barely restrain them.[23]

Andrews spent most of his time guarding six hundred Union officers held at the city hospital. His task was to see that the prisoners did not tunnel their way out of the building, a favored and at times successful means of escape. By this time, since entering the service three years before, the young soldier had fought in the battle of Olustee, Florida, and had skirmished with the Twenty-sixth New York Colored Troops up and down the Georgia coast. Of his comrades' eagerness to strip the shoes off fallen black soldiers, he noted, "You may know the boys wanted shoes pretty bad to take them off a dead Negro's feet." Now in Savannah, sharing with his messmates a diet of stewed, fried, and baked wharf rats, Andrews wrote of his resentment at the constant promenade of smartly dressed officers and well-to-do civilians in Forsyth Park: "While we ought not to envy others, it does look hard that we have nothing in common with those well-dressed people who seem to be enjoying life to the fullest extent while we are dragging out a miserable existence, but such is war." By mid-November, the return of groups of newly released Confederate prisoners of war, dirty, famished, and exhausted, only added to the city's misery.[24]

An Irish immigrant guarding Union prisoners told one of them, Lieutenant Abbott, "We is all your friends here in Georgia. Every Irishman will help yees to get off, if yees can only get out of here." He added that Confederate officers had deliberately assigned men like him to Savannah: "they dasn't send us to the front, for they know us." A German recruit from Wisconsin, Frederick Emil Schmitt, enjoyed cordial treatment from one of his southern compatriots, a Mr. Weber, "a genuine German" and foreman of a machine shop outside Savannah. Schmitt, an engineer, had jumped at the chance when Confederate authorities offered him employment; he donned a Confederate uniform as part of the deal. In the few weeks that he worked at the shop Schmitt came to know both the Jewish Weber, who introduced him to his wife and children, and a Mr. Smedborg, "a born Scandinavian" and a "Union man" at heart.[25]

In MID-DECEMBER, Schmitt noted "the disorder in the shop was on the increase, and the Negroes became more unruly." Indeed: by that time General William Tecumseh Sherman, his massive army, and several thousand black men, women, and children were camped on the outskirts of Savannah. After three and a half years of anxiously looking downriver toward the sea, Savannahians could hardly believe that they faced a siege launched from the state's interior. The long-dreaded Yankee invasion was at hand.[26]

The beginning of the end had come on September 2, when Atlanta surrendered to Sherman. Before they withdrew from the city, southern troops torched all the locomotives, cars, and machine shops in the Confederacy's railroad "turntable." The fall of Atlanta marked the capstone of Sherman's four-month campaign from southern Tennessee through northern Georgia, as the Union army forced the Confederates to retreat,

retreat some more, and finally abandon their last outpost: Atlanta, the gateway to all of Georgia and the seacoast beyond. After a six-week occupation, Union forces evicted the remaining civilians, burned what was left of the city, and embarked on a great march toward the southeast. Few people other than Sherman and his closest aides knew that their ultimate destination was Savannah. Wrote one soldier on November 15: "Started early this morning for the Southern coast, somewhere, and we don't care, so long as Sherman is leading us." Some officers did not know they were headed for the Forest City until three weeks later. Meanwhile, Savannahians had access to precious little information about the army's whereabouts; the *Republican*, which had a correspondent in Virginia, published more news about military operations in the northern reaches of the Confederacy than about the cataclysmic events in its own state.[27]

Certainly midsummer had produced alarming if vague accounts of Sherman's push south from Chattanooga to Kennesaw Mountain, northwest of Atlanta. Around this time, Colonel William B. Gaulden placed a notice in the paper for all men in Liberty, McIntosh, and Bryan counties between the ages of sixteen and sixty to report for duty, to "awake, arise! Shake the dew drops from the garments. The crisis of your fate has arrived." Gaulden listed his position as "Aide-de-Camp, Coast Guard," as if there were still a Georgia coast to guard. Learning that Sherman had moved his troops out of Atlanta in late November, Savannah whites reassured themselves that the army intended only a tentative foray into the heart of the state; some apparently believed that he had lost his way and was wandering aimlessly around the Piedmont. On December 1, the *Republican* opined that the general's movements "indicated anything but decision of purpose as to his destination." No doubt many had been "unduly alarmed" by wild rumors. To remain on the safe side, however, Mayor Arnold began to mobilize all remaining white men "not absolutely incapacitated from disease," the so-called shinplasters, men unfit for service, including the very old and the very young. "Our city is well fortified, and the old can fight in the trenches as well as the young; and brave forces can, behind entrenchments, successfully repel the assaults of treble their number." Fortified or not, the city apparently afforded no safe place for the mayor's considerable stash of alcohol, which he sent upcountry to Augusta: "The wines are above all price and I would dislike to see them sacrificed, independent of all pecuniary considerations," he wrote.[28]

In December, in response to the Confederacy's shifting fortunes, the *Morning News* took part in a region-wide debate over the arming of the slaves for Confederate service. The manpower shortage was critical; Governor Brown had recently called on local jails to open their doors and disgorge civilian prisoners, now that conviction of a crime amounted to a "permanent exemption from service." An unsigned article in the newspaper laid out the case for enlisting slaves in the army, an idea gaining credence within the highest echelons of the Davis administration. At this crucial point in its brief history, according to the author, the Confederacy should not allow the slave "to increase and fatten as an idle spectator of the rapid exhaustion of power which rules over him." In fact, military service would provide a system of discipline sorely needed by the black man: "There need be no fear of desertion and rebellion. The most dangerous position is that which he now occupies; freed from his ordinary restraints, without his ordinary supplies, idle, and agape for all the silly tattle of alarmists, or the lying seductions of indoctrinated negro emissaries." But rather than shoulder arms, the black man should be assigned "the most servile and laborious duties" so that he could relieve "weak, overworked white men" of the routine physical exertions necessary to any military campaign. The black Confederate would not receive his freedom in return; his reward would be the knowledge that "he has done nothing more than his duty, and is entitled to no special reward." A black man's compliance and eagerness to please—his "race"—suited him for military service after all.[29]

Eventually General Robert E. Lee and other Confederate leaders would argue for the enlistment of black men as soldiers, and for rewarding them with freedom. Although such arguments never became policy, they suggest the increasing desperation overtaking the South by late 1864. In Richmond, Jefferson Davis and his staff understood full well the significance of the fall of Atlanta. They were also fervently hoping that in the November elections the Democratic presidential candidate George McClellan would defeat Abraham Lincoln and go on to offer a peace plan favorable to the South. However, thousands of Union soldiers cast absentee ballots that assured Lincoln an Electoral College landslide, 212 votes to McClellan's 21. At the same time, the Republicans cemented their three-fourths majority in the U.S. Congress. In public, the Confederate president remained defiant, declaring of the South, "Nothing has changed in the purpose of its Government, in the indomitable valor of its troops, or in the unquenchable spirit of its people." Yet his administration was teetering on the verge of self-destruction. Farther south, Georgia was for all intents and purposes defenseless.[30]

The logistics of the three-hundred-mile March to the Sea are historic: a gigantic army of sixty-two thousand, split into two wings (one commanded by General Oliver O. Howard and the other by General Henry Slocum), forty miles wide, lumbering forward with ambulance trains, supply wagons, and cattle. Joining the march at various points were as many as fifteen thousand black men, women, and children, some of whom were workers but most refugees. In order to move swiftly and cover from six to twenty-one miles each day, the army lived off the land; General Judson Kilpatrick's cavalry scoured the countryside for food (approximately 2.7 million rations in all) and thereby made good on Sherman's pledge to make all of Georgia "howl."[31]

After months of hard fighting, the march represented a respite of sorts for the troops, "merry as crickets," who described it variously as "one big picknick" and as "a glorious old tramp" that encountered "no opposition deserving the name." A large number of soldiers kept journals of the four-week campaign, noting such details of their surroundings as the exotic live oak trees, the black fox squirrel, and the tasty ground melon. These men enjoyed some time to themselves, especially in the evening, when under more dangerous conditions they would have been tending to the dead and wounded and preparing for the next day's battle. Still, the first part of the march—those initial, sunny days of feasting off Kilpatrick's plunder of turkey, pork, and sweet potatoes—were later followed by two cold, rain-drenched weeks of slogging through the mud and swamps of lower Georgia and subsisting on unhulled rice. For the most part the army met little formal resistance; General Joseph Wheeler's cavalry provoked a few armed encounters, but the foe consisted of large numbers of elderly men and young boys, many shoeless and famished. Union foragers, especially the "bummers" who scouted for Kilpatrick's cavalrymen, risked their own lives, for some ran into southern bushwhackers and deserters inclined to hang, shoot, or slit the throats of Yankees detached from the main army. A battle near Macon claimed five hundred Union soldiers and twice as many Confederates, and the assault on Fort McAllister, on December 13, cost sixty Union casualties—a "picknick" compared to Gettysburg.[32]

For the vast majority of Georgia whites, the arrival of Sherman's men ("fleeing toward the coast" in the words of one overly optimistic Putnam County planter) was their first encounter with enemy combatants. Some welcomed them warmly—the German immigrant professing Union loyalties, the friendly folk offering "percimmon Beer." These people bitterly condemned the "Big men of the South" who had caused the war. By the time the marchers passed through Macon, that area of the state had its own peace movement: "The people of Georgia are tired of the War, which is daily depopulating our country, and bringing ruin upon a whole continent." More common were words of resignation tinged with defiance: "We are whipped but we hate you." Some areas had already endured raids by southern troops who then retreated, leaving barns and bridges smoldering, smokehouses stripped bare, and civilians wondering which army to fear most. Like the family whose backyard was appropriated by Union surgeons, who strewed the ground with severed limbs, many Georgians in Sherman's path did not resist; they endured.[33]

It was the Engineering Corps that maintained the forward movement of the army, bridging rivers, traversing swamps, and destroying Georgia's rail infrastructure. By this time, Union engineers had perfected a clawlike device that could twist a heated iron rail and bend it out of shape forever. Littering the wake of the advancing army were pieces of these twisted rails, charred wreckage called "Sherman's hairpins." Army "pioneers," or laborers, expended considerable muscle power constructing as many as several hundred pontoon bridges (platforms attached to flotation devices), some as many as a quarter mile long; innumerable fascines; and miles of corduroy roads made of lumber planks laid across sandy soil and wetlands. Officers filled daily reports with their boasts—a thousand-foot-long bridge repaired in three days; five miles of railroad destroyed in a day; the Ogeechee swamps overlaid with corduroy roads; vast expanses of quicksand, mud, and dense vegetation traversed.[34]

The army's success, then, depended to a considerable extent upon large numbers of men cutting wood, hewing and squaring timbers, constructing fascines, and assembling and disassembling pontoon boats. Sherman made a point of putting Confederate prisoners to work scouring for live mines and removing torpedoes from rivers. But because the campaign was so labor-intensive, he also encouraged the use of as many black men as "pioneers" and servants as the army could feed along the way. Convinced that blacks lacked the discipline and endurance to make good soldiers, the general adopted a wholly opportunistic, if not entirely cynical, policy: "I must have labor and a large quantity of it. I confess I would prefer 300 negroes armed with spades and axes than 1000 as soldiers." Black men were valuable to the extent that they could chop down trees, carry supplies, and cook for the white troops. General Slocum estimated that a total of fourteen thousand blacks marched with the army at some point, but many who did follow were forced behind and off the road, out of the way of soldiers and wagon trains. As for women, children, the elderly, and the infirm: these were people that neither side could use or feed in the last months of December 1864. Watching their "pampered" house servants and longtime field hands join up with Sherman, some slaveowners shrugged: "O, we are all glad of it, for your army has taken about all we have to live upon, and the less niggers we have to take care of the better for us."[35]

During the first week of December, a notorious incident at Ebenezer Creek, not far from Savannah, exposed the strategy of the Union army: an eager appropriation of black men's muscle power and a simultaneous denigration of the lives of black people who were deemed useless to the troops. With a rebel cavalry hard on their heels, General Jefferson C. Davis (not to be confused with the Confederate president) led his Fourteenth Corps over a pontoon bridge and then ordered it pulled up before scores of black refugees waiting on the other side could cross. Some plunged into the deep icy water and drowned. Others huddled on the banks, only to die at the hands of "Fighting Joe" Wheeler's cavalrymen. The "hellish slaughter" provoked "great indignation among the troops" (according to an Indiana physician), and received some attention in the northern press, though Sherman later justified the incident in terms of military necessity, and exonerated Davis. According to Sherman, the sympathy expressed for blacks by Davis's detractors "was not of pure humanity, but of *politics*."[36]

Nevertheless, many African Americans saw Union troops, no matter how crude, cruel, or indifferent, as a grand army of liberation. At the sight or sound of the approaching vast procession, thousands of black men, women, and children along the way came out into the open, eager to free themselves as the Yankees passed by. Some emerged from the slave quarters, others from nearby swamps where they had been hiding. To greet the invaders, some dressed in their finest clothes—the women in fancy bonnets, the men wearing a pair of the master's cast-off gloves. Mothers prepared for the trek ahead, balancing huge bundles on their heads, or carrying babies on their hips. People of all ages rushed to appropriate their masters' mule teams and wagons, piling them high with children, chickens, and household furniture. Still, for the most part, northern soldiers regarded the slaves with a combination of pity, contempt, and amusement: "The Darkies come to us from every direction. They are all looking for freedom but really don't seem to know what freedom means."[37]

Many refugees understood that they had a better chance of protection if they could prove useful to commanding officers and weary foot soldiers. Old and young men and women provided military intelligence; revealed hidden supplies and livestock; and offered to cook and wash for the troops, at times expecting or demanding payment in return. Many soldiers considered blacks worthy of interest only if they could contribute to the march—by bringing with them pack animals, by offering food and water, by cooking meals and washing clothes. One group of black people had ventured out from the swamps with forty mules and horses, assuming that the Yankees could make good use of them and hoping in some measure to advance the cause of freedom. Of this group an army chaplain noted, "They all seem to have the idea that we are sent down here to set them at liberty, or that the war is in behalf of the blacks." Other soldiers recorded in detail the caches of food, weapons, cash, and family heirlooms that blacks uncovered for the invaders. On the Jones family plantation in Burke County, Cato, a longtime family slave, pointed out the hiding place of sixteen mules and two horses, and the raiders went on to clean the place out of hogs, wagons, corn, rice, and potatoes, leaving barns and bales of cotton smoldering in their wake. "Disloyal" slaves were in the process of becoming freedpeople, persons of all ages "who had pointed out the places where the planters had secreted provisions, and who watched for rebels while the bummer secured his plunder," from sweet potatoes and slabs of bacon to jars of jelly, preserves, and honey.[38]

In mid-December, not far from Savannah, cold, wet troops camped at the sprawling Langdon Cheves plantation, grateful to find themselves on a piece of dry land in the middle of the freshet-soaked rice swamps. Cheves, an engineer for the CSA, had died at Battery Wagner in 1863. His widow abandoned the three-thousand-acre plantation, which then became the site of Confederate Camp Anderson. In the history of the march, the place gained iconic status when Sherman mounted the roof of its rice mill to watch the successful assault on Fort McAllister nearby. By the time Union forces arrived at the Cheves plantation, southern foragers had already carried off all the corn and cattle. Settling in for a few days' respite, a group of soldiers listened as a small number of blacks gathered around and told of the toil extracted from the two hundred Geechee men, women, and children who produced over ninety thousand bushels of rice a year. To prove her assertion of widespread chronic illness among the slaves, "a bright-looking Negress who had lost a right arm in a rice mill" showed a skeptical officer "a large cupboard or room . . . displaying an array of quinine bottles which she said they had to take in great doses." The officer noted, "I have been astonished to find how widespread amongst field hands, as well as house servants, the idea is that the Yankees are coming to set the captives free, and how long this feeling has existed."

Interviewed years later, many lowcountry blacks marked the beginning of their freedom from the time they first saw a Union soldier: "I was a slave until Sherman came."[39]

Camped with the Seventh Illinois Regiment near the Cheves estate, a surgeon remarked on December 11, "the darkies all seemed pleased enough—Guess they will not be so well satisfied when they come to loose [*sic*] by the soldiers all their chickens & other truck." Two days later Kilpatrick began a systematic foraging effort in Liberty County, where, in the words of Robert Q. Mallard, raiders "robbed servant and master with perfect impartiality." One man, neither servant nor master, was Tony Axon, the freeborn blacksmith who kept a shop near Riceboro. Taking his pay in provisions rather than cash, he had accumulated considerable property by December 1864. When the Yankees swept through the area, they seized his horses, wagons and buggies, cows, hogs, bushels of wheat and corn, a saddle, fodder, clothing—and all his blacksmith tools, his livelihood. Nearby, on Edward J. Delegal's plantation, troops carried off the goods that belonged to Tony and his wife, Nellie, together. The Axons' losses were exceptional only in degree. Tony Axon knew what was at stake in the conflict: "I rejoiced when I first heard of the war and I said thank God so that my wife and daughter could have the same privilege as I had." But like Axon, many rice-field workers in Liberty County saw a lifetime of hard work vanish into Yankee wagons, saddlebags, and stomachs during December and January—soon after harvesttime, when stocks of staples were greatest. Most soldiers refused to believe that black people possessed so much in the way of hogs, rice, livestock, lard; on the other hand, these white men did not really worry about who owned what, one way or the other.[40]

Liberty County whites suffered the loss of more than food, goods, and enslaved labor. For many, Kilpatrick's raids signaled the end of a familiar old world and the beginning of an ominous new one. At home with her daughter Mary (who was pregnant again) and her grandchildren, Mary Jones watched in horror as Kilpatrick's men stripped the family storehouses and destroyed books and heirlooms. She saw not famished men in her midst, but inhuman forms. One soldier "crouched like a beast over the fire. He was black and filthy as a chimney sweep. Indeed, such is the horrible odor they leave in the house we can scarcely endure it." In her eyes, the Yankees had metamorphosed into the degraded slaves they were professing to liberate. In her journal, Jones asked, "Do the annals of civilized—and I may add savage—warfare afford any record of brutality in extent and duration to that which we have suffered and which has been inflicted upon us by the Yankees?" The short answer to her question was, of course, yes. In the annals of civilized warfare, the Yankee raids of late 1864 and early 1865 were relatively benign: though they stomped through the house, yelling and cursing, the soldiers did no harm to the women of the Jones household. As a matter of policy at least, the troops engaged not in wanton destruction but in targeted destruction—factories, bridges, culverts, railroad lines and stations, lumber and rice mills, and the homes of well-known CSA politicians and in at least one case the home of an infamous prisoner-of-war tracker. Both Mary Jones's son-in-law, Robert Mallard, and her son Joseph were taken prisoners of war during Sherman's sweep through south Georgia, but the men were later released unharmed. The Yankees inflicted considerable damage on property, but unlike other conquering armies they did not massacre civilian men, women, or children.[41]

WHEN THE TWIN COLUMNS of General Slocum and General Howard began to converge outside Savannah in mid-December, they found much of the surrounding countryside underwater; the rebels had opened sluice gates in the rice fields and flooded the region with an overflow fed by freshets from nearby rivers. The First Michigan Engineers was forced to devise means of transporting not only men but also wagons, cattle, and horses across submerged rice fields and the swamps, lagoons, canals, and rivers that covered much of the area—with nary an intact bridge in sight. According to Howard, "Savannah almost defended itself by its bays, bogs, and swamps all around." The few patches of dry land consisted of an "impenetrable morass, vines and leaves." For years residents had feared their vulnerability to Yankee forces, but when the enemy came, the city's defenses turned out to be mainly natural, not man-made.[42]

Union troops dug in for a week, preparing for a climactic battle against what they believed was a numerous and well-fortified enemy. Meanwhile, in Savannah, the Confederate general William J. "Old Reliable" Hardee was preparing to evacuate his troops from the city. He had his men work feverishly to dump large stores of ammunition into the river and to construct a pontoon bridge stretching from Anderson's Wharf to Hutchinson's Island, in the middle of the Savannah River, and then on to the South Carolina shore. Hardee's bridge consisted of thirty immense fascines, each between seventy and eighty feet long, laid end to end and then covered with planks ripped from the city's docks. Foggy weather caused the work ships to run aground, stalling the project's progress. But finally, with Sherman just a few miles outside the city, Hardee organized his own march to move his 9,089 troops across the river. A few families followed in their private carriages. For two hours, Lieutenant Charles C. Jones oversaw the artillery barrage that covered the retreat. Left behind were seventy large guns, several thousand small arms, massive quantities of rice and cotton, and an unknown number of weary Confederate soldiers eager to give themselves up to the enemy. Still, Hardee considered his grand military procession, funereal though it was, a complete success. In 1866 he wrote to Charles, who was writing a book about the siege of Savannah, "Tho' compelled to evacuate the city, there is no part of my military life to which I look back with so much satisfaction." One evacuee, Sergeant William Andrews, remembered the scene differently: "Doors were being knocked down, guns were firing in every direction, the bullets flying over and around us. Women and children screaming and rushing in every direction." In the midst of chaos, some soldiers melted into the civilian population, "preferring being made prisoners to fighting any longer," in Andrews's words.[43]

At 3 a.m. on Wednesday, December 21, General John Geary with the Twentieth Corps of Slocum's division advanced to the western outskirts of Savannah and learned that in the absence of any defensive fortifications, the enemy was "hastily retreating." Meanwhile, informed by Hardee of the army's imminent evacuation, the city council had held an emergency meeting on Tuesday night. Mayor Arnold and the assembled aldermen resolved to save the city by surrendering it at the earliest possible moment. Their aim was to "secure such terms as would insure the protection to the persons and property of the citizens from the soldiers whose previous conduct filled the minds of all with a lively apprehension that slaughter and rapine would mark their entrance into the city."[44]

In the process of finding enough horses and buggies to convey them to the front, the mayor and a group of aldermen became separated, losing precious minutes hunting around for each other in rain and darkness. Finally, one party consisting of John O'Byrne, Robert Lachlison, and Christopher C. Casey came upon Union pickets, who escorted them to Geary. The three men explained that they had lost the mayor and the others en route to the front. They then proceeded to act as guides for Geary and his men, along the way picking up Arnold and the others. With this odd entourage, Geary's Twentieth marched into Savannah on West Broad Street, then to Bay Street, just as dawn was breaking. Though the night had been rainy, Geary remembered the troops' entrance into Savannah this way: "Before the sun first gilded the morning clouds, our

National colors, side by side with those of my own division, were unfurled from the Exchange and over the U.S. custom house."[45]

The sight produced some lasting memories, accurate or otherwise. Ben Graham had been a slave of a Baptist minister in Savannah. During the war he had accompanied his master to the front, an odyssey that took both of them to battles at Gettysburg and at Chickamauga, Tennessee. In the fall of 1864, Graham, now twenty-three, was in Washington County, Georgia, and when Sherman's troops passed through, he was one of the many who joined the army on its march to Savannah. Many years later he remembered Mayor Arnold running "down Bay Street wid a big white sheet tied to two poles and he was hollerin', 'Peace, peace, for God's sake, peace.' " Arnold probably conducted himself with considerably more dignity that early December morning, but Graham's impression had the ring of truth: masters brought low.[46]

With members of the city council watching from the portico of the Exchange, General Geary praised his troops and announced that "this beautiful city of the South" was now in Union hands. James Simms described the scene in biblical terms: the Yankees "had come for our deliverance, and the cry went around the city from house to house among the race of our people, 'Glory be to God, we are free!' Shout the glad tidings o'er Egypt's dark sea, Jehovah has triumphed, his people are free!'"[47]

Geary immediately set out to establish order in the city, "in which I had found a lawless mob of low whites and negroes pillaging and setting fire to property." In fact, famished people were in the process of seizing stores of food—rice, flour, sugar, and molasses—to save themselves from starvation. But Geary saw only chaos and crime. At noon on Wednesday the 21st, the provost marshal's guards were patrolling the streets of Savannah.[48]

Sherman himself entered the city the following day. By that time most of the rest of his grand army had arrived, greeted by, in his words, "the poor classes . . . grouped around, apparently well pleased with the change, for they had nothing to lose, and had suffered much during the war." The general immediately took up residence in Pulaski House, where Savannahians came to pay their respects; among the first supplicants were Mayor Arnold and Noble A. Hardee, a merchant and the brother of the retreating general. Within a day Sherman had accepted Charles Green's offer to occupy his magnificent mansion on Madison Square. (Green stayed, but tucked himself away in two rooms.) It was there that Sherman wrote his famous telegram to President Lincoln: "I beg to present you as a Christmas-gift the city of Savannah, with one hundred and fifty heavy guns and plenty of ammunition, also about twenty-five thousand bales of cotton."[49]

Over the next few days black Savannahians came to meet the famous general: "A constant stream of them, old and young, men, women and children, black, yellow and cream-colored, uncouth and well-bred, bashful and talkative—but always respectful and well-behaved," in the words of an aide, Major Henry Hitchcock. The general greeted them with his customary hearty greeting, " 'Well, boys,—come to see Mr. Sherman have you? Well, I'm Mr. Sherman—glad to see you.' " On December 23, some of the city's black ministers came "to pay their respects, and offer humble thanks for their deliverance from bondage," according to James Simms. The gruff general was delighted by the warm reception from people who told him, "Been prayin' for you all long time, Sir, prayin' day and night for you, and now, bless god, you is come."[50]

In the first few days of the occupation, the Bay became a "theatre of several magnificent reviews," the various regiments marching in formation with faded, tattered flags flying and brass bands playing. Sherman's goal was to make a "big showing," a "spectacle" that would suitably impress the citizenry—a gesture that Savannahians of all ages, black and white, could appreciate. Delia Rivers, a neighbor of Georgiana Kelley, recalled seeing the Union army for the first time: "I went to the Bay and I screeched and screamed until I hadn't any voice. I had no handkerchief with me when General Sherman came and I took my apron off and waved that."[51]

At the same time, the general was making clear his own priorities: "My first duty will be to clear the army of surplus negroes, mules, and horses." Beginning on December 24, a rapid series of orders established the principal goals of the occupation: "Families should be disturbed as little as possible in their residences, and tradesmen allowed the free use of their shops, tools, etc; churches and all places of amusement and recreation should be encouraged, and streets and roads made perfectly safe to persons in their pursuits." Sherman allowed the city council "to continue to exercise their functions," and he ordered the fire department, gasworks, and waterworks "kept in organization." Soldiers were to respect civilians and their private property (real and personal estate, excepting slaves). Unlike Atlanta, Savannah possessed no functional railroad hub, no critical factories or arsenals, and so no larger military or strategic significance. Sherman would spare the city and his men would partake of its pleasures, if only for a few weeks. According to one wealthy Savannahian, the occupation proved "a blessing in disguise" because the general "maintained good order."[52]

At first glance, the whites seemed compliant enough: they were "at least humble enough and heartily sick of war." On Sunday, Christmas Day, white men and women attended church services in the company of Union soldiers, "and mutual courtesy and respect were shown." Certainly it was not difficult for the victors and vanquished to reach some rough accommodation with each other; Sherman still had a war to win, and Arnold had a city to preserve. The general proved deferential to the sensitivities of the rebels, deeming it "wise, so far to respect the prejudices of the people of Savannah, not to garrison the place with negro troops. It seems a perfect buggery to them, and I know that all people are more influenced by prejudice than by reason." For his part, Arnold understood that in this new phase of the war—the political phase—a certain amount of cooperation with the occupiers might help restore the city's former glory, and quickly. On December 28, the mayor presided over a public meeting in Masonic Hall, which resolved "that laying aside all differences, and burying by-gones in the grave of the past, we will use our best endeavors once more to bring back the prosperity and commerce we once enjoyed."[53]

For all their political savvy, neither Sherman nor Arnold factored into their strategies the collective will of lowcountry African Americans. In the coming months the former slaves would swiftly transform the society and politics of Savannah and the surrounding region. And in the process few bygones would find a resting place in the grave of the past.

POSTBELLUM

CHAPTER NINE

The Way We Can Best
Take Care of Ourselves

O N THE MORNING of January 10, 1865, five hundred black children, ragged, shoeless, and shivering from the cold, assembled in the sanctuary of Savannah's First African Baptist Church. Spilling out into the street, they marched en masse through Franklin Square to the edge of the city market on Ellis Square, and on to an imposing three-story brick structure on St. Julian Street—their new school, the old Bryan Slave Mart. For residents along the way, leaning out windows and peering from doorways, this "army of colored children . . . seemed to excite feeling and interest, second only to that of Gen. Sherman's army," in the words of one observer. Then, in the building where traders had bought and sold slaves just a few weeks before, pupils took their seats on wooden benches, their feet dangling above the floor. Surrounded by remnants of the old regime—handcuffs, whips, paddles, sales receipts for slaves—and positioned in front of the auctioneer's desk, now occupied by their teacher, freed girls and boys commenced their classes. Surely the African-American community leaders who choreographed this grand school opening possessed a keen sense of the dramatic and the symbolic: black children would seize the streets, and they would transform the trappings of slavery into the means of their own liberation.[1]

Throughout the city, the day of jubilee echoed with defiance: a girl taunting her mistress by jumping up and down and chanting, "All de rebel gone to hell[;] Now Par Sherman come"; a boy, dressed in a baggy Yankee uniform and fortified with a bit of whiskey, refusing to leave a white woman's yard, "saying it was as much his as hers"; laundresses ceasing their labors and becoming freedwomen, "leaving some clothes on the line, some in the tubs, and the rest in the washroom." Many men and women filtered freedom through the prisms of family feeling and religious faith. Some thought first of "going *home*"—in other words, according to one man, "where my wife is." Queried by a northern soldier, fifty-year-old Nellie explained why she remained in Savannah: "This was my home. My children and friends and my husband were all here." For years she had lived with "a terrible mystery, to know why the good Lord should so afflict my people, and keep them in bondage,—to be abused, trampled down, without any rights of their own, with no ray of light in the future." She had always believed "that we were all of one blood,—white folks and black folks all come from one man and one woman," and now her faith was rewarded: "*I knew it—I knew it!*"[2]

With Sherman's triumphal entry into Savannah came a crush of humanity that overran and overwhelmed the city. In the public squares and on the outskirts, sixty thousand federal troops set up tents and cobbled together makeshift wooden shanties for themselves. The frantic effort to provision and house the huge army wreaked havoc on Savannah's population, black and white. By now accustomed to running roughshod over civilians, soldiers continued their forays into nearby Liberty County, but now in the city they also pillaged stores of chickens, hogs, and rice from skilled workers and tradesmen. The butcher Jackson Sheftall lost a lifetime's worth of accumulated possessions, edible and otherwise. Owners of modest homes could do little but watch as Sherman's men ripped off porches, tore down fences, and in some cases dismantled whole houses for firewood and building lumber. According to the truck farmers Moses Stikes and Binah Butler, "after the army came to Savannah . . . we had lost all we had." Recalling the men who raided a stable that she and her husband held "in common," Georgiana Kelley noted, "you can lock from cats and rats but you can't lock from Sherman's army."[3]

Still, the Kelleys and other longtime residents fared far better than the estimated eight thousand exhausted refugees now languishing in alleyways and on the docks. Many of these former slaves had followed Sherman's army out of the Georgia interior; others had fled from vengeful slaveowners nearby. And, too, more Confederate deserters were beginning to slip back into town. Typhoid, measles, and spinal meningitis swept through tenements and army camps. Hundreds of dead pack animals, Sherman's "seediest horses and sorriest mules," now littered the streets, and the stench of rotting carcasses filled the air. Within weeks of the occupation, by official count the United States scavenger department had picked up 568 dead animals, 8,311 carts of garbage, and 7,219 loads of manure from city streets.[4]

Four long years of war combined with the immense influx of soldiers and refugees meant that newcomers in early 1865 found not the elegant port of antebellum days, but a "miserable hole" full of dilapidated buildings, broken street lamps, rotting docks, and overgrown cemeteries. Banks stood empty, bankrupt, their mortgage and bond business gone the way of the Confederate dollar. The city's rail lifelines with the outside world—the Central linking Savannah with Macon, the Atlantic and Gulf reaching into Florida—were destroyed, a mass of smoldering "Sherman's hairpins." The Savannah River was obstructed by the Union's sunken "stone fleet," and by islands of mud and sand.[5]

From the beginning of the military occupation, Savannah's elite made strenuous efforts to preserve the city's normal operations. General Sherman cooperated by authorizing the council to continue, though with diminished authority. Mayor Arnold established three dozen ward committees headed by aldermen and other prominent leaders, most of them adamant Confederates—among others, George Wylly, John Foley, A. S. Hartridge, Octavus Cohen, and Christopher C. Casey. On New Year's Eve day, Casey, chief engineer of the fire department, presided over a review of the nine fire companies. Spectators—including journalists, soldiers, cotton speculators, missionaries, and government officials newly arrived in the city—all marveled at the "interesting and pretty spectacle" of fire engines "very neatly decorated with evergreens and National emblems." Almost 1,300 black and white firefighters attired in colorful if threadbare uniforms marched to the accompaniment of the singers of the Scipio Africanus Opera. A reporter for the *Philadelphia Inquirer* described "a whole Broadway full of immaculate blacks . . . old women and young protecting the rear and flanks of the ebony column, all marching through the city and chanting some unearthly song, not a word of which is intelligible to the uninitiated." In this case, what the Northerners found novel, native Savannahians found familiar, for good or ill.[6]

At the same time, in a dramatic break with the past, an emancipated community began to assemble in a series of mass meetings. During the afternoon of January 1 hundreds of black people—the women arrayed in turbans, brightly colored handkerchiefs, and beribboned bonnets—convened at First African. They sang traditional hymns that now resonated with the power of newfound freedom:

> *Blow ye, the trumpet, blow,*
> *The gladly solemn sound,*
> *Let all the nations know*
> *The year of jubilee has come.*

Among the several newcomer preachers speaking that day were the Reverend Mansfield French, the Union army chaplain; the Reverend James Lynch, missionary of the North-based African Methodist Episcopal Church; the Reverend William T. Richardson, education secretary of the American Missionary Association; and the Reverend John W. Alvord, secretary of the American Tract Society. Alvord told the throng that "he wanted them to begin to do for themselves, [for] they were not babes to be carried, or rocked in cradles, but men who could develop themselves, [and] now is the time for action." Over the next few years, black people in lowcountry Georgia would indeed engage in a struggle for self-determination, to the consternation of white authorities, French, and other Northerners no less than embittered rebels.[7]

The children's march revealed that Savannah's black clergy had wasted little time establishing a formal school system. Relegated to a minor role in the New Year's afternoon celebration, nine ministers and lay leaders, including William J. Campbell, Ulysses L. Houston, and James Porter, regrouped later in the day. Constituting themselves into an ecumenical executive committee, they formed the Savannah Education Association (SEA). The Reverend John Cox of Second African and James Porter reprised their leadership roles from the Emancipation Day "watch-meeting" exactly two years before and served as the president and secretary, respectively, of the new organization. On January 3, in front of a large crowd, the board met again at First African, conducted a public examination of applicants, and then formally appointed fifteen black teachers, ten women and five men. Among them were Margaret Denslow, Georgia Stewart, Abigail Small, and Samuel Whitfield. The committee also drafted and approved a constitution that provided for a school board and a finance committee, and set fees for SEA membership on a monthly (25¢), annual ($3), or lifetime ($10) basis. Many in the audience came forward in what one observer called "a *grand rush*. . . Much like the charge of Union soldiers on a rebel battery," depositing a total of $730 in membership fees on a table in front of the committee. Before long, the SEA had in place five different schools enrolling 1,000 of Savannah's 1,600 black children. The classes accommodated pupils of widely varying skills, since some youngsters had already studied reading, writing, arithmetic, and geography.[8]

Those first few days of January seemed to confirm an unbroken line of leadership among Savannah's black preachers, men who had led their congregations in slavery and would continue to do so in freedom. Certainly the traditional authority of the clergy, combined with the institutional structure that supported them, facilitated their ongoing and even renewed influence within black communities. Yet matters were not that simple. In some cases, new leaders rose quickly to positions of power. Among the original SEA teachers was Samuel Whitfield, absent from the written record of antebellum Savannah, but assertive in his community's nascent drive for autonomy from whites. Some newcomers aggressively sought influence within the established churches. Soon after arriving from Baltimore in late December, the Reverend James Lynch entered into negotiations with the Reverend William Bentley, pastor of Andrew Chapel. Lynch persuaded Bentley and the church elders to dissolve their affiliation with the (white) Methodist Episcopal Church South and join the African Methodist Episcopal (AME) Church. Celebrated with a joyful love feast on a Sunday morning in January, the move enriched the AME parent organization by 360 members and a building worth $20,000.[9]

However, it quickly became apparent that the churches were no longer the exclusive arenas of black organization: ways were opening in the schools, in the fields, in mutual-aid associations (old and new), on the docks, and in partisan politics for leaders of diverse backgrounds, personalities, and ideologies. One of the two school principals appointed by the SEA was James Simms; the other was veteran teacher James Porter. When he returned from Boston in early February, Simms claimed the mantle of leadership in the SEA and at least two other institutions. In Boston, he had joined an African-American order of Freemasonry—the Grand Lodge of Massachusetts, organized in the 1850s by the abolitionist Lewis Hayden—and he had also been ordained a Baptist clergyman during a service led by preachers of Boston's Baptist churches. Back in Savannah, the forty-one-year-old Simms introduced the Masons to Savannah blacks, and joined the ranks of the city's clergy. But in the process he found himself decidedly out of favor with his former mentor, William Campbell, who refused to acknowledge the upstart as a legitimate Baptist preacher. In response, Simms successfully sought a commission from a northern society, the American Home Baptist Mission Society (AHBMS), and began organizing and evangelizing among freedpeople in the Ogeechee rice district. During the spring of 1865, Simms delivered lectures to raise money for the SEA; the title of one of his talks was "The Dealings of God vs. the Dealings of the Nation upon the Negro Question." No doubt sensing (correctly) that Simms had political aspirations, Campbell persuaded the AHBMS to rescind Simms's commission. Yet of all postbellum Savannah leaders, Simms would write and speak

most poignantly about the need for blacks to break their long silence—
the silence of slavery, when "all moved along as empty pitchers, but the
glowing lamp of prayer was burning brightly in their hearts." While
emancipation united blacks, it also shattered traditional leadership patterns into myriad new channels of action.[10]

Nevertheless, to many white observers, the black community of early
1865 presented a united front, and a maddening one. When he arrived in
Savannah in mid-January, S. W. Magill, an agent of the American Missionary Association (AMA) and superintendent of its new schools, discovered to his chagrin that he was already too late to oversee formation of
the city's black school system. Formerly the pastor of the Second Congregational Church in Waterbury, Connecticut, Magill embodied the AMA's
twenty-six-year-old mission to claim unchurched souls for northern
Congregationalists and Presbyterians, or, if need be, to poach converted
souls from rival denominations. For the AMA, freedpeople's schools
were a means of proselytizing as much as they were the ends of a righteous war. Incredulous at the rapid formation of the SEA, Magill considered the system's managers "jealous and sullen" in their effort to protect
their prerogatives, as they extended their "spirit of exclusiveness" to all
whites and not just their former masters. Representatives of freedmen's
aid societies converging on Savannah, most notably the AMA and the
New York and New England branches of a Quaker group, the National
Freedmen's Relief Association (NFRA), together lamented the "rather
peculiar feeling among the colored citizens here, in regard to the management of the schools . . . There is a jealousy of the white man in this matter. What they desire is assistance without control."[11]

At least in their early negotiations with whites, freed preachers
appeared to represent a cohesive black community. On the evening of
January 12, twenty of the city's religious leaders (including the newcomer
James Lynch, but excluding Simms) held a historic "interview" with
Sherman and Secretary of War Edwin M. Stanton at the general's headquarters, the stately Green mansion. Sherman acquiesced in the "collo-
quy," but complained that Stanton "should have catechized negroes
concerning the character of a general who had commanded a hundred
thousand men in battle, had captured cities . . . and brought tens of
thousands of freedmen to a place of security." Participants included,
among others, the Reverends William Campbell, of First African; Ulysses
L. Houston, of First Bryan Baptist; William Bentley, of Andrew Chapel
(AME); and James Porter, of St. Stephens (Episcopal). The group elected
as their spokesman the sixty-seven-year-old Garrison Frazier, a native of

Granville County, North Carolina. Now retired, Frazier, a Baptist, was attached to no particular congregation.[12]

Answering the queries of Sherman and Stanton, Frazier expressed a consensus among black people throughout the lowcountry: "The way we can best take care of ourselves is to have land, and turn it and till it by our own labor . . . We want to be placed on land until we are able to buy it and make it our own." Freedom meant that black people now "could reap the fruit of our labor, take care of ourselves and assist the government in maintaining our freedom." Frazier acknowledged that the original purpose of the war was not to liberate the slaves; nevertheless, black people had offered up their silent but heartfelt prayers for the success of the northern army, and now their young men stood ready to take up arms for the Union and for freedom.[13]

Four days later Sherman issued his famous Special Field Order No. 15. The directive set aside the South Carolina and Georgia Sea Islands, plus a wide swath of coastline reaching thirty miles inland, from Charleston to the St. Johns River bordering Georgia and Florida, "for the settlement of the negroes now made free by the acts of war and the proclamation of the President of the United States." Almost immediately federal officials began to divide and assign to qualified blacks coastal lands "abandoned" by their white owners. Many people at the time, and many historians since, interpreted Special Field Order No. 15 as the federal government's support for black land ownership, at least in early 1865. The order gave rise to widespread anticipation among freedpeople all over the South that they would be able to settle on a small piece of land and support their families—the "plot of not more than (40) forty acres of tillable ground" stipulated in the directive. In fact, Sherman saw the order primarily as an effort to relocate large numbers of black women and children to the coast and islands while their menfolk remained in Savannah working for the army.[14]

Federal authorities had already devised a plan to meet the needs of the military. As early as January 4, Sherman and his officers instructed the army quartermaster to round up "all unemployed negroes" and set them to work cutting wood, building fortifications, and loading ships. White soldiers manhandled many refugees into service, and also reached into the surrounding countryside, promising field hands $12 a month for their labor. At the same time, bounty hunters preyed upon young freedmen, promising cash bonuses to substitutes who would enable individual northern states to meet their enlistment quotas during the waning weeks of the war. Thus as white Northerners completed their stint in the army in early 1865, black Southerners were mustered in to fill their places. (Northern black soldiers who enlisted in 1863 and 1864 had signed up for three years of service; although many yearned to return to their families at war's end, they would fill the ranks of the northern occupying army.) In Savannah, a few of Sherman's own soldiers decried the deceptive and violent tactics of these so-called "recruiters," men who sported fraudulent military insignia, and in some cases even kidnapped victims and smuggled them out of state. Yet many officials held that military service of any kind—not only shouldering arms but also cleaning streets—would provide black men with a strong dose of much-needed discipline.[15]

The black exodus out of Georgia's heartland in late 1864 had served the army's strategy well by diverting scarce labor resources from the Confederacy to the Union army. Now Sherman conceived a plan to deal with the people he no longer needed, people who constituted "a serious problem" as long as they remained in Savannah. Thus the corollary to the forcible appropriation of black men's labor was the forcible relocation to the Sea Islands of refugee women and children, the old, and the infirm. In January, missionaries at Port Royal, South Carolina, scrambled to provide rations for hundreds of desperate people hounded to the coast, including "old men of seventy and children of seven years [who] have kept pace with Sherman's advance, some of them for two months and over, from the interior of Georgia." The refugees brought with them little but "the clothing on their backs and the young children in arms."[16]

Ultimately, then, Special Field Order No. 15 grew out of the refugee problem, which, in the words of one Union officer, "left on our hands the old and feeble, the women and children," too many hungry mouths to feed in the city of Savannah. In addition, the order provided that "the young and able-bodied negroes must be encouraged to enlist as soldiers in the service of the United States, to contribute their share toward maintaining their own freedom, and securing their rights as citizens of the United States." The order made explicit the connection between military service for men and homesteads for their families, and it provided not for fee-simple titles, outright ownership of the land, but rather possessory titles that remained contingent on future political developments. The order itself remained "subject to the approval of the President." What came to be called the Sherman Reservation, then, was a means of draining Savannah of women, children, and the elderly while providing for enforced service among young men. This initial goal foreshadowed the order's troubled future.[17]

The forced out-migration of black women and children could hardly alleviate Savannah's distress. Sherman had seized all the rice warehoused in the city and ordered it distributed to the city's poor. During those first weeks of 1865 substantial aid also came from a most unlikely source: the North, including relief committees organized in Boston, New York, and Philadelphia. The day the schoolchildren marched in Savannah, residents of Boston were meeting in historic Faneuil Hall to express their sympathy for Savannah's plight, and launching a fundraising effort that yielded more than $30,000. Before the end of the month, the first supply ships had steamed south laden with salted and canned beef, fish, vegetables, turkeys, smoked hams, pork, lamb, and barrels of flour.[18]

Given the war's ongoing cost in blood and treasure, and the stubborn persistence of a mortally weakened Confederacy, this outpouring of generosity toward the South seems somewhat puzzling. However, correspondence between the Boston Relief Committee and Mayor Arnold suggests that northern textile interests were eager to resume trading with purveyors of upland and Sea Island cotton. New York and Boston merchants contemplated the fate of 38,000 bales of cotton still stored in Savannah warehouses, a cache worth an estimated $28 million. In a letter, members of the Boston committee put the matter frankly to Arnold: "The North was glad of the opportunity to relieve Savannah because it thought your people desirous of cooperating in rebuilding the walls of our national unity! For upon this the North is determined." The committee pointedly raised the issue of the stockpiled cotton and its ultimate disposition. More generally, though, many Northerners believed that, once the war was won and slavery abolished, little stood in the way of reconciliation; a common political and religious heritage would heal the wounds of a blood-drenched nation. Philadelphia fundraisers praised Savannah's leaders for surrendering so gracefully to Sherman—presumably a sign of the city's heartfelt remorse for its misguided support of the rebellion.[19]

On January 25, Arnold presided over a town meeting to offer up thanks to the city's northern benefactors. Assembling in the Exchange, a committee of leading white citizens passed resolutions of gratitude, noting that the Bostonians had recently met in Faneuil Hall, "the cradle of American liberty in the days of our common struggle for independence" and hence an appropriate venue "for the renewal of those ties which then bound Massachusetts and Georgia in a common bond." At the same time, the Savannah committee resolved to reject the role of a "conquered city." Since they were now presumably subject to the laws of the United States, "we ask the protection over our persons, lives, and property recognized by these laws"—a thinly disguised demand to retain their land

and slaves. Throughout the meeting, Arnold struck a decidedly conciliatory tone, at one point quoting Saint Paul: "Tribulation worketh
patience, and patience experience, and experience hope."[20]

Around this time an army officer, Charles C. Coffin, rendered in vivid
detail the "motley crowd" that congregated expectantly on a cold January
day at a supply distribution point. Coming together to partake of northern largesse were men and women, people of "all ages, sizes, complexions
and costumes," former slaves and "gray-haired old men of Anglo-Saxon
blood," together with "well-dressed women wearing crape for their husbands and sons who had fallen while fighting against the old flag." Coffin
described the scene as a "ragman's jubilee for charity," notable for the
clothing on display—dresses made out of old silks and satins and coarse
linsey-woolsey and gunny cloth; jackets fashioned from feed sacks and
crimson plush upholstery; garments rescued from the scavenger's heap,
and "hats of every style worn by both sexes, palm-leaf, felt, straw, old and
battered and well ventilated. One without a crown was worn by a man
with red hair, suggestive of a chimney on fire, and flaming out at the top!"
Despite the diversity of the crowd, it is not clear that blacks received their
fair share: one woman bitterly remarked of the aid, "Not a mouthful have
I had," though "all my life I have worked for [white people]."[21]

For many ordinary Savannahians, their suffering deepened on the
night of January 28, when a tremendous explosion rocked the city's Confederate arsenal, the storehouse for ammunition and fifty tons of gunpowder. For five hours three thousand shells rained down, igniting a raging
fire that consumed an estimated 125 wooden tenements inhabited by
hundreds of poor people, black and white. Of unknown origin, the conflagration claimed surprisingly few lives—less than a dozen—but exacerbated the critical housing shortage and widespread distress of the poor.[22]

The U.S. military prided itself on promoting an essentially benign
occupation—on treating the city's residents not as a vanquished enemy
but as wayward siblings. Army officials encouraged shopkeepers to open
their doors and civilians to go about their business, such as it was. Familiar routines begat public order, or so the theory went. Still, an emerging
"normality" masked deeper changes to the social fabric. The two newspapers resumed publication, but both were now controlled by northerners. S. W. Mason, former editor of a U.S. Army newspaper in Port Royal,
South Carolina, changed the name of that "fire-eating sheet," the *Savannah Morning News,* to the *Savannah Daily Herald.* John Hayes, a Massachusetts native and war reporter for the *New York Tribune,* assumed
editorship of the *Republican,* which became an outlet for the occupying

forces. The city theater once again offered entertainment, but attractions now included a performance by the Aeolian Opera Troupe of the Twenty-ninth Pennsylvania Volunteers and a lecture on "Pluck" by the journalist Mortimer Thomson, the persona non grata "Doesticks" who had covered the Pierce Butler slave auction six years before. Spectators thrilled to daily military parades, but marching now were U.S. regiments such as "the renowned Fifteenth Corps," pressing forward along the Bay "like a huge caterpillar of gorgeous colors slowly moving on innumerable legs to the strains of martial music." Composed of aldermen and a mayor elected the previous October, the city council began holding regular meetings on January 23. Sherman had shorn it of all its committees.[23]

Northern observers were convinced that segments of the immigrant Irish and German communities welcomed the Yankees and saw in the U.S. flag "an emblem of hope and a signal of salvation." Some soldiers found evidence of a Savannah "Union League," presumably a clandestine organization that had managed to weather the war and now offered its support to the conquering army. These Union sympathizers were not the only ones to offer their support to Sherman; even some of the old guard were impressed by the general's restraint and forbearance.[24]

Yet on the whole, die-hard rebels, men and women, waxed indignant about their captors, apparently indifferent to the fact that their ability to express their grievances openly was a sure sign of leniency among the occupiers. For example, Union military authorities had charged General Hugh W. Mercer with executing seven U.S. soldiers, prisoners of war recruited into the Confederate army. In response, his son, the attorney George, railed in public against army judges robed in "black garments of revenge" intent on hunting down Confederate leaders "like wild beasts" and offering a stricken people only "ruin and humiliation." (The general was later acquitted.) Damage done to the Catholic cemetery by Union fortification workers, expulsion from the city of the wives of Confederate officers, government seizure of Confederate cotton, orders mandating oath-taking—all of these prompted a torrent of angry letters to and defiant interviews with military authorities. Clergy felt free to denounce the occupation forces from the pulpit, and during a military-sponsored Washington's Birthday celebration on February 22, city officials refused to fly the U.S. flag above the Exchange in observance of the day.[25]

Some white men and women continued to decry what they considered Mayor Arnold's premature surrender of the city, whispering that he had descended into alcoholism and disgrace ("I hear Dr. Arnold has a small practice, drinks often—defends his course as the best he could do for Savannah—& has very little influence.") In fact, Arnold considered himself a realist; eager to reunite with the Union, he understood that slavery was dead and so was the Confederate cause. Though well acquainted with the virtues of "Northern energy and Northern capital," Arnold feared that both would "melt down" when exposed to Savannah's "semitropical climate." The reconstruction of Savannah and the South would have to be left to Southerners, now stripped of an estimated "two thousand millions" of dollars worth of slave property. (What the South owed black men, women, and children for generations of uncompensated labor, the mayor did not say.) The task of "reorganizing" black workers would "require a heart of a Philanthropist and the head of a Statesman," noted Arnold, qualities he believed he possessed in abundance.[26]

Still, even unrepentant rebels realized that to keep from starving they must do more than complain. After four long years of deprivation, elite white women demonstrated a great deal of initiative, entrepreneurial and otherwise. Some stood at basement windows selling tobacco, cakes, and pies to "whoever would buy"—mostly the greenback-toting conquerors. Well-to-do women soon found that almost any useful article could be used as currency. Some swallowed their pride and took in Yankee boarders. But others had their limits. Approached by an officer seeking lodgings, two white women lied and said their household consisted of eight children, all under the age of five: " 'Good God!' he cried, throwing up his hands. 'Eight under five! I'll go *anywhere* else!" Confronted by a soldier who demanded they relinquish one of their carriage wheels, the two carried it up four flights of stairs and hid it in the attic; later they decided to trade it for a supply of fresh beef. These women also marketed surplus milk from their lone cow, and sympathized with their neighbors who were "selling their ball dresses and cast-off finery to the negro women, one of our friends having sold an old silk for one hundred dollars."[27]

Through the winter and early spring, some whites truly believed that the war was still winnable, though the source of that hope is not immediately apparent. In January 1865 virtually the only Confederate force of any size still standing was Robert E. Lee's Army of Northern Virginia. Confederate money had lost all practical value while the northern economy continued to prosper and expand. In desperation, southern military and political officials began to consider seriously the possibility of arming slaves to counter depleted troop strength and plummeting morale. Lee himself favored granting eventual freedom to soldier slaves and their families, arguing that blacks were fully qualified for service: "Long habits of obedience and subordination, coupled with the moral influence which in our country the white man possesses over the black, furnish an excellent foundation for that discipline which is the best guarantee of military efficiency." The general admitted, however, that "our chief aim should be to secure their fidelity." Meanwhile, anticipating a Union victory that spring, the U.S. House of Representatives approved the Thirteenth Amendment to the Constitution, abolishing slavery.[28]

In a drenching rain on January 26, Sherman began to move the bulk of his army out of Savannah, heading north and preparing to confront the South Carolina traitors whom he and other Northerners considered ultimately responsible for all the blood shed over the previous four years. Among the Engineering Corps were some of the black "pioneers" who had joined the march in Georgia and would now ease the army's way through the Carolinas—a trek over 425 miles and numerous bridgeless rivers. In February President Lincoln met with a three-member southern peace commission, including the Confederate vice president, Alexander H. Stephens, to discuss possible conditions for the cessation of hostilities. The commissioners rejected Lincoln's demand for unconditional surrender and returned home. There they could read newspaper dispatches detailing the ruin of Charleston and the Union army's relentless march toward Virginia.[29]

Sherman's departure prompted black leaders to appropriate Special Field Order No. 15 for their own purposes; they were convinced that the directive vindicated their claim to the land they and their forebears had lived and slaved upon. The Reverend Ulysses L. Houston, a former slave, was the first of several black men who sought to establish independent colonies along the coast. On February 2, General Rufus Saxton had addressed a large community meeting at Second African Baptist Church on the city's east side. In his speech Saxton encouraged black families to settle on the coast and islands. Shortly thereafter Houston led a group of congregants to the Island of Skidaway, near the mouth of the Savannah River, and settled on land abandoned by Joseph F. Waring (brother of the suspect Confederate surgeon) and other wealthy planters. A butcher by trade, Houston carried four hundred animal hides to Skidaway, because, he declared, "I want to turn them into money, and purchase a portable saw-mill to cut out lumber for our houses." The group of 362 colonists, representing 99 households, divided five thousand of the island's most fertile acres into plots, numbered the plots, and then chose numbers from a hat as a way of assigning parcels. They also set aside land for a school and a church. The town plan suggested "Plymouth colony repeating itself . . . So blooms the Mayflower on the islands of the South Atlantic coast," in the words of one enthusiastic if overly optimistic observer.[30]

HEARING LARGELY GOOD news from the battlefront, and watching black people assert themselves and the planter elite grub for their daily bread, some newcomers to Savannah could not help gloating. Julia Marshall, an American Missionary Association teacher and a native of Williamsburgh (now part of Brooklyn), saw rebel women peddling their old clothes for cash and exclaimed, "What a *glorious* fall they have had—while the 'unbleached American Nobility' are on the topmost of fortune's ladder!" Marshall admitted "feeling more than usually *ugly* toward them . . . It would be pleasant, had I the power and *iron heel* strong enough to grind everyone of these Secessionists deep into the earth." Marshall's words might seem out of character for a young music teacher, but they conveyed the intense feelings of many northern aid workers laboring for the Union cause in Savannah and elsewhere. The life stories of several of the nine AMA teachers assigned to Savannah in the spring of 1865 indicate the backgrounds and motivations of many more (mostly) women to come.[31]

Sarah A. Jenness, age twenty-one, was the daughter of a prosperous Wolfeboro, New Hampshire, farmer. A Congregationalist, she had graduated from Abbott Female Academy, and even at a young age taught in a common (public elementary) school. In her application to the AMA, Jenness wrote that she hoped "to do something for those whom we have so long and deeply wronged." At the same time, she had to contend with opposition from her parents and friends "who consider her undertaking quite Quixotic." Another teacher, thirty-eight-year-old Mary K. Colburn of Worcester, Massachusetts, asked to be assigned with her friend Laura Capron; they would serve in Savannah together. Bereft of both parents and a permanent home, Colburn was living with her sister, the wife of a Union soldier, when she applied to go south. Bostonian Harriet C. Bullard had attended a female seminary in Holliston, Massachusetts. She had worked first as a milliner and then as a Bible missionary, inspired by "the runaway [slave Anthony] Burns," whose trial in her hometown had made a great impression upon her when she was only twelve years old. In a testimonial on her behalf, one writer revealed that Bullard's father, "an intemperate man" (now in the army), had deserted the family and left her mother impoverished.[32]

Fanny E. Miner, thirty-one, from Manchester, Vermont, spent only a few weeks in Savannah. The daughter of a former member of Congress, Miner applied to go south in August 1864, asking that the AMA provide her with traveling companions of "intelligence and refinement." According to AMA Superintendent S. W. Magill, the young woman shocked the other passengers on board a steamship en route to Georgia by "playing cards very constantly with officers of only casual acquaintance." Once in Savannah, she attended the theater with a soldier who was apparently "under the influence of drink" (added Magill, "but of this, she says, she was unaware"). She also insisted on promenading the streets with an officer, on Sunday evening no less. At first Magill was inclined to let her stay, since most of her indiscretions took place under the cover of darkness, sparing the AMA public embarrassment. But he soon thought better of it, and sent her home.[33]

Making do with makeshift classrooms and shortages of books and other supplies, the women found their duties alternately exhilarating and exasperating. In a letter reprinted in the AMA's monthly magazine, the *American Missionary,* and intended to appeal to potential donors, Mary Colburn highlighted the unique nature of her mission while at the same time stressing (in Magill's words) "the practicality of conducting a school, composed of these colored children, just as we do our northern schools." Assigned to the city's imposing Massie School, now run by the AMA, Colburn wrote that her greatest challenge initially was to tame restless beginners and instruct them in northern-style classroom decorum. Under the circumstances, they showed "encouraging progress" in settling down and learning reading, writing, spelling, geography, and arithmetic: "Restrained as they have hitherto been, and precluded from all opportunity of acquiring knowledge, it is truly wonderful that they are so tractable." The teacher also had her pet: "A quadroon has won my heart, by her uniform good behavior, and the zeal with which she applies her daily studies." Colburn concluded her letter by noting, "The future will unfold the capabilities of the African race, and disprove the assertion so often made, that they cannot be elevated to the standard of the white man."[34]

Despite promising reports from the classroom, in late February Magill was still fuming over the Savannah Education Association, this "radically defective organization" composed of preachers "jealous of their honor and influence"—"leading men among the negroes [who] . . . have started on the principle of managing things themselves and just having their white friends do inferior work as assistants in carrying out their ideas and wishes." Magill was especially irritated that the Reverend James

Lynch was spreading the word that the AMA "discriminated unfairly against col'd people, in respect to employing them as teachers, etc." Magill also lamented that the National Freedmen's Relief Association was supplying the SEA with much-needed cash for teachers' salaries.[35]

In the meantime, AMA teachers as well as black Savannahians relied upon the goodwill and public security offered by the army of occupation, which was increasingly composed of black soldiers. Wherever black troops were stationed, black women in particular gained a new protection from white harassment on the streets. On March 13, the battle-hardened Thirty-third U.S. Colored Troops (formerly the First South Carolina Volunteers) entered Savannah. Accompanying them was the young Susie Baker King, who had spent two years working for the troops as a teacher, laundress, nurse, gun cleaner, and cook of turtle-egg custards, among other jobs. Sherman had initially deferred to the sensitivities of white Savannahians by keeping black soldiers out of the city: "Prejudice, like religion, cannot be addressed," he believed. However, by mid-March, 2,300 soldiers from four black regiments were filling the places of demobilized white troops. Southern whites regardless of class reacted viscerally to what they saw as "the glitter, the show" of these uniformed blacks, whose "very presence . . . is an overflowing fount of evil." One white woman of modest means excoriated the black soldiers guarding the roads into Savannah who checked her produce bound for market—the "black nigger soldiers fur to stop a poor woman on the road . . . make me stand four hours in the hot sunshine, with the big, greasy corporal a settin' in a chair, and me a standin' up! O, them beasts!"[36]

The presence of Union troops overturned at least some antebellum conventions governing city streets. For one young white girl, Georgia Conrad, a particular incident would remain emblazoned on her memory: "one evening, coming home, as I was passing a narrow sidewalk, a huge Negro compelled me to take to the gutter, to escape coming in contact with him." Indeed, every day in the spring of 1865 made clear that Savannah's street life had been profoundly transformed. On their way to the city pumps for water, former mistresses, draped in black, picked their way through trash and debris, menaced by unmuzzled dogs and accosted by rowdy newsboys and bootblacks, black and white. These women shrank from the signs of changed times—poor people milling around the streets, with many of the men armed, refugees sleeping in doorways, men and boys bathing at the dock at the foot of Drayton and Abercorn streets "in a perfectly nude condition." Soon after occupying the city, Union officials had placed an American flag on the west side of Bull Street, forcing pedestrians either to walk under the flag or to cross the street and walk in front of the military barracks—a choice unacceptable to any southern white lady.[37]

But it was freedpeople who bore the brunt of brutal transformations. Early on, Union officers began to punish black men and women convicted of stealing by putting them in a ball and chains and forcing them to labor under armed guard on the streets. Enraged, black leaders formed a citizens' group headed by Houston and Simms and formally protested this form of public humiliation, pointing out that white thieves were fined, not set to work under slavelike conditions. Nevertheless, in the coming months, the mayor and other city judges would continue the practice, which, they believed, had much to recommend it: the chain gang provided a ready, cheap source of menial labor for cleaning streets; it alleviated overcrowding in the Chatham County jail; and it also reminded every pedestrian and cart driver in the city that "heavily ironed" freedpeople remained uniquely vulnerable to the various layers of law that governed the city in 1865.[38]

In a spring 1865 petition to military authorities, a black citizens' committee (including Garrison Frazier and Charles DeLaMotta, among others) charged military authorities with a range of abuses against the freed population. In response to the petition, a military board of inquiry took testimony from black witnesses who told of beatings and verbal abuse perpetrated by white soldiers, and of alleged petty criminals sent, in Simms's words, "unjustly . . . to the islands." Perhaps most dramatic were the accounts of black nurses, cooks, and custodians of the Freedmen's Hospital. (Soon after the occupation, military officials had converted the Savannah Poor House and Hospital into a hospital for freedpeople.) Employees rendered in graphic detail the sadistic practices of a white physician, an alcoholic army surgeon who strung patients up by their thumbs, turned the hose on ill men and women who had soiled themselves, and beat them with a whip and a bed slat. One nurse heard the doctor exclaim of black patients, "Let them die! I've plenty of coffins! There are too many of them." The doctor was quickly dismissed from his post, perhaps because the accounts of black witnesses were corroborated by white soldiers and nurses in the hospital. Whatever the reason, petitioners and witnesses alike had the satisfaction of successfully pressing their case against a white man in authority.[39]

The month of April marked the long-in-coming end of the war. On Sunday, April 9, Robert E. Lee surrendered his forces to General Ulysses S. Grant at Appomattox Courthouse in Virginia. Grant permitted a general dispersal of Confederate forces, allowing the men to keep their horses—a gesture that Lee predicted "will do much toward conciliating our people." That evening in Savannah, perhaps in response to this news, army officers conducted a "grand review" of black troops on the parade ground adjoining Forsyth Park. Despite a drizzle, the troops displayed "exactitude and precision [in their] movements and evolutions," presenting a sharp appearance in uniforms. Indeed, "not a cartridge box, not a belt, not a buckle was out of place." Such martial displays swelled the pride of all blacks, especially the men who had recently traded the rags of a slave for the uniform of a U.S. soldier. The war, at least the one fought on the conventional battlefield, was over.[40]

On April 14, ten days after he toured the defeated Confederate capital of Richmond, Abraham Lincoln lay dying, struck down by John Wilkes Booth. James Simms later recalled the horror that gripped the black community in the wake of the murder. For the first few months of 1865 the Union occupying forces had been "guarding the peace and liberty of all who prayed for the peace, unity, and prosperity of these United States; and this did the [black] churches with fervent zeal." And now an assassin's bullet had cut short the life of "this great and wonderfully-gifted man, whom God in his providence had raised up to be the great emancipator of our race in North America." The city's ministers "soon recovered their faith in God, and felt that what he commands is certainly wisest and best." But mingled with grief was fear. In Simms's words, "What did it mean? Was the question."[41]

Lowcountry whites remained "almost paralyzed here by the rapid succession of strange and melancholy incidents that have marked the last few weeks," according to Mary Jones's daughter-in-law Caroline, wife of Joseph: "the sudden collapse of our tried and trusted General Lee and his army . . . then the rumors of peace, so different from the rapturous delight of a *conquered* peace we all looked forward to; then the righteous retribution upon Lincoln." Caroline Jones believed that the president's death amounted to but "one sweet drop among so much that is painful." On April 16, Charles Lamar, former owner of the *Wanderer* and colonel of the Twenty-fifth Georgia Cavalry Regiment, was killed near Columbus, Georgia, one of the last men to fall in the service of the Confederacy. In early January, his father, Gazaway Bugg Lamar, had been one of the first men in Savannah to take the loyalty oath to the United States.[42]

On Saturday, April 22, Savannah memorialized Lincoln with an outdoor assembly of an estimated five thousand people. Stores closed their doors, dirges echoed through the streets, bells tolled, and minute guns fired in what the *Republican* (mistakenly) called "a universal feeling" of mourning for the slain president, "Lover of his Country, Lover of his Race." Buildings throughout the city and even the trees in Johnson Square, where the meeting was held, were draped in black. Organized by military officials, the gathering featured speeches by newly emboldened Georgia Unionists, most notably Amherst W. Stone, lately arrived from Atlanta. A former speculator in blockade runners, he now aspired to the position of U.S. attorney.[43]

Savannah's unrepentant white citizens tried to maneuver the lead in staging the Lincoln memorial rally. The committee on arrangements had invited the city's ministers, black and white, to attend and take their seats on the stand, but unexpectedly a group of whites backed up by northern white soldiers compelled the black clergy to move to the back of the crowd. Outraged, Simms later complained to military authorities: "We claim the right to mingle together with the whites on such public occasions." While he and other self-proclaimed "loyal citizens" were being forced to disperse, Mayor Arnold, the white clergy, and members of the city council grimly waited out the proceedings. Sharing the stand with them were representatives of the Union army and northern aid associations. The meeting officially expressed the city's "*horror* and detestation of these cruel, barbarous and unparalleled atrocities" and "resolved to pledge ourselves anew to the *great cause* for which [Lincoln] lived, worked, and *died*." Not far from Savannah in "this eaten-out country," Mary Jones was mourning not for Lincoln but for a way of life; she was negotiating with Jack, one of her former slaves, over his monthly wage; they settled on $25.[44]

In late April the state of Georgia, which had enlisted 120,000 men and sent 30,000 of them to their deaths over the previous four years, officially capitulated to Union authorities. In June, Savannah civic leaders, eager for "the speediest plan of restoring the State to her original condition in the Union," dispatched Mayor Arnold to Washington. There he met with the new president, Andrew Johnson, and pleaded for a restoration of local authority that would suppress "repeated depredations from bands of lawless men, whites and blacks," who were "subjecting the people of the State to the peril of famine and anarchy." Johnson (who impressed the mayor with "his looks, manners, and intellect") early indicated that he favored allowing the former Confederate states to reenter the Union quickly. In May the president recognized the state governments previously approved by Lincoln—Arkansas, Louisiana, Tennessee, and Virginia—and thereby acknowledged that no state need enfranchise blacks in order to gain his favor. He also extended amnesty to all Southerners who professed their loyalty to the United States; these men would have their land, but not their slaves, restored to them. The wealthiest Southerners, like prominent Confederate political officials and military leaders, would have to appeal personally to Johnson for a pardon. Though he opposed any dramatic moves that would lift the black population out of poverty and menial labor, the president relished the prospect of large numbers of vanquished planters coming to him on bended knee. One Tennessean who knew him well claimed, "If Johnson were a snake, he would lie in the grass to bite the heels of rich men's children."[45]

In the historical imagination, Sherman's burning of Atlanta has eclipsed his saving of Savannah as a dramatic sign of the impending Union triumph. The general's decision to destroy Atlanta's rail facilities served to announce his military strategy in marching to the sea—to impair the South's ability and will to continue fighting—even as his decision to spare the river port announced his generosity, born of recent victory. By allowing the Savannah mayor and council to remain in office and the municipal government to continue to function, Sherman made it possible for city authorities to engineer what they considered a remarkably smooth transition to peace, aided and abetted by Union occupiers. In their efforts to restore "order" to the city, Sherman and his troops thus earned the gratitude of former Confederates, even as the freedpeople, leaders and ordinary folk alike, denounced the brutality that "order" entailed. It was during those pivotal first months of 1865 that Union military officials put the city on a political path that it would not veer from for over one hundred years.

-✦❙ CHAPTER TEN ❙✦-

For I Have a Great Deal to Do

O NE DAY IN MARCH 1865, the Reverends Tunis G. Campbell and Hardy Mobley boarded a steamship in New York City bound for Savannah, and within a week or so they caught their first glimpse of the Forest City. In all likelihood the two clergymen already knew each other, and had planned to make the voyage together. Before the war, Campbell lived in New York, where he combined a successful career as caterer and hotel manager with evangelizing among the poor. It was there too that Mobley had established a small business after freeing himself (with the help of American Colonization Society supporters) and fleeing from Augusta, Georgia, in 1853. Now Campbell had received a commission from the federal government to work among the thousands of freed blacks along the Georgia coast. Mobley was returning to his native state under the auspices of the Union Congregational Church of Brooklyn to "labor for the improvement of his old neighbors who [had] been less fortunate than himself." Bringing with them their wives and children, and intending to start a new life among the newly freed slaves, the two men were in the vanguard of a large number of newcomers who would come south to the Georgia lowcountry after the war. These were black and white men and women animated by religious fervor, political and economic ambition, humanitarian sentiments, and, in many cases, a kaleidoscopic combination of these motives. Few were prepared for the contentious and often violent cauldron of postbellum southern religious and partisan politics.[1]

Congress was more willing than President Johnson to confront the practical implications of emancipation. In early March that body had created the Bureau of Refugees, Freedmen, and Abandoned Lands; its mandates included providing immediate aid in the form of rations and transportation to Southerners loyal to the Union, and overseeing the transition of 3.5 million Southerners from slavery to freedom. In Georgia, bureau agents focused on what they considered the linchpin of that transition: a new system of annual contracts between landowners and former slaves. Presumably the contracts would provide incentives for employers to treat their workers fairly. Named the bureau's first commissioner, General Oliver Howard in turn appointed General Rufus Saxton assistant commissioner for South Carolina, Georgia, and Florida. Deriving his authority from Special Field Order No. 15, Saxton was determined to distribute to the freedpeople any lands "abandoned" by white planters. To facilitate the settlement of the Georgia coastline, he named Tunis G. Campbell "governor" of Burnside, Ossabaw, St. Catherines, Sapelo, and Colonel's islands. But Campbell was not interested in enforcing annual contracts. His missionary work in South Carolina convinced him that the freedpeople would thrive not as field hands under the direction of northern cotton agents, but as members of self-sufficient colonies.[2]

In the North, Campbell had aggressively solicited aid from the New York branch of the National Freedmen's Relief Association and used the money to equip a party of several hundred freedpeople with seeds and government rations for a colony on St. Catherines. Within days of arriving on the island, he had established a tenuous state in miniature, with a government consisting of an eight-person senate, a twenty-person house of representatives, and a judicial system and a supreme court. To provide for the colony's defense, he organized a black militia. In words that reflected the posturing of other postbellum Georgia leaders, he boasted of his influence among the destitute refugees: "the people, as a general thing, are simple and childlike, and just now can be led in any direction, and they flock around me just like sheep: my name had gone before me years ago, and they will follow me anywhere."[3]

By late spring, 200 adults and 117 children had settled on St. Catherines. Campbell made a concerted effort to promote marriage, education, and collective independence among the settlers. The colony cultivated vegetables, sold wood to passing steamships, and gathered moss for the Savannah market. Despite its founder's promising combination of idealism and resourcefulness, the colony had a great deal of difficulty feeding itself. Among the crops planted first, only the melons would be ripe before July. The settlers' efforts to harvest shellfish and shoot game were hampered by U.S. sailors who harassed them from nearby gunboats, and by the increasing number of refugees streaming across St. Catherines Sound from the mainland. Bringing with them elderly kin and other dependents, many of these refugees had been evicted by coastal planters, who, as soon as the cotton crop was sown that spring, sent whole families away, "unpaid, to the islands." These men, women, and children had few possessions, and indeed many were "as innocent of clothing as Adam and Eve before they used fig leaves."[4]

Campbell's urgent letters to Freedmen's Bureau officials reveal that the colony could not hope for true self-sufficiency without the basic necessities he specifically requested: clothing, mules, lumber, plows, seeds, clocks, window sashes, medicine (quinine, castor oil, laudanum), guns, and ammunition. He also needed a sailboat and "a good horse as I have to go about a great deal . . . for I have a great deal to do." Campbell feared that outside influences would likely hinder his best efforts to get the colony on its feet; he especially dreaded purveyors of alcohol. At the same time, some of the original owners of St. Catherines were returning to claim their plantations and demand that the colonists accept wage labor in the cotton fields. Realizing that slavery-like field labor, paid or otherwise, would undermine the settlement, Campbell protested that "the facts are the men wanted to work for themselves after they came to the Island."[5]

The migration of refugees to St. Catherines and other islands was part of larger population movements throughout the lowcountry during the spring of 1865. Some freedpeople had been displaced from their homes, while others left eagerly, searching for loved ones, employment, safety, or the intense thrill of Savannah itself. By the summer many who had initially left or been forced off plantations in the winter were returning home. Blacks refugeed to the interior during the war years now constructed rude rafts and floated down creeks and streams into the Savannah and the Altamaha rivers—if not to a specific place, then to a general region laced with kin networks and marked by the graves of their forebears. Former slaves of the Butler family—those refugeed upcountry and even some sold at the great auction of 1859—made their way back to the Butler's Island and Hampton Point plantations. Transported to Early County by her master during the war, Dora Roberts remembered that "most of us wanted to come back to de place whar we libed befo'—Liberty County." Camping out on highways and near railroad stations, lowcountry freedpeople pinned their hopes on broken-down wagons and ailing mules to transport their families and modest belongings over many miles of war-torn territory. Yet white planters saw in this movement, in the words of Mary Jones, only "anarchy and rebellion," proof that the "negro race," completely dependent on whites, would soon die out.[6]

The Freedmen's Bureau's newly assigned assistant commissioner for Georgia, General Davis Tillson, also complained about the freedpeople's resistance to renewed labor in the rice and cotton fields. A brigadier general in the Union army, the Maine native was unaccustomed to anyone mocking his strategy or countermanding his orders. Seeing in regional migration only signs of social disorder, he complained that "colored people are impressed with the idea, that freedom means they can go anywhere they please, do as they please, and work when they please."[7]

Planters reclaimed abandoned homesteads only to find that black kin groups had taken up residence in the main house and begun working for themselves. In McIntosh County, one white family was shocked to discover "a goodly number of our old slaves had returned, and, without leave or license, simply considered it their privilege to come home, after they were scattered by Sherman's raid." In June 1865, Susan Kollock was relieved that her family's Whitebluff plantation was "not injured at all. Salt works all safe, every kettle in place." "But," she added, "the house is filled with our own negroes, who are using the old furniture we left there; the whole place has a decidedly *negro air*." Like other former slaveholders, Kollock descended into self-pity, denouncing blacks' "*injustice* to us in robbing us of our property."[8]

While Susan Kollock was seeking to reclaim her family's plantation, Samuel Boles, a self-described "Head Stevedore of Confidence," was writing to Union authorities and pleading the case of former refugeed slaves seeking to return to St. Catherines Island. Boles listed several reasons why this group deserved to settle there: "now those that wos taken away wos Born & Raise on that Iseland & there parent is still there . . . furthermore they has a knolledge of the Soil what it Can Produce . . . the houses & all improvement on the place is there labor . . . & these peoples knoes Evry thing In Regard to the plantation." Boles thus made a case based on blood-and-sweat equity—the right of people "that wos born Raise & give there labor there all there Life" to return to their homes and their kin.[9]

Many freed families set about providing for themselves by fishing and hunting for game. Others demonstrated a more entrepreneurial bent. Louis Manigault's brother Joseph reported that the blacks on his Savannah River plantations were "engaged in pulling down my large rice mill and barns, mill chimney, boilers, machinery &tc and transporting the same to Savannah for sale." On the islands freed people scraped up any remaining rice or cotton, hunted down cattle, and cut railroad ties, all things to sell in the city. Touring Savannah in July, U.S. General Carl Schurz observed the roads into the city clogged with "a good many colored people driving carts loaded with watermelons and different kinds of vegetables, while not a few were engaged in fishing the 'creeks' which separated the Sea Islands from the mainland." Schurz believed that "these pursuits are certainly not unprofitable, but they take away from the cotton and corn fields a considerable proportion of the labor force"—a connection not lost on the region's planters.[10]

By this time Savannah blacks had launched a two-pronged campaign for self-determination in their churches and schools, and for integration into the larger political process. Lacking the right to vote or run for political office, they used the only strategies available to them: petitioning, forming political organizations, and flexing their numbers in public (about 40 percent of the city's swollen population of 45,000). Early on, it became clear that the churches would seek to free themselves from white oversight. In the summer of 1865, James Simms and Samson Whitfield (a free man before the war, and possibly the father of SEA teacher Samuel Whitfield) were present when the newly independent First, Second, and Fourth African and First Bryan (formerly Third African) Baptist churches of Savannah met in Hilton Head; together with other area churches they formed the First Negro Baptist Association, encompassing Georgia and South Carolina.[11]

Regardless of their denominational affiliation, Savannah's black clergy scorned the evangelizing efforts of white denominations in general and the American Missionary Association in particular. AMA officials decided that they needed at least one black preacher to reach the large number of Baptists and Methodists, and so commissioned the recently arrived Reverend Hardy Mobley to labor in the Savannah vineyard. (While still in New York, in a move that was not unusual in these turbulent times, Mobley had readily switched his denominational allegiance— in his case from the Methodists to the Congregationalists.) Now in Savannah he set about fine-tuning his sermons, "preparing them with great caution," and impressing upon his listeners the fact that "freedom and education should go together." But in his campaign to bolster attendance at AMA schools at the expense of the SEA, Mobley earned only a "scurrilous attack" on himself from the native black clergy. His efforts to plant the seeds of a staid Puritan church, and the efforts of his successors, would find infertile soil in Savannah.[12]

The black community saw no contradiction in pursuing cultural self-determination and political integration simultaneously. In April, sixteen ministers, including Simms, presented a petition to the military occupation forces, charging recruitment abuses on the part of bounty hunters, and demanding the right to vote. In late May a group of black men established the Chatham County Colored Union League, a political organization defined by its support for the Union. Since the Republian Party did not yet exist in Georgia, a statewide network, or league, of Union clubs would serve as an opening wedge for it. Consisting of almost four hundred members at the outset, Savannah Colored Union clubs also gave voice to disenfranchised blacks. Among the founding members were the butcher Jackson Sheftall; King Solomon Thomas, teacher of a private school; and the teacher Samuel Whitfield. In June the club sent a petition "asking for the right to vote" to Senator Charles Sumner, one of a group of Republican lawmakers sympathetic to their demands. In response, Sumner assured the 350 petitioners, "The prejudice of caste and a false interpretation of the constitution cannot prevail against justice and common sense, both of which are on your side."[13]

About this time, a small number of whites formed a separate organization called the Georgia Union Club. Founders of the group included Amherst W. Stone as well as four-term alderman Henry Brigham and former Marine Bank director Edward Padelford (the participation of the latter two would be short-lived). The group also attracted the fervent support of *Republican* editor John E. Hayes, who used his columns to tout political reconciliation and commercial enterprise, with or without the support of the city's African Americans. Tellingly, his editorials riled both former Confederates and former slaves. By this time, S. W. Mason, proprietor of the *Daily Herald*, was embracing the tenets of white supremacy in his coverage of the city's daily news.[14]

On the morning of Tuesday, July 4, white Savannah was on edge as marchers massed for a grand parade. City council members warned darkly of impending violence, now that the Freedmen's Bureau had granted permission to black firemen not only to march but also to display the city-owned hand engine they used at fires. The parade was primarily a military affair, "a grand review of the garrison" that included all the black and white troops of occupation. But the black fire companies made a point of marching with 250 members of the Colored Union League. The sight of this emergent freed African-American community—firemen, political activists, and U.S. soldiers—proved too much for some white men and boys. And apparently northern white soldiers ("showing their old Five Points [i.e., street gang] spirit," in the words of Carl Schurz) sided with white "roughs" in a pitched battle with the black soldiers and firemen. Whites attacked the marchers with clubs and stones, and dragged the engine away from the firefighters. The drum major of the Thirty-third U.S. Colored Troops was critically wounded.[15]

At the end of the month, black leaders moved to reclaim the streets for their own purposes. Early on the morning of July 26, the city's various Colored Union League clubs came together to celebrate the anniversary of Liberian independence from the United States exactly eighteen years earlier. After a short march through the city's main thoroughfares, the procession headed toward the old Bilbo canal at the western edge of the city, and then halted in a grove of live oak trees. There a ladies' auxiliary had laden long tables with food and decorated the trees with banners that honored both the first Liberian president, Joseph J. Roberts, and the martyred Lincoln. In charge of the day's proceedings was Charles A. DeLaMotta, who was selling subscriptions to the American Colonization Society periodical, the *African Repository*, as he had been doing since 1849. Proudly on display was a new Liberian national flag; "Some collard Ladays," DeLaMotta noted, "made it with there own hands . . . 6 feet long and of the best Materiels." The band of the Thirtieth Maine Volunteers provided music for the festivities. The highlight of the day's proceedings was a speech by Simms, who expounded "upon the blessings of human liberty, urging his hearers to prove worthy of the great boon God had bestowed upon them." Thus in one celebration could Savannah blacks affirm their support for an all-black African state and at the same time reaffirm their drive for full citizenship rights at home.[16]

BY THE EARLY FALL of 1865 the city was showing signs of rebounding from the war years. The rebuilding of railroads proceeded apace as planters and merchants anticipated a full cotton harvest. Although Savannah whites did not like to admit it, much of the economic recovery was due to an infusion of cash supplied by the hated Yankees. Army officers rented lodgings and frequented soda parlors, taverns, and billiard halls, paying handsomely to do so; price-gouging was common among suppliers of services to occupying troops. And then in September Davis Tillson's arrival signaled an intensified Freedmen's Bureau presence in the city. He authorized the renting of rooms and buildings for offices and schools; the distribution of rations to the poor; and the hiring of local workers, including carpenters, painters, and masons, to renovate classrooms for black children. In addition, the new school year brought eleven AMA workers to the city, including superintendent Edwin A. Cooley (age thirty-four), and his wife, Ellen (both from Sunderland, Massachusetts), and, from Winchester, Connecticut, a sixty-four-year-old missionary, the Reverend Ira Pettibone, his wife, Louise (also sixty-four), and their teacher daughter, Mary Louise, twenty-five. The New England Freedmen's Aid Society was sponsoring sixteen teachers in Savannah, including ten hired by the SEA, among them Simms and Samuel Whitfield.[17]

The war's end unleashed a torrent of lawsuits that enriched the city's lawyers if no one else. Particularly prominent were property disputes pitting freedpeople against their former owners, and neighbors and family members against each other. Conflicts over ownership—whether of a horse or an expansive Sea Island plantation—kept local lawyers busy. Those willing to take the loyalty oath did not lack for clients rich and poor, black and white. Northern companies sought new or reestablished ties with Savannah merchants, creating mountains of paperwork in the form of rental contracts and partnership agreements. When city officials or private property owners moved to reclaim "abandoned" property from the Freedmen's Bureau, and when businessmen went bankrupt, they called upon a coterie of well-connected men, including former aldermen Solomon Cohen and Robert Lachlison, to represent them in court. A profusion of courts—the military provost's court; the military commission court; the Freedmen's Bureau courts; and, beginning in the fall of 1865, the reinstated Chatham County inferior and mayor's courts—all provided work welcomed by the city's lawyers.[18]

Meanwhile, the mayor and aldermen were gaining in confidence as they gradually resumed complete control of the city. Mayor Arnold's cooperative demeanor won him the respect of a succession of U.S. Army commanders, and he even secured a paid position as an assistant health commissioner. In late August Georgia's provisional governor, James Johnson, had authorized civil officers to resume their normal functions in all jurisdictions except control over black lawbreakers. As its first official order of business, the city council levied shipping fees, drayage licenses, property taxes, and other revenue-raising measures. In its relations with the military, the council used the city's deplorable physical condition as a basis for indignant protests: military slaughter pens in the city were polluting reservoirs of drinking water and clogging local waterways with effluvia and offal. In September, Arnold complained to a federal officer that "on Monday last I myself saw a dead cow or ox, floating in the [Savannah] River. From its size, it was evidently a Northern animal, but of course I cannot say whence it came." Army officials promised to rectify the situation.[19]

On September 4, soon after the council had had its customary powers restored, the city's black dockworkers struck for higher wages. Working for $1.50 a day (compared to the $3.00 earned by their white counterparts), they demanded a half-dollar increase in pay. Unable to convince everyone to walk off the job, some of the strikers shook their fists and brandished guns to intimidate co-workers. A U.S. officer arrived on the scene with a squad of soldiers and arrested the leaders. Appalled at the "insolent" strikers, Hayes of the Savannah *Republican* offered them "a little friendly, wholesome advice gratuitously." The contract between laborer and employer partook of a sacred nature, he maintained: "The laborer is everywhere worthy of his hire, but this does not justify the organizing of secret bands of men to extort by threats from their employers what they deem just compensation for their services." The workers had contracted to load and unload ships for $1.50 a day, and it was wrong of them now to "abandon" their employer. The "manly" course would be to give the employer fair notice and then search for another job.[20]

The next day the Colored Union League responded to Hayes's editorial, conceding that their "deluded brethren"—the militant ones—had "jeopardize[d] the great interests in the trial of Liberty and free labor now before the country." But members of the league also asserted that the sixty strikers "were among our best and most peaceful colored citizens." The league stressed the charged atmosphere in which the workers toiled, now that their wages were being undercut by large numbers of impoverished, desperate refugees: rural folk continued to stream into the port city, some pushed off plantations by whites who did not want to support them after the harvest, others now biding their time until what they hoped would be a general distribution of land at Christmastime. The strike was in fact an attempt by the "old citizens" to hold on to their jobs in the face of declining wages combined with rising rents and taxes. League members vowed to continue to organize, "whereby we may in the best manner avail ourselves of the means of enlightenment, of industry, of mutual help and protection."[21]

In midautumn came signs that former Confederates were poised to regain control over Georgia politics, as delegates from all over the state assembled for a constitutional convention in Milledgeville. The body had been charged by Congress to repeal the ordinance of secession, abolish slavery, and renounce the Confederate war debt, all in an effort to prepare the state for readmission to the Union. Only white men who had taken the loyalty oath or received personal amnesty from the president could vote for delegates. Meeting from October 27 until November 11, the three hundred convention members represented a truly conservative spirit; many had identified with the antebellum Whig party, and during the war most were too old, or lacking in a political constituency, to contribute to the Confederate cause as military officers. Not surprisingly, as a group they showed a studied indifference to black civil rights.[22]

On November 15, white voters throughout the state went to the polls and elected sixty-year-old Charles Jenkins as governor and a plethora of former Confederates as state legislators. The legislature also chose Georgia's new U.S. senators: Alexander H. Stephens, former CSA vice president, and Herschel V. Johnson, a former CSA senator. The state's delegation to the U.S. House would include prominent former Confederate military officers, most of whom were ineligible to take the loyalty oath. State legislators then proceeded to grant blacks the right to sue and be sued, to sign contracts, and to own property. Some laws—those outlawing vagrancy and enticement, and those providing for the "apprenticeship" of children—were rendered in color-neutral terms. Yet blacks still lacked the right to vote, run for office, sit on juries, or testify in cases that did not directly affect them as plaintiffs or defendants. Former governor Joseph E. Brown, wielding renewed political clout, showed little contrition for his part in the war, and eagerly set about adjusting to the new political realities. At the same time, he shared the views of most white leaders regardless of class, party, or ideology when he said he was convinced that "unless madness rules the hour, [blacks] will never be placed upon a basis of political equality with us . . . they are not competent to the task of self-government, much less to aid in governing a great nation of white people."[23]

On the first Wednesday in December Savannah held its first municipal election since the city's liberation. Outsiders like Carl Schurz were convinced that in this "hottest" of "rebel places" the "restoration of civil government is not yet possible." Indeed, the electorate was virtually identical to that of the antebellum and war years. And so it was not surprising that familiar leaders once again took the reins of power. Fifty-year-old Edward C. Anderson, captain of the blockade-running *Fingal*, was elected mayor, recalling his first stint in office eleven years before, when he had been called upon to lead the city after the disastrous yellow-fever epidemic. He would hold the office from 1865 to 1869. The council too evoked antebellum days: Robert Lachlison had served eight terms as an alderman since 1854, and George Wylly was elected to his fifth term in seven years. E. A. Soullard had served before and during the war. John Williams, John Villalonga, John F. O'Byrne, and Francis Gúe had sat on the council all four years of the war and won reelection to a fifth term in 1865. The tenacious Waring Russell remained the city jailer (as he would until 1884). Dominick O'Byrne resumed his duties as county ordinary, and Philip M. Russell Sr. (Waring's brother) retained his job as clerk of city council, a position he had held since 1849. These men were charged with restoring civil government and enforcing all laws on the books, with the exception of those that "conflict with the new status of the negro."[24]

At the same time, whites began to knit back together the web of fraternal, benevolent, social, and religious societies that served to unite white men and women regardless of ethnicity, class, and religion. The Savannah Benevolent Society, Odd Fellows, (white) Masons, Georgia Medical Society, Ladies of Episcopal Orphans Home, Seamen's Benevolent Society, Hibernian Society, Irish Union Society, Hebrew Benevolent Society, and Ladies of the Hebrew Congregation were among those voluntary organizations that survived the war. For the most part the white fire companies also remained intact. A new one, formed in the summer of 1865 and called the Metropolitan Fire Company, was composed of CSA veterans. Federal authorities had outlawed the rebellious volunteer militia companies, but at least some of them simply changed their names and called themselves "social" organizations. Hence the Oglethorpe Light Infantry became the Oglethorpe Light Club and under that title continued to march, purchase arms, and "monitor" the polls on election day.[25]

By way of either accommodating themselves to the new order or challenging it, some white leaders accepted positions as "citizen" or "civilian" Freedmen's Bureau agents. Speaking at the constitutional convention in late October, the bureau's Tillson expounded on the benefits of nonmilitary agents, especially whites possessing influence among the planter class. Some citizen agents were Northerners, clergymen or entrepreneurs renting land in the lowcountry. But the job of bureau agent was appealing to some former Confederates for several reasons: they could make money by charging fees to perform marriages and to certify labor contracts, they could have a hand in overseeing black workers who signed such contracts, and they could ingratiate themselves with federal authorities. Among the unlikely citizen agents in the Savannah region were William B. Gaulden, the anti-secessionist, pro-Confederate planter; Elias Yulee, a former major in the Confederate army; Augustus McIver, a schoolteacher and, during the war, a private in the Liberty County Independent Troop; Theodore P. Pease, a prominent Darien businessman;

Dominick A. O'Byrne, lawyer, judge, and former arbiter of slave runaway cases; and Levi Russell and his brother Philip, sons of the city clerk and judge Philip Russell Sr.[26]

During this period some of Savannah's most prominent citizens managed to retain, or reclaim, their magnificent fortunes, especially those with substantial commercial interests or real estate holdings in the city or in the North. In March 1865, Nellie Kinzie Gordon had moved back to Chicago, to be near her parents. Returning to Savannah from the war, her husband, William, reacted angrily to reports that Sherman had called upon her and conveyed best wishes from her uncle, General David Hunter: "What really galls me," wrote Gordon to his wife, "is that you should associate with my enemies upon any other terms than those politeness demands from every lady." In June, he was even more distressed to learn that his wife had traveled to Washington, D.C., to ask for Hunter's help with federal authorities so that she could arrange the sale of her husband's cotton stockpiled back in Savannah. Wrote William, "If you have availed yourself of his [Hunter's] protection, or used his name to get pay for your miserable cotton or to procure any other favor from the Yankee Government, I shall never forgive you so help me God!" Yet within a year, the cotton factorage firm of Gordon and Tison was prospering once again. Nellie and William reconciled their wartime differences, and William launched a successful postbellum career as a bank president and Georgia state legislator.[27]

However, the war left many other planters stranded, their wealth in cash and slaves now gone, their land useless without labor to till it. They found themselves enfolded by "the dark, dissolving, disquieting wave of emancipation," in the words of Mary Jones's brother John. Some former CSA officers scrambled to earn a little cash by opening a school for neighborhood children, by charging admission to a "Pic Nic and Chowder Party" on their once-grand estates, or by commandeering a wooden wagon to carry a bit of cotton to sell in Savannah. Some retained their business positions—Anderson, Screven, Cohen, and Villalonga as directors of the Atlantic and Gulf Railroad, for example—and prospered with the city's gradual recovery. Others parlayed their prewar family and political connections into jobs with new businesses, while still others made a graceful transition into the new world by drawing upon the skills they had learned in the army—such as operating a telegraph office—to earn a living after the war.[28]

At least these men had come home. Many households remained in mourning, overwhelmed by the loss of loved ones. The war had claimed the lives of a diverse group, including the city's elite and their sons—Francis S. Bartow, Thomas Purse Jr., Edward Padelford Jr.—but also Manuel Molina, a tobacco and cigar dealer, married with two children; and Edward Saussey, a carpenter who was living with his mother before he enlisted. Although between one-quarter and one-third of all Confederate soldiers lost their lives, the numbers killed in any one company could run as high as 40 percent or more. Companies G, H, and I of the Forty-ninth Georgia Regiment lost from 38 to 40 percent of their men either to disease or to battle wounds. Of a sample of the First Volunteer Regiment of Georgia, one-third died and one-quarter deserted. Certainly many grieving families never learned the fate of their loved ones—where or how they were killed, where or how they were buried.[29]

Some men returned bruised in body—maimed, missing a limb—and battered in spirit. The Oglethorpe Light Infantry had lost soldiers at First Manassas, Second Manassas, Sharpsburg, Thoroughfare Gap (Virginia), Gettysburg, Garnett's Farm and Malvern Hill (Virginia), Atlanta, Jonesboro (Georgia), and the Battle of the Wilderness (Virginia). Many men saw comrades in arms dismembered, blown to bits. And a good number witnessed an execution of a deserter, or knew someone who mutilated himself or committed suicide rather than go back to the front. Most of the veterans who came trickling home to Savannah in the late spring and early summer received the gratitude of a weary city, but others endured public ridicule and rumors of cowardice and disloyalty. It is unclear what happened to deserters like the twenty-eight-year-old German baker George Giebelhouse, who was married when he joined the Republican Blues early in the war, and then deserted after the fall of Fort Pulaski. And not all the wounded were returning soldiers; some women were now dealing with the horrors of war by relying on liberal doses of brandy and morphine. They too were suffering, as were the vanquished men who had returned home to an uncertain future.[30]

A number of white men parlayed their military service into postbellum political careers. Members of the German Volunteers such as immigrants Henry Blun, a commission merchant, and Conrad Weigand, owner of the Savannah Hotel, became active in fire department politics. In contrast, the lawyer George Mercer coped with the war's psychic scars by descending into depression and self-doubt as he watched his contemporaries profit from the gradual resuscitation of the city: "I hear of what lucky merchants and speculators are making, and look with almost a melancholy regret upon my dusty shelves, venerable tomes, and empty purse." Condemned to the "wearisomeness" of defending ordinary citizens in minor cases, Mercer cast an envious eye on "the lot of others," with their "lavish wealth, handsome establishments, &c." He watched as friends and neighbors were once again able to afford vacation trips to Europe, all the while tormented by the fact that he had spent a considerable part of the war in Savannah, far away from the " 'flashing of guns,' " enjoying "all the comforts of home," instead of "in that time of my country's peril . . . exposed to danger & hardship."[31]

If another privileged young lawyer, Charles Jones, shared similar regrets about his service far from the front lines, he did not dwell upon it in the fall of 1865. By that time most of the slaves on the Joneses' lowcountry plantations had departed for Savannah, the men responding to offers of railroad and military construction jobs. Arcadia was now home exclusively to former slaves, who "ruled there entirely" for the remainder of 1865. Out of necessity, Charles soon rolled up his sleeves, "earning his daily bread 'by the sweat of his brow,' " in the words of his wife, Eva. He began at Indianola, the family's Burke County plantation, scraping together six bales of cotton, which he took to Savannah "in a most primitive style." While her husband's hands turned "hard and burnt like a common laborer's," his wife set about "becoming a very efficient chambermaid and seamstress." Possessed of *"not a greenback,"* Jones nevertheless resisted taking the loyalty oath and busied himself with the challenges of his family's land-rich, cash-poor station in life.[32]

The extended Jones family contended with freedpeople who wanted to remain in their former quarters but work on their own, spurning contracts, credit, or promises of payment from their former owners. Faced with his own workers' "restiveness," the Reverend John Jones called in U.S. military forces, who "came promptly, and by use of the strap and sometimes a leather trace . . . restored order generally," rendering the offenders "thunderstruck that they should receive such treatment (and in some cases severe, even cruel) at the hands of their friends." Jones's sister Mary, widow of Charles Senior, remained at Montevideo, and she too "had been forced to call in the Yankees" when Cato, one of her former slaves, in her words, *"instigated"* a rebellion among the workers against the white overseer. According to his former mistress, Cato "has been to me a most insolent, indolent, and dishonest man; I have not a shadow of confidence in him, and will not wish to retain him on the place." However, eventually both Mary Jones and her son Charles were forced to rely on their former slaves to oversee the cultivation of the land. In January 1866, the Joneses removed the white overseer of Arcadia and gave control of the plantation to one of their former slaves, the enterprising Stepney, now Stepney West, who set about managing the work of members of his own extended family.[33]

In December 1865, Charles decided to pack up his family and move for good to New York City, where he had been offered a position— "a providential opening" in the law firm of his former mentor, John E. Ward. In explaining his decision to his distraught mother, he claimed that his chief concern was the health of his wife, Eva, and the fact that Savannah offered "but little prospect" for him now. Yet Charles's motives—and despair—went deeper. Gazing mournfully at the grave of his father, overrun with weeds, he could not abide this new way of life. The once-brash lawyer and Confederate officer was now having to auction his furniture and beg creditors for more time, and to bargain with blacks bent on appropriating their due—whether in coins or cotton—from their former owners. Claiming he could better provide for his mother from a distance in his new job, he put Arcadia and Maybank up for sale and took up residence in New York on East 16th Street, near his office on Broadway. There he assumed the role of "petitioner in favor of the plundered Confederate."[34]

Faced with stubborn resistance among lowcountry blacks to its labor policies, in September 1865 the Freedmen's Bureau tapped a man of stern principles to enforce the annual contract system: assistant commissioner Davis Tillson. That month President Johnson had ordered General Oliver O. Howard to rescind possessory titles to land now claimed by its former owners; blacks could remain on such lands only if they signed contracts. By this time 40,000 freedpeople had settled on approximately 400,000 acres of the Sherman Reservation, the Georgia Sea Islands and coastal area set aside for black settlement in early 1865. The bureau now aimed to remove many of these people, and to oversee labor contracts for the coming year among those who chose to stay. In December Howard petitioned his superiors for more military power to be used against the black settlers. During that month the bureau responded favorably to the land claims of twenty-five white plantation owners in the Sherman Reservation.[35]

Tillson was particularly alarmed at developments on the coast and the islands, where, he very much regretted, the region's natural bounty enabled freedpeople to support themselves without growing cotton or rice for the market: by fishing, gathering oysters, and foraging for berries, the people there might earn "a half straitened subsistence," but they would soon resort to stealing from whites to supplement their larder, he claimed. Therefore the area had the potential to become a magnet "for all the lazy, idle, loafing negroes of the state." Moreover, Tillson found himself contending with bureau agents and others who, he believed, were doing more to perpetuate the freedpeople's misguided sense of independence than to restore order in the area. Chief among these offenders was Tunis G. Campbell. By this time the St. Catherines colony consisted of 425 black settlers and their families, who claimed parcels all over the island. The colony's armed militia vowed to keep whites away from the freedpeople's fields.[36]

Tillson sought to eliminate any doubt about his own priorities when he announced that by January 10, 1866, all black workers must either sign labor contracts for the coming year voluntarily or be forced into such "contracts" by bureau agents. This move had the explicit approval of President Johnson. Soon Johnson would remove Rufus Saxton from his post, impatient with what he saw as the snail's pace of restoring Sea Island lands to their former owners.[37]

In late 1865, then, as Tillson assumed a monumental task of dispossession, he was hardly prepared for a direct challenge from a most unlikely source: a fearless black attorney utterly contemptuous of U.S. and southern officials. In late November, Aaron A. Bradley, fifty, the former Augusta slave who had spent the last three decades in the North, returned to his native state, armed with a law degree and a defiant attitude unlike anything Georgia whites had ever seen. During the war Bradley had remained in Boston and used his legal skills to file petitions with the Massachusetts legislature urging lawmakers to eradicate "the [legal] disabilities now resting on colored citizens." By the summer of 1865 he was openly denouncing President Johnson in print, crafting legal arguments that at different points cited the Articles of Confederation, the Constitution, the *Dred Scott* Supreme Court decision, and the Emancipation Proclamation. Bradley maintained that black men, as free people, clearly possessed the legal right to the franchise. He held that President Johnson, by his unseemly haste to readmit the rebel states to the Union, had betrayed the cause of freedom: "Although we conquered on the bloody field of battle, we complain of the Chief, in command of the army and navy of the United States, for ignominiously humiliating a great and powerful nation in the Executive chamber." In what would become his refrain over the next few years, Bradley concluded, "We demand protection against our friends."[38]

Drawn to the rich ferment of Savannah and the lowcountry—collective stirrings on the docks, on the streets, and in the fields—Bradley quickly set about attacking planters for seeking to return black laborers to a state of neoslavery, the mayor and military authorities for condemning black prisoners to work with ball and chain, and Freedmen's Bureau officials for colluding with their former enemies in denying fundamental justice to black citizens. Dressed smartly in a top hat and kid gloves, and adept at drawing street-corner crowds with impromptu speeches, the light-skinned, freckle-faced Bradley had no difficulty attracting attention to himself.

In early December Bradley spoke at a mass meeting held at the Second African Baptist Church. In his speech, he explicitly challenged the speaker who came before him, the elderly preacher Garrison Frazier, who had told his listeners, "You must not steal!" Bradley would have none of this conciliatory talk, so characteristic of black clergy before the war: speaking forcefully and directly, he maintained that since black people were the source of all wealth, they were not stealing when they took what they had earned. According to an alarmed Freedmen's Bureau agent who heard the speech, Bradley claimed that since the former Confederate states were now U.S. territories, black people had the right to occupy the plantations they had slaved upon. According to a *Republican* editorial, Bradley urged his listeners to *"resist, if necessary, at the point of a bayonet, all attempts on the part of the agents of the Freedmen's Bureau to dispossess or remove"* them from the lands they currently occupied. A few days after this public appearance, Bradley opened a school, which bureau officials promptly "suspended."[39]

By the end of the month military authorities had arrested, tried, and convicted Bradley for seditious and insurrectionary language. Among the witnesses against him was AMA superintendent Edwin A. Cooley, who privately referred to the lawyer as a "very insolent, pestilent fellow," and a "conceited demagogue of the barroom." Bradley proceeded to appeal his sentence of one year's confinement in Fort Pulaski directly to a number of federal officials, including Secretary of War Stanton and President Johnson himself. Winning release on parole, the attorney vowed to open another school.[40]

Despite the widespread fears among whites that landless blacks would stage a bloody uprising on December 25, the end of the year passed quietly throughout the region. Blow-outs resumed, signaling the beginning of a new social season cast in the old mold. In Savannah, controversy erupted only when the city council refused to grant a permit to black firemen for a parade on New Year's Day. Mayor Anderson assured the Freedmen's Bureau that he had no principled objection to the parade but rather "on the grounds that they will be likely to be interfered with by citizens—young men who may get intoxicated and interrupt them." The parade took place without the permit and without incident.[41]

Ten days later, Aaron Bradley was present when delegates from all over the state met in Augusta for a historic "Freedmen's Convention" and formed the Georgia Equal Rights Association. The purpose of the association was to press for full citizenship rights—freedom of travel and assembly, the right to vote, hold office, and sit on juries. The delegates formally welcomed "Lawyer Aaron A. Bradley" among the honored guests. The convention elected James Porter of Savannah its temporary chair, and Louis B. Toomer, a black teacher from the city, its secretary. Also among the Savannah delegates were Charles DeLaMotta and the Reverend Ulysses L. Houston. Taking the podium, Davis Tillson delivered a long-winded speech in which he advised the group to cultivate "kindly relations between yourselves and the white people," and to refrain from supporting universal suffrage. This last measure, he maintained, could only yield "mischievous consequences . . . highly injurious to society."[42]

Meanwhile, Bradley lost little time clashing with the other delegates over certain procedural resolutions, and, in an apparent violation of the terms of his parole, he made blanket criticisms of a number of federal officials, including Stanton and the deceased Lincoln. When word got back to Stanton, he gave Bradley a choice of one year in Fort Pulaski or a year in exile from the state. Bradley chose the latter course, but only after he had fired off an angry letter (in the form of a petition) to Howard. In it he blasted the Freedmen's Bureau court and its judge ("as Ignorant of Law as a Slave, and as Unjust as Nero to the Colored People"), the Savannah city marshal, and "a Possy of Irish Police Men" all bent on humiliating black citizens. This document was a signature Bradley effort, full of references to the law, history, and his own moral outrage. When Bradley went north, he left in his wake a trail of rattled officials, northern and southern whites united in their fear of this swaggering provocateur.[43]

Not all challenges to the old order came in the form of fiery denunciations of white people. Others, though just as far-reaching, were marked only by the shuffling of official forms and the scratching of Xs on paper. On January, 10, 1866, a group of freedmen and -women entered a building on Bryan Street near Drayton, bringing with them modest amounts of cash: the Freedman's Savings and Trust Company was opening its Savannah branch. The first depositors included Henrietta Saxton, still living with her former owners, John and Mary Stoddard; Madalina Parling, a cook who opened an account for her granddaughter Ida Post; Grant Sampson, a widower who worked as a teamster and served as deacon of the First Bryan Baptist Church; and Frank Thompson, a laborer and the single parent of three sons and three daughters. Congress had originally intended the bank as a means for black soldiers to save and safeguard their wages and their bounty money. And indeed, in Savannah, the list of depositors in the first few weeks read like a roll call of the occupying army, with several companies of the United States Colored Troops (USCT) represented—Edward King's unit, the Thirty-third, in addition to the Thirty-fourth and the 103rd, with men from as far away as Tennessee and Virginia. And many soldiers hailed from Savannah and the surrounding counties—Paul Potter, of Company C, Thirty-fourth USCT, was a former slave of James Potter, the master of the Simms family. Other depositors, civilians and soldiers alike, had once belonged to some of the most prominent families in the lowcountry, families with such last names as Cuyler, Jones, Maxwell, Habersham, and DeLyons. Within a few days of his arrival in the city, the bank's cashier, the Reverend I. W. Brincker-hoff (a Congregational minister), had become enmeshed in the social web of AMA teachers and bureau agents. With Cooley, he had testified against Aaron Bradley in the black attorney's December trial.[44]

About the same time Bradley made his appearance in Savannah, another former runaway arrived on the city's docks. Together with her daughter Louisa, Harriet Jacobs had secured a teaching commission from the New York Society of Friends. By now well-known for *Incidents in the Life of a Slave Girl,* her sensational account of hiding in a North Carolina attic for seven long years, Jacobs came to Savannah a seasoned worker among black refugees. She and her daughter had spent the last two and a half years of the war teaching and providing material relief for blacks in Alexandria, Virginia. The Jacobses' work there convinced them that the freedpeople would respond best to black teachers, men and women who understood that the impoverished former slaves were "quick, intelligent, and full of the spirit of freedom." Opening a school in January 1864, Louisa fully appreciated the potential of her pupils: "When I look at these bright little boys, I often wonder whether there is not some Frederick Douglass among them, destined to do honor to his race in the future." Given the chance, the freedpeople would provide for themselves, but this process would require time and patience.[45]

Though they paid for first-class tickets, Harriet and Louisa Jacobs were forced to travel to Savannah in the steerage compartment, and only after they strenuously protested did the captain of the steamship allow them to take their meals with the white passengers. When they disembarked at Savannah they were greeted by a distressing sight: clustered on the docks were freedpeople who had arrived a few days earlier from the islands of Ossabaw and St. Catherines, displaced by returning landowners. The miserable refugees "huddled around a few burning sticks, so ragged and filthy they scarce look like human beings." Nearby, black laborers went about their work—the men loading the ships and the women, paid 25¢ a day, separating good cotton fibers from bad. Gesturing toward the cotton bales packed for export and detritus scattered around the bluffs, one freedwoman exclaimed to the newcomers, "There you see our blood. Three hundred weight when the sun went down or three hundred lashes, sure!"[46]

The two teachers opened a school in the Freedmen's Hospital, now run by Major Alexander T. Augusta, an African-American surgeon whom they had met in Alexandria. Fearful of venturing outside the city, where a smallpox epidemic was raging, Harriet expressed admiration from afar for the work of James Simms, who was working as a Baptist missionary and labor agent among some four thousand freedpeople in the rice district between the Big and Little Ogeechee rivers, due west of Savannah in Chatham and Bryan counties. Though himself a product of the city, Simms understood the powerful historical forces at work in the lowcountry, and he believed that he could best shape labor relations in the countryside through his role as a "minister-missionary" to the people there. He observed that the freedpeople would try to remain rooted to the land, determined to honor their forebears—"their Fathers and Mothers [who] cleared those Swamps and Marshes, and Made them the Fruitful Rice Fields they are." Yet the bureau's annual contract system seemed to reduce freedpeople to neoslavery. During this season of contract negotiations, Harriet Jacobs decried the agreements drawn up specifically for rice hands; she believed their purpose was to strip black families of all semblance of self-sufficiency. Though approved by the bureau, the contracts were "very unjust. They [workers] are not allowed to have a boat or musket. They are not allowed to own a horse, cow, or pig. Many of them already own them, but must sell them if they remain on the plantations." At the end of the year, hands inevitably found themselves in debt to the landowner, beholden for rations and other supplies received on credit. Workers who left the plantation without permission of the owner, or who entertained friends or kin, faced cash fines of 50¢ a day or in some cases expulsion.[47]

It is possible that Simms, as an agent for the Ogeechee blacks, was able to moderate the provisions of a few contracts, the ones he helped negotiate. One signed in early 1866 by Clotaire S. Gay, owner of Rice Hope plantation, and thirty-four men and youths, is suggestive. The agreement at least allowed the workers to keep garden patches and stock animals since "they have families to support," and it also stipulated that "their said Agent James M. Simms . . . will represent them throughout said division seeing that it shall be justly made." But this contract also required that hands must not in any way show "disrespect and disobedience" to the landowner and "shall work faithfully upon the said plantation whether in cultivating the crop or in cutting wood and lumber always under the direction" of the landowner. It was around this time that Simms was warning Oliver O. Howard, head of the bureau in Washington, that the labor contracts signed by rice hands would "virtually enslave them" by leaving them mired in debt at the end of the year. Simms implored Howard to "Protect the Rights of these Poor Fellowmen of Mine, and now no longer Slaves but Loyal citizens to the government under Which We Live." The local bureau agent considered Simms "a rascal . . . making much mischief among the Freedmen." Perhaps Simms's personal style, which garnered him political support among blacks, antagonized white authorities. Despite his small stature, Simms, in the words of a Northern reporter, was able to accomplish much "by force of a subtle, keen intellect."[48]

As part of the original Sherman Reservation, the Ogeechee district was home to many blacks who sought to claim parcels of these fertile rice lands and then work them collectively. In the antebellum period, with slaves outnumbering whites by five to one (2,435 compared to 413), the area had produced 1.2 million pounds of rice annually. As early as March 1865, the Ogeechee Home Guard (black) militia had emerged on several plantations. Dozens of former slaves settled on hundreds of acres of lands that would gradually revert to their former owners—thirty families on 245 acres of J. R. Cheves's Grove Point plantation, fifty families on 641 acres of William and Robert Habersham's Grove Hill. In contrast, blacks were renting land from the owners of Wild Horn, Oriza, and Vallambrosia, the Burroughs, McCleod, and Heyward families, respectively. In the summer and fall of 1865, planters launched largely successful legal challenges to the blacks' possessory titles in the district. Bureau agents sought to ensure that the workers, once they were either evicted or reduced to wage labor, could claim the proceeds from crops grown that year. Yet in their "self-directed labor" and their tenacious hold on the land, Ogeechee blacks remained at odds with both planters and federal authorities. With the encouragement of leaders of the Savannah Colored Union League, especially James Simms and Moses Bentley, workers formed their own Union Club, which held meetings on Grove Point plantation.[49]

Bureau officials sympathetic to the freedpeople found their position full of frustrations in the remote, virtually all-black Ogeechee district. One agent described it as "this region of miasma, disease and death," before he decamped for the North in December 1865. He had charged $1 to each couple he married (fifty-five by November 1865), and a colleague managed to supplement his own income by selling whiskey; but even these moneymaking ventures were not enough to make up for what Northerners considered the debilitating climate of the area. Like other agents throughout the coastal region, they had a difficult time understanding the former slaves, who spoke rapidly in their pidgin language, Geechee.[50]

Where the Ogeechee had once been the center of a deadly system of task labor, it now became the center of freedpeople's arduous struggle for self-determination. The bodies of men and women there revealed the effects of slavery and four hard years of war. Workers of all ages bore painful scars on their backs from whippings. Their feet were ulcerated from toiling in freezing water, and many suffered from respiratory diseases. In the winter of 1865 and the following spring, cholera and smallpox spread through the region. The onset of cold weather caused much hardship among the elderly. Many of the men were off elsewhere, serving as soldiers or working for the military. Nevertheless, Ogeechee families together sought control over their own productive energies. Rather than pay a toll of seven out of every hundred bushels of rice to the Freedmen's Bureau—the fee for using a central rice threshing mill—the workers winnowed the rice by hand at home. Some resisted selling the rice altogether, "as they consider it the Lord's, given them to feed hungry mouths with." To the extent possible, they tried to negotiate for relatively favorable terms from a landowner.[51]

Thomas Clay Arnold, a wealthy planter, complained to the bureau at the end of December that the blacks on his Cherry Hill plantation "refused to contract with me *upon any terms*, for the ensuing year, and, also, refuse to leave the place, and threaten violent resistance to any effort to put them off the place." Workers throughout the region tried to negotiate the share of the crop (one-half versus one-third), and the presence of an overseer in the fields. Still, the people had only modest wants. A coachman for the Cheves family had always done "my duty religiously," he said, but his master would whip him nevertheless *"just because he could.*" Now the freedman wanted "a little strip of land for a garden where I can raise a few things jes to keep me along." According to one woman, "One meal a day and little bits of coffee and freedom is a great deal better than slavery."[52]

In the fall of 1865, two northern white women stepped into this volatile political scene. Esther W. Douglass of Brooksville, Vermont, and Frances Littlefield of Hallowell, Maine, preferred a rural outpost to the more comfortable circumstances of their Savannah co-workers. Before the war, the forty-one-year-old Douglass had wanted to evangelize among the Cherokee, but her mother would not allow her to go. By 1864, her mother was dead, leaving Douglass bound "by no family ties." In her application to the AMA, she professed her commitment to the freedpeople, but admitted that "a fondness for travel, and desire to see more of our country, come in also, as less worthy motives." She and Littlefield had taught together in Virginia before arriving in Georgia.[53]

Setting out from Savannah, the two women traveled the fifteen miles to the Ogeechee, and found themselves in a strange land littered with "the traces of war," downed trees and bleached animal bones. Though charmed by the moss-covered live oaks, they also feared that such exotic flora signified a "debilitating" climate. Nevertheless, they energetically set up housekeeping in the main residence of Grove Hill, which they dubbed "Spinster Hall," and opened a school they called "Ogeechee Institute." The white landowner uttered a scornful prediction: "Those women in there think they are doing something great but those children only learn like parrots. They will soon come to the bottom of their brains."[54]

Douglass and Littlefield found a warm welcome from people of all ages eager to learn. According to Littlefield, "An old uncle said to me, I hope we will use you well." The school, held in the parlor of their residence, drew children from seven neighboring plantations. On her first day Douglass was startled by the sight of "120 dirty, half naked, perfectly wild, black children crowded on the floor." She could hardly understand them, for "their language was to us, a confused jargon." With the exception of those raised as house slaves, the pupils had a hard time comprehending her as well. Supplied with only a few slates and some printed cards she tacked to the walls, Douglass nevertheless tried to uphold northern-style standards of punctuality and classroom decorum. But some children had to walk as far as six miles to school on cold winter mornings, wading barefoot through icy water, and they were frequently absent, "minding 'birds' or 'babies.' " The teachers also conducted a night school for adults; among their pupils was an elderly man who learned at home as well as at school, "catching his letters" from the schoolchildren each day.[55]

On a typical day the two women rose at five thirty in the morning, breakfasted on fried hominy, and conducted a round of home visits before school began. They checked up on elderly and crippled shut-ins, reading a few Bible verses and praying, handing out quilts and coats sent from the North, dispensing a teaspoon of painkiller mixed with sugar and hot water for a stomachache, camphor for cholera. With the help of Harriet Gaylord, another AMA teacher who regularly came out from Savannah, they sponsored an "industrial school," teaching women and girls how to cut patterns, baste, sew buttonholes, and make collars. On the weekends Douglass sought to establish a beachhead for Congregationalism on the plantation, where the worship services were "Episcopal in form," reflecting the denominational affiliation of the former master. She taught religious school, and, on Sunday morning, in the absence of the Reverend Ira Pettibone, conducted worship services. This last task caused her some apprehension, given the Congregational injunction against women preachers.[56]

The teachers also found time to write "begging" letters to solicit cash, used clothing, and garden seeds from the North. Like Harriet Jacobs, Douglass rejected the bureau's almost pathological fear that distribution of clothing and rations would render the people permanently dependent on private charity and the federal government: "They need help as they are just starting in life and in short time they can support themselves as well as they could themselves and 'massa' too."[57]

A description of the teachers preparing a Christmas dinner for the elderly on the plantation—a repast of beef soup with rice, and crackers and ginger cakes—echoes the labors of the antebellum plantation mistress, dispensing food and good cheer to her slaves. The teachers were delighted with their reward from the guests: a song of thanks praising Littlefield's dark eyes and Douglass's curly hair, followed by a little dance. And certainly some of the dialogue recorded by Douglass between herself and freedmen and -women resembles the deference ritual practiced under slavery. When she observed that a young man pounding rice was "hard at work I see," he replied, "O yes, Missus . . . work brings the greenbacks now . . . There's nothing better than greenbacks." Soon after the teachers went north for the summer, in May 1866, a pupil named James Grant appealed to AMA officials: "please to send them to the Grove Hill Plantation a gain for they have done so much good heare and

Have been so kind to the sick they we all feel that they are dear friends to us."[58]

One year after the official end of the war, both Mayor Anderson and Commissioner Tillson could take heart from a series of dramatic albeit divergent developments. By March 1866, the city had regained control of the Chatham County jail. The mayor's court had resumed operations, and U.S. troops were gradually withdrawing—2,600 in January alone. The Board of Education had reclaimed Massie School for the city's white children. Alexander H. Stephens was reassuring former Confederates that President Johnson was a true states' rights man and their ally in Reconstruction. In April, Johnson declared the rebellion officially over; he was eager to give power back to the states.[59]

For his part, Tillson and the men and women of the military–AMA–Freedmen's Bureau complex believed that their own work was progressing. In late 1865 the American Tract Society had made what the AMA's Cooley considered an ill-advised decision to keep the SEA alive with an infusion of much-needed cash. But by the spring the SEA was unable to pay its teachers regularly, forcing several to apply for commissions from the AMA. The end of the spring term marked the demise of the black-led group. On April 9, Cooley crowed in a letter to his New York superiors, "The field is now virtually our own . . . in having a [mission] house, school buildings, and no opposition." He was looking forward to reducing twelve former SEA teachers to the level of assistants for his own women teachers when AMA schools opened in the fall.[60]

At the same time, Washington lawmakers were preparing to defy the president. In February, Andrew Johnson vetoed two measures passed by the Republican-dominated Congress. The first was an extension of the Freedmen's Bureau, which, Johnson claimed, encouraged the former slaves to lead "a life of indolence" when they should be taking responsibility for their own lives. The second measure was a civil rights bill guaranteeing citizenship (though not the right to vote) to all non-Indian natives of the United States, as well as "full and equal benefit of all laws and proceedings for the security of person and property." The bill provided that federal rather than state courts would enforce its provisions. Johnson slammed the measure, arguing that "the distinction of race and color is by the bill made to operate in favor of the colored and against the white race." The president went further and made explicit his belief that black people should never gain citizenship rights, no matter how limited.[61]

In early 1866, increasingly contentious labor and political relations were roiling the coastal region. Tillson removed Tunis G. Campbell as a bureau agent in April, charging him with defrauding the government of taxes on the wood the St. Catherines colonists sold to passing steamships, and with paying people in "intoxicating liquours"—an accusation that Campbell, a longtime temperance reformer, heatedly denied. Though divided by war and politics, Anderson and Tillson could agree on certain fundamentals: that black people must continue to grow cotton under the supervision of whites, and that the law must deal decisively with troublemakers like Aaron A. Bradley and striking dockworkers. Susie Baker King recorded a speech made by her husband's commanding officer, Charles T. Trowbridge, when the Thirty-third U.S. Colored Troops were mustered out of service in early 1866. Trowbridge assured the men, "The prejudices which formerly existed against you are well-nigh rooted out." The freedpeople must now follow "paths of honesty, virtue, sobriety, and industry, and . . . a willing obedience to the laws of the land." Most former Confederates would have agreed with both the spirit and the particulars of this advice.[62]

These converging narratives suggest a certain harmony of interests between northern and southern whites, a harmony enshrined in the supremacy of law and order, variously defined. Federal legislation guaranteed an emerging set of fundamental rights for the freedpeople, but local officials felt free to interpret those rights according to custom, and in the interests of "public order." Indeed, former Confederates remained remarkably unapologetic—either for justifying the institution of bondage or for initiating a rebellion that claimed nearly 700,000 lives (not only those of soldiers, but also southern slaves and white civilians) to preserve it.

As black men and women mounted ever more aggressive challenges to shared assumptions among white authorities, they revealed that the tensions between federal prerogatives and local power, and between slavery and freedom, were by no means resolved. And so new battles were joined on the streets, on the docks, and in the fields.

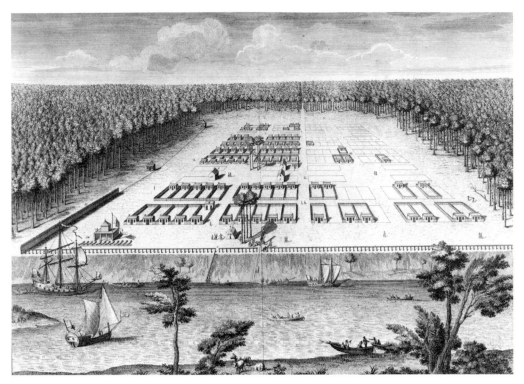

This 1734 view of Savannah looks south from Hutchinson's Island, across the Savannah River. The urban grid pattern reflects the idealism of Georgia's founders, who intended to create a settlement of hard-working householders of modest means. The colony also served a strategic military role, as a buffer between South Carolina to the north and a threatening mix of Spanish and Indians to the south. *(Courtesy Georgia Historical Society, item 1, 1361MP, General Map Collection)*

On the morning of April 12, 1851, a contingent of 150 federal and local law enforcement officials escorted the fugitive slave Thomas Simms to Boston's Long Wharf and a waiting ship that would return him to his master in Savannah. Persistent efforts on the part of the city's abolitionists to free Simms made the large show of force necessary. Simms, in the middle of a hollow square of police, is not visible in this drawing. *(Published in* Gleason's Pictorial Drawing-Room Companion, *May 10, 1851)*

LEFT: In his book *The Great South* (1875), Edward King included this drawing of a stone stairway leading down the bluff from Bay Street to the river and wharves below. A black woman carries a large bundle on her head in the customary West African manner. *(Courtesy Catherine Clinton)*

RIGHT: Photographed in 1867, this River Street scene was an enduring image emblematic of Savannah's nineteenth-century staple-crop export economy. Here a drayman stands next to his heavy wooden cart laden with bales of cotton, a load driven to the docks from the railroad depot in the northwestern part of the city. The top floors of these brick warehouses front Bay Street, on the bluff that runs parallel to the river. *(Courtesy Georgia Historical Society)*

The Gothic Revival–style Chatham County jail on the corner of Whitaker and West Hall Street was overcrowded from the time it was built in 1846 until it was demolished in 1888. Savannah's lively underground economy, based on petty crime and the provision of illicit goods and services, kept the jail full with black and white men and women of the laboring classes. *(Courtesy Georgia Historical Society, item 1, VM 1360 Cordray-Foltz Collection)*

A rare photograph showing an enslaved man and woman plowing a rice field in the vicinity of Savannah, c. 1855. The soft soil of the lowcountry swamps discouraged the use of horses, mules, or oxen to pull plows. The task-labor system on rice plantations did not lessen the danger or difficulty of field work for slaves of all ages, who remained vulnerable to deadly respiratory and waterborne illnesses.
(Courtesy Georgia Historical Society, item 1, 1361SG, Stereographic View Collection)

This engraving, titled "Rice Culture on the Ogeechee, near Savannah, Georgia," appeared in the December 12, 1865, issue of *Harper's Weekly*. Its montage of scenes illustrates the essential features of rice cultivation, including the intricate system of floodgates and ditches that allowed the fields to be flooded periodically with freshwater from nearby streams and rivers. Rice planters relied as much on the labor of enslaved women as on the labor of enslaved men.

LEFT: These Sapelo Island women are using mortar and pestle to hull rice, an arduous task. Beginning in the eighteenth century, Georgia planters exploited the knowledge and expertise of enslaved Africans skilled in the cultivation and processing of rice. Traditional African farming practices and tools remained characteristic of lowcountry rice production throughout the nineteenth century. *(Courtesy of Georgia Archives, Vanishing Georgia Collection)* RIGHT: Dr. Richard D. Arnold was a ubiquitous presence on the Savannah political scene for his entire adult life, serving in a remarkable number of elected and appointed positions related to city governance, health, and education. As mayor of Savannah, he surrendered the city to federal forces in December 1864. He remained an active leader in the postwar effort among whites to resist the demands of African Americans for full citizenship rights and full participation in city government. *(Courtesy Georgia Historical Society)*

Built in 1799, the City Exchange, located on Bay Street at the foot of Bull Street, served as Savannah's City Hall from 1812 until 1904, when the structure was demolished. City council meetings were held on the second floor. Aldermen watched from the portico when federal troops entered the city and marched down Bay Street on the morning of December 21, 1864.
(Courtesy Georgia Historical Society, item 594, 1361PH, General Photograph Collection)

This house on East St. Julian Street was once the home of Catherine Deveaux, an immigrant from Antigua. Here Deveaux's daughter Jane helped her teach a clandestine school for black children. Beginning in the 1830s, Jane Deveaux taught her own school for many years, spanning the period before, during, and after the Civil War. This structure is similar to houses owned by other relatively well-to-do free people of color. *(Courtesy Historic Savannah Foundation)*

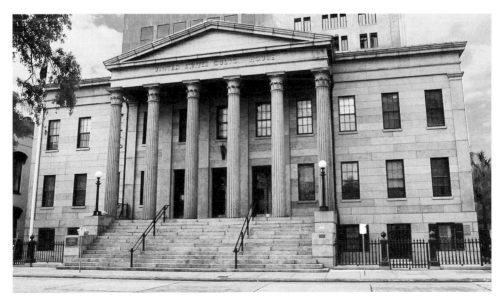

Symbol of an enduring but troubled federal presence in Savannah, the federal Customs House is centrally located on Bay Street. It was built in the Greek Revival style favored by antebellum architects of many kinds of public buildings, including banks, churches, and waterworks. After the Civil War, Republican presidents staffed the customs office with patronage appointees, among them black leaders such as James Simms and John Deveaux. *(Courtesy Historic Savannah Foundation)*

Built in 1821, Savannah City Market occupied the perimeter of Ellis Square and featured an open courtyard in the middle. Here white farmers and enslaved men and women from the surrounding countryside would come to sell fish, produce, and meat to Savannah customers, black and white. In 1874, a new two-story brick building replaced this wooden one. *(Courtesy Georgia Historical Society, item 1266, 1361PH, General Photograph Collection)*

LEFT: A Savannah African-American fireman posed for this portrait around 1856. Black men, enslaved and free, were an integral component of the city's firefighting force; free men of color received annual tax rebates, and slaves received cash stipends each time they responded to a call. Whites objected to the fact that their black counterparts also wore uniforms, a source of pride for all of the city's firefighters. *(Courtesy of Special Collections Department, Robert W. Woodruff Library, Emory University)* RIGHT: Black men and women hucksters were a common sight in Savannah. Peddling fresh vegetables, baked goods, and handcrafted items on city streets and between plantations, they demonstrated a strong entrepreneurial impulse common to enslaved workers and free people of color throughout the region. This impulse enabled some blacks to profit financially from Savannah's wartime distress. *(Courtesy Georgia Historical Society, item 4441, 1361PH, General Photograph Collection)*

First African Baptist Church, located at 23 Montgomery Street on Johnson Square, was completed in 1859 with donations of money and labor from members of its congregation and from African American supporters in the North. James Simms, a skilled carpenter, was among the congregants who worked on the structure, reported to be the first brick building owned by black people in Georgia. *(Courtesy of the Historic Savannah Foundation)*

LEFT: The Reverend Andrew C. Marshall served as pastor of Savannah's First African Baptist Church from 1826 until his death thirty years later, at age 100. During his tenure, the church enlarged not only the size of its Savannah congregation, but also its reach into surrounding rural areas. Estimates put the membership of First African at 4,000 by the 1850s. Marshall, like most other black preachers, worked at a wage-earning job; together with his sons, he operated a successful drayage business. *(E. K. Love,* History of the First African Baptist Church, *[1888])* RIGHT: In his roles as preacher, teacher, labor agent, state legislator, judge, and civil rights activist, the Reverend James Meriles Simms shaped the political and social landscape of the Georgia lowcountry during the Civil War era. Simms worked to advance the dual struggles of African-American political rights and economic freedom. Contemporaries agreed that he was a singularly eloquent and effective public speaker. He included this portrait of himself in his book, *The First Colored Baptist Church in North America* (1888).

LEFT: Pierce Butler, owner of two expansive estates in Glynn and McIntosh Counties, sold more than four hundred of his slaves in 1859, one of the largest slave auctions in the late antebellum period. Butler's need to pay off massive personal debts led to the violent separation of enslaved family members on the two plantations. After the Civil War, some of those sold during what their descendants called "the weeping time" found their way back to the lowcountry and their loved ones. *(Courtesy Historical Society of Pennsylvania)* RIGHT: Frances Kemble, an accomplished English actress, was married to the wealthy Pierce Butler. In 1838 and 1839 the couple lived together on the Butler holdings. She was horrified by the brutal treatment of the family's slaves by Butler, his overseer, and other whites. In 1846 she separated from her husband, and three years later they divorced. During the war she published her account of her southern sojourn, *Journal of a Residence on a Georgian Plantation, 1838–1839. (Courtesy Catherine Clinton)*

On November 8, 1860, white Savannahians rallied in historic Johnson Square to mark the election of Abraham Lincoln as president. The Nathaniel Greene monument (in honor of the Revolutionary War hero) is decorated with a banner that reads "Our Motto: Southern Rights, Equality of the States." *(Courtesy of Special Collections and Archives, Robert W. Woodruff Library, Emory University)*

This scene, published in *Frank Leslie's Illustrated Newspaper*, shows white Savannahians bidding farewell to Georgia troops en route to Virginia in the summer of 1861. The crowd is assembled in Monterey Square, site of a monument honoring Casimir Pulaski, a Polish military officer who died defending Savannah against a siege by the British in 1779. Georgia's Civil War governor, Joseph E. Brown, clashed with Confederate president Jefferson Davis over the deployment of the state's soldiers during the conflict.

LEFT: Charles C. Jones Jr. poses for a formal portrait in his military uniform. A lawyer by profession, Jones enlisted in August 1861 as a senior first lieutenant in the 1st Volunteer Regiment Georgia Artillery. In October 1862 he was appointed lieutenant colonel of artillery and served as chief of artillery at the siege of Savannah in December 1864, helping to evacuate Confederate troops as they fled the city across the river to South Carolina. *(Courtesy of the Hargrett Rare Book and Manuscript Library, University of Georgia)* RIGHT: This unidentified woman was an enslaved worker in the household of the Reverend Charles C. Jones. Despite their professed paternalism, the Joneses did not hesitate to sell workers whom they considered recalcitrant and resistant to plantation discipline, as was the case with the seamstress Phoebe, her husband, Cassius, and their children in 1856. *(Courtesy of the Hargrett Rare Book and Manuscript Library, University of Georgia)*

Labeled "Indiscriminate Flight of the Inhabitants," this engraving from a December 1861 issue of *Frank Leslie's Illustrated Newspaper* conveys the sense of panic felt by white Savannahians immediately after Union forces occupied Tybee Island at the mouth of the Savannah River. However, by the end of the month the federal navy had obstructed the lower reaches of the river, making an invasion by water unlikely. *(Courtesy Georgia Historical Society)*

This portrait, a copy based on the original, shows Eleanor Kinzie before she married William Washington Gordon II, son of a prominent Savannah family, in 1857. During the war, while her husband was serving as a Confederate officer, the Chicago native endured the taunts and insults of white Savannahians. They regarded her male kin fighting for the Union, including her uncle David Hunter, a general in the U.S. Army, as proof of her suspect loyalties. *(Courtesy Georgia Historical Society, item 5666, MS318, Gordon Family Papers)*

The Waring siblings, from left: Annie, James J., Joseph Frederick, George H., and William R., with their Aunt Annie Johnston. Planter and real estate speculator Dr. James J. Waring proved a steadfast if unlikely ally of Savannah's freedpeople. He clashed frequently with many white authorities, including Richard D. Arnold. *(Courtesy Georgia Historical Society, item 5, VM1360, Cordray-Foltz Collection)*

LEFT: A Northerner by birth, the Reverend Tunis G. Campbell believed that southern blacks would not be truly free until they could become independent of white landlords, clergy, teachers, and sheriffs. After the war, Campbell founded black colonies on the Georgia coast, one on St. Catherines Island, and the other in McIntosh County. He also served as a state legislator and Republican Party activist. Supported by the county's black majority, he became a magistrate and formidable political force until white officials forcibly removed him from office. RIGHT: Susie Baker King Taylor used this portrait of herself, in a post-war nurse's uniform, as the frontispiece to her memoir, *Reminiscences of My Life in Camp with the 33rd*, published in Boston in 1902. During the war she served as a teacher of southern black men recruited into the U.S. Army. Later she attempted to operate her own school for black children in Savannah, an effort that faltered in the face of competition from the American Missionary Association.

In the spring of 1863, Louis Manigault circulated this advertisement for Dolly, a valued cook and laundress, who had run away from the Manigault wartime residence in Augusta. Like many other masters, he attributed his slave's disappearance to a mysterious white man who had enticed her away. In fact, a Mr. Lewis, another slave, had begun to court Dolly, and it is likely she fled to be with him.

(Manigault Family Papers, Southern Historical Collection, University of North Carolina at Chapel Hill)

Frank Leslie's Illustrated Newspaper published this drawing in a March 1865 issue. The artist depicts the black men, women, and children who freed themselves by joining Sherman's army on the march from Atlanta to Savannah. In some cases the refugees appropriated the clothing, wagons, and horses of their former owners. The army put many of the able-bodied men to work clearing the army's path over rivers and through swamps.

This contemporary drawing suggests the frenzied and chaotic efforts of General William T. Sherman's foragers who raided plantations on their march from Atlanta to Savannah in late 1864. A black woman and her children stand by helplessly as soldiers round up, shoot, and wrestle to the ground pigs, sheep, and cattle. *(Author's collection)*

Built for British-born merchant Charles Green in 1851, this grand mansion in the Gothic Revival style quickly became a Savannah landmark. One foreign journalist noted with some understatement that the home's lavish interior furnishings, including Italian statuary and stained-glass windows, made it "an exception to the general run of Southern edifices." General Sherman used the mansion for his head-quarters during his one-month stay in Savannah beginning in December 1864. *(Courtesy Historic Savannah Foundation)*

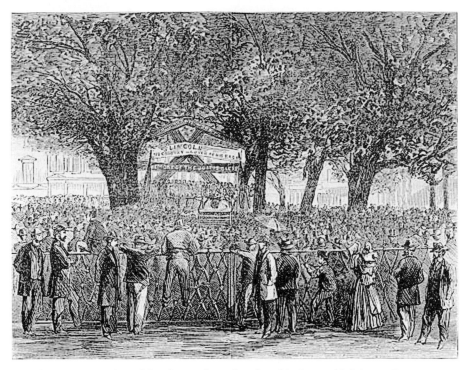

On April 22, 1865, an estimated five thousand people gathered in Savannah's Johnson Square to mourn slain president Abraham Lincoln. A banner stretched across the park reads "Lover of His Country, Lover of His Race." Not everyone in attendance was mourning Lincoln. Some local officials, in concert with occupying federal troops, attempted to keep James Simms and other black leaders away from the section at the front of the crowd designated for prominent white politicians and clergy.

LEFT: Born into slavery in 1812, the Reverend William J. Campbell served as an assistant to the Reverend Andrew C. Marshall. When Marshall died, Campbell assumed leadership of First African Baptist Church. He disapproved of other ministers who pursued political office and influence. A biographer noted admiringly that he "controlled the church, absolutely, for twenty-three years. . . . In most things he was law to the people, and from his decision no one dared to appeal." RIGHT: Born a slave in Charleston in 1822, Charles DeLaMotta was for many years an agent of the American Colonization Society in Savannah. In the 1840s, his wife, Martha, emigrated to Liberia, where she was, he said, "injoying hur freedom in a free land, which affords me much plesur." A member of First African, DeLaMotta continued to feud with the Reverend William J. Campbell. After the war DeLaMotta served as superintendent of the church's Sunday School, which employed seventeen teachers.

Built in 1833, the Chatham County Court House was located on the southeast corner of Wright Square. Georgia's original trustees stipulated that southeastern lots facing the squares should be occupied by structures devoted to public or religious purposes. After the war, the local Democratic Party often limited county balloting to a single box, the one in the courthouse. This practice helped to suppress the black vote by making voting difficult for rural freedmen, who had to travel long distances to cast their ballots. *(Courtesy Georgia Historical Society, item 601, 1361PH, General Photograph Collection)*

This scene in a Georgia cotton field sometime in the 1870s suggests the family economy characteristic of southern staple-crop agriculture in the postbellum period. Families of eight to ten children were not uncommon, and all family members labored in the fields during the busy harvest season. Sharecropping families received a share of the cotton they grew and picked, though many found themselves in debt to their landlords at the end of the year. *(Courtesy Georgia Historical Society, item 8, 1361PH, General Photograph Collection)*

WE WERE STOLEN SOLD AND BOUGHT TOGETHER FROM THE AFRICAN CONTINENT
WE GOT ON THE SLAVE SHIPS TOGETHER WE LAY BACK TO BELLY IN THE HOLDS OF THE
SLAVE SHIPS IN EACH OTHERS EXCREMENT AND URINE TOGETHER SOMETIMES DIED
TOGETHER AND OUR LIFELESS BODIES THROWN OVERBOARD TOGETHER TODAY WE ARE
STANDING UP TOGETHER WITH FAITH AND EVEN SOME JOY

MAYA ANGELOU

In the 1990s, teacher, journalist, and activist Dr. Abigail Jordan initiated a project to memorialize her forebears, and all enslaved workers, in Savannah. Completed in 2002, this memorial was designed by Dorothy Spradley, and its base includes an inscription by the poet Maya Angelou. The controversial seven-foot bronze statue is located on the Savannah riverfront, and constitutes one of the few sites where the city's history of slavery receives recognition. *(Photo courtesy of Chatham County–Savannah Metropolitan Planning Commission)*

CHAPTER ELEVEN

A Dream of the Past

I T WAS A FAMILIAR Sunday evening ritual: clusters of families and friends wending their way home through the streets and public squares after Sabbath services. And in April 1866, Savannah by moonlight was lovely, with "boughs of the groves, swept by the sea breeze, playing bo-peep with the stars," in the words of one enchanted visitor. But by now another Sunday evening scene had become all too familiar: routinely, brazen black and white prostitutes emerged out of the flickering gaslight shadows, and, according to William Wray, the chief of detectives, "ma[d]e night hideous by their lewd and lascivious behaviour." Throughout the center of town, sounds of crude blasphemies shattered the reverie of Sabbath night, rendering public space, for the faithful, profane.[1]

In the spring of 1866, few Savannah black workingwomen could claim the attention simultaneously of the chief of detectives, the mayor, and the head of the Freedmen's Bureau as well as the judge of its court; yet thirty-four-year-old Johanna Anderson managed to provoke the full spectrum of the city's white power structure simply by going to work. Anderson was not content to remain in the brothel she owned, the "*low assignation House*" through which "scores of young girls, white and black" circulated; instead, each night she walked the streets with her entourage of co-workers. (Missing from the detective's account was any mention of the white male customers responsible for Anderson's livelihood.) Possessed of some unspecified physical deformity, Anderson (according to a police report) had earned notoriety as "the most *depraved and abandoned character within* the City Limits." At some point she had apparently left her position as a (presumably free) servant in the household of a Cuban immigrant seamstress, where she was working in 1860. Savannah, like other ports, had never lacked for prostitutes; but beginning in the spring of 1865 Anderson and other women were responding to a renewed demand stimulated by a revived city full of soldiers, seamen, construction workers, counterfeiters, confidence men, and "roughs" from New York City. Of all the city's residents who made money from the ongoing process of Reconstruction, Anderson and her co-workers were among the most visible—and audible.[2]

Detective Chief Wray believed that white prostitutes were more redeemable—more "easily reached"—than their black counterparts, who seemed intent on making a mockery of local law enforcement and judicial systems. However, in the spring of 1866, white officials saw the problem of prostitution chiefly through the prism of recurring black performances staged in the middle of town. Arrested, jailed overnight, and hauled into court the next morning, the offending freedwomen paid their $5 fines and at nightfall returned to the streets, insulting passersby and "laugh[ing] at the punishment inflicted for their offense." With the jail full to overflowing, Mayor Anderson demanded that the Freedmen's Bureau send these black women "down to the Islands and bound out to the Farmers or other persons in need of servants"—a solution Davis Tillson thought justified by city vagrancy statutes. In the meantime, the women would continue to stage their defiance of white authorities.[3]

A detailed April 1866 police report offered titillating reading for the men who, in their official capacity, felt compelled to familiarize themselves with the case histories and physical descriptions of several "shameless colored prostitutes." Yet the distressing situation documented in the report was just one piece of a larger picture: The streets of Savannah, those in poor neighborhoods and even those surrounding the picturesque squares, were largely outside the control of any one person or institution. The same month that Detective Chief Wray was conducting his investigation, city officials took the unprecedented step of disbanding one of the black fire companies for "insubordination" toward white fire company officers. Contending with the "evil of concealed weapons," authorities lamented a spike in street violence in the months following the South's surrender. Simultaneously they confronted the bold if indirect protests of blacks of all ages who, deprived of any formal participation in the city's political system, sought to impress upon elites the power inherent in their numbers, and in their public commotion.[4]

By this time in parks and backyards, black men and women alike were insinuating themselves into the city's soundscape with their "Balls, Shoutings, Public Exhibitions, etc." The teacher Louisa Jacobs cited a new fearlessness among the black people she encountered in Savannah—

in their dress (the women were now wearing the elaborate veils denied them during slavery), and in their speech and public demeanor. Jacobs observed a young servant who, threatened by her former owner, responded to the white man with "fiery eye [and] quivering form . . . telling him that she was no man's slave; that she was as free as he." Two AMA teachers were horrified when a black boy burst into their classroom one day, pursued by a white man angered at the youth's comment "that he himself was as good *just as good* as any white boy!!" In front of a class of 150 frightened pupils, the man "caught his victim and vented his spirit and fury by pounding him with his fists to the full content of his *demon heart*," in the words of the Reverend Ira Pettibone.[5]

As black defiance provoked white rage, city officials set about perfecting legal strategies—stepped-up law enforcement on the streets, harsh sentences for offenders, new civil statutes—to ensure that black people remained literally in their proper "place." (Complicating this effort was the persistent unreliability of the city's foot patrolmen, who were just as likely to join in the carousing as to halt it. In 1866 the city promulgated 106 rules for the police; the order amounted to a litany of offenses committed by the officers, from taking bribes to drinking on the job.) Though suspicious of the motives of local whites, federal army and bureau officials remained respectful of what they considered the legitimate rule of law in the service of public order. By early 1866, city police were arresting disproportionately more black men and women compared to whites for a variety of offenses and on the slightest pretext. In addition to larceny, disorderly conduct, trespassing, and vagrancy, other criminal charges lodged against blacks included firing a pistol, "committing a nuisance," sleeping in a wagon, "being a suspicious person," malicious mischief, "having in possession a bar of soap he could not account for," disrespectful language toward a policeman, and "improper conduct." Serving as a Freedmen's Bureau court judge in early 1866, the former alderman Dominick O'Byrne routinely sentenced black petty-crime offenders to five or six months of hard labor "on streets and lanes with ball and chain." He also forced many to wear a "placard on back stating I am a thief, which *placard you must positively place on*."[6]

At the same time, street-side arrests and judicial hearings were becoming increasingly boisterous events, as black bystanders conducted loud, spontaneous protests. Mayor Anderson had to contend not only with raucous gatherings, like a "general pow-wow" one Saturday night in January, but also with the throngs of blacks who crowded into the mayor's court on Monday morning to offer their support for the dozens arrested.

It was unclear which was more annoying to officials, the late-night party or the disturbance in court that followed it. In May 1866, a crowd formed after the arrest of two black youths, George Washington and Henry Jackson, on charges of vagrancy. Taking note of the disruption, Mayor Anderson declared that "since a large crowd generally follows a prisoner through the streets when under the arrest by a policeman," he was now authorizing the police "to arrest, hereafter, all persons who may congregate about or follow a prisoner through the streets when under arrest." Anderson failed to mention that the city lacked the facilities to hold whole crowds of black hecklers.[7]

In late May, Rufus Saxton's successor, Major General James B. Steedman, paid a visit to Savannah and listened sympathetically to a number of prominent whites who argued that the key to a peaceful North–South reconciliation was the withdrawal of the federal government altogether from court cases involving blacks. The South could never recover a civil society, according to Judge William Law, as long as the Freedmen's Bureau continued to promote adversarial relations between blacks and whites and thereby hinder "the kindly relations which had always existed heretofore." Steedman himself was offended by what he perceived as discrepancies between locally controlled courts and bureau courts—with the latter much more lenient toward black criminals, he believed. Within a few months he would dismantle the bureau judicial system and throw blacks accused of major crimes back on the mercy of civilian courts.[8]

The city council tried to do its part to control the public comings and goings of the freed population. In June 1866, alderman Christopher C. Casey offered a resolution noting that Forsyth Park had been "set apart by the City of Savannah as a pleasure ground by the citizens thereof," but that "at present it is a public nuisance by the congregation of large numbers of negroes and the mutilation of benches and the destruction of the trees and shrubbery and the use of indecent and profane language to the exclusion of ladies and children." Claiming the "duty to abate all nuisances," the council voted to post guards at the gates of the park "and not admit the Negroes unless they are in charge of children of white persons." When Davis Tillson objected that the new statute discriminated against blacks, the councilors proceeded to close the park to everyone—in order "to preserve order and decency," they maintained.[9]

On July 9, a group of whites challenged the time-honored system that placed the city's black firefighters under the authority of the city-controlled Savannah Fire Department. At a mass meeting led by Henry Blun, a CSA veteran and first foreman of the Germania Company (composed of volunteers of German descent), members of the white fire companies called for a reorganization of the system, since the status of the black man "is changed, and [he] in no way [can] be depended upon to permanently maintain the position he has filled so satisfactorily to the citizens of Savannah in times past." At issue was the rule that the six white companies together were entitled to only ten ex officio representatives to the department, while the four black companies had thirty-five standing representatives (white men) with considerably more voting privileges. Eager to maintain control over all of the city's firefighters, the council rebuffed the demands of Blun and the others. As a result, periodic parades featuring the black men of Pulaski, Franklin, Columbia, and Tomochichi companies became even more of a provocation to white men and boys.[10]

Three days after this meeting of the white fire companies, in the early evening of July 12, a seemingly minor collision in the city streets escalated into a case of murder. Samuel Whitfield, SEA teacher and Union Club member, witnessed an altercation between two cartmen, a black man (unnamed in eyewitness accounts) and a white man named Lawrence Craney. Challenged over his right-of-way on the street, the black man allegedly called his antagonist "a rebel son of a bitch," prompting Craney to spring from his wagon and beat the other driver with such ferocity that Whitfield feared for the black man's life. With a friend, William Allen, Craney took off in his cart, followed by Whitfield and an angry crowd. Someone called out to Whitfield, who was armed, "Why don't you shoot him?" but Whitfield replied that his intention was to keep track of the two white men until a policeman could apprehend Craney. Soon after this exchange, Allen and Craney halted the wagon, and Allen pointed a revolver at Whitfield and shot him through the heart. The two white men then made their getaway, though "pursued by a crowd of negroes, uttering all sorts of threats." Within days, Allen had been tried for murder in magistrate's court, with one of the three judges, Philip M. Russell Sr., "stating that he would introduce no evidence whatever on behalf of the defense," since the case did not call for any. The jury agreed, declaring the case justifiable homicide and the defendant not guilty. Writing to members of the National Freedmen's Relief Association, James Simms concluded that all local courts "Will Surely Justify Any White Man in Beating or Killing a Colored Man on a Trivial Offence . . . Such is the State of Law and Justice here, and as we Patiently Worked and Waited the Deliverance of God from Bondage We Will Work and Trust that We Shall yet obtain Justice."[11]

Savannah's mix of defiant black cartmen, firefighters, and soldiers, combined with quick-to-anger white policemen and bystanders, was not unique among southern cities. Indeed, during the spring and summer of 1866 two other ports, New Orleans and Memphis, were the scenes of white street riots directed at blacks, though both of these melees took many more lives than the fatal encounter between Samuel Whitfield and William Allen. On May 1 in Memphis, the collision of two carts, one driven by a white man, the other by a black man, ignited a prolonged pitched battle between black veterans on the one hand and Irish policemen and firemen on the other. At the end of three days, forty-six blacks and two whites lay dead, and whole black neighborhoods lay in shambles. On July 30 in New Orleans, white policemen attacked black veterans who had gathered on the streets to support a new state constitutional convention, one that would extend the franchise to black men. The ensuing massacre led to the deaths of thirty-four blacks and three of their white allies. It was around this time that President Johnson embarked on a national campaign to discredit congressional Radical Republicans in favor of conservatives who wanted to restore complete power to local authorities.[12]

The brutality of Savannah's street politics thus differed in degree, but not in kind, from that of other southern cities. On July 13, the day after the Whitfield murder, NFRA teachers Louisa and Harriet Jacobs sought to return home to the North. Perhaps their trip had been long planned. Or it might have reflected their grief over the death of Whitfield, a fellow teacher sponsored by the northern aid group. Their host, Dr. Alexander T. Augusta, had recently resigned from the Freedmen's Hospital, and the city was clamoring for the return of the building so it could be used again for ailing white seamen. In any case, when the two women presented their first-class tickets on board the steamer *Leo,* they learned that they would have to travel in the steerage compartment if they traveled at all. Refusing, they found themselves ejected from the boat and forced to book passage on another vessel. Once they sailed north, they never again returned to Savannah.[13]

The fact that all black passengers faced humiliation and worse from streetcar conductors and steamship captains remained a source of considerable bitterness among Savannah blacks. After Edward King was mustered out of the army in February 1866, he and his wife, Susie, settled in Savannah, full of hope: "A new life was before us now," she wrote later, "all the old life left behind." Both husband and wife took a keen interest in a venture begun that year: a syndicate, financed by black veterans and other "colored citizens," formed to purchase a "a steamer of their own." Intended to run regularly between Savannah and Darien and to treat black and white passengers equally, the boat had not been in service long before it ran aground en route to Florida, damaged and permanently useless. The investors lost their money.[14]

In the fall of 1866 Baker King was teaching her own school on South Broad Street, charging each of the twenty pupils one dollar per month in tuition. Her husband, a "boss carpenter," discovered that few white employers wanted to hire a black veteran; he was trying to make a living working on the docks. A confluence of events would force the young teacher to close her school by the end of the year. In September, Edward King died, and shortly thereafter his widow gave birth to their child, a son. Meanwhile, it was becoming more difficult to attract tuition-paying pupils. The American Missionary Association dominated the field, endangering the survival of small, black-taught schools. Susie Baker King left Savannah in search of a teaching opportunity in the surrounding countryside. Now that the SEA had disbanded, Superintendent Cooley could afford to express grudging respect for the abilities and dedication of the city's black teachers; he ordered a world map for King Solomon Thomas, who taught thirty or forty youngsters in his private school, and he offered employment as assistants to some of the former SEA teachers (James Porter he considered "well educated for a Colored Person here, though not a very good disciplinarian in the schoolroom"). Still, Cooley now faced a new challenge: the Catholic church was planning to open a new school for black children in the fall.[15]

At the same time, unrest was engulfing the rice and cotton districts of Ogeechee, the coast, and the islands. In the city, whites could manipulate the law, but on the plantations, the rules were shaped less by police and local statutes than by landowners and the laborers themselves. Congress had recently capitulated to the president's insistence that all Sherman Reservation lands be returned to the original owners. But up and down the coast, black settlers forcefully laid claim to stocks of cattle they had tended since the war, to hogs running wild in the marsh, and to compensation for improvements on the land. Families and individuals lacking land warrants refused to go quietly. Still, under the bureau's rules of restoration, freedpeople had to be allowed to retain the proceeds of any harvest they produced. And it was this specific issue—the division of the fall 1866 crop—that crystallized the more fundamental question of who controlled the land. Reports from individual plantations and several of the islands suggest that each place was troubled in its own way, but that the threat of black assertiveness—"mutinies" among workers—ran deep throughout the region.[16]

In the Ogeechee, J. R. Cheves summoned the local Freedmen's Bureau agent to quell an uprising on his Grove Point plantation (the teachers Esther Douglass and Frances Littlefield had not yet returned from summer vacation). Cheves had berated his workers for their carelessness in the fields, but then "finally taking umbrage at my presence among them, they assembled as a *Landsturm*, surrounded my house & drowning my voice with violent, insolent & contemptuous denunciations declared there was no master on the plantation." Nearby, on another estate, two men and a woman had "conducted themselves with so much insolence" that the landowners were too frightened even to try to subdue them. In Liberty County, William L. Walthour faced violent resistance from workers who had been supplied "with sundry articles payable out of their crops," and who now, he maintained, owed the landowner a considerable part of their proceeds from the harvest to pay their debts.[17]

On the island of Ossabaw, black workers under contract were growing (in the words of a bureau official) "impudent and intractable," envious of their neighbors cultivating small plots on their own. A northern firm, McGill, Fly, and Middleton, resisted demands from their laborers for the unprecedented wage of $3 to $5 a day plus an increase in rations. On St. Simons, the bureau agent was caught between a northern planting firm intent on cheating its workers and individual black men resisting all discipline, "restless planets . . . [who] if not held under a steady rein will be sure to make trouble." On Sapelo Island, the bureau agent found that blacks had slaughtered over four hundred head of cattle, and then sold the hides; these workers vowed they would avoid signing contracts until Tunis Campbell came over from St. Catherines and oversaw the process. Many Sapelo freedpeople owned boats and they insisted on coming and going as they pleased; they refused to remain hard at work on the island for any sustained length of time. The freedman Toby Maxwell watched as the crop was divided and partners in a northern firm declared that "they owed the workers nothing at all for a year's labor." In this instance, the laborers who refused to add their cotton to the pile were arrested, sent to Fort Pulaski, and, under orders from Tillson, put to hard labor.[18]

White planters seized upon this regionwide turmoil as a reason to begin organizing themselves into vigilante bands called Regulators, Jayhawkers, and Black Horse Cavalry. By the fall of 1866, such groups had emerged in South Carolina, as well as in Liberty and McIntosh counties, Georgia, where blacks had organized militia companies and conducted a highly public drilling regimen. Limited by having too few men to cover too much territory, bureau agents and military officers were largely unsuccessful in apprehending men charged with "committing outrages on the freedmen." As one officer explained, "I believe the other parties against whom charges are filed in the Bureau cannot be easily arrested as the news of the arrival of any U.S. soldiers in their vicinity is sent to them at once by their confederates, and they escape to the swamps."[19]

In the face of widespread disorder, members of the bureau-military-missionary complex fell out with one another. In Liberty County, three Freedmen's Bureau agents engaged in a protracted, bitter feud that pitted the idiosyncratic William G. Gaulden against U.S. Army major J. Kearny Smith. Arrayed against both of these men was Georgia native Elias Yulee, a teacher and the elder brother of David Levy Yulee, former U.S. senator from Florida and member of the Confederate Congress. Gaulden, accused of molesting a young black girl he had "apprenticed" to himself, was later forced to resign from the bureau, though not before trying to mobilize local blacks on his own behalf and in opposition to his white neighbors. In a dramatic showdown outside a Liberty County court-house, Gaulden and Smith squared off against each other, an act of bravado on Smith's part that later cost him his job for conduct unbecoming a federal officer.[20]

At the same time, in Savannah, the freedpeople's persistent drive for autonomy in their religious and educational affairs continued to aggravate representatives of the AMA. Black preachers considered Hardy Mobley "unfit for the place," and so the AMA preacher remained "decidedly unpopular among the colored people." The Reverend Ira Pettibone and other AMA leaders were reaping an unwelcome harvest after the gradual disintegration of the SEA. In particular, Pettibone had taken offense at James Porter's stubborn, outspoken defense of the black school system, and decided not to offer him a commission, even as an assistant teacher in a classroom taught by a white woman. Within the mission home, Pettibone was contending with "friction" among teachers, most of whom were well-trained professionals and thus "independent thinkers" resistant to the pronouncements of an elderly minister who had never taught school himself. In October, Gilbert L. Eberhart, the Freedmen's Bureau education superintendent for Georgia, took up residence in Savannah and requested free room and board in the mission home as "remuneration for the services I may render the Association." Always pressed for funds, Pettibone felt awkward in the extreme as he contemplated the trade-offs between gaining political influence with Eberhart on the one hand and suffering financial "embarrassment" thanks to this free-loader on the other.[21]

If loyal Unionists could not count on each other after the war, neither could southern whites develop a fully united front against either southern blacks or northern whites. Developments in the fall and early winter of 1866 reminded the city's elite (if they had ever forgotten) that the black-white duality so integral to their own ideology was terribly flawed. It is true that the controversy surrounding the Savannah Fire Company suggests that the white laboring classes believed that they gained nothing, and lost much, by black emancipation. The influx of refugees depressed wages for unskilled labor, and the bravado of victorious black troops challenged the "manhood" of vanquished Confederates regardless of class. And for many of the poorest people the comfort of a white skin was cold indeed. A correspondent for the *New York Times* reported in the fall of 1866 that most Savannahians lived in "miserable wooden structures—some nothing more than shanties, that offend the eye and give an unmistakable evidence of poverty." With the start of the busy season, an in-migration of seamen and dock laborers drove up prices and created food shortages. The outskirts of town were rapidly filling up with what officials called "worthless refugees and vagabonds," blacks and whites alike. Many white men who had kept small stores or hawked food or newspapers after the war were losing out on the streets to enterprising boys of both colors. The high price of food and rent (the latter hovered in the vicinity of an exorbitant $25 a month for dilapidated lodgings for a single family) afforded no privileges to white men or women.[22]

War widows and their children in particular barely subsisted. Mobley was shocked to find that "Some of the most Extreme Cases of destitution, that I have met With" were "not among the Colored but the White People." He cited a mother with five children ages six to fifteen; she had lost her husband, three brothers, two brothers-in-law, and one son-in-law in the war. The conflict had claimed the lives of another woman's husband, her son-in-law and six brothers. Regardless of their political leanings, many well-to-do people regarded the struggles of impoverished whites with contempt. Hayes of the *Republican* saw in a group of impoverished white women only evidence of vice and moral degradation. He decried "their unseemly conduct in open day, and drunken revels at night especially [which], call loudly to the arm of the law to be stretched forth to arrest them in their evil course." Few elites, northern or southern, appreciated either the economic toll the war had taken on the city's most vulnerable populations, or, more generally, the plight of people living in a port with a seasonal economy, one that afforded meager opportunities for employment from May to October.[23]

During the summer and fall, as refugees evicted from the islands crowded into the city's poorest neighborhoods, a cholera epidemic in the outlying districts prompted a quarantine of all ships coming up the Savannah River. At one point the disease broke out on board the *San Salvador,* which was transporting nearly five hundred fresh New York City recruits for the Seventh Infantry stationed in Savannah. While the ship remained anchored at Tybee Island, the epidemic affected more than a hundred men and claimed fifty-five lives. About this time, nine soldiers lit out for the marsh, signaling a new crisis for local and federal officials alike: the proliferation of U.S. Army deserters throughout the region. In the city, growing numbers of jobless white workingmen, especially immigrants with names such as Wetzler and Alvinsleben, were joining the Union army. When they became disillusioned with discipline and routines, with moldy tobacco and spoiled beef, they headed for the swamps. If captured (more often than not drunk), they languished in the city jail for "safekeeping" until they could be retrieved by an officer. Fugitives from the military were now upholding Savannah's tradition as a nest of runaways.[24]

On October 6, two days before the annual municipal elections, a group of white mechanics met at a German hall, the Volks Garten, and called for the formation of a mechanics' and workingmen's association. The meeting had two purposes: to publicize the grievances of the city's white laboring classes, and to advance the candidacies of men who opposed the current city council and its policy of high taxes. The meeting resolved, "The mechanics and working men of Savannah were entirely crippled in means at the close of the late war, having nothing left but the labor of their hands by which to support themselves and their families." The crush of high rents and low wages, combined with a new round of taxes and licensing fees, had put a decent living well nigh out of the reach of many ordinary people. Among the speakers at the meeting were Dr. James Johnstone Waring, the inconstant Confederate surgeon, and Thomas Holcombe, a wholesale grocer, former alderman, and one-term mayor of the city during the war. Both Waring and Holcombe were eager to appeal to this potent political constituency.[25]

The municipal election, held on October 8, returned Mayor Anderson and seven experienced aldermen to office. But voters also chose five newcomers, and among them was the thirty-seven-year-old Waring. Over the next decade, he would cast himself as the champion of workingmen, black and white, a remarkable role for the scion of one of the town's most prominent families. After the cessation of hostilities he had set about rebuilding his real estate holdings throughout the city, and pursuing some measure of political influence. His advantages included his great personal wealth and his well-known brother Joseph, a former alderman now active in white fire department politics. Running on a ticket opposed to the mayor, James Waring was not squeamish about taking his place among colleagues who had gossiped freely about his loyalties during the war. At least three of the aldermen elected in 1866—Wylly, Gúe, and Villalonga—had been members of the council that rejected Waring's gift of rent proceeds in the spring of 1862. Yet right after the election of 1866 the physician offered to serve as chair of the Dry Culture Committee, and promised to cooperate with the mayor.[26]

Perhaps feeling vindicated in his lackluster support for the war, Waring deviated from the political party line drawn so rigidly by Savannah's wellborn. In early 1866 he had attended an ailing AMA teacher, Harriet Gaylord, who had been helping Esther Douglass and Frances Littlefield in the Ogeechee district. Gaylord found to her surprise that Waring was "a Christian gentleman and a firm friend of the colored people." In the course of several long conversations, Waring had told her (and she quoted directly) "that if we wanted to do the Freedmen a practical good we could not do it better than to provide them with farming utensils." The teacher herself felt emboldened to write to AMA headquarters, suggesting, "Give a colored man a hoe, spade & an ax and you set him on his feet, and in nine cases out of ten he will walk right on to self-dependence." Waring had rented out part of his holdings on Skidaway Island to blacks, encouraging them to work on their own.[27]

Waring and the rest of the council members were eager to return the port city to its former glory, now with the aid of new machines—steam engines to replace the hand pumps used by the fire companies, a dredging device to remove obstructions in the Savannah River. The aldermen established a permanent board of (white) education for Savannah and Chatham County, and took steps to bolster the police force by increasing the pay of individuals and adding more mounted officers. They also tentatively addressed the grievances of the white fire companies, for whatever the merits of the firefighters' claim to greater representation within the department, the dissidents represented a formidable voting bloc. At their December 26 meeting, the aldermen voted to turn over the city's new steam fire engine to the Oglethorpe company, noting that the petition in favor of such a move represented "almost one third of the property

holders in the city." Yet the council not only failed to reconsider the onerous taxes recently protested by the white mechanics; at the end of the
year, they added a $10 licensing fee for all longshoremen. Dockworkers
responded with outrage.[28]

WITH DISORDER threatening from all sides, the last person city and
Freedmen's Bureau officials wanted to see was a reinvigorated Aaron A.
Bradley. A recent Supreme Court decision, *Ex parte Milligan,* held that
military trials of civilians were unconstitutional, invalidating Bradley's
1865 conviction in Savannah. And swiftly moving events in Washington
revealed an upsurge in Radical Republican strength. The Republicans
emerged from the November 1866 congressional elections with a veto-
proof majority. The refusal of southern states to ratify the Fourteenth
Amendment, the bloodshed in New Orleans and Memphis, President
Johnson's claim that the rebels were sufficiently reconstructed to reenter
the Union: these developments propelled majorities in both the Senate
and the House toward concrete measures that would shore up the
Republican Party of the South and repudiate the conservative policies of
Johnson. Against this backdrop, Aaron Bradley made a dramatic reappearance in Savannah in December 1866.[29]

During his exile in the North, Bradley showed that he would not be
cowed by his brief but rocky tenure in Savannah. Writing to Freedmen's
Bureau commissioner Oliver O. Howard on behalf of landless freedpeople all over the South, he declared: "My great object is, to give you Backbone, as the Chief Justice of 4 millions of Colored people, and Refugees;
You can not, and must not, be a Military Tool, in the hands of Andrew
Johnson." Yet in the Georgia lowcountry Bradley ran up against a formidable, if diffuse, power structure composed of elected officials, planters,
employers, and the local bureau head, Davis Tillson.[30]

In early January, Bradley sent U.S. senator Benjamin F. Wade of Ohio
a public letter charging that Tillson "has not regard for the laws of the
United States, humanity, nor the laws of God." Bradley enumerated Tillson's crimes—evicting freedpeople from their lands "under duress,"
before they could harvest their crops, and lending his support to Waring
Russell, the Savannah jailer, who routinely whipped and placed in ball
and chain black men arrested on trumped-up charges. "We are governed
by laws not made by us, nor recognized by the Congress of the United
States," wrote Bradley. Tillson swiftly denied the accusations and denounced Bradley's tactics, which included, he said, advocating "open,

armed, and organized resistance to the authority of the United States." Nevertheless, in a blow to Tillson, Senator Wade asked Secretary of War Stanton to investigate Bradley's charges, noting, "I have no doubt his statements are true."[31]

Bradley understood that white officials were increasingly relying on legal strategies to thwart black people's struggle for control over their own lives. And so, soon after his arrival in Savannah, he applied for a license to practice law in Chatham County. In his petition to the Superior Court, the former slave paraphrased Article 4 of the U.S. Constitution—"full faith and credit shall be accorded each state to judicial proceedings of every other state"—and he drew upon an 1856 Supreme Court decision holding that any citizen traveling to another state is guaranteed "the rights of person, with all the *privileges and immunities* which belong to citizens of the state." Since persons of "the African race" were citizens, then the state of Georgia "could *not restrict them, or place the party in an inferior grade.*" However, Bradley, the "humble petitioner," was at the mercy of William B. Fleming, the formidable judge of the Eastern District Court of Georgia. Fleming had had a long career as a jurist, serving as judge of the city court of Savannah (1844–45), and in his current capacity as judge of the eastern circuit since 1853, with the exception of a wartime interlude. He had represented the lowcountry in the state's secession convention. The same day the sixty-four-year-old judge received Bradley's petition, he rejected it on the grounds that the laws of Georgia "do not authorize or contemplate the admission of persons of color to the Bar."[32]

Unfazed by Fleming's decision, Bradley hastened to the South Carolina side of the Savannah River, where trouble had erupted on Delta plantation. Delta's two owners, Charlotte and Isabella Cheves, had leased their plantation to a former Confederate officer, Captain A. S. Barnwell, for the coming year. The move triggered a rebellion among freedmen and -women who refused either to sign labor contracts with Barnwell or to leave the property. Though many of the workers had possessory certificates from the original Sherman Reservation grant, they now learned that such certificates were invalid and that they must abandon their homes and apply for new land warrants on St. Helena Island. By January 19, the Delta freedpeople's resistance had thrown the city of Savannah into a panic, with rumors that "this was but the beginning of a terrible slaughter—the first signal for a second Santo Domingo etc."[33]

On January 19, a local Freedmen's Bureau official, Captain Henry Brandt, took a small force of men with him to Delta, intending to establish order on the plantation. After "expostulating in vain" with what the

Savannah *Republican* called a "mob" of men, women, and children, Brandt withdrew from the plantation, but not before two hundred freed-people, armed with "muskets, clubs, and missles of every kind," had surrounded his "feeble force" of men. Within a few days a subsequent attempt by the officer yielded no better results, and in fact his presence "if anything, tended to increase the anger of the freedmen, who crowded together in solid phalanx, and swore more furiously than before that they would die where they stood before they would surrender claims to the land." One of the leaders claimed, "We have but one master now—Jesus Christ—and he'll never come here to collect taxes or drive us off." Backed by "women and children screaming," men in the crowd continued to fill "the air with oaths and imprecations." At one point "an old mulatto woman bearing a babe in her arms" rushed up to Brandt and begged him not to fire on the crowd. She said that Bradley had urged them "to resist at the point of the bayonet any attempt that should be made to eject them from the land." With his haughty demeanor and self-assured invocation of constitutional principles and legal dicta, the attorney had convinced a fair number of plantation workers that he was a potentially powerful advocate for them, and a formidable foe of white authorities.[34]

But not all former slaves fell in line behind Bradley. Apparently he had urged the Delta workers to sign a petition that he claimed would help them win back their land. He assessed each signatory one dollar; the fee was necessary to pay the postage to send the document to Washington, he said. At least one "aged negro" was skeptical, exclaiming, "Yes, sah! But dis chile can send dem ar petition to de city ob Washton for three cents"—that is, for the price of a stamp. Within the week a more effective show of military force temporarily defused the situation, with some blacks capitulating to the demand that they sign contracts and others deciding to leave for the coast. Nevertheless, Bradley could claim a victory: on January 23 Tillson resigned from the bureau.[35]

Tillson got out just in time. Urged on by Bradley, some of the dispossessed workers were returning to plantations up and down the Savannah River, their flatboats piled high with furniture and other belongings. White landowners fled to the city, and U.S. troops mobilized against the workers. In one incident, an officer responded to an attack by a musket-bearing black man by shooting and killing him. Within days a coroner's inquest had ruled the death justifiable self-defense. In keeping with his paper's anti–Radical Republican stance, a *New York Times* reporter summarized the Delta plantation "negro insurrection" and suggested the black workers in the rice swamps were "the most ignorant, the least intelligent, and the least civilized" of all freedpeople, easily duped "by the Bradley eloquence to which they have been listening for some time."[36]

Simultaneously another "outbreak," this one on the docks of Savannah, was consuming the energies of city and bureau officials. January 24 was the last day for all dockworkers to buy a license for $10 each; no employer would be able to hire a man who did not have one. The new fee hit black workers harder than their white counterparts, since blacks earned $1.25–$1.50 a day, and whites received wages twice as high. Regardless of color, most of the men could count on only six full months of work a year. To protest the "oppressive measure," about three hundred black and white men loading cotton and lumber stopped work. The next morning Detective Chief Wray led a contingent of police out onto the docks, causing panic among the longshoremen, most of whom still lacked licenses. Merchants and ship captains began to complain about the disruption to their business; they threatened to transport six thousand bales of cotton to Charleston to be loaded on vessels there. About eight hundred workers milled around the wharf area, now strangely quiet during what should have been the busiest time of the year. Up on the bay, black men in the new Workingman's Union Association, a "Stevedores Society," resolved "to maintain a firm stand for what they consider 'their rights.' "[37]

In contrast to the dockworkers' strike in September 1865, this one claimed the energies of white as well as black employees. And the issue revolved around an onerous new licensing fee and not a broken labor contract. For these reasons Hayes of the *Republican* praised the "manly spirit of open and universal opposition" to the "extortionate tax." For the time being, Mayor Anderson and his allies on the council remained unmoved by the mounting piles of cotton bales on the wharves, declaring on January 27 that "no more indulgence will be granted." At a special meeting the next day, though, the aldermen reconsidered, and, on a motion by James Waring, voted to reduce the cost of a license from $10 to $3. Anderson then tried to broker a compromise whereby the shipowners would advance the men the fee and deduct the sum from their future wages. However, on the 29th a large crowd assembled on the bluff, scorned the mayor's offer, and proceeded to block all streets leading down to the wharves. Losing patience, Anderson dispatched two-thirds of the city's police force to clear the passageways. The police proceeded to club black protesters, who were then "used rather roughly" when they resisted arrest. Into the middle of this altercation stepped Gilbert L. Eberhart, the bureau education chief, who reportedly yelled, "Why don't they arrest the white men?"—a cry considered so inflammatory that

Eberhart himself was arrested for his "remarks, which the authorities thought tended to increase the difficulty."[38]

The following day eight black men stood trial in mayor's court for "riotous conduct" during the strike—Stephen Bicket, Smart Haines, Peter Fields, Samy Young, S. Jenkins, Harris Miles, S. Donegal, and D. Whitfield. Convicted and unable to pay their fines of $50 each, they were remanded to jail and sentenced to hard labor for ninety days. On their way back to the jail, a large crowd of supporters followed along, alarming the police. In the coming days, other trials followed, including that of Nero Thomas, president of the Negro Stevedores Association, sentenced to pay a $100 fine and serve thirty days in jail for his role in the disturbance. The *Daily Herald* condemned "evil councilors" for leading black workers astray. Before this, according to the paper, blacks "would never have placed themselves in conflict with the local authorities, who are their friends."[39]

The uprisings on the Delta plantation and the docks of Savannah pointed more generally toward what Mary Jones termed a "January revolution" in early 1867. The beginning of a new contract year on the countryside, the imposition of new fees in the city—these measures provoked collective resistance among blacks and, in the case of the dockworkers' strikes, among whites similarly situated. For planters, New Year's brought what would become an annual, dramatic turnover in the labor force. On the Jones holdings, the "January revolution" was marked by the departure of field hands for neighboring plantations, and cooks and laundresses for Savannah. At the same time, Mary Jones greeted the new year with hope that the future would bring a measure of stability. With the freedman Stepney West overseeing Arcadia, "The place is well filled up with many valuable laborers, and it is hoped that they will do better this year than the last," the widow wrote to her daughter, Mary Mallard, on January 2. Yes, it would be impossible to produce a decent crop without reliable hands; but a new, "marvelous washing machine and a wringer" might compensate for the loss of a laundress.[40]

In cobbling together a sufficient workforce, Mary Jones was finding that black family ties caused her considerable aggravation. The authority of fathers, the attachments of husband to wife and parents to children—these relations revealed the "unreliable character of the laborers," in her eyes, and scuttled her best-laid plans for the crop in any one season. In light of her departed husband's strenuous attempts to impress upon his slaves the sacred bonds of marriage and family, Mary Jones's complaints about the strength of those bonds in the postwar period seem ironic, at the least. In her January 2 letter, she wrote, "Kate announced today that she must go with her husband next year. I hope to persuade her to the contrary." (Charles Junior had tried and failed to unite the enslaved couple during the war.) Around this time, the Joneses' Burke County Indianola plantation foundered at least in part because the blacks refugeed there during the war insisted on returning to networks of extended kin in Liberty County. In this and other decisions, "the women are the controlling spirits," according to Mary Jones. Before Charles and his wife, Eva, decided to move to New York City, they were looking for a good house servant; Mary suggested the freedwoman Tenah, but then acknowledged that Tenah's insistence on bringing along her expanding family could be "a burden in town."[41]

When Sam (now Sam Roberts) came back to Monte Video to claim his wife, Sue, their former mistress argued against it, reminding Sue of "Sam's want of fidelity to her, and the unjust and unkind manner in which he had often treated her." But despite so much work to be done—the washing of clothes and cutting of rice—Sue insisted on leaving and taking her niece Elizabeth. Mary Jones said if they were going to go, they must go immediately. And so when the white woman urged Sue to return "if she was ever in want or ill-treated," the freedwoman replied, "No Ma'am, I'll never come back, for you told me to go"—in this "saucy way," according to Jones, "perverting my remark." Mothers, brothers, and other kin periodically showed up at Monte Video to retrieve family members. And even when a family did stay put, their obligations to each other increasingly took precedence over the demands of their employer. On January 8, 1867, Jones noted of the freedman Gilbert, who soon after emancipation changed his last name from Jones to Lawson: "Gilbert will stay on his old terms, but withdraws Fanny and puts Harry and Little Abram in her place and puts his son Gilbert out to a trade. Cook Kate wants to be relieved of the heavy burden for two and wait on her husband."[42]

Two years after the end of the war, black households were still in flux, buffeted by unsettling political and economic forces. Some men and women appealed to local Freedmen's Bureau agents to help resolve family conflicts, many no doubt due to wartime upheaval; others indicative of the continued exploitation of black children by white men and women; and still others evidence of the timeless tensions between parents and children, husbands and wives. Freedmen's Bureau records contain details of many cases of black parents trying to regain custody of their children from whites who were holding them against their will, forcing them to work, and whipping or otherwise abusing them. But other complaints were less clear-cut. In February 1867, a Savannah bureau agent was dispatched to investigate the case of the freedwoman Dimock Johnson. She was trying to recover her daughter and son who, she charged, had been bound out to a white planter by a black man named Rand. Rand was the father of her son, but Rand and Dimock had not lived together for more than a decade, and therefore (Dimock claimed) he had no claim on his son, or on the girl, Dimock's daughter by another man.[43]

Few bureau officials were inclined or equipped to deal with sorting out relations among freedpeople's families, complicated as those relations often were by separations over long distances and periods of time. Around the time that Mary Jones was complaining of workers' kin ties, Antoinette and Abner Hargrave, a married couple nearby, were facing a crisis in their relations with each other. Antoinette appealed to the local bureau agent, Elias Yulee, and charged that her husband was abusing her and their children. Yulee told the woman that he would not look into the case until she had paid a $1 fee up front. In the meantime, Abner had taken into his possession four of their children, plus a cow, two hogs, and a wagon that his wife said was a gift from her father. Over the next few weeks, the Hargraves exasperated Yulee no end. Shortly after lodging her first complaint, Antoinette returned to the agent and "begged him off, & went lovingly home with [her husband]." In an endless cycle—a "*chronic* one*," in Yulee's words—the couple would separate and then reconcile shortly thereafter. Yulee was uncertain whether or not their problems fell within his purview; after all, he told his superior, Abner was entitled to exercise his authority over his family: "the beating of his children, not being beyond the law, I could not legally prohibit or I would be interfering with his paternal rights and duties." Moreover, the husband possessed admirable qualities; he was an energetic and hardworking fellow, if "rather violent in temper," and had to reckon with a "moody" wife who was "unwilling to work and [leading] his children into idle habits." Although Antoinette might be entitled to her wagon and livestock, she was not entitled to her children, in Yulee's view. And besides, the couple was trying his patience by failing to pay the stipulated fee of $1 per hearing. He decided to wash his hands of the whole affair.[44]

Family-reconstitution efforts help to account for the presence of large numbers of black people on rural back roads and footpaths for several years after the war. For whites accustomed to monitoring the movements of slaves so rigidly, the mere sight of an unfamiliar black person on a public thoroughfare could be infuriating. On a road near Riceboro, Liberty County, in February 1867, two young white men confronted a freedman,

Fortune James, and demanded to know where he was going, calling him "a damned black son of a bitch." James replied, "No where Sir," but the two white men attacked him, one striking him over the head and shoulders with a whip, the other threatening him with first a rifle and then a knife, and finally throwing a two-pound weight at him. Escaping with his life, James filed a complaint with a local Freedmen's Bureau agent.[45]

James's two assailants were Dunwody Jones, Mary Jones's twenty-five-year-old nephew, and thirty-year-old James Ross, also a resident of Liberty County. After service in the army—fighting Yankees, searching for Confederate deserters, guarding prisoners at Andersonville—Dunwody found himself at loose ends, reduced to running errands for his aunt Mary and trying to adjust to civilian life as a planter of modest means. Ross had enlisted early in the war as a private, but received a promotion to the rank of second lieutenant a year later. He was court-martialed in 1863 and, rather than stand trial, resigned. His superior officer described him this way: "Lieutenant Ross is under thirty years of age and by reason of his habits of intemperance, in which he cannot or will not control himself, *is wholly unfit and incompetent* to be an officer in the Confederate States army." Shortly thereafter Ross reenlisted in an independent cavalry unit. Sherman's men captured him in Liberty County in December 1864, and he spent the rest of the war in a federal prisoner of war camp in Maryland.[46]

At the hearing, Fortune James testified against the two men, prompting Jones to deny the charges and, in front of the bureau agent, scream at the black man, "Don't contradict me again or I'll put a ball in your head *now!*" And Ross too threatened James "that if you ever meet me in the road, or attempt to speak to me I'll plant a load of shot in you." The night of the hearing, Ross, Dunwody Jones, and a third white man, Charles Jones, assaulted another black man, Stuart Screven, whom they had encountered traveling along the Sunbury Mail Road. (This Charles Jones, twenty-three, was another cousin of Dunwody's, a CSA veteran, and stepson of the planter Thomas King of Liberty County.) They told Screven that they were "only 'funning' with" him, and indeed "they all laughed & were amused at his alarm." These young Confederate veterans were "knocking about the country" and tormenting black people traveling through the countryside.[47]

Bureau agents were too few to prevent random attacks on blacks throughout the lowcountry. Similarly, duplicitous planters also largely eluded the control of bureau officials. In the fall of 1866, Esther W. Douglass and Frances Littlefield returned to the Ogeechee district, where "the colored people welcomed us joyfully," alerted to the teachers' arrival because "Uncle Jack had seen us (though no word had been sent) in a *vision*." The welcoming party bore gifts of rice, peanuts, eggs, and potatoes. At the beginning of 1867, the people on Wild Horn plantation had signed a contract that allowed them to reserve a dwelling for the teachers—a stipulation the landowner, William Burroughs ("Mr. Rebel"), reluctantly agreed to. But as soon as the contract was signed, Burroughs evicted the two teachers. The freedpeople believed that the women represented a threat to the white man's authority; literacy would protect them from fraudulent settlements at the end of the year. The teachers prepared to leave.[48]

Their second season of teaching had inspired the two to be more outspoken in their condemnation of the credit system coming into favor with white planters in the Ogeechee district. Wrote Douglass of the annual settlement in December 1866: "Injustice and oppression are on every side & I do not see how these people can ever have any of their own." She summarized the cruel bargain: "They raise the rice that fills the pocket books of those in charge of the plantations but are told that the rations have taken even more than their share of the crop and so the next year begins with a debt." Plantation merchants were charging two times as much as supplies cost in Savannah. Planters routinely drove off workers after the harvest without paying them. And in one case, a landowner, sitting astride his horse and towering over a group of workers, flashed a roll of bills and promised to pay the men for loading a flatboat full of rice. When the work was finished, he turned and galloped away, yelling back to them, "Now you may whistle for your pay." No wonder, then, that many people did not want to sign a contract, for "they do not get anything but a little corn & meat for their year's work."[49]

Still, planters throughout the lowcountry experimented with a variety of contracts during the months and years after the war. In March, while Douglass and Littlefield were taking their leave of the Ogeechee (they had accepted new teaching assignments on Daufuskie Island, South Carolina), Louis Manigault decided to survey his family's Savannah River plantations on Argyle Island. Like other planters, he was eager to rent out rice lands that lay barren and ruined after the war, and he offered a deal to George P. Harrison, a neighbor. Harrison, a brigadier general in the CSA army and now Chatham County's representative to the state legislature, had taken over a number of plantations recently. In the spring of 1867, he was operating one, Monteith, with a "chain gang" of black men, punishing the recalcitrant ones by putting them in stocks. In agreeing to rent the

Argyle lands, Harrison said that he would not live on the island, but he would contract with five black foremen, four of whom were former Manigault slaves, to oversee daily operations on Gowrie and Hermitage. Harrison made little attempt to keep track of the plantation workers, noting that many of the men could pick up day jobs up and down the river, and that "a Negro frequently worked a few weeks on one place & changed locality with another in this way preventing being bound down to the same Plantation all year round." The contract signed by his workers revealed the relatively lax oversight favored by this absentee planter: "Little or no intercourse is held between Gen'l Harrison and the Mass of the Negroes, & provided the work is performed it is immaterial what Hands are employed the same or others."[50]

On March 22 Louis traveled west from Savannah, past the ruins of the Charleston and Savannah Railroad and the charred remains of barns, threshing mills, and houses torched by Sherman's soldiers. Accompanied by Harrison, Manigault found Gowrie plantation flooded by a recent freshet, the waters streaming through a broken trunk. Manigault pinned the blame on a former slave, a carpenter, saying he was guilty of "negligence and most likely malice" in not repairing the trunk sooner. Surveying the desolate area, once a "Village" but now a "wilderness," Manigault noted the loss of his outbuildings, including a kitchen and a stable, both built just before the war, and the burned-out rice pounding mill, also destroyed by Sherman's troops. Freedpeople had dismantled the buildings and sold every last brick in Savannah (for a total of $5), and had also disposed of all the parts of the steam-operated rice thresher, including anything made of iron. The bridges around the island they had ripped apart and used for firewood.[51]

Manigault was surprised to see so many of his former slaves on the island; he noted that just the day before he arrived, "Currie Binah," one of the original slaves his father, Charles, had purchased for Gowrie thirty-four years earlier, had died. On his list of "our former Negroes" was Nancy Hunt, wife of John, now a foreman for Harrison, and Nancy's brother Abel. Wrote Manigault next to Abel's name: "once almost crazy, after effects of Cholera," referring to the young man's fit of grief soon after he and his extended family were brought to the plantation in 1854. But the planter's conversations with people he had known for many years were now painfully awkward: "That former mutual & pleasing feeling of Master towards Slave and vice versa is now as a dream of the past." The women to whom he had formerly presented earrings, kerchiefs, shoes, and trinkets would now not even deign to acknowledge him as he passed their quarters. While the freedpeople on Argyle Island were piecing together a meager existence the best they could, Manigault mourned for the antebellum world he had lost. On his way back to Savannah he discovered that the black man who had driven him around the place "had stolen nearly every thing I had in the buggy, but I have never thought it worth my while to mention it to the General, as I have no doubt he has from his contact with Negroes annoyance enough."[52]

Like his neighbors, Louis Manigault professed shock that the crumbling of the old plantation order was so swift, so complete. He had apparently forgotten that prewar Argyle Island was no idyllic land of happy, healthy slaves. And so his lament for "That former mutual & pleasing feeling of Master towards Slave and vice versa" had a disingenuous, if not self-deluded, ring about it. The hard reality was that black men and women were laboring to reestablish family ties, to make a living on their own, and to participate fully in the civic life of the postbellum world. Two years after the war's end, freedpeople were poised to take advantage of new opportunities in the political realm in a way that would doubly confound their former masters and mistresses. For these whites, a dream of the past settled uneasily over the troubled lowcountry of the present.

CHAPTER TWELVE

To Have a Big Meeting, a Big Shooting, or Big Blood

W HILE LOUIS MANIGAULT was making his sentimental journey to Argyle Island, Congress was in the process of passing major military reconstruction legislation over the president's veto. By March 23, 1867, the Radicals had halted President Johnson's process of restoring the South to its essential antebellum political-economic configuration, and substituted their own plan of Reconstruction. Passed on March 2, An Act to Provide for the More Efficient Government of the Rebel States applied to all the former Confederate states with the exception of Tennessee; its centerpiece was the enfranchisement of black men. Since most northern states did not grant their black residents this right, the provision carried with it more than a whiff of hypocrisy. Still, many congressmen believed that, armed with the ballot, blacks could do their own work of Reconstruction: as voters, freedmen could elect lawmakers sympathetic to their plight (thereby protecting themselves against state-sanctioned violence) while at the same time laying the foundation of a nascent southern Republican Party. In the process black voters would relieve Congress and northern taxpayers of any responsibility for their welfare; "the ballot will finish the negro question . . . the ballot is the freedman's Moses," in the words of Senator Richard Yates of Illinois.[1]

The March 2 act and a supplementary law passed three weeks later mandated that new southern state constitutions be drawn up by special conventions whose delegates would be chosen by black voters and a reduced electorate of whites. Excluded from this latter group were men who had taken an oath of allegiance to the Union before the war and then served in an official CSA capacity during the war. Ordinary soldiers would thus be eligible to vote, along with CSA leaders who had not held a federal post before 1861. Congress ordered that the new state constitutions must enact universal manhood suffrage and ratify the Fourteenth Amendment. Finally, the South was divided into five districts, each under the authority of a military commander who would oversee voter registration and elections. General John Pope assumed authority in the Third Military District, which consisted of Georgia, Florida, and Alabama.[2]

These revolutionary measures ignited a firestorm of political organizing and speechifying in Savannah and the lowcountry. Between March 18 and April 1, two Republican-sponsored outdoor mass rallies in the city provided a forum for leaders of divergent factions now emerging from the crucible of black enfranchisement—factions that could not be reduced to a simple contest between blacks and whites, Northerners and Southerners, Republicans and Democrats. Among the speakers appearing at one or both rallies were four whites, Amherst W. Stone, Dr. Louis Falligant, Dr. Joseph W. Clift, and Dr. James J. Waring, and three prominent black leaders, James Porter and the Reverends Tunis G. Campbell and James M. Simms. The three-and-a-half-hour meeting held on April 1 in Chippewa Square attracted an audience estimated at seven thousand white and black men, women, and children, a sure sign that the tasks at hand—choosing delegates to the new state constitutional convention mandated by Radical Reconstruction and scheduled for December, and building the Republican Party in the lowcountry—would produce spectacles as much as partisan-political organizing. The crush of the immense crowd, the appearance of black and white men on the same platform: certainly a new day was dawning for all of Savannah.[3]

The speakers limned the broad outlines of political conflicts to come. Stone, a former resident of Atlanta and a Unionist during the war, spoke for those native southern white Republicans who wished to distance themselves from both Confederate diehards and from freedpeople demanding full and equal rights. His views helped to explain the existence of segregated black and white Union League clubs in Savannah and elsewhere in Georgia. Acknowledging that black men were in the process of gaining some measure of political influence, Stone said that "they must, however, prove themselves worthy of this great liberty." To the blacks who claimed they could not get justice from the courts he advised, "It was not the fault of the Courts that they lose their rights, but because they neglected to employ counsel." Judges would eventually prove fair, he predicted, but of necessity blacks "must make allowance for the prejudices of the [white] people."[4]

Falligant, a Savannah native and physician who had been educated in the North, was a former Confederate captain and aide to Argyle Island lessee General George P. Harrison. In the coming months he would take a lead in establishing so-called Colored Clubs that sought (and failed) to harness the electoral power of blacks in support of the self-interests of the former rebels. Falligant and others recapitulated antebellum arguments that black people must place their well-being in the hands of paternalistic white men. He also offered a novel argument for why the former slaves should now trust him and other former Confederates. Unrepentant about his support for the southern cause, Falligant said that the war had caused a "revolution, the first shot of which was the death-knell of slavery." By provoking war, planters could at least indirectly take credit for the abolition of slavery, and for that all black people should be grateful.[5]

Joseph Clift, a Harvard-educated Union army surgeon, had settled in Savannah after the war. Like other newcomers, he considered himself uniquely influential among the freedpeople: "The colored people in this Congressional district will vote for me for almost anything and many of the whites also," he bragged to American Missionary Association headquarters in April. Clift urged blacks to work hard and deposit their money in the Freedman's Bank. In contrast, James J. Waring declared his willingness to support the most basic struggles of black people. He said that he had foreseen "the very state of things now sought to be remedied by this assemblage, the war between capital and labor. Then labor was controlled and owned by capital; now labor is free and antagonistic to capital, and this antagonism will bring about good results." As a wealthy planter and avid speculator in real estate, Waring demonstrated that a person's ideological bent could not necessarily be inferred from color, income, or place of birth.[6]

At the rallies, Porter, Campbell, and Simms came to the fore as black leaders of this new world. All three invoked the hand of God during these perilous times, but none relied on the rhetorical indirection that had been the hallmark of black preachers before the war. Porter praised God for delivering the slaves from bondage, and went on to reject the idea of an "educated suffrage" (which would considerably diminish the number of black voters, many of whom were illiterate), declaring, "God deals justice to all, irrespective of race, color, or intelligence." Campbell claimed that "today his people stand up on the same footing as white men," exhorting his listeners to elect "only the best qualified, regardless of color." Of the three men, James Simms ("being loudly called for" at the April 1 meeting) offered the most pointed comments. The *Republican*, edited by John Hayes (still allied, though uneasily, with the Republican Party), gave this version of the speech:

> The white race had never understood or known us perfectly; because we have always dissimulated. This was a natural result of tyranny—of the tyranny of slavery. We are now free, but we are under no obligation to any man or set of men North or South. To God we owe our deliverance, and to Him be all the praise. We will support good men. We will elect men in our Municipal, State, and Federal relations, who are loyal, true, and tried. On short probation we will trust the Mayor and policemen, for we want it to be understood here and now that we want no bigoted Mayor and no brutal policemen; but we mean to have black aldermen and white aldermen, black policemen and white policemen, and we will mix the colors up like 'rum and [mo]lasses.' We will send no man to congress who is not loyal and who is not blind to color. When you go to the polls to vote be sure that your squad is commanded by a colored corporal, and one who can call the roll.

The white-supremacist *Savannah Daily Herald* transcribed the same speech this way:

> The white man has never known us perfectly. We have acted deceitfully, like other people similarly circumstanced would not. We must elect men who have our prosperity at heart. We intend to elect colored men for aldermen, and to have colored policemen. We will take them on probation, and if they do not do right, we will turn them out. We intend to have no more brutal policemen nor besotted Mayors. White and black shall constitute our police. We shall send to Congress men who are loyal, and, so help me God, I will vote for no man to represent me in Congress who is not blind to color. Don't trust a white man, for he is treacherous. It is safer to trust your own color. You've proved white men unworthy of trust, with but very few exceptions.

A reporter for the New Orleans *Tribune* (established in 1864 as the country's first daily black newspaper) offered yet another version of the speech:

> James Simms, a colored man, said that [whites] knew nothing of his race. Under the old system Negroes were compelled to use dissimula-

tion towards their masters. Now, for the first time, he could tell them the truth.

Colored men are not fools. They knew enough to fight right and they will vote right. I wish the white people to understand distinctly that we will not elect a Rebel Mayor or have any more *brutal policemen*.

Offices should be filled by both white and colored men who are capable of serving with honor. I would have white and colored alder-men and white and colored policemen and the sooner people know it the better. Some people might be surprised to see white and colored men working shoulder to shoulder in the political field—I am not.

The reporter noted, "It is impossible to describe the intense enthusiasm exhibited by the speaker and the proud look of triumph with which he alluded to the great change within a few years"—specifically, the differ-ence in circumstances between his brother Thomas, "the great fugitive, brought from Boston and dragged through the streets of Savannah to jail"—and himself, "introduced by a Southern gentleman to address a political gathering." (James was not in the habit of mentioning Thomas in his speeches.) The reporter concluded by noting James's "clear musi-cal voice, distinct enunciation and elegant style of delivery" which "impressed . . . and astonished" his listeners.[7]

Over the next few weeks Clift and Simms organized a petition drive that gathered five hundred signatures of black residents, calling for the removal of the mayor and aldermen "on the ground of malfeasance of office, and injustice to the colored people who were arraigned at the courts." In response, John Hayes lamented the fragmenting of Unionist political strength: "To us it is positively painful to witness the bristling armor in which the various little clans and cliques are clothing themselves as if preparing to enter a gladiatorial contest. Matters are strangely and sadly mixed."[8]

In accordance with the congressional Reconstruction acts, General Pope appointed a three-man registration board (consisting of two whites and one black) for each of Georgia's senatorial districts. As registrar of Savannah he named Clift, who within a few weeks would marry Julia Marshall, the AMA music teacher. For the second district Pope appointed two white men and Tunis G. Campbell. In December 1866, Campbell had left St. Catherines Island and founded a new colony in McIntosh County, renting land from Charles H. Hopkins. A wealthy planter who owned more than one hundred slaves yet opposed seces-sion, Hopkins would become active in the emerging lowcountry Republican Party. He rented Campbell his Belle Ville plantation in a deal that required the colony to pay regular cash installments toward the $15,000 purchase price. In relocating to McIntosh County, Campbell took with him people who had constituted the remnants of his St. Catherines settlement, such as Toby Maxwell, who were disillusioned with the contracts they had made with whites on the islands. The surnames of other Belle Ville colonists suggest many were former slaves of the large coastal planters—Spalding, Bryan, Bennett, Pinckney, and also Hopkins.[9]

On March 4, Toby Maxwell and "other Citizens, Farmers, & Laborers of Belle Ville, McIntosh County, Georgia" formed the Belle Ville Farmers Association, with Tunis G. Campbell as president, his son Tunis Jr. as vice president, and adopted son Edward E. Howard recording and corresponding secretary. Maxwell assumed the position of fence-viewer. Among the other officers were constable, road-master, "janitor of buildings," market inspector ("to see meats or vegetables are disposed for sale"), and hog and cattle overseer. In the spring of 1867, with Tillson out of the way, Campbell managed to convince the new Freedmen's Bureau regional head, J. Murray Hoag, to advance Belle Ville government-issued rations. By the summer a bureau agent was reporting that the colonists were "contented and hopeful of the future," with "a fine crop of corn and cotton" that promised them a measure of self-sufficiency by the fall.[10]

Whites had watched with alarm as Campbell set about organizing a Belle Ville militia, a rumored " 'secret order' of colored people" on the coast. Yet for all his efforts at "drilling, uniforming, [and] keeping up" such an organization, Campbell's intentions were clearly more political than military. Before long Mary Jones and her neighbors were taking note of his organizing activities as he traveled around the countryside, drawing in the curious with magic lantern shows and financing his budding political career with $1 admission fees. In April he held "a great mass meeting (political) of the freedmen" at Newport Church. "I am told there never was such a turnout in this county," Jones wrote to her daughter Mary. "They were addressed by Rev. Campbell [who] . . . urged them to hold fast to the Radicals and give the democrats a wide berth. This is the onward progress to (I fear) a war of races." What Jones saw as evidence of an impending race war, Campbell considered good politics. In May he served as a delegate to the Georgia Education (formerly Equal Rights and Education) Association, and the following month he attended an African Methodist Episcopal Church convention in Augusta.[11]

Campbell was among the lowcountry representatives to the first Georgia Republican state convention, held in Atlanta on July 4. Other delegates and their alternates representing Savannah were among the founding members of the Chatham County Republican Party; these included Amherst W. Stone, James J. Waring, Charles H. Hopkins, Joseph W. Clift, James Porter, James Simms, William Pollard, Ulysses L. Houston, Jackson Sheftall, Charles DeLaMotta, and Louis B. Toomer. In Savannah, the K. S. Baker Council No. 9, Union League of America, celebrated Independence Day with a parade. A highlight was the presentation of a "beautiful banner" by Louisa McIntosh on behalf of the "colored ladies" who had embroidered the flag on blue silk, with borders of gold fringe. Nevertheless, the *Republican* recorded the day's festivities by dwelling upon "the gross and illiterate harangues of the illiterate and would-be Moses of the colored race—Aaron Bradley": "This insolent brawler and disturber of the public peace, as usual, indulged in the worst kind of incendiary language." Not to be outdone, the *Daily Herald* called Bradley "this narrow-minded colored pettifogger," full of "donkey stupidity." By this time, 3,091 blacks and 2,240 whites had registered to vote in Savannah. Disenfranchised for the first time in their lives, a group of white leaders, including Judge William Law, George A. Mercer, Edward C. Anderson, Philip M. Russell Sr. and his son Levi, and Richard D. Arnold, marked the occasion by placing an ad in the *Daily Herald* protesting the fact they were not allowed to register, even though they had received personal pardons from President Johnson two years before.[12]

Bradley appealed to his own constituency, which included not only field hands on the surrounding rice plantations, but also black laborers in the city. In his role as black politician, he was unique in postwar Savannah, for he was not a preacher, nor did he lay claim to religious authority of any kind. His secular approach to politicking, combined with his outsider status, failed to win him many allies among equally ambitious and more established lowcountry black leaders. Bradley eschewed references to God or Divine Providence in favor of quotations from the Constitution or any of numerous other laws or regulations from the federal level on down to municipal statutes. At one point he helped coordinate an appeal sent to Freedmen's Bureau officials on behalf of the two hundred "colored laborers of the city of Savannah" protesting a new tax on "porters" and "stewards." The petitioners pointed out that the workers targeted by this tax "had no voice in enacting it": "notwithstanding 'all just laws derive their powers from the consent of the governed.'" Furthermore, many laboring men slapped with the tax were not porters or stewards at all, but common laborers legally exempt from such fees. The petitioners, with Bradley listed as their attorney, went on to quote Section 14 of the

Freedmen's Bureau Bill of July 11, 1866, and to call for the bureau to "extend military protection" to the black laboring classes, now faced with "*Starvation* and Threatened outrage" from the mayor of the city. In presenting himself as an advocate for illiterate rural and urban workers, and in meeting his adversaries head-to-head on the rule of law, Bradley positioned himself as a force to be reckoned with in future political contests.[13]

Over the next few weeks, the campaign for the upcoming state constitutional convention delegates became ever more divisive, as black and white leaders scrambled for the votes of black men, a majority of the new electorate. A number of black delegates to the Fourth of July Republican meeting remained in Atlanta to plot strategy for the next few months, a gathering coordinated by the Reverend Henry M. Turner. Born to free black parents in South Carolina, Turner was a minister in the African Methodist Episcopal Church and the first black U.S. Army chaplain, attached to the First United States Colored Troops in 1863. Representing a total of forty counties, the delegates convened for a day to hear Turner introduce a "dialogue" to be used as a means of organizing black voters. Campbell and Turner demonstrated the dialogue, with Turner taking the part of "the Freedman" asking questions and Campbell, "the true Republican," supplying the answers.[14]

Turner outlined an ambitious statewide effort that would take organizers into "our country churches, societies, leagues, clubs, balls, picnics, and all other gatherings, allowing one man to sit back in the audience and then read the questions and the other to stand up in the pulpit or some conspicuous part of the house and read the answers." Focusing on black men's responsibility to vote the Republican ticket, this political catechism could be memorized by "the uneducated masses," according to Turner. They could then recite it aloud before crowds all over the state. Indeed, Republican organizers quickly penetrated even remote rural counties, for planters were soon complaining that the registration drive interfered with a critical stage of cotton growing: weeding the crop. Political activities had thus "diverted the minds of the colored citizens from those rustic pursuits for which they are so distinguished, and which a base materialism values far above the right to vote," in the words of a *New York Times* reporter. At a time when black men, women, and children were supposed to be hard at work, chopping grass in the fields, they were listening instead to stump speeches and partaking of political instruction at all hours of the day and night.[15]

As Simms and Campbell embraced a newly inclusive political

process, they grew skeptical of what they considered Bradley's outrageous personal style and reckless rhetoric. And Bradley's successful appeal to rice hands throughout the coastal region threatened to spark a backlash among white officials, a reaction that might hamper black organizing efforts more generally. Indeed, some observers were drawing a distinction between "the country people" and the "conservative city colored people" (this latter group was also referred to as "the better class of blacks"). In mid-September the Colored Union League of Savannah denounced Bradley's plans to hold a mass outdoor meeting that would draw voters from the surrounding Effingham and Bryan counties, as well as Chatham. As reported by the *Republican*, the league, through its president, Jackson Brand, "repudiated" the "sentiments of the wiseacre and leading spirit of this proposed meeting, Aaron Alpeoria Bradley." Writing on behalf of the league, Brand charged that the attorney had "transcended the bounds of propriety, and brought reproach upon this council and the respectable colored men of this city." The council demanded Bradley's resignation as recording secretary, a position he had held for only a month.[16]

The circumstances surrounding the upcoming gathering, which Bradley called a "confiscation-homestead meeting," help to explain the efforts of league members to distance themselves from the irrepressible attorney. Throughout September, rumors flew that General Pope would capitulate to Bradley's recent tirades against the disloyal mayor and aldermen by removing all of the city officers and installing new ones. Bradley had spent days distributing posters announcing the meeting scheduled for Monday, September 30, at 11 a.m. in Chippewa Square. He also publicized his campaign platform, now that he had declared his candidacy for the constitutional convention: suffrage for "all blacks and poor white persons," whether or not they possessed property or literacy skills; an eight-hour workday, with overtime pay; and a 10 percent reduction in rents throughout the city. By this time Bradley faced the combined opposition of the white and black Union Clubs, the U.S. military and Freedmen's Bureau, and the mayor. But he was also in his element as brash truth-sayer, and he was determined to forge ahead with his plans for a mass rally. Rumor had it he said "that he intended to have a big meeting, a big shooting or big blood."[17]

Tensions escalated over the weekend, when several hundred black men, women, and children streamed in from the surrounding countryside. The women brought enough provisions for a two-day stay, and the men bore "clubs, or sharpened ramrods, or bars of iron, or sections of gaspipes, converted into canes." Though disenfranchised, mothers, wives, and sisters lent their support—in their numbers and their vocalizing—to the campaign on behalf of black political power. Even taking into account the *Daily Herald*'s bent toward melodrama, it was clear that the sight was spectacular: "the country negroes came in gangs, one large party armed with muskets, and parading through the streets in imitation of Sherman."[18]

On Monday morning, a formidable array of armed men ringed Chippewa Square: virtually the entire Savannah police force, along with U.S. troops and the mayor, sheriff, and other city officials. As a campaign rally, the meeting proved anticlimactic, for several advertised speakers failed to materialize and confusion mounted over who would share the convention delegate ticket with Bradley. He was in the process of passing the hat to recoup his expenses for the meeting when a black man (described by the *News and Herald* as "a Conservative Savannah negro") breached a line of bodyguards and threatened him, setting off a fight. At that point the combined military and police forces moved in, providing what some observers considered "a gratifying sight": "the company of blue-coats and a company of grey-coats, side by side, acting without the least disagreement." If nothing else, Bradley had brought U.S. troops and Savannah police together in common cause. The *Republican* later claimed these forces "prevented one of the bloodiest riots since the days of the New Orleans and Memphis massacres."[19]

The police arrested forty black men on charges of carrying concealed weapons and inciting a riot. Marched to the nearby army barracks, the prisoners inspired another predictable round of disturbances; two black women, Amelia Thompson and Maria Habersham, were later convicted and fined for "exciting conduct." The next morning the procession of prisoners again attracted a loud crowd, which the men then played to: Jim Habersham, arrested for "riotous conduct," called out defiantly for his rights, and Jim Harris, from Augusta, proclaimed his willingness to die for Aaron Bradley.[20]

Confusion reigned during the last month before the October 29–November 2 elections, as individual candidates tried to position themselves on ad hoc campaign tickets. In some cases, mass meetings were called; well-known speakers advertised; platform scaffolding erected; and patriotic bunting displayed—only to have a gathering cancelled at the last minute. Meanwhile, sidelined elites could not resist excoriating the turncoat white Republicans in their midst. After reading an anonymous letter to the *Daily Herald* labeling him a "Black Republican," James J.

Waring confronted the editor of the paper and extracted from him the name of the slanderer—Richard Arnold. Within a few days, Arnold had issued a public retraction, claiming his letter was "designed purely and solely for a political purpose," and not as a personal insult. Waring accepted the apology, but this was just the first volley in what would become a protracted feud between the two.[21]

Blacks, too, attacked other men of their color who did not adhere to what they considered a politics of group self-interest, in this case the Republican cause. On October 17, three freedmen stripped Aaron Hurt of his clothing, cut his hair, and smeared his body with hot tar and feathers. Hurt, a black carpenter from Columbus and an itinerant speaker paid by the Democratic Party, later said one of his assailants yelled, "—— —— you, I want to let you know that no Democrat will speak here." They had robbed him of his money, $3.50, as well as all his clothes. One of the accused attackers later confessed, saying, "We decided that it would not do to have an upcountry freedman come and intrude upon us that way." The following day the city council passed an ordinance stipulating that the mayor must approve in writing any assemblies after sundown, a measure clearly designed to thwart black voters' plans for nighttime meetings. Mayor Anderson was already on record denouncing torchlight processions "during the present excited state of the public mind" as conducive to "riot and conflagration."[22]

On October 21, a number of prominent leaders made a bid for the votes of field-workers when they agreed to share the platform with Bradley at a rally on the Parade Ground behind Forsyth Park. Among the participants were Joseph W. Clift, along with his younger brother Walter (a Republican activist attorney recently arrived in the city and "radical up to the handle"), Charles H. Hopkins, and Amherst W. Stone. Bradley called for support from "all Loyal League Men, Republican Clubs, and Fire and Axe Companies," indicating that this last category of black men was acting as a political group. Yet Bradley drew his greatest support from rural blacks who found his angry demand for land redistribution enormously compelling. At the meeting was a fine show of his constituents, men and women who had traveled to Savannah by steamers and plantation boats from the Georgia and South Carolina sides of the Savannah River.[23]

Beginning on October 29, the three-day election to choose eight delegates to the constitutional convention representing the state's First Senatorial District (Chatham, Bryan, and Effingham counties) attracted a total of 3,509 voters. Confiding to his diary, the attorney George Mercer con-

demned "this solemn farce of an election," which brought into the city so
many blacks from the surrounding countryside, including, apparently,
areas of South Carolina. Captain Henry C. Brandt of the Freedmen's
Bureau tried to convince the out-of-state would-be voters of their error,
without much success. Mercer sneered at the sight of "these ignorant
semi-savages clothed with a power which rightfully belongs only to the
wise and good." Elected were the white Northerners Asa L. Harris, Walter Clift, and Isaac Seeley (the three had recently arrived in Georgia from
Vermont, Massachusetts, and New York, respectively), and native white
Southerners Charles H. Hopkins, the Belle Ville colony's landlord;
W. H. D. Reynolds, and James Stewart. The African-American delegates
were Aaron A. Bradley and Moses H. Bentley.[24]

The overwhelmingly black electorate from the Second Senatorial District (Liberty, Tatnall, and McIntosh counties) sent as their representatives the Reverends Tunis G. Campbell and William A. Golding. As early
as 1865 Golding, a former slave, had complained to the Freedmen's
Bureau, "We are a working class of people and we are willing and
desirous to work for a fair compensation. But to return to work upon the
terms that are at present offered to us, would be we think going back to
the state of slavery." In total, the convention included 169 delegates, 37 of
them black.[25]

On December 9, delegates met in Atlanta and began their delibera-
tions, which lasted for three months. The convention approved a constitution that provided for the enfranchisement of black men, established a
public school system for white and black children (local authorities
would decide whether or not to segregate facilities), outlawed whipping
as a punishment for crime, and abolished imprisonment for debt (Campbell had offered the initial resolution). Not surprisingly for a convention
dominated by upcountry whites, delegates did not consider the issue of
redistributing land to the freedpeople. A majority of the white men voted
to defer action on a resolution that blacks be accorded equal treatment on
public transportation, and they also voted against a clause that would
have specifically guaranteed blacks the right to hold elective office. Black
delegates acquiesced in this last move, presumably on the assumption
that citizenship (signified by suffrage) by definition included the right to
run for office. Voters would ratify the document and elect representatives
to a reconstructed state legislature the following April.[26]

Whites at the convention aimed to cut short Aaron Bradley's budding
political career, and, with the help of blacks fearful of guilt by association,
they expelled him from the convention on February 12. Delegates exam-

ined documents showing that in 1856, officials in Suffolk County, Massachusetts, had revoked his attorney's license "for contempt of court and malpractice." Other documents purported to show that in 1861, a Brooklyn court had sentenced him to prison for two years for "seduction." Bradley denied both charges—whether the second was true or not is unknown—and launched a counteroffensive by claiming that many of the other delegates were themselves guilty of sexual offenses, including any former slaveholders in attendance who had abused their female slaves. Although it is clear that the expulsion of Bradley for past convictions, real or otherwise, had no basis in law or custom, the delegates voted unanimously "That Aaron A. Bradley, for gross insults offered to this Convention and its members thereof, be forthwith expelled from his seat in this body."[27]

Bradley's fate at the hands of the convention testifies to the outright hostility among many white Republicans, both Northerners and upcountry Georgians, toward the political demands of freedpeople. Though black voters formed the base of the emerging, if struggling, southern Republican Party, they also represented a threat to the tenets of white supremacy that a majority of whites, regardless of party, held sacred. In the fall of 1867, the letter writer "E. Y." (probably Elias Yulee, the citizen Freedmen's Bureau agent from Liberty County) wrote a piece for the Savannah *News and Herald,* asserting that the Republican Party was like a snake trying to swallow a whole catfish (that is, the black electorate), which, by extending its spiky fins, prevented the snake from either swallowing it or regurgitating it: "Such is the negro in the jaws of the party. They cannot get him up or down, and he is bound to kill them." The writer warned that by allying themselves with black voters, white Republicans would engage in an act of self-destruction, leaving the freedman, "poor fellow," at the mercy of the former rebels.[28]

Spurned by the Atlanta convention, Bradley returned to Savannah, where he learned that federal officials had thwarted his ongoing campaign to remove Mayor Anderson from office. The charges against the mayor were straightforward enough: he served as judge and jury in his own court and routinely punished blacks merely for acting as free citizens, criminalizing political activity by calling it "riotous and disorderly conduct." Bradley argued that Anderson's "oppressive acts have reached a point at which our indurence [*sic*] fails to be a virtue in freemen. Are we yet Slaves or are we free American citizens?" In January the War Department held that since the mayor and city council members had taken an oath of loyalty to the Union, their actions were beyond the reach of the military commander of the district (now General George Meade, who had recently replaced Pope). The ruling granted Anderson license to continue harassing Bradley, with the implicit support of federal authorities. Unlike Tunis G. Campbell, the black attorney could claim no church affiliation, let alone formal religious authority, and he found himself increasingly alienated from Savannah blacks and dependent on the support of lowcountry rice workers.[29]

In contrast, Campbell faced little or no opposition from other aspiring black or white leaders among the freedpeople of McIntosh County. At the same time, his success among black voters masked the increasingly vulnerable condition of his Belle Ville settlement. The summer months had brought a plague of problems—torrential rains and the cotton worm, a deepening debt to the Freedmen's Bureau for rations, a bill for past rent due Hopkins, the expense of food to be purchased and stockpiled for the winter. At the end of November the local bureau agent, J. Murray Hoag, visited the colony, which included sixty-one adults and forty-seven children, and submitted a report to his superiors: "I have the honor to report the enterprise an entire failure." The crop for the year amounted to 7,500 pounds of cotton and 400 bushels of corn, not enough to keep the colony going. The labor force consisted primarily of extended family members who worked the land together. Toby Maxwell had grown 900 pounds of cotton and 107 bushels of corn with his family, which included the single men Anthony and Samuel Maxwell. The Maxwell clan was at the upper end of production; some individuals managed to eke out only 35 pounds of cotton and 6 bushels of corn. (The crops were marketed through a commercial house co-owned by relatives of Julian Hartridge, a wartime representative to the Confederate Congress.) Like the St. Catherines colonists, Belle Villeans found it almost impossible to sustain a self-supporting collective.[30]

The 1867 end-of-year reckoning brought renewed anger and disappointment to many field laborers, as they found themselves in debt to any number of whites—the Freedmen's Bureau, a landlord (northern or southern), a furnishing (supply) merchant. But the year's more than a hundred successive days of rain had proved devastating for many white landowners as well. In early 1868, one of them, Mary Jones, decided on "the closing up of my life at home," and left Liberty County forever. Arcadia remained unsold, and the workers at Monte Video had produced an end-of-year profit of only $90—the proceeds from one bale of cotton and 20 bushels of corn. An accumulation of other woes had finally taken a toll on the beleaguered fifty-nine-year-old widow; on her feet all day at Monte

Video, she contended not only with unscrupulous overseers and the periodic appearances of "Yankee Negro" speakers, but also with angry field hands and servants, some of whom had the temerity to sue her for back wages in Freedmen's Bureau court. An encounter with the local agent, Elias Yulee, disgusted her, as she tried to negotiate with workers whose minds had evidently "been poisoned by someone," she thought. Moreover, Jones's neighbors were renting land to blacks, a move she believed "very injurious to the best interest of the community."[31]

Jones considered living with her son Charles and his family, but a visit to their new home in New York in the summer of 1866 had left her unwell and depressed. Her brother John had recently moved to Griffin, Georgia, and would eventually settle in Atlanta; in the meantime he was urging his sister to counsel his son, her nephew Dunwody, who was now for some unstated reason "in great trouble." But in January 1868 she moved to New Orleans, where her daughter Mary Mallard and her family lived; within a year they would be joined by Mary Jones's son Joseph, the physician, and his wife and children. Like Savannah, New Orleans suffered from periodic epidemics of yellow fever; and the Louisiana city had the added liability of a city government that included black aldermen—a state of affairs that Mary Mallard considered "beyond endurance." But Mary Jones went and stayed, surviving less than a year and a half in her new home. She died in April 1869.[32]

IN EARLY 1868, not all whites in Savannah and its environs reckoned their progress in terms of bales of cotton and bushels of corn. On New Year's Day, American Missionary Association workers sponsored a grand celebration marking the dedication of Beach Institute, an impressive two-story, eight-room frame school building, constructed at a cost of $13,000. (The Freedmen's Bureau and Alfred E. Beach, publisher of *Scientific American*, had provided most of the funding.) Inscribed over the doorway to the new school, through which as many as six hundred black children passed each day, were the words KNOWLEDGE WITH VIRTUE. The nine teachers included eight white women and one black woman, Emily Jackson. (One of the few blacks to receive an AMA commission in the city schools, Jackson had traveled south in 1866 under the sponsorship of the New York Society of Friends.) Also dedicated that day was a new AMA mission home for teachers, a $3,000 structure located near the school, the association's declaration of independence from cramped quarters in boardinghouses run by "irritable Irishmen." The ceremony included an opening prayer and a short speech by James Simms, and appearances by visiting dignitaries. A state Freedmen's Bureau official, John R. Lewis, reminded the freedpeople and their children that they "were not thoroughly emancipated or free until they emancipated themselves from vice and immorality, and became educated and fit to enjoy the rights which had been conferred upon them." Conspicuous for their absence were the city's white clergy, who had been invited but failed to attend.[33]

AMA operations remained contentious within the new mission home and school. The recently arrived superintendent was twenty-seven-year-old Orlando Dimick, the son of a Lyme, New Hampshire, blacksmith. Four years earlier Dimick had been a resident of "Camp Sorghum," a prisoner of war camp in Columbia, South Carolina. He managed to escape in 1864. Three years later he accepted a commission from the AMA and, accompanied by his wife, began work in Savannah. Young and impatient, Dimick proved to be a reluctant administrator. He chafed under the mountains of paperwork—"these puzzles"—required by both the AMA and the Freedmen's Bureau; "I am not an accountant by birth or education," he wrote in February 1868. He scrambled to accommodate finicky teachers who insisted on importing graham crackers, biscuits, and barrels of beef from the North. The Savannah mission home functioned as a way station for teachers en route to points in Georgia and Florida, and these "transient boarders" undermined his already overtaxed budget. Adding insult to injury, one of the female wayfarers arrived one morning and lost no time accepting a ride in a closed carriage with a man who had already "proven himself a most unfit representation of northern virtue." Accountant, school superintendent, boardinghouse operator, enforcer of personal morality, and representative of northern ideals deep in the heart of the former Confederacy: the young man could barely bear the strain.[34]

Anxiously, Dimick tried to gather support from Savannah blacks (in the form of a "soliciting Committee"), but that effort foundered on the shoals of "the political excitements" of the fall of 1867. He thought it would be a good idea to hire Louis B. Toomer in order "to quiet jealousy by showing that we [are] not exclusive in our choice of teachers," but his superiors in New York told him AMA finances would not permit it. Once again small private schools were springing up, stubbornly, even in the shadow of the now-formidable Beach Institute. In early 1868, James Porter was operating an "English Grammar School" out of his residence. The inimitable Jane Deveaux averaged thirty-five in her school, which was in session from 9 a.m. to 2 p.m. every day but Saturday. P. M. Middleton used rooms in Second African Baptist, while J. W. Randolph held class in the AME parsonage. Hezekiah Brown, a newcomer from the North, with teaching experience at Lincoln University in Pennsylvania, received permission from the Reverend Ulysses L. Houston to use his residence for "Brown's School," which offered orthography, grammar, geography, arithmetic, philosophy, and "English branches generally."[35]

Other worries plagued Dimick as well: Vague threats against the AMA caused him to lose sleep worrying whether the association's wooden school buildings were insured against arson. One of the teachers, Harriet M. Haskell, a graduate of Mount Holyoke College, flatly refused his order that she write "begging letters" to potential northern donors, claiming that she had enough work to do, especially considering that "labor among the Freedmen is telling upon my nervous system." Sarah Jenness challenged Dimick at every turn, and he considered her "not only very trying, but even *dangerous* to some who have not strength to resist [her] power." Though only twenty-three, she had seen several superintendents—Magill, Cooley, and Pettibone—come and go. Jenness's refusal of a desk assignment in New York City—she told headquarters she was "well contented and happy" in Savannah—caused Dimick to panic; he wired the New York office: "Refuses to come what shall I do please telegraph."[36]

And finally, Cornelia A. Drake was spreading dissension among coworkers who considered her "harsh and unkind" in her view that blacks' suffering stemmed from their own "improvidence" and "thriftlessness." She was convinced that the free distribution of food and clothing "does more harm than *real* good." Drake had recently adopted an eight-year-old orphan, Rose, and was planning to send the little girl north, though she agreed with the other teachers that "it would be a pity she should just be put in somebody's kitchen with only servants for her associates."[37]

AMA teachers in Savannah were learning that even commodious new classrooms and quarters could not mitigate rivalries and personal resentments. At the same time, rural teachers continued to labor as "pioneers" left largely to their own devices. Sponsored by the New York Society of Friends, Matilda Nevins, a black woman, had come to Georgia from Massachusetts in 1866 and had started a school at Strathey Hall on McAllisters plantation, in the Ogeechee. (By early 1868 blacks there were calling for Esther Douglass and Frances Littlefield to return.) Hettie Sabattie, who had lived in Savannah before the war as a free woman, taught in a series of schools on the coast and the islands, beginning in 1865. Nevins and Sabattie depended largely on the support of local black communities that, like others in Georgia, contributed labor for building houses and raised money for teachers' salaries through fairs and other fundraisers.[38]

In February 1868, Ellen E. Adlington, a thirty-four-year-old white woman from Weymouth, Massachusetts, was setting up her classroom in a cotton gin house in Camden County. Though at times the site of personal transcendence, the building itself was a primitive affair, without a chimney or a stove. As a result pupils suffered from the cold when they were not choked by "a glorious smoke." When Adlington gave one of her older pupils his first lessons in joining letters to form a word, he said, "I shall have to stand up first and shiver before I write it." Adlington boarded with an Ohio-born planter, Virgil Hillyer, who had recently come south from New York with his family and aspired to a career in Republican politics. Not far away one of her colleagues, Abbie Howe, was teaching on Bell plantation, establishing temperance societies—Life Guard of Temperance for the adults, Bands of Hope for the children. Howe confessed to her superiors at AMA headquarters, "What a study these people are! Ever pleasing, disappointing and puzzling us—strange inconsistencies!"[39]

In rural areas and along the coast, no less than in Savannah, black schooling remained highly politicized. Without the means to hire Louis B. Toomer in the city, Dimick urged him to go 80 miles down the coast to Brunswick and open a school there, but he refused, saying that his wife and children preferred to stay in Savannah and he did not want to leave them. The request for a Brunswick teacher had come from the local Freedmen's Bureau agent, Lieutenant Douglas L. Risley of the Forty-second U.S. Infantry. Risley was convinced that Brunswick needed a person who would not only teach the ABCs, but also "instruct the adults in their *rights, privileges, and duties.*" He was looking for a discreet young black man, someone who could board with a black family, withstand the scorn of whites, and gain the respect of the freedpeople. However, in the late fall of 1867, he got much less and much more than he bargained for when the AMA assigned two white teachers to Brunswick. Twenty-nine-year-old Sophia Russell, daughter of a Maine carriage maker, was a veteran AMA worker; she had taught in Hampton, Virginia, before coming to Georgia. Sarah H. Champney, thirty-nine, was also an experienced teacher; the daughter of a Massachusetts army surgeon, she had worked in Aberdeen, Mississippi. The two seemed to be adventurous enough; they preferred setting up housekeeping alone, for in Champney's words, "I have observed that w[h]ere a number live together there is more or less trouble." Unable to find their own lodgings, they at first consented to board with a northern man, but soon found him to be "a man of grossly intemperate habits." Within a few days they were sharing a room in the main house of Hofwyl plantation, a situation so unpleasant that Russell exclaimed, "It may be, after my warfare is ended, after I have left my cross, some soul from Hofwyl will meet me at God's right hand—if so Oh how rich, will be my reward!" Both teachers hated the food, especially the larded griddlecakes "with just enough flour to keep them from running away."[40]

Before long the two had opened a school in a pine barren infested with fleas and mosquitoes. Teaching 104 pupils between them, they reported their first impressions: The children "are very dull and stupid; might as well have been raised in Africa for all they know of real civilization to say nothing of Christianity." Though the women were experienced teachers of the freedpeople, they were unprepared either to understand or to appreciate the distinctive Ogeechee culture they encountered in lowcountry Georgia. The Brunswick blacks were, Russell opined, "the most ignorant & degraded of all this ignorant & degraded race"—"just like raw Africans." By January the teachers had moved to a new place, a boardinghouse owned by a white woman. This situation had its own liabilities, for Champney and Russell deeply resented the fact that northern money was being funneled to unreconstructed southern whites for room and board.[41]

But Champney expressed a deeper frustration: "I do not yet feel very much acquainted with the [black] people as we cannot have any of them coming to the house; nor are we allowed to visit them." Risley had put the teachers on notice that they should not interact with blacks outside the classroom, even on missions of mercy to individual households; he insisted that such a reckless move would only inflame the feeling of the whites and endanger the whole educational enterprise in Brunswick. Compounding the teachers' growing annoyance was the fact that, in late January, after an engagement of just three days, the thirty-year-old Risley had married a woman twenty years his senior, Mary F. Moore. The teachers claimed that Moore, a "southern reb . . . *still perfectly despises the negro, & loves the lost cause . . .*" In other words, Risley was becoming "southernized." Wrote Russell to AMA headquarters, "My cheeks burn with shame for the honor of the [U.S.] government."[42]

By early March, Champney and Russell had managed to set up housekeeping on their own, and they began clandestine after-dark visits within the neighborhood. Attending a local black church service, the two found themselves "quite agreeably surprised at the good order & quietness of the congregation & good sense & intelligence of the preacher." The people were "as still & attentive as any white congregation." And in just a few weeks their school had improved immeasurably, with pupils who now "would compare favorably with any white school of the same grade." Still, Risley absolutely forbade their nighttime ramblings—"for our own *protection*," they noted contemptuously. Once again they appealed to AMA headquarters: "tell us in writing whether you wish us to be governed by rebel ideas, or to labor to the best of our judgment for the good of the colored people." But New York officials informed them that they were in danger of disgracing the association and giving "its enemies occasion to speak evil of it."[43]

The heated letters penned by Champney and Russell betray no sense of the intense political campaigning for state and local elected offices that had overtaken the lowcountry in the spring of 1868. Nevertheless, the teachers' silence on the subject of politics raises a larger question: just how far could political transformations penetrate the lowcountry, alter the relation between worker and employer, and give hope to the landless black families struggling to survive? The next few months would provide some answers. In the meantime, as blacks plunged into the political maelstrom of 1868, few people, regardless of ideology, self-interest, or "race," seemed to doubt the revolutionary potential of the ballot box to transform the state of Georgia and obliterate its slaveholding past.

CHAPTER THIRTEEN

The Present Deranged System of Labor

MONDAY, APRIL 20, 1868, at Butler's Island plantation, just north of Darien: In the lush yard of the main house, huge magnolias flower in their springtime fullness, and commingled scents of orange and peach trees and roses fill the air. Out on the rice flats, redbirds, blue jays, and blackbirds flit over a vast expanse of two hundred acres, now ready for an initial planting timed to coincide precisely with the spring tides. At ten in the morning, though, this McIntosh County plantation is remarkable less for its natural beauty than for the stillness of its fields, now devoid of all human activity. On what should have been one of the busiest days of the spring planting season, the field hands have all left for Darien to cast their ballots on the first day of the four-day statewide elections for the governor, the state legislature, and Congress. The owner of the plantation can hardly believe it: "not a man left on the place, even the old half-idiot, who took care of the cows, having gone to vote with the rest." Work would have to wait.[1]

The tranquillity of Butler's Island that morning served as a fitting counterpoint to the feverish electioneering that had consumed so many Georgia freedpeople all spring. But where lowcountry blacks celebrated the birth of a new, raw democracy, the owner of Butler's Island saw only discord and a tragic waste of energy. And in fact, anticipating this breach in plantation discipline weeks before, Frances Butler had sought to plan accordingly and prevent it. The daughter of Pierce Butler and Frances Kemble, the thirty-year-old had grown increasingly agitated by the "political meetings and excitement of all kinds" that drew McIntosh County freedpeople into Darien. There whole families gathered at political rallies and heard what the white woman considered irresponsible harangues delivered by "Northern political agents," chiefly, apparently,

two Republican candidates for the state legislature, the Reverend Tunis
G. Campbell and Virgil Hillyer. And so the planter was determined to
keep her employees from rushing out on their fool's errand to the ballot
box. Convinced that the election would yield little more than an excuse
for her hands to abandon the fields for four long days during critical
planting time, she had told them "when the day for voting came [they]
must do all their day's work and vote afterwards." Her employees must
put in a full day's work in the fields until three in the afternoon, and only
then could they go to the polls; otherwise she would evict them all.[2]

Frances Butler and her father had traveled south from Philadelphia in
March 1866 to reclaim their family estates from the Freedmen's Bureau
agents who considered the lands "abandoned" after the war. The young
woman had no memory of her Georgia childhood; she was only a baby
when her parents stayed at Butler's Island in the winter of 1838. But now,
twenty-eight years later, Frances had returned to help her father oversee
plantation operations on the mainland and at Hampton Point on St.
Simons Island. She was pleasantly surprised to find that many of the Butler family's former slaves who had been refugeed inland during the war,
and even some who had been sold away in 1859, had found their way
back to their former homes; they resumed gardening, hunting, fishing,
and trading among themselves. Still, the determined Frances had no
patience for either the local white population, now so "conquered,
ruined, and disheartened," or the black people, with their "foolish and
extravagant ideas of freedom." With the help of a German maidservant
brought from Philadelphia, she opened up the main house on Butler's
Island and gave a portrait of Robert E. Lee pride of place over the mantel-
piece. Her father, however, did not seem to have his heart in the reclama-
tion effort, and in August 1867 he died (possibly of malaria). Frances
resolved to carry on without him, to make black people work, and to
make the Butler plantations *pay*.[3]

Returning to the land where their forebears had lived and died, Bram
and Juba, Carolina, Charity, and other freedpeople staked out small plots
of land for themselves. Butler marveled at "how completely they trust us,"
but she considered them ultimately inscrutable in word and deed.
Exhorted to work hard, harder than they had ever worked before, the former slaves responded, agreeably, "Dat's so, Missus; just as missus says."
And then they did just as they liked. Butler pitied the aged, crippled
Charity until she discovered that the woman was in the habit of walking
six miles nearly every day to sell eggs to a neighboring planter. Indeed,
Butler's Island blacks did their best to live on their own terms; they gath-

ered kin together and revived traditional worship services. Scraping together a little cash, a few managed to buy small plots of land in the sandy piney woods or on the outskirts of Darien. In early 1868 Butler insisted that all her employees sign a yearlong contract, but her rice hands only aggravated her with "long explanations, objections, and demonstrations." They would have their say, and she would listen.[4]

Frances Butler felt trapped. Like most planters, she believed white people incapable of surviving work in the rice fields, though some low-country labor agents were already recruiting foreigners (including a contingent of Germans in 1868) for just that purpose. And she worried that the poison of politicking was infecting the men and women on both her plantations. Given the intricacies of spring rice planting, she was in no mood to give her blessing to voters intent on taking a several-day outing to the Darien polls. In early April she appealed to General George Meade, a longtime friend of her father and now the Union officer who had recently assumed control of the Third Military District. She was relieved by Meade's affirmation of her rights as an employer; he told her that come election time, she could insist that her workers live up to their contractual obligations. Yet in a subsequent communication, Meade cautioned Butler that she would not "have the right to decide when your people shall vote." Agreeing that no doubt "the election will be a great nuisance," he nonetheless insisted she make reasonable accommodations for the inevitable delays the men would face at the polls. They would have to wait hours in line. They would have to respond to challengers who questioned the spelling of their names, and to registrars who insisted their names were missing from the polling list altogether.[5]

Beginning on April 20, Butler expected the worst—that her hands would go off to vote and then take a protracted holiday. For months the whole coastal region had been swept up in anticipation of the time when black men would join whites and vote on the proposed state constitution and for candidates for state and local office. In January, many lowcountry workers had refused to sign labor contracts, holding out hope that the election would lead to a widespread redistribution of land. Savannah Freedmen's Bureau agent J. Murray Hoag spoke for many other northern officials when he suggested an inverse relation between black well-being and electioneering in the countryside. Comparing what he considered the more quiescent freedpeople in the interior to those on the coast, he claimed of the former, "Their greater prosperity I attribute to the absence of political excitement, and false teachings of ambitious adventurers."[6]

It was true, apparently, that in the Ogeechee district west of Savannah, black men were spending a considerable amount of time politicking, drilling, and parading rather than laboring in the fields. In February, a plantation owner in the district, J. Motte Middleton, dismissed his resistant workers, and even convinced Hoag to send in a detail of U.S. soldiers "to prevent anticipated trouble in removing from the plantation freedmen refusing to contract." When the troops encountered a defiant black army veteran, thirty-three-year-old Solomon Farley, president of the local Union League, they promptly arrested him. Democrats warned that small Union Leagues scattered throughout the countryside had suddenly metamorphosed into formidable political machines. Alexander Stephens told a *New York Times* reporter, "The negroes are compactly organized, their 'leagues' reaching every corner of the State. They coerce and threaten any black man who does not join them." He concluded, "They are a unit politically."[7]

During the early spring, the whole city of Savannah appeared to move out-of-doors, as blacks and whites thronged the streets and squares in an endless round of political meetings, countermeetings, and public cele brations. The looming municipal elections, also scheduled for late April, intensified the already high level of excitement. The November before, white Democrats had boycotted elections of delegates to the constitutional convention, but this time around they decided not only to vote, but also to launch an aggressive appeal to black men—those alienated from the leadership of white and black Republicans, as well as those favoring a practical alliance with former Confederates. The city's local Republican ticket included a number of familiar faces. Running for U.S. Congress was Dr. Joseph W. Clift, his political ambitions apparently undiminished by the untimely death of his bride, the AMA music teacher Julia Marshall, in January. Aaron A. Bradley was a candidate for the state senate, James Porter and James M. Simms for the house of representatives, and Charles H. Hopkins for mayor.[8]

Throughout the South, former Confederates recoiled at events unfolding in Washington, where on February 24 the House of Representatives had voted to impeach President Andrew Johnson. The prospect of Radical Republicans usurping the power of the chief executive propelled whites into the partisan political fray of Savannah. One of them was Dr. Richard D. Arnold. By this time Arnold had done penance for what some considered his all-too-eager surrender of the city three years before. Now he cast off the cloak of cooperation with occupying federal military forces and presented himself to the white electorate as the shrewd champion of a new Democratic Party (also called the Conservative Party) poised to meet head-on the challenge posed by Radical Republicans, with their absurd notions of black equality. In January, the sixty-year-old Arnold announced that he was eschewing retirement in favor of forming a "Conservative Club" that would appeal to both whites and blacks. The club's purpose was to oppose "by all proper and legal means" the rule of "Deconstructionists," which Arnold deemed "the most stupendous wrong ever attempted to be inflicted on a civilized people." He even sought to enlist other white doctors in an effort to counter the Republican threat: In early February a fight had broken out between police and black Republicans at an outdoor rally, and several black men were injured. In response, Arnold urged Georgia Medical Society members not to provide medical care for members of the Union League "engaged in the late riot."[9]

Despite their bravado, Arnold and other whites watched nervously throughout the late winter and early spring as blacks seized any opportunity to march and speechify—the anniversary of Lincoln's birthday on February 12, which featured a parade of two black axe companies, the Union Lincoln Association, and the Second African Baptist Church Sunday school; the third anniversary of the creation of the Freedman's Savings Bank on March 5; a public gathering of Republican office-seekers on March 16. On March 24, at a rally for the new Conservative Party, Arnold appealed to black voters to "unite in one common effort to rescue our city government from the hands of unworthy men who seek in these disordered times to grasp it for their own selfish and iniquitous purposes." A putative mayoral candidate, John Screven—planter, railroad president, and former Confederate military officer—also delivered pointed remarks aimed at black listeners ("of whom there were many in the crowd," according to a reporter), noting that as a child he had played with many of them, and that "no colored man or woman could say that he had ever done them intentional harm."[10]

Savannah elites realized that they were in uncharted territory now that blacks were eligible to vote in city elections. The mayor and aldermen had managed to halt the state legislature's move to expand the city's boundaries, knowing that incorporating outlying poorer districts would tip the at-large system of elections in favor of the black population, and thus endanger a whole host of officeholders, from the mayor on down. They therefore responded with considerable relief when General Meade announced on March 26 that he was postponing municipal elections indefinitely. Meade feared that too many illegal black voters would overwhelm Savannah polling places and engulf the city in chaos. For now at least, the local government would remain largely insulated from black political influence.[11]

By this time Simms had created a new medium of black Republican expression: a newspaper called *Freemen's Standard*. (Joseph Clift provided financial backing for the venture, and Simms had used the money to purchase printing supplies during a trip to Boston the summer before.) In the first issue, published on February 15, Simms proclaimed the new publication "in the interests of the laboring classes"—a source of information, an "organ or tongue" of community leaders, and a "means of sounding 'the tocsin of alarm' in an emergency." Appearing irregularly during the spring, the *Freemen's Standard* condemned the kinds of routine law enforcement and judicial abuses that the two other papers in town took for granted, such as the roundup of innocent black citizens on trumped-up charges of "vagrancy" and the disruption of peaceful political meetings by armed police. The paper also covered matters of interest to the local community, such as the new Educational Board of Twenty-One to survey city schools; and ran ads for black businesspeople, including the grocer Absalom Sallans, saddle- and shoemaker March Davis, and barber and hairdresser Freeman Flournoy. The *Standard* lauded long-time community leader Jane Deveaux, proprietor of a clandestine antebellum school beginning in 1840 and still teaching children nearly three decades later. Notices in the paper exhorted men, women, and children to open accounts in the Freedman's Bank, and voters to make certain that their names were spelled correctly on official polling lists. Forced for so long to hold his tongue, Simms now embraced his new role as journalist. In one of the paper's editorials, titled "Hints for the Times: 'Soul Liberty,' " he wrote that the liberty of the soul is "more precious than liberty of the body." No doubt with black conservatives in mind, he proclaimed that the enslavement of the soul, when the body is free, "then is the most abject, debasing, and disgraceful of all bondage."[12]

Meanwhile, Aaron Bradley was handing out and tacking up posters throughout the city, warning whites: "If you Strike a Blow, the Man or Men will be followed, and the house in which he or they take shelter will be burned to the ground. TAKE HEED! MARK WELL! Members of the Union RALLY! RALLY! Rally!! For God, Life, and Liberty!" And rally he, and they, did, in Chippewa Square on April 6. This mass meeting was an urgent response to a mysterious group calling itself Savannah Division 90 of the Ku Klux Klan, with its leader identified only as the "Grand Cyclops for Georgia." The *Freemen's Standard* reprinted a copy of an ominous Klan warning to Republicans, with daggers and a coffin as illustrations. Still, Bradley and others knew full well that the source of the former rebels' real power lay not only in guns and pistols, but also in the manipulation of the everyday machinery of city government.[13]

The election itself represented a new chapter in the long history of Savannah street theater. On Monday, April 20, when the courthouse polls opened at 7 a.m., "the mass of the new enfranchised humanity began to surge, and . . . it was a life and death struggle as to who would get in and get squeezed." Black men turned out in large numbers not only because of the lively electioneering of the previous weeks, but also because Governor Rufus Bullock had suspended a state-sanctioned poll tax (the state legislature allowed such a tax if the proceeds went to public education). The *News and Herald* condemned the mass of impoverished, illiterate black voters, who, the paper claimed, flooded the city from South Carolina "to finish their hellish orgies . . . fresh from the banquet over the remains of a free constitutional government." The *Freemen's Standard* saw a different drama unfolding: whites came armed with sword canes, bowie knives, and revolvers in order to "intimidate and terrify the white and colored loyalists." Fistfights broke out between blacks and whites and between black Democrats and black Republicans. Wrote one white reporter at the end of the four-day election, "Glad are we that it's over, gladder still that such scenes will never again be witnessed in the beautiful city of Savannah."[14]

Down the coast, Frances Butler expressed amazement when her employees all returned to work on April 21, the day after they cast their votes; her fears had proved unfounded. Puzzled, she labeled blacks the "most effervescent people in the world"; one day they were "gesticulating wildly, talking so violently that no one on earth can understand one word they say," and the next day they were peaceably going about their tasks in the fields. Yet throughout the lowcountry, black voters had spoken in a way that was hard to ignore or misunderstand: returns from Chatham County suggested the near balance between blacks and whites in Savannah, with Republican candidates just barely besting their Democratic rivals (about 2,800 votes to 2,700 for each in the different contests). However, in the Ogeechee and outlying areas, the black majority overwhelmingly cast their ballots for the Republican candidates, ensuring their election. Voters sent Dr. Clift as their representative to Congress; the two Jameses, Simms and Porter, to the lower house of the state legislature, and Aaron A. Bradley to the state senate. A light-skinned veteran of the Massachusetts Fifty-fifth Regiment, South Carolina–born, Oberlin-educated Richard W. White, was elected clerk of the Savannah Superior Court.

The majority-black coastal counties sent a number of familiar Republican leaders to the state assembly—William Golding from Liberty, Virgil Hillyer from Camden, the Reverend Tunis G. Campbell, and his son Tunis Junior from McIntosh (father to the state senate, son to the house). The senior Campbell was also elected a justice of the peace for Darien. Statewide, voters narrowly approved the new constitution and elected Republican Rufus Bullock governor.[15]

The new state legislature had only a slim Republican majority, but it would soon become clear that partisan labels meant less than the overwhelming desire of all white men regardless of party to control officeholding and lawmaking throughout the state. Indeed, despite the near parity between white and black registered voters and despite gains in local offices, black Republicans were becoming more discouraged; in the legislature, whites outnumbered blacks 236 to 29. The statewide Republican Executive Committee remained all white. White politicians of both parties hailed the election as proof that black suffrage need not translate into black political power, as long as white men dominated in elective office. Frustrated with "moderate" white Republicans who claimed to have blacks' best interests in mind, Henry M. Turner remarked bitterly, "We are told, that if black men want to speak, they must speak through white trumpets; if black men want their sentiments expressed, they must be adulterated and sent through white messengers, who will quibble, and equivocate, and evade as rapidly as the pendulum of the clock."[16]

Savannah freedpeople understandably harbored doubts about the liberating potential of the political process. Many of the former rebels' rearguard actions were outside the control of the former slaves who were now voters. Fed up with Aaron Bradley's endless provocations, Mayor Anderson issued an order for the black man's landlady to evict him or she would be charged with running a brothel. The city council named new wards and streets after arch-Confederates (such as the clergymen Father Jeremiah O'Neill and the Reverend Stephen Elliott, and the wealthy businessmen Cuyler, Burroughs, Wylly, and Screven), and pressed black men and women into forced labor on the city streets. Arrested on the slightest pretext, freedpeople of both sexes and all ages lacked the resources to pay lawyers, and so, according to Amherst Stone, "are lodged in jail and stay there for months, without an examination." Meanwhile, jury verdicts were "more or less governed by prejudice."[17]

Indeed, the prospects of workers everywhere bore no discernible link to the ballot box. In the hinterland many field hands remained in virtual slavery, cheated out of their share of the crop at the end of the harvest season. Exploitative labor "contracts" afforded workers no protection against landowners who physically abused them. Those families that moved down the road at the end of the contract year were likely to find their new employer operating on the same principle of labor relations as their old: landed whites as a group lording over landless blacks. Local magistrates continued to "apprentice" black children to white "guardians." In Liberty County, children of impoverished or deceased parents found themselves bound to white women and men who promised to instruct their charges in "the art or mistery of agriculture" or in "the art or mistery of House service and husbandry." On the coast, workers struggled to leverage their muscle power into negotiating power during wage disputes. In the lumber industry near Darien, such disputes—"riots"—included equal numbers of black and white men, raftsmen and other workers employed by the Atlantic Steam Mill Company. Their variable fortunes depended less on legislative pronouncements and more on worker solidarity as it threatened employers' profit margins.[18]

In Savannah, white men of all classes continued to mend the sinews of community that had been damaged during the war. Now that militias were banned, the city's six white fire companies reemerged as a robust expression of white fraternity. On May 1 the "White Fire Company" of Savannah marked its first anniversary by sponsoring a grand parade that included guest companies from Charleston, Macon, Thomasville, and Augusta. A delegate from the Vigilant Company of Augusta thanked his hosts in a speech of unrepentant Confederate nostalgia: "Though the star that arose so resplendently upon the field of Manassas sank in gloom like the departed sun," he said, "it left its glory behind, and we are united in a common bond by its sacred memories." He was also polite, or politic, enough to gloss over Savannah's swift capitulation to Union military forces: "The past of your city is glorious."[19]

The firemen's parade on the first of May revealed more than just the growing power of "lost cause" rhetoric. That day the Washington Company proudly displayed its new steam fire engine, recently purchased with forty-eight hundred of the taxpayers' dollars. In 1868, the council would bestow $12,000 on the white companies for maintenance and for the purchase of new equipment. Deprived of public aid, their six black counterparts remained organized in four hand-engine companies and two axe companies. The all-white firemen's celebrations drew the support of the mayor and aldermen, who marched in the parades and toasted at the dinners in an elaborate show of white solidarity. The spectacle of fancy steam engines competing with each other to see which could throw water the greatest distance relegated black firemen to the sidelines.[20]

NEVERTHELESS, late spring also provided abundant evidence that most lowcountry freedpeople were investing in a new order of some promise. Black men had turned out in large numbers to vote. In Washington, the trial of the impeached president was moving toward an anticlimactic conclusion; though he won a narrow vote of acquittal, Johnson would have to yield to the Radicals for the remaining six months of his term. Perhaps justice would flow from the halls of Capitol Hill after all.

One measure of freedpeople's optimism, or at least their rootedness, was the difficulty faced by the American Colonization Society in its attempt to revive Savannah as a port of embarkation for emigrants bound for Liberia. Mindful of the historic hostility shown them by Savannah whites, ACS officials had moved their regional operations to Charleston in the first two years after the war. Nevertheless, some supporters from the antebellum period, including Charles DeLaMotta, resumed their roles as local ACS agents, distributing the *African Repository* and serving as liaisons between the society and potential emigrants. Skilled black workers remained the society's most active constituency, with their wives (unreasonably) expecting private quarters on board any Africa-bound ship.[21]

At the same time, postbellum developments revealed the ACS's difficulties in appealing to a free people. With the triumph of abolitionism, the main goal of the ACS had changed from recruiting American slaves as colonists to evangelizing among Africans, though the group decided to retain its old name. The schedule for sailings—in May and November—conflicted with the busiest seasons for growing rice and cotton, and with the Freedmen's Bureau system, which enforced yearlong contracts. Increasingly, blacks believed "they will have the South to themselves" someday, according to one white Savannah correspondent (though he himself thought such hopes were but a "pipe dream"). With each stage of political progress—military occupation of the South, the passage of the Reconstruction Acts, the impeachment of Johnson, state elections in April of 1868—many black men and women saw a glimmer of progress. They hoped to rebuild their lives in their own country, not in a foreign one.[22]

For their part, white landowners and employers in Georgia remained divided, with some protesting that ACS schemes were nothing more than

an effort to drain the South of its rural workforce, and others eagerly promoting the out-migration of troublesome would-be voters and landowners. Dependent on black men to build an indigenous southern
Republican Party, U.S. military officials and Freedmen's Bureau agents
united in their opposition to the ACS. Some Georgians, white and black,
saw an ACS commission as the ticket to a modest stipend; in July 1866
the Reverend Henry M. Turner promised ACS officials that he would be
speaking soon at a "large barbecue in favor of Liberia," and stressing
"that we will never get justice here . . . [and] that we are destined to be
missionaries to the millions of Africa."[23]

In early 1868 the ACS announced that the Liberian-bound *Golconda*
would make a stop in Savannah in May. By March it was clear that the
passengers would hail not from the city or the lowcountry, but from interior towns such as Sparta, Columbus, and Augusta, Georgia; Pound
Ridge, South Carolina; and even from as far away as Tennessee and Alabama. The list of promised emigrants from Augusta included a bricklayer, shoemaker, harness maker, pressman, carpenter, seamstress, and
two blacksmiths. Columbus was reportedly sending a party three hundred strong, organized by Philip L. Monroe, who planned to bring a
number of his extended kin. As late as April 15, Monroe was scrambling
to pack for the trip, requesting supplies from the perennially cash-
strapped ACS headquarters—bitters, glass pitcher and goblets ("for
administering the Lord's supper"), "Websters Dictionary unabridged +
any other valuable books you think I shall need now my dear sir." But as
the departure date drew near, a number of emigrants had a change of
heart and backed down because, according to at least some whites, "four
days of elections have demoralized the negro and made him hope for better things than Liberia." (In this instance, "demoralized" blacks were
those who resisted toiling in the fields.) In other parts of the state, too,
freedpeople reneged at the last minute, explaining they had decided to
plant crops and wanted to stay to harvest them in the fall.[24]

When he arrived in Savannah on April 24, ACS agent William Coppinger found that "much feeling prevails" against his group, largely
owing, he thought, to the tensions surrounding the just-concluded election. Taking a room at the Screven House Hotel, Coppinger managed to
find lodging for the emigrants at the Freedmen's Hospital, but he chafed
at paying $5 a day to store their belongings in a local warehouse. To meet
mounting food expenses, he appealed to a handful of sympathetic
wealthy white men, ACS contacts before the war. But he found that
"business South has passed into the hands of younger active men and

[so] to many of them I went direct, stating my mission and what I wanted." He finally persuaded I. W. Brinckerhoff, cashier at the Freedman's Bank, to cash a check. By the end of the month the expected 650 emigrants had dwindled to 450.[25]

During the first days of May, the long wait and intense heat began to take their toll on the restless emigrants. On May 9, panic broke out as increasing numbers began to talk of returning home. The *Golconda* finally arrived on May 15, but did not leave for three more days. In a replay of earlier years, the ship finally set sail, leaving in its wake an exhausted ACS agent on the verge of a nervous breakdown.[26]

During the anxious weeks he spent in Savannah, Coppinger had time to become acquainted with the Savannah black community. "The Savannah negroes have no idea of going to Liberia," he noted. And one of the main reasons was the city's rich associational life, with political organizations and mutual aid societies among its most public manifestations. By the spring of 1868, more than one hundred black-run organizations had opened accounts in the local branch of the Freedman's Bank groups affiliated with church congregations (for example African Methodist Episcopal Church Sabbath School, Zion Baptist Association); with the Union League or the Republican Party (Ladies Branch Republican Society, Union Republican Association, Young Union Lincoln Guards); and with specific kinds of workers (Wagoners Union Association, Portermen's Society, Longshoremen's Union Association). Many were apparently small mutual aid societies formed before the war to provide health and burial benefits to members, not only in the city proper but also in outlying areas (the Poor Saints societies of Springfield plantation, north of Savannah, and Skidaway Island). Some of the groups made loans, sponsored social events, and mediated disputes; together they formed a latticework of associations that facilitated political organizing in the city and its hinterland. Virtually all of the black Baptist, Episcopal, and AME churches were represented among Freedman's Bank depositors, as were the Oglethorpe Axe Company No. 2, the K. S. Baker Council No. 9 of the Union League of America, and the Eureka and Hilton Masonic Lodge. In the names of their associations, members expressed their determination to leave behind the degradation of slavery. Women were prominent in this effort. Of the more than 120 societies opening accounts in the bank by 1872, almost one-sixth had "ladies" in the title—the Ladies Union St. Paul's Society, the Young Ladies of Honor, and the Young Ladies Independent Star Society, among others.[27]

These groups, some small and ephemeral, others large and enduring, revealed that men and women, young and old, rich and poor, literate and illiterate, skilled and unskilled, assumed leadership roles in the black community of Savannah. The Daughters of Zion, for example, alternated between male and female presidents; the United Benevolent Association, John the Baptist Society, and Mary Magdalene Society included both men and women among its officers at any one time. In May 1868, Hammond C. Aves, a literate thirty-one-year-old carpenter, was serving as a secretary of the Poor and Needy Institution, while the illiterate midwife-nurse Georgiana Guard Kelly, age fifty, Richard Arnold's former ward, occupied the position of president. Officers of other groups included Robert Wight, a literate wagoner, president of the Macedonian Benevolent Society in the spring of 1868; and Chance Cuyler, age forty-seven, who, though illiterate, was treasurer of the Portermen's Society.[28]

Literacy seemed not to be a criterion for leadership in an array of societies, including the John the Baptist Society (the president was sixty-two-year-old Maria Johnson) and the Independent Elect Cherubim (the president was thirty-six-year-old Jerry Ferguson, a bricklayer), or a church congregation (Grant Simpson, a teamster, was deacon of the First Bryan Baptist Church). The Union Benevolent Society, sponsored by the Second African Baptist Church, had for its elected officers Ann Wilson, president; Lydia Edwards, vice president; Deana Boles, treasurer; and King Solomon Thomas, secretary. Wilson, fifty-three, was an illiterate laundress, but here she outranked Thomas, thirty-three, a prominent teacher and grocer in the city. Boles, fifty-one, had family connections: she was the daughter of a former, and the wife of the current, pastor of Second African.[29]

In a pattern not unlike that of the white community, a few black leaders formed an interlocking directorate among several associations. James M. Simms was active in a number of religious, political, and fraternal groups. Unsurprisingly, he linked black associational activity with political progress—whether the association was the Baptist Church, the Masons, the Republican Party, or any of the small mutual aid societies. It was around this time that Simms, as a member of the state legislature, pressed for a charter for a proposed black-owned bank called the Chatham Mercantile, Loan, and Trust Company, an effort that failed, though he proved prescient in his effort to challenge the Freedman's Bank. When he returned to Savannah from Boston in 1865, Simms founded a branch of the Masons, Eureka 11, which had received authorization from the Prince Hall Grand Lodge of Massachusetts in June 1866; within a few months the John T. Hilton Lodge No. 13 was also established. During this period

Simms served as district deputy grand master for Georgia, Florida, and Alabama. King Solomon Thomas too emerged as a citywide leader: he served as an officer in as many as seven organizations, including the Masons, the Union Benevolent Society, and the Macedonian Benevolent Society.[30]

Many of the groups coming to the fore after the war had existed in some form under slavery and owed their origins to traditional West African secret societies. Freemasonry, for example, with its multilevel progression of stages, was similar to African "making of the man" rituals and associations. In the United States, the organization was the largest black fraternal order, spanning time (beginning in the eighteenth century) and space (with semisecret lodges in the North and South). The Savannah Masons and other groups took full adavantage of the Freedman's Bank. It was less remarkable that some groups survived the transition from slavery to freedom, and some blossomed after freedom, than that so many put their trust—and money—in the bank. By 1868 it appeared to be a stable institution, one that not only facilitated traditional forms of mutual aid societies, but safeguarded those societies for the future as well.[31]

The social bonds created and sustained by clubs and mutual aid societies crisscrossed Savannah's black community, binding together a people whose family lives had been devastated by generations of enslavement and by four hard years of war. In opening their accounts, depositors had to list their potential heirs (nearest of kin), and in the process these men, women, and children revealed heartbreaking histories of forced family separation. Richard Chisholm, an illiterate engineer in a Savannah shipyard and a city resident for ten years, had lost contact with his father. His mother had died twenty-seven years before. A sister, Dolly, lived in Macon, and another, Bella, on the Flint River in Georgia. He did not know whether his children—formerly owned by an Alabama man—were alive or dead. In another case, Dorcas Whitfield, a native of North Carolina and now a widow, earned a living in postwar Savannah by knitting. She had made heroic efforts to keep track of her scattered family. Her father had died in 1823, but she thought that as of 1861 her mother was still living in Georgia. Dorcas's husband, Jim, had died in 1867. She believed that two of her four grown children were in the vicinity of Gainesville, Florida. Another one had last been heard of in 1865, living near Vicksburg, Mississippi.[32]

When the widow Mary McGill opened her account, she was working in the AMA mission home as a laundress for the teachers. Five of her children had died before she could name them. During the war ("after Fort Pulaski was taken") Mary's husband, Joseph, had passed away "on Mr. Jordan's Place up in Georgia." She believed her thirty-year-old son was now living in Albany, Georgia. She did not know the whereabouts of one of her daughters, who had been sold away twenty years before. Her other daughter Martha Ann had been a slave of a Dr. Clemens, who had sold her to a Mr. Swinton, living on an island near Charleston. For Richard Chisholm, Dorcas Whitfield, and Mary McGill, bereft of their blood kin, Savannah's rich associational life offered the social support of an extended family.[33]

Yet in a few cases family separations afforded a measure of comfort to husbands and wives. When James Simms opened one of several Freedman's Bank accounts in February 1868, he reported that his wife, Margaret, his daughters Susan, nineteen, and Isabella, fifteen, and his sister Cornelia Sikes were all living with his brother Thomas in Cambridgeport, Massachusetts. His mother, Minda, was living with him (James), and his sister Ann Bougher, four years older than he, also resided in Savannah. The Simms family would maintain its ties to Boston, where Thomas had achieved near-iconic status within the abolitionist community, and where James had received his credentials as both Baptist minister and Masonic leader. Indeed, James Simms kept in close touch with Boston Masonic leader Lewis Hayden, and throughout his life he retained fond memories of familiar Boston sights such as Bunker Hill, the Common, and the public library.[34]

A series of dramatic events in the summer of 1868 no doubt confirmed in Simms's mind the wisdom of keeping his family far from Savannah, at least for now. On July 21, the sons of two prominent white men fell out in a deadly barroom brawl. Isaac Russell, twenty-three, a deputy sheriff of the city and a constable of the county, and the son of Philip M. Russell Sr. (clerk of the city court and a fire department official), confronted William R. Hopkins, twenty-two, the recently elected tax receiver for Chatham County, who was the son of Republican politician Charles H. Hopkins. The younger Hopkins was no stranger to violent encounters. With his brother Charles Junior, William Hopkins had been arrested in June for brutally beating journalist John E. Hayes with a slingshot and loaded whip. At the time of the attack, the *Republican* editor was already in failing health, weakened after serving a three-month prison sentence (from February through April) for libeling attorney Solomon Cohen in his newspaper. The Hopkins brothers had mounted a successful defense against assault charges, claiming that Hayes had wounded himself falling into a signpost or an awning outside his office.[35]

Russell faced off with Hopkins in Frank Yaeger's barroom, at the corner of Jefferson and Minis, in the northwestern part of the city, the day after the city's Democrats had sponsored an immense torchlight parade in support of the party's candidates in the upcoming November election. Hopkins reportedly entered the store and, upon seeing Russell, denounced him as "one of those G——d d——d rebel sons of bitches" and began to pummel him on the head with the butt of his pistol. Russell pulled out his own gun and shot Hopkins four times.[36]

Savannah authorities were accustomed to trigger-happy sons of privilege getting into fights. But what transpired after Hopkins's murder that night truly frightened whites throughout the city. Word spread quickly that Hopkins had been shot, and a crowd of angry freedpeople soon gathered at Yaeger's store. They bore Hopkins's lifeless body to his father's house, and then proceeded as a group to the home of Russell Senior, whose son by this time had surrendered to authorities. The *News and Herald* reported that drumbeats echoing through the city (no doubt evoking the drumbeats of rebellious slaves) had summoned two to three thousand blacks to the street outside the Russell residence. Many of the men brandished axes, clubs, and guns and shouted, "We have fought in the war and know how to fight; let's kill the rebels . . . Kill every rebel that dares to shoot a Republican." Some of the axe wielders were in their firemen's uniforms. The next day the newspaper put the matter bluntly: "The assemblage of the negroes last night immediately after the tapping of the drum shows that they are organized and have given signals by which they can be collected at any point in a few moments. This state of affairs bode [*sic*] no good to our citizens." The ear-piercing demonstrations completely unnerved whites, including the widow Henrietta Wayne, who wrote, "I think things are now getting so unpleasant, negroes have so many privileges that I sometimes feel I would much rather live among Yankees than here." Still, the protests were peaceful; they produced much noise but no violence.[37]

Subsequent developments convinced the elder Philip Russell and others that it was time to outlaw the black firemen companies, now that they had apparently become the militant arm of the local Republican Party. On July 27 the black community hosted a Liberian independence day celebration, and welcomed firefighters from Macon, Beaufort, and Charleston. Many black men, women, and children took to the streets to watch the axe and engine companies parade "in their vari-colored uni-forms with flags flying and bands playing present[ing] a novel and impos-ing appearance." Neither the "novel and imposing appearance" of the marchers nor the recent arrest of four black men for the "riot" at the Rus-sell house could quell the fears of whites. In mid-August Edward Taylor, captain of Axe Company No. 2, felt compelled to write to the *News and Herald* and explain that the night of the disturbance members of the com-pany had been meeting to prepare for the July 27 festivities; just because Russell saw two men in uniform with axes "is not sufficient proof for charging upon these organizations with so serious an offense, and I think he will be unable to substantiate the charges."[38]

By late summer, in anticipation of the upcoming elections, both sides began to position themselves for a bitter campaign that would be fought not only in the streets and backrooms but in the courts and state legisla-ture. Charles Hopkins told Mayor Anderson that he could count on Hopkins's support if he wanted to run for the U.S. Senate; in return Anderson must deliver the Democrats for Hopkins in his bid for mayor. The Republicans, including black Republicans, appeared to be on the offensive. State lawmakers again proposed expanding the Savannah city limits in an effort to add blacks to voter registration rolls. In August, James J. Waring agreed to serve as surety for the bond that Richard W. White was required to post before he could assume his newly elected position as clerk of the superior court. (Setting a high security bond as a condition of holding office worked against potential black officials at every level of government.) Waring's generosity earned him the enmity of his fellow members of the Georgia Medical Society; they initiated pro-ceedings to expel him. Meanwhile, Aaron Bradley had returned to Savan-nah from Atlanta; alert to white legislators' intention to remove him from that body for his alleged moral turpitude, he had deprived them of the satisfaction by resigning. Bradley resumed his campaign among his low-country supporters and announced that he planned to run for the U.S. Congress; he was breaking with the Republican establishment in an effort to oust the incumbent, Joseph Clift.[39]

In September, white state legislators made a stunning move: they expelled all of the black members on the grounds that the state constitu-tion did not guarantee the right of blacks to hold office. Invoking the 1857 *Dred Scott* Supreme Court case, forty-six Republicans joined with thirty-seven Democrats to oust Simms, Porter, Turner, Campbell father and son, and twenty-four others from their legislative seats. Soon after the expulsion, the lawmakers decided to eliminate another legal ambiguity when they voted to prohibit all Georgia blacks from serving on juries.[40]

In the immediate aftermath of these moves came reports from Savannah that blacks in the Ogeechee district were "making warlike preparations"—"organizing into military companies, battalions, and regiments in obedience from 'Head Quarters,' " and throwing up pickets on the roads leading into the city. Later that month John E. Hayes died from the wounds he had received earlier in the summer; his paper, the *Republican*, was quickly bought by its former owner, the unrepentant secessionist James Sneed. And then the Georgia Medical Society officially stripped Waring of his membership on the grounds that in aiding and abetting the Republican cause, "his conduct was unworthy of a gentleman and & had forfeited his social standing." Richard Arnold paid Waring grudging tribute when he remarked that, if "Waring had not the hide of a Rhinoceros . . . he would have committed suicide before this."[41]

On October 6, Henry M. Turner called a convention of the expelled black legislators and their supporters in Macon. The purpose of the meeting was, in Simms's words, "to take under consideration our condition as a people; the outrages perpetrated upon us; the expulsion of our members from the state legislature; and the killing then going on in several of the counties, which had very much alarmed the colored people." The body aimed to petition Congress, pointing out that several dozen openly disloyal (i.e., former Confederate) legislators had ejected loyal black men from the positions to which they had been legally elected. Drawing 136 delegates from 83 Georgia counties, the convention formed a new (and ephemeral) group, the Civil and Political Rights Association. The brief existence of the association convinced many of Turner's critics that it amounted to little more than a scheme for him to support himself by charging the delegates membership fees.[42]

A week before the November 3 state and national elections, black men and women from the city and the surrounding countryside held a rally in Johnson Square, and a number of speakers emphasized the high stakes involved. Municipal elections were still in a state of suspension; voters would not elect a new mayor and council for another year. But the national election pitted the Republican Civil War hero Ulysses S. Grant against Horatio Seymour, former pro-slavery governor of New York. At the same time, regardless of party, the exclusively white candidates for the state legislature served as a rebuke to black citizenship aspirations. Simms declared "that the blacks had gained the right to vote by a revolution, and that it would take a bloodier revolution to take it away." With the *Freemen's Standard* now defunct, Simms's words no doubt received only imperfect transcription in the *News and Herald*, which quoted him as saying, "We will remain peaceable, law-abiding citizens if we may, but devilish, fighting citizens if we must." Indeed, "his whole speech breathed the spirit of the bravado and incendiary."[43]

On the morning of November 3, Savannah authorities opened the city's single polling place, in the Court House, where approximately one thousand black men were already waiting outside. In contrast to the April election, election officials now insisted that voters must present proof that they had paid a $1 voter registration fee before they could cast their ballots. Simms and other black leaders protested, pointing out that Governor Bullock had suspended the poll tax for this election, but they were rebuffed by the county ordinary, who claimed he knew nothing about the suspension. By this time Democratic challengers had crowded into the small polling place and threatened to turn away all men who could not prove with a written receipt that they had paid their taxes for the year 1867. Later estimates suggest that fully 90 percent of the black registered voters who sought to cast their ballots were prevented from doing so because of these challenges. Some employers had paid their workers' taxes and then deducted the money from their wages; in any case few black men possessed written documentation.[44]

Turned out of the courthouse, the angry voters regrouped on the street and sidewalk. At 8:15 about fifty white employees of the Central of Georgia Railroad arrived; they "said they must vote immediately and return to work," in the words of one observer, and a contingent of police began to push aside the restless crowd of blacks, making way for the newcomers. Suddenly shots rang out. In all, three blacks and three white policemen died. An estimated seventeen blacks were wounded. Simms and others called out to the crowd to retreat to a nearby church, but later in the afternoon many dispersed to their homes without voting. The melee outside the courthouse that morning was less a riot than a rout of black voters.[45]

Systematic intimidation of black voters was not limited to Savannah. Down the coast, between four and five hundred freedmen assembled early in the morning at the Camden County courthouse, only to learn that officials had spirited the ballot boxes to another place, Ward's Store. This way all whites could cast their votes "without being degraded" by the presence of blacks. By late morning the county ordinary had appeared at the courthouse and told the expectant men that they should find their way to Satilla Mills, more than a dozen miles distant, if they wanted to vote. Recalled one Republican, "There was a general break for the mill . . . and in good time, you can rest assured—old and young, lame, halt, and well, all on a double-quick."[46]

Out on the Ogeechee, three hundred black voters arrived early at the district's polling station; many were bearing pistols, clubs, and flintlock muskets. Pickets, calling themselves sheriffs, patrolled the surrounding area. By late morning the crowd had swelled in anticipation of hearing Aaron Bradley, who had promised to deliver a speech, but their mood turned fearful when Union League president Solomon Farley reported that whites were lying in wait and threatening to kill Bradley whenever he appeared. It was also rumored that white saboteurs had destroyed bridges in the surrounding area in an effort to keep men from getting to the polls. Adding to the tension were more than a dozen white men, including newspaper reporters and Democratic vote-challengers, who had arrived from Savannah to "observe" the election.[47]

Nevertheless, in the early afternoon Bradley made a triumphal appearance and spoke to a crowd estimated at one thousand men, women, and children. After his speech, the Ogeechee Home Guards formed a military escort and, together with a "great crowd," proceeded to accompany his carriage back to the city. Riding with Bradley that afternoon was the grocer-schoolteacher King Solomon Thomas, who possessed political aspirations of his own. The procession soon found its way impeded by a number of wrecked bridges; and then on the outskirts of the city the group was met by a posse of white men led by a Savannah police captain. The officer ordered Bradley and his entourage to disarm and disperse before proceeding further. The blacks balked, and someone fired a shot. During the ensuing gun battle, twenty-four-year-old Samuel S. Law, a member of the posse and the son of Judge William Law, fell dead. The next day an inquest found that Law "came to his death by gunshot wounds received at the hands of parties who were led on by one Aaron Alpeoria Bradley." At last white authorities had a chance to pursue Bradley and hold him accountable not only for the countless "incendiary" speeches he had delivered over the years, but for murder. But by this time the attorney had disappeared.[48]

For most Savannah whites, the deaths of Samuel Law and the three white policemen were but an unfortunate by-product of a glorious victory for Conservative/Democratic candidates. The twin strategies of intimidating black men and challenging their right to vote (because of unpaid taxes, variously defined) proved to be a winning combination. In the

November election Savannah Republican candidates for office received less than one-fourth the number they had won in April; though the city had 3,900 registered black voters on its rolls, Grant got only 400 votes. Liberty County, overwhelmingly black, gave 288 votes to Seymour, compared to only 207 for Grant; county election officials had rejected a legitimate Riceboro ballot box brought in by a group of black men as "illegal." Later, testifying before a congressional committee, Mayor Anderson dismissed charges of fraud and intimidation, assuring skeptics that "Negroes are regarded by us as children. We thus treat them with consideration and tenderness, placing them . . . under the equal protection of law." In his public testimony, John Screven, president of the Atlantic and Gulf Railroad, took a more aggressive stance and defended efforts to keep blacks from voting; whites in general, he said, "are strongly averse to giving the black people political power to which they are not entitled under the law, and for which they are not fitted by education, experience, or other just qualifications."[49]

If the election represented a turning point in lowcountry partisan politics—the beginning of the end of full black voting strength at the polls—it also highlighted an upsurge in armed resistance among pockets of lowcountry freedpeople. In December on St. Catherines Island, a black teacher was urging workers to defy white employers, and on Skidaway, armed freedmen were firing on white oystermen, vowing to keep them from entering the area. In response to these threats, a group of German-immigrant truck farmers southwest of Savannah formed patrols reminiscent of planters' efforts to monitor the nighttime comings and goings of slaves. Said one of the farmers, "Our duty as patrolmen was to guard our fields and the roads, and to see that everything was quiet on the roads." City officials authorized the vigilantes to arrest blacks for disturbing the peace, among other infractions. On December 5, patrolmen Frederick Brodbacker and Frederick Brickman were killed in a shoot-out with a group of black men who had denounced them, yelling, "You damned gardeners." Two of the original five defendants were later convicted and hanged for murder.[50]

Meanwhile, on the neck of land between the Big and Little Ogeechee rivers, black workers were making a last-ditch effort to control their own labor. The area just west of Savannah had long been a source of trouble for Chatham County whites, who routinely encountered black pickets shouldering muskets and shotguns on the road leading out of the city. By late 1868, the Ogeechee rice plantations that Esther Douglass and Frances Littlefield knew so well were now home to two well-organized, overlapping groups, the Home Guards and a Union League. These groups made the community's rallying cry of self-defense more than a rhetorical exercise. One leader, Jack Cuthbert, proclaimed that "the white people had commenced the thing with them, and that they [the blacks] intended to end it; that as long as they could see a man with straight hair that he should not stay in the Ogeechee." Black men and women had worked the land as slaves and now they would make it their own. Around this time, when an overseer started to tear down a shack on one plantation, a black man protested vigorously, claiming that he was coming back to live in that dwelling as soon as he received his forty acres.[51]

The Ogeechee rice hands had continued to chafe under Freedman's Bureau labor contracts that promised them only one-third of the crop after a year's hard work for a white man; these contracts bore the imprint of slavery, and the people would reject them if they had to "fight knee-deep in blood." As the end-of-year reckoning approached, disputes broke out between the workers and overseers over contract disputes. In late December the workers employed by J. Motte Middleton and others staged nighttime raids on the barns at Southfield and Prairie plantations, attacking watchmen and overseers and then, over a matter of days, loading an estimated six thousand bushels of rice (worth $12,000) on flatboats and floating them away to a hiding place on the river. The black men also ransacked Middleton's house and stripped it bare of books, clothing, bedding, and furniture. The employer would later profess his bewilderment at the uprising: "I have never beaten any of these people, and know not why they should have an antipathy toward me." On Wednesday, December 23, in response to a request by Middleton, Savannah local magistrate Philip M. Russell Jr. issued warrants for the arrest of seventeen workers for larceny and attempted murder. Unable to secure reinforcements from federal military officials, a Savannah sheriff, James Dooner, set out on the morning of December 29 to convince the men "by kindness and persuasion" to give themselves up. With Dooner were Middleton and two deputies, Emanuel Mendel and Julius Kauffman.[52]

Soon after arriving in the district, Dooner secured the cooperation of four of the accused freedmen he had managed to locate. They agreed to meet him later in the day at the railroad station and go with him to Savannah. But when the sheriff's party went on to New Hope plantation with the intention of arresting that "great rascal" Solomon Farley, they found more than they had bargained for. At first, Farley seemed compliant, handing over his shotgun—but then he suddenly dropped to his knee and began to scribble something on a piece of paper. After he handed the note to his wife, who was standing nearby, she hastened away. During a forced march to the train station (monitored closely by two freedwomen), Farley every once in a while lifted his hat from his head and twirled it in the air. The sheriff and his deputies soon understood the meaning of these signals: at midafternoon, when the white men arrived with their prisoner at the train station, they encountered a greeting party of two hundred angry blacks, the men armed with muskets, axes, and clubs. A large number of women, "with sticks and hatchets in their hands," began "inciting the men to acts of violence."[53]

Testifying later, Dooner recalled the tumultuous scene this way: The black men said "they had laws of their own, and did not care one damn for the sheriff." Julius Kauffman remembered the threats in similar, if more detailed, terms: "They said 'We don't care for the sheriff, neither for the state of Georgia, the Governor, nor for the President of the United States. We have our own laws here." For Middleton, however, the most frightening aspect of the moment was the women "all jabbering together like a pack of magpies. They were striking the ground with sticks, flourishing them in the air, and other things of that kind." But when they tried to talk to him, he told them, "I desired to speak to the men, and not to the women." Taking refuge in a nearby house, the white men soon decided that they had no choice but to surrender. When they finally emerged, a contingent of men under the command of Captain Green, head of the Ogeechee Home Guards, stripped them of their guns, arrest warrants, and money, and sent them on their way to Savannah, on foot. They walked five miles before a freight train picked them up and carried them back to the city.[54]

The headlines of the December 31 *Morning News* screamed, "OUTRAGEOUS CONDUCT OF THE OGEECHEE NEGROES... *Houses Plundered and Goods destroyed by the Blacks.* THEY DECLARE THAT THEY HAVE COMMENCED WAR. NO WHITE MAN TO BE PERMITTED TO LIVE ON THE OGEECHEE." That day Sheriff Dooner once again ventured out to the district, this time with a posse of twenty unruly men firing wildly from railroad cars. He quickly retreated to Savannah, convinced that they still stood no chance against so many insurrectionists, who by this time were sacking more barns and burning more houses. Back at the Ogeechee railroad station, a manifesto (reportedly the work of Solomon Farley) had "been posted in a conspicuous place" claiming that the sheriff had had no authority to arrest him, and in a cryptic coda, "If you should not see Me I will make my Appearance Just as Soon as the law Being Essued for the Right of all Classes & Color!!!! Yours, Ogeechee Until Death."[55]

In a surprising turnaround, within a couple of days, black leaders announced that they would surrender to a federal military officer but not to local civil authorities. And so by January 7, 1869, two companies of United States infantry had arrested sixty-eight prisoners and brought them into Savannah, where they were lodged in the Oglethorpe Barracks and turned over to local officials. Eight days later a pretrial hearing commenced; it lasted more than two weeks. Savannah whites could derive some satisfaction from the sight of a "hard looking crowd" of black men now subdued and on display daily at the courthouse.

As far as elites were concerned, the Ogeechee incendiaries seemed safely in the hands of the four presiding judges, including Philip M. Russell Sr. and his son Philip Junior. The defense team, consisting of James Johnson, U.S. district attorney, and prominent Republicans Henry S. Fitch and Amherst W. Stone, intended to show that the "Ogeechee Troubles" amounted to little more than an ordinary contract dispute. The prosecutor, former Confederate general Henry R. Jackson, promised to prove that the uprising constituted a violent insurrection flowing out of a secret conspiracy against established authorities. During the hearing, the prosecutors would focus on the Ogeechee Home Guards and the Union League, and on Farley's written message, his hat signal to his supporters, and periodic "telegraphic signs . . . made in the air"—presumably evidence of a plot conducted against a background of incessant nighttime drumbeating and daytime drilling. The prosecutors wondered aloud, Why did the Ogeechee rebels possess bayonets? Surely not for shooting sparrows or catching fish! Throughout the testimony, spectators thronged the courtroom, with black women bearing baskets of food for the prisoners to eat during breaks in the proceedings.[56]

The strategy of defense attorney Fitch was revealing. He scoffed at the notion that black people could organize any meaningful plot on their own. Of Captain Green he said: "The very face of the prisoner was a type of semi-civilization; his dress beggared description; he had no more understanding what insurrection meant than he did of the mystery of the Immaculate Conception." Fitch claimed that the case was really about "kleptomania" on the Ogeechee, where people aspired to "a kind of Indian reservation, a life of indolence and ease—no law, no sheriff's warrants," where people "would rather pilfer than plough."[57]

Dampening the long hearing's entertainment value was its price tag: the county would have to expend a tremendous amount of the taxpayers' money in order to meet the magistrates' and sheriff's bills of more than $6,300, and then spend many more thousands trying, lodging, and feeding the prisoners, who, of course, would shoulder none of the expenses. For their part, the aggrieved Ogeechee planters had little incentive to relegate large numbers of their workers to prison indefinitely. Called to the stand, three of the landowners downplayed the events on the rice flats of Chatham County. Middleton claimed he knew of no military organization in the area, though "there seemed to be something of a martial spirit pervading them." He said he took it as a routine fact that all of his hands—as many as 125 in the busy threshing season—carried muskets and shotguns to the fields with them. The hearing ended with the prisoners remanded to trial, which would begin in May. In a fitting end to the first phase of the proceedings, the *Morning News* ran an ad for Dotterer's Improved Rice Sowing Machine, patented in 1868, with its timely pitch: "In the present deranged condition of the system of manual labor it is important that planters avail themselves of the advantages of labor saving machinery in all possible cases."[58]

Black men and women in the Ogeechee attempted by force to gain control of their own productive energies and to seize the land their forebears had worked for generations. Northern officials and lowcountry whites were determined to thwart this effort, and also to deny the freedpeople the opportunity to acquire meaningful power through conventional political means. Yet it was highly unlikely that the political system would have proved responsive in any case to blacks' demands for compensation for generations of unpaid labor and untold suffering. Northern Republicans no less than southern Democrats held sacred the principles of private property and employers' prerogatives; under these conditions, former slaves in the lowcountry were left to ponder their options for the future. Together they continued to press against the forces of oppression, even as they also turned inward to nourish community institutions of family, school, and church.

CHAPTER FOURTEEN

You Will See Them Studying

ON JANUARY 6, 1869, just as the Ogeechee Rebellion was reaching its crisis point, Charles Colcock Jones Jr. delivered a lecture to an appreciative audience at the Georgia Historical Society. Though now living in New York and working as a lawyer, Jones managed to find time to research and write history books about the Georgia lowcountry. Indeed, like his former law-office colleague George Mercer, Jones felt more drawn to literary pursuits than to legal filings and motions in the courtroom. Over a thirty-year period Jones would publish substantial volumes at a rate that was impressive by any standard: histories of Augusta, Savannah, the Chatham Artillery, and Sherman's siege of Savannah; as well as biographies of Spanish explorer Hernando de Soto, Revolutionary War hero Major John Habersham, and Confederate navy commodore Josiah Tattnall. An amateur anthropologist and archaeologist, Jones also completed works on lowcountry myths and trickster tales, and on Indian tribes, their leaders, "dead towns," and "monumental remains" in Georgia.[1]

That day in January, Jones's listeners no doubt took some comfort in retreating, if only for an hour or two, to a time full of hope—the past, when all of Georgia's future lay before it. Now as fresh rumors and wild speculations emanated hourly from the Ogeechee, the historical society offered a refuge of sorts from immediate events that boded ill for the long term. Jones had chosen to speak about the subject of his latest book, published the fall before—Tomochichi, the *mico* (chief) of the Yamacraw Indians, who died in 1739 at the age of ninety-seven. In the early eighteenth century, Tomochichi had forged the Yamacraw out of groups of Creek and Yamasee Indians, settling his small band of two hundred people on the bluff above the Savannah River. It was there that James Oglethorpe, the founder of the colony of Georgia, founded Savannah in

1733. The elderly Indian leader quickly established friendly diplomatic and trade relations with Oglethorpe and other English colonists.

In his book, Jones detailed what he considered the admirable qualities of Tomochichi, "the first, the noblest, and the most influential friend the colony of Georgia ever had." According to Jones, the Indian "appreciated the fact of the superior power of the white race," and went out of his way to show the foreign interlopers "kindness and fidelity." A warrior of considerable physical strength, Tomochichi was nonetheless eager to accord white people the respect due them, bringing gifts of game and fish, and offering to protect them from the menacing Spanish to the south in Florida. Jones also wrote that not only did the chief openly express his gratitude to the benevolent Oglethorpe, but he also, frequently and in public, acknowledged that whites were more intelligent and more powerful than his own people. The Indian leader rejected the notion that the Yamacraw should convert to Christianity en masse; instead, he requested that they receive meaningful religious instruction, a request that was ultimately spurned by Methodist missionaries. In 1734 the chief traveled to England, where he met with the king and the Archbishop of Canterbury. Jones lauded the "vein of manhood" that ran through Tomochichi's life, a vein of "honor, of friendship, of generosity, of integrity, of courage, of fidelity, of love for his fellow-man, and of interest in whatever was elevating and of good report."[2]

Jones's paean to Tomochichi was a thinly veiled indictment of what he considered the ultimately disappointing, and in some cases perfidious, behavior of another dark-skinned, exotic group in Georgia: the freedpeople of the coastal region. By this time Jones was echoing his father, who had published his own book three decades earlier lamenting the shortcomings among Georgia slaves—their ingratitude toward their masters and mistresses, their dissembling and untrustworthiness, their resistance to Jones Senior's stern brand of Christianity. In his deference toward whites and his apparent willingness to cede power to them, Tomochichi demonstrated that distinctive peoples might, in their relative powerlessness, serve as allies and not antagonists of whites. To Jones and his friends, the uprising on the Ogeechee represented a disastrous chapter in the state's illustrious history, a betrayal of the implicit promise made by Tomochichi—that men of a darker hue would ultimately and eagerly embrace subordination to whites.

Jones arranged his talk to coincide with his annual visit from his home in New York City to the family's two plantations, each run by a former slave—Gilbert Lawson at Monte Video and Stepney West at Arcadia.

Jones was exasperated: the Monte Video workers had not met their individual quotas of cotton and corn for the year—four hundred pounds of cotton and ten bushels of corn for each man, three hundred pounds of cotton and eight bushels of corn for each woman, with the amounts for child workers prorated according to age. At Arcadia, the hands were supposed to turn over one-third of all the crops they grew to their landlord-employers. For the new year, 1869, Jones decided to institute a new contract system, one that would allow the workers on both plantations to pay rent in the form of cash, not crops, and enable the Joneses to retain ownership of the land free from the obligation of furnishing workers with seed and other supplies. Jones retained the former house slaves West and Lawson, in recognition of their skills as plantation managers, and on the theory that any outsiders, such as resident overseers, were more trouble than they were worth. Black fathers and husbands on the two plantations now gained some flexibility in the way they allocated the labor of family members, with men and older boys pursuing wage work off the farm in the winter season—on the Savannah docks, in the timber industry in Darien.[3]

Around this time, Frances Butler was facing her own annual reckoning on Butler's Island and Hampton Point. The first of the year—an unsettled and unsettling time combining "Christmas, politics, and pay-off"—had left her fearful for the future. The Ogeechee uprising to the north seemed to presage an imminent "general negro insurrection" along the coast. Matters were satisfactory on St. Simons Island, where the Butlers' former slave Bram was managing a workforce of fifty cotton field hands, including eight members of his family, all "working like machinery, and [giving] no trouble at all." But in the coming months an attack of caterpillars would ruin the crop and force Butler to rent parcels of land to individuals for cash instead of shares.[4]

Meanwhile, the rice workers on Butler's Island were in an uproar. Their persistent refusal to do the cold, disagreeable work of banking and ditching left Butler little choice but to hire "a gang of Irishmen" from Savannah for the winter months. She felt betrayed, now that the blacks' initial "expressions of affection and desire to work for me" had given way to "sullen unwillingness." Her employees "seemed to reach the climax of lawless independence"; they had taken to calling white people by their last names, and the men refused to take their hats off in the presence of a white woman. Butler kept a loaded pistol by her bed.[5]

As another precautionary measure, she convinced a local U.S. military officer to send troops to Butler's Island, but within a matter of days the small occupying force had done little but rile her workers, eat her stores of food, and strip her orange trees of their fruit. Butler knew that she could not count on civil authorities to bring order to the plantation: the local election had left the town of Darien and the county of McIntosh largely in the control of local blacks, who held the positions of ordinary, sheriff, superior court clerk, constable, and magistrate. The Reverend Tunis G. Campbell, together with his longtime supporters, had capitalized spectacularly on the four-to-one black-white ratio in the town. Butler knew that if she sent to Darien for help she would soon see a black sheriff on her doorstep. Still, she had decided against cooperating with her neighbors who spoke of investing large sums of money in bribing Campbell "to use his influence over our negroes to make them work for us." Instead, she was contemplating an effort to bring Chinese laborers to the lowcountry.[6]

Like freedpeople throughout the South, workers on the Butler and Jones holdings pressed their employers for schools, an issue that by this time had become just as contentious as negotiations over labor contracts. Charles Jones had remained firm in his decision to "*deny consent* to the establishment of a schoolhouse upon Arcadia land," on the assumption that "it would, in the present condition of things, be but an opening to complications, losses, etc. etc." In contrast, Butler had hired a young white college graduate, who soon decided that teaching black children was a task beneath him, and left. But because the school was so popular among her workers she hired another teacher, a black divinity student from Philadelphia. Listening in on the children's recitations one day, she was startled "to hear them rattle off the names of countries, lengths of rivers, and heights of mountains, as well as complicated answers to arithmetic."[7]

Four years after the war, black communities along the coast were struggling to provide elementary schooling for their children week to week, month to month. Funding came from diverse and largely unpredictable sources. The Freedmen's Bureau was winding down and offered only minimal aid to a dwindling number of places. Some schools stayed open with modest subsidies from local poor funds controlled by blacks or sympathetic whites. Other schools were receiving money from the Peabody Fund, founded by George F. Peabody, a wealthy northern merchant. And in the 1868–69 school year the American Missionary Association sponsored more than three dozen teachers in Savannah and throughout the coastal region. Although most of the AMA teachers were northern white women, by this time the association was also sending $15 a month to southern- and northern-born white and black men and women who worked in small schools scattered throughout the area. A few planters like Frances Butler believed building schools on their land was sound labor relations, but insisted that the teachers refrain from political "agitation."[8]

More and more schools were dependent on the support provided by the freedpeople themselves, including parents who contributed through either sponsorship or monthly tuition fees. Rural and small-town schools especially were precarious ventures, plagued by money problems and high rates of teacher turnover. Harriet Newell, a fifty-year-old white widow living in Liberty County, taught a school of ninety-six children with the help of her fourteen-year-old son; the two subsisted on squirrel and robin meat in the face of neighbors who condemned her for "teaching the 'black dogs.' " The well-organized community in Darien pledged their support of the local school, taught by a black woman, Savannah native Hettie Sabattie, in the fall of 1868; when she left on account of failing health, the AMA sent two northern white teachers to replace her. Along the coast, a number of black male teachers lurched from crisis to crisis. At Elliot's Bluff, north of St. Mary's, Anthony Wilson tried to make a living by teaching school. A former sawmill employee, he had lost a hand in a workplace accident; now he found himself threatened by another young man in the area who wanted his job and the paycheck that came with it. At the Grant School, located at the intersection of five rice plantations north of Brunswick, a newcomer from New York, James Snowden, took pride in his pupils, young and old. He reported to his AMA sponsors, "After day school I have walked out in the rice fields, where most of my night scholars work; there you will see them all with a spelling book in a bag around their necks, and every spare moment they have you will see them studying." At the same time, their former masters "were and are very much against their having a school."[9]

Douglas Risley, the Freedmen's Bureau agent in Brunswick, was no doubt pleased to welcome Snowden to the area. In the fall of 1868, Risley contended with two new AMA women teachers, replacements for Sarah Champney and Sophia Russell. The previous summer, Risley had warned AMA headquarters against returning his two nemeses to Brunswick; he wrote Russell directly and accused her of being "a morally jealous and disappointed woman, who naturally has an unfortunate propensity for gossip and strong appetite for scandal." Her propensities and appetites were evident in her attempt to "blacken" his character and that of his bride with rumors "that there was something wrong between

Mrs. R & myself before we were married." Rather than return to Brunswick, Champney and Russell decided to accept an assignment in the west Georgia town of Cuthbert for the coming year; upon arrival they received "there comes Hell" from the local white folks, a greeting the two women took in stride. At the same time, Brunswick's primitive conditions—both boarding and schooling—proved too rough for the newcomers, two other veteran AMA teachers. They had fled to Staunton, Virginia, by January 1869. Risley was again appealing to the AMA for "a *good colored man*"—one who could withstand, among other indignities, "sneers, frowns, opposition, ostracism, etc. etc"—and primitive living conditions and unpalatable, ill-cooked food.[10]

Another teacher in the Brunswick area confirmed the worst fears of whites when she set about forming "Grant Clubs" among blacks. Ellen E. Adlington had long been a boarder in the household of Virgil Hillyer, who was now representing Camden County in the state legislature. She marveled at the grapevine that appeared to connect all freedpeople in the area and facilitate political organizing: "These people are like telegraph wires[;] what one knows all knows." But while Hillyer was away in Atlanta, his business partner decided that the teacher had become too much of a liability to white Republicans in the area, and tried to cut off the funding for her school. In December 1868, Douglas Risley stepped in with some money from the Peabody Fund and saved it.[11]

In contrast to the countryside, where tiny one-room schools waxed and waned in response to funding and politics, Savannah boasted the imposing Beach Institute and a plethora of smaller black-run private schools. Yet in the spring of 1869 the institute was embroiled in fresh controversies. Fourteen people lived under the roof of the AMA mission home, now overseen by yet another superintendent. Thirty-seven-year-old Congregational minister Charles W. Sharp had worked for the AMA in West Virginia and North Carolina before bringing his wife, Helen, and his mother, Aphia, to Savannah. When he arrived he found to his dismay that the strong-willed veteran teacher Cornelia Drake already exerted considerable influence within the home, and she had little inclination to relinquish that control. Drake, in Savannah since 1865, had formed an alliance with a new teacher, Robert H. Gladding of Newport, Rhode Island, himself an aspiring superintendent. (Within a few months the two would marry.) Together Gladding and Drake began their own prayer meeting as a public challenge to Sharp's spiritual leadership. At the same time, two boarders, Captain J. Murray Hoag of the Freedmen's Bureau and his wife, also proved to be divisive forces; when William Jones, a black teacher from Hopeton, came to visit, the Hoags went out of their way to refuse to eat at the same table with him. Sharp wrote in exasperation to AMA headquarters, "the Captain and Mrs. H. have no *Christian interest* in our work . . . their influence is not helpful to the missionary spirit and religious life of those engaged in it."[12]

In January 1869, Robert Gladding decided on his own to turn out one hundred Beach Institute students who had not paid their tuition, about one-third of the total student body. Sharp was furious; no doubt it was he who formulated the petition that he and seven teachers signed, requesting that AMA headquarters reassign Gladding to some other place. Sharp was in the process of negotiating the treacherous waters of Savannah religious politics, and he feared that Gladding's precipitous move would squelch his effort to start the city's first Congregational church. Wrote Sharp in March 1869, "Every influence in Savannah, white and colored, is against us." Apparently unaware of the history of the AMA's failed proselytizing efforts—Hardy Mobley's thwarted missionary work in particular—Sharp professed shock that the city's black preachers were so opposed to his efforts: "The very idea of our going ahead, seems to provoke them to malice, and to the exercise of their ingenuity in stirring up prejudice and awakening suspicions."[13]

By this time Sharp had brought to Savannah a young black preacher, Robert Carter, a former slave of Georgia planter-politician Howell Cobb. Settling into his position, Carter switched denominations, from Presbyterian to Congregational. He began serving as "a connecting link" between Sharp and potential black congregants, especially young people resisting the "strong and even bitter pull" of their parents. Sharp found Carter useful not for his preaching but for his energy and his flexibility. In April 1869 the black man founded the First Congregational Church of Savannah; and when the handful of new members, presumably former Baptists, told Carter that they wished their children to be submerged during baptism, Carter replied obligingly that he would submerge them "or sprinkle [them], just as they like."[14]

The AMA was stepping up its proselytizing efforts at a time when smaller private black schools were closing and a Catholic order of nuns—the Sisters of St. Joseph, trained in France for African missions—was offering free classes for black children. Beach Institute provided regular classes and a full complement of teachers, and parents were inclined to support the school, especially if their children could avoid paying the tuition fees. One casualty of the AMA's size and reach was the thirty-year-old teacher Susie Baker King. After her husband, Edward, died in September 1866 she had moved from Savannah to Liberty County, where she taught a small school on her own. She soon found, however, that "country life did not agree with me," and returned to the city in 1868. There she lived with her widowed mother; her father, who had served on a federal gunboat during the war, had died in 1867. King opened a night school for adults, taking on a number of odd jobs in order to support herself and her baby son. But in the fall of 1868 Beach Institute began offering free night classes to adults, and she lost all her pupils. Leaving her two-year-old in the care of her mother, she began working as a live-in domestic servant for a white family.[15]

It was apparent by now that schools of all kinds had become deeply enmeshed in the city's religious rivalries. In October 1868, Bishop Augustin Verot renewed an effort to convince the city council to help pay the large expenses incurred by the Catholic school system. Verot timed his appeal well. In early 1869 the city's white politicians were already planning for the municipal elections to be held that fall, the first in two years. They could ill afford to alienate such a huge part of their constituency—Irish tradesmen and laborers. In one of his communications, the bishop began by reminding the aldermen that Catholics formed "a large portion of the population of the City, as appears from the internments in Laurel Grove and the Cathedral cemetery." One had no need to look as far as the burial grounds to find evidence of Catholic numerical strength: they constituted as much as one-quarter of the total white population (and a greater proportion of adult white men), and for the aspiring politician, they collectively presented an unforgettable appearance on election day. Verot pointed out that the Catholic schools spent a great deal of money to offer a free education for many poor children—the preceding year, $7,000 for 700 children. At the same time, Catholic taxpayers were subsidizing a public system from which they derived no discernible benefit. Their taxes and parochial tuition fees amounted to a "double burden."[16]

In 1867, when Verot first made this appeal, white politicians were nervous about funding separate schools based on the proportionate allocation of public funds: black taxpayers would not be far behind their Catholic counterparts in demanding money from the school board. Constitutional issues aside, at that point the Catholic proposal seemed impractical. But two years later the political landscape had shifted, and in the spring of 1869 the board again took up the question. This time all of the parties hammered out a compromise in time for the fall school term. Under the agreement, the Savannah board of education accepted financial responsibility for the Catholic schools. The board would retain current teachers who met its standards (vague as those might be), and it would permit the teachers to open classroom exercises with scripture and prayer and to use history books and other texts consistent with the Roman Catholic religion. In submitting this plan for approval by the council, the board recognized that the relation of the Catholic schools to the public schools was "one of great social and practical importance," and that all parties involved must "harmonize and cooperate" in a larger educational effort. Board members added that they stood ready and willing to provide for the schooling of all black children of the city, as soon as the state legislature authorized them to do so.[17]

In the spring of 1869, Savannah Democrats saw both promise and peril in myriad political developments at the local, state, and national levels. In March, the Republican Ulysses S. Grant took office as president. After holding hearings on the previous November's election in several southern states, including Georgia, Congress had refused to count Georgia's electoral votes and rejected the state's choices for U.S. senator, charging election fraud. At the same time, state lawmakers meeting in Atlanta had made two major decisions that their supporters considered both well reasoned and highly symbolic: the expulsion of the black legislators in the fall of 1868, and the rejection of the Fifteenth Amendment to the U.S. Constitution in March 1869. Barring renewed federal interference, the black vote seemed safely under control, the state Democrats in the ascendancy.[18]

For former Confederates, developments in and around Savannah were less reassuring. That spring, James Simms had received a federal appointment as a postmaster in Savannah, indicating that national Republicans, if not local ones, could still reach into city politics. In the summer the Republican Governor Bullock pardoned the six Ogeechee defendants after they had been tried, convicted, and sentenced to hard labor in Milledgeville. More disturbing to whites, though, was a test case initiated in Savannah and related to black officeholding. The case, focused on Richard W. White's election as clerk of the Chatham County superior court, was moving its way up through the state's court system. In February a jury for the Superior Court of the Eastern District of Georgia had ruled that since White was one-eighth black—"of African blood"— he was ineligible to hold office regardless of his election the previous November. However, in mid-June the Georgia Supreme Court (under the direction of Chief Justice Joseph E. Brown, the former governor) reversed that decision and decided in White's favor in *White v. Clements*.

William J. Clements was the white man who had lost the election to White. The black man's election was a special irritant for white authorities, because James J. Waring had posted his bond, required of all new officeholders.[19]

Although the supreme court justices diverged in their reasoning, all three agreed that the question turned ultimately on the provisions of Irwin's Code, the unified law code of the state of Georgia. A set of principles outlining citizenship rights, the code was drawn up by state legislators in 1863 and revised and included in the state's new constitution of 1868. The original code defined four categories of men residing in the state of Georgia: citizens (white men, who had the right to vote, sit on juries, and run for office); residents (recent in-migrants from other states who had not yet met the state's residency requirement for suffrage); aliens (nonnaturalized immigrants from other countries); and persons of color (anyone of at least one-eighth African descent, enslaved or free).

Because White looked white, his "race" remained a point of contention. In the original trial, he had refused to testify about it, claiming the question was irrelevant. One witness said that White "was reputed in the neighborhood to be a colored person." The registrar of voters testified that he had put a "c" (for "colored") next to White's name on a list that was posted in public and that White never challenged the list, presumably proof that he at least considered himself to be black. A white physician, a self-proclaimed expert in the "science of ethnocology," claimed that "science taught men the rules by which the race of man was ascertained," and it was his professional opinion that White was indeed black, though the doctor provided no specific reasons for that finding. In their opinion, the justices decided that White was a Negro for all intents and purposes: "Pedigree, relationship and race may be proven by evidence of reputation among those who know the person whose pedigree or race is in question." Race, then, was matter of "reputation" rather than bloodlines or physical appearance.[20]

Chief Justice Brown and a second justice agreed that, now that black men fell into the "citizenship" category, they possessed the "privileges and immunities" of that status. The 1868 constitution had granted black men the right to vote for candidates for office, which included the right to run for office and to serve if elected. The third justice held that blacks were now citizens, but that that status did not necessarily include the right to hold office. He argued that the legislators who originally approved Irwin's Code included officeholding in their definition of citizenship, but only because they understood the category of citizen to be restricted to

white men. Unlike voting, officeholding was an honor, not a right, conferred on specific categories of people. In order for a group explicitly
denied a right to gain it, the legislature must act affirmatively to grant it. In
the end, though, all three judges ruled that the lower court decision must
be reversed; the third apparently concurred on a technicality—that the
lower court had not fully considered the question of White's race.
Richard White assumed the office of clerk of Chatham County superior
court.[21]

While *White v. Clements* was still under review, Savannah authorities
were making plans to revolutionize the city's electoral process in order to
preserve the power of white men, this in anticipation of the upcoming
municipal elections. In March 1869, in keeping with the state law that
held poll taxes were legal as long as the funds they raised were spent for
educational purposes, the council provided for a city-election registration tax that would support the white schools. This fee would make voting a relatively expensive proposition for the majority of laborers, white
and black. (In short order Republican leaders would attempt to pay the
fees of their laboring-class constituents, suggesting they were following
the lead of their Democratic counterparts.) Not content to leave matters
at that, the council inaugurated a new system of representation, based on
municipal districts. On April 3 voters went to the polls to choose two
constables and one magistrate (justice of the peace) for each of four new
city districts and three outlying rural districts. Authorities created these
seemingly innocuous entities with a larger purpose in mind. Local
observers made careful note of the social composition of each district in
the city proper: The first and fourth included a substantial number of
blacks; the second and third district only a few. When the votes were tallied on April 4, three black men had won—James Andrews and Joseph
Habersham had been elected constables, and King Solomon Thomas a
magistrate, all in the Fourth District.[22]

Initiated by the Democratic Party as an internal reform, and then
approved by the council, the district system signaled a break from the traditional at-large municipal elections that diluted the power of any one of
the party's constituencies—in the antebellum period, Irish working-class
voters especially. However, in the late summer of 1869 the purposes of the
new system became clear. Now the Democratic (at times called Conservative) Party in each of the four districts would meet in early September and
nominate three candidates for the city council, and then a committee of
twenty-eight (seven people representing each of the four districts) would
decide on a single candidate for mayor. Voters cast their ballots for tickets

and not for individuals. (The Republicans lacked the tight party organization required to take advantage of the new plan.) In the end, the purpose of the district system, in the words of Democrats, was to "preserve the ancient fame and good name of the Forest City from misrule—and ruin," and, they might have added, from a black electorate that constituted nearly one-half of the city's total number of voters. The process, relying on district-level decisions to produce a single citywide ticket, would later become known as the white-primary system.[23]

On the evening of Wednesday, September 1, the self-proclaimed Conservatives in each of the four districts held a meeting to appoint a nominating committee. That day the *Morning News* reminded its readers of the momentous nature of the event, the first municipal election since the fall of 1867: "At no period in the political history of the city of Savannah, has the election of wise, prudent and trusty men for the offices of Mayor and Aldermen required greater foresight and discretion on the part of the citizens of Savannah, than at this apparent juncture." All white men must band together and once and for all banish the "designing men"—those "thorns in the flesh of the body politic, festering sores that break out ever and anon in the healthiest communities." The official Conservative ticket consisted of John Screven, the forty-two-year-old railroad official and Confederate veteran, for mayor, and a slate of twelve new faces for the city council slots. The demographic profile of the candidates had not changed much from antebellum days, dominated as it was by, in the words of the *Morning News,* "well-known gentlemen of the highest social and commercial standing"—lawyers, merchants, businessmen, and others "thoroughly identified with our people." Rounding out the ticket were two immigrants, forty-five-year-old Michael Lavin, a wealthy wholesale grocer who "has transferred his warm attachment for Erin to Savannah," and thirty-year-old German-born John Schwarz, an officer in the Germania Fire Company, a man who "by his strict attention to business has won the esteem of all classes."[24]

The Conservatives calculated that the voter-registration fee would depress the black vote and that the disarray of the Republicans would block any semblance of a Radical (Republican) ticket of candidates. But the system did not work perfectly this first time around. James J. Waring showed up uninvited at a Conservative rally and demanded to speak—an insult to the tenets of white solidarity—and he was shouted down before he could reach the podium. The need to maintain a united front in opposition to the Republicans prohibited debate within the ranks of the Conservatives; former mayor Edward Anderson, who had well-founded doubts about the fiscal probity of John Screven, held his tongue during the run-up to the election. And then at the last minute persons unknown circulated two "outside tickets," apparently intended to confuse Conservatives. One included Screven at the top for mayor, but then listed seven white independents for aldermen. The other put forth Charles H. Hopkins as a mayoral candidate with the same seven independents.[25]

In the weeks before the election, black men rushed to register, many apparently finding safety in numbers and kinship as they appeared before the city registrar. For example, all seven men appearing before the registrar on August 30 were black, three with the surname of Johnson and two with the surname of James. They included two carpenters and a gardener, a hostler, a fisherman, a laborer, and a bricklayer. Whites made light of the sight, claiming that clothes recently pilfered from washtubs and chickens plucked from the roost provided evidence of would-be voters stealing goods and livestock to sell for the dollar they needed to pay their registration fee. Indeed, the fact that "the black element takes such a lively interest in politics" remained profoundly troubling. In their zeal to play a full and active role in politics, freedpeople would continue to confound their former owners.[26]

Nevertheless, the Conservative ticket swept the October 11 election by a vote of three to one—Screven's 2,977 to Hopkins's 967—and all twelve of the official Conservative candidates won city council seats. In preparing for the election itself, Conservative leaders had worked with municipal authorities (of course the two groups overlapped to a large degree) and left nothing to chance. The city appointed one hundred special deputies to police the polls beginning at seven that morning. The Conservative party put together a "challenging committee" of seventy-five persons who would rotate in groups of three among the three ballot boxes at the courthouse. These men raised official objections to black voters whom, they charged, were ineligible to vote because they failed to meet residency or poll-tax requirements. Among the challengers at the ready were the jailer, Waring Russell; the deputy Julius Kauffman of Ogeechee Troubles fame; the attorney George A. Mercer; former mayor Anderson's son Edward Junior; and a host of past and current aldermen. An effort by Charles Hopkins to reserve one of the ballot boxes for black voters—"to prevent the possibility of *any trouble*"—was rebuffed by Philip M. Russell Sr., clerk of the city court, on October 8. The combined effects of a weakened and fractured Republican party leadership, black and white; the poll tax; and the Conservatives' show of official force at the polls that morning either prevented or discouraged many black men from voting. On the night of October 13 the Conservatives celebrated, in mayor-elect Screven's words, "the preservation of the municipal government in their own hands, and escaping the fate of our sister cities of Charleston, Mobile, Montgomery and New Orleans," all of which had black aldermen on their city councils. A torchlight procession attracted throngs of spectators and featured the familiar lineup of white fire companies (now representing their respective election districts), marching bands, and city officers and other dignitaries, all illuminated by the glare of blazing torches, rockets, and Roman candles.[27]

The election took place against a backdrop of regional labor politics that seemed to signal new forms of economic insecurity among black workers in Savannah and the surrounding lowcountry. Black longshoremen in Charleston had recently struck for an increase in wages, to $3 a day. Shipping interests vowed to replace the strikers with white men imported from the North and thus effect "a complete eclipse of the domineering spirit of negro equality." In the end, though, the workers did manage to extract a compromise from their employers, who agreed to pay them $2.50 per day, with 40¢ per hour for each hour worked after a 7:30 a.m. to 6 p.m. day. But meanwhile, planters throughout the lowcountry were threatening to populate the rice fields with Chinese immigrants, and promising that northern white men would ultimately abandon the freedpeople "when the rat-eaters arrive in sufficient numbers to become an element of political power."[28]

The mere mention of enlisting Chinese labor bespoke a dramatic, albeit gradual, coastal revolution apparent during the annual reckoning of December 1869. In the Georgia and South Carolina lowcountry, rice workers refused to perform the wet, cold, disagreeable labor in the wintertime fields, leaving ditches undug and canals unbanked. More generally, landowners who persisted in hiring a large number of cash tenants or sharecroppers could look forward only to a disruptive turnover among their workforces at the end of the year. Bad weather and a caterpillar infestation during the 1868 and 1869 crop seasons forced planters gradually to seek out new sources of income—truck farming, lumbering, repairing boats, producing naval stores, keeping bees for honey, growing sugar, starting a small hotel for northern tourists. Some black men were moving to Florida to find wage work in the railroad, turpentine, and timber industries. Those who could buy or squat on a small piece of sandy land tried to eke out a living by growing potatoes and corn and raising chickens to sell in the Savannah market. Some husbands and fathers agreed to work for a landowner Mondays and Tuesdays in return for the freedom the rest of the week to spend their time as they chose. These combined factors led to the eventual breakup of many plantations into small plots more suitable for truck farming than staple production, as landowners grew weary of coaxing Irish laborers out from the city for the winter season, and as grandiose schemes for importing Chinese laborers came to nothing.[29]

With the exception of small all-black enclaves such as Darien, black people possessed little formal power despite their "lively interest" in the political process. Effectively barred from all positions of influence in Savannah, and outvoted at the state level, they had no chance to effect meaningful changes in the way they were governed or the way their tax money was spent. And the demographic and political realities of Georgia discouraged even those few sympathetic white people from championing the cause of a group so vulnerable. So-called "moderate" Republicans showed more interest in facilitating economic development such as railroads than in addressing widespread landlessness among the former slaves.

Savannah blacks had plenty of cause to scorn their inconstant, self-proclaimed white allies. But one exception stood out: James J. Waring seemed bent on needling the white men of property and standing who under different circumstances would have gladly claimed the wealthy physician as their own. Throughout 1868 and 1869 Waring figured prominently in a number of political controversies. In a lengthy series of court proceedings, he successfully sued and won reinstatement in the Georgia Medical Society; his fellow physicians had sought to punish him for posting Richard White's bond. Before he lost his seat on the city council, Waring had to fend off a charge of corruption from his colleagues—that he was using his position on the Dry Culture Committee to enhance the value of his substantial real estate holdings in and around the city. Undeterred, he turned around and forced the council to initiate an inquiry into the jailer, Waring Russell, for paying as his deputy a man who was already on the police payroll. James Waring's startling appearance at the Conservatives' mass meeting on September 1—and subsequent letters defending himself to the editor of the *Morning News*— suggest a certain fearlessness, if not a self-destructive streak, in a man who had no realistic chance of furthering his own political ambitions, whatever they might have been.[30]

In DECEMBER Congress passed the Reorganization Act, which mandated that Georgia reseat the black legislators expelled in September

1868. Once again the recalcitrant state came under military rule to be "reconstructed" for a third time. Aaron Bradley returned to take his seat in the state senate, only to find himself at odds with Republican leaders, including the Reverend Tunis G. Campbell, who resented Bradley's apparent poaching of supporters on Campbell's home turf of McIntosh County. Over the next few months Bradley, Porter, and Simms would sponsor a variety of bills aimed at outlawing chain gangs, segregated public transportation, and voting and poll taxes. This last measure was approved in May 1870, only to be reversed by the new legislature seven months later.[31]

Bradley was now denouncing all white politicians, men who were "all *rebel tyrants*, who are continually rendering unfair decisions for the oppression of the colored race." Despairing of any meaningful legislative changes at the state level, in May 1870 he went to Washington to urge Congress to act on "chain-gang slavery in Georgia":

> Little girls and boys under ten years of age are sent to chain-gangs for [stealing] three potatoes or [for] singing Shoo-fly, with great locks and chains around their necks; colored bogusly-convicted women and men are let out for ten cents a day to do out-door work that should be done by honorable white and colored laborers at $1.50 per day, and never permitted to vote after it. Any colored person can be convicted for anything, and white men cannot be convicted for anything done to negroes.

Bradley declared, "We the colored people of Georgia will be heard," and with some attention-grabbing hyperbole, he even threatened that blacks would soon bolt the Republican Party, to appeal to "the Democracy [i.e., Conservatives], who are now anxious to do all for us we require."[32]

The chain-gang issue was emblematic of Savannah's new order. Elites believed that disorder in the streets hindered efforts to restore the city to its former glory and to present a welcoming public face to foreign visitors and potential business and real estate investors. In early 1870, the city observed the social season by playing host to well-heeled tourists, to a delegation of prominent southern businessmen, and to Robert E. Lee (in January). Five years after the end of the war, the city once again was enjoying the luxury of a revived social scene marked by glittering displays of excess. By all accounts the wedding of Octavus Cohen's daughter, who married her cousin, was "a magnificent affair," with the dresses of the lady guests surpassing any that the fashionable set had ever seen; a dinner that included "every delicacy that could be obtained"; and gifts of "silver, jewelry, sets of lace and many others too numerous to mention" in the words of one awestruck correspondent (Henrietta Wayne). The lavish Cohen wedding suggested that postwar prosperity had muted, at least for the time being, the prejudice toward the city's Jewish merchants during the war. And indeed, old and new forms of white fraternity—baseball teams no less than fire companies—suggested cross-class harmony among whites who were nevertheless divided by extremes of wealth and poverty.[33]

Still, as the city regained its prominence as a port, the sidewalks and public thoroughfares reflected the noisy restlessness and diversity of the population. Everyone, it seemed, regardless of age, sex, or skin color, was eager to partake of moneymaking opportunities, licit or otherwise. Prostitutes still plied their trade in the city parks and shouted obscenities to passersby. Little boys, black and white, raided corner grocery stores and picked the pockets of shoppers. The residents of Broughton Street awoke each morning at 6:30 to the sounds of "an *army* of people" marching and "making morning hideous, with informal screams" selling crabs, tomatoes, peaches, apples. "The 'squash boy,' the 'apple woman,' the 'crab man,' or the 'peach girl'" all added to "this infernal din, to which the braying of a jackass would be pleasant music." Still, some disturbers of the public peace were not out to make a living, just out to resist a little authority. U.S. soldiers, some drunkards and others deserters, assaulted passersby on the sidewalk and robbed hardworking shopkeepers. Dockworkers and others in the city's "floating population" continued to observe the end of a long workday with fistfights and knife fights in the streets. Black draymen persisted in careening around street corners with wagonloads of goods, making the thrill of driving fast a public health hazard. Black and white children took advantage of an evening concert in the park to pelt each other with pinecones, forcing indignant white women to move their seats or abandon the park altogether.[34]

During the spring of 1870 the city council made a concerted effort to address specific nuisances that offended the "respectable" classes. Over the next months, council members sought to regulate the storage of guano, fertilizer made out of the waste of seabirds and bats, so that whole neighborhoods would not be overwhelmed with the stench. Maintaining a sewage system that kept pace with rapid population growth remained an intractable problem, especially for a city constantly on yellow-fever alert. Residents were warned to refrain from beating their carpets in the squares and throwing their slops in the streets. Council members also sought to restrict the location of both permanent and temporary exhibits of exotic animals. With its "menagerie of wild beasts and reptiles on said premises, engendering foul smells and allowing snakes to escape from their confinement," the Nobles Museum on Broughton Street was "considered to be detrimental to the public health and safety of life."[35]

It was within this context—city leaders' preoccupation with public aesthetic issues—that the council initiated two new projects that affected Savannah's poorest and most vulnerable residents. In January the council took up the issue of the city jail, now an eyesore to the community. When it was built in 1845, the building occupied a pine barren; but now "it stands in the most attractive and rapidly improving part of Savannah"— the edge of Forsyth Park. This "dilapidated and wretched" structure, with its "grim walls [that] frowned upon our beautiful promenade," daily spewed forth "the painful and demoralizing spectacle of men in manacles going to their trial or punishment," a scene "darkly presented to the sight of the visitors to Forsyth Place of whom especially at this season of the year, are strangers." The city needed not only a new jail but a new jail in a new place.[36]

Two months later, the council took up another eyesore. Two recent cases of black people who had died "upon the public thoroughfares" provoked an outcry, with the police and private citizens appealing to Mayor Screven for action. The challenge, according to Screven, was how to get "the dying, the loathsome, and the unknown sick" off the streets and out of the public eye; the jail was full, and the poorhouse was reserved for ill seamen and other indigent whites. The mayor was skeptical of the suggestion that private persons be paid to care for black patients. He worried that eager benefactors (black in this case) would be "only too willing to undertake a pretended task for falsely earned compensation." Earlier in the year the council had rejected a request by a black leader, the Reverend Abraham Burke, that the city provide aid for infirm and aged black men and women. Burke, age fifty-two, was active in a number of local mutual aid societies, and he was eager to secure council assistance for a charitable effort organized by the black community. Instead, Screven favored a plan, which the council subsequently approved, to seek white philanthropists who would fund a shelter "without permitting an unwise extravagance in their management of the institution, or converting it into a home for the idle and malingering." In any case, the chief object was to "remove from the high-ways the pitiable objects which at once offend and appeal to the public humanity." These were people—or corpses—best removed from the sight and minds of whites.[37]

In reducing the welfare of the black population to a question of aesthetics, and likening lifeless bodies to so much street debris, white Savannah confronted the ironies of a post-emancipation society. Elites claimed that black people were childlike, unable to exercise judgment on their own, and then condemned them when they pursued schooling and a robust form of politicking and civic engagement. On the docks and in the streets, the white laboring classes responded eagerly to the cynical embrace of politicians who maintained that a white skin remained a badge of pride and superiority. As a result, freedpeople in the city of Savannah and in the lowcountry were forced to wonder where slavery ended and freedom began in a society only imperfectly transformed.

CHAPTER FIFTEEN

I Came to Do My Own Work

W HAT LITTLE WE KNOW of Irish-born Philip Carroll, federal census taker, suggests that he was a man of strong constitution. During a sweltering lowcountry summer, in 1870, he trudged around Savannah's central business and residential district, knocking on doors, and recording each person's name, place of birth, and property holdings. For some bits of information Carroll had to rely on his instincts: as an arbiter of "racial" designations, he had to categorize individuals as "white," "black," or "mulatto," though skin color alone was not always a reliable marker of social identity. Like other census takers that summer, Carroll further relied on his instincts and avoided canvassing certain back-alley neighborhoods that struck him as particularly unwelcoming. Yet for all the challenges of the job, the twenty-four-year-old must have felt some pride in his position as an assistant United States marshal. He was entitled to 2¢ for every name he wrote down, so his list of 7,880 men, women, and children (a little more than one-quarter of the city's total population of 15,166 whites and 13,069 blacks) earned him the respectable sum of $157—not bad for six weeks' work, though his illiterate compatriots probably took in just as much or more for a similar-length stint on the docks during the winter.[1]

On June 1, Philip Carroll began his first day on the job by recording his own household, headed by a successful Kentucky-born bookkeeper named Alvin B. Clark, thirty-one, husband of Jeannette, twenty-two, a native of Ohio, and father of four-year-old Mamie. In addition to the young census taker, the Clarks boarded another Kentucky-born book-keeper, Andrew B. Clark (also thirty-one, perhaps Alvin's twin). An eighteen-year-old black servant, Samuel Grant from South Carolina, lived in the house as well. That first day, after taking the Clarks' information, Carroll went next door, to the home of the black politician James Porter, "Member Legislature," and noted Porter's children—John, fifteen, Laura, thirteen, James R., eleven, and Elizabeth, seven, living at home with their father. Typical for Savannah at the time, the Porter household contained several persons who did not share the last name of the head, including Martha Artsen, sixty-seven; Richard D. Artsen, thirty-five, a carpenter and presumably Martha's son; a day laborer named Emanuel Wyatt, thirty, and Sarah Lancaster, fifteen. On July 16, a month and a half, 466 households, and 198 pages after he began, Carroll returned full circle to his own neighborhood, and ended his tally with a household next door to the Clarks. This one included two unmarried men: William Pierce, age twenty-seven, a white bookkeeper born in Kentucky, no doubt a friend of Carroll's landlord, and the wealthy Joseph W. Clift, thirty-six, Massachusetts native and "Member Congress."[2]

Although the fact was probably lost on Carroll, implicit on the pages of the census was high drama—stories of black families liberated from slavery. Even individual names were revealing. Among the four children of Samuel and Rebecka Young, both illiterate house servants, were two sons—one, born the year of the Emancipation Proclamation, they had named Moses; his younger brother, born two years later, they called Lincoln. (To honor a harbinger of freedom, they had chosen to call an older son, born in 1859, Gabriel.) And the composition of individual households suggests the strenuous efforts of laboring men to free their mothers, wives, and children from the generations-long burden of menial labor. Robert Young, a twenty-eight-year-old illiterate cotton-press worker, had recently served as president of the Sons of Zion society. He made enough money to allow his wife, Jane, to stay home and keep house, and their son John, age twelve, to attend school. Still, many families needed multiple breadwinners to sustain themselves. Fortune Campbell, an officer in the Zion Travellers Society, was working as a day laborer. His large household relied on the income of his wife, Susan, a laundress, and their three teenage sons, also employed as laborers. Under their roof were the Campbells' three younger children; an elderly woman, Catherine Campbell, probably Fortune's mother; Lilly Stewart, forty-two, a huckster, and Joseph Stewart, ten, probably Lilly's son.[3]

Some people who had been free before the war managed to survive and keep their families and property intact. The household of the successful brickmason Simon Mirault and his wife, Elizabeth, included their four children, in addition to a sixteen-year-old laborer and a twenty-nine-year-old dressmaker and her small son. The widowed Georgiana Kelley, a prominent church and mutual-aid society leader, retained the substantial house (worth an estimated $3,000) she had shared with her teamster husband, Jeremiah; but her household now included the Reynolds family—Jefferson, Lucretia, and their four children and a servant. Jane Deveaux, fifty-four, the schoolteacher of many years' standing, also owned her home; she was keeping house for her sons John, twenty-five, a clerk and local Republican activist, and Charles, nineteen, a barber; and for Eliza Lloyd, fifty-seven, "at home," and the teenager Florida Byrne, an apprentice dressmaker.[4]

The information collected by Philip Carroll and his co-workers provides a collective portrait of the black community, or at least the relatively stable portion of it. Black men were employed in fifty-eight occupations, ranging from cook and stevedore to cotton shipper, pilot, upholsterer, and bookbinder. The most common jobs were laborer, drayman, porter, teamster, carpenter, and bricklayer. Black women, 70 percent of whom were employed, were limited to jobs as midwives, cooks, seamstresses, nurses, and servants. Sixty-six proprietors owned among them twenty-seven different kinds of businesses. Throughout the community, literate blacks could be found in all kinds of jobs, including those of farmer, laborer, waiter, carpenter, undertaker, porter, tailor, butcher, painter, and whitewasher. No longer need a person be a schoolteacher or a preacher to be able to read the Bible or the *Morning News*.[5]

Individual households such as the Lawrences revealed the familial and group ties that bound Savannah freedpeople to each other. Elizabeth, forty-three, and John, forty-five, at one point served as president and secretary, respectively, of the John the Baptist Society. In the summer of 1870 John was working as a huckster and Elizabeth was keeping house. Living with them were their own children (a son, a butcher; and a daughter, a nurse); Justine Erwin, twenty, a laundress; and two children, Tina Barrett, eight, and Madeline Frazier, ten. Black households included an average of three persons who did not share the same surname as the head, suggesting a collective ethos that informed the postwar community. And together they were industrious: by the spring of 1870, three thousand account holders, either individually or as members of mutual-aid societies, had deposited a total of $415,781 in the Savannah branch of the Freedman's Bank. The drafts drawn on the bank by this time—worth more than $324,000—help to account for the $400,000 in property owned by Savannah blacks, a fourfold increase over 1860.[6]

The five years after the war had transformed the lives of whites as well as blacks. Specifically, the census revealed the return of at least some

Confederate veterans to the semblance of a normal family life and a measure of economic independence. A twenty-four-year-old grocery-store clerk named Henry Snyder had left the household of his mother and siblings to go to war in 1860; ten years later he was still working as a clerk, but now as the head of his own family, married with an eight-year-old stepdaughter. Similarly, Augustus LaRoche was eighteen in 1860, a student living with his parents; ten years later he was the head of his own household, married with a baby, and working as a timber inspector. The sons of the elite, including William C. Purse (in 1870 a bookkeeper), Philip M. Russell Jr. (notary public), and George Anderson and William Gordon (both cotton merchants) were thriving, no doubt due to their fathers' connections. These men had integrated themselves back into familiar social circles, and embarked on a new life.[7]

Household configuration reflected class status; unmarried laborers, male and female, found lodging in boardinghouses and private homes, while the wealthy employed many resident domestic servants. In 1870 Georgia Stewart, hired by the Savannah Education Association in January 1865, was no longer teaching; now she took in boarders, including a boat pilot, a huckster, and a blacksmith, and the families of these workers, as well as her own son, John, a watchman, his wife, Georgia, and their two children. The physician Richard Arnold, age sixty-two, presided over a large household in his impressive downtown residence, which was worth an estimated $10,000. His extended family included his only child, a daughter, Ellen, thirty-six, and her British-born husband, William Coscns, thirty-six, a fire insurance agent, and their children Margaret, twelve, Richard A., ten, and Georgia, three. Also living on the premises were eight black servants—John and Lizzie Martin, Solomon and Lizzie Black, and two children among them.[8]

One of Philip Carroll's co-workers, H. J. MacDonald, covered the area west of Forsyth Park, including the jail, where in August one Peter Ford, an illiterate thirty-five-year-old Irish immigrant, was being held for murder. The whereabouts of the other players in Ford's sensational crime were unknown. Ford had been a denizen of the rough neighborhood of Canuet's Row in the southeastern corner of the city. This was a place where blacks and whites lived "promiscuously," in the words of the *Morning News*, a place not acknowledged by respectable white people except in the records of mayor's court. On July 12, 1870, Ford shot dead a black man named Anthony Gordon, husband of Kate Heary, a mulatto. In her husband's absence, the woman had taken up with Ford, and when Gordon returned, Ford allegedly killed him. Adding to the melodrama, at one point Ford and Kate's sister "had been living together in a state of miscegenation," in the breathless words of a reporter. And so in late August the census taker found Ford in the county jail under the watchful eye of Waring Russell. Living under the same roof as the accused murderer were other black and white men and women, native-born and foreign-born, a predictable assortment of seamen, day laborers, washerwomen, and house servants. But here too were representatives from some of the more respectable trades—blacksmiths, plasterers, coopers, clerks, carpenters. Kate Heary herself eluded Savannah census takers.[9]

The county jail was not the only building in Savannah where whites and blacks encountered each other in rough equality as in antebellum days, promiscuously or not. Despite years of hand-wringing by public officials, clusters of brothels persisted in remarkably multicultural form. The neighboring houses run by Susan Dusenberry and Mary Norris, for example, consisted of white and black women ranging in age from sixteen to thirty-eight and hailing from Ireland, New York, and Georgia. In an annual report, city officials tried to categorize different groups of these women workers, estimating that 65 were living in brothels, 50 were making their living on the street, and 150 were serving men as "kept women."[10]

Prostitutes were a fixture in the city, but they were also emblematic of a larger issue that Savannah officials only reluctantly acknowledged. Despite whites' obsession with various forms of black public expression—politicking, marching, protesting—it was clear that the city had a "white" problem also. In 1870, foreign-born residents numbered 3,671, a 25 percent decline since 1860, a period during which the white population as a whole had increased. (At the same time, the fact that the census was taken in the summer means that immigrant wintertime dock workers were undercounted.) Prosperity in the North, combined with an emerging preponderance of black workers on the docks, slowed foreigners' in-migration to the Forest City. Still, like their black counterparts, white rowdies and "roughs" and other public nuisances continued to embarrass the city in the eyes of visiting merchants and wealthy tourists. When Mary Murphy refused to stop drinking, her prone body was too frequently a sidewalk obstruction; when common-law partners fell out in a noisy row, the city's reputation as an orderly place suffered accordingly. And these public displays of moral turpitude seemed intractable. The unfortunate Murphy, "known for a long time to every member of the city police," periodically received sentences that ranged from thirty days in jail to a stint scrubbing out the municipal offices in the Exchange, but no form of punishment reformed or deterred her.[11]

Around this time, groups of immigrant weavers and machine operatives bound for the new textile mills of Columbus, Georgia, were passing through Savannah; the state now led the South in the number of cotton mills and spindles. The mill operatives' brief appearance sparked a debate about the problem of joblessness among whites: Should Savannah promote manufactures as a way of sopping up the human detritus on the streets? In mid-August the Georgia Historical Society sponsored an open forum on distress among the white population, this "great and growing moral evil." Not surprisingly, participants in the meeting arrived at few conclusions: "The vastness of the subject, underlying as it must the whole strata of human society, politically, morally, and socially, of course carried the subject to various issues, and a great deal of interesting facts were elicited." Still, it was becoming impossible to ignore the plight of young whites like Thomas Plummer, a native of Brooklyn, sleeping in Chippewa Square and bereft of friends, money, and employment. The mayor released Plummer after he promised to return to New York "by the first steamer." But the fact remained that the city's seasonal economy, which left dockworkers idle for half the year or more, continued to produce hardship among whites as well as blacks.[12]

In September, elites created a new library specifically for white men; its purpose was to provide some means of self-improvement among striving members of the laboring classes, and to divert husbands, fathers, and sons from the city's grogshops and brothels. The temperance movement, which had achieved only limited success before the war, now began to gain favor among the self-consciously respectable tradesmen of the city. Among the officers of the newly formed Bartow Division of the Sons of Temperance were the unmarried George P. Gray, twenty-one, a store clerk and the son of a well-to-do wood merchant; and the family men Ely Otto, thirty-two, a printer, and Henry A. McLeod, thirty-three, a bookkeeper. In the fall of 1870 this division hosted others from Georgia to form a state organization, the Grand Division of the Sons of Temperance. Members of these groups were in the process of distancing and distinguishing themselves from the brawling, hard-drinking workers on the docks and railroads.[13]

By this time the Republican era of Georgia's postwar politics was coming to a close. On July 15 Congress readmitted the state to the Union for the third time in five years (the first time under Presidential Reconstruction in 1865, and the second time under Congressional Reconstruction in 1868) and approved state elections in December. That summer the federal government closed the state's last Freedmen's Bureau office. Dogged by charges of corruption, Republican governor Rufus Bullock had alienated prominent members of his own party, opening the way for Democrats to seize the initiative and close ranks under the banner of white supremacy. In the state's interior, the Ku Klux Klan was organizing what would be a final, concerted campaign to terrorize black voters, a campaign that would prove effective in suppressing—and in some areas eliminating—freedpeople's influence at the ballot box.[14]

In Savannah, black men and women confronted a grim reality: their near-total exclusion from the formal machinery of power. No black people served on the juries of any city, county, or state court; and the mayor, members of the city council, and the entire police force were all white. At the same time, within their own constricted world, blacks sought to advance their interests as individuals, parents, and members of religious and community groups. Their everyday struggles shifted the balance of power—modestly but perceptibly—away from white employers, missionaries, and law enforcement agents.

In November, city authorities decided they had to take strong measures against the black boys who were disturbing the downtown peace by "chunking rocks" with slingshots. Since the city no longer whipped blacks, the mayor declared that youthful offenders should receive their correction at the hands of "those having authority over them." Summoned to the stable behind the police barracks, the parents of Jack Williams were ordered to whip him themselves, but before his father could lift a hand, the boy's mother called out, "No chile ob mine is gwine to be whipped. Dese yer is 'mancipation times, an' I ain't gwine to stand it. We'll pay de money [fine] fust, but you shan't whip de chile no how. No you shan't!" The *Morning News* reporter described what he no doubt believed was a hilarious conclusion to the affair: Jack began to scream and curse his parents, enraging his mother, who exclaimed, "Cuss yer old daddy, will yer? Is dat de way you was raised?" She then held her son while her husband administered the flogging, a more potent dose of the lash than even the police sergeant had intended. Though Jack might not have appreciated its finer points, the principle of black parental authority was finding expression in the words and actions of freed mothers and fathers.[15]

As workers, black men and women sought to define their own priorities over and above the interests of the whites who hired them. For a domestic servant, the mere act of quitting a job was a means of retaining at least a modicum of control over his or her workplace; and sometimes a bidding war for the worker's services ensued. Mayor Anderson was annoyed to lose his servant Paul to the wealthy merchant Abraham Minis, who had a large household to maintain; Paul said that he could not get along with the cook employed in the Anderson household, but the mayor suspected it was Minis's offer of an additional $2 a month that made the difference to the servant. (Now a life insurance agent, Anderson was well situated; but with property worth $13,000, he could not compete with Minis, who reported $40,000 in real estate and personal property.) Anderson had to promise another servant, Nina, a raise of $5 a month, in the hope that she would not quit "to go into the country," as she had threatened to do. The intense demand for cooks and maids citywide translated into careless work in the parlor and the kitchen, and rapid turnover among black workers more generally. Henrietta Wayne retained little influence over her five live-in black servants, all of whom were necessary for her large household of seven family members and boarders. Writing to her stepmother, Wayne lamented, "Times are so different now. Servants have to be looked after or nothing is done right, I have to make changes of excellent servants"—including a valued house servant who quit to get married. This quiet domestic revolution reached into the innermost recesses of white family life.[16]

For the most part, black institution building proceeded out of the sight and earshot of the white community. White-controlled publications largely ignored the proliferation of black churches and mutual aid societies; the city directory failed to include them in lists of religious and charitable enterprises, and the local papers only occasionally alluded to local fundraising efforts. In 1870, the popularity of the Freedman's Bank among individuals and voluntary societies received only passing attention from Savannah whites when, in the spring, 787 depositors received their quarterly interest payments, ranging from 8¢ to $21 (on a total of $61,000 currently held by the bank). At the same time, public celebrations suggested the outlines of institutional bonds joining men to women, young to old, laborers to skilled workers, Savannah teachers to lowcountry field hands. When the freed community marked the ratification of the Fifteenth Amendment in the spring of 1870, the event attracted an estimated three thousand people from a broad swath of the coastal region, and showcased the Union League, the voluntary societies, the schools, and the churches, all in a huge procession that wended its way through the city.[17]

American Missionary Association officials scrambled to respond to freedpeople who were by no means uncritical of the association's schools. Though eager for their children to become literate, many parents remained decidedly ambivalent about the AMA. Two years after its completion, the imposing Beach Institute employed seven teachers and boasted an enrollment of three hundred children; but the school had still not secured a central place in the black community. Local religious leaders as well as parents cast a suspicious eye on the persistent proselytizing efforts of the AMA staff in general, and of Robert Carter in particular; he remained vocal in denouncing rival black preachers and in trying to win converts for the Congregationalists. Aiding Carter in his missionary efforts were U.S. Representative Joseph W. Clift, home from Washington, D.C., in the summer of 1870, and Isaac Brinckerhoff, cashier of the Freedman's Bank. These men felt compromised by their own missionary efforts, which, they believed, required them to "crouch . . . at the feet of ignorance and superstition"—that is, to appeal to black Baptists and Methodists.[18]

Almost all AMA teachers abandoned Savannah for the North each summer. When Philip Carroll canvassed the east side of the city in the summer of 1870, he found a skeleton staff at the mission home; two teachers, Kate Bent, twenty-six, of Massachusetts, and Lizzie Parsons, twenty-two, of New York, had stayed behind after their co-workers left in late spring. (Boarding with the two were Joseph Clift's brothers Walter, now the Savannah postmaster, and Edwin, a clerk in the post office.) At the end of the spring term, the home, a popular meeting place for northern visitors, had bustled with activity, creating problems for the recently arrived superintendent, Andrew N. Niles. This was the first AMA assignment for the forty-five-year-old bell manufacturer from East Hampton, Connecticut. He was soon complaining to his New York superiors that the home was "overrun with visitors at almost all hours of the day and night and in the 'ladies chambers.' " Before retiring at night he found in the downstairs hallway "the rack crowded with hats and not knowing where the *heads* were that belonged in them."[19]

As was usual after the summer interlude, several new AMA teachers arrived on the scene for the beginning of the new school year. Lizzie Parsons acknowledged the disruption caused by teacher turnover when she wrote that the parents of her pupils said to her, "We just get used to knowing our teacher, used to her ways—and she to ours, when she is sent somewhere else." In turn, the AMA's summertime absence allowed small private black schools to spring up all over the city. Black mothers especially appreciated summer school, at least through June, for then "the children are sure of care, and restrained from evil for at least five or six hours of the day," according to one teacher. But in the fall of 1870 Beach Institute postponed opening day for several weeks. The teachers were slow to arrive, or return, and Niles wanted black parents to get used to the idea that the AMA tuition of one dollar a month would be enforced for the coming year. With rents high, cotton prices low, and work slow, this fee was out of reach for most families; but AMA headquarters was adamant that even impoverished parents pay for their children's schooling.[20]

In the fall, the private black schools that had taken hold over the summer were posing a serious challenge to Beach Institute. Niles outlined the obstacles, "hindrances [that] like armed men close in on every side": "The first families scoff at the idea of sending their children to school with refugees—Others think the advances in tuition a Yankee trick to get their money—others think that a bill before the Legislature relating to education will relieve them of the necessity of paying *anything*—others think the colored people are competent to manage their own affairs in their own way." And then there was the issue of classroom instruction: Some parents preferred the smaller classes of the private schools, believing, according to one AMA teacher, that "they are getting more for their money for the reason that they have *more time spent on them*," and that the teachers were "*attending* to *them* [the children and parents] personally."[21]

The AMA continued to set a rigorous schedule for its teachers, who felt they were "terribly overworked." Abbie W. Johnson ran a successful used-clothing operation—her "rag department"—and also taught day school. She embraced the physical challenges in the classroom, where she had "*Cooks, Washers, & Ironers, Cigar makers, Cotton Pickers, Child minders, Nurses, Milk Carriers, toters of water*, and playful little Girls & boys." However, not every teacher was temperamentally suited for dealing with a "medley" of children every day. Some northern women sought only "a gay season at the South," a time of "mirth and trifling," in the words of Andrew Niles. But neither were their opposites necessarily suitable for the work. The superintendent pronounced Mary Hall, a new teacher that fall, "a most unfortunate lady for us"—rigid in her demeanor with the pupils and judgmental in her relations with her co-workers. Her department was "thinning out," as parents pulled their children out of her classroom and enrolled them elsewhere. Niles worried about her effect on the overall AMA enterprise: the parents, he wrote, "can't be turned off with second rate teachers."[22]

Just as black men and women sought to exercise some control over their children's schooling, they also sought to affirm their rights and their dignity as citizens of the city of Savannah. The result was a series of dramatic campaigns against city ordinances mandating segregated streetcars and voter-registration fees. The local streetcar company had announced a new policy that black ticket holders must use separate cars, and that those cars would run every forty-five minutes—that is, less frequently than cars carrying whites. On the morning of Friday, May 6, 1870, James Habersham, a constable in King Solomon Thomas's magistrate district, boarded a car just as it was leaving the Exchange and sat down with white passengers. The conductor quickly halted the car and ordered Habersham off, but the black man declared "that he would not get out; that his money was as good as white people's money, and he intended to ride on that car at all hazards." Within a few minutes two police officers had arrived on the scene; Habersham resisted arrest, "remarking that he would not be taken, that he was a state and County officer, and superior to the policemen." Appearing in court on May 9, he remained defiant, but the mayor decided to release him, admonishing him to "respect the rights of others"—in other words, to "respect" the "right" of whites to ride in their own exclusive cars.[23]

Aaron A. Bradley alluded to this incident soon after when he appeared at the Union League hall in Washington, D.C., and gave a speech condemning Georgia's white Republicans. Still under indictment in Chatham County for his alleged role in the killing of Samuel Law in November 1868, Bradley noted that before the war, black people could pay half fare to ride in passenger cars with whites; but now black passengers "must pay full fare and be huddled into a stock car." Though a state senator, Bradley was preoccupied with fending off the timeworn charges that he was ineligible to serve because of his conviction for "seduction" in New York, nineteen years before. Of his stubborn parrying with his tormentors, the *Atlanta Sun* noted, "he is the incubus that is torturing [white legislators] at all hours and under all circumstances. On all occasions he rises like the ghost of Banquo and obstinately refuses to [sit] down at any bidding." While in the capital, Bradley had petitioned the U.S. Supreme Court (unsuccessfully) to be allowed to argue cases before it.[24]

Throughout this period other members of the lowcountry delegation to the statehouse continued to press for legislation in the interests of their black constituents. In August, James Porter introduced an equal-accommodations bill in the state legislature, though the measure found no favor among white Republicans. Porter also joined with Tunis Campbell and James Simms to support passage of the so-called "Savannah

Bill," which would deny localities the authority to levy a voter-registration tax. Savannah Democrats charged that the bill, "this revolutionary scheme," was an ill-disguised attempt to encourage rural black South Carolinians to flood the city on election day.[25]

Looking ahead to the municipal elections in October, and under rhetorical assault from black legislators in Atlanta, the Savannah city council reaffirmed its prerogative to impose a poll tax. Aldermen had approved the $1 fee on March 17, 1869. On July 7, the city attorney, Edward J. Harden, felt compelled to render a formal opinion on the subject. The day before, Richard White, clerk of the superior court, had appeared unannounced at a council meeting, intending to demand that the registration ordinance be repealed. Accompanying White were James J. Waring and Isaac Seeley, a fifty-year-old native of Maine and a U.S. Post Office political appointee. White, Waring, and Seeley took their seats in the city council chambers and waited patiently for the conclusion of regular business so they could deliver prepared remarks. But abruptly, council members adjourned the proceedings before allowing the men to speak.[26]

Not surprisingly, the municipal elections of October resulted in a clean sweep of white Democrats, though it is unclear whether black leaders even fielded a slate for the city council. Black candidates for a number of other offices, including the board of city commissioners and the board of education, all went down to defeat. Still, the Conservatives' new system of choosing nominees at the district level was proving less than foolproof. Indignant at the challenge posed by a group of (white) upstarts, council incumbents put together their own ticket "embracing the tried and true spirit of the old Board." Another ticket featured "the strength of Young America in her mechanical, mercantile and commercial interests"— presumably immigrant laborers and shopkeepers. Despite opposition from Conservative Party leaders, several newcomers were elected to the council, among them Edward C. Anderson Jr., son of the former mayor. Christopher C. Casey, the onetime alderman who had helped surrender the city to Sherman in 1864, also claimed a seat on the new council; like Richard Arnold, he was enjoying a rebound in his public career.[27]

Aaron Bradley ventured back to Savannah in early October. No evidence linked him to the Law murder, and on October 13 the indictment against him was quashed. Anticipating the statewide elections in late December, he announced his candidacy to the U.S. Congress and denounced the incumbent, Joseph Clift, as well as every other city, county, and state Republican in sight, including Richard White (whom he labeled an "ineligible Indian"). Not surprisingly, then, Bradley played no role in the Chatham County Republican nominating convention, which was held in early November in a dimly lit hall above a Savannah alehouse. Prominent among the speakers were Charles H. DeLaMotta, Walter Clift, and Isaac Seeley, but ordinary people also took part; among them was Peter Houston, a forty-year-old dock laborer. For his part, Bradley was disgusted with biracial coalitions on any level. In campaigning against the party regulars, including the Clift brothers and Virgil Hillyer of Camden County, he demanded to know: "In places where the majority are colored, why should we seek to elevate a third-class white man over a *first-class* colored man?" To emphasize his point, he lambasted Freedman's Bank cashier I. W. Brinckerhoff, whose courtroom testimony had helped commit him to Fort Pulaski five years earlier.[28]

The prospect of the upcoming elections struck fear in the hearts of just about everyone. Democrats were worried about recent state legislation that prohibited challenges to voters at the polls. They railed against white Republicans, "negro traders" who supposedly trafficked in the votes of gullible blacks. Still, municipalities retained the right to impose voter registration taxes, and to set up ballot boxes where they wished; in most counties and towns, this meant a central polling place that would discourage rural folk from voting. At the same time, demographic changes seemed to favor black interests, at least countywide. Since the previous census, in 1860, Savannah had grown by 22 percent, but local officials had managed the city's boundaries so that 15,000 whites just barely outnumbered 13,000 blacks. In the same period, the county of Chatham had grown by a third—to about 40,000 people, 24,000 of them black. Yet overall, black and white Republicans saw what little influence they had left ebbing away, now that federal oversight of the state had ended.[29]

A week before the election, Bradley demonstrated that he could still put on a show. He had taken to appearing in public armed with a bowie knife and a derringer. On December 12, riding a "well-fed steed," and accompanied by a drum and string band, candidate Bradley began a grand procession at South Broad Street, marching through southside black neighborhoods up to the bay. As many as six hundred supporters followed along, halting before the Customs House to offer up three cheers for the U.S. flag and three more for President Grant, and then moved on to Whitfield Square. Along the way, Bradley distributed flyers, ending the procession with a rally to promote an independent Republican Association. He was hoping the new group would include Ulysses L.

Houston and James Simms, among other black leaders. Several up-and-coming activists—John Deveaux, twenty-five, a clerk and the son of veteran teacher Jane Deveaux, and James Johnson, twenty-eight, a South Carolina–born barber—agreed to appear with Bradley onstage. The attorney also entertained the crowd with a new composition, "The Laborer's Song": "Come united let us be / In setting all the Laborers free / Hurrah, hurrah, hurrah."[30]

For the first time in his life Bradley received what might be termed favorable coverage from the *Morning News.* By splitting from Clift, Campbell, and other Republican Party stalwarts, Bradley had the potential to divide the black vote; if the Democrats could remain united, they would undoubtedly triumph in the election in Savannah and Chatham County. This is probably what happened. Perhaps in an effort to avoid bloodshed, the city compromised with black leaders and opened two polling places on the morning of December 20, one at the courthouse on Wright Square and one in King Solomon Thomas's precinct. Though civil authorities lacked the legal means to challenge voters directly, they did encourage local police to arrest any black voters they suspected of coming into the city from South Carolina. With consecutive congressional seats up for grabs—one to serve out the rest of the Forty-first Congress, the other for the following session—Bradley had run for both, taking more than 2,100 votes away from Richard White (a candidate for the Forty-first) and Virgil Hillyer (for the Forty-second) out of more than 8,000 cast. Democrats won both seats. Though three white men were running against each other for sheriff, King Solomon Thomas lost by only 83 votes and came in second, suggesting that the ballot counting was less than fair and accurate.[31]

A prominent member of the Russell political dynasty, Philip Senior's son Isaac defeated James Porter for a seat in the state house of representatives, and Rufus E. Lester (the Democrat who had taken the place of the expelled Bradley in the state senate two years before) defeated James Simms for a senate seat. At the state level, of eighty-six contested house seats (one-half the total), seventy-one were won by Democrats, along with nineteen of twenty-two senate seats. The city of Savannah, the county of Chatham, and the state of Georgia had successfully staved off a five-year-long Republican challenge.[32]

During the holiday season of late 1870, elites celebrated the solidifying of Democratic power. Fashionable visitors thronged the streets, enjoying the mild weather, as trainloads of cotton arrived continuously from the interior. (Within a year, the river port would reach its historic high point in terms of the percentage of the nation's share of cotton it shipped from the South.) In anticipation of Christmas, local stores appealed to the well-heeled shopper looking for the latest in "grand action pianos," children's toys, and clothing imported from Europe: "Santa Claus has taken up his quarters at Thomas Bateson's store, corner Congress and Drayton." In preparation for the festivities, ladies could stop in at the salon of Madame L. Louis and have their hair dressed "in the highest style of art."[33]

The wives of Savannah bankers and cotton brokers mingled with the rest of the city on the morning of December 25 to watch the Mysterious Fantasticals, heralded by a brass band, gallop through the sandy streets on horseback. Young men outfitted themselves in costumes of "fantastic cut and color" now befitting the spirit of the times, with some of them mocking President Grant and Union general Benjamin F. Butler. On horseback or in bullock carts, and "followed by the young of all colors and sexes and conditions," the Fantasticals paused long enough to pose for a costume contest and to hold a jousting tournament, and then they rushed off again. The day's festivities also included a pigeon-shooting competition and "the Yankee innovation of a base-ball match." Throughout the city, people celebrated by attending church services or a Yamacraw cockfight, depending on individual preferences.[34]

Out in the countryside, New Year's brought the annual reckoning, and here former Confederates could take less comfort from the state of things. Up and down the coast and on the islands, where blacks represented fully 75 percent of the population, the most striking development was the breakup of the large antebellum plantations. Since 1860, in Chatham County, the number of farmers working from three to ten acres had grown from 24 to 203; in Camden County, from 3 to 189; in Liberty from 13 to 616. These small holdings grew at the expense of the largest estates. On the eve of the war, Camden County had boasted eighteen plantations of over 500 hundred acres; ten years later only six remained intact. In lower Georgia, in the course of the decade the average farm size declined from 885 acres to 240. These changes were not the result of impersonal economic forces, but of the determination of black men and women to own their own land and avoid work in the rice and cotton fields under the supervision of whites.[35]

These combined transformations signaled the appearance of a black peasantry, with families subsisting on a small plot and sending fathers and sons off to wage work in railroad camps or the Florida timber industry for part of the year. Grudgingly, white landowners accommodated themselves to the new order. In December 1870, when Frances Butler returned to Butler's Island from a trip to England, she found half of her hands gone, presumably for good. They were protesting her overseer, a man she admitted to be "very injudicious, and . . . far too hot-tempered to manage my people." Butler was still contemplating a workforce of Chinese laborers operating a new steam plow; but until those people or that machine materialized, she must make do with the labor she had. Unable to find a suitable replacement for her volatile overseer, she placed the plantation under the management of "negro captains." Meanwhile, her neighbors were abandoning planting altogether.[36]

Around this time, a federal initiative prompted black people throughout the lowcountry to contemplate the multiple meanings of the Civil War, and the limits of their newfound citizenship. In the spring of 1871, local representatives of the Southern Claims Commission began to take depositions from claimants who sought compensation for property losses suffered at the hands of Union soldiers during the war. Congress had authorized the commission to hear testimony from witnesses and, if a person's claim was judged legitimate, to grant him or her a cash settlement in recognition of any private property that the Union army had seized to supply the troops. Successful claimants had to prove that they had remained loyal to the Union throughout the conflict.[37]

Among Georgia lowcountry claimants, black men and women predominated. These claims testified to the devastating raids conducted in December 1864 and January 1865 by Sherman's men in the countryside surrounding Savannah, as well as his troops' rapacious appropriation of city residents' stores of food and other property. Former slaves of some of the region's most prominent planters took their place at the deposition table, an echo of the heyday of the lowcountry Rice Kingdom that had enriched Charles C. Jones Sr., James Potter, Edward J. Delegal, Joseph Quarterman, and many others. In Liberty County, a total of ninety-two claims, all but three initiated by black men and women, ranged in size from $49 to $2,290 (this highest amount was claimed by the politician William Golding); the average allowed claim amounted to $357.43. The claims process was cumbersome; in some cases litigation dragged on for more than ten years.[38]

On March 3, 1871, Virgil Hillyer began taking depositions in the case of Boson Johnson of Liberty County, claim number 15505. Eventually, Johnson would testify in his own behalf, and a number of witnesses would seek to corroborate his account. The witnesses included his wife, Nancy, their grown son Wallace, and Rhesa Floyd, an elderly white man who worked as a miller and lived near the Johnson family. In depositions taken over more than five years, the Johnson family would recount a fateful day in January 1865, when mounted federal soldiers raided the plantation of David Baggs.[39]

Boson Johnson's claim was not unlike that of other former slaves in this area of Georgia, and it revealed his family's pattern of property accumulation. According to Nancy, her husband was "always a hardworking man," laboring for himself each day after he completed his task in the field, and working on behalf of his family all day Sunday as well. The family claimed $514.50, compensation for a mare ("a good creature," in Nancy's words), 625 pounds of bacon, 60 pounds of lard, 12 bushels of corn (tied up in the children's undershirts "like bags" and carried off by soldiers), 8 bushels of rice, 7 meat hogs, 11 stock hogs, and 25 chickens. The soldiers had taken more—cloth, baskets, tubs, dishes, "two fine bed quilts," even her husband's clothes and her daughter's silk dress; but since these did not qualify as military supplies they were omitted from the formal claim.[40]

Before answering specific questions, witnesses had the opportunity to make a general statement. When she was interviewed by claims commissioners, Nancy Johnson told a dramatic story of the way the war had ended one chapter of her life and ushered in a new, uncertain one. For her, the raid was but a culmination of a series of dramatic encounters she had had with a number of different white people since the conflict began. She testified that at one point her family had sheltered a Yankee prisoner who "came to our house at night; we kept him hid in my house a whole day." The freedwoman could not help but be struck by the novelty of the situation: "He sat in my room. White people didn't visit our house then." Within a few days the Johnsons had spirited the fugitive to safety; but their master sent his own grandson to extract information from the couple about the man's whereabouts. Denying any knowledge of the soldier, Nancy Johnson said she chose to "tell a story" to save her husband's life. She feared he would be killed for hiding a Yankee.[41]

Nancy Johnson also told of feeding two rebel soldiers who had deserted their unit: these were "poor white people" who were "opposed to the war and & didn't own slaves & said they would rather die than fight." Toward the end of the war, David Baggs tacitly recognized that slavery was doomed. He came to Nancy Johnson and pleaded with her to stay: He said "if you won't go away & will work for us we will work for you." In response, the freedwoman said, "I told him if the other colored people were going to be free that I wanted to be." Baggs's wife took a different tack: Nancy Johnson left the plantation and upon her return the white woman "asked me if I came back to behave myself & do her work & I told her no that I came to do my own work." Enraged, Mrs. Baggs asked her "if I came back to work for her like a '*nigger*'—I told her no that I was free & she said be off then & called me a stinking bitch." To add insult to indignity, the white woman failed to pay the cash she had promised Nancy Johnson for weaving forty yards of dress cloth.[42]

Johnson gave a vivid account of the raid itself. Among the famished soldiers who arrived at the Baggs place that cold January day was the very same man she and her husband had earlier sheltered as a fugitive. While his frantic, ragged comrades were rooting around the slave quarters, shooting chickens and helping themselves to a pot of food and a pie, the soldier told her that he would try to prevent the men from burning her house, but that he could not keep them from taking everything the family owned. The raid lasted but one chaotic hour, though the soldiers remained camped nearby for two days. Johnson's fourteen-year-old son, Henry, sent by Baggs to the swamps to guard a wagon of provisions hidden there, disappeared with the Yankees the day they left. Said Nancy Johnson, "It didn't look like a Yankee person would be so mean."[43]

Johnson told her story knowing that, if her family was to prevail with the commissioners, she must above all prove her husband's loyalty to the Union. She had prefaced her remarks by saying of Boson, "He was a good Union man during the war. He liked to have lost his life standing up for the Union party. He was threatened heavy." The couple had few opportunities to aid the Union cause directly: "we were back in the country, but his heart was right & so was mine." Although the commission eventually awarded the family $155, less than a third of what they claimed, the award itself was testament to Nancy Johnson's compelling story.[44]

In a series of depositions and interviews, Nancy's husband, Boson, and son Wallace also recounted the raid. Before and during the war, Boson had worked in the sawmill on Baggs's property, and he acknowledged that he had neither cash nor property to contribute to the Union war effort: "I was a slave and had no chance anyway . . . I cast my influence on the Union side—being a slave I could not vote." He alluded to Henry, the son who vanished with the Union soldiers, saying that the boy had eventually served as a soldier in the Union army. But neither he nor Wallace made any mention of the rebel deserters that Nancy said they had taken in during the war. Wallace said that his father had helped "the Union prisoners when they came along," but he provided no details of what would surely have been an unforgettable encounter. In all likelihood, Nancy Johnson's story was a composite account of black people's contributions to the Union war effort—a story that she chose to tell on behalf of her husband's claim.[45]

It is possible that the Johnsons had benefited from the close counsel of their attorney, in this case one M. J. Denoghue, and that Nancy felt she had to compensate for her husband's candor when at one point he described the Union soldiers as abusive toward him: "they said shut up your head or we will put a bayonet through you." Unable to document either their loyalty to the Union or their ownership of the disputed goods, many claimants had to rely on advisers of various kinds to help them with reams of paperwork, a labyrinth of rules related to filing, and claims commissioners' unreasonable standards for proof of Union support. Indeed, the process proved a boon for a handful of local attorneys and federal officials. A small army of lawyers and notary publics received compensation for their efforts, and even a successful claimant might end up with only 10 percent of the final award. Virgil Hillyer, appointed special commissioner of claims, enlisted the support of his brother, Charles, as a lawyer; and Ellen E. Adlington, his boarder and an AMA teacher, as a witness for many of the claimants. Adlington in turn summoned her sister Amey from the North to help with the formalities. James M. Simms served as an attorney for some claimants and a witness for others, among them other former slaves of his own former owner, James Potter.[46]

Black deponents and interviewees faced the commissioners' intense skepticism about, first, their claims of owning substantial amounts of livestock and stockpiled food and, second, their loyalty to the Union. Indeed, many whites, especially Northerners, were inclined to believe that either black claimants were lying or "they were induced to consent to the filing of claims in their names and that the claims were substantially the creation of some interested party other than the nominal claimant." Among the suspected "interested parties" was Simms, who was portrayed as duping elderly women into filing wildly inflated claims. (He served as attorney for a number of successful claimants, including Toby Adams and Thomas Butler; the latter was also a former slave of James Potter.) Of the 3,447 claims filed in Georgia, only 764, or about 20 percent, were successful.[47]

It helped to have a prominent white advocate. Georgiana Kelley's claim was approved, probably because of the support of Ellen Cosens, the daughter of Kelley's former guardian, Richard D. Arnold. In her testimony, Kelley chose to highlight her role in the coordinated effort to feed the Union prisoners of war when they were being held in Savannah in the summer and fall of 1864. Other women claimants and witnesses also mentioned this act of mercy. Perhaps, like Nancy Johnson, they recognized a larger historical fact—blacks' support for the Union cause—and turned it into dramatic personal testimony. Rachel Bromfield told of carrying clothing and tobacco to the prisoners and of hiding five escaped prisoners in her boardinghouse for five months, all in defiance of bayonet-wielding rebels. Judy Rose said she hid a Union prisoner—"poor creater"—in her house for two weeks, until the Yankees entered the city and he could get away. Amelia Kimball reported that she brought cakes to the prisoners and later cooked and washed for the Union army of occupation.[48]

Like the Johnsons, some of the claimants were families of relatively modest means, while others were notable for their entrepreneurial spirit. The industrious Liberty County blacksmith Tony Axon, forty-eight, made a claim. Still working at his trade, Axon now had with him his wife Nellie, fifty-three, keeping house, and their two children. Former truck farmers Moses Stikes and Binah Butler, who had produced and sold foodstuffs during the war, were also successful in winning some compensation for their losses. But the well-to-do Sheftall family paid a price for their wartime activities, and their attorney, James Simms, could not win a settlement for any of them. Several members of this extended family had been free before the war, although as Emanuel Sheftall reminded interviewers, "I was born free but was most as much a slave as any other colored person til the Union army came in." Commissioners found ample reason to deny the claims of the Sheftalls, these "nearly white" persons. Jackson the butcher, son of a slave and a slaveowner, petitioned on his own behalf; others were heirs of the deceased family patriarch, Jackson's uncle Adam Sheftall, also a butcher. William Sheftall failed to defend himself against charges that he had labored for the Confederate army; he had served as a drummer for a volunteer unit of German immigrants (receiving $2 for every parade he marched in), and he had been forced to work on the fortifications at Fort Pulaski under armed guard. Claims commissioners held that he had provided the rebel cause with tangible support.[49]

Filing his extensive Chatham County claim for a total of nearly $4,000 in July 1871, Jackson Sheftall acknowledged that he had supplied butchered meat to the Confederate army; according to the commissioners, he had thus "made money by his service and rendered as much aid and comfort to the Confederacy as a white man under similar circumstances." Sheftall's story of helping Union prisoners of war escape through five different picket lines found no favor with the commissioners.

He had a hard time explaining how he had bought his wife and daughter from their owners in 1862, paying $2,600 in cash for the two of them. Concluded one commissioner, "There was no compulsion about the butchering business, but there was large profit in it, and for that the claimant went in zealously."[50]

The testimony offered up to the Southern Claims Commission was part of a larger project among various groups to shape the meaning and memory of the war. Black claimants did their best to prove their loyalty to the Union, arguing they had provided food and refuge for Union soldiers. At the same time, white Northerners began to promote reconciliation between whites of both sides; in early 1871 the family of Robert Gould Shaw made a gift of $1,000 so that the congregants of St. Andrews Parish in Darien could rebuild their church, which was burned in the raid of July 1863. White Savannahians were especially aggressive in using the war for their own political purposes. Beginning in 1870, the deaths of prominent former southern military officers—Josiah Tattnall (on June 15) and Robert E. Lee (on October 12)—unleashed a wave of nostalgia for the Confederacy. The arrival of the remains of thirty-two southern soldiers slain and buried at Gettysburg—to be reinterred in the city—was occasion for more processions, more speeches, more strewing of flowers upon graves.[51]

Complicating the Confederate memorial project were the raw clashes between the haves and have-nots in Savannah during the late winter and spring of 1871. Dockworkers and teamsters pressed their advantage, striking for higher wages during the busiest time of the season. Trouble also came from an unexpected quarter, when the city's largely Irish police force demanded an end to the system of compensation based on the fines exacted from the men and women they arrested and the courts convicted. (Out of a corps of 100 men, 61 were immigrants—57 from Ireland and 4 from Germany—and of the 36 who were born in the United States, many had Irish surnames.) The police, who had to furnish their own uniforms, wanted a set wage instead of 50 percent of the fines they collected from lawbreakers. They considered the present system objectionable for several reasons: it provided only an uncertain income for individual policemen; it required them to make a living by bringing charges against their compatriots; and it raised doubts about the veracity of the testimony of policemen on the stand, men who had much to gain from the conviction of anyone arrested on their word. When the city council debated the matter, the Irish-born John O. Ferrill, together with John Schwarz, a native of

Germany, led the fight in favor of the measure, but Mayor Screven broke a tie vote and the old method of compensation remained in place.[52]

The pay issue highlights the suspect nature of crime statistics, which indicate that a disproportionate number of blacks were arrested for stealing. Other "black" offenses included disorderly conduct, street fighting, appearing to be a "suspicious character," and "fast and reckless driving." Whites predominated in the "drunkenness" category. If Irish cops did show a distinct bias in overlooking their own lawbreaking kin and compatriots, and instead arrested mostly black men, women, and children for stealing, then they were complicit in perpetuating the widely held view among elites that freedpeople were thieves by nature. Yet in fact Savannah's underground economy, whereby poor people illicitly seized and distributed private property, was a biracial, multiethnic enterprise. Newspaper reports detail a remarkable range of pilfering, on every street and in every nook and cranny of every warehouse and private residence, dry-goods shop, bank, and even some churches. Youthful black and white pickpockets loitered on street corners awaiting their prey. Horse thieves and buggy thieves were adept at spiriting away large animals and conveyances in the blink of an eye. Shoplifters relieved storeowners of everything from farm tools to rolls of ribbon, and scavengers stripped gutters from houses and plucked cabbages from gardens. Among this cavalcade of thieves were wharf rats who stole small bits of cotton for resale, highway robbers who attacked travelers on the road, cat burglars who raided houses for jewelry and other loot, chicken thieves who shadowed backyard coops. Articles under the generic headline "Daring robbery" were a regular feature of the *Morning News*, with reporters torn between condemning the crime and admiring the remarkable ingenuity of the criminal.[53]

But these were only the small purveyors of crime; others engaged in its more lucrative forms. Fencers of stolen goods organized small armies of petty crooks, cardsharps plied their marks with "popskull" (a lethal form of cheap alcohol), and swindlers offered rigged games of chance to the gullible. The most successful of these thieves and con artists worked full-time to perfect their craft. For example, "the art and mystery of cotton stealing has been reduced to a science," according to the *Morning News* in early 1871, suggesting elaborate plans involving stakeouts and lookouts that emptied local warehouses of unknown quantities of the fiber each year. At the highest echelons of criminal enterprise were the forgers, smugglers, embezzlers, blackmailers, extortionists, and world-class counterfeiters, all of which Savannah, city of enterprise, had in abundance in the spring of 1871.[54]

When it came to spending money and promoting the city's interests, broadly defined, the city council maintained its priorities by favoring and funding public symbols and parks beautification. The city arranged a huge funeral for Josiah Tattnall at public expense, and paid $390.75 to commission a full-length portrait of Robert E. Lee. It appropriated $3.25 each for 153 tree boxes and $5.50 each for 20 benches to grace Forsyth Park, but cut back on the pay of city laborers employed on the streets, lanes, and parks, and refused to refund taxes to small businessmen who had overpaid. Well-to-do residents contending with foul-smelling businesses could count on a sympathetic hearing in council, but the people in poorer areas such as Yamacraw found no support when they complained about stinking fertilizer factories and foundry smokestacks befouling their neighborhoods.[55]

The council continued to grapple with the tension between economic development on the one hand and public order on the other, all within a context of pronounced white working-class political influence. In time-honored tradition, prominent politicians and former generals appeared as counsel for shopkeepers accused of selling liquor on Sunday, and for homeowners who threw garbage in the streets. In the summer of 1871 the council chambers were the site of an unusual proceeding against two brothel owners, Julia P. Holing and Lizzie Jandon. The women's lawyers utilized the familiar but in this case ultimately unsuccessful defense that the city had overstepped its authority in trying to shut down the two neighboring and enduring houses of prostitution. Still, Alderman Ferrill, ever sensitive to the wishes of his constituents, broke with the majority of his colleagues and voted to keep the houses in business, just as they had been as early as 1859.[56]

Through peace and war and then peace again, Savannah's underground economy remained a lively mix of black and white petty-commodity traders and purveyors of stolen goods and illicit services. In the early 1870s, blacks and whites were still mingling in back alleys and poor neighborhoods; just as in antebellum days, poor white men possessed a measure of political power in the form of the ballot, while black men still did not. The largely impoverished community of freedpeople thus sought to leverage whatever influence it did possess—in the form of numbers and moral outrage—in the service of justice.

CHAPTER SIXTEEN

When You Leave Set Fire to All the Houses

BY THE SPRING AND SUMMER OF 1871, certain black leaders were inclined to strike a bargain of convenience with white authorities in order to wrest Beach Institute from the American Missionary Association. Many black teachers, preachers, and politicians remained bitter over the demise of the Savannah Education Association five years earlier; now some sought to exact what they considered their due from the Congregational interlopers. In response, AMA superintendent A. N. Niles was seriously contemplating a move to another field of missionary labor, among the freedpeople of Atlanta or those of Talladega, Alabama, or the unchurched Chinese and Indians in the Far West. Though the AMA was still active in Georgia—sponsoring a total of fifty-two teachers there, more than in any other state in 1871—its effort in Savannah seemed stalled. Niles feared that some of the northern teachers assigned to the city were too old and frail, others indifferent to the cause. In May he complained to headquarters, "It is no holiday exercise to meet the varied tasks of a given number of maiden ladies of a certain or uncertain age." The superintendent found something new to worry about every day: a teacher who mismanaged small amounts of money entrusted to her, the chronic indebtedness of the mission home, the dilemma of receiving donations from a northern church earmarked for a palsied man whose story was concocted as a fundraising device. Eventually, Niles decided to stay in Savannah for the time being; he cited not the nobility of the mission, but the fact that he had invested $50 in carpets for the mission home and preferred not to abandon them.[1]

The persistent hostility of local black preachers left Niles feeling disoriented: "I am all afloat and cannot anchor." Of blacks who resisted the essence of New England church services, he remarked that they "have no conception of singing as an act of worship but are bent on a Banjo performance." The freedpeople as a group he found "impulsive" and unreliable—and he included his assistant Robert Carter in that assessment. In April Niles took some satisfaction from the dedication of the Beach Institute Chapel, and from a public expression of support signed by the Reverend William J. Campbell, pastor of First African Baptist, and two other black preachers. Of Niles they wrote, "He is all to us That *A Friend* Can be in this Lower World of Sorrow." But there is evidence to suggest that Niles was caught in the middle of a larger dispute among the city's black preachers and politicians. Over the next few months matters would heat up. When Niles appeared as a guest speaker at a black church, the minister's wife rose to denounce him for never hiring a black teacher at Beach Institute. Niles was able to cite one black woman whom he had employed as a teacher's assistant, to refute the embarrassing charge. Still, competition in the field of black education continued to wax and wane, with some black teachers capitalizing on the AMA's exclusive hiring policies by forming their own schools—and in one case appealing to the collective consciousness of the community by naming the school the African Union.[2]

NILES'S WOES were set against a backdrop of growing anxiety among northern liberals that "The South is yet Volcanic." In this view, so-called new leaders of the South had "all the malignity of the rebellion," and some new forms of malignity as well, as demonstrated by the ongoing terrorism unleashed by a variety of vigilante groups. Responding to Ku Klux Klan depredations in the South, congressional Republicans initiated formal hearings in the summer and fall of 1871. Witnesses detailed the wave of terror engulfing the state of Georgia—the daylight assassinations and nighttime whippings and killings, the death threats and the destruction of property. Not all lynch mobs bothered to disguise themselves or give themselves a name such as the KKK. Loose collections of white men representing in many cases a cross section of their own communities banded together to attack a wide range of people they considered social undesirables—blacks and whites living together; whiskey sellers; blacks who voted, or those who denounced cheating employers. Some planters broke with the vigilantes over tactics, which could provoke a mass exodus of workers out of a county or plantation district. To the alarm of employers, the Klan told freedpeople in Georgia's Tattnall County: "When you leave set fire to all the houses or gins and be sure they all burn down as it will save us the trouble of doing it." Klan activity created a pervasive climate of fear, especially in the cotton belt, where white-supremacist terrorists were the most murderous.[3]

The Georgia lowcountry was relatively free of vigilante groups, probably because poor blacks held such an overwhelming numerical advantage over well-to-do whites, and there were few middle-class or aspiring poor whites to be resentful of insubordinate freedpeople. Nevertheless, several well-known Savannah figures were featured among the witnesses at the 1871 congressional hearings on the KKK. Former mayor Edward C. Anderson issued bland assurances about the generosity of spirit with which former Confederates embraced their political rivals; "a law-abiding" city, Savannah was not only on the mend from the devastation of war, it was thriving, according to Anderson. "We receive northern men with the utmost kindness and are anxious that they shall come among us," he told the panel on July 14, 1871. (A few minutes later he was excoriating the same group of men as "the refuse of creation . . . unconciliatory in demeanor, arrogant, exacting, and as a general rule, ignorant.") Anderson told the panel that the city's biggest problem was the large number of "toughs" who flooded the city each winter. William W. Paine, representing Savannah and the First Congressional District in Washington, justified vigilantism and lynch law as necessary to hold arsonists and thieves accountable for their misdeeds. Joseph Brown, the former governor, who was serving as chief justice of the state's supreme court and as president of the Western and Atlantic Railroad Company, spoke for the small group of native whites uneasily aligned with the Republican Party. Most black people were "morally delinquent," according to Brown. He praised the generous landowners now offering their former slaves remunerative employment, rescuing them in the process from "idleness and dissipation, and thieving." He also approved of the expulsion of the black legislators two years earlier, claiming that poor whites were superior in character and industry to all blacks.[4]

The municipal election of October 1871 recapitulated the winning formula of the previous year. The Democrats' district nominations to the city council resulted in the triumph of the party ticket, with just one exception; a challenger, Alfred Haywood (a British-born merchant), bested one of the regulars. Opposition slates drew relatively few votes. Among their candidates were Irish challengers; a lone Republican, the ubiquitous James J. Waring; and a member of the old guard, George Wylly, former slave trader.[5]

Immune to the local partisan political process, distorted though it might be, were appointees who owed their jobs to Governor Bullock or the national Republican Party. By 1871 Democrats could focus their wrath on men they considered abject dupes of the northern Republicans—in particular the resilient James M. Simms, who maintained a solid grass-roots base of black support in Chatham County. Simms was useful to both northern Republicans and southern Democrats as an all-purpose symbol of all that was either noble or evil about the war and Reconstruction. In the spring of 1869 Senator Charles Sumner of Massachusetts had nominated Simms for the position of postmaster of Savannah. Around this time Simms and Henry M. Turner visited Sumner in Washington, and reported to him about Georgia's antidemocratic forces, which were gaining in power. During their visit, the senator showed the two men around the capital, taking them on a tour of the city's great monuments. Turner later remembered the day this way: "And to my astonishment the greatest statesman the sun ever shone upon, walked up between us and locked our arms, and proceeded through the streets and buildings as unconcernedly as if he had been in company with his senatorial colleagues; he thought no more of asking a black man to dine at his table, than he did of the whitest man on earth."[6]

Throughout the postwar period, Simms had maintained his connections with northern whites by traveling periodically to Boston, where he would appear before workers and Republican groups, condemning the "reign of terror" against blacks that prevailed in his home state. However, President Grant rebuffed Sumner's nomination of Simms, instead appointing Walter Clift, Joseph's younger brother, to the postmaster position. In its account of the incident, the *New York Times* suggested that Simms, as the brother of the famous fugitive Thomas, carried a great deal of moral weight with neoabolitionists. Indeed, said the *Times,* Senator Sumner had "sought to teach the chivalry of Georgia another humiliating lesson and thereby to add in this peculiar instance to the glory and revenge of Massachusetts."[7]

Ironically, what the nation's executive branch could or would not deliver to Simms, the governor of Georgia did. In January 1871 Simms accepted an appointment from Rufus Bullock just as the governor was losing favor quickly among white Republicans. Simms was named district judge of the First Senatorial District, a first for a black man and a source of considerable consternation among whites of all stripes in Savannah. The court itself was new, created by the state legislature to hear cases of higher value than those heard by the justice of the peace, who dealt with sums up to $100. The nomination immediately sparked an out-cry. Thomas R. Mills Jr., thirty-one, a lawyer and the son of a wealthy commission merchant, had applied to Bullock for the position of attorney general of the First Senatorial District. Simms had even written a letter to the governor on Mills's behalf, noting that the young man was "con-nected with one of the best families in this city, who have never been iden-tified in politics, but are merchants and ship-owners." Bullock accepted Mills's application, but word of Simms's appointment prompted the young lawyer to withdraw his name from consideration, and in a very public way. In a letter to Bullock (and presumably released to the press), Mills maintained, "I cannot for one second entertain the monstrous proposition of accepting [the post] under the embryo judge appointed for the position." Claiming that Bullock intended only to insult him, Mills concluded his letter by suggesting that Simms's appointment amounted to "a lasting memento of an attempt by a Governor of Georgia to soil and disgrace the judiciary of the State." Bullock responded by defending Simms, "a colored man possessed of a fair education, excellent moral character, and far more than ordinary natural ability." Bullock also cited Simms's performance in the state legislature, where he showed "a readi-ness, argument, and eloquence, which did great credit to himself as a member and to his race." This fulsome praise of the black man did noth-ing to mollify the wounded Mills, who believed he had his own dignity to preserve.[8]

Mills was not the only one to balk at Simms's appointment. In the wake of the announcement, members of the Savannah bar quickly assem-bled to declare that they would consider any court proceedings invalid until the new judge stepped down from the bench. They claimed that the governor could make an appointment without the senate's consent only if he were filling a vacancy; since this court was a new one, mandated by the constitution of 1868, it had no "vacancies" to fill. The committee con-cluded darkly that, if Simms did not withdraw, "there are adequate legal and constitutional remedies to prevent the consummation of such a pur-pose or attempt; which remedies they forbear to refer to more specifically for reasons obvious to this meeting." Signing the warning was a who's who of the Savannah legal establishment, including George A. Mercer, William B. Fleming, Dominick O'Byrne, John O. Ferrill, and Isaac Rus-sell. On March 7, when he convened the court for the first time, Simms was greeted by a large crowd of black well-wishers. His clerk pro tem, King Solomon Thomas, opened the proceedings by reading the law that had created the court. But the district attorney failed to appear, and local attorneys boycotted the proceedings. The new judge had little choice but to preside over the empty shell of a court.[9]

In 1871 Simms was fighting on several fronts. While local whites schemed to turn him out of his appointed judgeship, Democratic state legislators redistricted his court out of existence in early 1872. (Thereafter Simms would refer to himself, and be addressed by his supporters, alternately as "Reverend" and "Judge" Simms.) At the same time, rival black leaders were challenging his authority and that of his ally, Ulysses L. Houston, pastor of First Bryan Baptist Church and a representative in the state legislature. When Houston returned to the legislature in early 1870, he faced a rebellion from some members of his own six-hundred-member congregation; led by Deacon Alexander Harris, the dissidents held that clergy had no business diverting their energies from the Gospel to the earthly pursuit of political office. Simms himself admitted that the constitutional separation of church and state argued against preachers *qua* politicians, but, he wrote, "in the very nature of things in the past of our people it was unavoidable." (And in any case, church congregations provided ready-made institutional bases for many preacher-politicians.) Simms considered Harris a man with "a highly intelligent mind and indomitable will," though he found "his natural manner and way of acting . . . peculiarly repulsive." No doubt Harris returned the compliment. While Ulysses Houston was campaigning for reelection in 1870, Harris made his move and, over the next few months, engineered the preacher's ouster and had himself installed as the pastor of First Bryan. Siding with Harris was Simms's old foe, the Reverend William J. Campbell of First African Baptist.[10]

Through the spring, summer, and fall of 1871 the congregation— one camp pro-Harris, the other pro-Houston—dissolved into bitter infighting; charges flew that church locks had been changed, communion linens and vessels pilfered, and the police called at Harris's request to expel his enemies. In September Houston's supporters obtained an injunction barring Harris from interfering in church affairs, and the next month a panel of Baptist preachers went public with their support for Harris. These included three white men and the black preachers Samuel Boles and William J. Campbell. The fractious congregation was forced to endure a humiliating public airing of its feuding. But by the end of the year Houston's supporters had managed to recall him to the pulpit. To celebrate his friend's restoration to authority, Simms in January 1872 transferred his church membership from First African to First Bryan, though he knew he was joining a congregation still in a "feverish state of excitement."[11]

In the spring, the church formally expelled Harris's followers; eventually 337 people would leave. Many found a welcome in Campbell's First African Church. A partial list of those expelled suggests they were hardly rabble-rousers. Although it is difficult to compare them to the group that stayed, those who left represented Savannah's stable class of tradesmen and skilled workers. Most of the men were heads of household, the women housekeepers. These were the families of brickmasons, carpenters, butchers, wagoners, shipwrights, sausage makers, and porters. Among the group were Abigail Small, one of the original teachers hired by the Savannah Education Association, who now kept house for her husband, Sandy, who was a butcher, and four boarders; and Ann Stiles and Sarah Odingsells, members of prominent freeborn families. Whether the First Bryan dispute centered on politics, principles, or personality, it suggested that no matter how oppressive white rule, conflicts among blacks would continue to split the Savannah community. Indeed, it is doubtful that, in denominational terms at least, a single religious "black community" even existed.[12]

Simms could take grim satisfaction from Houston's reinstallation as preacher of First Bryan Baptist Church. The two had prevailed not only over Harris, but also over the committee of five—Campbell, Boles, and three whites—who had gone public with their criticism of the church. (Meanwhile, black congregants were not the only ones struggling with controversy. The venerable Christ Episcopal Church was caught up in its own scandal that spring, as Bishop Elliott's successor was forced to resign for "grossly immoral conduct," apparently with Savannah prostitutes.) Reluctantly, Simms had transferred his membership from a church that he had helped to build with his own hands; but in his view the nasty political climate that pitted principled black leaders against whites and their obsequious black supporters mandated flexibility in one's religious affiliation no less than in one's political allies.[13]

MEANWHILE, Washington, D.C., was consumed by debate over a proposed civil rights bill sponsored by Senator Sumner. The Massachusetts lawmaker was pushing for a measure that would guarantee all citizens equal access to a wide range of institutions, accommodations, and forms of public transportation—schools, juries, trains and streetcars, cemeteries, and even churches. The Senate passed a watered-down version of the bill, but the House killed it. At least Congress was confronting the issue of systemic, widespread segregation. Nevertheless, Georgia politics had a way of tamping down the optimism of blacks heartened by developments at the national level. By this time Simms had been stripped of his judgeship by a newly emboldened state legislature and a new Democratic governor, James M. Smith, determined to erase the vestiges of Radical Reconstruction. Increasingly, state-level politicians would seek control over those small pockets of black political influence, overriding local majorities in the process. Moreover, with the new governor's blessing, throughout the state, antebellum white militia companies were quickly reorganizing. Around this time Savannah began to herald the return of the Savannah Volunteer Guards, Chatham Artillery, Georgia Hussars, Republican Blues, Phoenix Regiment, Irish Jasper Greens, German Volunteers, DeKalb Riflemen, Oglethorpe Light Infantry, and Savannah Cadets (this last was a "regiment" of boys organized in May of 1861).[14]

In the early 1870s, the Reverend Tunis G. Campbell was learning the same lesson as Simms: that Democrats could manipulate local legal and legislative systems in new and creative ways. As justice of the peace in Darien since 1871, Campbell wielded unprecedented power, bolstered not only by his official position but by a local militia fiercely loyal to him, a political organization that encompassed the city and the surrounding rural area, and an array of other elected and appointed black officials. Some supporters, such as Toby Maxwell, had followed Campbell from the St. Catherines colony to Belle Ville and then on to Darien. In the summer of 1871, a white magistrate attempted to have Campbell arrested, only to back down when a crowd of three hundred armed blacks appeared inside and outside the courtroom, "acting in a very excited and threatening manner and evincing a demonstration to resist by force of arms his [Campbell's] imprisonment."[15]

As a judge in a busy seaport, Campbell had ample opportunity to redress what he considered the all-too-common grievances of exploited seamen. In July 1871, he charged Captain John Irvine of the English bark *Grace* with assault and battery and abusive language toward five black crewmen. Irvine claimed that the blacks were refusing to complete a voyage from New York City to France; the men countered that they had signed on only for the New York–Georgia leg of the trip. In consultation with a local attorney, Irvine persuaded the United States Commissioner in Savannah, Henry N. Wayne, to have Campbell and six other black officials arrested on a conspiracy charge. But a Savannah judge merely chastised Campbell for errors in judgment, and released him and his codefendants. The five seamen also went free.[16]

Soon after Governor Smith assumed office in December 1871, the state legislature took steps to dilute if not eradicate Campbell's power in McIntosh County. Lawmakers appointed a seven-person commission to oversee a wide range of public activities in the county, including tax collection, elections, and jury selection in criminal trials—generally "the official books and papers" of Tunis G. Campbell. The purpose of these maneuvers was to restore the county to all-white government. And then in January white McIntosh residents petitioned the state senate, charging Campbell with malfeasance in office. Democratic senators vowed to investigate Campbell for criminal behavior, try him, and then remove him from office. They were in no mood to tolerate a public official who reportedly traveled the state damning "the oppressive and iniquitous laws . . . [which] completely subjected the negroes to the whites." Campbell claimed that McIntosh blacks had "one resource left, which was dear to every freeman's heart and that was the musket and the Bayonet."[17]

The state commission held public hearings into Campbell's performance in office, highlighting embarrassing testimony from Campbell's adopted son, E. E. Howard, now estranged from his father. During the spring and summer of 1872, Campbell faced harassment in the form of a McIntosh County Superior Court indictment (charging him with falsely imprisoning a white man in 1871); and a stint in a Savannah jail, on charges that as a magistrate he had illegally officiated at a wedding between a black man and a white woman. Undeterred, Campbell took his seat in the state senate when it convened in July. There, between filing bills and offering resolutions in favor of workers' rights and black education, he fended off charges from the Committee on Privileges that he "was guilty of using disrespectful and slanderous language towards the Senate . . . guilty of trying to excite an insurrectionary spirit among the people of his district by advising them to resist a public law of the state with the bayonet."[18]

It was around this time that the *Morning News* referred to Campbell as that "monkey-faced evil spirit." The term was typical of those used by editors and reporters of the Savannah press to describe black politicians. And so at various points in his career, "Congo" Campbell, the "King of the Ashantees," was nothing more than a "gorilla." James Simms, church leader, state legislator, labor agent, attorney, editor, and judge, was branded that "miserable creature," and "nigger." James Porter, musician, educator, and state legislator, was merely a "tripe-visaged" miscreant. And Aaron A. Bradley was routinely referred to as the "Great Wahoo of the Ogeechee." The press also held up ordinary black people to ridicule, labeling black women workers as "a full force of Fifteenth Amendments," and black men "bullet headed" and "ebony bipeds." These terms of contempt and derision failed to curtail the political activity among black citizens.[19]

Indeed, freedpeople continued to maintain a lively political presence in the midst of discrimination and disfranchisement. At one point Savannah blacks rallied on Bay Street to protest proposed congressional legislation that would repeal the duty on rice and thus endanger the livelihoods of those still toiling in the coastal rice fields. Speaking to the crowd, Aaron Bradley promised that if the national Republicans enacted the change, "You and I will then stand together and fight against the capitalists, and those who may support them." The group signed a petition to send to the House Ways and Means Committee. This meeting and others included women as well as men, mothers with babies balanced on their hips, clapping and singing and dancing—to the strains of "Rally Round the Flag Boys" at one outdoor meeting of the Republican Central Committee in April.[20]

It was the congressional debate over proposed civil rights legislation that sparked a bloody streetcar protest in Savannah at the end of July 1872. Weeks before, anonymous letter writers had warned the streetcar company that blacks would attempt to integrate the cars; in response, the company ordered its conductors to ignore any attempts to disrupt service, and to accept the tickets of black passengers regardless of the car they boarded. The private company that ran the cars cared less about the principles of segregation than about possible disruptions to, and boycotts of, its services. At 10 p.m. on Saturday, July 27, apparently according to plan, a group of blacks boarded the white cars at the Exchange stop and rode to Liberty Street, where three white men forcibly ejected them. A crowd gathered immediately and blocked the cars from moving forward, and as one black man seized the bridle of one of the horses, a white man stepped forward, struck him in the face, and knocked him to the ground.[21]

The next morning an eerie quiet prevailed, boding trouble. At six that evening the protests resumed, with Richard W. White boarding a white car with women passengers, only to have a group of men throw him off. Within a few hours blacks were pelting the cars with bottles, and young white men were beating black protesters. The fighting continued on Monday, with Simms among the assaulted streetcar riders. That evening a crowd estimated at one thousand blacks and whites gathered from South Broad Street to Bryan and Whitaker, watching as the same scene was reenacted over and over—with blacks boarding a car and whites pitching them off. The brief appearance of a newly formed black militia, the Union Lincoln Guards, electrified the blacks, but the unarmed men simply marched past the scene. The agitation reached fever pitch, with one observer noting, "The women were particularly excited, and endeavored strenuously to encourage the men to take some violent course." At 8:15 p.m. the firing started, and when it was over three blacks lay dead and several had been wounded. Errant shots also wounded two white women and their children, who had been sitting on their front stoops on Bull Street north of Anderson.[22]

For whites, the real danger lay in the possibility of an all-out battle that could call out federal authorities. Both Mayor Screven and Chief of Police Robert H. Anderson were out of town, seeking cooler climes and leaving a vacuum in the white power structure. Yet the black demonstrators intended to do more than vent their frustrations against authorities. On Tuesday, Avery Smith, thirty-four, a Georgia-born employee of the federal Customs House and a carpenter by trade, initiated legal proceedings against three white men. Smith went to United States Commissioner Henry Wayne and demanded that charges be filed against the three, who, he claimed, had violated his civil rights on the evening of July 28 by throwing him off a streetcar. The essence of Smith's case was that a ticket to ride a streetcar constituted a contract between the passenger and the company, and that for a conductor to deny a black person a seat on any car represented an abrogation of that contract. Smith had tried to board the first car that came along, regardless of its "color." Lawyers for the three defendants countered that the cars assigned to blacks were equal in comfort and availability to those reserved for whites. In all of this, whites suspected a conspiracy more threatening than the staged protest itself. Truly alarming was testimony at the hearing initiated by Smith's complaint that $833 had been deposited in the local Freedman's Bank as a war chest "to test the case in the Courts and to pay the fare of such others as wished to ride in any cars of the Company."[23]

Commissioner Wayne announced his decision on August 4. He ruled that Congress had not conferred a "social privilege" upon blacks that would entitle them to integrated transportation or hotel facilities. He noted that the state of Georgia retained the prerogative to segregate these facilities—just as Maryland and Pennsylvania had done recently. Then Wayne turned on Smith and condemned him as "a deliberate violator of a legal regulation of the streetcar company, and *pro tanto*, a disturber of the public tranquility." He took Smith to task for his failure to give up his seat to a white woman on the car, and for taking advantage of spineless streetcar company owners who had acquiesced in the "duress of apprehension" instead of enforcing the law. According to Wayne, Smith, as an employee of the federal government and a relative newcomer to the city, "should have been the last to foment disturbance of the public peace, and not the firebrand of social discord." Granted, Wayne said, a "few native ruffians" had contributed to the disturbance, but their misdeeds paled in comparison to Smith's provocations. Finally, Wayne offered up a brief lecture to the court: "During her long history in connection with slavery, which was forced upon her, against her solemn protest, by her trustees in England, when a colony, Savannah has been noted among the cities of the South for the kindly relations, confidences, and friendships that existed between masters and slaves." The city need not tolerate this attack on its "custom," one so destructive of these "kindly relations."[24]

Wayne effectively squelched this round of streetcar protests, but the matter was far from settled. Meanwhile, competing for public attention was a raucous feud between city Republicans. By 1872 an explosive mix of groups vying for the soul of a beleaguered Republican Party had converged in Savannah. Among these were those relative old-timers determined to fight the good fight on the high-minded level of principle; but this faction—Bradley, Simms, White, and others—was already badly split. Complicating the picture were white and black Republicans recently arrived in the city to claim the spoils of party patronage in the Customs House, the federal courts, and the post office. Avery Smith was a night watchman in the Customs House, and other federal posts included a wide array of day watchmen, bailiffs, treasury agents, and clerks, in addition to the plum jobs of collector of customs and city postmaster. These positions became ever more precious as power receded from the grasp of Republicans on both the state and local level; after the state government fell into the hands of the Democrats in early 1872, federal patronage was one of the only means to shore up the Republican Party in the Democratic stronghold of Savannah.[25]

Bradley took the lead in condemning the "Custom House Ring" composed of federal appointees whom he considered greedy interlopers. And so by the spring of that year a cauldron of party members—some from the South, some from the North, some longtime Savannahians, others newcomers, some committed to black civil rights, others only to getting and keeping a job—was simmering at every meeting of the Republican Central Committee. Nor did Bradley have much affection for the Savannah blacks who managed to profit from patronage, including Simms and Charles DeLaMotta, rewarded in 1872 with jobs in the Customs House.[26]

Within a week of the streetcar hearings, the city once more had reason to ponder the "kindly relations" between blacks and whites. On August 13 two Savannah policemen went out to the Ogeechee to try to arrest a black man named Morgan Anderson who was accused of stealing. In the process they broke up a high-stakes card game and unleashed a gunfight; a black man, Butler King, fell mortally wounded. Meanwhile, another group of black men attacked a store owned by the white man who had brought charges against Anderson. Among those implicated in the attack was Caesar Waldburg, a leader of the Ogeechee Troubles in the winter of 1868–69. Whites were quick to see this latest disturbance as evidence of yet another "conspiracy," like its predecessor replete with secret signs, "raps," and signals, but this one organized by Richard White "and his negro and white allies in this city." What the busted-up card game revealed, however, was not a protopolitical rebellion along the lines of the previous uprising, but a spontaneous form of resistance to white authorities, in this case city police.[27]

IT WAS WITHIN this heated environment that the city braced for the upcoming state elections in October and national elections the following month. Complicating the political scene was a burgeoning controversy over the fate of Beach Institute. The AMA's Andrew Niles had contended with one aggravation after another during the 1871–72 school year. He feared that the opening of the St. Augustine Episcopal free school in Yamacraw would trigger mass defections of the mulatto children of skilled tradesmen currently enrolled in the institute. The northern teachers were flagging, and even their round-the-clock efforts could not keep up with the demand: many eager pupils were being turned away at the schoolhouse door, though they had been invited to come "with such a flourish of trumpets." At the same time, black parents were clamoring for smaller classes and more personal attention for their children. No matter that the AMA could not accommodate all Savannah's black children; Niles dreaded ceding any of them to a rival denomination.[28]

In late summer of 1872 a group of black leaders, including the baker William Pollard, Congregationalist missionary Robert Carter, Baptist leader Alexander Harris, and veterinarian William Cleghorn, began to press the AMA to turn over Beach Institute to the city. Niles saw a plot afoot, an attempt by "greedy" men, black and white, to run the AMA teachers out of town; he also regarded the move as part of a Catholic scheme to get black children into public schools taught by Catholic teachers: "If the Protestant hare sleeps the Catholic tortoise will overtake it," warned Niles. For their part, the AMA teachers maintained they would not be turned over to the city "like furniture." But they need not have worried on that score. Richard D. Arnold, chair of the Savannah Board of Education, was not interested in hiring the Northerners in any capacity. Conducting negotiations with AMA official E. M. Cravath, Arnold maintained that if the city gained control of the school building, Niles would have to go. As for the teachers, the board would examine each applicant and choose only those who demonstrated "scholarly competency and satisfactory moral character," presumably a test that few AMA workers could hope to pass. The exchange between Arnold and Cravath was something of a sensation, published in the local papers during August and September. Cravath rejected Arnold's terms.[29]

Nevertheless, in late November the city opened the first public school for black children on East Macon Street, not far from Beach Institute. The three-room structure made room for—apparently with difficulty—220 pupils; since the building belonged to the St. Stephen's congregation, it was perhaps not surprising that the church's longtime music director, the politician James Porter, was installed as its first principal. Seventeen-year-old Eliza Pollard, William's daughter, assisted a black teacher, a Mr. Mins. The other teacher was the seventy-year-old Elias Yulee, former Freedmen's Bureau agent, assisted by a white woman, Miss Maynard. Perhaps aware of what lay ahead, Bradley, Simms, and White played no public role in the transfer, which produced a cash-starved, segregated school system for black children.[30]

Black parents wanted the displacement of northern Congregationalists and the installation of black teachers in a tuition-free Beach Institute. Savannah city authorities could agree with at least the first half of this goal: they never tired of ridiculing the school and the Yankees who ran it. Once again in the public limelight, this time as hardnosed negotiator with the AMA, Arnold relished his new status as Savannah's elder statesman. By now he had regained the time and resources to travel to New York City and enjoy lavish dinner parties, imbibing stimulating conversation along with the wines and the perfect Madeiras. Arnold still fretted over sporadic outbreaks of yellow fever in Savannah, noting with some certainty that "in no instance has the yellow fever been of imported origin." Still, his greatest worry was the social disorder caused by the unruly freedperson, whom he compared to "the Wild untamed elephant of Africa."[31]

Savannah politics remained contentious throughout the fall. Ever vigilant to new strategies that would depress the black vote, the state legislature accommodated a request from the city council and changed the date of municipal elections from October to January, presumably in an effort to pad the registration rolls with Irish transients. The legislature also approved the extension of the terms of mayor and aldermen to two years, further insulating the city government from the popular will, unpredictable as that was. Black politicians refused to retreat in the face of such machinations. Now a former judge, James Simms filed suit against the state for nonpayment of services rendered during his brief stint on the bench. In September Aaron Bradley renewed his denunciations of police abuse and the exclusion of blacks from juries; he also initiated a public campaign to appeal to "all true Irishmen and German laboring Democrats," on the theory that their interests were the same as those of the wage-earning freedpeople. Bradley advised blacks to go to the polls with hatchets, which were more effective "at close quarters" than pistols. Meanwhile, with some effort, Republicans attempted to put aside their differences for the sake of the upcoming elections. Meetings included a diverse lineup of state luminaries, including Henry M. Turner and John E. Bryant (a leader of the state's Republican Party), now serving as federal officeholders in Savannah; John Deveaux, among other ambitious young men; White, Simms, and other stubborn fighters; and working-class party activists attired in their drayman's aprons.[32]

Nevertheless, the elections of fall 1872 suggested that by this time white Democrats had perfected a winning formula for long-term success at the polls. During the contest for state officers, the newly revived volunteer militias, including the Georgia Hussars and the Savannah Sabre Club, made a show of force in the streets. The chief of police went out of his way to mobilize a large number of officers who set up a virtual military encampment around the courthouse, the only polling place in town. These officers were quick to arrest Josiah Grant, twenty-nine, a black carpenter, for exhorting voters to resist white intimidation, and they were quick to use their clubs on John Bryant, who declared the election a fraud (he was later charged with inciting a riot and carrying two loaded derringers in his pockets). In the courthouse, a crowd of whites forcibly prevented Avery Smith from voting; the local *Republican* later blamed Smith himself, saying that he had failed to vote because of his own " 'obstinacy' and 'want of perseverance.' " During the day, another Republican, Savan-

nah port collector James Atkins, presented the local tax collector with
$800 in cash, money to pay the poll taxes of 800 black voters, but the city
official declared "he did not do business in that way."[33]

When the ballots were tallied (after the Democrats' own fashion), it
appeared that lowcountry Republican voting strength had declined precipitously over the last four and a half years. Where Governor Bullock
had garnered 4,471 votes in Chatham County in 1868, the Republican
candidate in 1872 won only 891; in Glynn County the drop was from 510
votes to 387; in Camden from 511 to 13. In Liberty County, where white
officials rejected two ballot boxes brought in by blacks, the Republican
tally dropped from 711 to 0. Only in the Campbell stronghold of McIntosh County did the Republican vote increase, from 446 in 1868 to 563 in
1872.[34]

The November presidential election recapitulated many of the same
polling-day strategies, though this time federal troops joined with the
local police to heighten the tension. The sight of the commander of federal troops, in Union blue, arrayed alongside the officer of a police force
uniformed in Confederate gray was all the more significant given that the
two men had been classmates at West Point before the war. Bradley held
forth at East Hall, denouncing the election as fraudulent and urging his
listeners "to burn the city of Savannah in revenge for what he claimed to
be an outrage upon his rights and that of others." Throughout the day,
gunshots punctured the air, panicking the voters.[35]

Over the next few days, Savannah election officials rejected the three
boxes holding the ballots of the overwhelmingly black Chatham County
voters who lived outside the city. Charles DeLaMotta and James Porter
lodged a formal protest, arguing that the boxes must be received and
counted, but to no avail. Later, George Dolly, a thirty-two-year-old cotton
sampler, filed charges against a number of prominent Democratic poll
challengers, including Christopher C. Casey, Isaac Russell, and Louis
Falligant, saying that they had turned him away at the courthouse and
denied him the opportunity to vote. The white men countered that they
believed Dolly had already voted earlier in the day and so were within
their rights to stop him. Savannah, together with the rest of the state, went
overwhelmingly for the Democratic/Liberal Republican presidential candidate Horace Greeley; concerned with President Grant's growing reputation for corruption, some white Republicans had bolted their own
party. Nevertheless, U. S. Grant was reelected. The three Republicans the
state sent to Congress that fall would be the last of the party to represent
Georgia in Washington for more than a century. One of the successful

Democratic candidates was Alexander Stephens, former Confederate vice president, who was chosen to represent the state's Eighth Congressional District.[36]

Around this time, Charles C. Jones decided to subdivide Arcadia plantation and sell it off in parcels of twenty-five acres each. Over the years Jones had been worn down by his failure to attract a buyer who would keep the plantation intact, and by the lack of profit accruing from the labor of the black families renting parcels from him. Now he rewarded his former slave, the manager Stepney West, with a ninety-acre lot; West would pay $270 over three years and receive title to the land in 1875. Populating the lowcountry were an increasing number of families who eked from the soil a mean subsistence of corn, potatoes, and peas. Seven years after emancipation some household heads, like Joseph Stevens of Liberty County, owned their own homesteads—in Stevens's case a sixty-acre farm cut out of the "Old Tom Gill place." But by this time the thirty-eight-year-old freedman and his wife, Julia, thirty-three, had little hope of accumulating much more than what they already possessed: a horse and a wagon, a cow and a calf, three hogs, bed linens and bedsteads, a spinning wheel for cotton, cooking utensils, clothing, and a Bible and a few schoolbooks. The parents of seven children ranging in age from one to twelve, Joseph and Julia pieced together a patchwork living for their family. Perhaps the sons and their father would eventually seek jobs in Savannah during the winter, when work was slack on the farm but busy on the docks of the river port. In the daily struggles of the Stevens family were revealed both the promise and the betrayal of the years following emancipation.[37]

Over the next generations, a lowcountry peasantry would preserve the outlines of the West African culture that had shaped the lives of Rice Kingdom slaves before the war. But not all black people chose to stay in the land of their forebears. Ever since Beach Institute had put her small school out of business, the young widow Susie Baker King had been living in Savannah with her son. (Her grandmother Dolly Reed was making a comfortable living as a dry-goods store owner and a laundress.) In 1872, Baker King managed to win a claim for the bounty promised her husband when he enlisted in the Union army a decade before; she promptly deposited the sum of $100 in the Savannah branch of the Freedman's Bank. The fall of that year she found a job as a laundress for the family of Charles Green, the wealthy British-born merchant who had played host to General Sherman in December 1864. Now Green, the owner of the United Hydraulic Cotton Press Company and president of the Savannah

Chamber of Commerce, could count on the faithful service of a former schoolteacher, paid to wash the family's clothing. In her twenty-four years, Susie King had witnessed firsthand, and had shaped, the revolutionary changes that had transformed the lowcountry. In 1874 she would leave the city forever and move to Boston, the haven that beckoned to Thomas Simms the year after she was born. There she would do battle on behalf of the legacy bequeathed to all Americans by the sacrifices of her deceased husband and other black veterans of the Civil War.[38]

Those Peaceful, Powerful Weapons

V ISITING SAVANNAH in the late autumn of 1873, a British journalist, Edward L. King, discovered a bustling city that, at least on the surface, evoked the busy season in 1854 when Thomas Simms stowed away on the *Gilmore*. The streets were still unpaved, and so despite all its commercial activity, the town's center remained oddly quiet: "There is little noise of wheels or clatter of hoofs in the upper town; the streets are filled with a heavy black sand over which dray and carriage alike go noiselessly." Luxuriating in the mild weather, King surveyed the river docks, where hundreds of bales of cotton were piled high against a backdrop of "a forest of masts; a mass of warehouses, not unhandsomely grouped; cotton-presses, surrounded by active, chattering toilers." Mingling together were sailors, dray drivers, rice-mill workers, and longshoremen, as of old. Savannah's economy still ran on cotton. All day and night the trains rumbled down from the upcountry and into the Central of Georgia depot, bearing the fluffy white harvests of Georgia, Alabama, and Tennessee. At the same time, the port continued to suffer from a less than satisfactory river route; some of the wartime obstructions remained, despite expensive, seemingly endless dredging projects. Still, the city exuded privilege and prosperity during the annual high-society season's round of boat races, parties, and military displays.[1]

King observed that the political upheaval accompanying emancipation had left intact traditional forms of power—white over black, rich over poor. By this time, however, as a result of the enfranchisement of black men, the means of power had undergone some notable modifications: now the ballot box loomed large over the political landscape. And so it was striking that, out of a population of 15,000 whites and 13,000 blacks, only 400 black men were registered to vote, less than 10 percent of those eligible. Indeed, noted King, "The negroes no longer have any voice whatever in political matters, and are not represented in the City Government." Local and state authorities had perfected a number of tactics to keep black men from voting. During county and citywide elections, officials set up only one ballot box, situated downtown; this policy did much to depress the vote of rural blacks, some of whom lived a dozen or more miles away. Authorities refrained from collecting the poll tax, and then prevented blacks from casting ballots, claiming they had not paid the tax. Blacks who did pay their taxes found their votes invalidated by officials who charged the men were not properly registered, or that they had voted under "false names." In the mid-1870s, according to a *New York Times* reporter, official Democratic challengers made a point of asking the brave black voter who did venture to the polls "all sorts of questions, legal and illegal, as to his age and occupation, his place of birth, as to his property, if he has any, if he has paid his taxes, if he is a resident of the district, &c." This litany of queries discouraged many men from waiting a long time in line to vote.[2]

At the state level, the legislature was little more than an arm of the Democratic Party. Lawmakers nearly eliminated the black vote altogether when, in 1877, they made the poll tax cumulative, requiring voters to show proof they had paid all previous years' fees, not just the ones due that year, thus ensuring that voting would remain an expensive proposition, well out of the reach of ordinary workingmen; in turn, registrars possessed a great deal of leeway in deciding who should cast a ballot. The tactics employed by whites in Savannah found favor all over Georgia, where blacks endured "sneaking midnight intimidation" and threats of violence if they showed an interest in voting. In November 1876, the same *New York Times* reporter concluded that Georgia blacks "are just as far from the ballot box as they were in the days of slavery." Between 1873 and 1882, the state was represented in Congress by former Confederate vice president Alexander Stephens. He was elected governor in 1882. Nevertheless, along the coast, the majority-black counties of McIntosh, Camden, and Liberty continued to send black representatives to the state legislature as late as 1901, and blacks in McIntosh elected blacks to a variety of local offices into the 1890s.[3]

Throughout the last quarter of the nineteenth century, James M. Simms wrestled with the central dilemma that all African Americans in the South would confront over the next one hundred years: How could a group disenfranchised, and hence not the constituency of any particular politician or party, achieve basic citizenship rights—to vote, send their children to public school, and live without the constant fear of harassment or bodily harm? Though not always unified, Savannah's blacks continued to employ a variety of strategies that capitalized on their formidable numbers, their clout as consumers of city services and as swing voters in local elections, and their claim to moral authority, all in an effort to agitate for full integration into the body politic. Complicating this project was the persistent lack of fearless (and necessarily reckless) white allies in the spirit of James J. Waring. Too, the persistent divide between the impoverished masses of people on the one hand, and a small but influential professional class on the other, continued to weaken a black community that was arrayed against whites who could, under certain circumstances, embrace a common "white" identity.

Through much of the 1870s, Simms remained active in the near-moribund Republican Party, and from 1872 to 1878 he was rewarded for his loyalty with a job as inspector at the U.S. Customs House. Nevertheless, he, Henry M. Turner, and James Porter were in the process of withdrawing from state politics, dominated as it was by white Democrats running roughshod over not only blacks but also the dwindling number of white Republicans. In a speech in Atlanta in 1876, South Carolina politician Wade Hampton declared, "Democracy in the South means peace." By that he meant that the Democrats must crush their opponents once and for all and thereby purge politics of partisan strife and violence. In response, Turner renewed his efforts to promote emigration plans that would take blacks out of Georgia, to other parts of the South or to Liberia. He also embraced the pulpit more fully as a means of influence, and in 1880 assumed the post of bishop of the Georgia African Methodist Episcopal Church.[4]

During this period, Simms served as a featured speaker at a remarkable variety of processions, mass meetings, and celebrations that brought Savannah blacks together. Each New Year's Day, the community sponsored an Emancipation Day grand procession of black militias, mutual aid societies, and church groups, culminating with speeches by established leaders. And those leaders, together with ordinary people, remained ever vigilant to specific forms of injustice. When Chatham County began its takeover of black schools (including, finally, Beach Institute in 1875), the move turned out to be little more than a ploy to keep those schools small and strapped for cash; in 1873 the city board of education spent $64,000 for white schools and $3,000 for their black counterparts, ensuring that more than half of all black youngsters (3,600 out of a total school-age population of 5,600) would not even find a seat in a classroom. Blacks conducted a series of "indignation meetings" to protest this misappropriation of their tax dollars, and it was the school issue that prompted Simms, Porter, Charles DeLaMotta, John Deveaux, and Louis B. Toomer to form what they called the City Executive Committee. Its purpose was to nominate black candidates for municipal office. This initiative yielded only modest successes; Toomer and others won election as magistrates of local city districts, but blacks remained excluded from the mayor's office, the city council, juries, and the police force. By the end of the century, the city boasted nine schools, including a high school, for white children, and relegated a fraction of the total number of black children to just three schools, all in various states of disrepair. Such was the bitter legacy of the rise and rapid fall of the Savannah Education Association years earlier; white control of black schools had become a means of starving black educational efforts nigh unto death.[5]

On March 18, 1874, more than 4,000 black men, women, and children gathered in and around St. Phillips AME Church to mourn the death of Senator Charles Sumner, who had died seven days before. Turner and Simms delivered eulogies in Sumner's honor, and James Porter directed a choir of singers from all of the city's churches. For Simms, the occasion carried almost unbearable poignancy: Sumner first won election to the Senate in the wake of the Thomas Simms affair, in the spring of 1851; later, the Massachusetts senator considered James his protégé of sorts, nominating him for the short-lived municipal judgeship in 1871. At the service, Simms spoke at length, recounting Sumner's compelling life story, and calling upon the mourners to "contemplate those peaceful, powerful weapons[—]argument, logic, and truth[—]by which he has achieved such glorious victories for us." Simms ended with the hope that a new generation of black people might find inspiration, as he had as a young man, "walking through the city of Boston, where Charles Sumner was born, admiring [the city's] grandeur as shown in her thrift and wealth."[6]

Beginning in 1870, Sumner's insistent sponsorship of a congressional civil rights bill capped a two-decade career of agitating forcefully for freedom and justice for African Americans. His death represented the end of an era when white men at the highest reaches of political power spoke out for equal rights. Within a year, the Civil Rights Act of 1875 would become law, but for only less than a decade. It stipulated that "all persons within the jurisdiction of the United States shall be entitled to the full and equal enjoyment of all accommodations, advantages, facilities and privileges of inns, public conveyances on land or water, theaters, and other places of public amusement . . . applicable alike to citizens of every race and color, regardless of any previous condition of servitude." Yet soon after the law's passage, whites in Savannah began an incremental campaign to segregate blacks and whites in public places—at open-air water fountains, in the toilets in the federal post office, in the major assembly halls and theaters throughout the city, on the streetcars. On a Monday evening in April 1876, well-dressed black patrons arrived at the Savannah Theatre to hear a concert presented by the Braham Musical Concert, only to find themselves, for the first time in history, forced to take their seats in the upstairs gallery, away from the white patrons seated below. Black leaders condemned this "malicious outrage upon decency and common sense," but the municipal regulation stood.[7]

Four months after the Sumner memorial service, the black community gathered together again to mourn, this time for the Freedman's Bank, which closed its doors on July 2, 1874, bankrupt. Among the aggrieved depositors was Susie Baker King's grandmother Dolly Reed, who had amassed a considerable sum through many years of marketing goods and working as a servant and laundress. Wrote her granddaughter:

> in that bank she had placed her savings, about three thousand dollars, the result of her hard labor and self-denial before the war, and which, by shrewdness and care, she kept together all through the war. She felt it more keenly, coming as it did in her old age, when her life was too far spent to begin anew; but she took a practical view of the matter, for she said, "I will leave it all in God's hand. If the Yankees did take all our money, they freed my race; God will take care of us."

On July 9, at a meeting of the bereft depositors, Simms lauded the original purposes of the bank, which he associated with Lincoln, the great emancipator. But Simms was also unsparing in his condemnation of the fraudulent bookkeeping practices and questionable investments that led to the bank's failure. Efforts to expose those abuses came too late for hundreds of investors—not only individuals such as Dolly Reed, but the many small mutual aid and benevolent associations that crisscrossed the Savannah black community. The average depositor lost $48, a meager but hard-earned reward for countless bales of cotton toted, barrels of rice loaded, cauldrons of laundry scrubbed, meals for white folks cooked. For years, bank officials had touted the Savannah branch as a glowing success story, and now in the mid-1870s its failure represented one more sorry example of the federal government's betrayal of freedpeople all over the South.[8]

Still, neither disfranchisement nor the collapse of the Freedman's Bank could hinder the continued growth and expansion of black institutions. By the 1870s, Savannah had become a center of Georgia Freemasonry, boasting two active lodges, Eureka 11 and John T. Hall No. 13. The vitality of these branches owed much to the personal relationship between Simms and Lewis Hayden, the Boston activist and former fugitive slave who had helped to secure the original charter for the black Masons of Savannah. In 1874 Hayden published a tract in the form of an open letter to "Hon. Judge Simms"; in it the Bostonian offered a lengthy defense of black Masons against the white group's efforts to deny their legitimacy. Wrote Hayden, "The dark day of slavery is fast passing away, and as its shadows recede, it is our duty, as colored men, who were the subjects of oppression, to advance toward light and knowledge." In 1872, the forty-nine-year-old Simms relinquished the post of grand master of Savannah Masons to Louis B. Toomer, thirty-eight, who served in the position for two years. Toomer's successor was John Deveaux, a rising star among black leaders; Deveaux remained grand master for nine years.[9]

In 1875, with Louis M. Pleasant, the twenty-nine-year-old Deveaux founded a newspaper called the *Colored Tribune*; the following year its name was changed to the *Savannah Tribune*. The paper provided not only a clear voice for Savannah's black professional class, but also an organ for what was left of the local Republican Party, and an advertising outlet for the city's black small-business owners. (Its conciliatory motto was culled from Lincoln's Second Inaugural address: "With malice toward none, with charity toward all.") In 1880, Deveaux and his wife, Fanny, and their three small children were living next door to Richard W. White, his wife, Annie, and their four children; both men were enjoying the fruits of Republican patronage, Deveaux as a clerk in the Customs House, White as a U.S. Post Office official. Deveaux was neither a preacher nor a veteran of the postwar political battles; but he represented an unbroken line of activism that stretched back to his maternal grandmother, Catherine, a native of Antigua, who with her daughter Jane had conducted a clandestine black school in her home in the first decades of the nineteenth century.[10]

On June 16, 1874, whites dedicated Savannah's first Confederate war memorial. A lofty structure of Canadian sandstone (donors eschewed any "Yankee" materials), the monument was erected in Forsyth Park with contributions from the Ladies Memorial Association. The original structure depicted two female figures, "Judgment" and "Silence," rendered in marble. Captain George A. Mercer, who in his younger years struggled with fear of public speaking, delivered the main address to an immense crowd. Nevertheless, white opinion-makers were disappointed with the design of the memorial, prompting a renovation that replaced the two female figures with a larger-than-life-size sculpture of a Confederate soldier. An inscription, etched into one side of the base, read, "Come from the four winds, O breath, and breathe upon these slain, that they may live" (from Ezekiel 37:9). The withdrawal of the last federal troops from the city the same year as the memorial's dedication represented the closing of the wartime era.[11]

Even as whites aggressively memorialized the past, they were forced to revisit a painful chapter in their antebellum history. In the summer and fall of 1876, Savannah again suffered an epidemic of yellow fever, raising the specter of the widespread devastation that had occurred twenty-two years earlier. Between August and November 1876, more than 1,066 white people died from the fever. In an echo of the events of 1854, public officials set upon each other, after first issuing public denials that the fever had made a reappearance. Once again a stricken city burned tar fires in the squares and gratefully accepted charity from donors, north and south. Once again men and women followed the injunctions of street-corner peddlers and newspaper advertisers, imbibing whiskey and mustard seed as preventive measures, only to succumb to the illness.[12]

Among the victims of *Aedes aegypti* this time was the physician Richard D. Arnold, who expired in the very room where he had been born sixty-eight years before. Arnold neared the end of his life still bewildered by the fever's virulence, and baffled by its causes, "an intricate subject not susceptible of a very satisfactory solution," he lamented. Unaware of the way a mosquito could transmit the disease from an infected person to another victim, Arnold had always argued strenuously against the idea that the fever was contagious, "because I do not believe in it and because the unfounded belief in it creates undue panic, needlessly obstructs commerce, interrupts communication between sister cities, and cuts short the ordinary charities of social life." In the end, Arnold, the inveterate booster, could save neither Savannah nor himself from the elusive killer.[13]

The physician-politician James J. Waring provided what was perhaps a fitting coda to the 1876 epidemic by reprising his postbellum attacks on the municipal authorities; now he charged Mayor Edward C. Anderson with criminal neglect of the city's health. Meanwhile, a distracted Anderson agonized over municipal budgetary shortfalls; the city's mounting indebtedness was the result of profligate spending initiated by his predecessor, John Screven, who pursued a number of costly projects, including a new market, a new drainage and sewer system, and renewed river dredging. Screven had forged ahead with these plans despite warning signs of large budget deficits. The tax base remained static, a recession in 1873 had damaged business interests, and the local economy continued to depend exclusively on the processing and transporting of rice, timber, and cotton. Anderson had been reelected in late 1873 to clean up this financial mess; one of his more unpopular solutions was to raise taxes on draymen and real estate owners. By cutting the police force and by floating bonds, the city managed to stabilize its finances in the early 1880s, but at the cost of the grandiose plans for "progress" that had marked the decade before.[14]

In the late nineteenth century James M. Simms simultaneously entered the ranks of Savannah's revered elders and embarked on a new life for himself. In 1876 he helped organize "a national convention of colored citizens" held in Nashville, Tennessee, in early April. (His brother Thomas was probably still living in that city.) At some point he began work on a book, *The First Colored Baptist Church in North America*, a history of First Bryan (formerly Third African) Baptist church. Simms sought to reclaim for the church the mantle of authority conferred by Andrew Bryan, founder of the first independent black Baptist church in the United States, and uncle of Andrew Marshall, revered pastor of First African. In recounting the history of the church's leadership and congregation, Simms joined with other black leaders around the country who sought, through such publications, to highlight religious institution-building as a significant force in black nineteenth-century life, a force that spanned slavery and freedom. Here in Simms's book, published in 1888, was the story of the ideal of equality among all people, spiritual and earthly; of a heroic struggle among blacks to control their own churches apart from whites; of preachers who boldly assumed positions of political leadership in the momentous days of Reconstruction; of fights and feuds among black congregants over the very soul of the community. Simms thus closely linked the history of the church to the history of emancipation. He cited a "mysterious Providence" that permitted the forced migration and enslavement of native Africans, but also eventually wrought "good out of evil" as their descendants emerged into the bright light of freedom.[15]

The publication of Simms's book marked his bid for renewed clerical authority at the same time he was opening a new chapter in his personal life. In January 1886, his mother, Minda Campbell, died in Savannah in her ninety-fourth year; obituaries identified her as "the mother of Tom Sims, the fugitive slave, whose trial in Boston created a great excitement." In December 1889, James, now sixty-six and presumably a widower (after the death of his wife, Margaret), remarried. He and his second wife, Priscilla Holmes, began a new family with the birth of James Junior in 1890, followed by Wendell P. in 1891, David in 1893, and Plutarch and Priscilla in 1895. The elder Priscilla died in 1895, perhaps giving birth to the twins; her namesake died in June of the following year. Despite these family tragedies, Simms remained active in community affairs, renowned especially for his rhetorical gifts; in 1895 a young admirer hailed him as the "Son of Boanerges [god of thunder], quick, brainy, shrewd, brilliant at repartee."[16]

In contrast to his Savannah counterparts, the Reverend Tunis G. Campbell managed to retain some local Republican influence within an overwhelmingly Democratic state. But he too eventually fell victim to whites' high-handed and cynical tactics. In January 1875, a McIntosh County grand jury convicted Campbell on trumped-up charges of "malpractice in office." This move prompted hundreds of Campbell's constituents to stage an angry protest outside the county courthouse. In short order, 326 men and 189 women sent a petition to President Grant, demanding that the president provide if not justice then federal troops, and if not troops then guns, so that the town's black people might defend themselves. Campbell languished in jail for 256 days while his appeals were rejected by a series of local and state courts. Finally, on a bitterly cold day in January 1876, white authorities roused the sixty-three-year-old from his cell, handcuffed and chained him, and transported him to Savannah, where he was marched through the streets and then sent to Washington County. There he was put to work on a chain gang to labor on a plantation owned by T. J. Smith, a white man. The Reverend Henry M. Turner, James Simms, and John Deveaux were among the seventeen black leaders who urged the governor to release Campbell, but the prisoner served a full year of forced labor on the Smith plantation. During this time his wife, Harriet, stayed in Atlanta, where she sold medicines, and picked blackberries and strawberries to earn money so that she could send her husband clothing, cakes, and pickled eggs while he was confined. Of the convict-labor farm Campbell later wrote, "If a man could not stand the work, then he was reported, and of course beaten. Women were treated in the same manner." Upon his release, Campbell moved to

Washington, D.C., where he continued to condemn the state of Georgia as "the Empire State of Rascality."[17]

In Washington, it is possible that Campbell crossed paths with a number of notables who had shaped Civil War–era Savannah. In 1877, Charles Devens, who from 1849 to 1853 had served as U.S. marshal for the District of Massachusetts, was appointed attorney general of the United States. Devens had long regretted his own role in returning the young fugitive Thomas Simms to slavery in 1851, and twenty-six years later he atoned for his official actions and appointed Simms, now forty-nine, a messenger in the Justice Department. The appointment ignited a minor controversy when the famous abolitionist Wendell Phillips denounced Devens as a "slave hound" for his role in the black man's rendition to Georgia. Devens's friends countered that "he had raised sufficient money to purchase Simms, from his owner, and made him a free man." In an April, 1877, interview (with the *Nashville American*), Simms broke his long silence about the dramatic events surrounding his escape from slavery. And he stated "definitely and positively that the war and not Gen. Devens freed him." Simms served in the messenger post until 1881, and then resumed work as a bricklayer in the capital.[18]

Other former slaves settled in Washington. After leaving Savannah in 1866, Harriet Jacobs launched a campaign to raise money to build a home for Savannah's poorest blacks, orphans, and the elderly. That effort took her as far away as London, but it never came to fruition. The year Thomas Simms received his Justice Department job, Jacobs also moved to Washington, where she operated a boardinghouse, first for whites, and then for well-to-do blacks. Her daughter Louisa finally received a stable if modest income with her appointment as assistant matron of the National Home for Relief of Destitute Colored and Women, in Washington, in 1898. The following year, mother and daughter visited Edenton, North Carolina, the place of their enslavement, hoping that the weather would improve Harriet's failing health; but they quickly returned to Washington. In the words of a friend, Harriet found Edenton "a forlorn place, . . . the place of her suffering for years." She would remain in Washington for the rest of her life.[19]

Scattering after their stint in Savannah and the lowcountry, most AMA workers returned to the North, but some continued to labor in association-sponsored schools and missions. Mary Colburn went on to work in a Chinese mission in California. Frances Littlefield left Daufuskie Island, her post-Ogeechee assignment, for Talladega, Alabama, where she taught in black schools for most of the 1870s. Her co-worker, Esther

Douglass, continued teaching in Alamance, North Carolina. Sarah Champney only reluctantly abandoned Brunswick, but she had a difficult time finding a place that suited her, moving from Newton to Albany in Georgia, then on to Aberdeen, Mississippi, and Brenham, Texas, in the course of her teaching career. Following his brief, frustrating tenure in Savannah, Hardy Mobley took his family and settled in New Iberia, Louisiana, where they maintained a precarious existence and tried to sustain an AMA church and school among freedpeople who wanted no "Congregationers here." James Porter's sojourn was more successful. He served for a few years as the first black schoolteacher hired by the city of Savannah. Eventually he left the Episcopal Church and in 1879 became an ordained minister in the African Methodist Episcopal denomination, which assigned him to successive posts in Florida, Mississippi, Arkansas, Bermuda, and Canada. In Yazoo, Mississippi, he worked as a principal in an AME-sponsored school, and wrote a book, *English Grammar for Beginners.*[20]

Aaron A. Bradley eventually left the lowcountry as well. In 1874 he ran unsuccessfully for Congress from the rice districts of South Carolina; four years later he was still giving speeches in Savannah. In October 1878, white newspapers were reporting, with time-honored contempt, "Aaron Alpeoria Bradley, the old negro Wahoo, made a speech in Savannah Saturday evening in favor of Democracy." Two years later Bradley departed for St. Louis, and there he quickly set about soliciting clients and getting into trouble with hostile judges. In April of 1882 the state's Court of Appeals threw out the conviction of a man he had defended, granting the man a new trial "on the grounds of the 'ignorance and imbecility' of his counsel." Bradley died that October—remarkably, of natural causes. According to the *Morning News*, he collapsed on a city street, penniless. Within days of his death St. Louis blacks took up a collection that saved him from a pauper's grave, suggesting that he had made his mark on that community soon after arriving. Among other apparently newsworthy aspects of his life, including his appearance—light-skinned, with long curly hair—the *Morning News* observed, "He was denied permission to practice at the bar of Chatham County on account of rascalities." With his command of constitutional law, his loyal following among lowcountry rice hands, and his defiant demeanor, Bradley had embodied the freedpeople's most potent, if ultimately unsuccessful, challenge to white supremacy.[21]

In Savannah, as in other cities throughout the South, white elites sought to consolidate their power over the white laboring classes and at the same time counter a rising generation of black activists who had been born after slavery. This neo-confederate project received the implicit blessing of the federal government, which had largely withdrawn from the South in favor of state and local control over matters related to politics, schooling, and labor relations. In 1883 the U.S. Supreme Court declared Sumner's Civil Rights Act of 1875 unconstitutional, and thirteen years later, in *Plessy v. Ferguson,* the Court put its official stamp of approval on ordinances that separated whites from blacks on streetcars and in schools.

Meanwhile, in Savannah, black people were enduring a multitude of commemorations that glorified the secessionists' cause. The former Confederate president, Jefferson Davis, made a triumphant appearance in the city in May 1886, and received a hero's welcome from the seventy thousand civilians and uniformed soldiers who lined his parade route. A reporter for the *Boson Daily Globe* listed the dignitaries present, from the governor of the state to county and city officials, and judged all the day's speeches, receptions, and banquets a rousing success. The parade especially constituted "a most inspiring spectacle": "The marching and evolutions of all the companies was remarkably fine, and the display the best and most extensive since Sherman's army came marching to the sea." The following day, Davis spoke to the white schoolchildren of the city, offering a paean to southern white motherhood and to the martyrs slain in the war to defend "the noblest people who have graced the pages of history." At the end of the century, the (white) former antagonists in the war seemed to close a final breach when U.S. Army militia joined with local Savannah military companies to honor the southern dead on Confederate Memorial Day, April 26. Elsewhere in Georgia, black veterans found themselves unwelcome at U.S. Memorial Day ceremonies, which had been refashioned to pay tribute exclusively to white men, dead and living, on both sides of the conflict.[22]

It was the black chapters of a national veterans' group, the Grand Army of the Republic (GAR), that memorialized sacrifices by African-American soldiers. At a ceremony in Boston in 1887, black veterans charged "that American citizens of African descent . . . are today in large portion of this great nation denied justice in the courts, deprived of the exercise of the elective franchise, the victims of mob violence, an unprotected and outraged people." The year before, Susie Baker King (remarried to a Bostonian, Russell Taylor, forty-nine, a Georgia-born "shore man") had helped to organize the Women's Relief Corps, an auxiliary to the GAR. She remained outspoken in her opposition to southern apologists, including the Daughters of the Confederacy, who seemed bent on erasing the brutality of slavery from the memory of the nation. In her book, *Reminiscences of My Life in Camp* (1902), she recorded her memories of a girlhood in Savannah—"the heart-rending scenes . . . thirty or forty men, handcuffed, and as many women and children, come every first Tuesday of each month from Mr. Wiley's [Wylly's] trade office to the auction blocks." Learning that southern white women were objecting to a new play based on Harriet Beecher Stowe's abolitionist novel *Uncle Tom's Cabin*, she asked, "Do these Confederate Daughters ever send petitions to prohibit the atrocious lynchings and wholesale murdering and torture of the negro?"[23]

In Savannah, the Robert Gould Shaw post of the GAR celebrated Emancipation Day with a parade of aging veterans as well as the uniformed members of voluntary black militias. These groups included, by the 1890s, the Forest City Light Infantry, Chatham Light Infantry, Savannah Hussars, Union League Guards, Georgia Artillery, and Lone Star Cadets. (However, in 1905 the Georgia state legislature outlawed all black militias.) Like other black GAR branches throughout the South, the Shaw post was segregated, and although membership in it carried great prestige within the black community, the group possessed little in the way of larger political influence. In 1890, only about 27 percent of all black Civil War veterans were still alive, compared to about 55 percent of their Confederate and white Union counterparts. Black veterans' relatively high mortality rates suggested that they were poorer and received less adequate medical care than whites. And government-sponsored discrimination followed them and their families throughout their lives: While about 90 percent of white Union applicants received federal pensions, only 75 percent of black applicants did. Similarly, 84 percent of widows of white soldiers received pensions, but only 61 percent of widows of black soldiers did. Many black men and women were too poor to travel to cities to fill out the requisite documents; lacking identification papers, they could neither meet official requirements nor persevere in the face of long delays imposed by indifferent clerks and pension officials.[24]

In the 1880s and 1890s, Savannah's social division of labor showed little change compared to the mid-nineteenth century. Black men continued to dominate the jobs of laborer, drayman, porter, bricklayer, and cotton sampler. At the same time, black skilled craftsmen, especially in the building trades, were being displaced by the white men favored by large construction companies. Black women labored as laundresses, cooks, nurses, and domestic servants; the demand for skilled seamstresses declined as ready-made clothing and sewing machines became more affordable among whites. The city's industries remained primarily extractive and processing—cotton presses, rice mills, and sawmills. In 1900, Savannah still lacked the substantial black middle class characteristic of larger southern cities. For example, Atlanta, though violently repressive, possessed a more diversified economy, and more institutions of higher learning for black people, than Savannah. It was in Atlanta in the 1890s, at the AMA-founded Atlanta University, that W. E. B. DuBois provided aggressive leadership in political activism, scholarly research, and literary and cultural expression.[25]

The lowcountry only gradually moved away from antebellum patterns of economy and agriculture. As late as 1879 Georgia was still producing almost one-quarter of all rice grown in the United States, but two decades later the proportion was 4.5 percent, signaling the demise of the Rice Kingdom and the rise of its eager competitor, Louisiana. In the fall of 1873 Frances Butler married a young English clergyman and amateur minstrel-show performer, James Leigh; shortly thereafter the couple took up residence on the Butler plantations in Georgia. Frances tried creative approaches to her own labor problem; at one point she was employing Irish immigrant ditchers; English carpenters, blacksmiths, and laborers; and black carpenters and field hands. In desperation, a neighboring planter experimented briefly with imported Chinese labor, prompting Frances Leigh to remark that the islands now represented "four quarters of the globe, as we have inhabitants on them from Europe, Asia, Africa, and America," and a plethora of religions, including Christianity, Confucianism, "and I know not what besides." Yet the planter and her neighbors had little choice but to accommodate themselves to the fact that black men and women eschewed working for whites in favor of a bare subsistence, owning a small piece of land, and fishing and hunting to support themselves. She believed the workers were now "quite satisfied with that, not yet having learned to want things that money alone can give." In early 1877 the Leighs left Georgia and settled in England, where Frances began work on her book, *Ten Years on a Georgia Plantation Since the War*. Published in 1882, it offered simultaneously a bitter rebuke to her mother's heartfelt abolitionism and a tribute to her father's raw pursuit of making money from rice and cotton hands, enslaved and free.[26]

Upon the death of his father, Charles, in 1875, Louis Manigault took over Gowrie plantation on Argyle Island. Unable to force blacks to do muck work, within a year he too hired Irish hands to clean ditches and repair banks in the winter months; across the Savannah River, a great strike among South Carolina's coastal blacks in 1876 had doomed that state's rice economy. By the early 1880s, many Georgia black rice workers had become transients, performing specialized seasonal labor, cultivating modest crops on their own land, fishing, selling wood and chickens in Savannah, and then working part of the week for planters. Soon after, the state's rice industry expired. In the place of the great plantations appeared a number of industries—timber, naval stores such as rosin and turpentine, cattle ranching, seafood processing, and truck farming. In oyster-shucking plants and lumberyards, black workers sang the work songs of their enslaved forebears: "This time another year / I may be gone / In some lonesome graveyard / O Lord how long!" A new form of seasonal employment came from tourism, fueled by the wealth of northern magnates, including Andrew Carnegie, J. P. Morgan, and Henry Ford, as well as extended families with the names of Rockefeller, Astor, Pulitzer, and Vanderbilt.[27]

In 1877, Charles C. Jones had brought his family back from New York City to Georgia and settled in an elegant mansion outside Augusta. Determined to sell off his family's lowcountry holdings, Jones was stymied. Though his brother Joseph wanted to keep Monte Video and Maybank in the family, no serious white buyers appeared on the scene, and the black tenants were producing more crops for themselves and fewer staples for their landlords. As a result, Charles had to continue to rely on former family slaves to manage the lands in his absence. Charles's son Edgeworth began to oversee the estate in 1893 and in the process signaled the end of the paternalist ethos the Jones family had so long prided themselves upon; instructing Niger Fraser, their agent on Monte Video, Edgeworth told him, "Squeeze every coffer you can out of the renters."[28]

DURING THE LAST decade of the nineteenth century, the Populist Party challenge to entrenched Democratic interests in Georgia bypassed the lowcountry; calls for a nascent alliance of black and white debtors resonated in the upcountry and the Cotton Belt in a way it did not among small farmers on the coast. Yet Savannah blacks engaged in their own forms of protest during this period. Between 1891 and 1906, they launched two major citywide efforts against exploitative wage rates and the onslaught of Jim Crow segregation. Both of these episodes—a strike among dockworkers, and a boycott of streetcars—exposed the strength and the weakness of the black community as workers and consumers. With a large number of impoverished laborers and only the bare bones of a middle class, black Savannah could mount but not sustain a meaningful challenge to the city's white elites.[29]

On September 27, 1891, an estimated 1,500 black dockworkers struck shipping and railroad companies to win recognition of the Laborers' Union and Protective Association (LUPA), and to secure overtime pay and higher wages—a raise of 5¢ over the current rate of 15¢ an hour. The work stoppage bore all the signs of a long-planned effort: the strike fund amounted to a reported (though probably exaggerated) $5,000, leaders welcomed the strikers and the public to rousing daily meetings in the local Odd Fellows Hall, and supporters raised money by sponsoring "balls" and other entertainments. Officers of the LUPA urged union members to refrain from violence and remain steadfast in the face of inevitable provocations from the police. Yet only two days had passed before Central Railroad officials began to bring in black and white strike-breakers from the surrounding countryside. The company even appealed to a group of Milledgeville excursionists, in town for a holiday, telling them that ample job opportunities awaited them on the docks. By this time a committee composed of the mayor and representatives from the employers and the workers was meeting regularly. The strikers stated their case simply: "the men were not paid enough for their labor, and . . . lately it had been the custom to start gangs to work at the Central wharves unloading cars a while before the quitting hour, and compel the men to continue the work until the freight was out"—and not pay them for the extra work.[30]

The employers then offered a rate of 20¢ an hour for overtime, but no increase in regular pay, a proposal the strikers rejected. Now warehouse and yard workers, porters, draymen, and samplers joined the stoppage, and demanded wage increases from their own employers. Meanwhile, white and black men from as far away as the Carolinas were pouring into the city and taking the place of the strikers. On October 3, a group of prominent black leaders advised the strikers to capitulate. One of them was a carpenter foreman named D. B. Morris, president of the Archery Club and the Mystic Tie of Arabs, two mutual aid societies that included some of the strikers as members. He told the workers "that they were injuring themselves by staying away from work and at the same time injuring the city . . . that they would starve themselves out first" before they would "starve the railroads out." In the end, the employers gained a significant victory, withdrawing the pay increase and refusing to recognize the union. Many members of the LUPA were discharged in favor of white and black strikebreakers. Referring to the multitudes of desperate men of both colors in the countryside, one railroad manager claimed, "We could have put 10,000 men here as easily as 1,000." He added, "There are hundreds of negroes in South Carolina, North Carolina, and Virginia waiting now for the Savannah trains anxious to come here for work."[31]

Eight years later a new ordinance mandating the segregation of city streetcars brought black Savannahians (now 52 percent of the city's total population of about 86,000) together in collective outrage. After the protests of 1872, the head of the largest streetcar company, Savannah Electric, determined that separation of blacks and whites was too expensive to maintain; he feared that a black-led citywide boycott would cripple his company. For several years thereafter the cars remained integrated. An 1891 state law mandated streetcar segregation "as much as practicable," and local companies took those words to mean they could exercise considerable discretion in their operations. In 1899, Savannah blacks successfully forced one company to repeal a new segregation policy imposed on a line that ran from the city to the small coastal town of Warsaw. However, in mid-September 1906, the council passed an ordinance requiring separate cars, and the president of the Savannah Electric Company acquiesced. Mass protests followed, with a group of black professionals urging people to stay off the streetcars. The *Savannah Tribune* told readers, "Let us walk! Walk! And save our nickels . . . Do not trample on your pride by being 'jim crowed.' Walk!" Members of the black clergy exhorted their congregants to walk to work rather than patronize the segregated cars. Over the next seven months, black boycotters cost Savannah Electric an estimated $50,000, despite police efforts to harass them and the private hack drivers who gave them rides.[32]

The protesters held out until March 1907, when the company initiated a series of novel strategies to break the backbone of the boycott. Savannah Electric agents began to put pressure on faculty and other state employees who worked at a local black college, Georgia Industrial. The company also made substantial contributions to the Colored Orphans Home in order to win over black clergy, and sponsored high-profile black entertainment acts at a venue it owned outside Savannah, Lincoln Amusement Park, which was accessible only by rail. Combined, these efforts managed to wear down the boycotters; the example set by ministers and other men of standing, who led the way onto the segregated lines, had a powerful impact on the rest of the community.[33]

. . .

GRADUALLY THE CIVIL WAR generation passed away, during the height of state-sanctioned terrorism and segregation, from the late 1880s through the first two decades of the twentieth century. James J. Waring died in 1888; Tunis G. Campbell in 1891; Charles C. Jones and Fanny Kemble, 1893; Harriet Jacobs, 1899; Frances Butler Leigh and Susie Baker King Taylor, 1910; James Porter, Henry M. Turner, and Esther Douglass, 1915; and Eleanor Kinzie Gordon, 1917. James M. Simms died in Savannah in 1912 at the age of eighty-nine. His brother's fate is unknown even, apparently, to members of the extended Simms family. In 1985 a student researching the life of Thomas interviewed James's grand-children and concluded, "Not very much is known about Thomas Simms' last years, for he did not keep in contact with his relatives."[34]

During World War I, many lowcountry blacks began to make a power-ful political statement, voting with their feet against the humiliating tac-tics of Jim Crow. In 1916, railroad labor recruiters descended on Savannah, and promised good wages for those willing to make the trip north. Alarmed, city officials authorized the police to intimidate would-be migrants, arresting them at the train station for "loitering," but failing to stanch the flow of refugees from poverty and violence. For those who remained behind, the rhythm of life, especially in rural areas, changed lit-tle over the next half century. In the 1920s ox-drawn carts still predomi-nated in coastal areas and on the islands. Honoring their Gullah-Geechee heritage, the black peasantry lived in wooden cabins under the shade of live oaks; abiding by custom, mothers swept clean their front yards, tended small vegetable gardens, and marketed chickens and eggs in Savannah. Their husbands and children fished and crabbed in the sur-rounding creeks and streams. Young people sought out wage work on the docks, in sawmills, in warehouses and hotels, especially during the busy months from September through December. For the elderly as well, cash wages, modest though they might be, were crucial to sustaining a liveli-hood on the land, to paying taxes and mortgages and purchasing fertilizer and clothing. By this time many families were living on plots of thirteen acres or less, barely enough to maintain a family of any size.[35]

In Savannah, Yamacraw and other poor neighborhoods were notori-ously congested, dirty, and noisy at all hours of the night and day. For those who preferred to avoid drinking and fighting, the city offered little in the way of wholesome entertainment: "All you can do is to go to a movie n' drink a bottle of soda pop," noted one resident. Church and social gatherings provided the main forms of respectable recreation. Like coastal farmers, city workers were cash-poor. A ten-hour day on the docks earned a man only $1.80, so it was no wonder that many hoped to board one of the steamers that would take them to Philadelphia, New York, or Boston, a twentieth-century variation on Thomas Simms's bid for freedom in 1851.[36]

Beginning in the late nineteenth century, scholars and folklorists "discovered" lowcountry African traditions in religion, culture, and music. In 1888 Charles C. Jones published *Gullah Folktales from the Georgia Coast*, a recounting of trickster tales combined with a eulogy for the antebellum Georgia rice country, "where generous hospitality and a patriarchal civilization abode." A number of amateur and professional folklorists and anthropologists publicized the distinctive Gullah and Geechee languages, art forms, worship services, and medical practices. Lydia Parrish, a northerner who first visited the Sea Islands in 1912, recorded traditional hymns and work songs in *Slave Songs of the Georgia Sea Islands* in 1942. In the 1930s, the linguist Lorenzo Turner catalogued 3,000 African names and words among lowcountry South Carolina and Georgia blacks.[37]

During the Great Depression, the Federal Writers Project (FWP) employed men and women to study folk beliefs in Savannah and the coastal region, and the result was *Drums and Shadows: Survival Studies Among the Georgia Coastal Negroes* (1940). This work, and the material collected between 1936 and 1940 by a northern clergyman, Harry Middleton Hyatt, revealed little difference between the culture of the Savannah black laboring classes and that of the farm folk on the coast and in the surrounding countryside. In Yamacraw, FWP interviewers noted that, even with the presence of Baptist and Methodist churches, "Ghosts are everyday experiences. Root doctors are in constant demand." Among the poorest people especially, the line between slavery and the twentieth century seemed unbroken for subjects such as eighty-year-old Martha Page, who remembered her African grandfather vividly, and who had throughout her life contended with the witches that he had warned about: "Some ub em could make yuh disappeah, he say, an some could fly all round duh elements an make yuh do anyting dey wants yuh tuh do. Wen I growd up, I discobuh dat plenty uh duh tings gran tell me is sho nuff true." The FWP interviews were just part of a long series of ongoing efforts to document the distinctive culture in the lowcountry; in the decades that followed, ethnomusicologists and documentary filmmakers would continue to find the region rich in African artistic and oral traditions.[38]

. . .

FOUNDED IN 1917, Savannah's local branch of the National Association for the Advancement of Colored People (NAACP) fell on hard times during the 1920s and 1930s. But by the end of the Great Depression decade a newly formed Young Men's Civic Club had launched a voter-registration drive, despite the taunts of a local registrar: "If I read a long paragraph as fast as I can read, I bet you can't write it." And then in the 1940s, the Reverend Ralph Mark Gilbert, a graduate of the University of Michigan and the newly installed pastor of First African Baptist, infused the local NAACP with renewed purpose. From 1942 to 1950, he served as its president and oversaw a burst of local organizing, in which more than forty branches were started throughout Georgia. His efforts resulted in a concerted black voter-registration drive, which overcame the tenacious white primary system in Savannah. Voters began to elect white reformers, and the first black Savannah policeman donned his uniform in 1947. Redeeming the failed promise of Reconstruction a century earlier, other "firsts" followed, but only in the wake of intense pressure from leaders such as Westley W. ("W. W.") Law, the head of the NAACP in the 1960s, as well as the larger black community: the first integrated public schools (1963), the first black person to represent Savannah in the Georgia legislature since the early 1870s (in 1968), the first black city council member (1970), the first black mayor (1995), the first black majority on the council in this majority-black city (1999). Savannah also sent to the U.S. Supreme Court the first justice fluent in Geechee: Clarence Thomas, born in Pin Point, to the south of the city, and appointed to the court in 1991.[39]

Due to the efforts of the Historic Savannah Foundation (formed in 1955), by the 1970s the city had begun to draw large numbers of tourists who came to admire the restored homes of wealthy and notable men and women. Perennial favorites included the birthplaces of Juliette Gordon Low, daughter of William and Eleanor Gordon and in 1912 founder of the Girl Scouts; and Johnny Mercer, composer, musician, and grandson of George A. Mercer. Harking back to antebellum days, the city continued to sponsor elaborate St. Patrick's Day festivities, including a parade that was drawing as many as 300,000 spectators in the early twenty-first century. By this time the city was hosting many visitors who had read journalist and magazine editor John Berendt's *Midnight in the Garden of Good and Evil.* A publishing phenomenon, the 1994 book sold three million copies in 101 languages and remained on the *New York Times* bestseller list for 216 consecutive weeks. Berendt's story focused on a sensational murder—or accidental shooting—that took place in 1981, in the house designed for Hugh W. Mercer (George's father) in 1860. "The book," as local residents called it, proved a boon to the city's economy. Tax revenues from the lodging industry jumped by 25 percent in the two years after the publication of *Midnight*, and the phenomenon spawned a plethora of streetcar and walking tours, as well as a remarkable variety of memorabilia ("Midnightabilia") ranging from T-shirts to candles to refrigerator magnets.[40]

Nevertheless, Savannah's effort to attract tourists came at the expense of black neighborhoods, including historic Currytown on the west side—its homes, churches, businesses, and entertainment district. The Historic Savannah Foundation focused on restoring downtown mansions and town houses to their former glory—residences that included those built in the antebellum period by enslaved tradesmen such as the bricklayer Thomas Simms and his brother James, a carpenter. Yet the historic preservation effort went hand in hand with urban renewal projects that leveled parts of the city that white authorities deemed potentially damaging to the tourist trade. Evoking mid-nineteenth-century concerns, whites reduced the issue of black economic distress to one of aesthetics; in this view, poor neighborhoods ringing downtown were a cause for concern because they were unsightly. In response, black activists charged that city officials cared more about the appearance of buildings than the welfare of people. In the early 1980s W. W. Law led the fight to create and preserve black historic areas, with their impressive range of architectural styles, including the Beach Institute Historic Neighborhood Association on the east side. Charging that the revitalization of the downtown did significant damage to the integrity of the black community, Law and other leaders sought to link the city's African-American history to its plans for the future, an effort formally acknowledged by the city with subsequent subsidies to the association.[41]

In the early twenty-first century, Savannah is a city of 133,000 people, 57 percent of them black. It boasts the fourth most active port in the United States; the nation's largest registered Urban Landmark Historic District (2.5 square miles); and a tourist industry that attracts 6 million visitors a year, employs 14,000 people, and brings in $1.4 billion annually. Despite its mixed economy, with jobs in the port, aerospace, and manufacturing sectors, as well as health care and higher education, the city remains poor. Its poverty rate of 22 percent is about one-third greater than the national average, and violent crime remains a stubborn fact of life. In certain key respects Savannah's geographical configuration retains the outlines of its postbellum years, with a large impoverished black population segregated in the areas that border the city on the east and west. In a wide-ranging interview in early 2007, Mayor Otis S. Johnson mentioned another characteristic of the city that echoed the nineteenth century: residents still looked for "any excuse to have a parade." (Johnson was the first black Savannahian to graduate from the University of Georgia, in 1967.) En route to the mayor's office, the visitor ascends to the second floor of the city hall, where a magnificent rotunda features the portraits of past mayors, including Richard D. Arnold, Charles C. Jones Jr., and Edward C. Anderson.[42]

Conducted by bus, the Negro Heritage Trail Tour, sponsored by the King-Tisdell Cottage Foundation, Inc., includes places of interest to the student of Civil War–era Savannah. James M. Simms is buried in Laurel Grove South Cemetery; no doubt he chose the inscription on his own gravestone, which highlights his position as first Grand Master of the Ancient Free and Accepted Masons of Georgia. Other stops on the tour include the neighborhoods of Yamacraw and Currytown, First and Second African and First Bryan Baptist churches, the Massie School, and the house where Jane Deveaux taught. These sites, though, cannot match the mass appeal of tours devoted to ghosts and gardens. The *Morning News* notes, "Despite a growing demand for black history tourism, Savannah's rich African-American past has not yet been fully promoted."[43]

And in fact, most visitors come to view the beautiful homes and moss-draped live oaks and in the process revel in the romance of a bygone era. In the early twenty-first century, retracing the steps of Alexis de Tocqueville, French writer Bernard-Henri Lévy confessed, "I love Savannah. I love the way the inhabitants love their town. I love the gesture, for instance, of those officers who in 1864 wanted to surrender to General Sherman rather than see Yankee troops sack the city." (Richard D. Arnold, arguably the man who saved the city in 1864, would not be pleased at his erasure from history.) Lévy praises "the enchantment of Savannah"—"this feeling you have of walking around in a greenhouse, almost a bubble, a minuscule and fragile island protected from barbarian invasions." And so, because of its "Old South beauty," Lévy writes, if he had to live in any American city "it's Savannah I choose."[44]

Part of the challenge in bringing to life the city's African-American history is the fact that antebellum buildings offer only mute testimony to the thousands of rice and cotton slaves whose labors built and paid for those buildings. Yet memorializing the life and labors of enslaved low-country men and women remains a thorny political issue. In 1991, Dr. Abigail Jordan, a graduate of the University of Georgia and a Savannah educator and journalist, responded to the conspicuous lack of any monument in the city to her enslaved forebears. She organized a committee and a petition drive to push officials for some sort of tangible representation of the historic roots of Savannah's African-American community. As a result, a memorial was completed in 2002, but not before the very idea of such a project had ignited protests over its form, location, and inscription. Designed by local sculptor Dorothy Spradley, the seven-foot bronze statue stands near the visitors' center on River Street, which runs parallel to the body of water that bore shiploads of Africans to the slave markets of Savannah. The statue depicts a father, mother, daughter, and son clothed in modern dress, with broken shackles at their feet. At its base is an inscription written by poet Maya Angelou. The initial version read:

WE WERE STOLEN, SOLD AND BOUGHT TOGETHER FROM THE AFRICAN CONTINENT. WE GOT ON THE SLAVE SHIPS TOGETHER. WE LAY BACK TO BELLY IN THE HOLDS OF THE SLAVE SHIPS IN EACH OTHERS EXCREMENT AND URINE TOGETHER, SOMETIMES DIED TOGETHER AND OUR LIFELESS BODIES THROWN OVERBOARD TOGETHER.

When the wording was first proposed, the city council objected because it seemed too stark, too grim a greeting for the many tourists strolling along the riverfront. Angelou then agreed to add a line:

TODAY WE ARE STANDING UP TOGETHER WITH FAITH AND EVEN SOME JOY.

Savannahians thus partook of a larger debate among southern states hoping to promote and profit from "atrocity heritage" and its variation, "slavery tourism." One cannot help but wonder what James Simms would have had to say about the inscription and the ensuing controversy; well into the twentieth century, family lore had it that Simms "would speak out on anything[;] he was not diplomatic at all."[45]

The generations-old legacy of slavery had by this time devolved into a war of words: How best to preserve among the living the stories and sufferings of those long dead? Down on River Street, the African-American monument encapsulated the ironies of memorializing slavery in a place where many people preferred to avert their eyes from a statue with a distressing message. Rendering in words the shocking history of slavery was difficult enough. It was no wonder then that the bitter legacies of that history—the persistent poverty among blacks in Savannah, and throughout the country—received even less attention from Americans determined to scrub from the present the hard truths of the past.

MAYORS AND ALDERMEN OF THE CITY OF SAVANNAH

ELECTED 1853-72

Dec. 12, 1853
John E. Ward, Mayor
Isaac Brunner
Solomon Cohen
Montgomery Cumming
Charles Ganahl
Edwin E. Hertz
Alexander R. Lawton
John N. Lewis
John Mallery
Dominick A. O'Byrne
James P. Screven
Samuel Solomons
Robert D. Walker

Dec. 11, 1854
Edward C. Anderson,* Mayor
Peter W. Alexander
Robert A. Allen
Gilbert Butler
George W. Garmany
Thomas H. Harden
Edwin E. Hertz
John N. Lewis
John Mallery
Alvin N. Miller
James G. Rodgers
Charles W. West
John R. Wilder

Dec. 10, 1855
Edward C. Anderson,* Mayor
Robert A. Allen

Richard D. Arnold
William S. Basinger
Richard Bradley
Aaron Champion
Solomon Cohen
John M. Cooper
John J. Kelly
Robert Lachlison
Dominick A. O'Byrne
John F. Posey
Robert D. Walker

Dec. 8, 1856
James P. Screven, Mayor
Richard D. Arnold
William S. Basinger
Aaron Champion
Solomon Cohen
John G. Falligant
James B. Foley
George A. Gordon
Robert Lachlison
Alvin N. Miller
John F. Posey
Thomas Purse
Robert D. Walker

Oct. 19, 1857
Richard Wayne, Mayor (died in office)**
Francis Blair
John G. Falligant
James B. Foley
James E. Godrey

411

George A. Gordon
Noah B. Knapp
John F. Posey
John Richardson
William R. Symons
Thomas M. Turner
Claudius C. Wilson
William Wright

June 27, 1858
Thomas M. Turner, Mayor (elected by
   Council)

Oct. 18, 1858
Thomas M. Turner, Mayor
Francis Blair
John Boston
John P. Dellannoy
John G. Falligant
James B. Foley
Martin J. Ford
John M. Guerard
Thomas Holcombe
Noah B. Knapp
John F. Posey
John F. Tucker
George W. Wylly

Oct. 17, 1859
Richard D. Arnold, Mayor***
Jourdon P. Brooks
Wallace Cumming
William M. Davidson
Charles C. Jones Jr.
Phineas M. Kollock
Robert Lachlison
Abraham Minis
John P. W. Read
John Richardson
Francis M. Stone
J. Frederick Waring
John F. Wheaton

Oct. 15, 1860
Charles C. Jones Jr., Mayor
John W. Anderson
W. F. Brantley
Henry Brigham
Isaac Brunner
Solomon Cohen
William M. Davidson

Robert Lachlison
John McMahon
John P. W. Read
John Richardson
E. A. Soullard
John F. Wheaton

Oct. 21, 1861
Thomas Purse, Mayor (elected by council
   since no candidate received a majority of
   votes cast)
Isaac Brunner
Francis L. Gúe
Robert Lachlison
John F. O'Byrne
Hiram Roberts
James M. Schley
A. A. Solomons
E. A. Soullard
John F. Tucker
J. L. Villalonga
John Williamson
George W. Wylly

Oct. 20, 1862
Thomas Holcombe, Mayor
Henry Brigham
Francis L. Gúe
William Hunter
Robert Lachlison
Joseph Lippman
John F. O'Byrne
Hiram Roberts
E. A. Soullard
Thomas M. Turner
J. L. Villalonga
Edward C. Wade
John Williamson

Oct. 19, 1863
Richard D. Arnold, Mayor
Henry Brigham
Christopher C. Casey
Henry C. Freeman
Francis L. Gúe
Robert Lachlison
Joseph Lippman
John F. O'Byrne
Hiram Roberts
J. L. Villalonga
Edward C. Wade

John Williamson
George W. Wylly

Oct. 17, 1864
Richard D. Arnold, Mayor
Henry Brigham
Christopher C. Casey
Henry C. Freeman
Francis L. Gúe
Robert Lachlison
Joseph Lippman
John F. O'Byrne
Hiram Roberts
J. L. Villalonga
Edward C. Wade
John Williamson
George W. Wylly

Dec. 11, 1865
Edward C. Anderson,* Mayor
Christopher C. Casey
John Cunningham
John C. Ferrill
Francis L. Gúe
John R. Johnson
Robert Lachlison
John McMahon
John F. O'Byrne
James M. Schley
E. A. Soullard
John Williamson
George W. Wylly

Oct. 15, 1866
Edward C. Anderson,* Mayor
Henry Brigham
William H. Burroughs
H. A. Crane (died in office)
Martin J. Ford
George C. Freeman
Francis L. Gúe
William Hunter
Mathias H. Meyer
Charles C. Millar
Alvin N. Miller
J. L. Villalonga
Edward C. Wade
James J. Waring

Oct. 16, 1867
Edward C. Anderson,* Mayor (served until
  Oct. 1869)

Henry Brigham
William H. Burroughs
Martin J. Ford
Francis L. Gúe
William Hunter
Mathias H. Meyer
Charles C. Millar
Alvin N. Miller
Frederick W. Sims
J. L. Villalonga
Edward C. Wade
James J. Waring

1868 (no city election)

Oct. 18, 1869
John Screven, Mayor
R. J. Davant
William M. Davidson
Alfred Haywood
Michael Lavin
George N. Nichols
James O'Byrne
John Schwarz
Andrew M. Sloan
Moses J. Solomons
E. A. Soullard
William H. Tison
Augustus P. Wetter

Oct. 17, 1870
John Screven, Mayor
Edward C. Anderson Jr.
Christopher C. Casey
John R. Dillon
John O. Ferrill
Robert H. Footman
Alfred Haywood
Michael Lavin
Mathias H. Meyer
George N. Nichols
John T. Ronan
John Schwarz
Moses J. Solomons

Oct. 16, 1871
John Screven, Mayor (served until Jan. 27,
  1873, after state legislature increased terms
  of mayor and aldermen to two years)
George Cornwell
John O. Ferrill

Robert H. Footman   William McLeod
Marmaduke Hamilton   Mathias H. Meyer
Alfred Haywood   Francis J. Ruckert
William Hunter   John Schwarz
Michael Lavin   Christopher White

* Also served 1873–77
** Also served 1844–45, 1848–53
*** Also served 1842–43, 1851–52
Source: Thomas Gamble, Jr., *A History of the City Government of Savannah, Ga., from 1790 to 1901* (Savannah, Ga.: City Council, 1900), pp. 5–22.

SAVANNAH BLACK SOCIETIES
OPENING DEPOSIT ACCOUNTS
IN THE FREEDMAN'S BANK,
1866–72

Abercorn Baptist Church
African Methodist Episcopal Church
  Sabbath School
Axe Co. No. 1
Axe Co. No. 2
Baptist Church, Ogeechee
Benevolent Daughters of Savannah Society
Benevolent Sons of Savannah, Georgia
Bonds of Love
Charitable Progress Society
Children of Edom Society
Colored Enterprise Association
Daughters of Consolidated Baptist
  Missionary Convention
Daughters of Zion
Eureka and Hilton Masonic Lodge
Everspring Club
First African Baptist Church Sabbath
  School
First Bryan Baptist Church
  Building Committee
First Congregational Church of Savannah
Forest City Light Infantry
Franklin Engine Company
Free Will Union Benevolent Society
Good Samaritans
Gospel Messenger
Independent Elect Cherubim
Independent Union Star Association
John the Baptist Society
King Star Brothers
Ladies and Girls Social
Ladies Branch United Republican Society
Ladies Charitable Union Society
Ladies Christian Association

Ladies EJC Branch
Ladies Laurel Club
Ladies Relief Association for Widows and
  Orphans of Savannah
Ladies Star of Bethlehem
Ladies Union
Ladies Union League
Ladies Union No. 1 Society
Ladies Union Socialize Society
Ladies Union St. Paul's Society
Langston Division Vanguard of Freedom
Laurel Union Association
Liberty Independent Society
Loan Association
Longshore Imported Benevolent Society
Longshoremen's Union Association
Macedonian Benevolent Society
Mary Magdalene Society
Mortality Association of Methodist
  Episcopal Church
Mt. Vernon Union Association
Nightingale Society
Oglethorpe Axe Company No. 2
Old Hundred Society
Only Star of Gospel Messenger
Poor and Needy Institution
Poor Saints Society of Skidaway Island
Poor Saints Society of (Woodville)
  Springfield Plantation
Portermen's Society
Pulaski Rising Star Association
Pulaski Union Association
Rising Star of Bethlehem Light of East
  Savannah
Savannah Hussars

Savannah Volunteers
Saxton Institute
Second African Baptist Church
  Pic-Nic Committee
  Pulpit Committee
Sisters Prayer Meeting Benevolent
  Association
Skidmore Club
Social Club
Sons and Daughters of Jerusalem
Sons and Daughters of Mary Magdalene
Sons and Daughters of St. Matthew
Sons of Zion
South Carolina Mutual Aid Association
St. Benedict's Benevolent Society
St. Paul's Benevolent Association
St. Stephens Elementary Sunday School
St. Stephens Episcopal Church
  Sewing Circle
Star of Bethlehem
Third African Baptist Church Building
  Fund
Union Association
Union Benevolent Society
Union Convention
Union League of America, K. S. Baker
  Council No. 9
Union Republican Association
Union Star Club
United Benevolent Association

United Benevolent Brothers
United Republican (Independent) Sons
  Association
United Star Association
Vocalist (Combination) Association
Wagoners Union Association
Walkers Union Association
Warden's Committee, Second African
  Baptist Church
Warren Institution
Workingmen's Friendly Association
Workingmen's Union Society
Wrestling Jacob (Progress) Society
Wrestling Jacob Society—Liberty County
Young Charitable Progressive Society
Young Independent Elect Cherubim
Young Ladies of Honor
Young Ladies Independent Social Society
Young Ladies Independent Star Society
Young Ladies Loving Society
Young Ladies of St. Cecelia Society
Young Men's Brotherhood Association
Young Men's Lincoln Guards
Young Men's Redemption Society
Young Men's Union Bible Society
Young Nightingales
Young Union Lincoln Guards
Zion Baptist Association
Zion the Rising Sun Society
Zion Travellers Society

Source: Records of the Freedman's Savings and Trust Co., Savannah Branch (M817), Records of the Office of the Comptroller of the Currency, Record Group 101, National Archives.

ACKNOWLEDGMENTS

I owe a profound debt of gratitude to the John D. and Catherine T. MacArthur Foundation, which provided crucial financial support for this project. Brandeis University also provided support in the form of a leave from teaching. I am grateful to a number of generous friends and colleagues who read and commented on the manuscript in various forms, either in whole or in part: Dennis Aftergut, Tim Borstelmann, Ruth Feldstein, Ellen Fitzpatrick, Michele Gillespie, Jane Kamensky, Kenneth Kusmer, John Lifter, Elaine Tyler May, Clarence Mohr, Mark Smith, and Michael Willrich.

I would also like to acknowledge several individuals who shared information, insights, and relevant pictures or printed matter they encountered as a result of their own work: Catherine Clinton, Roy E. Finkenbine, Michael T. Gilmore, Jessica Lepler, and Hilary Moss. A number of people went out of their way to provide myriad kinds of research and administrative assistance. At Brandeis, I relied on Judy Brown and Dona Delorenzo in the Department of History, and on Evan Simpson, assistant manager of access services, and Ralph Szymczak, instructional support staff, both in Goldfarb Library. I would also like to acknowledge the help of Randall Burkett, curator of African-American Collections, Woodruff Library, Emory University; Dale Couch of the Georgia Department of Archives and History in Atlanta; Michael P. Musick, archivist at the National Archives in Washington, D.C.; Leslie P. Rowland, co-editor and project director of the Freedmen and Southern Society Project at the University of Maryland; and the staffs of the Amistad Research Center at Tulane University; Southern Historical Collection, University of North Carolina, Chapel Hill; Duke University Rare Book, Manuscript and Special Collections Library; Widener Library, Harvard University; and the Waltham, Massachusetts, branch of the National Archives and Record Administration.

I would also like to acknowledge the following collections for allowing me to cite from unpublished materials in their possession: Amistad Research Center at Tulane University, New Orleans; the Rare Book, Manuscript, and Special Collections Library, Duke University; Georgia Historical Society, Savannah; Atlanta University Archives, Robert W. Woodruff Library of the Atlanta University Center, Atlanta; and Southern Historical Collection, Wilson Library, the University of North Carolina at Chapel Hill.

In Savannah, I appreciated the efforts of the knowledgeable staff of the Georgia Historical Society. Special thanks to W. Todd Groce, president and chief executive officer, and Stan Deaton, vice president for programs and scholarship. In the society's historic library reading room, Jewell Anderson, Kathryn Donahue, Stephany Kretchmar, Nora Lewis, Mary Murphy, and Lynette Stoudt all fielded many requests for books, manuscript collections, reels of microfilm, photocopies, maps, photographs, and other materials. Cassie Dolecki of the Historic Savannah Foundation kindly reproduced photographs of several historic buildings. Although I presented parts of this book to a number of different audiences, I would like to single out the symposium organized by Paul Pressly, director of the Ossabaw Educational Alliance, in Savannah in February 2008. The symposium, on the Atlantic World and African American Life and Culture in the Georgia Lowcountry, provided me with an opportunity not only to discuss my work, but also to meet and talk with descendants of the Gullah-Geechee people whose struggles I seek to recount in these pages.

On a single memorable day in Savannah I had the good fortune to speak with Dr. Otis S. Johnson, mayor of the city, in the morning, and to find that the Reverend Charles Lwanga Hoskins was my African-American Heritage Trail tour guide in the afternoon. I venture to say that few Savannahians know more than these two men about the city's black community, past or present. I appreciate their willingness to share their research and their memories with me.

My editors at Knopf, Ash Green and his successor Andrew Miller, offered thoughtful comments on the manuscript. Their efficient editorial assistant, Sara Sherbill, helped guide me through the intricacies of publication, and my copy editor, Susanna Sturgis, did a superb job with the manuscript. I would also like to thank Geri Thoma, my agent, who believed from the beginning that the story of Civil War–era Savannah was worth telling.

Friends and members of my extended family have followed the progress of my "Savannah book" with great interest. I am fortunate to have such a warm and supportive family, anchored by my mother, Sylvia P. Jones, and my in-laws, Rose and Albert Abramson. I would like to acknowledge Ellen Fitzpatrick, Karin Lifter, and Nina Tumarkin for their long-lasting friendship. Since I began research on this book, Sarah and Anna Abramson have configured their own lives as researchers, writers, and scholars, and I am proud of the new places where their passions and talents have taken them. Over the last few years, Jeffrey Abramson has been working on his own book, but he not only read and commented on my manuscript with his characteristic insight and rigor, he also found himself living with Savannah in conversations over breakfast, on walks around Lake Waban, and, happily for both of us, visits to the Forest City. Every day I celebrate our enduring partnership, which began with a conversation at a library card catalog many years ago.

In the course of my career I have taught many undergraduates and graduate students, as well as alumni groups, continuing education students, and K–12 teachers outside the classroom. To thank all of my students for their enthusiasm and their openness to learning about American history, and for teaching me in return, I dedicate this book to them.

NOTES

Abbreviations Used

ACS   Records of the American Colonization Society
AHR   *American Historical Review*
AM   *American Missionary*
AMA   Archives of the American Missionary Association
ASF   Arnold and Screven Family Papers
BAP   Black Abolitionist Papers
BDA   *Boston Daily Advertiser*
BDG   *Boston Daily Globe*
BDWC   *Bangor Daily Whig and Courier*
BRFAL   United States Bureau of Refugees, Freedmen, and Abandoned Lands, Record Group 105, National Archives, Washington, D.C. M798: Records of the Assistant Commissioner for the State of Georgia; M799: Records of the Superintendent of Education for the State of Georgia; M1903: Records of the Field Offices for the State of Georgia
CC   Minutes of the Savannah City Council
CWH   *Civil War History*
DCH   *Daily Cleveland Herald*
DNI   *Daily National Intelligencer*
DU   Duke University
EAW   Edmund Asa Ware Records
ECA   Edward C. Anderson Papers
EWD   Esther W. Douglass Papers
FB, GHS   Unprocessed Freedmen's Bureau Collection, Georgia Historical Society
FDP   *Frederick Douglass' Paper*
FMC   Federal Manuscript Census, Population Schedules
FR   *Freedmen's Record*
FSSP   Records of the Freedmen and Southern Society Project
FST   Records of the Freedman's Savings and Trust Co., Records of the Office of the Comptroller, Record Group 101, National Archives
GHQ   *Georgia Historical Quarterly*
GHS   Georgia Historical Society, Savannah, Georgia
GSA   Georgia State Archives, Atlanta, Georgia
HF   Harden Family Papers

JFG   Jeremy Francis Gilmer Papers
JFW   J. F. Waring Papers
LDI   *Lowell Daily Citizen*
NA   National Archives, Washington, D.C.
NF   *National Freedman*
NS   *North Star*
NYT   *New York Times*
ORUCA   *The War of the Rebellion: A Compilation of the Official Records of the Union and Confederate Armies*
ORUCN   *Official Records of the Union and Confederate Navies In the War of the Rebellion*
RDA   Richard D. Arnold Papers
RG   Record Group (National Archives, Washington, D.C.)
RG 101 Savannah Branch, Records of the Freedman's Savings and Trust Bank (M816, reel 8) and index (M817, reel 2), Records of the Comptroller of the Currency, National Archives
RG 109 War Department Collection of Confederate Records, National Archives
RG 233 Records of the United States House of Representatives, National Archives
RG 393 Records of the U.S. Army Continental Commands, 1821–1920, National Archives
SCC   Case Files, Southern Claims Commission. Records of the Third Auditor, Allowed Case Files, Records of the U.S. General Accounting Office, Record Group 217, National Archives, Washington, D.C.
SDH   *Savannah Daily Herald*
SDMN   *Savannah Daily Morning News*
SDN   *Savannah Daily News*
SDNH   *Savannah Daily News and Herald*
SDR   *Savannah Daily Republican*
SHC   Southern Historical Collection, Manuscripts Department, Wilson Library, University of North Carolina at Chapel Hill
SLG-D   *St. Louis Globe-Democrat*
SMN   *Savannah Morning News*
SNH   *Savannah News and Herald*
SR   *Savannah Republican*
ST   *Savannah Tribune*

PROLOGUE

1. *SDMN*, Feb. 22, 1851; Parrish, *Slave Songs of the Georgia Sea Islands*, p. 206.
2. "she . . . been": *SR*, Feb. 22, 1851; *SDMN*, Feb. 22, 1851.
3. "the late disgraceful": *SDMN*, Feb. 24, 1851; ibid., Feb. 17, 1851.
4. "Boston riot": *SR*, Feb. 18, 1851; *"The City of Boston"*: ibid., Feb. 22, 1851; ibid., Feb. 24, 1851.
5. The story of Henry is taken from an article, "Caught," in the Savannah *Georgian*, March 25, 1850.
6. "national": *SDMN*, Feb. 24, 1851.
7. *SDMN*, April 9, 1851; *Liberator*, April 11, 1851; "bowed": Parker, "Boston Kidnapping: A Discourse to Commemorate the Rendition of Thomas Sims," p. 38; Charles Francis Adams, *Richard Henry Dana: A Biography*, vol. 1 (Boston: Houghton Mifflin, 1890), p. 192; Lois E. Horton, "Kidnapping and Resistance: Antislavery Direct Action in the 1850s," in Blight, ed., *Passages to Freedom*, pp. 162–65; Schwartz, "Fugitive Slave Days in Boston," pp. 191–212.

8. *SDMN*, April 10, 1851; Levy, "Sims' Case," pp. 39–74; Campbell, *Slave Catchers*. The Simms (full) siblings, children of the slaves Minda (sometimes Minta) Campbell and James Simms, include Ann (born in 1820), Cornelia (1826), James Meriles (1822), and Thomas (1824). There is some evidence that their mother also had a son, Samuel Campbell (1819), by Toby Campbell (presumably a slave).

   For information about the extended Simms family in Savannah, see 1860 FMC, Georgia, Chatham County, Savannah, p. 128; 1870, p. 46; 1880, 16th District, p. 7; 1900, 1st Militia District, p. 23; Savannah Branch, FST; Edmund West, comp., *Family Data Collection: Individual Records* (Provo, Utah: Generations Network, 2000). All three of these sources are available online and fully searchable through http://www.ancestry.com.

9. R. J. M. Blackett, " 'Freemen to the Rescue': Resistance to the Fugitive Slave Law of 1850," in Blight, ed., *Passages to Freedom*, pp. 133–47; Horton and Horton, *In Hope of Liberty,* pp. 230–31, 253–54; "like the beasts": William Craft in "Report of the Great Anti-Slavery Meeting, Held April 9, 1851, in the Public Room, Broadmead, Bristol, to Receive the Fugitive Slaves, William & Ellen Craft" (Bristol, England: James Ackland, 1851), p. 7.

10. Levy, "Sims' Case."

11. *SDMN*, April 10, 1851; *Liberator*, April 11, 1851; "in the character": *SDMN*, April 12, 1851; "he was there": *Liberator*, April 11, 1851; "blow-out . . . whirl": Waring, *Cerveau's Savannah*, pp. 44–45; Fraser, *Savannah in the Old South*, p. 175.

12. *SDMN*, April 9, 1851, and April 10, 1851; *SR*, April 8, 1851; *SLG-D*, April 10, 1877.

13. *SDMN*, April 12, 1851; "were out of the way": *SR*, April 10, 1851. See also the account in "Trial of Thomas Sims, on an Issue of Personal Liberty, on the Claim of James Potter, of Georgia, Against Him, as an Alleged Fugitive from Service," pp. 46–47.

14. "deeply . . . board": *SR*, April 10, 1851. Lois E. Horton describes a fugitive slave case in 1836, when Eliza Small and Polly Ann Bates arrived in Boston on board the brig *Chickasaw* captained by a Mr. Eldridge ("Kidnapping and Resistance," p. 154).

15. Fraser, *Savannah in the Old South*, pp. 1–41; John W. Reps, "C2 + L2 = S2? Another Look at the Origins of Savannah's Town Plans," in Harvey H. Jackson and Phinizy Spalding, eds., *Forty Years of Diversity: Essays on Colonial Georgia* (Athens: University of Georgia Press, 1984), pp. 101–51; Bannister, "Oglethorpe's Sources for the Savannah Plan," pp. 47–62.

16. Weaver, "Foreigners in Ante-Bellum Savannah," pp. 1–17; Rousey, "From Whence They Came to Savannah," pp. 305–36; Foster, *Wayside Glimpses, North and South*, p. 109; Adams, *South-Side View of Slavery*, pp. 15–16; Pearson, "Captain Charles Stevens and the Antebellum Georgia Coastal Trade," pp. 493–96; Haunton, "Savannah in the 1850s," pp. 100–104; Eisterhold, "Savannah: Lumber Center of the South Atlantic," pp. 526–43; Fraser, *Savannah in the Old South*, p. 244; Hunt, "Organized Labor," p. 185.

17. Burke, *Pleasure and Pain*, pp. 20–27, 73; Waring, *Cerveau's Savannah*; Henry L. Cathell Diary, SHC; *Liberator*, April 11, 1851; Horton and Horton, *In Hope of Liberty*, p. 123; David W. Blight, ed., *Narrative of the Life of Frederick Douglass, An American Slave*, 2nd ed. (Boston: Bedford/St. Martin's, 2003), pp. 110–16; *SDMN*, April 15, 1851; *Georgian*, March 25, 1850.

18. *Liberator*, April 11, 1851; *SDMN*, April 12, 1851; Fraser, *Savannah in the Old South*, p. 214.

19. Levy, "Sims' Case"; *SDMN*, April 12, 1851.

20. "The abolitionists": *SDMN*, April 15, 1851; Levy, "Sims' Case"; "Trial of Thomas Sims."

21. Horton and Horton, *In Hope of Liberty*, p. 120; Robboy and Robboy, "Lewis Hayden," pp. 591–613; *Liberator*, April 11, 1851; *FDP*, April 17, 1851; "Whether we": Higginson, *Cheerful Yesterdays*, pp. 143–44; *FDP*, April 17, 1851.

22. "In this spirit": Shaw quoted in Levy, "Sims' Case," p. 60.

23. "this moral earthquake": Broderick, ed., *Henry David Thoreau: Journal*, vol. 3: *1848–1851*, p. 203; "Our officers": Charles Francis Adams, *Richard Henry Dana: A Biography* (New York: Houghton, Mifflin, 1890), p. 193. See also Troy Duncan and Chris Dixon, "Denouncing the Brotherhood of Thieves: Stephen Symonds Foster's Critique of the Anti-Abolitionist Clergy," *CWH* 47 (June 2001): 97–117; *SDMN*, April 9, 1851.

24. "Let . . . heart": *FDP*, April 17, 1851; "brood . . . dead!": Parker quoted in Levy, "Sims' Case," p. 67; "The southern planter": [Speech delivered at Tremont Temple, April 8, 1851] *Slavery: Letters and Speeches of Horace Mann* (Miami: Mnemosyne Publishing Co., 1969; orig. pub. 1853), p. 45; "the gurgling": Thoreau, *Journal*, vol. 3, pp. 208–209. See also Smith, *Listening to Nineteenth-Century America*, pp. 172–94.

25. *SR*, April 18, 1851; "the Boston": *William Lloyd Garrison, 1805–1879, The Story of His Life Told by His Children*, vol. 3: *1841–1860* (New York: Century Co., 1889), p. 328.

26. "In no trial": legislation quoted in Levy, "Sims' Case," p. 50; "Have we got": *SDMN*, April 12, 1851; "transfer": *Liberator*, April 11, 1851. The white activist Abby Folsom tried to address a mass meeting at Tremont Temple on April 8, only to be "forcibly ejected" from the church. See *SR*, April 15, 1851.

27. "Sims": *SDMN*, April 16, 1851; Higginson, *Cheerful Yesterdays*, p. 144; *SDMN*, April 17, 1851. For a contemporary drawing of the forced march to Long Wharf, see *Gleason's Pictorial Drawing-Room Companion*, May 10, 1851.

28. CC Minutes, April 24, 1851. See also ibid., May 8, 1851.

29. "The fiery": *SDMN*, April 14, 1851; "gas let off": *SDMN*, April 12, 1851; "not been influenced": *SDMN*, April 22, 1851; ibid., April 24, 1851. On proslavery ideologues' objection to abolitionists' speaking freely about slavery, see Gilmore, "Free Speech and the American Renaissance," pp. 90–113.

30. Savannah Unit, Federal Writers' Project, *Savannah River Plantations*, pp. 246–48; Clifton, ed., *Life and Labor on Argyle Island*, pp. i-x.

31. Sullivan, *Early Days on the Georgia Tidewater*; Stewart, *"What Nature Suffers to Groe"*; "They . . . blood": Marion Tinling, ed., *The Correspondence of Three William Byrds of Westover, Virginia, 1684–1776*, vol. 2 (Charlottesville: University Press of Virginia, 1977), pp. 487–88; Codrina Cozma, "John Martin Bolzius and the Early Christian Opposition to Slavery in Georgia," *GHQ* 88 (Winter 2004): 457–76.

32. Clifton, ed., *Life and Labor on Argyle Island*, p. xv; Savannah Unit, Federal Writers' Project, *Savannah River Plantations*, p. 233; Sam B. Hilliard, "Antebellum Tidewater Rice Culture in South Carolina and Georgia," in Gibson, ed., *European Settlement and Development in North America*, pp. 91–115; Greenberg, "Creating Ethnic, Class, and Southern Identity in Nineteenth-Century America," p. 47; Stewart, *"What Nature Suffers to Groe,"* p. 196; Gomez, *Exchanging Our Country Marks*, pp. 102–104; Wood, *Black Majority*.

33. Haunton, "Savannah in the 1850s"; Green, "A Preliminary Investigation of Black Construction Artisans"; Jones, *Historic Savannah;* "very": *SDMN*, April 26, 1851; Byrne, "The Hiring of Woodson, Slave Carpenter of Savannah," pp. 245–63.

34. "to satisfy": *SR*, April 21, 1851; Levy, "Sims' Case," p. 69; Pressly, "Northern Roots of Savannah's Antebellum Elite," pp. 157–99; Lanman, *Adventures in the Wilds*, p. 102. The *Republican* listed the last names of the agents who escorted Simms to Savannah: Riley, Byrne, Russell, Clarke, Cooledge, Sawin, True, and Dolliver. The 1850 FMC lists all the persons in the Boston area with those last four names as native-born New Englanders.

35. Stewart, *"What Nature Suffers to Groe,"* pp. 94–99, 136, 172, 178; Young, "Ideology and Death on a Savannah River Rice Plantation," pp. 673–706; Dusinberre, *Them Dark Days,* pp. 48–84; Huggins, *Black Odyssey*.

36. "ring shouts": Savannah Unit, Georgia Writers' Project, *Drums and Shadows*, p. 168; "goes ahead": ibid., p. 63; Stewart, *"What Nature Suffers to Groe,"* p. 179. On the magic

hoe stories, see Joyner, *Remember Me*, p. 55; *Drums and Shadows*, pp. 63, 79, 99, 110, 111, 137, 168; Jones, *Gullah Folktales from the Georgia Coast*. On African roots of lowcountry religious practices among blacks, see Kuyk, *African Voices in the African American Heritage*; Creel, *"A Peculiar People"*; Johnson and Jersild, eds., *"Ain't Gonna Lay My 'Ligion Down"*; Gomez, *Exchanging Our Country Marks*.

37. "by industry and economy," "liberty of trading": Alexander Steele, Chatham County claim no. 229, SCC. See also Thomas Butler, Chatham County claim no. 6053, SCC (Butler was represented by James M. Simms in the proceedings); Penningroth, *Claims of Kinfolk*; Armstrong, "From Task to Free Labor," pp. 432–47; Morgan, "Work and Culture," pp. 563–99. See also the testimony of Charles Jess in Ira Berlin, et al., eds., *Freedom*, Series 1, Vol. 1, *Destruction of Slavery*, pp. 143–45.

38. Haunton, "Savannah in the 1850s," pp. 7–12; Haunton, "Law and Order in Savannah," pp. 1–24; "he would have": "An Interesting Narrative: The Story of the Fugitive Sims," *NYT*, April 26, 1863, p. 3. It is possible that the thirty-nine-lash maximum was based on biblical injunctions. See Deuteronomy 25:2–3 and 2 Corinthians 11:24.

39. "quick, brainy": Obituary of James Porter, *ST*, Nov. 13, 1895; "continued . . . defiant": Love, *History of the First African Baptist Church*, p. 175; Fraser, *Savannah in the Old South*, p. 73; Hoskins, "The Trouble They Seen," p. 65.

40. "*The North:*" *SDMN*, April 26, 1851; Burke, *Pleasure and Pain*, p. 5; Foster, p. 105; "tormented": *SDMN*, April 25; ibid., April 22 and 23, 1851.

41. Quarles, *Black Abolitionists*, p. 207; Yellin, *Harriet Jacobs*, p. 110; Groover, *Fugitive's Gibraltar*, pp. 227–28; Slaughter, *Bloody Dawn*.

42. Kollock, ed., "Letters of the Kollock and Allied Families," Pt. 2, pp. 42–43; Shryock, *Georgia and the Union in 1850*, p. 315; Arnold letter to the editor of the *SR*, June 19, 1851.

43. "the white race": *SR*, April 2, 1867; "Loath": James M. Simms to O. O. Howard, Savannah, Feb. 3, 1865, Washington Headquarters, Records of the Commissioner, series 15: Letters Received, S-97 1865 (FSSP A-5161); "His clear, muscial voice": *New Orleans Tribune*, April 13, 1867.

44. Jones, *Soldiers of Light and Love: Northern Teachers and Georgia Blacks, 1865–1873* (Chapel Hill: University of North Carolina Press, 1980).

45. "God is no respecter": Andrew Bryan quoted in Simms, *First Colored Baptist Church*, p. 37.

CHAPTER ONE

1. "How changed": Rev. Mr. Crumley, pastor of Savannah Methodist Church, *SMN*, Sept. 5, 1854. See also his letter to the editor, *SMN*, Sept. 20, 1854; and letter from Mother [Anna Moodie Johnstone Waring?] to Dear Children, Clarksville, Ga., Sept. 14, 1854, Box 1, Folder 5, JFW Papers, GHS.

2. Usinger, "Yellow Fever from the Viewpoint of Savannah," pp. 143–56; Fraser, *Savannah in the Old South*, pp. 297–301; "my . . . credit": Shryock, ed., *Letters of Richard D. Arnold*, pp. 69–71; Pressly, "Northern Roots of Savannah's Antebellum Elite," pp. 187–90.

3. Mackie, *From Cape Cod to Dixie and the Tropics*, p. 115; King, *Great South*, p. 362; Lanman, *Adventures in the Wilds*, p. 100.

4. Sam B. Hilliard, "Antebellum Tidewater Rice Culture in South Carolina and Georgia," in Gibson, ed., *European Settlement and Development in North America*, pp. 91–115; Stewart, *"What Nature Suffers to Groe"*; Shryock, ed., *Letters of Richard D. Arnold*, pp. 1–9, 28; Fraser, *Savannah in the Old South*, p. 210; Schwartz, *Birthing a Slave*.

5. "who do not": *SMN*, Aug. 30, 1854; "the reputation": Ward quoted in Haunton, "Savannah in the 1850s," p. 293; "go out": *NYT*, Aug. 30, 1854; Kollock, ed. "Letters of the Kol-

lock and Allied Families, 1826–1884," Pt. 3, p. 139; Fraser, *Savannah in the Old South*, pp. 199, 227, 297.

6. Pavich-Lindsay, ed., *Anna*, pp. 248–52; *SMN*, Sept. 6, 1854; Haunton, "Savannah in the 1850s," pp. 293–302; CC Minutes for the months of August and September 1854.

7. On the origins of the Dry Culture Committee, see Savannah Unit, Federal Writers' Project, "Plantation Development in Chatham County," p. 324.

8. Johnson, *Black Savannah*, pp. 73–76. On the relative immunity of West Africans to malaria, yellow fever, and other mosquito-borne diseases, see Wood, *Black Majority*; Pollitzer, *Gullah People and Their African Heritage,* pp. 69–73. Savannah physicians owned a relatively large number of enslaved women, presumably pressed into service as nurses. See Goldin, *Urban Slavery in the American South*, p. 24.

9. *SMN*, Sept. 9, 11, 1854; *SR*, Sept. 9, 1854 (article reprinted in *NYT*, Sept. 13, 1854).

10. "Dreadful . . . away": House, ed., *Planter Management and Capitalism in Ante-bellum Georgia*, pp. 120, 255–60.

11. Berlin et al., *Destruction of Slavery*, pp. 150–54; Penningroth, *Claims of Kinfolk*, pp. 91–95.

12. *SMN*, Sept. 15, 1854; Screven, "Savannah Benevolent Association."

13. Fraser, *Savannah in the Old South*, pp. 298–99.

14. "Stampede . . . harvest": Shryock, ed., *Letters of Richard D. Arnold*, p. 69.

15. "a great enemy": *SR*, Sept. 4, 1854; *SMN*, Sept. 11, 19, 1854. See for example S. N. Harris, "Report on the Treatment of Some Cases of Cholera Occurring on Savannah River," *Charleston Medical Journal and Review* 4 (1849): 581–85, and Juriah Harriss, "What Constitutes Unsoundness in the Negro?" *Savannah Journal of Medicine* 1 (Sept. 1858): 145–52; (Jan. 1859): 289–95; 2(May 1859): 10–16. For a biography of Wildman, see Myers, ed., *Children of Pride*, pp. 1730–31.

16. "some of her sisters": Shryock, ed., *Letters of Richard D. Arnold*, p. 70; "Get up Dinah": Parrish, *Slave Songs of the Georgia Sea Islands*, p. 117. See also ibid., p. 28; Schwartz, *Birthing a Slave,* pp. 60, 110, 120; Fett, *Working Cures*; John M. Janzen, "Ideologies and Institutions in Precolonial West Equatorial African Therapeutics," and Gloria Waite, "Public Health in Precolonial East-Central Africa," both in Feierman and Janzen, eds., *Social Basis of Health and Healing in Africa*, pp. 195–211 and 212–31; Mitchell, *Hoodoo Medicine*, p. 38.

17. "wiseacres . . . prejudiced": Shryock, ed., *Letters of Richard D. Arnold*, p. 71; "here . . . effect": Adams, *South-Side View of Slavery,* p. 26.

18. "went off": Shryock, ed., *Letters of Richard D. Arnold*, p. 69; Interview with George Carter, in Rawick, ed., *American Slave*, Supplement Series 1, Vol. 3: *Georgia Narratives*, Part 1, pp. 150–66; "unchristian": *SMN*, Oct. 2, 1854; "stranger . . . scoundrel": ibid., Sept. 15, 1854; ibid., Sept. 19, 1854.

19. "adventurers . . . DEATH!!!": *SMN*, Oct. 11, 1854.

20. *SMN,* Oct. 27, 1854; Haunton, "Savannah in the 1850s," pp. 288–89; "Let us try": Pavich-Lindsay, ed., *Anna*, p. 267; "unaccountable": CC Minutes, Nov. 11, 1854; "depot . . . pride?": *SMN*, Sept. 4, 1854; "the epidemic": Shryock, ed., *Letters of Richard D. Arnold*, p. 71; Farley, "Mighty Monarch of the South," pp. 56–70.

21. CC Minutes for fall 1854.

22. "the peace and order . . . ungodly planters": Mallard, *Plantation Life Before Emancipation*, pp. 105–107; Starobin, ed., *Blacks in Bondage*, p. 42; Jones, *Religious Instruction of the Negroes*. See also Mathews, "Charles Colcock Jones and the Southern Evangelical Crusade," pp. 299–320; Clarke, *Wrestlin' Jacob*, pp. 40–41; Clarke, *Dwelling Place*, pp. 140–51.

23. Myers, ed., *Children of Pride*, p. 88; Clarke, *Dwelling Place*, pp. 337–38.

24. "The Angel": Myers, ed., *Children of Pride*, p. 89; "weeping . . . dead": ibid., p. 104.

25. Clifton, ed., *Life and Labor on Argyle Island*, pp. 191–92; Parrish, *Slave Songs*, p. 37; Creel, *"A Peculiar People,"* pp. 54–55.

26. "uninterrupted": Foster, *Wayside Glimpses*, p. 105; "to do": Shryock, ed., *Letters of Richard D. Arnold*, p. 71; "It is awful . . . irritation": Chamerovzow, ed., *Slave Life in Georgia*, pp. 186–87; Pruneau, "All the Time Is Work Time."

27. Dusinberre, *Them Dark Days*, pp. 48–83. See also K. David Patterson, "Disease Environments in the Antebellum South," and Todd L. Savitt, "Black Health on the Plantation," in Leavitt and Numbers, eds., *Sickness and Health;* Pruneau, "All the Time Is Work Time," pp. 253–306.

28. Dusinberre, *Them Dark Days*, p. 53; Stewart, *"What Nature Suffers to Groe,"* pp. 138–46; Schwartz, *To Birth a Slave*, pp. 129–39.

29. "Slaves": Clifton, ed., *Life and Labor on Argyle Island*, p. 190; see also p. 195.

30. Clifton, ed., *Life and Labor on Argyle Island*, pp. 187, 226; Dusinberre, *Them Dark Days*, pp. 60–63; Young, "Ideology and Death on a Savannah River Rice Plantation," pp. 673–706.

31. "Slaves no longer": Clifton, ed., *Life and Labor on Argyle Island*, p. 190. See also Dusinberre, *Them Dark Days*, pp. 58–61.

32. Shryock, *Georgia and the Union in 1850*; Pressly, "Northern Roots of Savannah's Antebellum Elite."

33. This discussion of class relations draws on the following works for points of comparison between Savannah and other, larger, more industrialized southern cities: Towers, *Urban South*; Gleeson, *Irish in the South*; Wells, *Origins of the Southern Middle Class*; Silver, "A New Look at Old South Urbanization," pp. 140–72; Berlin and Gutman, "Natives and Immigrants, Free Men and Slaves," pp. 1175–1200.

34. Petit jury lists, Ordinary/Superior Court Records, Chatham County, GSA. Two juries convened over the 1859–60 period, and consisting of twenty-four persons located in the 1860 FMC for Georgia, Chatham County, Savannah, included one each of a shipping master, policeman, carpenter, telegraph operator, railroad agent, gardener, watchman, peddler; two each of painters, clerks, grocers; four laborers; and six merchants.

35. "The Mayor": Shryock, ed., *Letters of Richard D. Arnold*, p. 39; Haunton, "Law and Order in Savannah," pp. 1–24; Lockley, "Trading Encounters Between Non-Elite Whites and African Americans," pp. 25–48.

36. "In a twinkling": quoted in Weaver, "Foreigners in Ante-bellum Savannah," p. 8; Shoemaker, "Strangers and Citizens," p. 291; Thigpen, "Aristocracy of the Heart," p. 535; Haunton, "Savannah in the 1850s," p. 198.

37. Haunton, "Savannah in the 1850s," pp. 197–99.

38. Fraser, *Savannah in the Old South*, pp. 306–307; Haunton, "Law and Order in Savannah"; CC Minutes for 1854–55.

39. Lockley, "Trading Encounters."

40. Biographical information on the defendants from the 1860 FMC, Georgia, Chatham County, Savannah, p. 299 (Dunn); p. 335 (Gleason); p. 316 (McAuliffe).

41. "stated": CC Minutes, April 5, 1855; "enticing . . . peers": ibid., Sept. 6, 1855. Biographical information on the attorneys from Myers, ed., *Children of Pride*, pp. 1464–65, 1591–92; 1540; and 1860 FMC (Georgia, Chatham County).

42. "the Irish": Myers, ed., *Children of Pride*, p. 181; "What a religion . . . revolution": ibid., p. 519.

43. "never": Campbell, "Sufferings of the Rev. T. G. Campbell," p. 5. See also Sidbury, *Becoming African*, pp. 13–14, 168–70.

44. "to africa": "Letters of Negroes Addressed to the American Colonization Society"; "friends": William McLain quoted in Gifford, "The African Colonization Movement in Georgia," p. 137; Miller, "Georgia on Their Minds," pp. 349–62; Richardson, " 'Labor Is

Rest to Me Here in This the Lord's Vineyard,' " pp. 5–6; Butchart, " 'We Best Can Instruct Our Own People,' " p. 31; *Slavery and the Peculiar Solution*; Sidbury, *Becoming African*, pp. 9, 68–75.

45. "injoying hur freedom": "Letters of Negroes Addressed to the American Colonization Society," p. 40; Miller, "Georgia on Their Minds"; Burin, *Slavery and the Peculiar Solution*, p. 111.

46. *SR*, May 17, 1849; "that . . . dissatisfaction": *SR*, May 17, 1849, June 6, 1849; Johnson, *Black Savannah*, pp. 13–14, 151–53.

47. Letter from D. F. Willard, Columbus, Ga., Dec. 14, 1854, letter from C. C. Jones, Riceboro, Dec. 28, 1854, container 136, pt. 2; letter from C. Hines, Hinesville, Ga., Sept. 27, 1854, container 135, pt. 2, microfilm reels 74 and 75 respectively, ACS; Gifford, "African Colonization Movement in Georgia," pp. 74–75.

48. "looked . . . buy": Cato Keating, Liberty County claim no. 20689, SCC.

49. "as living was cheap": Tony Axon, Liberty County claim no. 21472, SCC.

50. Johnson, *Black Savannah*, pp. 85–132.

51. Johnson, *Black Savannah*, pp. 65, 76, 80–82, 115, 157; Schweninger, "Prosperous Blacks in the South," p. 35; CC Minutes, Jan. 25, 1855; *SMN*, Aug. 3, 1855.

52. "List of Free Persons of Color Registered for the Year 1855," *SMN*, Aug. 2, 1855; Lightner and Ragan, "Were African American Slaveholders Benevolent or Exploitative?" pp. 535–58; Durett, "Free Blacks in Selected Georgia Cities, 1820–1860," pp. 38–40. Lightner and Ragan suggest that the larger the slaveholdings owned by a free person of color, the more likely the slaves were exploited as workers and not held as family members. Cf. Woodson, *Free Negro Owners of Slaves*.

53. "I'd rather live": Bodichon, *American Diary*, pp. 128–29; "it is hardly": ibid., p. 120.

54. "a great many": "Letters of Negroes Addressed to the American Colonization Society," p. 301; Gifford, "The African Colonization Movement in Georgia," p. 205.

CHAPTER TWO

1. Bancroft, "Census of the City of Savannah [1848]"; Jones, ed., *Historic Savannah*, pp. viii–xvii. See also McInnis, *Politics of Taste in Antebellum Charleston*.

2. Nichols, *Early Architecture of Georgia*, pp. 48, 243, 276, 277; Lane, *Architecture of the Old South*, pp. 11–15; Morrison, *John S. Norris*.

3. "the progress": CC Minutes, March 22, 1855; Lee and Agnew, *Historical Record of the City of Savannah*, p. 167; Griffin, "Savannah, Georgia, During the Civil War," pp. 13, 35; Haunton, "Savannah in the 1850s," p. 95; Savannah Hospital Papers, Board of Managers Minute Book, GHS.

4. Haunton, "Law and Order in Savannah," p. 19; Williams, "Travel in Ante-bellum Georgia as Recorded by English Visitors," p. 197; Bremer, *Homes of the New World*, Vol. 2, p. 457. See also Murray, *Letters from the United States, Cuba, and Canada*, pp. 226–27.

5. "the expense . . . State": Beveridge and McLaughlin, eds., *Papers of Frederick Law Olmsted*, Vol. II: *Slavery and the South, 1852–1857*, pp. 201–202.

6. "in the application": *SMN*, March 8, 1855; "freedom shriekers": *SMN*, May 5, 1858.

7. Fraser, *Savannah in the Old South*, pp. 275–76; Haunton, "Savannah in the 1850s," pp. 326–42.

8. Johnson, *Black Savannah*, pp. 3, 25, 126–30, 176–78.

9. Wright, *A Brief Historical Sketch of Negro Education in Georgia*, pp. 18–20; Johnson, *Black Savannah*, pp. 12, 21, 26, 110, 127–30, 172; Hoskins, *Black Episcopalians in Savannah*, p. 14.

10. "with our books . . . trades": Taylor, *Reminiscences of My Life in Camp*, pp. 29, 5.

11. Ibid., pp. 26–27. See also Catherine Clinton's introduction to a recent edition of Taylor's

Reminiscences (Athens: University of Georgia Press, 2006), p. xiii; Fraser, *Savannah in the Old South*, p. 287.

12. "such a gibberish": Henry L. Cathell Diary, Folder 1851–2, 1856, entry dated Nov. 27, 1851, SHC. See also Mackie, *From Cape Cod to Dixie and the Tropics*, p. 115; Royall, *Mrs. Royall's Southern Tour*, vol. 2, p. 86; Wood, *Women's Work, Men's Work*, pp. 80–100; Burke, *Pleasure and Pain*, pp. 9–10.

13. "structure": Harn, "Old Canoochee-Ogeechee Chronicles," Pt. 3: Life Among the Negroes," pp. 147–48; "as one would": Royall, *Mrs. Royall's Southern Tour*, vol. 2, p. 86; Burke, *Pleasure and Pain*, pp. 19, 17.

14. On the politics of sound in the antebellum South, see Smith, *Listening to Nineteenth-Century America*, pp. 19–91, and White and White, *Sounds of Slavery*.

15. "fast life": Wylie, ed., *Memoirs of Judge Richard H. Clark*, p. 78; "the gathering": Gamble, *Savannah Duels and Duellists*, p. 211; "Cheap enough": Parsons, *Inside View of Slavery*, p. 49; Bell, "Ease and Elegance, Madeira and Murder," pp. 551–76; Smith, *Listening to Nineteenth-Century America*.

16. Hawes, ed., "Memoirs of Charles H. Olmstead," p. 405; "drown[ed]": *SMN*, March 30, 1857; Thigpen, "Aristocracy of the Heart," pp. 120–23; Shoemaker, "Strangers and Citizens."

17. Byrne, "Burden and Heat of the Day," pp. 194–95; Johnson, *Black Savannah*, p. 120; Durett, "Free Blacks in Selected Georgia Cities, 1820–1860," p. 44; "Report of Chief Fireman" in "Report of James P. Screven, Mayor of Savannah . . . 1854" (Savannah, Ga.: E. J. Purse, 1857), pp. 29–31.

18. "as the sound": Conrad, "Reminiscences of a Southern Woman, Pt. 3," p. 257; *SMN*, May 31, 1856.

19. "the largest": Adams, *South-Side View of Slavery*, p. 23; "placed": Conrad, "Reminiscences of a Southern Woman, Pt. 3," p. 257.

20. "conduct": CC Minutes, July 12, 1855; Johnson, *Black Savannah*, p. 135; Fraser, *Savannah in the Old South*, p. 293.

21. "rough element": quoted in Fraser, *Savannah in the Old South*, p. 293; "the fierce . . . collision": CC Minutes, July 24, 1856.

22. "Freedom": quoted in Haunton, "Savannah in the 1850s," p. 225; Weaver, "Foreigners in Ante-bellum Savannah," p. 11. Timothy Lockley argues that "pro-shopkeeper councils" were elected in 1857 and 1858, and that "anti-shopkeeper councils" were those that took office in 1859 and 1860. See "Trading Encounters Between Non-Elite Whites and African Americans in Savannah," p. 46.

23. Clifton, ed., *Life and Labor on Argyle Island*, pp. 198–219.

24. "a slippery": ibid., p. 219. See also ibid., pp. 217–18.

25. "You can't": ibid., p. 211; "a Charleston woman": ibid., p. 203; "visiting": ibid., p. 207. See also pp. 204, 211.

26. The contract is reprinted in Lane, ed., *Neither More nor Less than Men*, pp. 126–27; "Keep him": Clifton, ed., *Life and Labor on Argyle Island*, p. 210. See also Wiethoff, *Crafting the Overseer's Image*, p. 88.

27. For descriptions of the planting season, see Stewart, *"What Nature Suffers to Groe,"* pp. 87–150. For the gender division of labor in the fields see Pruneau, "All the Time Is Work Time," pp. 79–81.

28. "George's Betty": Clifton, ed., *Life and Labor on Argyle Island*, p. 232; "if they think . . . uselessly": ibid., p. 230. See also Joyner, *Down by the Riverside*; Schwalm, *A Hard Fight for We*, pp. 47–74.

29. "Judy": ibid., p. 198; "runaway . . . home": Thomas, *Memoirs of a Southerner*, pp. 14, 15–16.

30. "foul mouthed": *SMN*, June 2, 1856; "Ability . . . about": *SMN*, Aug. 2, 1856.

31. "nigger . . . rampant": *SMN*, June 6, 1856; Campbell, *Sufferings of the Rev. T. G. Campbell*, pp. 5–6.
32. "the political": letter of J. Windsor Smith, April 23, 1856, Container 143, Pt. 1, Reel 79, ACS.
33. "stop this shipping": letter of McLain, June 4, 1856, Container 143, Pt. 2, Reel 79, ACS; Gifford, "American Colonization Movement in Georgia," pp. 78–89.
34. "can it be": quoted in Burin, *Slavery and the Peculiar Solution*, p. 140. See also ibid., pp. 114, 135.
35. "a very common": Myers, ed., *Children of Pride*, p. 240. See also ibid., pp. 240–42; Clarke, *Dwelling Place*, pp. 347–61.
36. "running . . . peers": Myers, ed., *Children of Pride*, p. 242; "to make": ibid., p. 241.
37. "bad words": Starobin, ed., *Blacks in Bondage*, p. 52; Clarke, *Dwelling Place*, p. 350.
38. "size": Myers, ed., *Children of Pride*, p. 245; "a house servant": ibid., p. 246.
39. "in the least": ibid., p. 257. See also ibid., p. 269.
40. "politics . . . streets": ibid., pp. 247–48. See also *SMN*, Nov. 4, 1856.
41. Starobin, *Industrial Slavery in the Old South*, p. 17; Siegel, "Artisans and Immigrants in the Politics of Late Antebellum Georgia," p. 228; Hunt, "Organized Labor," p. 178. See also *SMN*, Dec. 5, 1856.
42. "Greatest . . . people": *SMN*, Dec. 5, 1856.
43. See coverage of the convention in *SMN*, beginning Dec. 8, 1856. "Slavery was": *SMN*, Dec. 11, 1856; "abominable": Myers, ed., *Children of Pride*, p. 273; Wender, "Southern Commercial Convention at Savannah," pp. 173–91.
44. "as the more": *SMN* Dec. 16, 1856; Johnson, *Black Savannah*, pp. 11–19, 58; Love, *History of the First African Baptist Church*, pp. 55–58; Sidbury, *Becoming African*, pp. 68–72.
45. Sermon quoted in Simms, *First Colored Baptist Church*, p. 247. See also Ernest, *Liberation Historiography*; White and White, *Sounds of Slavery*, pp. 55–71, 120–44.
46. "an immense . . . coffin": *SMN*, Dec. 16, 1856.
47. "when I . . . funeral": Love, *History of the First African Baptist Church*, p. 165; Simms, *First Colored Baptist Church*, pp. 32–33, 64.
48. *SMN*, Dec. 16, 1865.

CHAPTER THREE

1. Clifton, ed., *Life and Labor on Argyle Island*, p. 189; *SMN*, Dec. 27, 1856; Hawes, ed., "Memoirs of Charles H. Olmstead," p. 380; Kollock, ed., "Letters of the Kollock and Allied Families," p. 60; Conrad, "Reminiscences of a Southern Woman," Pt. 3, p. 257. See also Davis, *Parades and Power*, p. 105.
2. "a devil . . . feathers": *SMN*, Dec. 27, 1856. Thomas Murtagh, a laborer born in Mayo, Ireland, was married to Ellen, 29 (in 1856), from the same county. Their sons included John, 9, James, 7, Michael, 3, and Thomas, 1. See 1860 FMC for Georgia, Chatham County, Savannah, p. 34.
3. "tamper . . . guard": Rev. R. Q. Mallard to Mary Sharpe Jones, in Myers, ed., *Children of Pride*, p. 284; "having": planter quoted in Lockley, *Lines in the Sand*, p. 129; Buckingham, *Slave States in America*, p. 131; Lyell, *Travels in North America*, Vol. 1, p. 169.
4. Pavich-Lindsay, ed., *Anna*, p. 323; "give out": Myers, ed., *Children of Pride*, p. 179. On lowcountry Georgia slave music and dances, see Savannah Unit, Georgia Writers' Project, *Drums and Shadows*; Hazzard-Gordon, *Jookin': The Rise of Social Dance Formations in African-American Culture*, p. 19; Parrish, *Slave Songs of the Georgia Sea Islands*, pp. 16, 56, 108.
5. "the sports": quoted in Genovese, *Roll, Jordan, Roll*, p. 576; "careless": House, ed., *Planter Management and Capitalism in Ante-bellum Georgia*, p. 127; "Christmas":

Manigault quoted in Dusinberre, *Them Dark Days*, p. 186; Smith, *Slavery and Rice Culture in Low Country Georgia*, p. 191; Fraser, *Savannah in the Old South*, pp. 45, 94, 171. See also White and White, *Sounds of Slavery*.

6. Stewart, *"What Nature Suffers to Groe,"* p. 102; Cheryll Ann Cody, "Cycles of Work and of Childbearing: Seasonality in Women's Lives on Low Country Plantations," in Gaspar and Hine, eds., *More than Chattel*, pp. 61–78; Savannah Unit, Georgia Writers' Project, *Drums and Shadows*; Turner, *Africanisms in the Gullah Dialect;* Wood, *Black Majority*. Also, see the 1998 film *The Language You Cry In: Story of a Mende Song,* a documentary about Joseph Opala, an anthropologist at the University of Sierra Leone, who traced a Mende-language song from the Georgia rice fields (in Harris Neck) to its origins in Senehun Ngola, Sierra Leone. The song is still sung in West Africa today. See also *Drums and Shadows*, pp. 24, 32, 162 and passim for African words and phrases. See also Penningroth, *Claims of Kinfolk*; Wood, *Women's Work, Men's Work*; Ramey, " 'She Do a Heap of Work,' " pp. 707–34; Pollitzer, *The Gullah People and Their African Heritage*.

7. "churning . . . them": Mallard, *Plantation Life Before Emancipation*, p. 26; White and White, *Sounds of Slavery*.

8. "conscience": Myers, ed., *Children of Pride*, p. 271; "there may": ibid., p. 306; "the revelation": ibid., p. 310.

9. "sold for spite": Starobin, ed., *Blacks in Bondage*, p. 55; Clarke, *Dwelling Place*, pp. 359–61.

10. "how the game": Myers, ed., *Children of Pride*, p. 309; Starobin, ed., *Blacks in Bondage*, p. 57. On the sewing machine, see Myers, ed., *Children of Pride*, p. 282.

11. Thomas, *Memoirs of a Southerner,* p. 30; "bigoted . . . damned": Shryock, ed. *Letters of Richard D. Arnold*, p. 86.

12. "of exceeding": quoted in Groover, *Sweet Land of Liberty*, p. 37; "all together": Clifton, ed., *Life and Labor on Argyle Island*, p. 239; Mallard, *Plantation Life Before Emancipation*, pp. 42, 105.

13. "the social glass": Myers, ed., *Children of Pride*, p. 564.

14. "that he should": ibid., pp. 566–67; "language": ibid., p. 566; "the truth is": ibid., p. 389.

15. "easily . . . motives": Harn, "Old Canoochee—Ogeechee Chronicles: Life Among the Negroes," p. 149; "queer": Thomas, *Memoirs of a Southerner*, p. 13; "deception . . . themselves": Jones, *The Religious Instruction of the Negroes in the United States*, p. 110; "familiar": Mallard, *Plantation Life Before Emancipation*, p. 28.

16. Murray, *Letters from the United States, Cuba, and Canada*, p. 212; "I lubs": Beveridge and McLaughlin, eds., *The Papers of Frederick Law Olmsted*, Vol. 2: *Slavery in the South, 1852–1857*, p. 224; White and White, *Sounds of Slavery*, pp. 79–80.

17. "false": Parsons, *Inside View of Slavery*, p. 31; "well, how . . . unhappy:": Bodichon, *An American Diary, 1857–58*, p. 125; Adams, *South-Side View of Slavery*, pp. 30–31.

18. "eternal": Clifton, ed., *Life and Labor on Argyle Island*, p. 291; "the Negroes . . . away," ibid., pp. 247, 246. See also Stevenson, *Life in Black and White*, pp. 23, 255; Christopher Morris, *Becoming Southern: The Evolution of a Way of Life; Warren County and Vicksburg, Mississippi, 1770–1860* (New York: Oxford University Press, 1995), p. 63; Creel, *"A Peculiar People,"* p. 345.

19. "difficulty . . . disquietude": Jones, *Gullah Folktales from the Georgia Coast*, p. 171. See also Schwartz, *Birthing a Slave*, p. 147; Penningroth, *Claims of Kinfolk*, pp. 102–103; Creel, *"A Peculiar People,"* p. 277; Kuyk, *African Voices in the African American Heritage*, p. 99; Parrish, *Slave Songs*, p. 33; Mary Arnold Twining, "Time Is Like a River: The World View of the Sea Island People," in Twining and Baird, eds., *Sea Island Roots*, pp. 89–125.

20. Gomez, *Exchanging Our Country Marks*, pp. 98–101; Diouf, *Servants of Allah*; Twining, "Time Is Like a River."

21. Gifford, "African Colonization Movement in Georgia," p. 200; Johnson, *Black Savannah*, p. 24; Simms, *First Colored Baptist Church*, p. 108.

22. "infernal . . . vexed": Myers, ed., *Children of Pride*, pp. 37–38; Schwartz, "Fugitive Slave Days in Boston," p. 209; Robboy and Robboy, "Lewis Hayden," p. 606.

23. Gifford, "The African Colonization Movement in Georgia," p. 137; Reidy, "Aaron A. Bradley," pp. 281–82; Richardson, " 'Labor Is Rest to Me Here in This the Lord's Vineyard,' " pp. 5–20. In 1850, Bradley was living in Boston's Fifth Ward (1850 FMC, Massachusetts, Suffolk County, Boston, p. 205); in 1860 he was boarding with a black family in the city's Sixth Ward (p. 252). The 1861 Boston Directory listed him as "counselor." See *The Boston Directory* (Boston: Adams, Sampson and Co., 1861). See also "A Colored Lawyer," *NS*, April 21,1848; "Court Calendar," *BDA*, Feb. 12, 1856; "Affairs in and About the City," *Boston Daily Atlas*, Oct. 6, 1856; "A Colored Brother," *LDCN*, Oct. 20, 1856; "Conference of Zion Church," *Liberator*, June 24, 1859.

24. "I resolved . . . race": Jacobs quoted in Yellin, *Harriet Jacobs*, pp. 49, 134.

25. "wild spirit": Myers, ed., *Children of Pride*, p. 374; Griffin, "Savannah, Georgia, During the Civil War," pp. 15–32; Bell, *Major Butler's Legacy*, pp. 319–22.

26. Bell, *Major Butler's Legacy*, pp. 280–81; Clinton, ed., *Fanny Kemble's Journals*.

27. "I pity them": Kemble quoted in Clinton, *Fanny Kemble's Civil Wars,* pp. 121–22; Bell, *Major Butler's Legacy*, p. 281; Schwartz, *Birthing a Slave*, p. 176.

28. Quoted in Bell, *Major Butler's Legacy*, p. 312.

29. "a wild": quoted in Parks, *Joseph E. Brown of Georgia*, p. 44; "Mr.": ibid., p. 11.

30. Newspapers quoted in ibid., p. 29. See also p. 39.

31. "thrilling . . . polished": quoted in ibid., p. 49.

32. "have determined": *SMN*, Oct. 10, 1857; *SMN*, Oct. 13, 1857; CC Minutes, Oct. 19, 1857. See the biographies of Screven, Wright, John Richardson, and George A. Gordon in Myers, ed., *Children of Pride*, pp. 1672–73, 1737, 1657, 1531.

33. "guilty of negligent": CC Minutes, Nov. 26, 1857; "suffer[ed]": ibid., Nov. 30, 1857; ibid., May 13, 1858.

34. "drunkenness . . . terrors": CC Minutes, Sept. 4, 1856; "jail and yard": *SR*, Feb. 24, 1858. See also interview with George Carter in Rawick, ed., *American Slave*, Supplement Series 1, Vol. 3, *Georgia Narratives*, Part 1, p. 157; Byrne, "Slave Crime in Savannah, Georgia," pp. 352–62.

35. Haunton, "Law and Order in Savannah," pp. 16–17; Bowden, *History of Savannah Methodism from John Wesley to Silas Johnson*, pp. 107–108; Sweat, "Free Negro in Antebellum Georgia," p. 129; Wade, *Slavery in the Cities*, pp. 44–45. See also Berlin, *Slaves Without Masters;* Johnson, "Free Blacks in Antebellum Savannah," pp. 418–31.

36. Durett, "Free Blacks in Selected Georgia Cities," pp. 1–17; Johnson, *Black Savannah*, pp. 15, 26, 27, 100, 113, 117; Foner, ed., *Freedom's Lawmakers*, p. 110; Goldin, *Urban Slavery in the American South*, pp. 20–24.

37. Lockley, *Lines in the Sand*, p. 74; Goldin, *Urban Slavery in the American South*, p. 15; Shoemaker, "Strangers and Citizens"; CC Minutes, March 4, 1858, Jan. 24, 1856. For Stegin, Blun, and Basler, see 1860 FMC, Georgia, Chatham County, Savannah, pp. 313, 22, 155.

38. Bancroft, "Census of the City of Savannah." For Jaudon and Fall, see 1860 FMC, Georgia, Chatham County, Savannah, p. 274; for Cleghorn see p. 276. This analysis of 1860 free households is the result of analyzing data for 1,600 (out of 3,200) households based on information in the Genealogical Committee of the Georgia Historical Society, comp., *1860 Census of Chatham County, Georgia*.

39. For the Cleghorn household, see 1860 FMC, Georgia, Chatham County, Savannah, p. 276 (Fourth District). The composition of free black households is calculated by the method described in the previous note.

40. Lockley, *Lines in the Sand*, p. 74; Shoemaker, "Strangers and Citizens," p. 21; Johnson, "Free African-American Women in Savannah," pp. 260–83; CC Minutes, March 4, 1858, Jan. 24, 1856; "is also fond": Kollock, ed., "Letters of the Kollock and Allied Families," Part 2, p. 46; "little . . . sphere": ibid., p. 49; Bodichon, *American Diary*, p. 128. For McCann and McAuliffe, see 1860 FMC, Georgia, Chatham County, Savannah, pp. 58, 287.

41. "on accent": Simms, *First Colored Baptist Church*, p. 86; Hoskins, "The Trouble They Seen," p. 62. In the summer of 1860, William H. Sikes was living with Margaret Simms; he was listed by the census taker as a porter in a shoe store. See 1860 FMC, Georgia, Chatham County, Savannah, p. 128.

42. Simms, *First Colored Baptist Church*; Hoskins, *Out of Yamacraw and Beyond*, p. 45.

43. Buckingham, *Slave States in America*, p. 135; "to attach . . . themselves": Clifton, ed., *Life and Labor on Argyle Island*, p. 271.

44. "the extensive": Harris, *Plain Folk and Gentry in a Slave Society*, p. 60; "the negro": Preamble quoted in Stephanie M. H. Camp, "Pleasures of Resistance," p. 571; "practical": Beaufort, South Carolina, planters quoted in Forret, *Race Relations at the Margins*, p. 112; "it has": ibid., p. 68.

45. Lockley, *Lines in the Sand*, pp. 76–85, 24–26; Harn, "Old Canoochee-Ogeechee Chronicles: Life Among the Negroes," pp. 47–55; Harn, "Old Canoochee Backwoods Sketches," Pt. 1: Old Canoochee Plantation," pp. 77–80.

46. "high cheek bones . . . temper": Beveridge and McLaughlin, eds., *Papers of Frederick Law Olmsted*, Vol. 2: *Slavery and the South, 1852–1857*, p. 212; Burke, *Pleasure and Pain*, p. 80.

47. "an outcast": Manigault quoted in Wiethoff, *Crafting the Overseer's Image*, p. 88; "elated . . . Man": Clifton, ed., *Life and Labor on Argyle Island*, p. 250.

48. "always be a man": CC Minutes, Nov. 27, 1858; Mallard, *Plantation Life Before Emancipation*, p. 40.

49. Goldin, *Urban Slavery in the American South*, pp. 19–23. The figures on bookkeepers are based on the 1860 Federal Manuscript Census for the city of Savannah, available in printed form, *1860 Census of Chatham County, Georgia*.

50. Fraser, *Savannah in the Old South*, p. 248; Goldin, *Urban Slavery in the American South*, pp. 20–25.

51. "Recreant": *SMN*, April 2, 1858.

52. *SMN*, Feb. 17, 1858, July 24, 1858.

53. Ibid., April 5, 1868; "Every white man": ibid., May 26, 1858; "ruling race . . . cause": ibid., May 27, 1858; "the brand": ibid., May 29, 1858. See also Towers, *Urban South and the Coming of the Civil War*.

CHAPTER FOUR

1. "confessedly"; CC Minutes, July 1, 1858 (from an article published in the *SR*, June 29, 1858).

2. *SR*, June 29, 1858. See also the biography in Myers, ed., *Children of Pride*, pp. 1718–19.

3. "most . . . *Negroes*": Myers, ed., *Children of Pride*, p. 426; "with their own": CC Minutes, July 1, 1858, and *SR*, June 29, 1858; "it was a spectacle": ibid.

4. "underswell . . . class": Adams, *South-Side View of Slavery*, p. 44. See also Foster, *Wayside Glimpses*, p. 52; Davis, *Parades and Power*, p. 168.

5. "no American city": Jones, *History of Savannah, Georgia*, p. 388; "step enlivened": Adams, *South-Side View of Slavery*; Buckingham, *Slave States in America*, p. 125; Shoemaker, "Strangers and Citizens," p. 354; Franklin, *The Militant South, 1800–1861*, pp. 22, 75; Stiles, *Marse George*; Waring, *Cerveau's Savannah*, pp. 30–31.

6. Franklin, *Militant South*, pp. 121–24; *SMN*, Dec. 31, 1856, Nov. 10, 1857, Jan. 4, 1858, March 17, 1859; Shryock, ed., *Letters of Richard D. Arnold*, pp. 54–57.

7. "knowing her . . . Americanism": Shryock, ed., *Letters of Richard D. Arnold*, pp. 91–92.

8. Rousey, "From Whence They Came to Savannah," p. 311; Haunton, "Savannah in the 1850s," p. 324; Pressly, "Northern Roots of Savannah's Antebellum Elite," pp. 157–99.

9. Gordon, "Eleanor Kinzie Gordon," pp. 179–96; Anderson, "Eleanor Kenzie [sic] Gordon," pp. 163–69.

10. See the biographical sketches in Myers, ed., *Children of Pride*, p. 1588.

11. Wells, *Slave Ship Wanderer*; "That is the advantage": June Hall McCash, *Jekyll Island's Early Years*, p. 163; Calonius, *Wanderer*.

12. Wells, *Slave Ship Wanderer*; McCash, *Jekyll Island's Early Years*, pp. 152–88; Davis, "Buchanian Espionage, " pp. 271–78.

13. "dangerous man . . . lawlessness": Myers, ed., *Children of Pride*, p. 479; "the people": *SR*, Feb. 15, 1859; "are known to be": ibid., Feb. 17, 1859.

14. "was a man": Wylie, ed., *Memoirs of Judge Richard H. Clark*, p. 95; "abundance . . . richer": quoted in Siegel, "Artisans and Immigrants in the Politics of Late Antebellum Georgia," p. 229; "more susceptible": quoted in Takaki, *Pro-Slavery Crusade*, pp. 115–16.

15. Rousey, "From Whence They Came to Savannah"; Byrne, "The Burden and Heat of the Day," pp. 204–207; Shoemaker, "Strangers and Citizens"; Weaver, "Foreigners in Antebellum Savannah," pp. 1–17.

16. Gillespie, *Free Labor in an Unfree World*; Goldin, *Urban Slavery in the American South*, p. 29; Johnson, "William Harris Garland," pp. 41–56.

17. Gillespie, *Free Labor in an Unfree World*, pp. 159–61; Shoemaker, "Strangers and Citizens," pp. 271–72, 293, 319; Burke, *Pleasure and Pain*, p. 81; *SMN*, Dec. 31, 1856; Siegel, "Artisans and Immigrants in the Politics of Late Antebellum Georgia."

18. "one which should": Myers, ed., *Children of Pride*, p. 469.

19. Taylor, *Reminiscences of My Life in Camp*, p. 140; Fraser, Jr., *Savannah in the Old South*, pp. 310–11; Hoskins, *Out of Yamacraw and Beyond*, p. 12.

20. "sheer folly": Sidney George Fisher, quoted in Bell, *Major Butler's Legacy*, p. 324; "a rough": Mortimer Thomson, "What Became of the Slaves on a Georgia Plantation?" *New York Daily Tribune*, March 9, 1859; *New York Semi-Weekly Tribune*, March 11, 1859.

21. "weeping time": Bell, *Major Butler's Legacy*, p. 614.

22. "brothers & sisters": Sidney George Fisher, quoted in ibid., p. 325.

23. Ibid., pp. 325–40; Bancroft, *Slave-Trading in the Old South*, pp. 222–36.

24. "soundness": Fett, *Working Cures*, pp. 15–35; "The Negroes": Thomson, "What Happened to the Slaves on a Georgia Plantation?"; "Pull off her rags": quoted in Bell, *Major Butler's Legacy*, p. 338; Bancroft, *Slave-Trading*, p. 332. See also Johnson, *Soul by Soul*.

25. Thomson, "What Became of the Slaves on a Georgia Plantation?"; Bell, *Major Butler's Legacy*, pp. 339–40; Bancroft, *Slave-Trading*, pp. 232–36; Piacentino, "Doesticks' Assault on Slavery," pp. 196–203.

26. "While the article": *SMN*, March 15, 1859; ibid., May 29, 1860; "devoutly": quoted in Bell, *Major Butler's Legacy*, p. 331; Jung, "Outlawing 'Coolies,' " pp. 677–701.

27. "the citizens": *SMN*, May 31, 1859; "an intelligent fellow": ibid., Oct. 11, 1858; ibid., Aug. 3, 1857; ibid., June 8, 1859.

28. "richly" and "at a little distance": John Stoddard, quoted in Haunton, "Savannah in the 1850s," pp. 366, 317; "to ride": quoted in ibid., p. 366; Patricia K. Hunt, "The Struggle to Achieve Individual Expression Through Clothing and Adornment: African American Women Under and After Slavery," in Morton, ed., *Discovering the Women in Slavery*, pp. 227–39.

29. "dulled": Bodichon, *American Diary*, p. 123; "Slaves with broadcloth . . . impunity": Adams, *South-Side View of Slavery*, pp. 29–30.

30. "the Democracy . . . delight": *SMN*, Oct. 8, 1859; Fraser, *Savannah in the Old South*, p. 308.

31. "these insane . . . blood": *SMN*, Oct. 22, 1859; Reynolds, *John Brown*, p. 429.

32. "Now, if it is deemed": Brown quoted in McPherson, *Battle Cry of Freedom*, p. 209; "wandering or strolling": quoted in Mohr, *On the Threshold of Freedom*, p. 14; "too free": *SMN*, Dec. 3, 1859.

33. "Safety-valve": letter of Robert Campbell, Augusta, Jan. 14, 1860, and clipping of article to Augusta *Chronicle and Sentinel* (Jan. 10, 1860), Container 158, pt. 1, reel 88, ACS.

34. "they said . . . me": letter of McLain, Savannah, April 27, 1860; Container 159, pt. 1, reel 89; "God has thus far": letter of Alfred Cuthbert, Jr., Feb. 6, 1860, container 158, pt. 1, reel 88, ACS. On the "Cuthbert Conspiracy," see Gifford, "African Colonization Movement in Georgia," pp. 152–61.

35. "turned out . . . wretchedly,": Clifton, ed., *Life and Labor on Argyle Island*, p. 266; "all sorts": ibid., p. 278.

36. "a man . . . unruly": ibid, p. 285; "preach them": ibid., p. 286; ibid., pp. 291–93; Wiethoff, *Crafting the Overseer's Image*, p. 121.

37. "this I have . . . negro": ibid., p. 300.

38. "bolters": "Documents: From the Autobiography of Herschel V. Johnson, 1856–1867," *AHR* 30 (Oct. 1924): 315.

39. "To her yoke": *SMN*, March 19, 1860; Mohr, *On the Threshold of Freedom*, p. 8.

40. "this Republican . . . want to be": Shryock, ed., *Letters of Richard D. Arnold*, p. 168; Pressly, "Northern Roots of Savannah's Antebellum Elite," pp. 187–90.

41. Myers, ed., *Children of Pride*, p. 592; Clifton, ed., *Life and Labor on Argyle Island*, p. 301.

42. "A more painful . . . Balls": Clifton, ed., *Life and Labor on Argyle Island*, pp. 301–302; "a John Brown": Reynolds, *John Brown*, pp. 11–12, 471.

CHAPTER FIVE

1. "Our Military Visitors," *NYT*, July 21, 1860, p. 1. The steamer was apparently the same vessel mentioned in the beginning of the Prologue.

2. Ibid.

3. Ibid; "General City News," *NYT*, July 20, 1860, p. 8.

4. "somewhat inclined": Myers, ed., *Children of Pride*, p. 597; "Their strategy . . . [cigars]": "The Savannah Republican Blues," *NYT*, July 23, 1860, p. 8; "Both were . . . property": "The Dinner to the Blues," *NYT*, July 24, 1860, p. 8.

5. "to elope . . . freedom": *NYT*, July 23, 1860, p. 8; Advertisement, J. Gurney & Son, *NYT*, July 28, 1860, p. 5; "a visit . . . pleasure: "Departure of the Savannah Blues, *NYT*, July 26, 1860, p. 8.

6. "a morbid": Mercer Diary, July 10, 1859, p. 175, GHS; "very late hours . . . good": ibid., July 1860, p. 8.

7. On the nominating conventions of 1860, see McPherson, *Battle Cry of Freedom*, pp. 213–33.

8. "stumping the state": "Political Miscellany," *NYT*, August 1, 1860, p. 3; "I am sorry": Shryock, ed. *Letters of Richard D. Arnold*, p. 96; Fraser, *Savannah in the Old South*, p. 316.

9. "unjust": *SR*, July 31, 1860; "A Southern Strike!" *NYT*, July 17, 1860, p. 4; "Bread Excitement in Savannah, Geo," *NYT*, July 17, 1860, p. 6.

10. "a most": "The Late Conflagration," *SMN*, Aug. 2, 1860; "without a pass . . . city": *SR*,

July 31, 1860; "the Crackers . . . watched": Clifton, ed., *Life and Labor on Argyle Island,* pp. 305, 303; Mohr, *On the Threshold of Freedom,* pp. 20–26.

11. "whose antagonism": CC Minutes, Sept. 27, 1860; ibid., July 5, 1860; "professional": ibid., Aug. 2, 1860; ibid., Aug. 16, 1860; ibid., Oct. 11, 1860; "Our citizen": "Report of R. D. Arnold, Mayor of the City of Savannah . . . 1860" (Savannah, Ga.: John M. Cooper & Co., 1860), p. 4; CC Minutes, Oct. 11, 1860.

12. "negroes . . . neighborhood": CC Minutes, June 21, 1860; "march an' drill": Interview with George Carter, in Rawick, ed., *American Slave,* Supp. Series 1, Vol. 3, *Georgia Narrs,* p. 160.

13. "tampering . . . view": Myers, ed., *Children of Pride,* p. 624; "avoid excitement": ibid., p. 628.

14. "pledge . . . do it": Freehling, *Road to Disunion,* Vol. 2, p. 409; "to purchase": CC Minutes, Nov. 7, 1860.

15. "perfect turmoil": Mrs. G. J. Kollock in Kollock, ed., "Letters of the Kollock and Allied Families," Part 3, p. 155; Savannah-Chatham County Board of Education, "The Debatable Lands: Native Americans in Coastal Georgia" (n.p., n.d.), p. 16. On the rattlesnake as a symbol of the patriots' revolutionary cause, and the secessionists' cause, see Fischer, *Liberty and Freedom,* pp. 75–84, 308–11.

16. "I am a Union man . . . state": Freehling, *Road to Disunion,* Vol. 2, p. 411; "Magnificent": CC Minutes, Nov. 11, 1860; Haunton, "Savannah in the 1850s," pp. 156, 168; Freehling, *Road to Disunion,* Vol. 2, pp. 406–13.

17. "I trust . . . ruinous": Myers, ed., *Children of Pride,* p. 627–28; "he would be": Shoemaker, "Strangers and Citizens," pp. 363–64; "Popery": Myers, ed., *Children of Pride,* p. 634; "one mind": Mrs. G. J. Kollock in Kollock, ed., "Letters of the Kollock and Allied Families," Pt. 3, p. 155; Greenberg, "Creating Ethnic, Class, and Southern Identity in Nineteenth-Century America," pp. 262–68.

18. "Stagnant state . . . hospital": CC Minutes, Nov. 21, 1860; "the Irish drayman": Mercer Diary, Nov. 29, 1860, pp. 38–39, GHS; "The Secession Movement," *NYT,* Jan. 17, 1861, p. 9; Entry for December 1860, Savannah Hospital Papers, Minute Book of Board of Managers, Savannah Poor House and Hospital, GHS. See also the letter from Henrietta J. Wayne to "Dear Mama" [her stepmother], Savannah, December 3, 1860, HF Papers, DU.

19. "Report of R. D. Arnold, Mayor . . . 1860," pp. 33, 4, 8; "not disposed": Roberts, quoted in Bryan, *Confederate Georgia,* p. 58.

20. "all the rowdies": Augusta J. Kollock, in Kollock, ed., "Letters of the Kollock and Allied Families," Part 4, p. 230; "minutemen": "Affairs in Savannah," *NYT,* Jan. 16, 1861, p. 2. On the Ribero incident, see Clifton, ed., *Life and Labor on Argyle Island,* p. 315; "What's in the Wind?" [Letter to Editor], *NYT,* Feb. 9, 1861, p. 3; "Southern Outrages on British Subject," *NYT,* July 30, 1861, p. 5; Shryock, ed., *Letters of Richard D. Arnold,* p. 98; Mohr, *On the Threshold of Freedom,* p. 43; Fraser, *Savannah in the Old South,* pp. 316–17. A carpenter, Joseph W. Ribero, 31, was listed in the 1860 census for Chatham County, where he was born. His English-born wife was 28; their two daughters, 2 and 10, were born in Savannah. He did not have "B" (for black) or "M" (for mulatto) after his name, suggesting that he was very light-skinned. (See 1860 FMC, Georgia, Chatham County, Savannah, p. 272). The census taker in Chelsea in 1870 listed all four family members as white. See the 1870 FMC, Massachusetts, Suffolk County, Chelsea, p. 394.

21. "The most imposing . . . Confederacy": *SR,* Dec. 27, 1860; "the custom . . . manners": Mercer Diary, Dec. 27, 1860, p. 42, GHS.

22. Candler, ed., *Confederate Records of Georgia,* Vol. 2, pp. 15, 14; "with drums beating": Olmstead, in Hawes, "The Memoirs of Charles H. Olmstead," p. 388; "I found the

life . . . planters": Mercer Diary, Jan. 19, 1860, p. 47, GHS; Durham, ed., *Confederate Yankee*, p. xxxvii; Freehling, *Road to Disunion*, Vol. 2, p. 481.

23. "We are": Augusta J. Kollock, in Kollock, ed., "Letters of the Kollock and Allied Families, 1826–1884," Pt. 4, p. 229; Bryan, *Confederate Georgia*, p. 15; Johnson, *Toward a Patriarchal Republic*, pp. 39–41.

24. "fights": Augusta J. Kollock, in Kollock, ed., "Letters of the Kollock and Allied Families," Pt. 4, p. 231; Hawes, ed., "Memoirs of Charles H. Olmstead," Pt. 5, p. 389; Wm. H. C. Whiting in *ORUCA*, Series 1, Vol. 1, pp. 318–19; *SR*, Jan. 24, 1861.

25. "are as familiar . . . insubordinate": "Affairs in Savannah," *NYT*, Jan. 16, 1861, p. 2; "have very generally . . . others": Clifton, ed., *Life and Labor on Argyle Island*, p. 313.

26. "to market": CC Minutes, Jan. 2, 1861; "or in a vital part": Clifton, ed., *Life and Labor on Argyle Island*, p. 314; Mohr, *On the Threshold of Freedom*, pp. 50–67.

27. Griffin, "Savannah, Georgia, During the Civil War," p. 100; Candler, ed., *Confederate Records of Georgia*, Vol. 2, p. 26.

28. "Our new government": Stephens, quoted in McPherson, *Battle Cry of Freedom*, p. 244.

29. "double": *SMN*, March 25, 1861; Johnson, *Toward a Patriarchal Republic*; "anarchical spirit . . . justice": Mercer Diary, Feb. 9, 1861, March 30, 1861, pp. 55–65, GHS.

30. "Fortunately, no one": Gordon, quoted in Gordon, "Eleanor Kinzie Gordon," p. 187.

31. "tieing up": Mercer Diary, April 23, 1860, p. 73, GHS; "The barbette gun": Myers, ed., *Children of Pride*, p. 683. See also ibid., p. 664; Fraser, *Savannah in the Old South*, p. 323; Thomas, *Memoirs of a Southerner, 1840–1923*, p. 34; Griffin, "Benevolence and Malevolence in Confederate Savannah," pp. 347 68.

32. "Your opinions": Henderson, *Oglethorpe Light Infantry*, p. 5. On Brown's position, see his correspondence with the CSA secretary of war in April and May 1861: Candler, ed., *Confederate Records of Georgia*, Vol. 3, pp. 35–90; Parks, *Joseph E. Brown*, pp. 110–28.

33. This discussion is based on names and other information included in the following sources: Henderson, *Roster of the Confederate Soldiers of Georgia*; Folsom, *Heroes and Martyrs of Georgia*, p. 157; Roddy, *The Georgia Volunteer Infantry*. For the households of the men listed, see 1860 FMC, Georgia, Chatham County, Savannah, as compiled by the Genealogical Committee of the Georgia Historical Society, *1860 Census of Chatham County, Georgia*, pp. 14 (Basinger); 335 (Scriven); 356 (Stiles); 291 (Padelford); 327 (Russell); 353 (Stegin); 130 (Fleck); 147 (Giebelhouse); 256 (Blun); 14 (Basler); 154 (Grace).

34. Ibid., pp. 93 (Davis); 4 (Anderson); 287 (Olcott); 350 (Snyder); 58 (Marmelstein); 213 (LaRoche); 305 (Purses).

35. "a strong . . . paupers": "Report of Charles C. Jones, Jr., Mayor of the City of Savannah . . . 1861" (Savannah, Ga.: John M. Cooper & Co., 1861), p. 19; "From Savannah," *NYT*, April 24, 1861, p. 1.

36. Bell, *Major Butler's Legacy*, p. 345; "the poor fellows . . . law": Myers, ed., *Children of Pride*, pp. 672–73.

37. Russell, *My Diary North and South*, p. 85; "camp . . . other": *SMN*, Sept. 2, 1861; Myers, ed., *Children of Pride*, p. 1571, 688, 690–91, 693; "I shall go": E. R. Harden to My Dear Mother, Savannah, April 28, 1861, HF Papers, DU.

38. Andrews, *Footprints of a Regiment*, pp. 2–7; Walker, *Hell's Broke Loose in Georgia*.

39. "an old-fashioned": Thomas Barrow quoted in Lane, ed., *"Dear Mother: Don't Grieve About Me,"* p. 15; "the deepest sand . . . edifices:" Russell, *My Diary North and South*, p. 80.

40. "I rather revolted": Russell, *My Diary North and South*, p. 85; "letting loose": "A Remarkable Case of Binocular Vision," *NYT*, May 21, 1861, p. 2; "marked interposition": "Report of Charles C. Jones, Jr., Mayor . . . 1861," p. 3.

41. "great caution . . . freedom": Simms, *First Colored Baptist Church*, pp. 130–33; "De . . . Yankees": Dusinberre, *Them Dark Days*, p. 273.

42. "Yes . . . freedom": Taylor, *Reminiscences of My Life in Camp*, p. 32; Hahn, *A Nation Under Our Feet*, pp. 46–48.

43. "it was thought": *SR*, June 11, 1861; "public": *SMN*, May 9, 1861, and *SR*, June 11, 1861; Fraser, *Savannah in the Old South*, pp. 323–24; Mohr, *On the Threshold of Freedom*, pp. 64–66, 309. The names of the free men and women of color are listed in *SMN*, July 3, 1861, and July 26, 1861. For biographical information see Genealogical Committee of the Georgia Historical Society, *1860 Census of Chatham County, Georgia*, p. 248 (Mirault/Marot); p. 196 (Jones); p. 98 (Deveaux/Devereaux); p. 201 (Kelley/Kelly); p. 97 (Densler).

44. CC Minutes, May 22, 1861; Screven, "The Savannah Benevolent Association," p. 35; Minutes of the Committee of Thirteen, Chapter 8, Vol. 388, Miscellaneous Minutes, Central Committee, Savannah, 1861, RG 109.

45. "a mulatto": Myers, ed., *Children of Pride*, p. 742; Clarke, *Dwelling Place*, pp. 395–97, 403–405, 475.

46. "a bad citizen": CC Minutes, Sept. 11, 1861.

47. "It seems": Myers, ed., *Children of Pride*, p. 722; "young men . . . steel": Sermon in Folder 303, Box 24, J. F. Waring Papers, GHS; Myers, ed., *Children of Pride*, p. 724; *SMN*, July 29, 1861; Fraser, *Savannah in the Old South*, pp. 325–26. See also Coopersmith, *Fighting Words*, pp. 72–73.

48. "spies . . . impossible": *SMN*, Aug. 24, 1861; "reign of terror": "Direct from Georgia," *NYT*, Sept. 1, 1861, p. 2; "I am a rattlesnake . . . etc.": Taylor, *Reminiscences of My Life in Camp*, p. 32.

49. DeCredico, *Patriotism for Profit*, p. 39; Savannah Unit, Federal Writers' Project, "Plantation Development in Chatham County," pp. 326–27; Fraser, *Savannah in the Old South*, pp. 307, 326; Myers, ed., *Children of Pride*, p. 748; Griffin, "Savannah, Georgia," pp. 44–46; Coddington, "Activities and Attitudes of a Confederate Business Man," pp. 3–36.

50. See the biography of Purse in Myers, ed., *Children of Pride*, p. 1650. On the state election see Parks, *Joseph E. Brown*, pp. 157–69; Bryan, *Confederate Georgia*, pp. 34–36.

CHAPTER SIX

1. "Mechanics . . . bayonet": Candler, ed., *Confederate Records of of Georgia*, Vol. 2, p. 199; W. G. Gill in *ORUCN*, Series 1, Vol. 12, p. 83; Wells, *Slave Ship Wanderer*, pp. 84-85; Bryan, *Confederate Georgia*, p. 70.

2. Mercer Diary, May 30, 1861, pp. 95–96, GHS; "some": Wiley, ed., "Confederate Letters of John W. Hagan," Pt. 1, p. 176; "brackish . . . diet": Andrews, *Footprints of a Regiment*, pp. 9–10; Folsom, *Heroes and Martyrs of Georgia*, p. 158.

3. Andrews, *Footprints of a Regiment*, p. 11; Chap. 8, Vol. 29, Miscellaneous Records of Employees and Property, Signal Office, Savannah, 1862–64, p. 70, RG 109.

4. "no Yankee": Louis Manigault in Clifton, ed., *Life and Labor on Argyle Island*, p. 327; "Providence": King, ed., "Rebel Lawyer," p. 214; "low swampy": Mercer Diary, June 23, 1862, p. 41, GHS.

5. "in the rain": Mercer Diary, Aug. 9, 1862, p. 45, GHS; "take a scrub": Mrs. E. F. Neufville in Kollock, ed., "Letters of the Kollock and Allied Families," Pt. 4, p. 243; "prepared for": Myers, ed., *Children of Pride*, p. 1096. See also MacKethan, ed., *Recollections of a Southern Daughter*, p. 63.

6. Mohr, *On the Threshold of Freedom*, pp. 122–23; Hoole, *Vizetelly Covers the Confederacy*, pp. 67–68; Mercer Diary, Sept. 4, 1861, p. 114, GHS.

7. "mounting": "Savannah in a Fright," *NYT*, Dec. 12, 1861, p. 2; "are not cattle": SMN, Dec. 10, 1861; Berlin, et al., eds., *Freedom*, Series 1, Vol. 3, *Wartime Genesis of Free Labor*, p. 122; Fraser, *Savannah in the Old South*, p. 327; Torian, ed., "Antebellum and War Memories of Mrs. Telfair Hodgson," p. 354.

8. "Something more": Jeremy F. Gilmer to Dear Loulie, Nashville, Nov. 28, 1861, JFG Papers, SHC; "It is a dreadful": Henrietta Wayne to Dear Mama H, Savannah, Dec. 6, 1861, HF Papers, DU; "the worst people": Mercer Diary, April 23, 1863, p. 95, GHS; Coddington, "Activities and Attitudes of a Confederate Business Man," pp. 3–36.

9. Myers, *Children of Pride*, pp. 802, 792; Fornell, "Civil War Comes to Savannah," pp. 252–54; F. W. Pickens in *ORUCN*, Series 1, Vol. 12, p. 828; Myers, ed., *Children of Pride*, p. 794; Neblett, "Major Edward C. Anderson and the C.S.S. *Fingal*," pp. 132–58; Luraghi, *History of the Confederate Navy*.

10. "quite a Panic . . . escape": Clifton, ed., *Life and Labor on Argyle Island*, p. 320; "the art": Henrietta Wayne to Dear Mama H, Savannah, Oct. 14, 1861, HF Papers, DU.

11. "If they have": Myers, ed., *Children of Pride*, p. 987; "many of her": Simms, *First Colored Baptist Church*, p. 132; "This war": Clifton, ed., *Life and Labor on Argyle Island*, p. 320; Mohr, *On the Threshold of Freedom*, pp. 102–108; Penningroth, *Claims of Kinfolk*, pp. 4–5, 221–22.

12. King, ed., "Rebel Lawyer," p. 87; Bryan, *Confederate Georgia*, p. 69; Myers, ed., *Children of Pride*, p. 790; Lee and Agnew, *Historical Record of the City of Savannah*, p. 82; Harden, *Recollections of a Long and Satisfactory Life*, pp. 97–98; "From Charleston and Savannah," *NYT*, Dec. 20, 1861, p. 3.

13. Mercer Diary, Jan. 12, 1862, p. 174, GHS; "soft . . . earth": Q. A. Gillmore in *ORUCA*, Series 1, Vol. 14, p. 321; Mohr, *On the Threshold of Freedom*, pp. 99–119; Hayes, ed., *Samuel Francis DuPont*, Vol. 1; Higginson, *Army Life in a Black Regiment*; "Letters of Dr. Seth Rogers, 1862, 1863," pp. 338–98.

14. CC Minutes, Jan. 5, 1862, and Feb. 12, 1862; Q. A. Gillmore in *ORUCA*, Series 1, Vol. 14, p. 328; "knew every foot": Hayes, ed., *Samuel Francis DuPont* (henceforth *DuPont Letters*), Vol. 1, p. 306; "thoroughly acquainted . . . upon": John Rodgers and Q. A. Gillmore in *ORUCA*, Series 1, Vol. 14, pp. 324–25; Mohr, *On the Threshold of Freedom*, p. 84; Johnson, *Black Savannah*, p. 164.

15. "a native . . . useful": *ORUCN*, Series 1, Vol. 12, pp. 432–33. The 1860 FMC Manuscript Census for Georgia, Chatham County, Savannah (p. 288), lists a William Bar, 22, a laborer and native of Clare, Ireland, boarding with an Irish-born grocer and his family.

16. "the earliest . . . and pain": Myers, ed., *Children of Pride*, p. 845.

17. "I find everybody": Edward Harden to Dear Mother, Savannah, April 17, 1862, HF Papers, DU; McPherson, *Battle Cry of Freedom*, pp. 431–32.

18. An account of the event, by Felix Gregory DeFontaine, is reprinted in Merrill, comp., "Personne Goes to Georgia," pp. 202–11, and in Moore, ed., *Rebellion Record*, pp. 74–75. See also Fornell, "Civil War Comes to Savannah," p. 259; Bryan, *Confederate Georgia*, pp. 138–39.

19. "low, petty . . . command": Myers, ed., *Children of Pride*, p. 894; Pemberton in *ORUCA*, Series 1, Vol. 14, p. 502; "most notoriously . . . camp"; Mercer Diary, Jan. 18, 1862, pp. 177–79, GHS. See also Clifton, ed., *Life and Labor on Argyle Island*, p. 333.

20. "Medicine": Kollock, ed., "Letters of the Kollock and Allied Families," Pt. 2, p. 44. For a biographical sketch of J. J. Waring, see Myers, ed., *Children of Pride*, p. 1714.

21. "He is a spy": Letter from Charles C. Jones Sr., Maybank, Oct. 5, 1861, in Folder 43, JFW Papers, GHS; Myers, ed., *Children of Pride*, p. 766; CC Minutes, Dec. 18, 1861, July 16, 1862; Griffin, "Benevolence and Malevolence in Confederate Savannah," p. 357. For details of the charges against Waring, and of his attempt to reclaim his good name, see Folder 43, "Spy Charges," Box 4, JFW Papers, GHS.

22. Gordon, "Eleanor Kinzie Gordon," pp. 186–87. See also Robertson, ed., "Northern Rebel," pp. 477–517; Anderson, "Eleanor Kenzie Gordon," pp. 163–69.

23. "to arm": Berlin, et al., eds., *Freedom*, Series 3, *Wartime Genesis of Free Labor*, p. 97; "50,000 pairs": Miller, *Lincoln's Abolitionist General*, p. 97.

24. "the floor": Montfort quoted in Berry, *All That Makes a Man*, p. 223; Myers, ed., *Children of Pride*, pp. 876–77; Fraser, *Savannah in the Old South*, pp. 330–31; Meaney, "Prison Ministry of Father Peter Whelan," pp. 4–11; Drummond, *Confederate Yankee*, pp. 3–37; "disgrace": Coopersmith, *Fighting Words*, p. 92.

25. "horrid hole": Robertson, ed., "Northern Rebel," p. 487; "A strange": *SMN*, May, 1862; Robert H. May [Mayor of Augusta] to Joseph E. Brown, Feb. 11, 1862, in Candler, comp., *Confederate Records of Georgia*, Vol. 3, p. 159; Bragg et al., *Never for Want of Powder*; Escott, *Military Necessity*, pp. 79–82. Giebelhouse was a soldier in the German Volunteers of Savannah. He is listed in the 1860 FMC, Georgia, Chatham County, Savannah, p. 28.

  See also Morgan, *Planters' Progress*, pp. 48–49; Henderson, *Roster of the Confederate Soldiers of Georgia*, Vol. 1, p. 202. See George W. Raines in *ORUCN*, Series 1, vol. 14, p. 532, on Augusta "as of vital importance to the Confederacy, being the great center of the inland communication between the States of the East and West . . . " For a biography of Hugh W. Mercer, see Myers, ed., *Children of Pride*, p. 1623.

26. See Lincoln's response in Berlin et al., eds., *Freedom*, Series 1, *Destruction of Slavery*, pp. 124–25; "heretofore capable . . . guard": Berlin, et al., eds., *Wartime Genesis of Free Labor*, p. 190; Miller, *Lincoln's Abolitionist General*, pp. 93–119; McPherson, *Battle Cry of Freedom*, pp. 499, 503.

27. Taylor, *Reminiscences of My Life in Camp*, pp. 32–37.

28. For accounts of life in the colony see ibid.; Heard, "St. Simons Island During the War Between the States," pp. 249–72; Bell, *Major Butler's Legacy*, pp. 359–61; Mohr, *On the Threshold of Freedom*, pp. 71–83; and material from *ORUCN* and *ORUCA* listed below. See also Hahn, *Nation Under Our Feet*, pp. 72–73. On Port Royal, see Rose, *Rehearsal for Reconstruction*.

29. These names, statistics, and occupations are based on compilations by Dorothy Elwood as part of the Civil War Sailors Database, a partnership between Howard University, the Department of the Navy, and the National Park Service. See http://www.itd.nps.gov/cwss/sailors_index.html ("Black Georgia-Born Sailors in the Union Navy").

30. "practically free . . . daring": Hayes, ed., *DuPont Letters*, Vol. 2, p. 69; E. Lanier in *ORUCN*, Series 1, Vol. 12, p. 727; S. W. Godon in ibid., p. 633; S. W. Godon in *ORUCN*, Series 1, Vol. 13, p. 633; Bullard, *Cumberland Island*, pp. 151–60.

31. Berlin et al., eds., *Destruction of Slavery*, p. 146; S. W. Godon in *ORUCN*, Series 1, Vol. 13, pp. 19–21; Mohr, *On the Threshold of Freedom*, pp. 73–75; Emilio, *Brave Black Regiment*, p. 45.

32. "self-supporting": S. W. Godon in *ORUCN*, Series 1, Vol. 12, p. 689; "great dislike": Hayes, ed., *DuPont Letters*, Vol. 2, p. 71; "to plant": ibid., p. 634; "idleness . . . rate": S. W. Godon in *ORUCN*, Series 1, Vol. 13, p. 144.

33. "We tried": Hayes, ed., *DuPont Letters*, Vol. 2, p. 70; "tariff of prices": J. R. Goldsborough in *ORUCN*, Series 1, Vol. 13, p. 159; "hoops, calicoes": ibid., p. 195.

34. "finely": S. W. Godon in *ORUCN*, Series 1, Vol. 13, p. 143; "children presented": French quoted in Mohr, *On the Threshold of Freedom*, pp. 82–83; Taylor, *Reminiscences of My Life in Camp*, p. 37; Penningroth, *Claims of Kinfolk*, pp. 170–72.

35. Taylor, *Reminiscences of My Life in Camp*, pp. 41–42, 38; Mohr, *On the Threshold of Freedom*, p. 81.

36. Berlin et al., eds., *Freedom*, Series 1, Vol 3, *Wartime Genesis of Free Labor*, pp. 41, 48; Berlin et al., eds., *Freedom*, Series 2, *Black Military Experience*, pp. 37–41; Taylor, *Remi-*

niscences of My Life in Camp, p. 41; Mohr, *On the Threshold of Freedom*, pp. 84–85; Johnson, *Black Savannah*, p. 163; *ORUCA*, Series 1, Vol. 14, pp. 377–78, 1020–21, 429–30.

37. "Your Uncle John . . . on": Myers, ed., *Children of Pride*, p. 929; "noncombatants": Pen. G. Watmough in *ORUCN*, Series 1, Vol. 13, p. 196; "inteligent . . . enemy": Court martial transcript in Berlin et al., eds., *Destruction of Slavery*, p. 785; Groover, *Sweet Land of Liberty*, pp. 45–47.

38. The petition, which includes all quotations, was signed by R. Q. Mallard, T. W. Fleming, and E. Stacy on behalf of "Committee of Citizens of 15 Dis. Lib County." See Berlin et al., eds., *Freedom*, Series 1, Vol. 1, *Destruction of Slavery*, pp. 795–98.

39. Ibid. See also *ORUCA*, Series 2, Vol. 4, p. 954.

40. "planters": Mallard, *Plantation Life Before Emancipation*, p. 45; "we must have": Joseph M. White in Berlin et al., eds., *Destruction of Slavery*, p. 700; Byrne, "Burden and Heat of the Day," pp. 323–24; Mohr, *On the Threshold of Freedom*, pp. 122–24; Bryan, *Confederate Georgia*, p. 132; Drago, *Black Politicians and Reconstruction*, p. 1.

41. Mercer Diary, Aug. 19, 1862, p. 50, GHS; "river . . . remedies": Myers, ed., *Children of Pride*, pp. 878–82; "an opportunity": planter quoted in O'Donovan, *Becoming Free in the Cotton South*, pp. 79–80. See also Jones, *American Work*, pp. 232–42.

42. "as a city": "Report of Thomas Purse, Mayor of the City of Savannah . . . 1862," p. 3; *SMN*, Jan. 8, 1863.

43. "little of the poetry": Mercer Diary, June 15, 1862, p. 40, GHS; "energetic . . . spade": C. C. Jones Jr., in Myers, ed., *Children of Pride*, p. 931; Chapter 6, Vol. 648, Medical Department, Letters Sent and Letters, Orders, and Circulars Received, General Hospital #1, Savannah, 1862–4, p. 16 (Oct. 7, 1862), RG 109. See also Myers, ed., *Children of Pride*, p. 857; CC Minutes, March 26, 1862; Byrne, "Burden and Heat of the Day," pp. 308–12. For a biography of Holcombe, see Myers, ed., *Children of Pride*, p. 1552.

44. Mayor's Report, 1862. On other city expenses, see, for example, CC Minutes for October and November, 1862.

45. C. G. Memminger, 1862 entry in Savannah Hospital Papers, Minute Book of the Board of Managers, Savannah Poor House and Hospital, GHS.

46. Henrietta Wayne to My Dear Mama H, Savannah, Feb. 24, 1863, HF Papers, DU; "nefarious . . . themselves": Mercer Diary, Nov. 21, 1862, p. 75, GHS; Myers, ed., *Children of Pride*, p. 978. See also the advertisements in the *Savannah Morning News* and the *Republican* where upcountry planters offer parcels of land for sale to refugeeing low-country planters.

47. Berlin, et al., eds., *Freedom*, Series 1, Vol. 1, *Destruction of Slavery*, pp. 31, 36, 38; "Who, then": Simms, *First Colored Baptist Church*, p. 133; "fiendish . . . population": Myers, ed., *Children of Pride*, p. 967; McPherson, *Battle Cry of Freedom*, pp. 502–505, 545, 557–58.

48. The day's proceedings were described by the Reverend Frederic Denison in *Shot and Shell*, pp. 120–27.

49. "prove . . . streams": R. Saxton in *ORUCA*, Series 1, Vol. 14, pp. 189–90; Higginson, *Army Life in a Black Regiment*, p. 33; Emilio, *Brave Black Regiment*, pp. 36–37.

50. "a number": W. T. Truxton in *ORUCN*, Series 1, Vol. 13, p. 299.

51. "their conduct" : J. H. Stimpson, ibid., p. 301; "several guns": L. West, ibid., p. 300; "Black Georgia-Born Sailors in the Union Navy"; Bullard, *Cumberland Island*, p. 138, 155–58; Mohr, *On the Threshold of Freedom*, pp. 81–82.

CHAPTER SEVEN

1. CC Minutes, Dec. 31, 1862; Simms, *First Colored Baptist Church*, pp. 134–35.

2. "the tongue . . . heaven": Simms, *First Colored Baptist Church*, p. 134; "that God . . .

proclamation": "Obituary of Rev. James Porter," *ST*, Nov. 13, 1895; Hoskins, "The Trouble They Seen," p. 30. See also Smith, *Listening to Nineteenth-Century America,* pp. 239–43.

3. "a thousand . . . sing!": Higginson, *Army Life in a Black Regiment*, p. 59.

4. "nothing": "Letters of Dr. Seth Rogers, 1862, 1863," pp. 340–41; Higginson, *Army Life in a Black Regiment*, p. 61; "not served . . . relish": Taylor, *Reminiscences of My Life in Camp*, p. 49; "Interesting from Port Royal," *NYT*, Jan. 9, 1863, p. 2. The thirty-nine-year-old Rivers was literate, and a slave, coachman, and president of an antebellum black mutual aid association in South Carolina. See Penningroth, *Claims of Kinfolk*, pp. 102–103; and Budiansky, *Bloody Shirt,* pp. 51–2.

5. "filled": Myers, ed., *Children of Pride*, p. 1007; *SR*, Jan. 1, 1863; McPherson, *Battle Cry of Freedom*, pp. 570–90.

6. "be received": quoted in John David Smith, "Let Us All Be Grateful That We Have Colored Troops That Will Fight," in Smith, ed., *Black Soldiers in Blue*, p. 1; National Park Service, "The Civil War Sailors Database," http://www.itd.nps.gov/cwss/sailors_trans.htm; Berlin et al., eds., *Freedom*, Series 2, *Black Military Experience*, pp. 1–36, 46–61; Abbott, "Massachusetts and the Recruitment of Southern Negroes," pp. 197–210; Taylor, *Reminiscences of My Life*, p. 138.

7. *SR*, Jan. 10, 1863, Jan. 3, 1863.

8. "apprehension": *SR*, Jan. 3, 1863; Fraser, *Savannah in the Old South*, p. 335. See *SR* for July 2, 1863, for advertisements for deserters, notices that cover fully one-half of the first page.

9. "safe": Savannah Police Department, Jail Register, 1862–1869, Vol. 4, GHS.

10. Hayes, ed., *DuPont Letters*, Vol. 1, pp. 306–308; "The slaves": Adams, ed., *On the Altar of Freedom*, p. 27; Drummond, *Confederate Yankee*, pp. 21–22; Thomas, *Memoirs of a Southerner*, p. 35.

11. "premium": Mohr, *On the Threshold of Freedom*, p. 182; Byrne, "Burden and Heat of the Day," pp. 318–21; Records of the Engineer Department, Chap. 3, Vol. 7 1/2, Register of Letters Received, 1861–1863, RG 109.

12. "I would": Tony Axon, Liberty County claim no. 21472, SCC; Boson Johnson, Liberty County claim no. 15505, SCC; Parsons, "Anthony Odingsells," pp. 218–19.

13. Penningroth, *Claims of Kinfolk*, p. 82; "a pretty": Georgiana Kelley, Chatham County claim no. 15586; Rachel Bromfield, Chatham County claim no. 13361; John Cuthbert, Chatham County claim no. 18096; Furgus Wilson, Camden County claim no. 15215; Moses Stikes and Binah Butler, Chatham County claim no. 17563, SCC; Johnson, *Black Savannah*, p. 162.

14. Claim of Jackson B. Sheftall, Claims Disallowed by the Commissioner of Claims, Southern Claims Commission, Records of the United States House of Representatives, 1871–1880, RG 233; Johnson, *Black Savannah*, pp. 117, 157.

15. City of Savannah, Clerk of Council, Registers of Free People of Color, Vol. 5, GHS.

16. Massey, *Refugee Life in the Confederacy*, p. 15; Myers, ed., *Children of Pride*, pp. 1529–30; "a sumptuous repast": Waring, ed., "Charles Seton Henry Hardee's Recollections of Old Savannah," pp. 34–35; Bryan, *Confederate Georgia,* p. 268; Henrietta Wayne to My Dear Mama H, Savannah, Feb. 24, 1863, HF Papers, DU.

17. "crowd . . . superiors": *SR* quoted in Green, "Theatre and Other Entertainments," pp. 103–104. See also ibid., pp. 23, 557–67; Griffin, "Savannah, Georgia, During the Civil War," pp. 238–42.

18. "Fredericksburg": Green, "Theatre and Other Entertainments," p. 557; "a bountiful": MacKethan, ed., *Recollections of a Southern Daughter*, p. 68; "grand . . . occasion": *SR*, Feb. 22, 1863; H. J. Wayne to My Dear Mother, Savannah, Jan. 14, 1863; and H. J. Wayne to My Dear Mama H, Savannah, Feb. 24, 1863, HF Papers, DU.

19. "to satisfy": Admiral S. F. DuPont, Feb. 18, 1863, *ORUCN* Series 1, Vol. 13, pp. 671–72; "that he was": J. Griffin, "Benevolence and Malevolence in Confederate Savannah," p. 355; Greenberg, "Savannah's Jewish Women and the Shaping of Ethnic and Gender Identity," pp. 765–68; Schultz, *Women at the Front*, pp. 32–44, 82–101, 118–19.

20. "acting most nobly," "we shall be ruined": Henrietta Wayne to My Dear Mama H, Savannah, Jan. 14, 1863; "grand affair . . . times": ibid., April 4, 1863, HF Papers, DU.

21. For Ehrlich, see CC Minutes, Feb. 25 and April 8, 1863; and 1860 FMC for Georgia, Chatham County, Savannah, p. 24. See also Williams and Williams, " 'Women Rising,' " pp. 49–83; "spirit . . . necessity": "Report of Savannah Mayor Thomas Holcombe . . . for the Year Ending 30th of September, 1863" (Savannah, Ga.: E. J. Purse, 1863), pp. 4–5.

22. "All indications": *SR*, Feb. 6, 1863; Mohr, *On the Threshold of Freedom*, pp. 124–25; "you may rest . . . labor": Berlin et al., eds., *Destruction of Slavery*, p. 715; D. B. Harris, April 19, 1863 in *ORUCA*, series 1, Vol. 14, p. 902.

23. "drinking . . . God of battles": Myers, ed., *Children of Pride*, pp. 1034–35; "William": ibid., p. 1022; "hopeful, cheerful words": ibid., p. 1975. See also ibid., p. 1041.

24. "loneliness": ibid., p. 1068; "sainted . . . knew": ibid., p. 1057; "I like this kind": ibid., p. 1571; Clarke, *Dwelling Place*, pp. 425–26. For a biography of Dunwody, see Myers, ed., *Children of Pride*, p. 1571.

25. Johnson, *Black Savannah*, p. 159; Simms, *First Colored Baptist Church*, p. 191.

26. "Department of Gen. Dix," *NYT*, April 25, 1863, p. 4; "An Interesting Narrative: The Story of the Fugitive Sims," *NYT*, April 26, 1863, p. 3; *New Orleans Times*, Jan. 9, 1865; "The Draft in Massachusetts," *NDI*, Aug. 1, 1863.

27. Byrne, "Burden and Heat of the Day," pp. 162, 268–69; *SMN*, April 13, 1863; Mohr, *On the Threshold of Freedom*, pp. 207–209; Savannah Police Department Jail Records, Vol. 4, GHS; CC Minutes, June 17, 1863.

28. "erect . . . free?": Higginson, *Army Life in a Black Regiment*, pp. 234–35; Denison, *Shot and Shell*, p. 210; "when de moon . . . sing": "Letters of Dr. Seth Rogers," p. 394.

29. Mohr, *On the Threshold of Freedom*, p. 85; Hahn, *Nation Under Our Feet*, pp. 92–94; Berlin et al., eds., *Black Military Experience*, pp. 40, 55, 57–60, 86, 366, 403, 406, 495, 518–19, 522–27, 535–37; Blatt, Brown, and Yacovone, eds., *Hope and Glory*.

30. Yellin, *Harriet Jacobs*, pp. 168–69; Foner, *Freedom's Lawmakers*, pp. 228–29; Robboy and Robboy, "Lewis Hayden," p. 609. For information on Richard W. White, discharged from Company D of the Fifty-fifth Massachusetts as a commissioned sergeant, see *Civil War Service Records* (Provo, Utah: Generations Network, 1999) (database online at ancestry.com).

31. "it can be": Capt. Reuben D. Mussey in Berlin et al., eds., *Black Military Experience*, p. 406; Keith Wilson, "In the Shadow of John Brown: The Military Service of Colonels Thomas Higginson, James Montgomery, and Robert Shaw in the Department of the South," in Smith, ed., *Black Soldiers in Blue*, pp. 306–35; Scharnhorst, "From Soldier to Saint," p. 309; Duncan, *Where Death and Glory Meet*; "Indian . . . Rebellion": Duncan, ed., *Blue-Eyed Child of Fortune*, pp. 339, 356. On the execution, see ibid., p. 362; and Emilio, *A Brave Black Regiment*, pp. 48–49; Looby, ed., *Complete Civil War Journal and Selected Letters of Thomas Wentworth Higginson*, pp. 158–59.

32. "meditative . . . body": Higginson, *Army Life in a Black Regiment*, pp. 78–79.

33. "that I believed . . . endurable": Ibid., pp. 97–98; Higginson, Feb. 1, 1863, in Berlin et al., eds., *Black Military Experience*, pp. 522–27; "Letters of Dr. Seth Rogers," p. 353.

34. "a negro . . . savages": W. S. Walker, April 20, 1863, *ORUCA*, Series 1, Vol. 14, p. 903; "a natural King": Higginson, *Army Life in a Black Regiment*, p. 78; Mrs. E. F. Neufville, Feb. 9, 1863, in Kollock, ed., "Letters of the Kollock and Allied Families," Pt. 4, p. 249; Hahn, *Nation Under Our Feet*, p. 95; Budiansky, *Bloody Shirt*, p. 52.

35. "he had been": "Letters of Dr. Seth Rogers," p. 369; ibid., p. 365; Berlin et al., eds., *Black Military Experience*, pp. 41, 126–27.

36. Campbell, *Sufferings of the Rev. T. G. Campbell*; Johnson, *Black Savannah*, p. 163; Fraser, *Savannah in the Old South*, pp. 328–29.

37. "to organize": Duncan, *Freedom's Shore*, p. 16; Rose, *Rehearsal for Reconstruction*.

38. "nearly all": Taylor, *Reminiscences of My Life in Camp*, p. 52; Hahn, *Nation Under Our Feet*, pp. 91–92, 113; Jones, *American Work*, pp. 286–96; Higginson, *Army Life in a Black Regiment*, p. 120; "he would": "Letters of Dr. Seth Rogers," p. 346; Clinton, ed., *Reminiscences of My Life in Camp*, pp. xxi–xxii.

39. Higginson, *Army Life in a Black Regiment*, p. 120; Taylor, *Reminiscences of My Life in Camp*, pp. 55–86; "these . . . men": Duncan, ed., *Blue-Eyed Child of Fortune*, p. 351; "pretty": Shaw quoted in Emilio, *Brave Black Regiment*, p. 42; Burchard, *One Gallant Rush*, pp. 102–13.

40. "this was": quoted in Emilio, *Brave Black Regiment*, p. 42. See also Burchard, *One Gallant Rush*, p. 108.

41. "stink . . . ground": Adams, ed., *On the Altar of Freedom*, p. 30; "upon unarmed . . . valor": "The War in Georgia: The Destruction of Darien," *NYT*, June 28, 1863, p. 2; David Demus (Co. K, 54th Massachusetts) to Mary Jane Demus, June 18, 1863, Demus and Christy Family Letters, The Valley of the Shadow, http://valley.vcdh.virginia.edu/personalpapers/collections/franklin/demus.html.

42. On the controversy, see Duncan, *Where Death and Glory Meet*, pp. 92–99; Coulter, "Robert Gould Shaw and the Burning of Darien, Georgia," pp. 363–73; "from their fatal": *Republican* quoted in Coopersmith, *Fighting Words*, pp. 149–50. On the "narrative" of David, see Mercer Diary, Feb. 25, 1863, p. 85, GHS; White and White, *Sounds of Slavery*, pp. 72–80.

43. "fiendish": Mercer Diary, June 17, 1863, p. 114b, GHS; "the mercy": Moore, ed., *Rebellion Record: A Diary of American Events*, Vol. 6, p. 195.

44. "perfectly": Shaw quoted in Duncan, *Where Death and Glory Meet*, pp. 98–99; "children . . . lived": "Letters of Dr. Seth Rogers," p. 338; "the proclamation": Higginson, *Army Life in a Black Regiment*, p. 108; "the world's": ibid., p. 51.

45. "gunboat fund": Myers, ed., *Children of Pride*, p. 867; Mercer Diary, June 17, 1863, p. 113, GHS.

46. McPherson, *Battle Cry of Freedom*, pp. 653–63; Habersham, *Ebb Tide*, p. 34.

47. "You say you will": Lincoln quoted in McPherson, *Battle Cry of Freedom*, pp. 686–87; "We have": Emilio, *Brave Black Regiment*, pp. 102–103; Wise, *Gate of Hell*.

48. "sentimental . . . states": Kemble quoted in Dusinberre, *Them Dark Days*, pp. 224–25; "there is nothing": Bell, *Major Butler's Legacy*, p. 378; Clinton, *Fanny Kemble's Civil Wars*, pp. 178–79.

49. Bell, *Major Butler's Legacy*, pp. 492–93.

CHAPTER EIGHT

1. CC Minutes, June 3, 1863, July 15, 1863; "grasping along": ibid., Oct. 7, 1863; "defenseless": ibid., July 20, 1863; *SR*, July 1, 1863.

2. MacKethan, ed., *Recollections of a Southern Daughter*, pp. 64–67; Myers, ed., *Children of Pride*, p. 984; Conrad, "Reminiscences of a Southern Woman," Pt. 5, p. 409; "unadulterated . . . income": *SMN*, April 2, 1863; Surgeon General circular, April. 2, 1862, Ch. 6, Vol. 648, Medical Department, Letters Sent and Letters, Orders, and Circulars Received, General Hospital No. 1, Savannah, 1864; Records of the Engineer Department, p. 2, RG 109; Schwartz, *Birthing a Slave*, p. 291; *SR*, July 2, 1863.

3. Wright, "Letters of the Bishop of Savannah," pp. 103–105.

4. "stampedes": Myers, ed., *Children of Pride*, p. 1137; "he has quite": ibid., p. 1100. See also ibid., pp. 1109, 1611.

5. Ibid., pp. 1104, 1114, 1199, 1506–7.

6. "There is Mr. Lewis . . . Yankees": quoted in Dusinberre, *Them Dark Days*, pp. 166–67.

7. Myers, ed., *Children of Pride*, p. 1545; Griffin, "Benevolence and Malevolence in Confederate Savannah," pp. 363–64; "as the quest": CC Minutes, Oct. 29, 1863; "for I detest": Henry Graves in Lane, ed., *"Dear Mother: Don't Grieve About Me,"* p. 278; *SMN*, Oct. 31, Nov. 2, 1863; Parks, *Joseph E. Brown of Georgia,* p. 252.

8. Denison, *Shot and Shell*, pp. 210–11.

9. Ibid., p. 213. On minstrel shows in the antebellum North, see David Roediger, *The Wages of Whiteness: Race and the Making of the American Working Class* (London: Verso, 1999); and Eric Lott, *Love and Theft: Blackface Minstrelsy and the American Working Class* (New York: Oxford University Press, 1993).

10. Dennison, *Shot and Shell*, pp. 208–209. On whites' responses to African-American religious-musical forms, see White and White, *Sounds of Slavery*, pp. 30–37, 97–144.

11. Ibid., pp. 213, 223; "He will have": Berlin et al., eds., *Black Military Experience*, p. 364.

12. James C. Beecher in Berlin et al., eds., *Black Military Experience*, p. 493. See also ibid, p. 633.

13. James Henry Gooding in ibid., pp. 385–86; Adams, ed., *On the Altar of Freedom*, pp. 117–24.

14. Ibid., pp. 392–93; Hayes, ed., *DuPont Letters*, p. 20n; Donald Yacovone, "The Fifty-fourth Massachusetts Regiment, the Pay Crisis, and the 'Lincoln Despotism,' " in Blatt et al., eds., *Hope and Glory*, pp. 35–51.

15. "It is not": Higginson, *Army Life in a Black Regiment,* p. 268; Berlin et al., eds., *Black Military Experience,* pp. 366–67; Emilio, *Brave Black Regiment,* p. 49.

16. "daring": "Department of the South," *NYT*, May 8, 1864, p. 8; Williams and Williams, " 'Women Rising,' " pp. 76–77; CC Minutes, April 20, 1864.

17. Williams and Williams, " 'Women Rising,' " p. 56; "the hardy wayworn . . . inheritance": Joseph E. Brown to Major General Howell Cobb, May 20, 1864, in Candler, ed., *Confederate Records of Georgia*, Vol. 3, p. 545.

18. Andrews, *Footprints of a Regiment,* "mob". CC Minutes, April 20, 1864, "free market". *SR*, April 22, 1864; Mercer Diary, Nov. 21, 1862, p. 75, GHS.

19. Adams, ed., *On the Altar of Freedom*, p. xxxi.

20. Marvel, *Andersonville*, pp. 176, 204–206; Ruhlman, *Captain Henry Wirz*, pp. 147–50; "the ghastly": Clarke, *Dwelling Place*, p. 426; Walker, *Hell's Broke Loose in Georgia*.

21. Fraser, *Savannah in the Old South,* pp. 336–37; "There must be": *ORUCA*, Series 2, Vol. 7, p. 788; "Level as a pancake": Schmitt, "Prisoner of War," p. 90; Griffin, "Benevolence and Malevolence," pp. 365–66.

22. "They seemed": Abbott, *Prison Life in the South*, p. 86; "ride past . . . help the prisoners": Georgiana Kelley, Chatham County claim no. 15586, SCC. See also Rachel Bromfield, Chatham County claim no. 13361; and Judy Rose, Chatham County claim no. 15867, SCC.

23. "citizens": Kelley, *What I Saw and Suffered in Rebel Prisons*, pp. 73–75, 81; "between 500": Andrews, *Footprints of a Regiment*, p. 150. See also *SR,* Nov. 14, 1864; Fraser, *Savannah in the Old South*, pp. 336–37.

24. Abbott, *Prison Life*, p. 100; "You may know": Andrews, *Footprints of a Regiment*, p. 151; "While we ought": ibid., p. 149; Jeremy F. Gilmer to Mrs. J. F. Gilmer, Nov. 17, 1864, JFG Papers, SHC.

25. "We is all . . . us": Abbott, *Prison Life in the South*, p. 96; "a genuine German . . . man": Schmitt, "Prisoner of War," p. 91. Smedborg was probably James R. Smedburg, 30, an iron and brass founder born in New York, married with a wife born in Connecticut. He

enlisted in Company G, First Infantry Regiment, Georgia, in April 1862. See Historical Data Systems, comp., *American Civil War Soldiers* (database online at ancestry.com); Genealogical Committee of the Georgia Historical Society, comp., *1860 Census of Chatham County, Georgia,* p. 345.

26. "the disorder": Schmitt, "Prisoner of War," p. 92; Young, "Two Years at Fort Bartow," pp. 253-64.

27. Bailey, *War and Ruin,* p. 21; "Started early": Clark, ed., *Downing's Civil War Diary,* p. 229.

28. "awake": *SR,* July 27, 1864; "indicated . . . alarmed": *SR,* Dec. 1, 1864; "not absolutely . . . number": *SR,* Dec. 19, 1864; "The wines": Shryock, ed., *Letters of Richard D. Arnold,* p. 112; "From Atlanta to Savannah," p. 192.

29. "permanent": Joseph E. Brown to General Assembly, Nov. 10, 1864, Candler, ed., *Confederate Records of Georgia,* Vol. 2, pp. 781–82; "to increase . . . reward": *SMN,* Dec. 10, 1864.

30. McPherson, *Battle Cry of Freedom,* pp. 804–805; "Nothing has changed": Davis quoted in ibid., p. 806.

31. For overviews, see, for example, Bailey, *War and Reunion;* Kennett, *Marching Through Georgia.*

32. "merry": "From Atlanta to Savannah," p. 189; "one big picknick": Osborn, ed., "Sherman's March Through Georgia," p. 326; Padgett, ed., "With Sherman Through Georgia and the Carolinas," p. 55; "John Van Duser Diary of Sherman's March from Atlanta to Hilton Head," p. 229; Wills, *Army Life of an Illinois Soldier;* Bradley, *Star Corps;* "The Great March," *NYT,* Dec. 20, 1864, p. 3.

33. "fleeing": Joseph Addison Turner quoted in Huff, ed., " 'A Bitter Draught We Have Had to Quaff," p. 324; "percimmon Beer": Black, ed., "Marching with Sherman Through Georgia and the Carolinas," p. 455; "Big men": Bradley, *Star Corps,* p. 186; "The people . . . you": *SR,* Sept. 14, 1864; Padgett, ed., "With Sherman Through Georgia," p. 59; Bryan, ed., "Georgia Woman's Civil War Diary," pp. 201–203; Carter, ed., *Diary of Dolly Lunt Burge,* pp. 158–64; Parks, *Joseph E. Brown of Georgia,* pp. 314–15.

34. *ORUCA,* Series 1, Vol. 44, pp. 68–330; Padgett, ed., "With Sherman Through Georgia," p. 61; Grimsley, *Hard Hand of War,* pp. 190–204; Howard, *Autobiography,* Vol. 2, pp. 86–100; Gray, "March to the Sea," pp. 111–38; Harden, *Recollections of a Long and Satisfactory Life,* pp. 119–20.

35. "I must have": Fellman, *Citizen Sherman,* p. 158; "O, we are all": Bradley, *Star Corps,* p. 187; Wells, *Army Life of an Illinois Soldier,* p. 332; H. W. Slocum, Jan. 9, 1865, *ORUCA,* Series 1, vol. 44, p. 159; Bailey, *War and Ruin,* pp. 93–95; Mohr, *On the Threshold of Freedom,* pp. 90–91; Padgett, ed., "With Sherman Through Georgia," p. 61; "John Van Duser Diary," pp. 234–35. See also Clarence L. Mohr, "The Atlanta Campaign and the African American Experience in Civil War Georgia," in Gordon and Inscoe, *Inside the Confederate Nation,* pp. 272–94.

36. Bailey, *War and Ruin,* pp. 92–95; "hellish slaughter . . . troops": Athearn, ed., "An Indiana Doctor Marches with Sherman," p. 419; Angle, ed., *Three Years in the Army of the Cumberland,* pp. 352–55; "was not": Sherman, *Memoirs,* p. 725.

37. "The Darkies": Winther, ed., *With Sherman to the Sea,* p. 136. For accounts of Sherman's army, see the interviews with elderly black men and women in the 1930s: Rawick, ed., *The American Slave,* Vol. 12, *Ga. Narrs.,* Pt. 1, pp. 247–48, 343–44; Pt. 2, pp. 112–13; Supp. Series 1, Vol. 3, *Ga. Narrs.,* Pt. 1, pp. 162–63; Vol. 4, *Ga. Narrs.,* Pt. 2, p. 401.

38. "They all seem": Bradley, *Star Corps,* p. 188; MacKethan, ed., *Recollections of a Southern Daughter,* pp. 71–72; "who had pointed . . . plunder": Coffin, *Four Years of Fighting,* p. 399; Clarke, *Dwelling Place,* p. 433; Hargis, "For the Love of Place," p. 833.

39. Sherman, *Memoirs*, pp. 671–80; Smith, *Slavery and Rice Cultivation in Low Country Georgia*, p. 219; "a bright-looking . . . existed": Quaife, ed., *From the Cannon's Mouth*, pp. 370-71; "I have been": see, for example, Cato Keating, Chatham County claim no. 20689, SCC. See also Brown, *"Our Connection with Savannah,"* p. 17.

40. "the darkies": *Diary of E. P. Burton, Surgeon*, p. 47; "robbed servant": Mallard, *Plantation Life Before Emancipation,* p. 210; "I rejoiced": Tony Axon, Liberty County claim no. 21472, SCC. See also other Liberty County claims, SCC; Berlin et al., eds., *Destruction of Slavery*, Series 1, Vol. 1, pp. 143-54; Penningroth, *Claims of Kinfolk*, pp. 69–78.

41. Myers, ed., *Children of Pride*—the quotes are on pp. 1237 and 1242; "From Atlanta to Savannah," see pp. 1220–48. For an example of scholars who share Jones's outrage, see George A. Rogers and R. F. Saunders Jr., "The Scourge of Sherman's Man in Liberty County, Georgia," *GHQ* 60 (Winter 1976): 356–69.

42. *ORUCA*, Series 1, Vol. 44, p. 71; "Savannah almost": Howard, *Autobiography*, Vol. 2, p. 94; "impenetrable": F. H. West, Dec. 29, 1864, *ORUCA*, Series 1, Vol. 44, p. 268; Padgett, ed., "With Sherman Through Georgia," pp. 61–62; Bauer, ed., *Soldiering*, pp. 197–98; Wills, *Army Life of an Illinois Soldier*, pp. 334-35.

43. "Tho' compelled": Hughes, *General William J. Hardee*, p. 270; Hughes, "Hardee's Defense of Savannah," pp. 43–67; "Doors . . . longer": Andrews, *Footprints of a Regiment*, pp. 154–55; Waring, ed., "Charles Seton Henry Hardee's Recollections of Old Savannah," pp. 20–24; Robert Walker Groves, "Beaulieu Plantation," *GHQ* 37 (1953): 207; "Savannah Ours," *NYT*, Dec. 26, 1864, p. 1; "Further Details," *NYT*, Dec. 28, 1864, p. 1; "From Savannah," *NYT*, Jan. 2, 1865, p. 1; Fraser, *Savannah in the Old South*, p. 339.

44. "hastily": John W. Geary, Jan. 6, 1865, *ORUCA*, Series 1, Vol. 44, p. 279; "secure": Lee and Agnew, *Historical Record of the City of Savannah*, p. 96.

45. "before the sun": John W. Geary, Jan. 6, 1865, *ORUCA*, Series 1, Vol. 44, p. 281; Lee and Agnew, *Historical Record*, pp. 96–97; Angle, ed., *Three Years in the Army of the Cumberland*, p. 368.

46. "Ben Graham," in Blassingame, ed., *Slave Testimony*, p. 636.

47. "this beautiful": Geary quoted in Lee and Agnew, *Historical Record*, p. 97; "had come": Simms, *First Colored Baptist Church*, p. 137; Quaife, ed., *From the Cannon's Mouth,* p. 370; *Harper's Weekly*, Jan. 14, 1865.

48. "in which I": John Geary, Jan. 6, 1865, *ORUCA*, p. 280; "From Atlanta to Savannah," p. 198.

49. "the poor": Conyngham, *Sherman's March Through the South*, p. 293; "I beg to present": Sherman, *Memoirs*, p. 711.

50. "A constant stream . . . you": Howe, ed., *Marching with Sherman*, p. 202; "to pay . . . come": Simms, *First Colored Baptist Church*, p. 202; "Further Details," *NYT*, Dec. 28, 1864, p. 1; Sherman, *Memoirs*, pp. 646–723.

51. "theatre": Hight, *History of the Fifty-eighth Regiment of Indiana Volunteer Infantry*, p. 251; "big showing": Clark, ed., *Downing's Civil War Diary*, p. 242; "spectacle": Angle, ed., *Three Years in the Army of the Cumberland*, p. 370. "I went": Georgiana Kelley, Chatham County claim no. 15586, SCC.

52. "My first duty": Sherman, *Memoirs*, p. 677; "Families . . . organization": ibid., pp. 713–14; "a blessing . . . order": Thomas, *Memoirs of a Southerner*, p. 53; "Victory! Sherman at Savannah," *NYT*, Dec. 19, 1864, p. 1.

53. "at least humble": Padgett, ed., "With Sherman Through Georgia," p. 62; "and mutual": "The Moral Aspect in Georgia," *NYT*, Dec. 31, 1864, p. 4; "wise, so far": William T. Sherman, Dec. 31, 1864, *ORUCA*, Series 1, Vol. 44, p. 842; "that laying aside": Lee and Agnew, *Historical Record*, p. 99.

CHAPTER NINE

1. "army . . . army": W. T. Richardson to M. E. Strieby, Savannah, Jan. 2, 1865, AMA Archives. Available on microfilm, the AMA letters are arranged chronologically, by state of origin. See also Hoskins, *Out of Yamacraw and Beyond*, p. 12.

For other accounts of the children's march and the new use of the Old Bryan Slave Mart, see Coffin, *Four Years of Fighting*, p. 435; Trowbridge, *The Desolate South*, pp. 271–72; Wright, *Brief Historical Sketch of Negro Education in Georgia*, p. 18; "From Savannah," *Anglo-African*, Feb. 11, 1865.

2. "All de rebel . . . hers": Howard, *In and Out of the Lines*, pp. 204, 194; "leaving": Caroline A. N. Lamar, quoted in Byrne, " 'Uncle Billy' Sherman Comes to Town," p. 94; Howard, *Autobiography of Oliver Otis Howard*, Vol. 2, p. 189; "going home": J. W. Alvord, "Negro Industry," *AM* (Nov. 1865): 248; "This was my home . . . It": Coffin, *Four Years*, p. 415; Smith, *Listening to Nineteenth-Century America*, pp. 230–43.

3. Chittenden, *Personal Reminiscences*, pp. 260–61; Myers, ed., *Children of Pride*, pp. 1238–47; Cato Keating, Chatham County claim no. 20689; "after the army": Moses Stikes and Binah Butler, Chatham County claim no. 17563; "you can look": Georgiana Kelley, Chatham County claim no. 15586, SCC; Jackson B. Sheftall, Report no. 9, Office 623, Records of the United States House of Representatives, 1871–1880, Claims Disallowed by Commissioners of Claims, RG 233; E. C. Anderson to Dearest Sarah, Charleston, S.C., January 11, 1865, ECA Papers, SHC.

4. Howard, *In and Out of the Lines*, p. 208; Powers, *Afoot and Alone*, p. 51; Lee and Agnew, *Historical Record of the City of Savannah*, p. 133.

5. "miserable": Gatell, ed., "A Yankee Views the Agony of Savannah [John M. Glidden]," pp. 429–31; Carter, *When the War Was Over*, p. 137; DeCredico, *Patriotism for Profit*, pp. 115–21; W. T. Sherman, Savannah, Dec. 31, 1864, in *ORUCA*, Series 1, Vol. 44, p. 843; Nichols, *Story of the Great March*, p. 105.

6. "interesting . . . uninitiated": *Anglo-African*, Jan. 28, 1865; "General Order No. 2 [Dec. 24, 1864]": *SR*, Jan. 4, 1865. The ward committees are listed in *SR*, Jan. 4, 1865. For an overview of the U.S. Army occupation of the city between December 1864 and June 1865, see Griffin, "Savannah, Georgia, During the Civil War," pp. 276–99.

7. "Blow ye": Pepper, *Personal Recollections of Sherman's Campaigns*, p. 290; Coffin, *Four Years*, p. 21; "he wanted": W. T. Richards to M. E. Strieby, Savannah, Jan. 2, 1865, AMA Archives.

8. "a *grand rush*": W. T. Richardson to M. E. Strieby, Savannah, Jan. 2, 1865; W. T. Richards to M. E. Strieby, Savannah, Jan. 10, 1865, AMA Archives; "General Sherman and the Freedmen," *FR* 1 (March 1865): 33; "Schools in Savannah, Ga.," *FR* 1 (May 1865): 72; Hoskins, "The Trouble They Seen," p. 30; "Colored Free Schools," *NF* (July 1865): 197–98; "Rev. James Porter," *ST*, Nov. 13, 1895; Williams, *Self-Taught*. See also Butchart, *Northern Schools, Southern Blacks, and Reconstruction*.

9. *FR* 1 (Dec. 1865): 203; *FR* 2 (Jan. 1866): 15; James Lynch, "Highly Important from Georgia," *Christian Register* (Feb. 4, 1865): 1; "From Savannah," *Anglo-African*, Feb. 11, 1865; Gaines, *African Methodism in the South*, pp. 5–6. Gaines reports that Lynch made "secret arrangements . . . to take out the church" (p. 5).

10. "all moved": Simms, *First Colored Baptist Church*, pp. 134, 135–36, 190–92; Thomas, *First African Baptist Church of North America*, pp. 77–81. Hoskins gives the title of Simms's talk in "The Trouble They Seen," p. 31. See also "Letter from W. C. Gannett," *FR* 1 (June 1865): 92; Drago, *Black Politicians*; Holt, "Georgia Carpetbaggers," pp. 72–86.

11. "jealous . . . exclusiveness": S. W. Magill to AMA, Savannah, Feb. 3, 1865; "spirit": report of S. W. Magill, June 1865, AMA Archives; "rather peculiar": "Letter from W. C.

Gannett," *FR* 1 (June 1865): 92; Butchart, *Northern Schools, Southern Blacks, and Reconstruction*, pp. 173–75.

12. For a transcript, see Berlin et al., eds., *Freedom*, Series 1, Vol. 3, *Wartime Genesis of Free Labor*, pp. 332–38; Howard, *Autobiography*, Vol. 2, pp. 189–93; "should have": Sherman, *Memoirs*, pp. 723–32.

13. "The way . . . freedom": Berlin et al., eds., *Freedom*, Series 1, Vol. 3, *Wartime Genesis of Free Labor*, pp. 334–35.

14. For the order, see ibid., pp. 338–40. See also Cimbala, *Under the Guardianship of the Nation*, pp. 166–92.

15. "all unemployed": *SR*, Jan. 4, 1865; Boyle, *Soldiers True*, pp. 508–509; Byrne, " 'Uncle Billy' Sherman Comes to Town"; Andrews, *South Since the War*, p. 382; Mansfield French to J. B. Stedman, Augusta, Sept. 5, 1865, AMA Archives; H. H. Hine to C. C. Sibley, Savannah, March 24, 1867, Letters Received, Reel 15, S1040 BRFAL-GA (M798), RG 105. See also House Executive Documents, 39th Congress, 1st sess., no. 70 (serial 1256), p. 348; Shaffer, *After the Glory*, pp. 23–24, 120.

16. "a serious": Boyle, *Soldiers True*, p. 508; "old men": Pearson, ed., *Letters from Port Royal*, p. 508; "The Freedmen of Georgia," *FR* 1 (Feb. 1865): 26; Schwalm, *A Hard Fight for We*, pp. 125–26.

17. "left on our hands": Boyle, *Soldiers True*, pp. 508–509; "the young . . . President": Berlin et al., eds., *Freedom*, Series 1, Vol. 3, *Wartime Genesis of Free Labor*, pp. 338–39. See also Cimbala, *Under the Guardianship of the Nation,* pp. 166–92. See also Oubre, *Forty Acres and a Mule*, pp. 46–71.

18. CC Minutes, April 4, 1866; Dyer, "Northern Relief for Savannah During Sherman's Occupation," pp. 457–72; Lee and Agnew, *Historical Record of the City of Savannah*, pp. 100–101; Chittenden, *Personal Reminiscences*, pp. 548–49; "Affairs in Savannah," *NYT*, Jan. 15, 1865, p. 1; Byrne, " 'Uncle Billy' Sherman Comes to Town," p. 100; Dyer, "Northern Relief"; CC Minutes, Jan. 25, 1865.

19. Smith, "Cotton from Savannah in 1865," pp. 495–512; "The North": H. O. Briggs and Henry D. Hyde to Richard D. Arnold, Boston, March 8, 1865, RDA Papers, SHC; CC Minutes, March 3, 1865.

20. "the cradle . . . bond": "Savannah and Boston: Account of the Supplies Sent to Savannah" (Boston, 1865), pp. 30–31; Shryock, ed., *Letters of Richard D. Arnold*, p. 119; "conquered city . . . hope": *ORUCA*, Series 1, Vol. 47, pp. 166–68.

21. Coffin, *Four Years of Fighting*, pp. 406–407, 417.

22. Ibid., pp. 418–19; Lee and Agnew, *Historical Record of the City of Savannah*, p. 101; Gatell, ed., "A Yankee Views the Agony of Savannah," p. 431; Chittenden, *Personal Reminiscences*, p. 363; Howard, *In and Out of the Lines*, p. 200.

23. *SDH*, Jan. 2, 1865; *SR*, Jan. 4, 1865; "fire-eating": *SDH*, Jan. 11, 1865; Talmadge, "Savannah's Yankee Newspapers," pp. 66–73; *SR*, Jan. 2, 1865; "the . . . music": Pepper, *Personal Recollections*, pp. 288–89; Connolly, *Three Years in the Army of the Cumberland*, p. 371; Abbott, "Republican Party Press in Reconstruction Georgia, 1867–1874," p. 726.

24. "an emblem": Pepper, *Personal Recollections*, p. 286; Thomas, *Memoirs of a Southerner*, pp. 53–54; Howard, *In and Out of the Lines*, pp. 192, 204.

25. "black garments . . . humiliation": Mercer Diary, June 11, 1865, p. 231, GHS; *SR* Dec. 18, 1865; Hight, *History of the Fifty-eighth Regiment of Indiana Volunteer Infantry*, p. 456; *SDH*, Feb. 5, 1865; "Sherman's Occupation of Savannah: Two Letters," pp. 109–14; Edward C. Anderson to Dearest Sarah, Charleston, Jan. 2, 1865, ECA Papers, SHC. On the damage done to the Catholic cemetery by fortification workers, see the correspondence between Maj. Gen. Gillmore and Bishop Augustin Verot in *ORUCA*, Series 1, vol. 47, pp. 202–205; "From Atlanta to Savannah," p. 199 and n. 18.

26. "I hear": H. B. to John Screven, Augusta, April 15, 1865, ASF Papers, SHC; "Northern energy . . . statesman": Shryock, ed., *Letters of Richard D. Arnold*, pp. 124, 116–17.

27. "whoever would": Avary, *Dixie After the War*, p. 155; "Good God. . . . dollars": Howard, *In and Out of the Lines*, pp. 180, 182, 183, 185, 186; Aunt L. to Lou [Mrs. J. F. Gilmer], Savannah, Jan. 10, 1865, JFG Papers, SHC. See also King, "Fanny Cohen's Journal of Sherman's Occupation of Savannah," pp. 415–16.

28. "Long habits . . . fidelity": "Memoranda on the Civil War [letter from Gen. Robert E. Lee to Rep. Andrew Hunter, Jan. 11, 1865]," *Century Magazine* 36, New Series, 14 (1888): 600–601; McPherson, *Battle Cry of Freedom*, pp. 807–30; H. B. to John Screven, Savannah, April 15, 1865, ASF Papers, SHC.

29. McPherson, *Battle Cry of Freedom*, pp. 819–30; Campbell, *When Sherman Marched North from the Sea*.

30. "I want . . . coast": "Georgia: The Bone and Sinew of the South," *NF* 1 (April 1, 1865): 82–83; Hoskins, *Out of Yamacraw*, p. 51; "Register of Land Titles: Skidaway Island," Reel 36, BRFAL-GA (M798); Coffin, *Four Years of Fighting*, p. 425; Hoskins, "The Trouble They Seen," p. 28.

31. "What a glorious . . . earth": "Georgia," *AM* (June 1865): 123. On the northern teachers, see Jones, *Soldiers of Light and Love*; Ronald E. Butchart, "Perspectives on Gender, Race, Calling, and Commitment in Nineteenth-Century America," pp. 15–32.

32. "to do something": Sarah A. Jenness to George Whipple, Andover, Mass., July 1, 1864; "who consider": Phoebe F. McKean to George Whipple, Andover, Mass., Dec. 10, 1864; Mary K. Colburn to M. E. Strieby, Worcester, Mass., Dec. 24, 1864; "the runaway": Harriet C. Bullard to M. E. Strieby, Boston, Mass., May 1864; "an intemperate man": Rev. John L. Grover, testimonial, May 1864, AMA Archives.

33. "intelligence": F. E. Miner to M. E. Strieby, Manchester, N.H., Aug. 2, 1864; "playing cards . . . unaware": S. W. Magill to AMA, Savannah, April 5, 1865, AMA Archives.

34. All quotes from "Georgia," *AM* (July 1865): 159–60.

35. "radically": S. W. Magill to AMA Secretaries, Savannah, to AMA, Feb. 2, 1865; "jealous . . . wishes": S. W. Magill to AMA Secretaries, Savannah, Feb. 26, 1865; "discriminated": S. W. Magill to AMA Secretaries, Savannah, Feb. 6, 1865, AMA Archives.

36. Taylor, *Reminiscences of My Life in Camp*, pp. 108, 90–91; "Prejudice": W. T. Sherman, Savannah, Dec. 31, 1864, *ORUCA*, Series 1, Vol. 44, p. 841; Byrne, " 'Uncle Billy' Sherman Comes to Town," pp. 107–108; "the glitter . . . evil": Letter to the editor of the *National Intelligencer*, Jan. 6, 1866, in House Executive Docs., 39th Cong., 1st sess., no. 70 (serial 1256), pp. 348, 352; "black": Powers, *Afoot and Alone*, p. 52; Shaffer, *After the Glory*, pp. 24–26.

37. "one evening": Conrad, "Reminiscences of a Southern Woman," Pt. 5, p. 410; Howard, *In and Out of the Lines*, pp. 204, 211; *SR*, June 12, 1865; "in a perfectly": *SDH*, June 16, 1865; Stiles, *Marse George*, p. 18; H. B. to John Screven, Augusta, April 15, 1865, ASF Papers, SHC.

38. *SDH*, March 18, 1865; Ira Pettibone to W. E. Whiting, Feb. 22, 1865, AMA Archives; George Crabtree to W. W. Deane, Brunswick, July 25, 1866, Unregistered Letters Received, Reel 25, BRFAL-GA (M798); Houston et al. to Gillmore, Department of the South, series 4109, Letters Received (H-153 1865), RG 393, Records of United States Army Continental Commands, NA (FSSP C-1342).

39. Houston et al. to Gillmore (see previous note); Savannah Poor House and Hospital Minute Book of Board of Managers, Savannah Hospital Papers, GHS.

40. "will do much": McPherson, *Battle Cry of Freedom*, p. 849; "grand review . . . place": *SDH*, April 11, 1865; Shaffer, *After the Glory*, p. 18.

41. Simms, *First Colored Baptist Church*, pp. 139–40.

42. Myers, ed., *Children of Pride*, p. 1268. See the brief biography of Charles Lamar in ibid., p. 1588; Father to Mrs. J. F. Gilmer, Richmond, Virginia, Jan. 20, 1865, JFG Papers, SHC.

43. "a universal": *SR*, April 24, 1865; Dyer, *Secret Yankees*, pp. 221–23.

44. "We claim . . . citizens": testimony of Simms, "Proceedings of a Military Board . . . May 8, 1865" in response to Houston et al. to Gillmore, Department of the South, Series 4109, Letters Received, RG 393, Records of United States Army Continental Commands, National Archives (H-163 1865) (FSSP C-1342); "*horror*": *SDH*, April 24, 1865; "this eaten-out country": Myers, ed., *Children of Pride*, p. 1263.

45. Diary of Joseph Frederick Waring, April 30, 1865, JFW Papers, GHS; "the speediest": *SDH*, May 10, 1865; "repeated . . . anarchy": *ORUCA*, Series 1, vol. 47, p. 595; "his looks": Shryock, ed., *Letters of Richard D. Arnold*, p. 122; Foner, *Reconstruction*, pp. 180-83; "If Johnson": Isham Harris quoted in Carter, *When the War Was Over*, p. 24.

CHAPTER TEN

1. Nieman, *To Set the Law in Motion*; Duncan, *Freedom's Shore*, pp. 20–29; Hardy Mobley to George Whipple, Savannah, Jan. 16, 1866, AMA Archives; "labor for": *AM* (April 1865): 90. For a theoretical perspective on "foreign founders," see Honig, *Democracy and the Foreigner*.

2. Duncan, *Freedom's Shore*, pp. 20–29; Cimbala, *Under the Guardianship of the Nation*, pp. 166–93.

3. Campbell, *Hotel Keepers, Head Waiters and Housekeepers' Guide*, pp. 8–10; Campbell, *Sufferings of the Rev. T. G. Campbell*, pp. 7–8; "the people": "Georgia: Sapolow Island," *NF* (June 1, 1865): 149; Duncan, *Freedom's Shore*, pp. 26–28; Cimbala, *Under the Guardianship of the Nation*, pp. 31, 50, 178.

4. "unpaid . . . leaves": "A List of Planters in Southern Georgia Who Have Sent Away the Freedmen Unpaid, to the Islands," FB, GHS.

5. "a good horse . . . to do": T. G. Campbell to A. P. Ketchum, Saint Catherines North End, June 2, 1865; "the facts": T. G. Campbell to A. P. Ketchum, Saint Catherines North End, July 17, 1865, FB, GHS.

6. Leigh, *Ten Years on a Georgia Plantation Since the War*, pp. 9–10; "most of us": Dora Roberts interview, in Rawick, ed., *American Slave*, Vol. 13: *Ga. Narrs.*, Pt. 4, p. 208; Powers, *Afoot and Alone*, pp. 61–62; Litwack, *Been in the Storm So Long*; "anarchy": Myers, ed., *Children of Pride*, p. 1247; Hoffman, "From Slavery to Self-Reliance," pp. 8-42; Jones, *The Dispossessed*, pp. 13–44.

7. Copy of Tillson speech dated Oct. 27, 1865, with letter from Armand Lefils to Davis Tillson, McIntosh County, Dec. 10, 1865, Unregistered Letters Received, Reel 24, BRFAL-GA (M798).

8. "a goodly number": Thomas, *Memoirs of a Southerner*, p. 57; Stiles, *Marse George*, p. 19; "not injured . . . property": Kollock, ed., "Letters of the Kollock and Allied Families," Pt. 5, pp. 317–18; Savannah Unit, Georgia Writers' Project, "Whitehall Plantation," Pt. 3, *GHQ* 26 (June 1942): 140.

9. Samuel Boles to Birge, June 16, 1865, Savannah, Subassistant Commissioner, Series 1022: Records of the Assistant Adjutant General Relating to the Restoration of Property in the Savannah Area, RG 105. Document reproduced in Hahn et al., eds., *Freedom*, Series 3, vol. 1: *Land and Labor, 1865*.

10. "engaged": Joseph Manigault to H. F. Sickles, Savannah, Dec. 16, 1865, FB, GHS; "a good many . . . force": Mahaffey, ed., "Carl Schurz's Letters from the South," p. 253; Morgan, "Work and Culture," p. 596; Nelson Bronson to W. W. Deane, Savannah,

May 11, 1866; John C. Dickson to "Gen," Sapelo Island, Sept. 22, 1866, Unregistered Letters Received, Reel 25, BFRAL-GA (M798).

11. Simms, *First Colored Baptist Church*, pp. 141–42.

12. "preparing": Hardy Mobley to S. S. Jocelyn, Savannah, June 30, 1865; "freedom . . . attack": E. A. Cooley to Samuel Hunt, Nov. 3, 1865, AMA Archives; Richardson, " 'Labor Is Rest to Me Here in the Lord's Vineyard,' " pp. 7–9; Richardson, "Failure of the American Missionary Association," pp. 261–83.

13. "asking for . . . side": *SR*, July 26, 1865; *SR*, June 1, 1865; *SMN* June 1, 1865; Drago, *Black Politicians*; Cimbala, *Under the Guardianship of the Nation*, pp. 67, 69, 97, 113, 212; Matthews, "Negro Republicans in the Reconstruction of Georgia," pp. 145–49; Cason, "Loyal League in Georgia," pp. 126–53.

14. *SDH*, June 1, 1865, Oct. 4, 1865; Abbott, "Republican Press," p. 727.

15. *SR*, July 6, 1865; Shryock, ed., *Letters of Richard D. Arnold*, p. 122; "a grand": *SR*, July 6, 1865; *SDH*, July 5, 1865; "showing": "Carl Schurz's Letters from the South," p. 245.

16. "Some . . . Materiels,": C. A. DeLaMotta to "Reven and Dear Sir," Savannah, Oct. 6, 1865, Container 181, Reel 98, ACS; "upon the blessings": *SR*, July 27, 1865.

17. Carter, *When the War Was Over*, pp. 140–41. On the Freedman's Bank see Osthaus, *Freedmen, Philanthropy, and Fraud*. The *Freedmen's Record* of December 1865 lists Savannah black teachers sponsored by the New England Freedmen's Aid Society: James M. Simms, Mrs. Georgia Stewart, Mrs. Margaret Denslow, Mrs. Abigail Small, Amanda Miller, Gertrude Henderson, Claudia Ward, Jane Nuttall, Mr. Whitfield, Robert Jones.

18. See, for example, H. F. Sickles to Cap't., Savannah, Nov. 16, 1865; H. Sickles to Cap't., Savannah, Nov. 20, 1865, Unregistered Letters Received, Reel 24, BRFAL-GA (M798); CC Minutes, Jan. 24, 1865.

19. CC Minutes, Aug. 23, 1865; "on Monday": CC Minutes, Sept. 6, 1865; ibid., Oct. 23, 1865; Letter to C. W. Reynolds, Savannah, Aug. 14, 1866, p. 31, Pt. 5, Post of Letters Sent, July 1866–Sept. 1870, RG 393.

20. *SR*, Sept. 5, 1865. Hayes titled his news story/editorial "Insolent Interference of Negroes with Free Labor." See also Stanley, *From Bondage to Contract*.

21. *SR*, Sept. 6, 1865.

22. Conway, *Reconstruction of Georgia,* pp. 40–49; Wynne, *Continuity of Cotton*, pp. 1–6; Carter, *When the War Was Over*, pp. 66–85. Delegates from the lowcountry included D. C. Scarlett, E. N. Atkinson, Verbanus Dart, James Couper, J. B. Mallard, H. F. Horne, J. K. Middleton, Armand Lefils. Source: Unregistered Letters Received, c. Dec. 15, 1865, Reel 24, BRFAL-GA (M798).

23. "unless madness": Brown quoted in Conway, *Reconstruction of Georgia*, p. 55; Foner, *Reconstruction*, pp. 196, 246. For the constitution of 1865, see Candler, ed., *Confederate Records of Georgia*, Vol. 4, "Journal of the Convention Held at Milledgeville."

24. "hottest . . . possible": "Carl Schurz's Letters from the South," p. 343; *SR*, Nov. 1, 1865. For a brief biography of Anderson, see Myers, ed., *Children of Pride*, p. 1452. See also Gamble, *History of the City Government of Savannah*, pp. 3–25; Greenberg, "Creating Ethnic, Class, and Southern Identity in Nineteenth-Century America," pp. 242–45.

25. Gamble, *History of the City Government of Savannah*, pp. 235–39; Lee and Agnew, *Historical Record of the City of Savannah*, pp. 153–54; Harden, *Recollections of a Long and Satisfactory Life*, p. 122.

26. Cimbala, *Under the Guardianship of the Nation*, pp. 57–64; Davis Tillson to W. B. Gaulden, Oct. 19, 1866, Letters Sent, Reel 4, BRFAL-GA (M798); Rapport, "Freedmen's Bureau as a Legal Agent for Black Men and Women," pp. 27–29; Thigpen, "Aristocracy of the Heart," pp. 641–44; E. C. Anderson to Davis Tillson, Savannah, Jan. 26, 1866, Unregistered Letters Received, Reel 25, BRFAL-GA (M798); Eugene Pickett to

Douglas Risley, May 20, 1867, Letters Sent, Reel 5, BRFAL-GA (M798); Greenberg, "Becoming Southern," pp. 55–75. For brief biographies of Gaulden, McIver, and Yulee, see Myers, ed., *Children of Pride*, pp. 1526–27, 1609, 1738. For Tillson's speech to the convention, see Candler, ed., *Confederate Records of Georgia*, Vol. 4, pp. 45–47.

27. "What really . . . God!": W. W. Gordon quoted in Robertson, ed., "Northern Rebel," pp. 514–15; Carolyn J. Stefanco, "Poor Loving Prisoners of War: Nelly Kinzie Gordon and the Dilemma of Northern-Born Women in the Confederate South," in Inscoe and Kenzer, eds., *Enemies of the Country*, pp. 148–71.

28. "Carl Schurz's Letters from the South," p. 244; Aunt L to Mrs. J. F. Gilmer, Savannah, Jan. 10, 1865, JFG, SHC; "the dark": Myers, ed., *Children of Pride*, p. 1292; Thomas, *Memoirs of a Southerner*, pp. 52–53; MacKethan, ed., *Recollections of a Southern Daughter*, p. 91; CC Minutes, Feb. 6, 1867; Waring, ed., "Charles Hardee's Recollections of Old Savannah," p. 27; Harden, *Recollections*, p. 116; Wiley, ed., *Recollections of a Confederate Staff Officer*, pp. 306–307; Henrietta Jane Harden to Mary Ann Harden, Savannah, June 10, 1865, HF Papers, DU.

29. Folsom, *Heroes and Martyrs of Georgia*, p. 123; Faust, " 'Dread Void of Uncertainty' " and *This Republic of Suffering*, pp. 211–49.

30. Brown, *"Our Connection with Savannah"*; Henrietta Wayne to My Dear Mother, Savannah, March 29, 1868, HF Papers, DU.

31. "I hear . . . hardship": Mercer Diary, March 30, 1866, p. 5; June 10, 1866, p. 8, July 1, 1866, p. 15, GHS.

32. "ruled": Myers, ed., *Children of Pride*, p. 1319; "earning": p. 1273; "in a most": p. 1276; "hard and burnt": p. 1276; "becoming . . . *greenback*": p. 1280; MacKethan, ed., *Recollections of a Southern Daughter*, pp. 91–92.

33. "restiveness . . . friends": Myers, ed., *Children of Pride*, p. 1292; "had been forced . . . place": ibid., p. 1296; Hargis, "For the Love of Place," p. 833.

34. "a providential . . . prospect": Myers, ed., *Children of Pride*, p. 1306; "petitioner": ibid., p. 1358; Hargis, "For the Love of Place," p. 833; Clarke, *Dwelling Place*, pp. 456–58.

35. For a brief biography of Tillson, see Myers, ed., *Children of Pride*, p. 1703; Howard, *Autobiography*, Vol. 2, pp. 215–49; Cimbala, *Under the Guardianship of the Nation*, pp. 167–76; Trowbridge, *Desolate South*, pp. 492–501; Oubre, *Forty Acres and a Mule*, p. 57.

36. "a half straitened . . . state": Davis Tillson to O. O. Howard, Savannah, Jan. 1, 1866, Letters Sent, Reel 1, BRFAL-GA (M798); Cimbala, *Under the Guardianship of the Nation*, pp. 172, 181; Duncan, *Freedom's Shore*, pp. 29–31; House Executive Docs., 39th Cong., 1st sess., no. 70 (serial 1256), pp. 319–33.

37. Cimbala, *Under the Guardianship of the Nation*, pp. 137–44; Foner, *Reconstruction*, pp. 161–63.

38. Reidy, "Aaron A. Bradley," pp. 281–85; "Although . . . friends": "The Elective Franchise," *Anglo-African* (Aug. 12, 1865); "the [legal]": "Mass. Legislature," *BDA*, Nov. 18, 1863. Bradley opened a savings account at the Savannah Branch of the Freedman's Bank in 1867 and gave his age as fifty-one. See records of the Savannah Branch, FST.

39. "You must": *SR*, Dec. 13, 1865; *"resist"*: ibid., Dec. 12, 1865; "suspended": H. F. Sickles to Davis Tillson, Savannah, Dec. 7, 1865, Unregistered Letters Received, Reel 24, BRFAL-GA (M798). On the "conservative and conciliatory . . . outlook and approach" of many black clergy during Reconstruction, see Montgomery, *Under Their Own Vine and Fig Tree*, pp. 157–59.

40. *SR*, Dec. 13, 1865; "very insolent . . . barroom": E. A. Cooley to Samuel Hunt, Savannah, Jan. 2, 1866, AMA Archives; Reidy, "Aaron A. Bradley," p. 268; H. F. Sickles to Tillson, Savannah, Dec. 7, 1865, Unregistered Letters Received, Reel 24, BRFAL-GA (M798).

41. H. F. Sickles to Davis Tillson, Dec. 29, 1865, Unregistered Letters Received, Reel 24, BRFAL-GA (M798); Carter, *When the War Was Over*, pp. 192–201; Magdol, *Right to the Land*, p. 169.

42. "kindly relations": p. 9; "mischievous": p. 8; in "Proceedings of the Freedmen's Convention of Georgia"; Reidy, "Aaron A. Bradley," pp. 286–87; Conway, *Reconstruction of Georgia*, pp. 72–73; Drago, *Black Politicians*, pp. 27–28.

43. Winfield et al. to O. O. Howard, Savannah, Jan. 27, 1866, Washington Headquarters, Records of the Commissioner, Letters Received (W-46 1866), RG 105, BRFAL, NA (FSSP A-433).

44. Savannah Branch (M816, Reel 8), FST.

45. quick": quoted in Yellin, *Harriet Jacobs*, p. 167; "When I look": ibid., p. 179; "Jacobs School," *FR* (March 1865): 41.

46. "huddled": Yellin, *Harriet Jacobs*, p. 191; "There you see": Lucy Chase quoted in Swint, ed., *Dear Ones at Home*, p. 186. See also *SDH*, Nov. 11, 1865; "From Savannah," *FR* (Jan. 1866): 3–4; House Executive Docs., 39th Cong., 1st sess., no. 70 (serial 1256), p. 352; Swint, ed., *Dear Ones at Home*, p. 80.

47. "their Fathers": J. M. Simms to "General," enclosure in Tillson to "General," Letters Sent, Correspondence, Office of the Assistant Commissioner, Georgia, entry 626, BRFAL (FSSP A-5161); "very unjust": Yellin, *Harriet Jacobs*, p. 196; Montgomery, *Under Their Own Vine and Fig Tree*, p. 157.

48. "they have families . . . direction": contract signed on Jan. 16, 1866, between Clotaire S. Gay "and the undersigned Freedmen," FB, GHS; "virtually . . . Live": James M. Simms to O. O. Howard, Feb. 3, 1866, Savannah, series 15: Letters Received, S-97 1865 (FSSP A-5161), RG 105, BRFAL, NA; "a rascal": J. Kearny Smith to W. W. Deane, Savannah, Oct. 17, 1866; J. Kearny Smith to W. W. Deane, Oct. 8, 1866, FB, GHS; "by force": "The South," *BDA*, Aug. 3, 1867.

49. Bell, " 'Ogeechee Troubles,' " pp. 377–78; Cimbala, *Under the Guardianship of the Nation*, pp. 169–72, 338–40; Stewart, *"What Nature Suffers to Groe"*; Charlotte Cheves to Davis Tillson, Savannah, Oct. 7, 1865; W. W. Deane to Davis Tillson, Savannah, Oct. 15, 1865; Report from the Reverend W. H. Tiffany, Grove Hall Plantation, Dec. 1, 1865; A. P. Ketchum to Cap't., Savannah, June 15, 1866, Unregistered Letters Received, Reel 25, BRFAL-GA (M798).

50. "this region": W. H. Tiffany to H. F. Sickles, Ogeechee District, Nov. 27, 1865, FB, GHS; "List of Marriages Performed by Rev. T. H. Tiffany, Ogeechee District, Georgia," ibid.; Cimbala, *Under the Guardianship of the Nation*, pp. 179–80.

51. "as they consider": Hattie Gaylord to Samuel Hunt, Grove Hill Plantation, Feb. 1, 1866, AMA Archives.

52. Bell, "Ogeechee Troubles," p. 381; Cimbala, *Under the Guardianship of the Nation*, p. 171; "refused": Thomas Clay Arnold to H. F. Sickles, Dec. 27, 1865, FB, GHS; Esther W. Douglass to Samuel Hunt, Feb. 1, 1866, AMA Archives; "my duty . . . slavery": Hattie Gaylord to Samuel Hunt, Grove Hill Plantation, Feb. 2, 1866, AMA Archives. For a brief biography of Thomas Clay Arnold, see Myers, ed., *Children of Pride*, p. 1455.

53. "by . . . motives": Esther W. Douglass to George Whipple, Brooksville, Vt., Sept. 1, 1864; Frances Littlefield to George Whipple, Boston, Dec. 12, 1864, AMA Archives.

54. "the traces": Esther W. Douglass, "Joy in Service—My Life Story," No. 1, p. 11, EWD; "debilitating": Esther W. Douglass to Samuel Hunt, Dec. 27, 1865; Frances Littlefield to Samuel Hunt, Grove Hill Plantation, Dec. 30, 1865, AMA Archives; "Those women": No. 2, "Grove Hill, Chatham County, Georgia, Oct. 1865," EWD.

55. "An old uncle": Frances Littlefield to Samuel Hunt, Grove Hill Plantation, Dec. 30, 1865,

AMA Archives; "120 dirty . . . jargon": No. 2, "Grove Hill, Chatham County, Georgia, Oct. 1865," p. 13, EWD; "minding . . . letters": Esther W. Douglass to Mrs. E. A. Adams, Grove Hill Plantation, EWD.

56. Esther W. Douglass to Mrs. E. A. Adams, April 14, 1866, EWD; Esther W. Douglass to Samuel Hunt, Grove Hill Plantation, Feb. 1, 1866, AMA Archives; "Episcopal": Ira Pettibone to George Whipple, Savannah, Jan. 26, 1866; E. W. Douglass to Samuel Hunt, Grove Hill Plantation, April 3, 1866, AMA Archives.

57. "They need help": Frances Littlefield to Samuel Hunt, Grove Hill Plantation, Feb. 1, 1866, AMA Archives.

58. "hard at work . . . greenbacks": Esther W. Douglass to Samuel Hunt, Grove Hill Plantation, Feb. 1, 1866, AMA Archives; "please . . . to us": James Grant to George Whipple, Grove Hill Plantation, May 30, 1866, AMA Archives; Penningroth, *Claims of Kinfolk*, p. 157.

59. Byrne, " 'Uncle Billy' Sherman Comes to Town," pp. 91–116; Conway, *Reconstruction in Georgia*, pp. 75–79; Foner, *Reconstruction*, pp. 239–51.

60. "The field": E. A. Cooley to George Whipple, Savannah, April 9, 1866, AMA Archives.

61. "a life": Johnson quoted in Foner, *Reconstruction*, p. 248; "full and equal": ibid., p. 243; "the distinction": Johnson quoted in ibid., p. 250.

62. Duncan, *Freedom's Shore*, p. 102; Cimbala, *Under the Guardianship of the Nation*, pp. 181–83; Trowbridge quoted in Taylor, *Reminiscences of My Life in Camp*, p. 115–18.

CHAPTER ELEVEN

1. "boughs": "Southern Jottings and Journeyings," *NYT*, April 1, 1866, p. 1; "ma[d]e": William Wray to E. C. Anderson, April 2, 1866, Unregistered Documents, Letters Received, Reel 29, BRFAL-GA (M798).

2. "Report of Notorious Prostitutes," attached to Wray's letter to Anderson (see n. 1). Johanna Anderson was listed as a servant in the 1860 FMC, Georgia, Chatham County, Savannah, p. 321. She was living with Elizabeth Bartello, thirty-five-year-old Cuban-born dressmaker, and five children, all born in Cuba, but with last names different from Bartello's.

3. Ibid. Soon after the beginning of the military occupation, black men and women had complained to Union officials about white soldiers patronizing a brothel owned by a white woman on Farm Street, in a black neighborhood; the patrons abused civilians and "occasioned great disturbance," according to Delia Grant, a neighbor of the establishment. "easily reached": William Wray to E. C. Anderson, Savannah, April 2, 1866, Unregistered Documents, Letters Received, Reel 29, BRFAL-GA (M798); news clipping [account of prostitutes in Freedmen's Court]; Testimony of Delia Grant, Proceedings of a Military Board . . . May 8, 1865, in response to Houston et al. to Gillmore, April 25, 1865, Department of the South, series 4109, Letters Received, H-163 1865, RG 393, Records of United States Army Continental Commands, National Archives (FSSP C-1342); "laugh[ing] . . . servants": E. C. Anderson to J. Kearny Smith, Savannah, Aug. 9, 1866, FB, GHS; Davis Tillson to E. C. Anderson, Savannah, April 13, 1866, Letters Sent, Reel 2, BRFAL-GA (M798).

4. "shameless": E. C. Anderson to J. Kearny Smith, Savannah, April 9, 1866, FB, GHS; "insubordination": Hoskins, "The Trouble They Seen," p. 22; "evil": E. C. Anderson to W. W. Deane, Savannah, Aug. 27, 1867, Unregistered Letters Received, Reel 25, BRFAL-GA (M798).

5. "Balls": Jan. 24, 1866; newspaper clipping, E. C. Anderson Diary, Book 1 (clippings), GHS; "fiery eye": "From Savannah," *FR* (March 1866): 55–56; "that he him-

self . . . *heart*": "Georgia: From Rev. Ira Pettibone," *AM* (April 1866), p. 80; Perdue, "Negro in Savannah," pp. 22–23. See also Gilbert L. Eberhart, Savannah, Dec. 17, 1866, Letters Received, Reel 14, BRFAL-GA (M798).

6. "on streets . . . *on*": Dominick O'Byrne, Savannah, Feb. 1, 1866, Unregistered Letters Received,Reel 25, BRFAL-GA (M798). Charges culled from reports of mayor's court and Freedmen's Court in *SR* and *SDH*. See also Savannah Police Department Jail Register, 1862–1869, Vol. 4, GHS; Carter, *When the War Was Over*, pp. 128–29; "Rules, Regulations and Ordinances, for the Government of the City Police of Savannah."

7. "general": newspaper clipping, April 24, 1866, E. C. Anderson Diary, Book 1, GHS; "since a large": *SDNH*, July 10, 1866. On April 2, 1866, the *Savannah Daily News* changed its name to the *Savannah Daily News and Herald*, which in turn changed its name to the *Savannah Morning News* on Sept. 20, 1868.

8. "the kindly": "Gen. Steedman's Tour," *NYT*, May 25, 1866, p. 5; "The South," *NYT*, May 19, 1866, p. 8; "The Freedmen's Bureau," *NYT*, May 22, 1866, p. 4.

9. "set apart . . . persons": CC Minutes, June 27, 1866; Davis Tillson to Savannah City Council, in CC Minutes, July 12, 1866; "to preserve": CC Minutes, July 25, 1866; Henrietta J. Wayne to "My Dear Sister," Savannah, July 20, 1866, HF Papers, DU.

10. "is changed": *SDNH*, July 10, 1866; Gamble, *History of the City Government of Savannah*, p. 275.

11. "Will Surely": James M. Simms to Miss Stevenson, *FR* (Sept. 1866): 167–68; *SDNH*, July 14, 1866; *SDR*, July 14, 1866; Yellin, *Harriet Jacobs*, pp. 200–201. Account of incident taken from *SDNH* of July 17 and 18, 1866.

12. Foner, *Reconstruction*, pp. 261–64; Shaffer, *After the Glory*, pp. 33–38, 43, 71–72; Hogue, *Uncivil War*, pp. 31–52.

13. Yellin, *Harriet Jacobs*, pp. 200–201; E. C. Anderson to Davis Tillson, Savannah, March 29, 1866, Board of Health Commissioners' Report to the Mayor, Savannah, March 28, 1866, Unregistered Letters, BRFAL-GA (M798); Savitt, "Politics in Medicine," p. 52.

14. Taylor, *Reminiscences of My Life in Camp*, pp. 123–24. See also *SDR*, July 3, 1867; J. V. deHamil to C. C. Sibley, Macon, May 18, 1867, Letters Received, Reel 14; newspaper clipping, c. July 3, 1867, Letters Received, Reel 17, BRFAL-GA (M798).

15. Taylor, *Reminiscences*, pp. 124–27; "well educated": E. A. Cooley to S. Hunt, May 11, 1866, AMA Archives. See also E. A. Cooley to S. Hunt, Savannah, Jan. 16, 1866, AMA Archives.

16. J. Kearny Smith to W. W. Deane, Savannah, Aug. 20, 1866, Letters Received, Reel 13; J. Murray Hoag, July 20, 1867, Savannah, Letters Received, Reel 14; Nelson Bronson to W. W. Deane, Savannah, Sept. 13, 1866, Unregistered Letters Received, Reel 25; F. J. Foster to Davis Tillson, Nov. 9, 1866, Unregistered Documents (Letters Received), Reel 26, BRFAL-GA (M798); Cimbala, *Under the Guardianship of the Nation*, pp. 182–85; Oubre, *Forty Acres and a Mule*, pp. 57–58.

17. "finally taking": J. R. Cheves to Davis Tillson, Sept. 14, 1866, Unregistered Documents, Letters Received, Reel 25; "conducted": Nelson Bronson to W. W. Deane, Savannah, Sept. 13, 1866, ibid.; "with sundry": Elias Yulee to Davis Tillson, Walthourville, Sept. 27, 1866, Reel 29, ibid., BRFAL-GA (M798); Cimbala, *Under the Guardianship of the Nation*, p. 184.

18. "impudent": Bronson Nelson to W. W. Deane, Savannah, Sept. 13, 1866, Unregistered Documents, Letters Received, Reel 25; J. Kearny Smith to S. W. Deane, Savannah, Aug. 20, 1866, Letters Received, Reel 13; John C. Dickson to Davis Tillson, Sapelo Island, Sept. 22, 1866, Unregistered Documents, Letters Received, Reel 26; "restless": William F. Eaton to Davis Tillson, St. Simons Island, Unregistered Documents, Letters Received, Reel 26, BRFAL-GA (M798); "they owed . . . nothing": Maxwell and Tillson quoted in Duncan, *Freedom's Shore*, p. 34.

19. "Savannah," *NYT*, Aug. 29, 1866, p. 4; "committing . . . swamps": M. A. Cochran to W. W. Deane, Savannah, Sept. 13, 1866, p. 49 of Pt. 5: Post of Savannah Letters Sent, July 1866 to Sept. 1870, RG 393, NA; Conway, *Reconstruction of Georgia*, pp. 64–65; Report of Davis Tillson in Lane, ed., *Standing Upon the Mouth of a Volcano*, pp. 52–57; "Washington News," *NYT*, April 9, 1866, p. 5.

20. The correspondence related to the Smith-Gaulden-Yulee feud and the Smith-Gaulden confrontation is extensive. See Reel 80, BRFAL-GA (M1903); correspondence from the summer of 1866, Letters Sent, Reel 3, and Letters Received, Reel 13, BRFAL-GA (M798).

21. "unfit . . . people": Sarah A. Jenness to Samuel Hunt, Savannah, Oct. 22, 1866; "friction . . . thinkers": Ira Pettibone to Samuel Hunt, Savannah, Oct. 22, 1866; "remuneration": G. L. Eberhart to Samuel Hunt, Augusta, Oct. 22, 1866, AMA Archives.

22. "miserable": "Paris in the South," *NYT*, Sept. 3, 1866, p. 8; "worthless": "Report of Edward C. Anderson, Mayor . . . 1867," p. 15; CC Minutes, July 6, 1865; Simms, "A Comment on Savannah in 1866," pp. 459–60.

23. "Some of the most": Hardy Mobley to George Whipple, June 4, 1866, AMA Archives; "their unseemly": *SDR*, March 18, 1867.

24. See correspondence dated July 26, 1866, and July 31, 1866, Pt. 5, Post of Savannah, Letters Sent, July 1866 to Sept. 1870, pp. 7, 12; and List of Recruits in Savannah (Aug. 4, 1867), Pt. 5, Post of Savannah, Georgia, Entry 5, Special Orders, 1867–1877, RG 393, NA; Savannah Jail Registers, 1866–67, GHS.

25. *SDNH*, Oct. 6, 1866.

26. For a list of mayors and aldermen throughout this period, see Appendix I of this book, with information drawn from Gamble, *History of the City Government*, pp. 3–22; *SDNH*, July 29, 1868.

27. Hattie E. Gaylord to George Whipple, Savannah, Jan. 22, 1866, AMA Archives.

28. CC Minutes, Oct. 31, 1866, Nov. 28, 1866, Jan. 23, 1867; "almost one third": CC Minutes, Dec. 26, 1866; *SDR*, Jan. 28, 1867; Orr, *History of Education in Georgia*, p. 208.

29. Reidy, "Aaron A. Bradley," p. 287; Foner, *Reconstruction*, pp. 261–71.

30. Bradley quoted in Reidy, "Aaron A. Bradley," p. 287.

31. The exchange of letters is reprinted in *SDR*, Jan. 23, 1867.

32. "full faith . . . Bar: *SDR*, Jan. 18, 1867. For a brief biography of Fleming, see Myers, ed., *Children of Pride*, p. 1522.

33. "this was but": *SDR*, Jan. 21, 1867.

34. Ibid. See also "The Recent Troubles with the Freedmen on the Sea Islands of South Carolina," *NYT*, Jan. 27, 1867, p. 6; Reidy, "Aaron A. Bradley," pp. 289–92; *SDR*, Jan. 21, 1867.

35. "aged . . . cents": *SDR*, Jan. 22, 1867.

36. *SDR*, Jan. 23, 1867; "negro . . . some time": "Georgia," *NYT*, Feb. 25, 1867, p. 1.

37. "oppressive": *SDR*, Jan. 25, 1867; "Stevedores . . . rights": *SDR*, Jan. 26, 1867; *SDR*, Jan. 29, 1867; Swint, ed., *Dear Ones at Home*, p. 185; Hunt, "Organized Labor," pp. 182–4.

38. "manly . . . granted": *SDR*, Jan. 28, 1867; *SDR*, Jan. 29, 1867; CC Minutes, Jan. 23, 1867, Jan. 28, 1867; "used": *SDNH*, Jan. 30, 1867; *SDR*, Jan. 29, 1867; "Why . . . difficulty": *SDR*, Jan. 30, 1867.

39. "riotous": *SDR*, Jan. 31, 1867; "evil . . . friends": *SDH*, Jan. 30, 1867. See also *SDR*, Jan. 31, 1867; Feb. 1, 1867; "Georgia," *NYT*, Feb. 25, 1867, p. 1; *NYT*, Feb. 10, 1867, p. 1; *National Workman*, Feb. 9, 1867.

40. "January revolution . . . wringer": Myers, ed., *Children of Pride*, p. 1365.

41. "unreliable": ibid., p. 1340; "Kate": ibid., p. 1365; "the women": ibid., p. 1310; "a burden": ibid., p. 1291.

42. "Sam's . . . remark": ibid., p. 1303; "Gilbert will stay": ibid., p. 1370; Hargis, "For the Love of Place," pp. 825–28.

43. On the Dimock Johnson case, see the case referred to George Walbridge, Savannah, Feb. 11, 1867, Letters Received, Reel 15, BRFAL-GA (M798). See also Charles F. Sawyer to C. C. Sibley, Savannah, June 22, 1867, Letters Received, Reel 19, BFRAL-GA (M798); Cimbala, *Under the Guardianship of the Nation*, pp. 194–203; Rebecca Scott, "The Battle over the Child: Child Apprenticeship and the Freedmen's Bureau in North Carolina," *Prologue* 10 (Summer 1978): 101–13; and Apprenticeship/Indenture Records, 1800–1930, Ordinary/Superior Court Records, Liberty County, GSA.

44. Report of Elias Yulee, Walthoursville, Dec. 1866, Letters Received, Reel 15; "begged . . . habits": Elias Yulee to Davis Tillson, Walthoursville, Dec. 14, 1866, Letters Received, Reel 15, BRFAL-GA (M798); Rapport, "Freedmen's Bureau as a Legal Agent for Black Men and Women," pp. 39–41. On wife abuse among freed couples, see Penningroth, *Claims of Kinfolk*, pp. 176–77, 182.

45. Report of H. J. Larsen, Savannah, March 12, 1867, Letters Received, Reel 16; H. J. Larsen to John E. Hosmer, Savannah, March 12, 1867, Unregistered Documents, Letters Received, Reel 16; Testimony taken by O. H. Howard (deposition of T. Golden, Chatham County, Feb. 14, 1867), Letters Received, Reel 14, BRFAL-GA (M798).

46. For brief biographies of Jones and Ross see Myers, ed., *Children of Pride*, pp. 1571, 1666. See also Charles H. Hopkins to Sibley, Savannah, Aug. 26, 1867, Unregistered Documents, Letters Received, Reel 18, BRFAL-GA (M798).

47. "Don't . . . contradict you," "knocking": Testimony taken by O. H. Howard, Feb. 14, 1867, Letters Received, Reel 14; "only": Deposition of Smart Screven taken by J. J. Larsen, Savannah, March 12, 1867; "they all": H. J. Larsen to John E. Hosmer, March 12, 1867, Unregistered Documents, Letters Received, Reel 16, BRFAL-GA (M798). For a brief biography of this Charles Jones, see Myers, ed. *Children of Pride*, pp. 1568–69.

48. "the colored people": Esther W. Douglass, "Joy in Service—My Life Story," p. 15; Esther W. Douglass to E. A. Adams, Savannah, Feb. 25, 1867, EWD; Esther W. Douglass to Theodore Adams, Wild Horn Plantation, Feb. 16, 1867, EWD; Bell, " 'Ogeechee Troubles,' " p. 382.

49. "Injustice . . . debt": Esther W. Douglass "[1866]," Dec. 24, 1866 entry; "Now you": Esther W. Douglass, "Joy in Service—My Life Story," p. 18, EWD; "they do not": Esther W. Douglass, "No. 2 [Wild Horn Plantation, 1867]."

50. "chain gang": Larson to William H. Bullock, Esq., Savannah, May 17, 1867, pp. 5, 336, Post of Savannah Letters Sent, July 1866–Sept. 1870, RG 393; "a Negro . . . others": Clifton, ed., *Life and Labor on Argyle Island*, pp. 363–64; Young, "Ideology and Death on a Savannah Rice Plantation," pp. 704–705.

51. Quotations on pp. 367–69 in Clifton, ed., *Life and Labor on Argyle Island*, p. 357.

52. Quotations are on pp. 361 and 365, ibid.

CHAPTER TWELVE

1. Yates quoted in Foner, *Reconstruction*, p. 278.

2. Ibid., pp. 271–91.

3. For coverage, see "Colored Mass Meeting in Savannah," *NYT*, April 2, 1867, p. 1; *SDNH*, March 19, 1867; ibid., April 2, 1867; *SDR*, March 19, 1867.

4. *SDNH*, March 19, 1867. On Stone, see Dyer, *Secret Yankees*, pp. 219–35.

5. *SDR*, March 20, 1867. For a biography of Falligant, see *Cleave's Biographical Cyclopaedia of Homeopathic Physicians and Surgeons,* http://www.homeoint.org/history/cleave/f/falligantla.htm.

6. "The colored people": Joseph W. Clift to E. P. Smith, Savannah, April 29, 1867, AMA

Archives; "the very . . . results": *SDR*, April 2, 1867. On Clift see Shadgett, *Republican Party in Georgia*, p. 11.

7. "educated . . . color": *SDNH*, March 19, 1867. For the three versions of Simms's speech: "The white race": *SDR*, April 2, 1867; "The white man": *SDNH*, April 2, 1867; "James Simms": New Orleans *Tribune*, April 13, 1867. The *Tribune* transcript is included in Sterling, ed., *The Trouble They Seen*, pp. 107–108.

8. *SDR*, May 29, 1867.

9. On the Belle Ville colony, see documents in the Georgia Historical Society's Unprocessed Freedmen's Bureau Collection (FB, GHS), including a list of freedpeople receiving rations from J. Murray Hoag in the summer of 1867, and for the calendar year 1867. See also Cimbala, *Under the Guardianship of the Nation*, p. 288 (n. 35); Duncan, *Freedom's Shore*, pp. 35–43. C. H. Hopkins to J. Murray Hoag, Savannah, March 12, 1867, Letters Received, Reel 15; C. H. Hopkins to C. C. Sibley, Savannah, March 21, 1867, Letters Received, Reel 15; C. C. Sibley to "General," Macon, March 13, 1865, Letters Received, BRFAL-GA (M798). For a brief biography of Charles H. Hopkins, see Myers, ed., *Children of Pride*, pp. 1553–54.

10. "Declaration of Belle Ville Farmers' Association, March 4, 1867," in FB, GHS; George Walbridge to J. Murray Hoag, March 22, 1867, Letters Sent, Reel 5; "contented . . . cotton": Charles H. Holcombe to C. C. Sibley, Hinesville, June 13, 1867, Letters Received, Reel 15, BRFAL-GA (M798); "Statement of Account Between U. S. and Belleville Colony of Freedmen," FB, GHS.

11. "secret . . . up": Eugene Pickett to Elias Yulee, Dec. 19, 1866; "a great . . . races": Myers, ed., *Children of Pride*, p. 1379; Duncan, *Freedom's Shore*, p. 45.

12. "beautiful . . . language": *SDR*, July 5, 1867; *SDNH*, July 3, 1867; "this narrow-minded": *SDNH*, July 6, 1867; *SDR*, July 3, 1867; Reidy, "Aaron A. Bradley," p. 290. On Louis Toomer, see Foner, *Freedom's Lawmakers*, pp. 213–14.

13. See "Petition to the Asst. Commissioner by James Mackey & 200 Others": Georgia BRFAL (M798), Reel 36, Unbound Miscellaneous Papers," RG 105; also http://freedmensbureau.com/georgia/savannahpetitoin.htm. ("petitoin" [*sic*]).

14. Turner letter in Abbott, "Black Ministers and the Organization of the Republican Party," p 33. On Turner, see Foner, *Freedom's Lawmakers*, pp. 215–16; Berlin et al., eds., *Freedom*, Series 2: *Black Military Experience*, pp. 309, 311–12, 661, 759, 761, 770, 359–61, 626–27, 756–57; Redkey, "Black Chaplains in the Union Army," pp. 331–50; "The South," *BDA*, Aug. 3, 1867.

15. "our country churches . . . masses": Turner letter in Abbott, "Black Ministers," p. 33; "diverted": "Affairs in Georgia," *NYT*, July 16, 1867, p. 2.

16. "the country people . . . blacks": "Demagogue at the South," *NYT*, Oct. 3, 1867, p. 4; "repudiated . . . city": *SDR*, Sept. 19, 1867.

17. "all blacks . . . blood": *SDNH*, Oct. 1, 1867; ibid., Sept. 30, 1867. The quotation is from an affidavit signed by James B. Habley and Richard H. Oglesby.

18. "clubs . . . Sherman": *SDNH*, Oct. 1, 1867; *SDNH*, Sept. 30, 1867; "Affairs in Georgia," *NYT*, Aug. 31, 1867, p. 1.

19. "a Conservative . . . disagreement": *SDNH*, Oct. 1, 1867; "prevented": *SDR*, Oct. 1, 1867; "Riot in Savannah," *NYT*, Oct. 1, 1867, p. 5.

20. "exciting . . . riotous conduct": *SDNH*, Oct. 2, 1867.

21. On the Waring-Arnold feud, see the exchange of letters in *SDNH*, Oct. 21, 1867; "designed": R. D. Arnold to James J. Waring, Savannah, Oct. 9, 1867, JFW Papers, GHS.

22. "——you . . . way": *SDNH*, Oct. 21, 1867; ibid., Oct. 18, 1867; "during": "Political Matters—Torchlight Procession Prohibited in Savannah," *NYT*, Oct. 14, 1867, p. 1.

23. "radical": *SDNH*, Oct. 22, 1867; "all Loyal League": *SDR*, Oct. 22, 1867.

24. "Georgia," *NYT*, Nov. 1, 1867, p. 1; "this solemn farce . . . good": Mercer Diary, Nov. 3, 1867, pp. 34–35, GHS; "Condition of the Freedmen on the South Carolina Coast," *NYT*, Nov. 13, 1867, p. 2. Convention delegates are listed in Candler, ed., *Confederate Records of Georgia*, Vol. 6, pp. 1020–27.

25. Golding quoted in Foner, ed., *Freedom's Lawmakers*, p. 88; Rogers and Saunders, "American Missionary Association in Liberty County," pp. 304–15; Coulter, "Henry M. Turner," pp. 371–410; Groover, *Sweet Land of Liberty*, p. 217. Golding was the slave of W. B. Gaulden's father, Jonathan Gaulden.

26. "Affairs in Georgia," *NYT*, Dec. 7, 1867, p. 2; Conway, *Reconstruction of Georgia*, pp. 154–55; Duncan, *Entrepreneur for Equality*, p. 25.

27. "for contempt": Candler, ed., *Confederate Records of Georgia*, Vol. 6, pp. 547–49, 577; "That Aaron": ibid., p. 962; "Georgia: The Reconstruction Convention," *NYT*, Feb. 17, 1868, p. 8.

28. *SDNH*, Oct. 9, 1867.

29. "riotous": "The Case of the Negro Bradley in Savannah," *NYT*, Jan. 7, 1868, p. 1; "oppressive": Bradley quoted in Reidy, "Aaron A. Bradley," p. 291; "Affairs in Georgia," *NYT*, Aug. 31, 1867, p. 1.

30. "I have the honor": J. Murray Hoag to C. C. Sibley, Savannah, Nov. 30, 1867; "Rations Issued to People of Belleville Colony, McIntosh County, Georgia, 1867"; "Tabular Statement of Belleville Affairs, 1867," FB, GHS.

31. "the closing": Myers, ed., *Children of Pride*, p. 1422; "Yankee Negro": ibid., p. 1382; "been poisoned": ibid., p. 1340; "very injurious": ibid., pp. 1308–9. See also ibid., pp. 1305, 1340.

32. "in great trouble": ibid., p. 1413; "beyond": ibid., pp. 1390–91. See also ibid., pp. 1354, 1422–23.

33. "Beach Institute," *AM* (July 1868): 145–46; *AM* (April 1869): 73–74; O. E. Dimick to E. P. Smith, Savannah, Jan. 3, 1868.

34. "Camp Sorghum": O. W. Dimick to E. P. Smith, March 7, 1866; "these . . . education": O. W. Dimick to E. P. Smith, Savannah, Feb. 15, 1868; "transient": O. W. Dimick to E. P. Smith, Savannah, Nov. 1, 1867; "proven": O. W. Dimick to E. P. Smith, Savannah, March 10, 1868, AMA Archives.

35. "soliciting": O. W. Dimick to E. P. Smith, Savannah, Nov. 5, 1867; "the political": O. W. Dimick to E. P. Smith, Savannah, Nov. 1, 1867; "to quiet": O. W. Dimick to E. P. Smith, Savannah, Nov. 11, 1867, AMA Archives; "English": *Freemen's Standard*, March 7, 1868. For a list of the other schools and teachers, see *Freemen's Standard*, Feb. 15, 1868.

36. "labor": Harriet M. Haskell to E. P. Smith, Savannah, Nov. 28, 1867; "not only": O. W. Dimick to E. P. Smith, Savannah, Nov. 18, 1867; "well": S. A. Jenness to E. P. Smith, Savannah, Nov. 25, 1867; "Refuses": Telegram from O. W. Dimick to E. P. Smith, Savannah, Nov. 25, 1867, AMA Archives. Louis B. Toomer first applied for a commission from the AMA in March 1866, when the SEA "failed to meet its obligations to her teachers." See Toomer to Samuel Hunt, Savannah, March 20, 1866, AMA Archives.

37. "harsh . . . good": Cornelia A. Drake to George Whipple, Savannah, Jan. 27, 1868; "it would be": Cornelia A. Drake to George Whipple, Feb. 27, 1868, AMA Archives; "Aiding the Freedmen," *AM* (Dec. 1864): 292.

38. O. W. Dimick to E. P. Smith, Savannah, Oct. 14, 1867; O. W. Dimick to E. P. Smith, Savannah, March 7, 1867, AMA Archives. Neven was sometimes listed as Matilda Nevers; see *FR* (May 1866): 103, and (June 1866): 123; Johnson, "A Black Teacher and Her School in Reconstruction Darien," pp. 90–105. Hettie Sabattie is listed in *FR* as a teacher on Sapelo Island in January and April 1866 and in Darien in June 1866. On local funding of schools, see Jones, *Soldiers of Light and Love*, p. 62; and Sharon Ann Holt, *Making Freedom Pay*.

39. "a glorious smoke . . . write it": Ellen E. Adlington to E. P. Smith, Berne Plantation, Crooked River, Camden County, Feb. 28, 1868; Ellen E. Adlington to E. P. Smith, Berne, March 31, 1868; "What a study": A. E. Howe to E. P. Smith, "Bell," March 31, 1868, AMA Archives.

40. O. W. Dimick to E. P. Smith, Savannah, Dec. 23, 1867, AMA Archives; "instruct": Douglas R. Risley to C. C. Sibley, Brunswick, Aug. 8, 1867, Letters Received, Reel 14, BRFAL-GA (M798); Report of Gilbert L. Eberhart to C. C. Sibley, Atlanta, July 30, 1867, Letters Received, Reel 17, BRFAL-GA (M798); "I have observed": Sarah Champney to E. P. Smith, N. Bridgewater, Mass., Aug. 11, 1868; "a man": Douglas R. Risley to E. P. Smith, Brunswick, Nov. 28, 1867; "it may be": Sophia Russell to E. Smith, Brunswick, Nov. 13, 1867; "with just": Sophia Russell to E. P. Smith, Brunswick, Nov. 12, 1867, AMA Archives.

41. "are very dull": Sophia Russell and Sarah H. Champney, Freedmen's Bureau Monthly Teachers' Report for Nov. 1867, Hofwyl Plantation, Glynn County, Reel 21, Freedmen's Bureau Education Records (M799); "the most ignorant": Sophia Russell to E. P. Smith, Brunswick, Nov. 12, 1867; Sophia Russell to E. P. Smith, Brunswick, Jan. 31, 1868, AMA Archives.

42. "I do not": Sarah Champney to E. P. Smith, Brunswick, Jan. 1, 1868; "southern . . . government": Sophia Russell to E. P. Smith, Jan. 31, 1868; Sarah Champney to E. P. Smith, Brunswick, Jan. 31, 1868, AMA Archives.

43. "quite . . . grade": Sophia Russell to E. P. Smith, Brunswick, March 1, 1868, AMA Archives; "for our own . . . people": Sophia Russell to E. P. Smith, Brunswick, April 15, 1868; "its enemies": Sophia Russell to George Whipple, Brunswick, May 7, 1868, AMA Archives.

CHAPTER THIRTEEN

1. "not a man": Leigh, *Ten Years on a Georgia Plantation*, p. 59.
2. "political . . . agents": ibid., p. 51; "when": ibid, p. 52.
3. "conquered . . . freedom": ibid., pp. 1–2; Owen Wister, Philadelphia, Dec. 20, 1867, Letters Received, Reel 20, BRFAL-GA (M798); Bell, *Major Butler's Legacy*, pp. 255–310, 406–15.
4. "how completely": Leigh, *Ten Years on a Georgia Plantation*, p. 28; "Dat's so": ibid., p. 29; "long explanation": ibid., p. 44.
5. *SNH*, Jan. 27, 1868; "have the right . . . nuisance": Leigh, *Ten Years on a Georgia Plantation*, pp. 56–57.
6. Circular, O. O. Howard, Jan. 17, 1868, Reel 20; Charles Holcombe to C. C. Sibley, Hinesville, March 5, 1868, Reel 20; "Their greater": J. Murray Hoag to C. C. Sibley, Savannah, Reel 21, Letters Received, BRFAL-GA (M798).
7. Cimbala, *Under the Guardianship of the Nation*, pp. 190–91; Bell, " 'Ogeechee Troubles,' " pp. 384–85; "to prevent": J. Murray Hoag to Maurice Maloney, Savannah, Feb. 29, 1868, FB, GHS; "The negroes . . . politically": "Alexander H. Stephens of Georgia on Public Affairs," *NYT*, Feb. 23, 1868, p. 3; Shadgett, *Republican Party in Georgia*, p. 15. See also Charles R. Holcombe, Hinesville, March 4, 1868, Letters Received, Reel 20, (M798), BRFAL-GA.
8. For an obituary of Julia Marshall Clift, see *AM*, March 1868, p. 63.
9. Foner, *Reconstruction*, pp. 333–36; "by all . . . people": *SNH*, Jan. 10, 1868; "A Colored Mass Meeting in Savannah," *NYT*, Feb. 5, 1868, p. 8; "engaged": Extracts from Minute Book of the Georgia Medical Society, Jan. 8, 1868–May 31, 1871, in JFW Papers, GHS.
10. "unite . . . harm": *SDNH*, March 25, 1868; "A Conservative Meeting at Savannah, Georgia," *NYT*, March 25, 1868, p. 5.

11. Leigh, *Ten Years on a Georgia Plantation*, pp. 53–54.

12. "is in the interests . . . vagrancy": *Freemen's Standard*, Feb. 15, 1868; ibid., April 24, 1868; ibid., April 4, 1868; "Hints . . . bondage": March 7, 1868; *LDC*, Aug. 5, 1867.

13. "If you": "An Incendiary Document in Savannah," *NYT*, April 2, 1868, p. 5; *SDNH*, April 2, 1868; "Grand Cyclops": *Freemen's Standard*, April 4, 1868; *SDNH*, April 7, 1868.

14. Conway, *Reconstruction of Georgia*, pp. 175–76; "the mass": *SDNH*, April 21, 1868; "to finish": ibid., April 24, 1868; "intimidate": *Freemen's Standard*, April 22, 1868; "Glad": *SDNH*, April 24, 1868.

15. "most effervescent . . . say": Leigh, *Ten Years on a Georgia Plantation*, p. 61; "Southern Elections," *NYT*, April 26, 1868, p. 8; Drago, *Black Politicians*, pp. 175–81; *SDNH*, April 29, 1868; Foner, *Freedom's Lawmakers*, pp. 228–29.

16. Conway, *Reconstruction in Georgia*, p. 161; "We are told": Turner quoted in Drago, *Black Politicians*, p. 59.

17. *Freemen's Standard*, April 24, 1868; "are lodged . . . prejudice": "Condition of Affairs in Georgia," p. 43 (testimony taken in late 1868 and early 1869); CC Minutes, Feb. 10, 1868.

18. "the art . . . husbandry": Liberty County Apprenticeship Records, Drawer 29, Microfilm Reel 37, GSA; Charles Sawyer, Haylcondale, Ga., April 6, 1868, Letters Received, Reel 20; telegram from Correll Bros. to C. C. Sibley, Savannah, Feb. 2, 1868, ibid.: correspondence re: Huger plantation, March 1868, ibid., Letters Received, BRFAL-GA (M798); Cimbala, *Under the Guardianship of the Nation*, pp. 157–65; Joseph P. Gilson, Darien, April 21, 1868, Reel 21, Letters Received, BRFAL-GA (M798); Rapport, "Freedmen's Bureau as a Legal Agent for Black Men and Women," pp. 35–37.

19. *SDNH*, May 1, 1868.

20. Report of Mayor E. C. Anderson for 1868–69; Owens, "Negro in Georgia During Reconstruction," p. 112.

21. Charles DeLaMotta to Reven and Dear Sir, Savannah, Oct. 6, 1865, Reel 99, Pt. 1; William Coppinger, Columbus, Ga., Oct. 14, 1867, Reel 101, ACS.

22. "they will have . . . dream": H. A. Crane to William McLain, Savannah, Jan. 9, 1866, Reel 98; Frank Simpson to My Dear Sir, Columbus, Ga., March 16, 1867, Reel 100; E. M. Pendleton to Coppinger, Sparta, Ga., March 18, 1867, Reel 100, ACS.

23. "large": H. M. Turner to Mr. Coppinger, Macon, July 18, 1866, Reel 100; Robert Logan, LaGrange, Ga., Nov. 21, 1865, Reel 98, ACS.

24. "for adminstering . . . sir": Philip Monroe, Columbus, Ga., April 15, 1868, Reel 102; W. L. McLain to Sir, Washington, D.C., March 26, 1868, Reel 101; R. Campbell to Coppinger, Augusta, Ga., April 28, 1868, Reel 102; E. M. Pendleton to Dr. McLain, Sparta, Ga., Feb. 11, 1868, ACS. See also Coppinger correspondence from Charleston, S.C., October and November 1866; E. M. Pendleton to Coppinger, Sparta, Ga., April 11, 1868, reel 102; "four days": ibid., April 24, 1868, Reel 102, ACS.

25. "much feeling . . . wanted": William Coppinger, Savannah, April 27, 1868, Reel 102; ibid., April 30, 1868, Reel 102, ACS.

26. Coppinger Correspondence for May 2–18, 1868, Reel 102, ACS.

27. "The Savannah": William Coppinger, Savannah, May 9, 1868, Reel 102, ACS; Hahn, *A Nation Under Our Feet*, p. 415. This list of associations is culled from records of the Savannah Branch, FST, Reel 8 (M816), RG 101; Index to Deposit Ledgers in Branches of the Freedman's Savings and Trust Company, 1865–1874, Reel 2 (M817), RG 101. See also Schwartz, *Birthing a Slave*, p. 308; Penningroth, *Claims of Kinfolk*, p. 117; Perdue, "The Negro in Savannah," pp. 156–57; Blassingame, "Before the Ghetto: The Making of the Black Community," pp. 475–77.

28. Savannah Branch, FST, Reel 8 (M816), and Index, Reel 2 (M817), RG 101.

29. Ibid.

30. Ibid.; Hoskins, "The Trouble They Seen," p. 64.

31. Savannah Branch, FST, Reel 8 (M816) and Reel 2 (M817) RG 101; Gomez, *Exchanging Our Country Marks*, pp. 98–101. See also "Letter from Lewis Hayden . . . to Hon. Judge Simms"; Sidbury, *Becoming African in America,* pp. 73–75.

32. Savannah Branch, FST, Reel 8 (M816), and Index, Reel 2 (M817), RG 101.

33. Ibid.; "after . . . Georgia": Record 499, Savannah Branch, FST, Reel 8 (M816), RG 101.

34. See Record 526, Savannah Branch, FST, Reel 8 (M816), RG 101; "Memorial Services: Tribute to the Hon. Charles Sumner," p. 31; "Local Matters About Town," *BDA,* Jan. 28, 1869.

35. *SDNH,* June 17, 1868; Gamble, *Savannah Duels and Duellists,* pp. 240–42; Abbott, "Republican Press in Reconstruction Georgia," p. 739.

36. *SDNH,* July 22, 1868, July 23, 1868.

37. "We have fought": *SDNH,* Aug. 11, 1868; "The assemblage": ibid., July 22, 1868; "I think": Henrietta Wayne to My Dear Mama H, Savannah, July 28, 1868, HF Papers, DU.

38. "in their . . . appearance": *SDNH,* July 28, 1868; "is": ibid., Aug. 14, 1868; ibid., Aug. 12, 1868.

39. *SDNH,* July 29, 1868; J. J. Waring File, JFW Papers, GHS; Shryock, ed., *Letters of Richard D. Arnold,* pp. 141–42; Folder, Chatham County, Grand Jury Chatham County, Savannah, "City Limits," GSA; E. C. Anderson to My Dearest Sarah, Savannah, July 16, 1868, ECA, SHC. See also Hahn, *Nation Under Our Feet,* p. 256; Coulter, "Aaron Alpeoria Bradley," Pt. 1, pp. 15–41; Pt. 2, pp. 154–74; Pt. 3, pp. 264–306.

40. Drago, *Black Politicians,* pp. 49–53; Conway, *Reconstruction of Georgia,* pp. 166–67; Coulter, "Aaron A. Bradley," Pt. 1, p. 16; Thompson, *Reconstruction in Georgia,* pp. 211–15.

41. "making warlike . . . Quarters": *SDNH,* Aug. 14, 1868; "his conduct . . . this": Shryock, ed., *Letters of Richard D. Arnold,* pp. 141–42; "Condition of Affairs in Georgia," p. 88; Gamble, *Savannah Duels and Duellists,* p. 243; Lee and Agnew, *Historical Record of the City of Savannah,* p. 192; Abbott, "The Republican Party Press in Reconstruction Georgia," pp. 745–47.

42. Drago, *Black Politicians,* p. 53; "to take": Simms testimony, "Condition of Affairs in Georgia," pp. 10–11.

43. *SMN,* Oct. 28, 1868; McPherson, *Battle Cry of Freedom,* pp. 560, 592.

44. Simms testimony, "Condition of Affairs," p. 8; Drago, *Black Politicians,* pp. 76–77.

45. "said they must": J. Murray Hoag testimony in "Condition of Affairs in Georgia," p. 55; *SMN,* Nov. 4, 1868; "Report of Outrages Committed upon Freedmen, State of Georgia," Jan. 1 to Nov. 15, 1868, Reports, Reel 32, BRFAL-GA (M798).

46. "without": William T. Spencer testimony in "Condition of Affairs in Georgia," pp. 76–77.

47. *SMN,* Jan. 22, 1869.

48. "great": *SMN,* Jan. 21, 1869; "came": *SMN,* Nov. 5, 1868; Jan. 23, 1869; *SMN,* Nov. 4, 1868.

49. "illegal": *SMN,* Nov. 6, 1868; "Negroes . . . law": E. C. Anderson testimony, "Condition of Affairs in Georgia," p. 179; "are strongly": Screven testimony, ibid., p. 228.

50. "our duty": *SMN,* Dec. 21, 1868; "You": *SMN,* Dec. 17, 1868; *SMN,* June 22, 1869.

51. "the white people": *SMN,* Jan. 21, 1869; ibid., Jan. 20, 1869; Bell, " 'Ogeechee Troubles' "; Cimbala, *Under the Guardianship of the Nation,* pp. 190–91; Lane, ed., *Standing Upon the Mouth of a Volcano,* pp. 79–89.

52. "fight": *SMN,* Jan. 21, 1869; *SMN,* Jan. 20, 1869; "I have never": ibid.; "by kindness": *SMN,* Dec. 29, 1869; *SMN,* Dec. 29, 1868. This account is taken from the trial of the Ogeechee defendants, held in Savannah, January 1869, as reported in the *SMN.*

53. "great": *SMN*, Dec. 29, 1868; *SMN*, Jan. 18, 1869; "with sticks": *SMN*, Jan. 18, 1869; "inciting": *SMN*, Jan. 19, 1869.

54. "they had": *SMN*, Jan. 16, 1869; "They said": *SMN*, Jan. 18, 1869; "all jabber-ing . . . women": *SMN*, Jan. 20, 1869; Drago, "Militancy and Black Women," pp. 838–40. In *Claims of Kinfolk*, Penningroth calls this a form of female "loud talking" (p. 184). For accounts in the *NYT*, see, for example, "The Troubles in Georgia," Jan. 1, 1869, p. 1; "Lawless Negroes," Jan. 4, 1869, p. 1.

55. *SMN*, Dec. 31, 1868, and Jan. 2, 1869; Bell, " 'Ogeechee Troubles,' " pp. 386–87.

56. "hard": *SMN*, Jan. 16, 1869; "telegraphic": *SMN*, Jan. 19, 1869.

57. *SMN*, Jan. 28, 1869.

58. "there seemed": *SMN*, Jan. 20, 1869, Feb. 1, 1869, Feb. 2, 1869, Jan. 19, 1869.

CHAPTER FOURTEEN

1. For a sampling of Jones's books, see *Historical Sketch of the Chatham Artillery During the Confederate Struggle for Independence* (1867); *Historical Sketch of Tomo-chi-chi, Mico of the Yamacraws* (1868); *Antiquities of the Southern Indians, Particularly of the Georgia Tribes* (1873); *The Siege of Savannah in December, 1864, and the Confederate Operations in Georgia and the Third Military District of South Carolina . . .* (1874); *The Dead Towns of Georgia* (1878); *The Life and Services of Commodore Josiah Tattnall* (1878); *History of Georgia* (1883); *Negro Myths from the Georgia Coast, Told in the Vernacular* (1888); *Memorial History of Augusta, Georgia* (1890); *Biographical Sketches of the Delegates from Georgia to the Continental Congress* (1891).

2. Jones, *Historical Sketch of Tomo-chi-chi*, pp. vi–vii, 17, 109.

3. *SMN*, Jan. 6, 1869; Hargis, "For the Love of Place," pp. 825–64.

4. "Christmas": Leigh, *Ten Years on a Georgia Plantation*, p. 70; "general": ibid., p. 71; "working": ibid., p. 76.

5. "a gang": ibid., p. 70; "expressions": ibid., p. 70; "seemed": ibid., p. 72.

6. "to use": ibid., pp. 73, 71–72, 80; Drago, *Black Politicians*, p. 82; Duncan, *Freedom's Shore*.

7. "*deny*": Myers, ed., *Children of Pride*, p. 1363; "to hear": Leigh, *Ten Years on a Georgia Plantation*, p. 85.

8. Douglas G. Risley, Savannah, Oct. 24, 1868, AMA Archives; E. P. Smith to E. A. Ware, New York, July 22, 1868, EAW; William P. Vaughn, "Partners in Segregation: Barnas Sears and the Peabody Fund," *CWH* (Sept. 1964): 260–74.

9. "teaching": Harriet Newell to E. P. Smith, McIntosh Station, Georgia, Feb. 23, 1870, AMA Archives; Myers, ed., *Children of Pride*, pp. 1633–34; Johnson, "A Black Teacher and Her School in Reconstruction Darien," pp. 90–105; Douglas G. Risley to E. P. Smith, Brunswick, Sept. 28, 1868; William Jones to E. P. Smith, Hopeton, Dec. 31, 1868; Douglas G. Risley to E. P. Smith, Brunswick, Dec. 31, 1868; "After day school . . . school": James R. Snowden, Glynn Co., March 15, 1869, AMA Archives; James R. Snowden, Glynn Co., March 1869 Freedmen's Bureau Monthly Teachers Report, Records of the Georgia Superintendent of Education, 1865–1870, Reel 23, BRFAL-GA (M799).

10. "a morally jealous . . . married": Douglas G. Risley to Sophia E. Russell, Brunswick, July 9, 1868; Annie R. Wilkins and Margaret Burke to E. P. Smith, Brunswick, Nov. 27, 1868; "a *good*": Douglas G. Risley to E. P. Smith, Savannah, Oct. 20, 1868; "sneers": Douglas G. Risley to E. P. Smith, Brunswick, Oct. 5, 1868, AMA Archives.

11. "These people": E. E. Adlington to E. P. Smith, Berne, Aug. 1, 1969; William T. Spencer to Douglas G. Risley, Brunswick, Feb. 23, 1869; William T. Spencer, Berne, Dec. 3, 1868, E. E. Adlington to E. P. Smith, Berne, Dec. 9, 1868, AMA Archives.

12. Helen B. Sharp to E. P. Smith, Savannah, Jan. 21, 1869; ibid., May 17, 1869; C. W. Sharp to E. P. Smith, Savannah, Jan. 29, 1869, April 16, 1869, April 30, 1869; "the Captain": C. W. Sharp to E. P. Smith, Savannah, May 6, 1869, AMA Archives.

13. "Every . . . suspicions": C. W. Sharp to E. P. Smith, Savannah, March 26, 1869; C. W. Sharp to E. P. Smith, Savannah, July 21, 1868; Jan. 19, 1869, Jan. 21, 1869, AMA Archives; C. W. Sharp to E. A. Ware, Savannah, March 17, 1869, EAW.

14. Owens, "Negro in Georgia During Reconstruction," p. 143; "a connecting": C. W. Sharp to E. P. Smith, Jan. 11, 1869; J. A. Rockwell to E. P. Smith, Macon, Jan. 10, 1869; C. W. Sharp to E. P. Smith, Savannah, Jan. 7, 1869; "strong": C. W. Sharp to E. P. Smith, April 20, 1869; "or sprinkle": Robert Carter to E. P. Smith, June 15, 1869, AMA Archives; Richardson, "Failure of the American Missionary Association."

15. Taylor, *Reminiscences of My Life in Camp*, p. 127; Alvord, "Letters from the South, Relating to the Condition of Freedmen," p. 13.

16. Harden, *History of Savannah and South Georgia*, Vol. 1, pp. 469–70; "a large . . . burden": CC Minutes, Dec. 9, 1868; ibid., Oct. 28, 1868.

17. Report of Mayor John Screven, 1869–1870, p. 19; CC Minutes, Aug. 18, 1869.

18. Conway, *Reconstruction of Georgia*, pp. 138–39, 182.

19. Bell, " 'Ogeechee Troubles,' " p. 393; *SMN,* Feb. 5, 1869, April 2, 1869, June 18, 1869; "Telegraphic," *BDWC*, May 5, 1869.

20. *SMN,* June 18, 1869; Conway, *Reconstruction of Georgia,* pp. 167, 186.

21. *SMN,* June 18, 1869.

22. CC Minutes, March 3, 1869; *SMN,* April 3, 1869, April 4, 1869.

23. "preserve": *SMN*, Aug. 31, 1869; *SMN*, Aug. 13, 1869.

24. "at no period . . . communities": *SMN*, Sept. 1869; Myers, ed., *Children of Pride*, pp. 1672–73; "well-known . . . classes": *SMN*, Sept. 9, 1869. For Lavin and Schwarz, see 1870 FMC, Georgia, Chatham County, Savannah, pp. 157 and 174.

25. *SMN*, Sept. 24, 1869; "outside": *SMN*, Sept. 27, 1869, Oct. 11, 1869, Aug. 31, 1869, Sept. 1, 1869.

26. Savannah voter registration lists, microfilm 11735–39, GSA; "the black element": *SMN*, Oct. 2, 1869.

27. "to prevent": *SMN*, Oct. 9, 1869; *SMN*, Oct. 4, 1869; "the preservation": *SMN*, Oct. 14, 1869; CC Minutes, March 3, 1869; *SMN*, Oct. 13, 1869. Bradley was still out of town. In November he gave a speech in New York City. See "Colored Labor Meeting," *NYT*, Nov. 17, 1869, p. 8.

28. "a complete eclipse": *SMN*, Oct. 7, 1869; "when the rat-eaters": *SMN*, Oct. 11, 1869; Oct. 9, 1869.

29. Leigh, *Ten Years on a Georgia Plantation*, pp. 67–68; Schwalm, *Hard Fight for We*, p. 222; Armstrong, "From Task to Free Labor," p. 443; Morgan, "Work and Culture," pp. 563–99; Waring, "Striving Seventies in Savannah," p. 163; Brooks, *Agrarian Revolution in Georgia*, pp. 31, 100; DeLeon, "Ruin and Reconstruction of the Southern States," p. 23; Bullard, *Cumberland Island*, pp. 165, 262; Alvord, "Letters from the South," pp. 11–12; Hargis, "For the Love of Place," pp. 854–64.

30. *SMN*, May 18, 1868, Aug. 31, 1869; J. J. Waring file, JFW Papers, GHS; CC Minutes, Aug. 26, 1869.

31. Drago, *Black Politicians*, p. 149; Reidy, "Aaron A. Bradley," pp. 281–308; Coulter, "Aaron A. Bradley," Pt. 3, pp. 265–77; Duncan, *Freedom's Shore*, pp. 69–73; Campbell, *Sufferings of the Rev. T. G. Campbell*, pp. 12–13.

32. *SMN*, May 26, 1870.

33. Henrietta Wayne to My Dear Mama H., Savannah, Dec. 21, 1868, HF Papers, DU.

34. "an *army* . . . music": *SMN*, July 22, 1870, April 26, 1870; CC Minutes, May 11, 1870; "floating": Report of Mayor John Screven, 1869–1870, pp. 7–8.

35. "menagerie": CC Minutes, May 11, 1870; CC Minutes, Oct. 25, 1871, Feb. 2, 1870, May 26, 1870, June 18, 1870, July 7, 1870.
36. "it stands . . . strangers": CC Minutes, Jan. 24, 1870.
37. "upon the public . . . humanity": CC Minutes, March 2, 1870; Annual Report of Mayor John Screven, 1869–1870, p. 16; CC Minutes, Jan. 24, 1870, Feb. 2, 1870. For the Burke household, see 1870 FMC, Georgia, Chatham County, Savannah, p. 132.

CHAPTER FIFTEEN

1. *SMN,* May 6, 1870, June 4, 1870. One of the other three assistant marshals in the city, A. Leers, a thirty-eight-year-old native of Germany and a clerk by profession, requested or was assigned a much larger area to canvass—12,400 names, which yielded $248.50. For Leers and Carroll, see 1870 FMC, Georgia, Chatham County, Savannah, pp. 7, 1.
2. Household information gleaned from the 1870 FMC, Savannah. Page numbers are listed for individual households. For the Clark and Porter households, see p. 1. For Pierce and Clift, see p. 198.
3. Samuel Young, Robert Young, and Campbell households: 1870 FMC, Savannah, pp. 110, 106, 107. Information about membership in community associations comes from the records of the Savannah Branch, FST, Reel 8 (M817), RG 101.
4. Mirault, Kelley, Deveaux households: 1870 FMC, Savannah, pp. 29, 73, 151.
5. "In the South," *NYT,* Jan. 3, 1871, p. 3; Blassingame, "Before the Ghetto," pp. 465–67.
6. Lawrence household: 1870 FMC, Savannah, p. 46; Perdue, "Negro in Savannah, 1865–1900," pp. 157, 166; Blassingame, "Before the Ghetto," p. 468; U.S. BRFAL, *Ninth Semi-Annual Report on Schools* (Washington, D.C.: Government Printing Office, 1870), p. 66; Osthaus, *Freedom, Philanthropy, and Fraud,* pp. 125–26.
7. Snyder, LaRoche, Purse, Russell, Anderson, and Gordon households: 1870 Census, Savannah, pp. 53, 183, 23, 82, 166, 75.
8. Perdue, "Negro in Savannah," p. 166; Stewart, Arnold households: 1870 FMC, Savannah, pp. 148, 40.
9. Waring Russell household (jail): 1870 FMC, Savannah, pp. 193–95; "had been living": *SMN,* July 12, 1870. Carroll and his co-workers either avoided these areas, found no one at home when they called, or received only incomplete or misleading information from those who were at home in the city's poorest neighborhoods.
10. *SMN,* Nov. 12, 1870; "kept women": "Report of John Screven, Mayor . . . for the Year Ending Sept. 30, 1871" (Savannah, Ga.: Savannah Morning News Steam-Power Press, 1871), p. 42; Dusenberry and Norris households: 1870 FMC, Savannah, pp. 7, 6.
11. "known": *SMN,* July 20, 1870.
12. "great . . . elicited": *SMN,* Aug. 16, 1870; "by": *SMN,* July 23, 1870.
13. *SMN,* Oct. 3, 1870; Gray, Otto, and McLeod households: 1870 FMC, Savannah: pp. 42, 146, 96. Black churches were also sponsoring temperance efforts. See Gaines, *African Methodism in the South,* pp. 31–32.
14. Conway, *Reconstruction of Georgia,* pp. 188–95; Cimbala, *Under the Guardianship of the Nation,* pp. 217–28; John E. Reed, "What I Know of the Ku Klux Klan," Pt. 1, *Uncle Remus's: The Home Magazine* (Jan. 1908): 21–26; Pt. 2 (Feb. 1908): 60–61; Pt. 3 (March 1908): 92–95; Pt. 3 (cont.) (April 1908): 122–23; *Testimony Taken by the [U.S. Congress] Joint Select Committee to Inquire into the Condition of Affairs,* Georgia testimony, Vols. 1, 2 (hereafter *Testimony Taken*).
15. *SMN,* Nov. 21, 1870.
16. "to go into": E. C. Anderson to My Dear Sarah, Savannah, Aug. 4, 1868, ECA Papers, SHC; "Times are": Henrietta Wayne to My Dear Mother, Savannah, May 8, 1870, HF

Papers, DU. For the Minis household see the 1870 FMC, Savannah, p. 159; for the Andersons, see p. 167.

17. *SMN*, Jan. 5, 1870, April 13, 1870.

18. Robert Carter to E. P. Smith, Savannah, Sept. 11, 1870; "crouch": A. N. Niles to E. M. Cravath, Savannah, Oct. 26, 1870, AMA Archives.

19. 1870 Census, Savannah, p. 34; "overrun . . . them": A. N. Niles to E. M. Cravath, Savannah, May 19, 1870, AMA Archives.

20. "We just get": Lizzie Parsons to M. E. Strieby, Savannah, Sept. 22, 1870; "the children": M. H. Hall to E. M. Cravath, Savannah, May 4, 1871; A. N. Niles to E. M. Cravath, Savannah, Nov. 28, 1870, AMA Archives.

21. "hindrances . . . way": A. N. Niles to E. M. Cravath, Savannah, Oct. 28, 1870; "they are": Abbie Johnson to E. M. Cravath, Savannah, Nov. 28, 1870, AMA Archives.

22. "terribly": A. N. Niles to E. M. Cravath, Savannah, Nov. 15, 1870; "rag . . . boys": Abbie Johnson to E. M. Cravath, Savannah, Nov. 28, 1870; "a gay season trifling": A. N. Niles to E. M. Cravath, Savannah, Nov. 2, 1870; "a most . . . teachers": A. N. Niles to E. M. Cravath, Dec. 12, 1870, AMA Archives.

23. "that he would . . . policemen": *SMN*, May 7, 1870; "respect": *SMN*, May 10, 1870.

24. "must pay": *SMN*, May 25, 1870; Coulter, "Aaron Alpeoria Bradley," Pt. 3, pp. 271–74; "he is the incubus": quoted in ibid., p. 273; *DCH*, April 6, 1870.

25. *SMN*, 135; "this revolutionary": *SMN*, Aug. 25, 1870; Duncan, *Freedom's Shore*, pp. 69–72; Drago, *Black Politicians*, pp. 96–100.

26. Drago, *Black Politicians*, p. 149; CC Minutes, July 7, 1870; *SMN*, July 7, 1870.

27. Perdue, "Negro in Savannah," p. 101; *SMN*, Oct. 4, 1870, Oct. 5, 1870; "embracing . . . interests": *SMN*, Oct. 11, 1870, Oct. 13, 1870.

28. Coulter, "Aaron Alpeoria Bradley," Pt. 3, pp. 277–82; "ineligible . . . man": *SMN*, Dec. 5, 1870; *SMN*, Nov. 11, 1870. For Peter Houston, see 1870 FMC, Savannah, p. 70. The census lists Houston with Charlotte, 27, keeping house; Edward, 16, a laborer; Peter, 14, a cart driver; Henry, 9, at school; and Pompey Butler, 31, a drayman.

29. "negro": *SMN*, Dec. 20, 1870; A. N. Niles to E. M. Cravath, Dec. 12, 1870, AMA Archives; *SMN*, Nov. 23, 1870; *SMN*, Dec. 16, 1870; Blassingame, "Before the Ghetto," p. 464.

30. "well-fed . . . hurrah": *SMN*, Dec. 13, 1870; *Testimony Taken*, Vol. 2, pp. 975–81.

31. *SMN*, Dec. 22, 1870, Dec. 23, 1870, Dec. 24, 1870, Dec. 26, 1870, Dec. 28, 1870, Dec. 29, 1870.

32. *SMN*, Dec. 13, 1870; *SMN*, Dec. 14, 1870.

33. "grand . . . art": *SMN*, Dec. 24, 1870; Waring, "Striving Seventies in Savannah," p. 163; Waring, "Notes and Documents: Savannah of the 1870s," pp. 62–64; Greenberg, "Creating Ethnic, Class, and Southern Identity," p. 47.

34. "fantastic . . . match": "In the South," *NYT*, Jan. 3, 1871, p. 3; Somers, *Southern States Since the War*, pp. 62–102.

35. Brooks, *Agrarian Revolution in Georgia*, p. 187.

36. Leigh, *Ten Years on a Georgia Plantation*, p. 90.

37. Moore, "Sherman's 'Fifth Column,' " pp. 382–409; Penningroth, *Claims of Kinfolk*.

38. Moore, "Sherman's 'Fifth Column' "; Morgan, "Ownership of Property by Slaves," p. 405; Penningroth, *Claims of Kinfolk*.

39. Liberty County Claims, SCC.

40. For Nancy Johnson's testimony, claim of Boson Johnson, see also Berlin et al., eds., *Freedom*, Series 1, Vol. 1, *Destruction of Slavery*, pp. 150–54.

41. Ibid.

42. Ibid.

43. Ibid.

44. Ibid.

45. "I was a slave": Boson Johnson, claimant's deposition; "the Union": testimony of Wallace Johnson, claim of Boson Johnson, Liberty County claim no. 15505, SCC.

46. "they said": claimant's deposition, claim of Boson Johnson; Alexander Steele, Chatham County claim no. 229, SCC; Penningroth, *Claims of Kinfolk*, p. 76.

47. "they were induced": report of agent denying claim of Hagar Stevens of Liberty County (report no. 9, office 637); Records of United States House of Representatives, 1871–1880, *Claims Disallowed by Commissioners of Claims*, RG 233. Simms was Stevens's attorney. See also Chatham County claims of Toby Adams, no. 3928, and Thomas Butler, no. 6053, SCC.

48. Georgiana Kelley claim, Chatham County claim no. 15586, SCC; Rachel Bromfield, Chatham County claim no. 13361; Judy Rose, Chatham County claim no. 15867; Rosanna Houston, testimony for Primus Wilson, Chatham County claim no. 20708; testimony of Ellen Cosens, claim of Georgiana Kelley, Chatham County Claims, SCC.

49. Moses Stikes and Binah Butler, Chatham County claim no. 17563, SCC; "I was born": testimony of Emanuel Sheftall (report no. 9, office 622); "nearly": claimant Jackson B. Sheftall (report no. 9, office 623), Claims Disallowed, RG 233.

50. "made money . . . zealously": Jackson B. Sheftall claim, denied by R. B. Avery, Special Agent, Claims Disallowed, RG 233.

51. *SMN*, Jan. 11, 1871; CC Minutes, Oct. 12, 1870; *SMN*, June 15, 1871; *SMN*, Aug. 23, 1871; "Robert E. Lee," *NYT*, Oct. 14, 1870, p. 1.

52. "Strike of the Cotton Stevedores' Employes [*sic*] of Savannah, Ga," *NYT*, Nov. 7, 1870, p. 1; Mayor's Report, 1870–71; CC Minutes, Dec. 6, 1871, and Dec. 16, 1871, Dec. 26, 1871; *SDR*, April 5, 1871.

53. "suspicious . . . driving": Mayor's Report, 1870–71, p. 41; "Daring": *SMN*, May 15, 1871; *SDR*, Aug. 16, 1872. Other examples have been culled from *SMN*, 1870–71.

54. "the art": *SMN*, Jan. 14, 1871; "Reported Extensive Forgeries in Savannah," *NYT*, May 30, 1870, p. 5; *SMN*, Jan. 26, 1871, Feb. 6, 1871, April 19, 1871.

55. CC Minutes, March 29, 1871, June 15, 1871, July 10, 1871, Aug. 2, 1871, Oct. 25, 1871; Kollock, "Letters of the Kollock and Allied Families," Pt. 5, pp. 324–25.

56. CC Minutes, Dec. 7, 1870, June 14, 1871, July 5, 1871; 1859 Savannah City Directory, http://www.rootsweb.com/~gachath2/1859SavCityDir.html.

CHAPTER SIXTEEN

1. "It is no holiday": A. N. Niles to E. M. Cravath, Savannah, May 3, 1871, AMA Archives; "The Indian As He Is," *AM* (March 1871): 59; A. N. Niles to E. M. Cravath, Savannah, April 11, 1871; A. N. Niles to E. M. Cravath, Savannah, April 20, 1871; A. N. Niles to E. M. Cravath, Savannah, April 17, 1871, AMA Archives.

2. "I am all . . . impulsive": A. N. Niles to Pike, Savannah, April 14, 1871; "have no conception": A. N. Niles to E. M. Cravath, Savannah, April 23, 1871; A. N. Niles to E. M. Cravath, May 17, 1871; "he is all": Petition from "Ministers and leading men," including William J. Campbell, C. O. Fisher, M. L. Simpson, Robert Carter, et al., Savannah, April 3, 1871; A. N. Niles to E. M. Cravath, Oct. 9, 1871, AMA Archives; Richardson, "Failure of the American Missionary Association," pp. 261–83; Hoskins, "The Trouble They Seen," p. 34.

3. "The South . . . rebellion": "The South Is Yet Volcanic," *AM* (Feb. 1871): 37; "When you leave": *Testimony Taken*, Vol. 2, p. 851; Drago, *Black Politicians*, p. 145.

4. Hahn, *Nation Under Our Feet*, p. 276; "a law-abiding . . . toughs": E. C. Anderson testimony, *Testimony Taken*, Vol. 1, pp. 177–78; William W. Paine testimony, ibid.,

pp. 190–93; "morally . . . idleness": Joseph E. Brown testimony, ibid., Georgia, Vol. 2, p. 816; see also ibid., pp. 811, 822.

5. *SMN*, Sept. 30, 1871, Oct. 7, 1871, Oct. 10, 1871.

6. "Memorial Services: Tribute to the Hon. Charles Sumner," pp. 15–16; Angell, "Black Minister Befriends the 'Unquestioned Father of Civil Rights,' " pp. 29–30.

7. "reign": *NYT*, Jan. 30, 1869, p. 1; "sought": "Washington: The Rejected Colored Nominee," *NYT*, May 7, 1869, p. 1.

8. "From the Atlanta *New Era*. The Colored Judge—Interesting Correspondence," *Daily Columbus Enquirer*, Feb. 8, 1871.

9. Perdue, "Negro in Savannah, 1865–1900," pp. 67–68; T. G. Campbell, testimony, *Testimony Taken*, Georgia, Vol. 2, pp. 859–60; "there are": *SMN*, Jan. 27, 1871, March 8, 1871, April 14, 1871; "Through the South, Savannah—A City of Parks," *NYT*, April 22, 1871, p. 2.

10. "in the very": Simms, *First Colored Baptist Church*, p. 151; "a . . . highly repulsive": ibid., pp. 152–53; "Through the South," *NYT*, April 22, 1871, p. 2.

11. "feverish": Simms, *First Colored Baptist Church*, p. 173. See also ibid., pp. 168–70.

12. Ibid., pp. 185–86. For Small, Stiles, and Odingsells, see 1870 FMC, Georgia, Chatham County, Savannah (hereafter 1870 FMC, Savannah), pp. 36, 130 (Stiles and Odingsells were part of the same household).

13. "grossly": Henrietta Wayne to My Dear Mother, Savannah, May 26, 1872, HF Papers, DU.

14. "The Personal Reminiscences of William Starr Basinger, 1827–1910," p. 290, GHS; Foner, *Reconstruction*, pp. 504–505, 532–34, 550, 552; Conway, *Reconstruction of Georgia*, pp. 201–202.

15. "acting": quoted in Duncan, *Freedom's Shore*, p. 88; Tunis G. Campbell, *Sufferings of the Rev. T. G. Campbell*, pp. 13–14; *SMN*, Jan. 11, 1872; Drago, *Black Politicians*, pp. 82, 178.

16. Tunis G. Campbell testimony, *Testimony Taken*, Vol. 2, p. 849; Duncan, *Freedom's Shore*, p. 78; "The Case of the British Bark Grace—Decision of the United States Commissioner," *NYT*, Aug. 23, 1871, p. 8.

17. "the oppressive": *SMN*, Jan. 11, 1872; Duncan, *Freedom's Shore*, p. 84; "one resource": ibid., p. 89; Campbell, *Sufferings of the Rev. T. G. Campbell*, p. 14.

18. "was guilty": Duncan, *Freedom's Shore*, p. 93.

19. See, for example, "monkey-faced": *SMN*, Sept. 18, 1872; "King": *SMN*, Nov. 11, 1871; "miserable": *SMN*, Jan. 27, 1871; "nigger": *SMN*, March 8, 1871; "Great Wahoo": April 16, 1872, *SMN*. In his series of articles, "Aaron A. Bradley, Georgia Negro Politician During Reconstruction Times," Coulter includes, with apparent relish, many of the epithets used by papers around the state to describe the attorney.

20. "You and I": *SMN*, Jan. 23, 1872; "Rally": *SMN*, April 16, 1872.

21. *SMN*, July 29, 1872.

22. "The women": ibid., July 30, 1872; Drago, "Militancy and Black Women in Reconstruction Georgia," p. 840.

23. *SMN*, July 31, 1872; "to test": *SMN*, Aug. 3, 1872; *SMN*, July 29, 1872. For Avery Smith, see 1870 FMC, Savannah, p. 37.

24. *SMN*, Aug. 5, 1872.

25. Shadgett, *Republican Party in Georgia*, p. 40; *SMN*, April 16, 1872.

26. *SMN*, Dec. 30, 1871.

27. "conspiracy": *SMN*, Aug. 21, 1872; "raps": *SMN*, Aug. 27, 1872; "and his negro": *SMN*, Aug. 14, 1872. See also *SMN*, Aug. 15, 1872.

28. A. N. Niles to E. M. Cravath, Savannah, Nov. 9, 1871; "with such": A. N. Niles to E. M. Cravath, Savannah, Nov. 14, AMA Archives; Hoskins, "The Trouble They Seen," p. 34.

29. Perdue, "Negro in Savannah," pp. 140–42; *SMN*, Sept. 28, 1872; A. N. Niles to E. M.

Cravath, Oct. 5, 1872; "if the Protestant": A. N. Niles to E. M. Cravath, Oct. 9, 1872; "like furniture": A. N. Niles to E. M. Cravath, Savannah, Feb. 20, 1872, AMA Archives; Shryock, ed., *Letters of Richard D. Arnold*, p. 163.

30. Mayor's Report for 1871–72; Owens, "Negro in Georgia During Reconstruction," p. 177; Gamble, *History of the City Government of Savannah*, pp. 285–86; Hoskins, *Black Episcopalians in Savannah*, p. 20; Perdue, "Negro in Savannah," p. 145.

31. "in no instance": Shryock, ed., *Letters of Richard D. Arnold*, p. 154; "the": ibid., p. 152. See also ibid., p. 150.

32. *SMN*, Sept. 3, 1872; "all true Irishmen": Sandy Mills, letter to the editor, *SMN*, Aug. 31, 1872; "at": *SMN*, Oct. 4, 1872, Sept. 6, 1872. Fall municipal elections of 1872 were pushed back to January 1873. See Gamble, *History of the City Government*, p. 6.

33. Angell, "A Black Minister Befriends the 'Unquestioned Father of Civil Rights' "; *SMN*, Oct. 3, 1872; Shadgett, p. 45; "obstinacy . . . perseverance": "The Greeleyite Outrages in Georgia," *NYT*, Oct. 8, 1872, p. 4; Oct. 12, 1872, AMA Archives; "he did not": *SMN*, Oct. 3, 1872. For Grant see 1870 FMC, Savannah, p. 108.

34. *SMN*, Oct. 7, 1872; "Affairs in Georgia," *NYT*, Oct. 8, 1872, p. 5; "Georgia: The Late Election—Unprecented [*sic*] Frauds—Intimidation, Violence, and Murder . . . ," *NYT*, Oct. 9, 1872, p. 2.

35. *SMN*, Nov. 6, 1872; "to burn": *SMN*, Nov. 8, 1872.

36. *SMN*, Nov. 7, 1872, Nov. 8, 1872, Nov. 11, 1872; Shadgett, *Republican Party in Georgia*, pp. 46–48. For George Dolly, see 1870 FMC, Savannah, p. 223.

37. Hargis, "For the Love of Place," p. 839; "Want and Waste," *AM* (Aug. 1871): p. 171; Stevens household, Liberty County Ordinary Homestead Exemptions, 1872, Reel 41, GSA; *Testimony Taken*, Vol. 2, p. 940. For the Stevens household, see also 1870 FMC, Liberty County, p. 48.

38. Taylor, *Reminiscences of My Life in Camp*, pp. 127–29; Shaffer, *After the Glory*, pp. 169–94.

EPILOGUE

1. King, *Great South*, p. 362.

2. "The negroes": ibid., p. 369; "false": R. F. Markham to M. E. Strieby, Savannah, Jan. 3, 1876, AMA Archives; "all sorts": "The Peace in Georgia," *NYT*, Nov. 3, 1876, p. 2; Drago, *Black Politicians*, p. 155; "Leaves of Travel": *NYT*, Feb. 7, 1875, p. 4.

3. R. F. Markham to M. E. Strieby, Savannah, Dec. 22, 1875, AMA Archives; "sneaking . . . slavery": "The Peace in Georgia," *NYT*, Nov. 3, 1876, p. 2; Dittmer, *Black Georgia*, pp. 98–99.

4. Drago, *Black Politicians*, pp. 157–59; "Democracy": "The Peace in Georgia," *NYT*, Nov. 3, 1876; Foner, *Freedom's Lawmakers*, p. 2; Redkey, *Black Exodus*, pp. 24–31.

5. "Emancipation Day," *NYT*, Jan. 2, 1874; Perdue, "Negro in Savannah," pp. 103–106, 143, 180; "indignation": Sterling, ed., *Trouble They Seen*, p. 302; *ST*, Jan. 30, 1892, and Feb. 15, 1896; Brundage, *Southern Past*, pp. 69–72.

6. "Memorial Services: Tribute to the Hon. Charles Sumner," pp. 30–31; Angell, "Black Minister Befriends the 'Unquestioned Father of Civil Rights,' " pp. 27–58.

7. *ST*, April 22, 1876.

8. "in that bank": Taylor, *Reminiscences of My Life in Camp*, p. 27; Perdue, "Negro in Savannah," p. 104, Osthaus, *Freedmen, Philanthropy, and Fraud*, pp. 173–200, 206–207.

9. "The dark day": "A Letter from Lewis Hayden, of Boston, Massachusetts, to Hon. Judge Simms, of Savannah, Georgia"; Drago, *Black Politicians*, pp. 91–98; Perdue, "Negro in Savannah," pp. 99, 110; Dittmer, *Black Georgia*, pp. 91–94; Hoskins, "The Trouble They Seen."

10. For the White and Deveaux households, see the 1880 FMC, Georgia, Chatham County, Savannah, p. 40 (Supervisor's District 3).

11. For a photo of the monument and an account of its history see http://www.geocities .com/Heartland/Pines/3093/pager.html.

12. Waring, "Epidemic at Savannah, 1876."

13. Ibid.; Gamble, *History of the City Government of Savannah*, pp. 287–340; Usinger, "Yellow Fever from the Viewpoint of Savannah," pp. 143–56; "because I do not": Shryock, ed., *Letters of Richard D. Arnold*, pp. 155, 9. See also Crosby, *The American Plague*.

14. Denmark, " 'At the Midnight Hour,' " pp. 350–90.

15. Simms, *First Colored Baptist Church*, pp. 13–14. See the broadside dated March 9, 1876, and signed by Turner, Simms, and J. F. Lang, calling for a convention in Nashville, Emory Library Manuscript Collection.

16. Wright, *Brief Historical Sketch of Negro Education in Georgia*, pp. 38–39; "the mother": "Death of an Aged Negress," *Macon Weekly Telegraph*, Jan. 21, 1886, p. 4; "son of": "Obituary [of James Porter]," *ST*, Nov. 3, 1895; Andres, "Life of James Meriles Simms," May 23, 1985, typescript in GHS.

17. "malpractice": Duncan, *Freedom's Shore*, p. 104; "If a man": Campbell, *Sufferings of the Rev. T. G. Campbell and His Family*, p. 26; *ST*, Jan. 15, 1876, May 20, 1876. See also Duncan, *Freedom's Shore*, pp. 105–09.

18. "Devens and Sims," *NYT*, April 11, 1877, p. 4; *Washington, D.C., Directory, 1890 and 1891* (database online) (Provo, Utah: Generations Network, Inc., 2000); "Simms' Slavery," *SLG-D*, April 10, 1877. Simms was living at 733 11th St. Northwest.

19. "a forlorn place": quoted in Yellin, *Harriet Jacobs*, p. 252.

20. "Congregationers": Richardson, " 'Labor Is Rest to Me Here in This the Lord's Vineyard,' " p. 17; Hoskins, *Black Episcopalians in Georgia*, pp. 61–62; Foner, *Freedom's Lawmakers*, p. 173; "Obituary," *ST*, Nov. 3, 1895. The post-Savannah careers of the AMA teachers are charted through the addresses on their letters to AMA officials.

21. "Aaron Alpeoria Bradley": "Political Notes," *NYT*, Oct. 21, 1878, p. 5; "He was denied": *SMN*, Oct. 25, 1882; Reidy, "Aaron A. Bradley," p. 300; Coulter, "Aaron Alpeoria Bradley," Pt. 3, pp. 301–303.

22. "a most inspiring . . . sea": "Soldiers at Savannah," *BDG*, May 4, 1886, p. 1; "Davis to the Children," ibid., May 5, 1886, p. 5; Shaffer, *After the Glory*, pp. 173–77; Blight, *Race and Reunion*; Brundage, "Race, Memory, and Masculinity," pp. 150–51. See also Clark, *Defining Moments*, pp. 130–37, 165–67, 202–204.

23. "that American": Shaffer, *After the Glory*, p. 162; "the heart-rending": Taylor, *Reminiscences of My Life in Camp*, p. 139. In the 1900 Federal Manuscript Census for Massachusetts, Suffolk County, Boston, Susie and Russell L. Taylor were living in a boardinghouse that included Susie Greene, 19, Russell's niece, and a number of black lodgers, including people born in Georgia, Virginia, Massachusetts, and Canada (Precinct no. 5, 10th div., p. 16).

24. Brundage, "Race, Memory, and Masculinity," p. 151; Shaffer, *After the Glory*, pp. 64, 121–23, 56, 206, 132, 137; *ST*, Feb. 15, 1896.

25. Harris, *Deep Souths*, pp. 78, 103, 143; Perdue, "Negro in Savannah," p. 190; Jones, *American Work*, pp. 222–45.

26. Stewart, *"What Nature Suffers to Groe,"* pp. 193–242; "four quarters": Leigh, *Ten Years on a Georgia Plantation*, pp. 124–25; "quite": quoted in Harris, *Deep Souths*, p. 16. See also ibid., pp. 101–103.

27. Monroe Work, "The Negroes of Warsaw, Georgia," *Southern Workman* 37 (January 1908): 29–40; Robert B. Outland III, *Tapping the Pines*; "This time": Parrish, *Slave Songs of the Georgia Sea Islands*, p. 220.

28. "Squeeze": Edgeworth quoted in Hargis, "For the Love of Place," p. 856.

29. Harris, *Deep Souths*, pp. 83–118; C. Vann Woodward, *Tom Watson*.

30. "the men": "The Savannah Wharf Workers' Strike, 1891" (based on *Savannah Morning News* accounts) in Foner and Lewis, eds., *Black Worker*, Vol. 3, p. 377.

31. "that they were": ibid., p. 395; "We could . . . work": ibid., pp. 403–404. See also Dittmer, *Black Georgia*, p. 28.

32. "as much as": Meier and Rudwick, "Boycott Movement Against Jim Crow Streetcars," p. 756; "Let us walk": quoted in Campbell, "Profit, Prejudice, and Protest," pp. 197–231.

33. Campbell, "Profit, Prejudice, and Protest," p. 227; Perdue, "Negro in Savannah," pp. 44–64. See also Kousser, *Shaping of Southern Politics*, pp. 41, 218–21; Harris, *Deep Souths*, p. 345; Dittmer, *Black Georgia*, p. 10.

34. "Not very much": Sanford E. Edwards Sr., "Thomas Simms' Quest for Freedom," May 23, 1985, p. 9, typescript in GHS vertical biographical file.

35. Harris, *Deep Souths,* pp. 217, 348–52.

36. "All you can": Kiser, *Sea Island to City*, pp. 137–38.

37. Hargis, "For the Love of Place," pp. 839–64; "where generous": Jones, *Gullah Folktales from the Georgia Coast*, p. 155; Parrish, *Slave Songs of the Georgia Sea Islands*; Lorenzo Dow Turner, *Africanisms in the Gullah Dialect*.

38. "Ghosts . . . true": Savannah Unit, Georgia Writers' Project, *Drums and Shadows*, pp. 23–24.

39. "If I read": quoted in Harris, *Deep Souths*, p. 308; Jones, ed., *Historic Savannah*, pp. 202–203; Hoskins, *Out of Yamacraw and Beyond*, pp. 130–38. See also ibid., pp. 254, 288. On Gilbert and the civil rights movement in Savannah, see the following New Georgia Encyclopedia entry: "Ralph Mark Gilbert Civil Rights Museum" (http://www .georgiaencyclopedia.org/nge/Article.jsp?id=h-2734&hl-y) and other entries, including "National Association for the Advancement of Colored People," "Black Voter Registration Drive," and "Civil Rights Movement."

40. "Savannah," New Georgia Encyclopedia (http://georgiaencyclopedia.org/nge/Article .jsp?id=h-1056&sug=y) and other entries, including *Midnight in the Garden of Good and Evil*.

41. Brundage, *Southern Past,* pp. 255–69, 287–91.

42. Daniel Machlara, "How Savannah Brought New Life to Its Aging Port," *Wall Street Journal*, Aug. 22, 2005, pp. A1, A4; Brundage, *Southern Past,* p. 269. Interview with Mayor Otis S. Johnson, February 21, 2007. Notes in author's possession.

43. "Despite": "Owens-Thomas House Adds a New Interpretation to Its History," *SMN*, Feb. 21, 2007. I am indebted to my tour guide, the Reverend Charles Lwanga Hoskins, historian and political activist.

44. Bernard-Henri Lévy, "In the Footsteps of Tocqueville," Pt. 4, *Atlantic,* Oct. 2005, p. 97, and *American Vertigo*.

45. Alderman, "Coastal Heritage as a Contested Landscape"; " would speak": newspaper article by Erik A. Andres, clipping from the *Savannah Evening Press*, in vertical biographical files, GHS. See also the relevant essays in Horton and Horton, eds., *Slavery and Public History*, especially James Oliver Horton, "Slavery in American History: An Uncomfortable National Dialogue," pp. 35–56; Edward T. Linenthal, "Epilogue: Reflections," pp. 213–24. On Dr. Abigail Jordan and her effort to erect the monument, see the article "Fighting the Good Fight," by Jason Peevy, in the University of Georgia publication *Profiles* 83 (March 2004).

SELECTED BIBLIOGRAPHY

PRIMARY SOURCES

NEWSPAPERS

Anglo-African
Bangor (Maine) Daily Whig
    and Courier
Boston Daily Advertiser
Boston Daily Atlas
Boston Daily Globe
Christian Register
Daily Cleveland (Ohio) Herald
Daily National Intelligencer
Frederick Douglass' Paper
Freedmen's Record
Freedmen's Standard

Liberator
Lowell (Massachusetts) Daily Citizen
National Freedman
National Workman
New York Times
North Star
Savannah (Daily) Morning News
Savannah Daily (News and) Herald
Savannah (Daily) Republican
Savannah Tribune
St. Louis Globe-Democrat

MANUSCRIPT COLLECTIONS AVAILABLE ON MICROFILM

American Colonization Society Records. Papers in the Manuscript Division of the Library of Congress.

American Missionary Association Archives. Amistad Research Center, Tulane University, New Orleans, Louisiana.

Records of Ante-bellum Plantation Records from the Revolution Through the Civil War. Series J. Edited by Kenneth Stampp. Frederick, Md.: University Publications of America, 1989–1993.

Black Abolitionist Papers, 1830–1865. Edited by George E. Carter and C. Peter Ripley. Sanford, N.C.: Microfilming Corp. of America, 1981.

MANUSCRIPT AND TYPESCRIPT COLLECTIONS

AMISTAD RESEARCH CENTER AT TULANE UNIVERSITY, NEW ORLEANS, LOUISIANA

American Missionary Association Archives.
Esther W. Douglass Papers.

THE RARE BOOK, MANUSCRIPT, AND SPECIAL COLLECTIONS LIBRARY, DUKE UNIVERSITY, DURHAM, NORTH CAROLINA

Harden Family Papers.

Charles S. Powell, "War Tales, 1861–1865" (typescript).

GEORGIA HISTORICAL SOCIETY, SAVANNAH, GEORGIA

Andres, Erik A. "The Life of James Meriles Simms." Typescript in Vertical Biographical File.

Edward C. Anderson Diary.

Richard D. Arnold Papers.

Basinger, William Starr. "The Personal Reminiscences of William Starr Basinger, 1827–1910," Rare Book Typescript.

John McLaughlin Papers.

Mercer Family Papers, 1848–1965.

Savannah Poor House and Hospital Records.

Savannah Police Department and Jail Records.

J. F. Waring Papers.

United States Bureau of Refugees, Freedmen, and Abandoned Lands, Unprocessed Collection.

NATIONAL ARCHIVES AND RECORDS ADMINISTRATION, WASHINGTON, D.C., AND COLLEGE PARK, MARYLAND

Freedmen and Southern Society Project. University of Maryland.

NATIONAL ARCHIVES RECORD GROUPS

Records of the Bureau of Refugees, Freedmen, and Abandoned Lands. Record Group 105.

Records of the Field Offices for the State of Georgia (M1903).

Records of the Assistant Commissioner for the State of Georgia (M798).

Records of the Superintendent of Education for the State of Georgia (M799).

Records of the Freedman's Savings and Trust Company, Savannah Branch, Records of the Office of the Comptroller of the Currency. Record Group 101.

Indexes to Deposit Ledgers in Branches of the Freedman's Savings and Trust Company, 1865–1864 (M817).

War Department Collection of Confederate Records. Record Group 109.

Southern Claims Commission Approved Claims, 1871–1880: Georgia, Records of the United States General Accounting Office, Record Group 217 (M1658).

Records of the U.S. House of Representatives, 1871–1880. Record Group 233.

Records of United States Army Continental Commands, 1821–1920. Record Group 393.

GEORGIA DEPARTMENT OF ARCHIVES AND HISTORY, ATLANTA, GEORGIA

Record Group 1: Executive Department

Reconstruction Oath Books

Reconstruction Returns of Voters

Record Group 4: Department of Archives and History, County Records

Ordinary/Superior Court Records

Apprenticeship/Indenture Records, 1800–1930

Free Persons of Color Registers, 1780–1865

Petit Jury Lists

County Records for Bryan, Chatham, Liberty, McIntosh
Chatham County, Savannah, City of
  Annual Reports of the Superintendent of Public Schools, 1866–68.
  City Council Minutes
  Clerk of Council
  Registers of Free People of Color
  Jail Records
  Mayor's Court
  Mayor's Annual Reports
  Peddler's Licenses
  Voter Registration Lists

ATLANTA UNIVERSITY ARCHIVES, ROBERT W. WOODRUFF LIBRARY OF THE ATLANTA UNIVERSITY CENTER, ATLANTA

Edmund Asa Ware Records.

SOUTHERN HISTORICAL COLLECTION, WILSON LIBRARY, THE UNIVERSITY OF NORTH CAROLINA AT CHAPEL HILL

Edward C. Anderson Papers.
Richard D. Arnold Papers.
Arnold and Screven Family Papers.
Henry L. Cathell Diary.
Jeremy Francis Gilmore Papers.

GEORGIA STATE GOVERNMENT PUBLICATIONS

Allen D. Candler, ed. *The Confederate Records of the State of Georgia.*
  Vol. 2: *State Papers of Governor Joseph E. Brown Relating to the Public Defense, the Organization and Equipment of Troops, Provision for the Family of Soldiers, etc., 1860 to 1865.* Atlanta: Chas. P. Byrd, 1909.
  Vol. 3: *Official Correspondence of Governor Joseph E. Brown, 1860–1865.* Atlanta: Chas. P. Byrd, 1910.
  Vol. 4: *Introduction to Reconstruction Records, General Orders Covering Reconstruction, 1867–1868.* Atlanta: Chas. P. Byrd, 1911.

U.S. GOVERNMENT DOCUMENTS AND PUBLICATIONS

"Condition of Affairs in Georgia," 40th Congress, 3d sess., House of Representatives, Misc. Doc. no. 52, 1869.
Official Records of the Union and Confederate Navies in the War of the Rebellion. 30 vols. Washington, D.C.: Government Printing Office, 1894–1922.
Report of the Commission on the Bureau of Refugees, Freedmen, and Abandoned Lands, Dec. 1865, 39th Cong., 1st sess., House Executive Doc. No. 11.
Testimony Taken by the Joint Select Committee to Inquire into the Condition of Affairs in the Late Insurrectionary States: Georgia. Vols. 1 and 2. Washington, D.C.: Government Printing Office, 1872.
United States Bureau of the Census. Manuscript Population Schedules. National Archives, Washington, D.C. Available on microfilm and online (ancestry.com)
War of the Rebellion: A Compilation of the Official Records of the Union and Confederate Armies. Series I, vols. 1–53; series II, vols. 1–8; Series III, vols. 1–5; Series IV, vols. 1–3. Washington, D.C.: Government Printing Office, 1880–1901.

PRIMARY PUBLISHED MATERIALS
BOOKS

Abbott, Allen O. *Prison Life in the South: At Richmond, Macon, Savannah, Charleston, Columbia . . . During the Years 1864 and 1865.* New York: Harper and Bros., 1865.

Adams, Nehemiah. *South-Side View of Slavery: Three Months at the South, in 1854.* New York: Negro Universities Press, 1969; orig. pub. 1854.

Adams, Virginia Matzke, ed. *On the Altar of Freedom: A Black Soldier's Civil War Letters from the Front* [James Henry Gooding]. Amherst: University of Massachusetts Press, 1991.

Andrews, Sidney. *The South Since the War: Fourteen Weeks of Travel and Observation in Georgia and the Carolinas.* Boston: Houghton Mifflin, 1971; orig. pub. 1866.

Andrews, W. H. *Footprints of a Regiment: Recollections of the 1st Georgia Regulars, 1861–1865.* Atlanta: Longstreet Press, 1992.

Avary, Myrta Lockett. *Dixie After the War.* New York: Doubleday, Page & Company, 1906.

Bancroft, Frederic. *Slave-Trading in the Old South.* Baltimore: J. H. Furst Company, 1931.

Bauer, K. Jack, ed. *Soldiering: The Civil War Diary of Rice C. Bull, 123rd New York Voluntary Infantry.* San Rafael, Calif.: Presidio Press, 1977.

Berlin, Ira, Barbara J. Fields, Thavolia Glymph, Joseph P. Reidy, and Leslie S. Rowland, eds. *Freedom: A Documentary History of Emancipation, 1861–1867*, Series 1, Vol. 1: *The Destruction of Slavery.* Cambridge: Cambridge University Press, 1985.

Berlin, Ira, Joseph P. Reidy, and Leslie Rowland, eds., *Freedom: A Documentary History of Emancipation, 1861–1867*, Series 2, *The Black Military Experience.* Cambridge: Cambridge University Press, 1982.

Berlin, Ira, Thavolia Glymph, Steven F. Miller, Joseph P. Reidy, Leslie S. Rowland, and Julie Saville, eds. *Freedom: A Documentary History of Emancipation, 1861–1867.* Series 1, Vol. 3: *The Wartime Genesis of Free Labor: The Lower South.* Cambridge: Cambridge University Press, 1990.

Beveridge, Charles E., and Charles Capen McLaughlin, eds. *The Papers of Frederick Law Olmsted.* Vol. 2: *Slavery and the South, 1852–1857.* Baltimore: Johns Hopkins University Press, 1981.

Blassingame, John, ed. *Slave Testimony: Two Centuries of Letters, Speeches, Interviews, and Autobiographies.* Baton Rouge: Louisiana State University Press, 1977.

Bodichon, Barbara Leigh Smith. *An American Diary, 1857-8.* Edited by Joseph W. Reed Jr. London: Routledge & Kegan Paul, 1972.

Boggs, Marion Alexander, ed. *The Alexander Letters, 1787–1900.* Athens: University of Georgia Press, 1980. Orig. pub. 1910.

Boyle, John Richards. *Soldiers True: The Story of the One Hundred and Eleventh Regiment Pennsylvania . . .* New York: Eaton & Mains, 1903.

Bradley, George S. *The Star Corps: Or Notes of an Army Chaplain, During Sherman's Famous "March to the Sea."* Milwaukee: Jermain & Brightman Printers, 1865.

Bremer, Frederika. *The Homes of the New World: Impressions of America.* 2 vols. New York: Harper & Brothers, 1854.

Broderick, John C., ed. *Henry D. Thoreau, Journal.* Vol 3: *1848–1851.* Princeton, N.J.: Princeton University Press, 1990.

Buckingham, James Silk. *The Slave States in America.* London: Fisher Son, 1842.

Burke, Emily. *Pleasure and Pain: Reminiscences of Georgia in the 1840s.* Savannah, Ga.: Beehive Press, 1991; orig. pub. 1850.

Campbell, Tunis G. *The Sufferings of the Rev. T. G. Campbell and His Family in Georgia.* Washington, D.C.: Enterprise Publishing Company, 1877.

———. *Hotel Keepers, Head Waiters, and Housekeepers' Guide.* Boston: Coolidge and Wiley, 1848.

Carter, Christine Jacobson, ed. *The Diary of Dolly Lunt Burge, 1848–1879*. Athens: University of Georgia Press, 1997.

Chamerovzow, L. A., ed. *Slave Life in Georgia: A Narrative of the Life, Sufferings, and Escape of John Brown, a Fugitive Slave Now in England*. 2nd. ed. Freeport, N.Y.: Books for Libraries, 1971.

Chittenden, L. E. *Personal Reminiscences, 1840–1890*. New York: Richmond, Croscup & Co., 1893.

Clark, Olynthus B., ed. *Downing's Civil War Diary*. Des Moines: Historical Department of Iowa, 1916.

Clifton, James M., ed. *Life and Labor on Argyle Island: Letters and Documents of a Savannah River Plantation, 1835–1867*. Savannah, Ga.: Beehive Press, 1978.

Clinton, Catherine, ed. *Fanny Kemble's Journals*. Cambridge: Harvard University Press, 2000.

——, ed. *Reminiscences of My Life in Camp: An African American Woman's Civil War Memoir by Susie King Taylor*. Athens: University of Georgia Press, 2006; orig. pub. 1902.

Coffin, Charles C. *Four Years of Fighting: A Volume of Personal Observations*. Boston: Ticknor and Fields, 1866.

Commons, John R., et al., eds. *A Documentary History of American Industrial Society*. 10 vols. Cleveland: Arthur H. Clark Company, 1910.

Connolly, James A. *Three Years in the Army of the Cumberland: The Letters and Diary of Major James A. Connolly*. Edited by Paul M. Angle. Bloomington: Indiana University Press, 1959.

Conyngham, David Power. *Sherman's March Through the South, with Sketches and Incidents of the Campaign*. New York: Sheldon & Co., 1865.

Denison, Frederic. *Shot and Shell: The Third Rhode Island Heavy Artillery in the Rebellion, 1861–1865*. Providence: Published for 3rd R.I. Heavy Artillery Veterans Association.

Diary of E. P. Burton, Surgeon 7th Reg. Ill. 3rd Brig. 2nd Div. 16 A.C. Des Moines, Iowa, 1939.

Drummond, Edward William. *A Confederate Yankee: The Journal of Edward William Drummond, a Confederate Soldier from Maine*. Edited by Roger S. Durham. Knoxville: University of Tennessee Press, 2004.

Duncan, Russell, ed. *Blue-Eyed Child of Fortune: The Civil War Letters of Colonel Robert Gould Shaw*. Athens: University of Georgia Press, 1992.

Folsom, James Madison. *Heroes and Martyrs of Georgia: Georgia's Record in the Revolution of 1861*. Macon, Ga.: Burke, Boykin & Company, 1864.

Foner, Philip, and Ronald E. Lewis, eds. *The Black Worker: A Documentary History from Colonial Times to the Present*, vol. 3. Philadelphia: Temple University Press, 1978.

Foster, Lillian. *Wayside Glimpses, North and South*. New York: Rudd and Carleton, 1860.

Gaines, Wesley. *African Methodism in the South; Or, Twenty-five Years of Freedom*. Chicago: Afro-American Press, 1969; orig. pub. 1890.

Genealogical Committee of the Georgia Historical Society, comp. *The 1860 Census of Chatham County, Georgia*. Easley, S.C.: Southern Historical Press, 1980.

Grimshaw, William H. *Official History of Freemasonry Among the Colored People of North America*. New York: Negro Universities Press, 1969; orig. pub. 1903.

Habersham, Josephine Clay. *Ebb Tide: As Seen through the Diary of Josephine Clay Habersham, 1863*. Edited by Spencer Bidwell King Jr. Athens: University of Georgia Press, 1958.

Hahn, Steven, Susan E. O'Donovan, John C. Rodriguez, and Leslie Rowland, eds. *Freedom: A Documentary History of Emancipation, 1861–1867*, Series 3, Vol. 1: *Land and Labor*. New York: Cambridge University Press, 2001.

Harden, William. *Recollections of a Long and Satisfactory Life*. New York: Negro Universities Press, 1968; orig. pub. 1934.

Hayes, John D., ed. *Samuel Francis DuPont: A Selection from His Civil War Letters*. Vol. 1, *The Mission: 1860–1862*. Vol. 2, *The Blockade: 1862–1863*. Ithaca, N.Y.: Cornell University Press, 1969.

Hedley, F. Y. *Marching through Georgia: Pen-Pictures of Every-Day Life*. Chicago: Donahue, Henneberry & Co., 1890.

Higginson, Thomas Wentworth. *Army Life in a Black Regiment*. New York: Collier Books, 1962; orig. pub. 1870.

———. *Cheerful Yesterdays*. New York: Arno Press, 1968; orig. pub. 1899.

Hight, John J. *History of the Fifty-eighth Regiment of Indiana Volunteer Infantry*. Princeton, N.J.: Press of the Clarion, 1895.

House, Albert Virgil, ed. *Planter Management and Capitalism in Ante-bellum Georgia: The Journals of Hugh Fraser Grant, Ricegrower*. New York: Columbia University Press, 1954.

Howard, Frances Thomas. *In and Out of the Lines: An Accurate Account of Incidents During the Occupation of Georgia by Federal Troops, 1864–65*. New York: Neale Publishing, 1905.

Howard, Oliver O. *Autobiography of Oliver Otis Howard, Major General, United States Army*. 2 vols. New York: Baker and Taylor, 1907.

Howe, M. A. DeWolfe, ed. *Marching with Sherman: Passages from the Letters and Campaign Diaries of Henry Hitchcock*. Lincoln: University of Nebraska Press, 1995.

Hughes, Nathaniel Cheairs, Jr. *General William J. Hardee: Old Reliable*. Baton Rouge: Louisiana State University Press, 1965.

Johnson, Robert Underwood, and Clarence Clough Buel, eds. *Battles and Leaders of the Civil War*. 4 vols. New York: The Century Co., 1887–88.

Jones, Charles C. *The Religious Instruction of the Negroes in the United States*. Savannah, Ga.: Thomas Purse, 1842.

Jones, Charles C., Jr. *Gullah Folktales from the Georgia Coast*. Athens: University of Georgia Press, 2000; orig. pub. 1888.

———. *Historical Sketch of Tomo-chi-chi, Mico of the Yamacraws*. Albany, N.Y.: J. Munsell, 1868.

———. *History of Savannah, Georgia: From Its Settlement to the Close of the Eighteenth Century*. Syracuse, N.Y.: D. Mason and Co., 1890.

Kelley, Daniel G. *What I Saw and Suffered in Rebel Prisons*. Buffalo, N.Y.: Thomas, Howard, and Johnson, 1868.

King, Edward. *The Great South*. Baton Rouge: Louisiana State University Press, 1972; orig. pub. 1875.

King, Spencer Bidwell, Jr. *Rebel Lawyer: Letters of Theodorick W. Montfort, 1861–1862*. Athens: University of Georgia Press, 1965.

Kiser, Clyde V. *Sea Island to City: A Study of St. Helena Islanders in Harlem and Other Urban Centers*. New York: AMS Press, 1967; orig. pub. 1932.

Lane, Mills, ed. *"Dear Mother, Don't Grieve About Me: If I Get Killed, I'll Only Be Dead"*: *Letters from Georgia Soldiers in the Civil War*. Savannah, Ga.: Beehive Press, 1977.

———. *Neither More nor Less than Men: Slavery in Georgia, A Documentary History*. Savannah, Ga.: Beehive Press, 1993.

———. *Standing upon the Mouth of a Volcano: New South Georgia, A Documentary History*. Savannah, Ga.: Beehive Press, 1993.

Lanman, Charles. *Adventures in the Wilds of the United States and British American Provinces*, vol. 2. Philadelphia: J. W. Moore, 1856.

Lee, F. D., and J. L. Agnew. *Historical Record of the City of Savannah*. Savannah, Ga.: J. H. Estill, 1869.

Leigh, Frances Butler. *Ten Years on a Georgia Plantation Since the War, 1866–1876*. Savannah, Ga.: Beehive Press, 1992; orig. pub. 1883.

Looby, Christopher, ed. *The Complete Civil War Journal and Selected Letters of Thomas Wentworth Higginson*. Chicago: University of Chicago Press, 2000.

Love, E. K. *History of the First African Baptist Church, from Its Organization, January 20th, 1788, to July 1st, 1888*. Savannah, Ga.: The Morning News Print, 1888.

Lyell, Charles. *Travels in North America*. 2 vols. London: John Murray, 1845.

MacKethan, Lucinda H., ed. *Recollections of a Southern Daughter: A Memoir by Cornelia Jones Pond of Liberty County*. Athens: University of Georgia Press, 1998.

Mackie, J. Milton. *From Cape Cod to Dixie and the Tropics*. New York: G. P. Putnam, 1864.

Mallard, Robert Q. *Plantation Life Before Emancipation*. Richmond, Va.: Whittet and Shepperson, 1892.

Moore, Frank, ed. *The Rebellion Record: A Diary of American Events*. 11 vols. New York: G. P. Putnam, 1861–1863; D. Van Nostrand, 1864–1868.

Murray, Amelia M. *Letters from the United States, Cuba, and Canada*. New York: Negro Universities Press, 1969; orig. pub. 1856.

Myers, Robert Manson, ed. *The Children of Pride: A True Story of Georgia and the Civil War*. New Haven, Conn.: Yale University Press, 1971.

Nichols, George Ward. *The Story of the Great March from the Diary of a Staff Officer*. Williamstown, Mass.: Corner House, 1972; orig. pub. 1865.

Parrish, Lydia. *Slave Songs of the Georgia Sea Islands*. Hatboro, Pa.: Folklore Associates, 1965; orig. pub. 1942.

Parsons, Charles Grandison. *Inside View of Slavery: Or, a Tour Among the Planters*. Boston: J. P. Jewett and Co., 1855.

Pavich-Lindsay, Melanie, ed. *Anna: The Letters of a St. Simons Island Plantation Mistress, 1817–1859*. Athens: University of Georgia Press, 2002.

Pearson, Elizabeth Ware, ed. *Letters from Port Royal Written at the Time of the Civil War*. Boston: W. B. Clarke, 1906.

Pepper, George W. *Personal Recollections of Sherman's Campaigns: In Georgia and the Carolinas*. Zanesville, Ohio: Hugh Dunne, 1866.

Powers, Stephen. *Afoot and Alone: A Walk from Sea to Sea by the Southern Route*. Hartford, Conn.: Columbian Book Co., 1884.

Quaife, Milo, ed. *From the Cannon's Mouth: The Civil War Letters of General Alpheus S. Williams*. Detroit: Wayne State University Press, 1959.

Quarles, Benjamin. *Black Abolitionists*. New York: Oxford University Press, 1969.

Rawick, George P., ed. *The American Slave: A Composite Autobiography*. Supplement Series 1. 12 vols. Westport, Conn.: Greenwood Press, 1977.

Royall, Anne M. *Mrs. Royall's Southern Tour*. 3 vols. Washington, D.C: T. D. Clark, 1830–31.

Russell, William Howard. *My Diary North and South*. Edited by Fletcher Pratt. New York: Harper and Brothers, 1954.

Savannah Unit, Georgia Writers' Project, Work Projects Administration. *Drums and Shadows: Survival Studies Among the Georgia Coastal Negroes*. Athens: University of Georgia Press, 1986; orig. pub. 1940.

Sherman, William Tecumseh. *Memoirs of General W. T. Sherman*. New York: Literary Classics, 1990.

Shryock, Richard H., ed. *Letters of Richard D. Arnold, M.D., 1808–1876*. Papers of the Trinity College Historical Society, Double Series XVIII–XIX. Durham, N.C.: Seeman Press, 1929.

Simms, James M. *The First Colored Baptist Church in North America*. New York: Negro Universities Press, 1969; orig. pub. 1888.

Somers, Robert. *The Southern States Since the War, 1870–1*. London: Macmillan, 1871.

Starobin, Robert S., ed. *Blacks in Bondage: Letters of American Slaves*. New York: New Viewpoints, 1974.

Sterling, Dorothy, ed. *The Trouble They Seen: Black People Tell the Story of Reconstruction.* Garden City, N.Y.: Doubleday, 1976.

Stiles, Margaret Vernon. *Marse George: Memories of Old Savannah.* Evans Print Co., n.d., n.p.

Swint, Henry L., ed. *Dear Ones at Home: Letters from Contraband Camps.* Nashville, Tenn.: Vanderbilt University Press, 1966.

Taylor, Susie King. *Reminiscences of My Life in Camp with the 33rd U.S. Colored Troops.* New York: Markus Wiener, 1988; orig. pub. 1902.

Thomas, Edward J. *Memoirs of a Southerner, 1840–1923.* Savannah, Ga., 1923.

Tower, Philo. *Slavery Unmasked: Being a Truthful Narrative of Three Years' Residence and Journeying in Eleven Southern States.* Rochester, N.Y.: E. Darrow and Brothers, 1856.

Trowbridge, John T. *The Desolate South, 1865–6.* Boston: Little Brown, 1956; orig. pub. 1866.

Turner, Lorenzo Dow. *Africanisms in the Gullah Dialect.* Chicago: University of Chicago Press, 1949.

West, Edmund, comp. *Family Data Collection: Individual Records.* Provo, Utah: The Generations Network, 2000.

Wills, Charles W. *Army Life of an Illinois Soldier, Including a Day-by-Day Record of Sherman's March to the Sea.* Washington, D.C.: Globe Printing, 1906.

Wilson, Henry. *History of the Rise and Fall of the Slave Power in America.* 2 vols. Boston: James R. Osgood, 1874.

Winther, Oscar O., ed. *With Sherman to the Sea: The Civil War Letters, Diaries, and Reminiscences of Theodore Freylinghuysen Upson.* Baton Rouge: Louisiana State University Press, 1943.

Wright, Richard R. *A Brief Historical Sketch of Negro Education in Georgia.* Savannah, Ga.: Robinson Printing, 1894.

Wylie, Lollie Belle, ed. *Memoirs of Judge Richard H. Clark.* Atlanta: Franklin Printing, 1898.

ARTICLES AND PAMPHLETS

Alvord, J. W. "Letters from the South, Relating to the Condition of Freedmen." Washington, D.C.: Howard University Press, 1870.

Athearn, Robert G. "An Indiana Doctor Marches with Sherman: The Diary of James Comfort Patten." *Indiana Magazine of History* 49 (Dec. 1953): 405–22.

Bancroft, Joseph. "Census of the City of Savannah together with Statistics Relating to the Trade, Commerce, Mechanical Arts and Health of the Same . . . " Savannah, Ga., 1848.

Bell, Whitfield J., Jr., ed. "Diary of George Bell: A Record of Captivity in a Federal Military Prison, 1862." *Georgia Historical Quarterly* 22 (June 1938): 169–84.

Berger, Mrs. Homer H. "Sherman's Occupation of Savannah: Two Letters." *Georgia Historical Quarterly* 50 (March 1966): 109–15.

Black, Wilfrid W., ed. "Marching with Sherman through Georgia and the Carolinas: The Civil War Diary of Jesse L. Dozer." *Georgia Historical Quarterly* 52 (Dec. 1968): 308–36.

Bryan, T. Conn, ed. "A Georgia Woman's Civil War Diary: The Journal of Minerva Leah Rowles McClatchey, 1864–65." *Georgia Historical Quarterly* 51 (June 1867): 197–216.

Conrad, Georgia Bryan. "Reminiscences of a Southern Woman." *Southern Workman* 30 (1901), Pt. 2: 167–71; Pt. III: 252–57; Pt. IV: 357–59; Pt. V: 407–11.

DeLeon, Edwin. "Ruin and Reconstruction of the Southern States: A Record of Two Tours in 1868 and 1873." *Southern Magazine* 14 (March 1874): 287–309.

Force, Manning F. "From Atlanta to Savannah: The Civil War Journal of Manning F. Force." *Georgia Historical Quarterly* 91 (Summer 2007): 185–205.

Gatell, Frank Otto, ed. "A Yankee Views the Agony of Savannah." *Georgia Historical Quarterly* 43 (Dec. 1959): 428–31.

Harn, Julia E. "Old Canoochee-Ogeechee Chronicles." *Georgia Historical Quarterly* 16. Pt. 2: "Life over the River-Canoochee-Ogeechee." (March 1932): 47–55. Pt. 3: "Life Among the Negroes" (June 1932): 146–51. Pt. 4: "Life at Taylor Creek" (Sept. 1932): 232–39.

———. November 15, 1864–January 3, 1865. "Old Canoochee Backwoods Sketches." *Georgia Historical Quarterly* 22. Pt. 1: "Old Canoochee Plantation." (March 1938): 77–80. Pt. 2: "Native Characteristics" (June 1938): 192–99; Pt. 3: "John Benton" (Sept. 1938): 292–93.

Harris, S. N. "Report of the Treatment of Some Cases of Cholera Occurring on Savannah River." *Charleston Medical Journal and Review* 4 (1849): 581–85.

Hawes, Lilla Mills, ed. "The Memoirs of Charles H. Olmstead." *Georgia Historical Quarterly* 42. Pt. 1 (Dec. 1958): 389–408; 43. Pt. 2 (March 1959): 60–74; Pt. 3 (June 1959): 170–86; Pt. 4 (Oct. 1959): 261–81; Pt. 5 (Dec. 1959): 378–90; 45. Pt. 10: (March 1961): 42–56.

Huff, Lawrence, ed. " 'A Bitter Draught We Have Had to Quaff': Sherman's March Through the Eyes of James Addison." *Georgia Historical Quarterly* 72 (Summer 1988): 306–26.

James, Josef C. "Sherman at Savannah." *Journal of Negro History* 39 (Jan. 1954): 127–36.

"The John Van Duser Diary of Sherman's March from Atlanta to Hilton Head." Edited by Charles J. Brockman Jr. *Georgia Historical Quarterly* 53 (June 1969): 220–40.

King, Spencer B., Jr., ed. "Fanny Cohen's Journal of Sherman's Occupation of Savannah." *Georgia Historical Quarterly* 41 (Dec. 1957): 407–16.

———. "Rebel Lawyer: The Letters of Lt. Theodorick W. Montfort, 1861–3." *Georgia Historical Quarterly* 49 (June 1965): 200–16.

Kollock, Susan M. "Letters of the Kollock and Allied Families, 1826–1884." *Georgia Historical Quarterly* 34. Pt. 2 (March 1950): 36–63; Pt. 3 (June 1950): 126–56; Pt. 4 (Sept. 1950): 227–57; Pt. 5 (Dec. 1950): 313–27.

"A Letter from Lewis Hayden of Boston, Massachusetts, to Hon. Judge Simms of Savannah, Georgia." Boston: Committee on Masonic Jurisprudence, Prince Hall Grand Lodge, 1874.

"Letters of Negroes Addressed to the American Colonization Society." *Journal of Negro History* 10 (April 1925): 154–311.

"Letters of Dr. Seth Rogers, 1862, 1863." *Massachusetts Historical Society Proceedings* 63 (Oct. 1909–June 1910): 337–98.

Mahaffey, Joseph H., ed. "Carl Schurz's Letters from the South." *Georgia Historical Quarterly* 35 (Sept. 1951): 222–57.

"Memorial Services: Tribute to the Hon. Charles Sumner, held in St. Phillip's A.M.E. Church, Savannah, Georgia, March 18th, 1874." Savannah, Ga.: D. G. Patton, 1874.

Merrill, James M., comp. "Personne Goes to Georgia: Five Civil War Letters." *Georgia Historical Quarterly* 43 (June 1959): 202–11.

Osborn, George C. "Sherman's March Through Georgia: Letters from Charles Ewing to his Father Thomas Ewing." *Georgia Historical Quarterly* 42 (Sept. 1958): 323–27.

Padgett, James A. "With Sherman Through Georgia and the Carolinas: Letters of a Federal Soldier." *Georgia Historical Quarterly* 33 (1949): 49–81.

Parker, Theodore. "The Boston Kidnapping: A Discourse to Commemorate the Rendition of Thomas Simms . . . by Theodore Parker." Boston: Crosby, Nichols and Co., 1852.

"Proceedings of the Freedmen's Convention of Georgia, Assembled at Augusta, January 10th, 1866." Augusta, Ga.: Loyal Georgian, 1866.

Robertson, Mary D., ed. "Northern Rebel: The Journal of Nellie Kinzie Gordon, Savannah, Ga., 1862." *Georgia Historical Quarterly* 70 (Fall 1986): 477–517.

"Rules, Regulations and Ordinances, for the Government of the City Police of Savannah." Savannah, Ga.: Daily Advertiser, 1866.

"Savannah and Boston: Account of the Supplies Sent to Savannah with the Last Appeal of Edward Everett . . ." Boston: John Wilson and Son, 1865.

Schmitt, Frederick Emil. "Prisoner of War: Experiences in Southern Prisons." *Wisconsin Magazine of History* 42 (Winter 1958–59): 83–93.

Screven, John. "The Savannah Benevolent Association." Savannah, Ga.: Morning News Print, 1896.

"Sherman's Occupation of Savannah: Two Letters." *Georgia Historical Quarterly* 50 (March 1966): 109–14.

Simms, L. Moody. "A Comment on Savannah in 1866." *Georgia Historical Quarterly* 50 (Dec. 1966): 459–60.

Torian, Sarah Hodgson. "Notes and Documents: Ante-Bellum and War Memories of Mrs. Telfair Hodgson." *Georgia Historical Quarterly* 27 (1943): 350–56.

"Trial of Thomas Sims, on an Issue of Personal Liberty, on the Claim of James Potter, of Georgia, Against Him, as an Alleged Fugitive from Service." Boston: W. S. Damrell & Co., 1851.

Waring, James J. "The Epidemic at Savannah, 1876. Its Causes—The Measures of Prevention." Savannah Morning News Steam Printing House, 1879.

Waring, Martha Gallaudet. "Charles Seton Henry Hardee's Recollections of Old Savannah." Pt. 2. *Georgia Historical Quarterly* 13 (March 1929): 13–48.

———. "The Striving Seventies in Savannah." *Georgia Historical Quarterly* 20 (June 1936): 154–71.

Waring, Thomas Pinckney. "Savannah of the 1870's." *Georgia Historical Quarterly* 20 (March 1936): 52–64.

Wiley, Bell Irvin. "The Confederate Letters of John W. Hagan." Pt. 1. *Georgia Historical Quarterly* 38 (June–Sept. 1954): 170–200.

Wright, Willard. "Letters of the Bishop of Savannah, 1861–1865." *Georgia Historical Quarterly* 42 (March 1958): 93–106.

Yulee, Elias. "An Address to the Colored People of Georgia." *Savannah Republican,* 1868.

SECONDARY PUBLISHED MATERIALS

BOOKS

Ash, Stephen V. *When the Yankees Came: Conflict and Chaos in the Occupied South, 1861–1865.* Chapel Hill: University of North Carolina Press, 1995.

Bailey, Anne J. *War and Ruin: William T. Sherman and the Savannah Campaign.* Wilmington, Del.: Scholarly Resources, 2003.

Bancroft, Frederic. *Slave Trading in the Old South.* Baltimore: Furst Co., 1931.

Bell, Malcolm, Jr. *Major Butler's Legacy: Five Generations of a Slaveholding Family.* Athens: University of Georgia Press, 1987.

Berlin, Ira. *Slaves Without Masters: The Free Negro in the Antebellum South.* New York: Random House, 1974.

Berry, Stephen W. *All That Makes a Man: Love and Ambition in the Civil War South.* New York: Oxford University Press, 2003.

Blatt, Martin, Thomas J. Brown, and Donald Yacovone, eds. *Hope and Glory: Essays on the Legacy of the Fifty-fourth Massachusetts Regiment.* Amherst: University of Massachusetts Press, 2001.

Blight, David W., ed. *Passages to Freedom: The Underground Railroad in History and Memory.* Washington, D.C.: Smithsonian Books, 2004.

———. *Race and Reunion: The Civil War in American Memory.* Cambridge, Mass.: Harvard University Press, 2001.

Bowden, Haygood S. *History of Savannah Methodism from John Wesley to Silas Johnson.* Macon, Ga.: Burke, 1929.

Bragg, C. L., et al. *Never for Want of Powder: The Confederate Powder Works in Augusta, Georgia*. Columbia: University of South Carolina Press, 2007.

Brooks, Robert Preston. *The Agrarian Revolution in Georgia, 1865–1912*. Westport, Conn.: Negro Universities Press, 1970; orig. pub. 1914.

Brown, Russell K. *"Our Connection with Savannah": History of the First Battalion Georgia Sharpshooters, 1862–1865*. Macon, Ga.: Mercer University Press, 2004.

Brundage, W. Fitzhugh. *The Southern Past: A Clash of Race and Memory*. Cambridge, Mass.: Harvard University Press, 2005.

Bryan, T. Conn. *Confederate Georgia*. Athens: University of Georgia Press, 1953.

Budiansky, Stephen. *The Bloody Shirt: Terror After Appomattox*. New York: Viking, 2008.

Bullard, Mary R. *Cumberland Island: A History*. Athens: University of Georgia Press, 2005.

Burchard, Peter. *One Gallant Rush: Robert Gould Shaw and His Brave Black Regiment*. New York: St. Martin's Press, 1965.

Burin, Eric. *Slavery and the Peculiar Solution: A History of the American Colonization Society*. Gainesville: University Press of Florida, 2005.

Burton, Orville Vernon, and Robert C. McMath, Jr. *Toward a New South? Studies in Post–Civil War Southern Communities*. Westport, Conn.: Greenwood Press, 1982.

Butchart, Ronald E. *Northern Schools, Blacks, and Reconstruction: Freedmen's Education, 1862–1875*. Westport, Conn.: Greenwood Press, 1980.

Calonius, Erik. *The Wanderer: The Last American Slave Ship and the Conspiracy That Set Its Sails*. New York: St. Martin's Press, 2006.

Campbell, Jacqueline Glass. *When Sherman Marched North from the Sea: Resistance on the Confederate Home Front*. Chapel Hill: University of North Carolina Press, 2003.

Campbell, Stanley W. *The Slave Catchers: Enforcement of the Fugitive Slave Law, 1850–1860*. Chapel Hill: University of North Carolina Press, 1970.

Carey, Anthony Gene. *Parties, Slavery, and the Union in Antebellum Georgia*. Athens: University of Georgia Press, 1997.

Carter, Christine Jacobson. *Southern Single Blessedness: Unmarried Women in the Urban South, 1800–1865*. Urbana: University of Illinois Press, 2006.

Carter, Dan T. *When the War Was Over: The Failure of Self-Reconstruction in the South, 1865–1867*. Baton Rouge: Louisiana State University, 1985.

Cimbala, Paul A. *Under the Guardianship of the Nation: The Freedmen's Bureau and the Reconstruction of Georgia, 1865–1870*. Athens: University of Georgia Press, 1997.

Clark, Kathleen Ann. *Defining Moments: African American Commemoration and Political Culture in the South, 1863–1913*. Chapel Hill: University of North Carolina Press, 2005.

Clarke, Erskine. *Dwelling Place: A Plantation Epic*. New Haven, Conn.: Yale University Press, 2005.

———. *Wrestlin' Jacob: A Portrait of Religion in Antebellum Georgia and the Carolina Low Country*. Tuscaloosa: University of Alabama Press, 1979.

Clinton, Catherine. *Fanny Kemble's Civil Wars*. New York: Simon and Schuster, 2000.

Conway, Alan. *The Reconstruction of Georgia*. Minneapolis: University of Minnesota Press, 1996.

Coopersmith, Andrew Seth. *Fighting Words: An Illustrated History of Newspaper Accounts of the Civil War*. New York: W. W. Norton, 2004.

Cornelius, Janet Duitsman. *"When I Can Read My Title Clear": Literacy, Slavery, and Religion in the Antebellum South*. Columbia: University of South Carolina Press, 1991.

Coulter, E. Merton. *Thomas Spalding of Sapelo*. Baton Rouge: Louisiana State University Press, 1940.

Creel, Margaret. *"A Peculiar People": Slave Religion and Community-Culture Among the Gullahs*. New York: New York University Press, 1988.

Crosby, Molly Caldwell. *The American Plague: The Untold Story of Yellow Fever, the Epidemic That Shaped Our History*. New York: Berkley Books, 2006.

Crow, Jeffrey, and Flora J. Hatley, eds. *Black Americans in North Carolina and the South*. Chapel Hill: University of North Carolina Press, 1984.

Davis, Susan G. *Parades and Power: Street Theatre in Nineteenth-Century Philadelphia*. Philadelphia: Temple University Press, 1986.

DeCredico, Mary A. *Patriotism for Profit: Georgia's Urban Entrepreneurs and the Confederate War Effort*. Chapel Hill: University of North Carolina Press, 1990.

Diouf, Sylviane. *Servants of Allah: African Muslims Enslaved in the Americas*. New York: New York University Press, 1998.

Dittmer, John. *Black Georgia in the Progressive Era, 1900–1920*. Urbana: University of Illinois Press, 1977.

Drago, Edmund L. *Black Politicians and Reconstruction in Georgia: A Splendid Failure*. Athens: University of Georgia Press, 1992.

Duncan, Russell. *Entrepreneur for Equality: Governor Rufus Bullock, Commerce, and Race in Post–Civil War Georgia*. Athens: University of Georgia Press, 1994.

———. *Freedom's Shore: Tunis Campbell and the Georgia Freedmen*. Athens: University of Georgia Press, 1986.

———. *Where Death and Glory Meet: Colonel Robert Gould Shaw and the 54th Massachusetts Infantry*. Athens: University of Georgia Press, 1999.

Dusinberre, William. *Them Dark Days: Slavery in the American Rice Swamps*. Athens: University of Georgia Press, 2000.

Dyer, Thomas G. *Secret Yankees: The Union Circle in Confederate Atlanta*. Baltimore: Johns Hopkins University Press, 1999.

Emilio, Luis F. *A Brave Black Regiment: History of the Fifty-fourth Regiment of Massachusetts Volunteer Infantry, 1863–1865*. New York: Arno Press, 1969; orig. pub. 1894.

Ernest, John. *Liberation Historiography: African American Writers and the Challenge of History, 1794–1861*. Chapel Hill: University of North Carolina Press, 2004.

Escott, Paul D. *Military Necessity: Civil-Military Relations in the Confederacy*. Westport, Conn.: Praeger, 2006.

Faust, Drew Gilpin. *This Republic of Suffering: Death and the American Civil War*. New York: Alfred A. Knopf, 2008.

Feierman, Steven, and John M. Janzen, eds. *The Social Basis of Health and Healing in Africa*. Berkeley: University of California Press, 1992.

Fellman, Michael. *Citizen Sherman: A Life of William Tecumseh Sherman*. New York: Random House, 1995.

Fett, Sharla M. *Working Cures: Healing, Health, and Power on Southern Slave Plantations*. Chapel Hill: University of North Carolina Press, 2002.

Fischer, David Hackett. *Liberty and Freedom*. New York: Oxford University Press, 2005.

Fitzgerald, Michael W. *Urban Emancipation: Popular Politics in Reconstruction Mobile, 1860–1890*. Baton Rouge: Louisiana State University Press, 2002.

Flynn, Charles L., Jr. *White Land, Black Labor: Caste and Class in Late Nineteenth-Century Georgia*. Baton Rouge: Louisiana University Press, 1983.

Foner, Eric. *Freedom's Lawmakers: A Directory of Black Officeholders During Reconstruction*. New York: Oxford University Press, 1993.

———. *Reconstruction: America's Unfinished Revolution, 1863–1877*. New York: Harper and Row, 1988.

Foner, Philip, and Ronald Lewis, eds. *The Black Worker: A Documentary History from Colonial Times to the Present*. 4 vols. Philadelphia: Temple University Press, 1978.

Forret, Jeff. *Race Relations at the Margins: Slaves and Poor Whites in the Antebellum Southern Countryside*. Baton Rouge: Louisiana State University Press, 2006.

Franklin, John Hope. *The Militant South, 1800–1861*. Cambridge, Mass.: Harvard University Press, 1956.

Fraser, Walter J., Jr. *Savannah in the Old South*. Athens: University of Georgia Press, 2003.

Freehling, William H. *The Road to Disunion*. Vol. 2, *Secessionists Triumphant, 1854–1861*. New York: Oxford University Press, 2007.

Gamble, Thomas, Jr. *A History of the City Government of Savannah, Georgia, from 1790 to 1891*. Savannah, Ga.: City Council, 1900.

———. *Savannah Duels and Duellists, 1733–1877*. Savannah, Ga.: Review Publishing and Printing, 1923.

Gaspar, David Barry, and Darlene Clark Hine, eds. *More Than Chattel: Black Women and Slavery in the Americas*. Bloomington: Indiana University Press, 1996.

Genovese, Eugene D. *Roll, Jordan, Roll: The World the Slaves Made*. New York: Pantheon, 1974.

Gibson, James R., ed. *European Settlement and Development in North America: Essays on Geographical Change in Honor and Memory of Andrew Hill Clark*. Toronto: University of Toronto Press, 1978.

Gillespie, Michele. *Free Labor in an Unfree World: White Artisans in Slaveholding Georgia, 1789–1860*. Athens: University of Georgia Press, 2000.

Gleeson, David T. *The Irish in the South, 1815–1877*. Chapel Hill: University of North Carolina Press, 2001.

Goldin, Claudia Dale. *Urban Slavery in the American South, 1820–1860: A Quantitative History*. Chicago: University of Chicago Press, 1976.

Gomez, Michael A. *Exchanging Our Country Marks: The Transformation of African Identities in the Colonial and Antebellum South*. Chapel Hill: University of North Carolina Press, 1998.

Gordon, Lesley J., and John C. Inscoe, eds. *Inside the Confederate Nation: Essays in Honor of Emory M. Thomas*. Baton Rouge: Louisiana State University Press, 2005.

Greenberg, Amy S. *Cause for Alarm: The Volunteer Fire Department in the Nineteenth Century*. Princeton, N.J.: Princeton University Press, 1998.

Griffith, Louis Turner, and John Erwin Talmadge. *Georgia Journalism, 1763–1950*. Athens: University of Georgia Press, 1951.

Grimsley, Mark. *The Hard Hand of War: Union Military Policy Toward Southern Civilians, 1861–1865*. Cambridge: Cambridge University Press, 1995.

Groover, Robert Long. *Sweet Land of Liberty: A History of Liberty County, Georgia*. Roswell, Ga.: W. H. Wolfe Associates, 1987.

Grover, Kathryn. *The Fugitive's Gibraltar: Escaping Slaves and Abolitionism in New Bedford, Massachusetts*. Amherst: University of Massachusetts, 2001.

Gudmestad, Robert H. *A Troublesome Commerce: The Transformation of the Interstate Slave Trade*. Baton Rouge: Louisiana State University Press, 2003.

Hahn, Steven. *A Nation Under Our Feet: Black Political Struggles in the Rural South, from Slavery to the Great Migration*. Cambridge, Mass.: Harvard University Press, 2003.

Harden, William. *A History of Savannah and South Georgia*, vol. 1. Atlanta: Cherokee Publishing Company, 1969, originally published in 1913.

Harris, J. William. *Deep Souths: Delta, Piedmont, and Sea Island Society in the Age of Segregation*. Baltimore: Johns Hopkins University Press, 2001.

———. *Plain Folk and Gentry in a Slave Society: White Liberty and Black Slavery in Augusta's Hinterlands*. Middletown, Conn.: Wesleyan University Press, 1985.

Hazzard-Gordon, Katrina. *Jookin': The Rise of Social Dance Formations in African-American Culture*. Philadelphia: Temple University Press, 1990.

Henderson, Lillian. *Roster of the Confederate Soldiers of Georgia, 1861–1865*, vol. 1. Hopeville, Ga.: Longina and Porter, 1959.

Henderson, Lindsey P. *The Oglethorpe Light Infantry: A Military History*. Savannah: The Civil War Centennial Commission of Savannah and Chatham County, 1961.

Hettle, Wallace. *The Peculiar Democracy: Southern Democrats in Peace and Civil War*. Athens: University of Georgia Press, 2001.

Hogue, James Keith. *Uncivil War: Five New Orleans Street Battles and the Rise and Fall of Radical Reconstruction*. Baton Rouge: Louisiana State University Press, 2006.

Holt, Sharon Ann. *Making Freedom Pay: North Carolina Freedpeople Working for Themselves, 1865–1900*. Athens: University of Georgia Press, 2000.

Honig, Bonnie. *Democracy and the Foreigner*. Princeton, N.J.: Princeton University Press, 1996.

Hoole, William Stanley. *Vizetelly Covers the Confederacy*. Tuscaloosa, Ala.: Confederate Pub. Co., 1957.

Horton, James Oliver, and Lois E. Horton. *In Hope of Liberty: Culture, Community and Protest Among Northern Free Blacks, 1700–1860*. New York: Oxford University Press, 1997.

———, eds. *Slavery and Public History: The Tough Stuff of American Memory*. New York: New Press, 2006.

Hoskins, Charles Lwanga. *Black Episcopalians in Georgia: Strife, Struggle, and Salvation*. Savannah, Ga.: Hoskins, 1980.

———. *Black Episcopalians in Savannah*. Savannah, Ga.: St. Matthew's Episcopal Church, 1983.

———. *Out of Yamacraw and Beyond: Discovering Black Savannah*. Savannah, Ga.: Gullah Press, 2002.

Huggins, Nathan I. *Black Odyssey: The Afro-American Ordeal in Slavery*. New York: Pantheon, 1977.

Hughes, Nathaniel Cheairs, Jr. *General William J. Hardee: Old Reliable*. Baton Rouge: Louisiana State University Press, 1965.

Inscoe, John, and Robert C. Kenzer, eds. *Enemies of the Country: New Perspectives on Unionists in the Civil War*. Athens: University of Georgia Press, 2001.

Johnson, Alonzo, and Paul Jersild, eds. *"Ain't Gonna Lay My 'Ligion Down": African American Religion in the South*. Columbia: University of South Carolina Press, 1996.

Johnson, Michael P. *Toward a Patriarchal Republic: The Secession of Georgia*. Baton Rouge: Louisiana State University Press, 1977.

Johnson, Walter. *Soul by Soul: Life Inside the Antebellum Slave Market*. Cambridge, Mass.: Harvard University Press, 1999.

Johnson, Whittington B. *Black Savannah: 1788–1864*. Fayetteville: University of Arkansas Press, 1996.

Jones, Carmie M., ed. *Historic Savannah: A Survey of Significant Buildings in the Historic Districts of Savannah, Georgia*. 3rd. ed. Savannah, Ga.: Historic Savannah Foundation, 2005.

Jones, Jacqueline. *American Work: Four Centuries of Black and White Labor*. New York: W. W. Norton, 1998.

———. *The Dispossessed: America's Underclasses from the Civil War to the Present*. New York: Basic Books, 1992.

———. *Soldiers of Light and Love: Northern Teachers and Georgia Blacks, 1865–1873*. Chapel Hill: University of North Carolina Press, 1980.

Joyner, Charles W. *Down by the Riverside: A South Carolina Slave Community*. Urbana: University of Illinois Press, 1984.

———. *Remember Me: Slave Life in Coastal Georgia*. Atlanta: Georgia Humanities Council, 1989.

Kennett, Lee. *Marching Through Georgia: The Story of Soldiers and Civilians During Sherman's Campaign*. New York: HarperCollins, 1995.

King, Spencer B., Jr. *Darien: The Death and Rebirth of a Southern Town*. Macon, Ga.: Mercer University Press, 1981.

Kousser, J. Morgan. *The Shaping of Southern Politics: Suffrage Restriction and the Establishment of the One-Party South, 1880–1910.* New Haven, Conn.: Yale University Press, 1974.

Kuyk, Betty M. *African Voices in the African American Heritage.* Bloomington: Indiana University Press, 2003.

Lane, Mills. *Architecture of the Old South.* New York: Abbeville Press, 1993.

———. *Times That Prove People's Principles: Civil War in Georgia.* Savannah, Ga.: Beehive Press, 1993.

Leavitt, Judith, and Ronald L. Numbers, eds. *Sickness and Health in America: Readings in the History of Medicine and Public Health.* 2nd ed. Madison: University of Wisconsin Press, 1985.

Litwack, Leon F. *Been in the Storm So Long: The Emergence of Black Freedom in the South.* New York: Alfred A. Knopf, 1978.

Lockley, Timothy. *Lines in the Sand: Race and Class in Lowcountry Georgia, 1750–1860.* Athens, Ga.: University of Georgia Press, 2001.

Luraghi, Raimondo. *A History of the Confederate Navy.* Annapolis, Md.: Naval Institute Press, 1996.

Magdol, Edward. *A Right to the Land: Essays on the Freedmen's Community.* Westport, Conn.: Greenwood Press, 1977.

Marvel, William. *Andersonville: The Last Depot.* Chapel Hill: University of North Carolina Press, 1994.

Massey, Mary Elizabeth. *Refugee Life in the Confederacy.* Baton Rouge: Louisiana State University Press, 1964.

McCash, June Hall. *Jekyll Island's Early Years, from Prehistory Through Reconstruction.* Athens: University of Georgia Press, 2005.

McFeely, William S. *Yankee Stepfather: General O. O. Howard and the Freedmen.* New Haven, Conn.: Yale University Press, 1968.

McInnis, Maurie Dee. *The Politics of Taste in Antebellum Charleston.* Chapel Hill: University of North Carolina Press, 2005.

McPherson, James M. *Battle Cry of Freedom: The Civil War Era.* New York: Oxford University Press, 1988.

Miller, Edward A. *Lincoln's Abolitionist General: The Biography of David Hunter.* Columbia: University of South Carolina Press, 1997.

Mitchell, Faith. *Hoodoo Medicine: Sea Islands Herbal Remedies.* Berkeley, Calif.: Reed, Cannon, and Johnson, 1978.

Mohr, Clarence L. *On the Threshold of Freedom: Masters and Slaves in Civil War Georgia.* Athens: University of Georgia Press, 1986.

Montgomery, William E. *Under Their Own Vine and Fig Tree: The African-American Church in the South, 1865–1900.* Baton Rouge: Louisiana State University Press, 1993.

Morgan, Chad. *Planters' Progress: Modernizing Confederate Georgia.* Gainesville: University Press of Florida, 2005.

Morrison, Mary Lane. *John S. Norris: Architect in Savannah, 1846–1860.* Savannah, Ga.: Beehive Press, 1980.

Morton, Patricia, ed. *Discovering the Women in Slavery: Emancipating Perspectives of the American Past.* Athens: University of Georgia Press, 1996.

Nichols, Frederick Doveton, and Frances Benjamin Johnston. *The Early Architecture of Georgia.* Chapel Hill: University of North Carolina Press, 1957.

Nieman, Donald. *To Set the Law in Motion: The Freedmen's Bureau and the Legal Rights of Blacks, 1865–1868.* Millwood, N.Y.: KTO Press, 1970.

O'Donovan, Susan E. *Becoming Free in the Cotton South.* Cambridge, Mass.: Harvard University Press, 2007.

Orr, Dorothy. *A History of Education in Georgia*. Chapel Hill: University of North Carolina Press, 1950.

Osthaus, Carl R. *Freedmen, Philanthropy, and Fraud: A History of the Freedman's Savings Bank*. Urbana: University of Illinois Press, 1976.

Oubre, Claude F. *Forty Acres and a Mule: The Freedmen's Bureau and Black Land Ownership*. Baton Rouge: Louisiana University Press, 1978.

Parks, Joseph H. *Joseph E. Brown of Georgia*. Baton Rouge: Louisiana State University Press, 1977.

Penningroth, Dylan C. *The Claims of Kinfolk: African American Property and Community in the Nineteenth-Century South*. Chapel Hill: University of North Carolina Press, 2003.

Pollitzer, William S. *The Gullah People and Their African Heritage*. Athens: University of Georgia Press, 1999.

Powell, Lawrence N. *New Masters: Northern Planters During the Civil War and Reconstruction*. New Haven, Conn.: Yale University Press, 1980.

Quarles, Benjamin. *Black Abolitionists*. New York: Oxford University Press, 1969.

Rabinowitz, Howard N. *Southern Black Leaders of the Reconstruction Era*. Urbana: University of Illinois Press, 1982.

Redkey, Edwin S. *Black Exodus: Black Nationalist and Back-to-Africa Movements, 1810–1910*. New Haven, Conn.: Yale University Press, 1969.

Reynolds, David S. *John Brown, Abolitionist*. New York: Alfred A. Knopf, 2005.

Roddy, Ray. *The Georgia Volunteer Infantry, 1861–1865*. Kearny, Neb.: Morris Publishing, 1998.

Rose, Willie Lee. *Rehearsal for Reconstruction: The Port Royal Experiment*. New York: Vintage, 1964.

Rosenbaum, Art. *Shout Because You're Free: The African American Ring Shout Tradition in Coastal Georgia*. Athens: University of Georgia Press, 1998.

Rubin, Saul Jacob. *Third to None: The Saga of Savannah Jewry, 1733–1983*. Savannah, Ga., 1983.

Ruhlman, Fred. *Captain Henry Wirz and Andersonville Prison: A Reappraisal*. Knoxville: University of Tennessee Press, 2006.

Savannah Unit, Federal Writers' Project, Works Progress Administration of Georgia. *Savannah River Plantations*. Savannah, Ga.: Georgia Historical Society, 1947.

Schultz, Jane E. *Women at the Front: Hospital Workers in Civil War America*. Chapel Hill: University of North Carolina Press, 2004.

Schwalm, Leslie A. *A Hard Fight for We: Women's Transition from Slavery to Freedom in South Carolina*. Urbana: University of Illinois Press, 1997.

Schwartz, Marie Jenkins. *Birthing a Slave: Motherhood and Medicine in the Antebellum South*. Cambridge, Mass.: Harvard University Press, 2006.

Shadgett, Olive Hall. *The Republican Party in Georgia from Reconstruction Through 1900*. Athens: University of Georgia Press, 1964.

Shaffer, Donald R. *After the Glory: The Struggles of Black Civil War Veterans*. Lawrence: University Press of Kansas, 2004.

Shryock, Richard Harrison. *Georgia and the Union in 1850*. Durham, N.C.: Duke University Press, 1926.

Sidbury, James. *Becoming African in America: Race and Nation in the Early Black Atlantic*. New York: Oxford University Press, 2007.

Slaughter, Thomas P. *Bloody Dawn: The Christiana Race Riot and Racial Violence in the Antebellum North*. New York: Oxford University Press, 1991.

Smith, John David, ed. *Black Soldiers in Blue: African American Troops in the Civil War Era*. Chapel Hill: University of North Carolina Press, 2002.

Smith, Julia. *Slavery and Rice Culture in Low Country Georgia, 1750–1860.* Knoxville: University of Tennessee Press, 1985.

Smith, Mark. *Listening to Nineteenth-Century America.* Chapel Hill: University of North Carolina Press, 2001.

Stanley, Amy Dru. *From Bondage to Contract: Wage Labor, Marriage, and the Market in the Age of Slave Emancipation.* New York: Cambridge University Press, 1998.

Starobin, Robert S. *Industrial Slavery in the Old South.* New York: Oxford University Press, 1970.

Stevenson, Brenda. *Life in Black and White: Family and Community in the Slave South.* New York: Oxford University Press, 1996.

Stewart, Mart. *"What Nature Suffers to Groe": Life, Labor, and Landscape on the Georgia Coast, 1680–1920.* Athens: University of Georgia Press, 1996.

Sullivan, Buddy. *Early Days on the Georgia Tidewater: The Story of McIntosh County and Sapelo.* McIntosh County Board of Commissioners, 1990.

Takaki, Ronald T. *A Pro-Slavery Crusade: The Agitation to Reopen the African Slave Trade.* New York: Free Press, 1971.

Towers, Frank. *The Urban South and the Coming of the Civil War.* Charlottesville: University of Virginia Press, 2004.

Twining, Mary A., and Keith E. Baird, eds. *Sea Island Roots: African Presence in the Carolinas and Georgia.* Trenton, N.J.: Africa World Press, 1991.

Wade, Richard C. *Slavery in the Cities: The South, 1820–1860.* New York: Oxford University Press, 1964.

Walker, Scott. *Hell's Broke Loose in Georgia: Survival in a Civil War Regiment.* Athens: University of Georgia Press, 2005.

Waring, John Frederick. *Cerveau's Savannah.* Savannah, Ga.: Georgia Historical Society, 1973.

Wells, Jonathan Daniel. *The Origins of the Southern Middle Class, 1800–1861.* Chapel Hill: University of North Carolina Press, 2004.

Wells, Tom Henderson. *The Slave Ship Wanderer.* Athens: University of Georgia Press, 1968.

Westwood, Howard C. *Black Troops, White Commanders and Freedmen During the Civil War.* Carbondale: Southern Illinois University Press, 1992.

White, Shane, and Graham J. White. *The Sounds of Slavery: Discovering African American History Through Songs, Sermons, and Speech.* Boston: Beacon Press, 2005.

Wiethoff, William E. *Crafting the Overseer's Image.* Columbia: University of South Carolina Press, 2006.

Williams, Heather. *Self-Taught: African-Amerian Education in Slavery and Freedom.* Chapel Hill: University of North Carolina Press, 2005.

Wise, Stephen R. *Gate of Hell: The Campaign for Charleston Harbor.* Columbia: University of South Carolina Press, 1994.

———. *Lifeline of the Confederacy: Blockade Running During the Civil War.* Columbia: University of South Carolina Press, 1988.

Wood, Betty. *Slavery in Colonial Georgia, 1730–1775.* Athens: University of Georgia Press, 1984.

———. *Women's Work, Men's Work: The Informal Slave Economies of Lower Georgia.* Athens: University of Georgia Press, 1995.

Wood, Peter. *Black Majority: Negroes in South Carolina from 1670 Through the Stono Rebellion.* New York: Alfred A. Knopf, 1974.

Woodson, Carter G., comp. *Free Negro Owners of Slaves in the United States in 1830.* Washington, D.C.: Association for the Study of Negro Life and History, 1924.

Wright, Richard R. *A Brief Historical Sketch of Education in Georgia.* Savannah, Ga.: Robinson Printing, 1894.

Wynne, Lewis Nicholas. *The Continuity of Cotton: Planter Politics in Georgia, 1865–1892.* Macon, Ga.: Mercer University Press, 1986.

Yellin, Jean Fagan. *Harriet Jacobs: A Life.* New York: Basic Civitas Books, 2004.

ARTICLES AND PAMPHLETS

Abbott, Richard. "Black Ministers and the Organization of the Republican Party in the South in 1867: Letters from the Field." *Hayes Historical Journal* (1986): 23–35.

———. "Massachusetts and the Recruitment of Southern Negroes, 1863–1865." *Civil War History* 14 (Sept. 1968): 197–210.

———. "The Republican Party Press in Reconstruction Georgia, 1867–1874." *Journal of Southern History* 61 (Nov. 1995): 725–60.

Alderman, Derek H. "Coastal Heritage as a Contested Landscape: The Politics of Remembering Slavery in Savannah, Georgia." *Proceedings of the 14th Biennial Coastal Zone Conference*, New Orleans, La., July 2005.

Anderson, Mrs. Clarence Gordon. "Eleanor Kenzie [*sic*] Gordon." *Georgia Historical Quarterly* 42 (1958): 163–69.

Angell, Stephen W. "A Black Minister Befriends the 'Unquestioned Father of Civil Rights': Henry McNeal Turner, Charles Sumner, and the African-American Quest for Freedom." *Georgia Historical Quarterly* 85 (Spring 2001): 27–58.

Armstrong, Thomas F. "From Task to Free Labor: The Transition Along Georgia's Rice Coast, 1820–1880." *Georgia Historical Quarterly* 64 (Winter 1980): 432–47.

Bannister, Turpin C. "Oglethorpe's Sources for the Savannah Plan." *Journal of the Society of Architectural Historians* 20 (May 1961): 47–62.

Bell, Karen B. " 'The Ogeechee Troubles': Federal Land Restoration and the 'Lived Realities' of Temporary Proprietors, 1865–1868." *Georgia Historical Quarterly* 85 (Fall 2001): 375–97.

Bell, Malcolm. "Ease and Elegance, Madeira and Murder: The Social Life of Savannah's City Hotel." *Georgia Historical Quarterly* 76 (Fall 1992): 551–76.

Berlin, Ira, and Herbert G. Gutman. "Natives and Immigrants, Free Men and Slaves: Urban Workingmen in the Antebellum American South." *American Historical Review* 88 (Dec. 1983): 1175–1200.

Blassingame, John W. "Before the Ghetto: The Making of the Black Community in Savannah, Georgia, 1865–1880." *Journal of Social History* 6 (1973): 463–88.

Brown, David H. "Conjure/Doctors: An Exploration of a Black Discourse in America, Antebellum to 1940." *Folklore Forum* (1990): 3–46.

Brundage, W. Fitzhugh. "The Darien 'Insurrection' of 1899: Black Protest During the Nadir of Race Relations." *Georgia Historical Quarterly* 74 (Summer 1990): 234–53.

———. "Race, Memory, and Masculinity: Black Veterans Recall the Civil War," in Joan E. Cashin, ed. *The War Was You and Me: Civilians in the American Civil War*. Princeton, N.J.: Princeton University Press, 2002.

Butchart, Ronald E. "Perspectives on Gender, Race, Calling, and Commitment in 19th-Century America: A Collective Biography of the Teachers of the Freedpeople, 1862–1875." *Vitae Scholasticae* 13 (Spring 1994): 15–32.

———. " 'We Can Best Instruct Our Own People': New York African Americans in the Freedmen's Schools, 1861–1875." *Afro-Americans in New York Life and History* (Jan. 1988): 27–49.

Byrne, William A. "The Hiring of Woodson, Slave Carpenter of Savannah." *Georgia Historical Quarterly* 77 (Summer 1993): 245–63.

———. "Slave Crime in Savannah, Georgia." *Journal of Negro History* 79 (Autumn 1994): 352–62.

———. " 'Uncle Billy' Sherman Comes to Town: The Free Winter of Black Savannah." *Georgia Historical Quarterly* 79 (Spring 1995): 91–116.

Camp, Stephanie M. H. "The Pleasures of Resistance: Enslaved Women and Body Politics in the Plantation South, 1830–1861." *Journal of Southern History* 68 (Aug. 2002): 533–72.

Campbell, Walter E. "Profit, Prejudice, and Protest: Utility Competition and the Generation of Jim Crow Streetcars in Savannah, 1905–1907." *Georgia Historical Quarterly* 70 (Summer 1986): 197–231.

Cason, Roberta F. "The Loyal League of Georgia." *Georgia Historical Quarterly* 20 (June 1936): 125–53.

Coddington, Edwin B. "The Activities and Attitudes of a Confederate Business Man: Gazaway B. Lamar." *Journal of Southern History* 9 (Feb. 1943): 3–36.

Coulter, E. Merton. "Aaron Alpeoria Bradley, Georgia Negro Politician During Reconstruction Times." *Georgia Historical Quarterly*. Pt. 1: vol. 51 (March 1967): 15–41; Pt. 2: vol. 51 (June 1967): 154–74; Pt. 3: vol. 51 (Sept. 1967): 264–306.

———. "Henry M. Turner: Negro Preacher-Politician During the Reconstruction Era." *Georgia Historical Quarterly* 48 (Dec. 1964): 371–410.

———. "Robert Gould Shaw and the Burning of Darien, Georgia." *Civil War History* 5 (Dec. 1959): 363–73.

———. "Tunis G. Campbell, Negro Reconstructionist in Georgia," Pt. 2. *Georgia Historical Quarterly* 52 (June 1968): 17–52

Davis, Robert Ralph, Jr. "Buchanian Espionage: A Report on Illegal Slave Trading in the South in 1859." *Journal of Southern History* 37 (May 1971): 271–78.

Denmark, Lisa L. " 'At the Midnight Hour': Economic Dilemmas and Harsh Realities in Post–Civil War Savannah." *Georgia Historical Quarterly* 90 (Fall 2006): 350–90.

Drago, Edmund L. "Militancy and Black Women in Reconstruction Georgia." *Journal of American Culture* 1 (Winter 1978): 838–44.

Dyer, John P. "Northern Relief for Savannah During Sherman's Occupation." *Journal of Southern History* 19 (Nov. 1953): 457–72

Eisterhold, John A. "Savannah: Lumber Center of the South Atlantic." *Georgia Historical Quarterly* 57 (Winter 1973): 526–43.

Escott, Paul D. "Joseph E. Brown, Jefferson Davis, and the Problem of Poverty in the Confederacy." *Georgia Historical Quarterly* 61 (Spring 1977): 59–71.

Farley, M. Foster. "The Mighty Monarch of the South: Yellow Fever in Charleston and Savannah." *Georgia Review* 27 (Spring 1973): 56–70.

Faust, Drew Gilpin. " 'The Dread Void of Uncertainty': Naming the Dead in the American Civil War." *Southern Cultures* (Summer 2005): 8–32.

Fornell, Earl W. "The Civil War Comes to Savannah." *Georgia Historical Quarterly* 43 (Sept. 1959): 248–60.

"From Atlanta to Savannah: The Civil War Journal of Manning F. Force, November 15, 1864–January 3, 1865." *Georgia Historical Quarterly* 91 (summer 2007): 185–205.

Gilmore, Michael T. "Free Speech and the American Renaissance." *Raritan* (Fall 2006): 90–113.

Gordon, George Arthur. "Eleanor Kinzie Gordon: A Sketch." *Georgia Historical Quarterly* 1 (Sept. 1917): 179–96.

Gottlieb, Manuel. "The Land Question in Georgia During Reconstruction." *Science and Society* 3 (1939): 356–88.

Gray, Tom S., Jr. "The March to the Sea." *Georgia Historical Quarterly* 14 (June 1930): 111–38.

Greenberg, Mark I. "Savannah's Jewish Women and the Shaping of Ethnic and Gender Identity, 1830–1900." *Georgia Historical Quarterly* 82 (Winter 1998): 751–74.

———. "Becoming Southern: The Jews of Savannah, Georgia, 1830–1870." *American Jewish History* 86 (1998): 55–75.

Griffin, J. David. "Benevolence and Malevolence in Confederate Savannah." *Georgia Historical Quarterly* 49 (Dec. 1965): 347–58.

Hargis, Peggy G. "For the Love of Place: Paternalism and Patronage in the Georgia Lowcountry, 1865–1898." *Journal of Southern History* 70 (Nov. 2004): 825–64.

Haunton, Richard H. "Law and Order in Savannah, 1850–1860." *Georgia Historical Quarterly* 56 (Spring 1972): 1–24.

Heard, George Alexander. "St. Simons Island During the War Between the States." *Georgia Historical Quarterly* 22 (Sept. 1938): 249–72.

Hoffman, Edwin D. "From Slavery to Self-Reliance: The Record of Achievement of the Freedmen of the Sea Island Region." *Journal of Negro History* 41 (Jan. 1956): 8–42.

Holt, Thomas C. "Georgia Carpetbaggers: Politicians Without Politics." *Georgia Historical Quarterly* 72 (Spring 1988): 72–86.

Hoskins, Charles L. "The Trouble They Seen: Profiles in the Life of Col. John Deveaux, 1848–1909." Published by the author, Savannah, Ga., 1989.

Hughes, N. C., Jr. "Hardee's Defense of Savannah." *Georgia Historical Quarterly* 47 (March 1963): 43–67.

Hunt, Monica. "Organized Labor Along Savannah's Waterfront: Mutual Cooperation Among Black and White Longshoremen, 1865–1894." *Georgia Historical Quarterly* 92 (Summer 2008): 177–99.

Johnson, Dudley S. "William Harris Garland: Mechanic of the Old South." *Georgia Historical Quarterly* 53 (Spring 1969): 41–56.

Johnson, J. G. "Notes on Manufacturing in Ante-Bellum Georgia." *Georgia Historical Quarterly* 16 (1932): 214–31.

Johnson, Whittington B. "A Black Teacher and Her School in Reconstruction Darien: The Correspondence of Hettie Sabattie and J. Murray Hoag, 1868–1869." *Georgia Historical Quarterly* 75 (Spring 1991): 90–105.

———. "Free African-American Women in Savannah, 1800–1860: Affluence and Autonomy amid Adversity." *Georgia Historical Quarterly* 76 (Summer 1992): 260–83.

———. "Free Blacks in Antebellum Savannah: An Economic Profile." *Georgia Historical Quarterly* 64 (Winter 1980): 418–31.

Jung, Moon-Ho. "Outlawing 'Coolies': Race, Nation, and Empire in the Age of Emancipation." *American Quarterly* 57 (Sept. 2005): 677–701.

Levy, Leonard W. "Sims' Case: The Fugitive Slave Law in Boston in 1851." *Journal of Negro History* 35 (Jan. 1950): 39–74.

Lightner, David L., and Alexander M. Ragan. "Were African American Slaveholders Benevolent or Exploitative? A Quantitative Approach." *Journal of Southern History* 21 (Aug. 2005): 535–58.

Lockley, Timothy J. "Trading Encounters Between Non-Elite Whites and African Americans in Savannah, 1790–1860." *Journal of Southern History* 66 (Feb. 2000): 35–48.

Mathews, Donald G. "Charles Colcock Jones and the Southern Evangelical Crusade to Form a Biracial Community." *Journal of Southern History* 41 (Aug. 1975): 300–20.

Matthews, John M. "Negro Republicans in the Reconstruction of Georgia." *Georgia Historical Quarterly* 60 (Summer 1976): 145–64.

Meaney, Peter J. "The Prison Ministry of Father Peter Whelan, Georgia Priest and Confederate Chaplain." *Georgia Historical Quarterly* 71 (Spring 1987): 1–24.

Meier, August, and Elliott Rudwick. "The Boycott Movement Against Jim Crow Streetcars in the South, 1900–1906." *Journal of American History* 55 (March 1969): 756–75.

Miller, Randall M. "Georgia on Their Minds: Free Blacks and the African Colonization Movement in Georgia." *Southern Studies* 17 (Winter 1978): 349–62.

Moore, John Hammond. "Sherman's 'Fifth Column': A Guide to Unionist Activity in Georgia." *Georgia Historical Quarterly* 68 (Fall 1984): 382–409.

Morgan, Philip. "The Ownership of Property by Slaves in the Mid-Nineteenth-Century Low Country." *Journal of Southern History* 49 (Aug. 1983): 399–420.

———. "Work and Culture: The Task System and the World of Lowcountry Blacks, 1700 to 1880." *William and Mary Quarterly*, 3rd series, 39 (Oct. 1982): 563–99.

Neblett, Thomas R. "Major Edward C. Anderson and the C.S.S. *Fingal.*" *Georgia Historical Quarterly* 52 (June 1968): 132–58.

Otto, John Solomon. "Slavery in a Coastal Community: Glynn County (1790–1860). *Georgia Historical Quarterly* 63 (Winter 1979): 461–68.

Parsons, Joseph. "Anthony Odinsells: A Romance of Little Wassaw." *Georgia Historical Quarterly* 55 (Summer 1971): 208–21.

Pearson, Charles E. "Captain Charles Stevens and the Antebellum Georgia Coastal Trade." *Georgia Historical Quarterly* 75 (Fall 1991): 485–506.

Piacentino, Edward J. "Doesticks' Assault on Slavery: Style and Technique in the Great Auction Sale of Slaves, at Savannah, Georgia." *Phylon* 48 (3rd Qtr. 1987): 196–203.

Pressly, Paul M. "The Northern Roots of Savannah's Antebellum Elite, 1780–1850s." *Georgia Historical Quarterly* 87 (Summer 2003): 157–99.

Ramey, Daina L. " 'She Do a Heap of Work': Female Slave Labor on Glynn County Rice and Cotton Plantations." *Georgia Historical Quarterly* 82 (Winter 1998): 707–34.

Rapport, Sara. "The Freedmen's Bureau as a Legal Agent for Black Men and Women in Georgia, 1865–1868." *Georgia Historical Quarterly* 73 (Spring 1989): 26–53.

Redkey, Edwin S. "Black Chaplains in the Union Army." *Civil War History* 33 (Dec. 1987): 331–50.

Reidy, Joseph P. "Aaron A. Bradley: Voice of Black Labor in the Georgia Lowcountry." In Howard N. Rabinowitz, ed., *Southern Black Leaders of the Reconstruction Era*. Urbana: University of Illinois Press, 1982.

Richardson, Joe M. "The Failure of the American Missionary Association to Expand Congregationalism Among Southern Blacks." In Donald G. Nieman, ed., *Church and Community Among Black Southerners, 1865–1900*. New York: Garland Publishing, 1994.

———. " 'Labor Is Rest to Me Here in This the Lord's Vineyard': Hardy Mobley, Black Missionary During Reconstruction." *Southern Studies* 22 (Spring 1983): 5–20.

Robboy, Stanley J., and Anita W. Robboy. "Lewis Hayden: From Fugitive Slave to Statesman." *New England Quarterly* 46 (Dec. 1973): 591–613.

Rogers, George A., and R. Frank Saunders, Jr. "The American Missionary Association in Liberty, County, Georgia: An Invasion of Light and Love." *Georgia Historical Quarterly* 62 (Winter 1978): 304–15.

Rogers, W. McDowell. "Free Negro Legislation in Georgia Before 1865." *Georgia Historical Quarterly* 16 (March 1932): 27–37.

Rousey, Dennis C. "From Whence They Came to Savannah: The Origins of an Urban Population in the Old South." *Georgia Historical Quarterly* 79 (Summer 1995): 305–36.

Savannah Unit, Federal Writers' Project, Works Progress Administration of Georgia. "Plantation Development in Chatham County." *Georgia Historical Quarterly* 22 (Dec. 1938): 305–30.

———. "Part 3: Colerain Plantation." *Georgia Historical Quarterly* 25 (June 1941): 120–40.

Savitt, Todd L. "Politics in Medicine: The Georgia Freedmen's Bureau and the Organization of Health Care, 1865–1866." *Civil War History* 28 (1982): 45–64.

Scharnhorst, Gary. "From Soldier to Saint: Robert Gould Shaw and the Rhetoric of Racial Justice." *Civil War History* 34 (1988): 308–22.

Schwartz, Harold. "Fugitive Slave Days in Boston." *New England Quarterly* 27 (June 1954): 191–212.

Schweninger, Loren. "Property Owning Free African-American Women in the South, 1800–1870." *Journal of Women's History* 1 (Winter 1990): 13–44.

———. "Prosperous Blacks in the South, 1790–1880." *American Historical Review* 95 (Feb. 1990): 31–56.

Siegel, Fred. "Artisans and Immigrants in the Politics of Late Antebellum Georgia." *Civil War History* 27 (Sept. 1981): 221–30.

Silver, Christopher. "A New Look at Old South Urbanization: The Irish Worker in Charleston, South Carolina, 1840–1860." In Samuel M. Hines, ed., *South Atlantic Urban Studies*, Vol. 3 (Charleston: University of South Carolina Press, 1980): 141–72.

Smith, George Winston. "Cotton from Savannah in 1865." *Journal of Southern History* 21 (Nov. 1955): 495–512.

Talmadge, John E. "Savannah's Yankee Newspapers." *Georgia Review* 12 (Spring 1958): 66–73.

Usinger, Robert L. "Yellow Fever from the Viewpoint of Savannah." *Georgia Historical Quarterly* 28 (Sept. 1944): 143–56.

Wallenstein, Peter. "From Slave South to New South: Taxes and Spending in Georgia from 1850 Through Reconstruction." *Journal of Economic History* 36 (1976): 287–90.

———. "Rich Man's War, Rich Man's Fight: Civil War and the Transformation of Public Finance in Georgia." *Journal of Southern History* 50 (Feb. 1984): 15–42.

Weaver, Herbert. "Foreigners in Ante-bellum Savannah." *Georgia Historical Quarterly* 37 (March 1953): 1–17.

Wender, Herbert. "The Southern Commercial Convention at Savannah, 1856." *Georgia Historical Quarterly* 15 (1931): 173–91.

Williams, Jack K. "Travel in Ante-bellum Georgia as Recorded by English Visitors." *Georgia Historical Quarterly* 33 (1949): 191–205.

Williams, Teresa Crisp, and David Williams. " 'The Women Rising': Cotton, Class, and Confederate Georgia's Rioting Women." *Georgia Historical Quarterly* 86 (Spring 2002): 49–83.

Young, Jeffrey R. "Ideology and Death on a Savannah River Rice Plantation, 1833–1867: Paternalism Amidst 'a Good Supply of Disease and Pain.' " *Journal of Southern History* 59 (Nov. 1993): 673–706.

Young, Rogers W. "Two Years at Fort Bartow, 1862–1864." *Georgia Historical Quarterly* 23 (Sept. 1939): 253–64.

UNPUBLISHED PAPERS, M.A. THESES, PH.D. DISSERTATIONS, AND TYPESCRIPTS

Bellows, Barbara. "Tempering the Wind: The Southern Response to Urban Poverty, 1850–1865." Ph.D. diss., University of South Carolina, 1983.

Butchart, Ronald E., and Melanie Pavich. "The Invisible Teachers: Southern Women in the Freedmen's Schools, 1861–1876." Paper presented at the Annual Meeting of the Southern Historical Association, Atlanta, November 2005.

Byrne, William A. "The Burden and Heat of the Day: Slavery and Servitude in Savannah, 1733–1865." Ph.D. diss., Florida State University, 1979.

Clark, J. B. "Fire Protection in the Old South." 2 vols. Ph.D. diss., University of Kentucky, 1957.

Durett, Dan. "Free Blacks in Selected Georgia Cities, 1820–1860." M.A. thesis, Atlanta University, 1973.

Gifford, James M. "The African Colonization Movement in Georgia, 1817–1860." Ph.D. diss., University of Georgia, 1977.

Green, Elvena Marion. "Theatre and Other Entertainments in Savannah, Georgia, from 1810 to 1865." Vols. 1 and 2. Ph.D. diss., University of Iowa, 1971.

Green, Venus. "A Preliminary Investigation of Black Construction Artisans in Savannah from 1820 to 1860." M.A. thesis, Columbia University, 1982.

Greenberg, Mark I. "Creating Ethnic, Class, and Southern Identity in Nineteenth-Century America: The Jews of Savannah, Georgia, 1830–1880." Ph.D. diss., University of Florida, 1997.

Griffin, James David. "Savannah, Georgia, During the Civil War." Ph.D. diss., University of Georgia, 1963.

Haunton, Richard H. "Savannah in the 1850s." Ph.D. diss., Emory University, 1968.

Hyatt, Harry Middleton. "Hoodoo-Conjuration-Witchcraft- Rootwork." 2 vols. Memoirs of the Alma Egan Hyatt Foundation, 1970.

Mercer, George A. "Diary of George A. Mercer." Copied from the original given by John H. Mercer, Los Angeles, for permanent preservation in the Southern Historical Collection, 1963, University of North Carolina, Chapel Hill.

Owens, James Leggette. "The Negro in Georgia During Reconstruction, 1864–1872." Ph.D. diss., University of Georgia, 1975.

Perdue, Robert E. "The Negro in Savannah, 1865–1900." Ph.D. diss., University of Georgia, 1971.

Pruneau, Leigh Ann. "All the Time Is Work Time: Gender and the Task System on Antebellum Lowcountry Rice Plantations." Ph.D. diss., University of Arizona, 1997.

Shoemaker, Edward M. "Strangers and Citizens: The Irish Immigrant Community in Savannah, 1837–1861." Ph.D. diss., Emory University, 1990.

Snyder, Holly. "A Sense of Place: Jews, Identity, and Social Status in British North America, 1654–1831." Ph.D. diss., Brandeis University, 2000.

Sweat, Edward F. "The Free Negro in Ante-Bellum Georgia." Ph.D. diss., Indiana University, 1957.

Thigpen, Thomas Paul. "Aristocracy of the Heart: Catholic Lay Leadership in Savannah, 1820–1870." Ph.D. diss., Emory University, 1995.

ONLINE SOURCES

Ancestry.com: United States Federal Census (database online). Provo, Utah: The Generations Network, Inc., 2003.

Henry David Thoreau, "Slavery in Massachusetts, 1854." http://www.sacred-texts.com/phi/thoreau/slavery.txt.

New Georgia Encyclopedia. http://www.georgiaencyclopedia.org/nge/.

National Park Service. "The Civil War Sailors Database." http://www.itd.nps.gov/cwss-/sailors_trans.htm.

"Black Georgia-Born Sailors in the Union Navy." http://ftp.rootsweb.com/pub/usgenweb/ga/military/civilwar/sailors[1–3].txt. Compiled and formatted by Dorothy Elwood.

INDEX

A NOTE ABOUT THE AUTHOR

Jacqueline Jones teaches at the University of Texas–Austin, where she holds the Walter Prescott Webb Chair of History and Ideas, and the Mason Gentry White Professorship in Southern History. She has published seven books, among them *Labor of Love, Labor of Sorrow,* which won the Bancroft Prize in American history. She has also been awarded the Taft Prize in American labor history, the Spruill Prize in American southern women's history, the Brown Prize in African-American women's history, and the Gustavus Myers Prize in the history of American race relations. She was the recipient of a MacArthur Fellowship in 1999. She lives in Austin, Texas.

A NOTE ON THE TYPE

This book was set in a typeface called Bulmer. This distinguished letter is a replica of a type long famous in the history of English printing which was designed and cut by William Martin about 1790 for William Bulmer of the Shakespeare Press. In design, it is all but a modern face, with vertical stress, sharp differentiation between the thick and thin strokes, and nearly flat serifs. The decorative italic shows the influence of Baskerville, as Martin was a pupil of John Baskerville's.

Composed by North Market Street Graphics, Lancaster, Pennsylvania

Printed and bound by Berryville Graphics, Berryville , Virginia

Map of Civil War–era Savannah by David Lindroth, Inc.

Book design by Robert C. Olsson